Bernard Shaw

The One-Volume Definitive Edition

Michael Holroyd

Chatto & Windus
LONDON

This edition first published 1997

1 3 5 7 9 10 8 6 4 2

Bernard Shaw by Michael Holroyd was originally published in four volumes, Volume 1 *The Search for Love 1856–1898*, Volume 2 *The Pursuit of Power 1898–1918*, Volume 3 *The Lure of Fantasy 1918–1950*, Volume 4 (Epilogue) *The Last Laugh* by Chatto & Windus

and reprinted by Penguin Books Ltd in 1990, 1991, 1992, 1993.
This present edition is a substantial abridgement, with revisions, of the complete work by the author.

First published in the United Kingdom in 1997 by
Chatto & Windus Limited
Random House, 20 Vauxhall Bridge Road
London SW1V 2SA

Random House Australia (Pty) Limited
20 Alfred Street, Milsons Point, Sydney
New South Wales 2061, Australia

Random House New Zealand Limited
18 Poland Road, Glenfield
Auckland 10, New Zealand

Random House South Africa (Pty) Limited
Endulini, 5a Jubilee Road,
Parktown 2193 South Africa
Random House UK Limited Reg. No. 954009

A CIP catalogue record for this book
is available from the British Library

ISBN 0 7011 6279 1

Index by Vicki Robinson

Printed and bound in Great Britain by
Mackays of Chatham PLC, Chatham, Kent

CONTENTS

CONTENTS

LIST OF ILLUSTRATIONS

ACKNOWLEDGEMENTS

The many people and institutions that helped me to prepare the original four volumes of my Shaw biography are comprehensively listed in those volumes, and I take this opportunity to renew my thanks to them all. I have continued reading *The Annual of Bernard Shaw Studies* in the United States and *The Shavian* in Britain, as well as new publications about G.B.S. and his contemporaries, and to keep an eye out for Shaw manuscript material coming up at auction, so as to make necessary adjustments to my text in this abridgement. I owe special thanks to Sarah Johnson who transcribed my increasingly illegible marginalia on to immaculate discs; to my editor Alison Samuel who has continued walking in my steps and issuing corrections when I put a foot wrong; and to Howard Davies who queried anything queryable in this revised narrative.

MICHAEL HOLROYD
Porlock Weir, December 1996

ILLUSTRATIONS

1, 3 Courtesy of the British Library, London. 2 Courtesy of Archibald Henderson, *Man of the Century*, Appleton, Century, Crofts, New York, 1956. 5, 24 Courtesy of the Dan H. Laurence Collection, University of Guelph Library, Guelph, Ontario. 6, 12 Courtesy of Dan H. Laurence, *Bernard Shaw: Collected Letters*, Vol. 1, Max Reinhardt Ltd, London, 1965. 7, 10, 13 Courtesy of the National Portrait Gallery, London. 8 Courtesy of the National Trust, 9 Courtesy of the Fales Library, New York University Library, New York. 11 Courtesy of John Kelly (ed.), *Yeats Letters*, Vol. 1, Oxford University Press, 1986. 14 Courtesy of the Burgunder Collection, Cornell University Library, New York. 15, 18, 26 Hulton Getty (Picture Library), London. 16 Courtesy of Mary Shenfield, *Bernard Shaw: A Pictorial Biography*, Thames & Hudson, London, 1962. 17 Courtesy of the Trustees of the Victoria & Albert Museum, London. 19 Courtesy of the Sir Barry Jackson Trust, Birmingham. 20 Courtesy of Allan Chappelow, *Shaw the Villager and Human Being*, Charles Skilton, London, 1961. 21 Pictorial Parade Inc. 22 Courtesy of Allan Chappelow, *Shaw 'The Chucker-Out'*, George Allen & Unwin, London, 1969. 23 Courtesy of *Smithsonian* Magazine, Washington DC. 25 Courtesy of London of School of Economics and Political Science, British Library of Political and Economic Science, and the Society of Authors, London. Front endpaper Courtesy of Mander & Mitchenson Theatre Collection, Beckenham. Back endpaper Photo by Vandamm.

PREFACE

In the late 1960s the Shaw Estate decided to commission a new biography of G.B.S. Previous biographies had been 'partial', usually written by friends of Shaw, and the time had come for 'an assessment of the man in his period'. Shaw's executor, the Public Trustee, had recently relinquished his control of the publication and production arrangements for Shaw's works and set up an independent Committee of Management composed of nominees from the Estate's three residuary legatees (the British Museum and Royal Academy of Dramatic Art in London, and the National Gallery of Ireland in Dublin). Its first chairman, Sir John Wolfenden, director and principal librarian of the British Museum, took advice as to who should write Shaw's life from an eminent biographer and incunabulist at the museum, and my name came up. So the Society of Authors (which acted as agent for the Shaw Estate) was asked to sound me out.

I was then thirty-four, had published a biography of Lytton Strachey the previous year and already agreed to write a biography of Augustus John. But this invitation surprised me. I was more accustomed to appeals from people wanting me *not* to write about their friends and members of their family. Perhaps, it occurred to me, I was becoming respectable. The feeling was not altogether comfortable. In fact, I was terrified. To my eyes G.B.S. appeared as a gigantic phenomenon with whom I felt little intimacy. At the same time he presented a challenge I really ought to accept. Nevertheless I hesitated. I had heard that Shaw used to write ten letters every day of his adult life and that correspondents kept his letters. I knew he had composed over fifty plays, that his collected works extended over almost forty volumes (and were well exceeded by his uncollected writings), and that there were libraries of books about his work and huge deposits of unpublished papers around the world. I suspected that with his shorthand and his secretaries G.B.S. could actually write in a day more words than I could read in a day. Since he lived into his mid-nineties, writing vigorously almost to the end, this was an alarming speculation. I therefore prevaricated, replying that while I would in principle be delighted to write Shaw's Life, I could not in practice begin until I had finished *Augustus John*.

To my surprise the Society of Authors was undeterred by this delay. I did not begin my research until early in 1975 when I went to Dublin. I lived in Rathmines, strategically placed between a convent and a barracks, and a mile or so from Shaw's birthplace in Synge Street. Intermittently

I worked at the National Library of Ireland (to which Shaw had donated the manuscripts of his novels) and I visited Dalkey where he had passed his happiest hours while growing up. I also met a number of writers – John O'Donovan, Monk Gibbon, Vivian Mercier, Arland Ussher, Terence de Vere White – who encouraged me. Yet, however hard I try, I cannot account for my time in Ireland very coherently. The atmosphere was thick with goodwill. There was almost no one who, even when they had no information at all, would not be prepared to volunteer something over a jar or two. People I had never heard of came to advise me that they knew nothing, and then stayed on awhile. Many wrote letters to the same effect: some hopefully in verse; others more prosaically enclosing business cards. And everyone pressed in on me so warmly that I was moved to reply with such politeness that my replies elicited answers to which I felt bound to respond. One lady (whom I had never met) eventually enquired whether we had ever had an affair, the crucial part of which had escaped her. I was swimming in the wake of the great Shaw legend, swimming and almost drowning.

The writing of my book, which took me all over the world, must have tested the patience of the Shaw Estate to its utmost. But the extra time I was obliged to spend with Shaw helped to give me that sense of intimacy I had found lacking at the beginning of my research and which I believe is an essential ingredient for the writing of biography. Between Shaw's work and his life, I found, moved an unexpected current of passion which I sought to navigate. I felt eventually as if I were breaking a Shavian code, the alpha and omega of his dramatic style (so assertive yet so reticent), and was picking up subtle themes that, to gain an immediate public, he orchestrated for trumpet and big drum.

Many people had come to think of the legendary G.B.S. as having only ink in his veins. I began to dismantle this literary superman and replace him with a more recognizable if still uncommon human being. I wanted to demythologize him without reducing him. Behind the public phenomenon was hidden a private individual, intermittently glimpsed, who gave G.B.S. his concealed humanity. He covered up his vulnerability with dazzling panache; I have tried to uncover it and show the need he had while alive for such brilliant covering. He became the saint of the lonely and a fugleman for those who were out of step with their times. He gave them a heartening message. For every disadvantage, in Shavian terms, becomes a potential asset in disguise. The art of life therefore is the art of heroic paradox.

The paradox continues into our own times. G.B.S. is in his element by virtue of still being heroically out of step. I had already noticed, with respect to my previous biographies, how quickly a prevailing mood could change and how unpredictable these changes sometimes were. In the 1960s I had been assailed by a good deal of homophobic mail after my *Lytton Strachey* was published; but when a rewritten version of that book came out twenty-five years later I received no hate mail at all. On the other hand Augustus John, generally seen in the mid-1970s as an adventurous heterosexual character who might have emerged from the pages of Fielding's *Tom Jones*, attracted much greater puritan censoriousness twenty years later, mostly from men who, though responding to the rise of feminism, put me in mind of Dr Johnson's attack on *Tom Jones*.

By the end of the 1980s most people expected there would soon be a Labour Government in Britain. But the country did not embrace change as the United States appeared to be trying to do by turning from the Republicans to the Democrats. Instead it was preparing to dig in against the rest of Europe over what was to be a radically retrogressive period. We returned to past battlefields. Many of the political campaigns in which Shaw took part, and which had been manifestly won, were being fought out again a hundred years later, and with opposite results. The break-up of the Soviet Union, the 'end of communism' and of 'history', the spread of privatization across the world and the rise of nationalism, the fear in Britain of the very word 'socialist' (as frightening as 'liberal' in the United States) were to make Shaw's beliefs deeply unfashionable. While Oscar Wilde's once-faded aestheticism was being revitalized and revived by modernists, Shaw's persistent progressiveness had become dated. Yet being thoroughly out of fashion, wilfully marching in an alternative direction, was a Shavian speciality – and perhaps a useful one. Many pages which I wrote as a contribution to social history now appear to me, as I reread them, to have gained a peculiar relevance to our contemporary politics.

'Trust your genius rather than your industry,' Shaw advised his biographer St John Ervine. In preparing this abridgement, which was planned and contracted for over ten years ago, I have done away with all signs of industry by following the example of Leon Edel's abridged Life of Henry James and eliminating reference notes. I have also trusted to my instinct while reducing ninety-four years of Shaw's hectic life, and more than fifteen years of my own work, into a form that a general reader can get through in a matter of weeks or days. I have weeded out errors I detected in earlier versions, and occasionally added a passage founded on recent Shaw scholarship. What I have aimed at is something equivalent in biographical narrative to the 'revolver shooting' of Shaw's own dramatic dialogue where 'every line has a bullet in it and comes with an explosion'. Undoubtedly this technique reveals a rather different G.B.S. from the one conveyed by my original armada of volumes. It is for readers rather than myself to say what the difference is. All I can say is that it emerges from this synthesis, rather than being premeditated or imposed.

When infiltrating the work of his biographers with concealed autobiography, Shaw sacrificed something of his own life so that these 'partial' biographies might act as endorsements to his political ideas. Treating the Gospels as early examples of biography, he noted in the Preface to *Androcles and the Lion* how St Matthew ('like most biographers') tended to 'identify the opinions and prejudices of his hero with his own', while St John used biography as a record of the 'fulfilment of ancient Jewish prophecies'. Since Shaw's death, biographical technique has grown more ingenious and the range of subject matter has expanded so that biography embraces most human experience, insofar as it is recoverable, and accepts it as fit for publication. So far as I am aware, I do not specifically identify my opinions with Shaw's, nor have I used his life to record the fulfilment or non-fulfilment of socialist predictions. My deepest involvement is with biography itself and its never-ending love-affair with human nature, and my aim has been to come a little nearer a biographical ideal described by Hugh Kingsmill as 'the complete sympathy of complete detachment'.

ONE

I

FERMENTING GENEALOGY

> Eternal is the fact that the human creature born in Ireland and brought up in its air is Irish.
>
> 'Ireland Eternal and External', *New Statesman* (30 October 1948)

Bernard Shaw died on 2 November 1950. For almost a decade interviewers had been recording his emphatic farewells. All were rehearsing for the time when G.B.S. could no longer have the last word, and when it arrived actors appeared nostalgically on new-fangled television sets; writers spoke without interruption on the wireless; statesmen round the world uttered their prepared addresses in newspapers.

The critic Eric Bentley bought several of these papers, but 'what I was reading made me sick', he wrote. '. . . Such mourning for Shaw was a mockery of Shaw . . . Grasping the first occasion when Shaw was powerless to come back at them, the bourgeoisie brayed and Broadway dimmed its lights.' To Bentley's mind it was the final acceptance of Shaw at the expense of all Shaw stood for.

Shaw had asked that his ashes should be mixed inseparably with those of his wife, which had been kept at Golders Green Crematorium, and then scattered in their garden. In the Dáil a proposal was made to convey them back to Ireland and place them beside Swift's at St Patrick's Cathedral in Dublin. For having lived his first twenty years in Ireland, Shaw felt 'a foreigner in every other country'. But it was only outside Ireland that he was recognized as Irish. As the Taoiseach John Costello said, 'Bernard Shaw never forgot his Irish birth.' Yet he had set out in his writings to give himself a new birth: a re-creation. He claimed to be as indigenous as the half-American Winston Churchill or a half-Spaniard such as Éamon de Valera, both excellent examples of cross-breeding. 'I am a typical Irishman; my family come from Yorkshire,' he assured G. K. Chesterton who, typically English, confirmed that 'scarcely anyone but a typical Irishman could have made the remark'.

*

The Shaws made no secret of being aristocrats. No Shaw could form a social acquaintance with a Roman Catholic or tradesman. They lifted up their powerful Wellingtonian noses and spoke of themselves, however querulously, in a collective spirit (as people mentioning the Bourbons or Habsburgs) using the third person: 'the Shaws'.

The family had come from Scotland, then moved to England. In 1689 Captain William Shaw slipped from Hampshire into Ireland to fight in the Battle of the Boyne. He was rewarded with a large grant of land in Kilkenny. There, as landed gentry, the Shaws hunted, shot and fished.

Most successful was Robert Shaw, who entered the Irish Parliament, founded the Royal Bank and in 1821 was made a baronet. His cousin Bernard (grandfather of G.B.S.) also seemed set for success. On 1 April 1802, aged thirty, he married the daughter of a clergyman, Frances Carr, who over the next twenty-three years gave birth to fifteen children. As High Sheriff of Kilkenny, Bernard spent much of his time in the country and neglected his Dublin business, with the result that his partner absconded with his money. Bernard woke up to find himself penniless, collapsed, and died in his sleep. His widow had to apply for help to Sir Robert. The banker-baronet was a wealthy man. 'Unlike the typical Shaw, he was plumpish and had the appearance somewhat of a truculent bear disturbed out of a doze.' He was hopelessly in love with Frances who, though disdaining his offers of marriage, accepted rent free 'a quaint cottage, with Gothically pointed windows' at Terenure. From here she launched her sons and daughters on the world 'in an unshaken and unshakeable consciousness of their own aristocracy'.

Like most large families, these Shaws were not exclusively teetotallers. We see them through the eyes of G.B.S. Of his four aunts, Cecilia (Aunt Sis), the eldest, was a temperate maiden lady. She had been pronounced dead when a child and placed in a coffin; but, climbing out, lived on into her nineties, 'a big, rather imposing woman, with the family pride written all over her'. Aunt Frances, a gently nurtured lady, drank secretly over many years before, submitting to it openly, she passed away. Charlotte Jane ('Aunt Shah') married an irreproachable man connected with a cemetery. Aunt Emily, exceeding in nothing but snuff, married a scholastic clergyman, William George Carroll, who, but for his temper (it was said), would have been a bishop.

'I know as much about drink as anybody outside a hospital of inebriates,' G.B.S. later wrote. His knowledge had come largely from his father and some uncles. Two of his uncles were unknown to him, having emigrated to the Antipodes and 'like Mr Micawber, made history there'. A third, Robert, was blinded in his youth and 'never had an opportunity of drinking'. Uncle Henry was the rich man of the family, able to afford two wives and fifteen children. But he invested his money in a collapsing coal mine and before his death became mentally unstable.

The other three brothers, including Shaw's father, were alcoholics. Uncle Barney (William Bernard) and Uncle Fred (Richard Frederick) both died in the family mental retreat, Dr Eustace's in the north of Dublin. The youngest, Uncle Fred, didn't drink until he married a girl named Waters. His drinking bouts then grew excessive but he gave up alcohol altogether once his wife left him to live in London. He was reputed to be ungenerous (he worked in the Valuation Office) and, in retirement, 'harmlessly dotty'.

Uncle Barney was an inordinate smoker as well as a drunkard. He lived a largely fuddled life until he was past fifty. Then, relinquishing alcohol and tobacco simultaneously, he passed the next ten years of his life as a teetotaller, playing an obsolete wind instrument called an ophicleide. Towards the end of this period, renouncing the ophicleide, he married a lady of great piety, and fell completely silent. He was carried off to the family asylum where, 'impatient for heaven', he discovered an absolutely original method of committing suicide. It was irresistibly amusing and no human being had yet thought of it, involving as it did an empty carpet bag. However, in the act of placing this bag on his head, Uncle Barney jammed the mechanism of his heart in a paroxysm of laughter – which the merest recollection of his suicidal technique never failed to provoke among the Shaws – and the result was that he died a second before he succeeded in killing himself. The coroner's court described his death as being 'from natural causes'.

'Drink is the biggest skeleton in the family cupboard,' G.B.S. told one of his cousins. But he did not leave this skeleton in its cupboard. He had a choice of making the Shaw drunkenness into 'either a family tragedy or a family joke', and he chose the joke. So, in the bookshop window of his works, we may see a cabaret of Shavian aunts and uncles with a chorus of inebriate cousins, and at the centre, a wonderfully hopeless chap, second cousin to a baronet, George Carr Shaw, G.B.S.'s father.

2

AN IRISH MARRIAGE

> Fortunately I have a heart of stone: else my relations would have broken it long ago.
>
> Shaw to Rachel Mahaffy (6 June 1939)

The story of George Carr Shaw's life was simple. He would tell you it had evolved as the retribution for an injury he had once done a cat. He had found this cat, brought it home with him, fed it. But next day he had let his dog chase it and kill it. In his imagination this cat now had its revenge, seeing to it that he would have neither luck nor money. He was unsuccessful because of this cat; unskilled, unsober, and unserious too.

Between the ages of twenty-three and thirty he had been a clerk at a Dublin ironworks, but in 1845 he lost this job. By means of family influence he landed up with a perfectly superfluous post at the Four Courts, a job without duties or responsibilities. Unfortunately, it was one of the first of such positions to be abolished in the legal reforms of the early 1850s, for which 'outrage' George Shaw received a pension of £44 a year. There were opportunities in Dublin for a wholesale corn-merchant (retail trade was impossible for a Shaw). But George Shaw needed capital. Until now he had walked by himself, a gentleman who was no gentleman, and all places were alike to him. He was in his thirty-eighth year and had recently come in contact with a twenty-one-year-old girl, Lucinda Elizabeth Gurly, called 'Bessie'. She was short, thin-lipped, with the jaw of a prize-fighter and a head like a football; but she had an attractive inheritance. George Carr Shaw felt drawn to her. 'It was at this moment,' G.B.S. records, 'that some devil, perhaps commissioned by the Life Force to bring me into the world, prompted my father to propose marriage to Miss Bessie Gurly.'

*

The master-spirit among Bessie's forebears had been her maternal grandfather, a country gentleman of imposing presence whose origin was so obscure that he was understood to have had no legal parents. But he lived *en grand seigneur* on his property of over two thousand acres in Kilkenny and at a place called Whitechurch to the south of Dublin. Each week he would drive in to a little pawnshop in Winetavern Street, one of the poorest quarters of the city. The name on the door was Cullen, an employee, under cover of whose identity John Whitcroft made his money.

The squire-pawnbroker wanted respectability by blood. On 29 December 1829 his daughter Lucinda married a ginger-whiskered squire from Carlow named Walter Bagnall Gurly, who was then living nearby at Rathfarnham. 'He was a wiry, tight, smallish handknit open-air man,' G.B.S. remembered, able to make his own boats and to ride the most ungovernable horses; an ingenious carpenter, dead shot, indefatigable fisherman: in short, 'able to do anything except manage his affairs, keep his estate from slipping through his fingers'.

In ten years of marriage they had one daughter and a son. Then, on 14 January 1839, Mrs Gurly died. Bessie was nine. She was placed under the care of her great-aunt, Ellen Whitcroft, a terrible hump-backed lady. This spidery creature taught her how to dress correctly, to sit motionless and straight; how to breathe, pronounce French, convey orders to servants. She was schooled in harmony and counterpoint, playing the piano 'with various coins of the realm on the backs of my hands, also with my hair which I wore in two long plaits down my back, tied to the back of my chair, also with a square of pasteboard hung on my neck by a string pretty much as pictures are hung . . . in order to prevent me looking at my hands'.

By a programme of constraints and browbeatings, she was 'educated up to the highest standard of Irish "carriage ladies" '. She never said anything coarse, loved flowers more than human beings and walked through the streets seeing nobody. Her aunt intended a great destiny for her – something that because of her deformity she had never achieved herself: marriage into the nobility. With these superior expectations, Bessie was floated into Dublin Society where she encountered the sinking George Carr Shaw.

Secretly Bessie detested her aunt and everything that, masquerading as education and religion, had made her childhood miserable. It was now that George Carr Shaw drifted forward to make his bid for Aunt Ellen's property by proposing marriage to her niece.

He was not a romantic figure. Almost twice her age, he had a weak mouth, one squinting eye and a number of epileptic ways. 'If any unpleasant reflection occurred to him, he, if in a room, rubbed his hands rapidly together and ground his teeth. If in a street, he took a short run.' He was an unconvivial man, with little interest in women. Drink and money were his world.

But Bessie, who had fallen out with her father, overlooked the squinting eyes, the grinding teeth, and took stock only of George Carr Shaw's social position and the prospects such a proposal offered of a better life. Yet this was to be a marriage of two blind people, each treating the other as guide dog. 'Money in marriage is the first and, frequently, the only passion,' wrote St John Ervine of nineteenth-century Irish marriages. G.B.S.'s parents married for money and were to live impecuniously ever after.

Aunt Ellen had tolerated George Carr Shaw as Bessie's chaperon because of his well-connected harmlessness. To be with Shaw was an alibi for almost anything; never before had he been known to take an initiative. So now Aunt Ellen declared the marriage impossible. Then, when none of her objections prevailed, she revealed that Shaw was a known drunkard – in any event it was notorious in the family. Bessie knew how to deal with this. She went round to Shaw and asked him; and he confessed that all his life he had been a bigoted teetotaller. But he did not tell her that he was a teetotaller who drank.

So the marriage went ahead. Aunt Ellen had one more card to play: she disinherited her niece. This was undeniably a serious blow to Shaw. Needing money to take advantage of a business opportunity from his brother Henry, he sold his pension for £500 and used this capital to buy a partnership in a corn-merchant business with his brother's ex-partner, George Clibborn. It was a start – to be supported after his marriage by his wife's own money and whatever could be regained of Aunt Ellen's inheritance. It could have been worse.

This was a good summer for Walter Bagnall Gurly. On 25 May 1852 he married his second wife who, two months before, had given birth to their first daughter; and twenty-three days later, at the same church, St Peter's in Aungier Street, he attended the wedding of his daughter and George Carr Shaw. As a wedding gift, Aunt Ellen had sent the couple a bundle of IOUs signed by Gurly – which he seized and burnt. Better still was the marriage settlement he had insisted on their signing a few hours before the ceremony. Bessie's personal assets were listed as 'one thousand two hundred and fifty-six pounds Nine shillings and two pence Government three and a quarter per cent Stock'. All this, together with income to be derived from her father's first marriage settlement and from the will of her pawnbroker grandfather, was transferred by deed to two trustees. The effect of this was to ensure that the inheritance would remain Gurly-money, never the Shaw-money it would otherwise have become. So George Carr Shaw had gained a wife and lost a fortune.

When they drove off after the wedding, George Carr Shaw turned to kiss his bride. She felt so disgusted that she was still protesting more than thirty years later. 'The rebuff must have opened his eyes a little too late,' their son judged, 'to her want of any really mately feeling for him.'

3

DEVIL OF A CHILDHOOD

> William Morris used to say that it is very difficult to judge who are the best people to take charge of children, but it is certain that the parents are the very worst.
>
> Shaw to Nancy Astor (21 August 1943)

They had chosen Liverpool for their honeymoon, and here their first child was conceived. It was nearly the end of their marriage. Years later,

Mrs Shaw told her son that, opening her husband's wardrobe, she had 'found it full of empty bottles'. The truth had tumbled out. 'I leave you to imagine,' wrote G.B.S., 'the hell into which my mother descended when she found out what shabby-genteel poverty with a drunken husband is like.'

They returned to Dublin and moved into 'an awful little kennel with "primitive sanitary arrangements"', 3 Upper Synge Street – a road of eleven small squat houses which runs round the corner from Harrington Street. Here their three children were born: Lucinda Frances, called Lucy, on 26 March 1853, Elinor Agnes, nicknamed 'Yuppy', two years later; and, on 26 July 1856, their son George Bernard, 'fifty years too soon', he calculated.

It was a difficult delivery, a vaginal breech birth that was carried out at Upper Synge Street by Dr John Ringland, Master of the Combe Lying-In Hospital, who had been called in by Bessie's general practitioner.

In his nursery days he was called Bob; by the time he had grown into his holland tunic and knickerbockers he had become 'Sonny'; it was not until he was reborn the child of his own writings in England that he developed the plumage of 'G.B.S.'

We first see Bob at the age of one. 'The young beggar is getting quite outrageous,' his father writes proudly to Bessie who was staying with her family. 'I left him this morning roaring and tearing like a bull.' He could eat his hat, vomit up currants, annoy his teeth and make a jigsaw of unread newspapers. But his chief accomplishment was to go off on marvellous walking expeditions from Papa to Nurse (who was threatening a breakdown) and back again. From his bed he plunged head-first onto the floor; and from the kitchen table he cascaded through a pane of glass without 'even a *pane* in his head'.

Once domesticated, this bull of a boy soon became the sedate Sonny. The most affectionate sound in Synge Street was his father's jokes. From their talks, Sonny was let in on the secret of how his father had saved the life of Uncle Robert – 'and, to tell you the truth, I was never so sorry for anything in my life afterwards'. It became a game between them, almost an intimacy, that the son should provoke his father to such exhibitions.

In a letter to his wife, George Carr Shaw had written of 'a Mill which Clibborn & I are thinking of taking at Dolphin's Barn . . . Wont it be great fun and grandeur to find yourself when you come back the wife of a dusty Miller, so be prepared to have the very life ground out of you . . .' Bessie was not amused: he never did anything positive. 'You are out for once in your life,' he told her. 'We *have* taken the Mill.'

Dolphin's Barn Mill was on the country side of the canal. Sonny, who sometimes walked there with his father and sisters before breakfast, used to play under the waterwheel by the millpond and in the big field adjoining the building. 'The field had one tree in it, at the foot of which I buried our dead dog. It was quite wild. I never saw a human soul in it.' On the front of Rutland Avenue was a Clibborn & Shaw warehouse, one corner of which had been made into a shop where corn, wheat, flour and locust beans were surreptitiously retailed to the villagers. But they did not prosper. Once, when the firm was almost ruined by the bankruptcy of a debtor, Clibborn wept openly in their office, while Shaw retreated to a corner of the warehouse and cried with laughter at the colossal mischief of it all.

It was this sense of mischief that Sonny loved, and that G.B.S. believed he inherited. But planted in so many of Papa's comedies were seeds of disaster. When pretending to fling his son into the canal, he almost succeeded: and a suspicion began to crawl into Sonny's mind. He went to his mother and whispered his awful discovery, 'Mama: I think Papa's drunk.' 'When is he ever anything else?' Bessie retorted with disgust.

*

Though he transferred the responsibility for his desolate childhood to his father, the central character in this scene had been his mother. Bessie was a grievously disappointed woman. She believed, and persuaded her son to believe, that 'everybody had disappointed her, or betrayed her, or tyrannized over her'. From this time onwards Sonny began to see his father through his mother's eyes, as a man to imitate, but in reverse. It suited George Carr Shaw's temperament to play along. When he caught Sonny pretending to smoke a toy pipe, he entreated him with dreadful earnestness never to follow his example. In this special Shavian sense, George Carr Shaw became a model father.

Of his mother, G.B.S. once admitted, 'I knew very little about her.' This was partly because she did not concern herself with him. Her own childhood had been made miserable by bullying, but Bessie never bullied; she made her son miserable by neglect. 'She was simply not a wife or mother at all.' Needing her attention, he found with dismay that he could do nothing to interest her. In her eyes he was an inferior little male animal tainted with all the potential weaknesses of her husband.

In his books and letters, G.B.S. places his mother on a carpet of filial loyalty, and he invites every potential biographer to pull it from beneath her feet. His American biographer, Archibald Henderson, scrupulously overlooking this invitation, received in red ink a brusque rebuff: 'This sympathy with the mother is utterly false. Damn your American sentimentality!'

In a rare moment of emotion, G.B.S. wrote to Ellen Terry of his 'devil of a childhood, Ellen, rich only in dreams, frightful & loveless in realities'. But looking directly at such bleakness was too painful. Usually he put on the spectacles of paradox. This paradox became his 'criticism of life', the technique by which he turned lack of love inside out and, attracting from the world some of the attention he had been denied by his mother, conjured optimism out of deprivation.

The fact that neither of his parents cared for him was, he perceived, of enormous advantage. What else could have taught him the value of self-sufficiency? He was spared, too, by their unconcealed disappointment in each other, from lingering illusions about the family. It was remarkable how these paradoxical privileges began to multiply once he became skilled at the game. From his observations he soon deduced the wonderful impersonality of sex, and the kindness and good sense of distancing yourself from people you loved.

'The fact that I am still alive at 78½ I probably owe largely to her [Bessie's] complete neglect of me during infancy,' G.B.S. confided to Marie Stopes. ' . . . It used to be a common saying among Dublin doctors in my youth that most women killed their first child by their maternal care . . . motherhood is not every woman's vocation.' G.B.S. believed that his mother preferred her daughters, in particular the red-haired Yuppy, who wilted under her slight attentions. As a child she developed a goitre; only the fortunate absence of medical aid enabled nature to perform a cure. Then at the age of twenty-one, assisted by a sanatorium of doctors, she died of tuberculosis. It could be no accident either that Lucy, Bessie's second favourite, was to die next following a long period of anorexic ill-health, seven years after her mother's death. She 'suffered far more by the process than I did,' G.B.S. wrote of their upbringing, 'for she . . . was not immune, as I and my mother were, from conventional vanities'.

There was no feuding at Synge Street. The house was small, but so far as possible they treated one another like furniture. 'As children,' G.B.S. explained, 'we had to find our own way in a household where there was no hate nor love.' Sonny's own way led him to the conclusion that nature had intended an element of antipathy as a defence against incest. Happily his family had been well dosed with this preventative.

G.B.S. believed that he had inherited from his parents qualities that they had found incompatible but which, in expiation, he must reconcile within himself. Only by marrying opposites, through paradox or a dialectical process of synthesis, did he feel that he could fulfil his moral obligation to optimism and a better future. In place of the warring of envy and class, he was to substitute a Hegelian policy of inclusiveness. But to include everything in his sights he was obliged to fly his balloon of words into a stratosphere of hypothesis where, in all its thin remoteness, his vision became complete.

He writes of a strangeness 'which made me all my life a sojourner on this planet rather than a native of it . . . I was at home only in the realm of my imagination, and at my ease only with the mighty dead.' It is this voice from the living dead that, despite the marvellous cadence, chilled his audience. In the lost childhood of Sonny the philosophy of G.B.S. was conceived. 'What else can I do?' he had asked. He strove to bring the world into harmony with his lonely nature, but the world reacted subconsciously to what was suppressed as well as to what he proclaimed. He could see everything but touch little. For what he had done was replace the first loveless reality with a dream. 'I very seldom dream of my mother,' he told Gilbert Murray;

> 'but when I do, she is my wife as well as my mother. When this first occurred to me (well on in my life), what surprised me when I awoke was that the notion of incest had not entered into the dream: I had taken it as a matter of course that the maternal function included the wifely one; and so did she. What is more, the sexual relation acquired all the innocence of the filial one, and the filial one all the completeness of the sexual one . . . if circumstances tricked me into marrying my mother before I knew she was my mother, I should be fonder of her than I could ever be of a mother who was not my wife, or a wife who was not my mother.'

Only in his imagination was such completeness possible.

Most of the time Sonny and his sisters were abandoned to the servants – 'and *such* servants, Good God!' The exception was 'my excellent Nurse Williams' who left while Sonny was still very young. But what could you expect on £8 a year? 'I had my meals in the kitchen,' G.B.S. recalled, 'mostly of stewed beef, which I loathed, badly cooked potatoes, sound or diseased as the case might be, and much too much tea out of brown delft teapots left to "draw" on the hob until it was pure tannin. Sugar I stole . . . I hated the servants and liked my mother because, on one or two rare and delightful occasions when she buttered my bread for me, she buttered it thickly instead of merely wiping a knife on it . . . I could idolize her to the utmost pitch of my imagination and had no sordid or disillusioning contacts with her. It was a privilege to be taken for a walk or a visit with her . . .'

Occasionally Bessie would take him to see Aunt Ellen, hoping that the old lady would feel sufficiently attracted to leave him her property. Sonny seemed mesmerized by this strange little hump-backed lady with her pretty face and magical deformity. One Sunday morning Papa announced that she was dead, and Sonny ran off to the solitude of the garden to cry, terrified that his grief would last for ever. When he 'discovered that it lasted only an hour,' wrote G.B.S., 'and then passed completely away', he had his first taste of realism.

Shaw was unable to tolerate feelings of sadness. 'People who cry and grieve never remember,' he wrote. 'I never grieve and never forget.' Sadness was a poison to his system and before absorption it had to be converted into something else. His attitude to death was the most extreme example of this manufacture of cheerfulness. Papa, he saw, 'found something in a funeral, or even in a death, which tickled his sense of humor.

' . . . the sorest bereavement does not cause men to forget wholly that time is money. Hence, though we used to proceed slowly and sadly enough through the streets or terraces at the early stages of our progress, when we got into the open a change came over the spirit in which the coachmen drove. Encouraging words were addressed to the horses; whips were flicked; a jerk all along the line warned us to slip our arms through the broad elbow-straps of the mourning-coaches, which were balanced on longitudinal poles by enormous and totally unelastic springs; and then the funeral began in earnest. Many a clinking run have I had through that bit of country at the heels of some deceased uncle who had himself many a time enjoyed the same sport. But in the immediate neighbourhood of the cemetery the houses recommenced; and at that point our grief returned upon us with overwhelming force: we were able barely to crawl along to the great iron gates where a demoniacal black pony was waiting with a sort of primitive gun-carriage and a pall to convey our burden up the avenue to the mortuary chapel, looking as if he might be expected at every step to snort fire, spread a pair of gigantic bat's wings, and vanish, coffin and all, in thunder and brimstone.'

In this way, Sonny began to laugh pain out of existence. Detachment from the fear of death was a step towards Shavian invulnerability in life. His death-anxiety was transferred into a fear of poverty (which, with a little courage and thought, we could eliminate), and any sediment of apprehension absorbed into a hygienic campaign against earth burial. Freed from escapist fables of personal immortality, death became an intensely democratic process. We began to die when more people wished us dead than wished us alive. Many a colleague, on the death of a wife, son or mother, was to find himself in receipt of Shaw's feeling congratulations. 'Rejoice in his memory; and be radiant,' he instructed Edith Lyttelton after the death of her husband. ' . . . Dying is a troublesome business: there is pain to be suffered, and it wrings one's heart; but death is a splendid thing – a warfare accomplished, a beginning all over again, a triumph. You can always see that in their faces.'

4

THE MAGICIAN APPEARS

I am an Irishman without a birth certificate.

Shaw to Denis Johnston (1 April 1938)

Sometime after her marriage Bessie was raised up into a new world of 'imagination, idealization, the charm of music, the charm of lovely seas' by a mysterious intruder, called Lee, one of the originals of George du Maurier's Svengali. He was a 'mesmeric conductor and daringly original teacher of singing,' G.B.S. records. It was the extraordinary effect he produced on Bessie that impressed her son. Sonny watched him closely.

There was something gypsy-like about his appearance. His face 'was framed with pirate-black whiskers' and he wore his luxuriant black hair long. He had a deformed foot and limped with peculiar elegance. But it was the confidence with which he asserted his heterodox opinions that Sonny noticed more than anything else. He noticed too the way his mother listened, the way she came alive under Lee's spell.

Sonny did not like Lee, but he could not help admiring him. He was, it seems, about six years old when his mother introduced this stranger into Synge Street. But, 'as his notion of play was to decorate my face with moustaches and whiskers in burnt cork in spite of the most furious resistance I could put up, our encounter was not a success; and the defensive attitude in which it left me lasted, though without the least bitterness, until the decay of his energies and the growth of mine put us on more than equal terms'.

G.B.S. never knew when Lee and his mother met. Lee claimed to have been born in Kilrush, County Clare, the natural son of Colonel Crofton Moore Vandeleur, MP. When he was a boy he had fallen down a flight of stairs. His wound was badly dressed, and though he wore his lameness 'as if it were a quality instead of a defect', he was left with a lifelong animosity towards orthodox medical science. He had never been to school and had 'nothing good to say of any academic institution'. Instead he provided himself with the title 'Professor of Music' and went on to pioneer a revolutionary discipline of voice training which he called 'the

Method'. He was more than a singing teacher: he was a philosopher of voice. Music, he would tell Sonny, was his religion.

But there were some facts of Lee's career that Sonny never heard. He had been born in 1830, the elder of two sons of Robert Lee, coalman, and his wife Eliza. At the age of eight he was living at 4 Caroline Row in Dublin and attending the Christian Brothers' O'Connell School nearby. In the school records his name is given as George Lee, and his brother's as William. This was a Catholic school, and it was here he took violin lessons and instruction in singing. On 9 January 1843, Robert Lee died. By 1851, the family was living at 2 Portobello Place. Less than two years later they had moved to 16 Harrington Street. Between 1851 and 1853 the family must have found some money – possibly from Colonel Vandeleur on the coming of age of George and William. The rateable value of 2 Portobello Place had been £5 10s., that of 16 Harrington Street was £34. It was in 1852 also that Lee founded his Amateur Musical Society, taking some sort of professional rooms for a year or two at 11 Harrington Street on the opposite side of the road. From nowhere in the published writings or letters of G.B.S. can it be inferred that Lee started his musical society and set up as singing teacher within a few months of Bessie's marriage to George Carr Shaw; nor is it clear that 2 Portobello Place was about two hundred yards from the Shaws in Synge Street, that 16 Harrington Street was some one hundred and twenty-five paces distant, and that two houses only separate Sonny's future birthplace from Lee's professional chambers.

Sonny sometimes speculated as to whether he might have been Lee's natural son; and G.B.S. was aware of other people's speculations. 'About G.B.S.'s parentage,' wrote Beatrice Webb in her diary for 12 May 1911. 'The photograph published in the Henderson Biography makes it quite clear to me that he was the child of G. J. V. Lee – that vain, witty and distinguished musical genius who lived with them. The expression on Lee's face is quite amazingly like G.B.S. when I first knew him.'

That Shaw may have had an unconscious wish to be the son of the remarkable George Lee and not of the miserable George Carr Shaw is possible. His campaign to demonstrate that he was George Carr Shaw's son was conducted primarily in defence of his mother. He was to model himself on Lee because of the extraordinary effect Lee had produced on Bessie and, in a number of three-cornered relationships, he was to play out the presumed asexuality of their liaison by refusing to compromise his own chastity. The themes of consanguinity and illegitimacy recur obsessively in his plays, but it is the emotional independence of the woman that is stressed. Eliza's parting from Professor Higgins in *Pygmalion* to marry Freddy Eynsford-Hill is Shaw's restatement of Bessie's economic attachment to Lee who is seen as a means to her self-sufficiency. In logic,

Sonny should have been Lee's son. But as Shaw demonstrated in his most deliberately pleasant play, *You Never Can Tell*, remarkable children were frequently born to incompatible parents.

But G.B.S. had to be certain. So he obliterated the ambiguous Christian name he shared with George Lee and George Shaw, using only the initial G. 'Professionally I drop the George,' he told an editor. 'Personally I dislike it.' 'Don't George me,' he would growl at people who made this mistake. He would remain George only to his family.

By finding a use for the knowledge of harmony and counterpoint hammered into her in her youth, Lee gave Bessie 'a Cause and a Creed to live for'. She became the chorus leader and general factotum of his musical society.

Lee's life had changed in those years. On 6 March 1860 his mother died, and two years later, on 7 May 1862, his brother William also died, aged twenty-seven, and was buried near Robert and Eliza Lee in the Roman Catholic Glasnevin Cemetery. His death brought Lee 'to the verge of suicide'. Since life outside music seemed to offer little to either Lee or Bessie, they became wedded to 'the Method'.

In his Preface to *London Music* G.B.S. touches on a peculiar aspect of this story. 'Lee soon found his way into our house, first by giving my mother lessons there, and then by using our drawing-room for rehearsals.' He presents Lee as a man apart, 'too excessively unlike us, too completely a phenomenon, to rouse any primitive feelings in us'. Because he was a cripple 'marriage and gallantry were tacitly ruled out of his possibilities, by himself, I fancy, as much as by other people. There was simply no room in his life for anything of the sort.' What little we know about Lee contradicts this view of the man. His Byronic limp was a focus of romantic interest; at least two women in his musical society, and possibly Sonny's sister Yuppy, fell in love with him. Later in life he made advances to Lucy Shaw and ended his days running a sort of night-club in London where he carried on an affair with his housekeeper. G.B.S. does not conceal this. But he presents it as a late-flowering sentimentalism that bloomed when, having been seduced by the capitalist atmosphere of 'overfed, monied London', he proved unfaithful to 'the Method' and had been dropped by Bessie.

To disinfect the relationship from all sexual implication, he built Bessie into 'one of those women who could act as matron of a cavalry barracks from eighteen to forty and emerge without a stain on her character'. 'To the closest observation' she was 'so sexless' that it was a wonder how she could have conceived three children. He could only guess that George Carr Shaw, when drunk, had forced himself on her and that to this operation he owed his existence. 'I was just something that had happened to them,' he bleakly concluded. Such a beginning, which explained his mother's neglect, was preferable to having the Lee–Bessie association 'unpleasantly misunderstood'. George Carr Shaw 'was Papa in the fullest sense always,' he wrote, 'and the dynamic Lee got none of the affection Papa inspired'. His arguments reflect the urgent need Shaw felt to make his case, in the light of what was to happen next between Lee and his mother.

5

MÉNAGE À TROIS

> We must reform society before we can reform ourselves . . . personal righteousness is impossible in an unrighteous environment.
>
> Shaw to H. G. Wells (17 May 1917)

Two experiences, both visual, dominate Sonny's early years. The first was his sight of the Dublin slums. 'I saw it and smelt it and loathed it.' His nurse would take him to the squalid tenements of her friends, or lead him off to a public house and (it is suggested) add to her £8 a year by picking up soldiers at the barracks. Shaw's lifelong hatred of poverty was born of these lonely days of slumming.

On being asked, at the age of seventy-five, to name the happiest hour of his life, Shaw was to answer: 'When my mother told me we were going to live on Dalkey Hill.' In 1864, two years after his brother's death, Lee moved from Harrington Street to 1 Hatch Street. He proposed a new arrangement: to lease a cottage on Dalkey Hill, nine miles south of Dublin, and to share it with the Shaws. Torca Cottage, into which they all moved in 1866, had four reasonably-sized rooms, a back room for Sonny, and a kitchen and pantry into which they squeezed the servant's bed. The front garden overlooked Killiney Bay, and the back garden Dublin Bay.

'I owe more than I can express to the natural beauty of that enchanting situation commanding the two great bays between Howth and Bray Head,' Shaw remembered towards the end of his life, 'and its canopied skies such as I have never seen elsewhere in the world.' In the miserable Synge Street house, opposite a big field blotted out by hoardings and behind 'the bare dark walls, much too high . . . too high to be climbed over', Sonny had felt a prisoner. At Torca he became 'a prince in a world of my own imagination'. His playground was Killiney Hill, a wonderland of goat-paths and gorse slopes down which he would run to the sandy shore and into the sea. But the beauty of Dalkey, taking him out 'of this time and this world', delayed his development. 'With a little more courage & a little more energy I could have done much more; and I lacked these because in my boyhood I lived on my imagination instead of on my work.'

The work of G.B.S. was a product not so much of his happy memories of Dalkey but of his visits to the Dublin slums which, 'with their shocking vital statistics and the perpetual gabble of its inhabitants', reflected the unhappiness Sonny seldom escaped. 'An Irishman has two eyes,' Shaw told G. K. Chesterton. One was for poetry, the other for reality. As Sonny grew into an adult the Dalkey eye closed. This is why, at his most serious, G.B.S. always seems to be winking.

After a year at Dalkey, Lee and the Shaws agreed to extend the *ménage à trois* to Hatch Street, while they continued to occupy Torca Cottage for summer holidays. 'The arrangement was economical,' G.B.S. explained, 'for we could not afford to live in a fashionable house, and Lee could not afford to give lessons in an unfashionable one.' Lee paid the rent for all of them – the rateable value being £35 – in addition to the costs at Dalkey. The amalgamation gave the Shaws a well-appointed three-storeyed house. 'Being a corner house it had no garden,' Shaw remembered; 'but it had two areas and a leads. It had eight rooms besides the spacious basement and pantry accommodation as against five in Synge St.' The hall door was in one street and the windows (with one exception) were in another. The exception, a window over the hall door and near the roof, was Sonny's bedroom where, his friend Edward McNulty remembered, 'there was barely room for anything but his bed'.

Like his mother Sonny was dazzled by Lee and adopted many of his startling ideas – sleeping with the windows open, eating brown bread instead of white and parading his disdain for doctors, lawyers, academics, clergymen. Lee filled the house with music and banished family prayers. In the Synge Street days, George Carr Shaw, as sole head of the household, had sent his children to Sunday School where genteel Protestants aged five to twelve, well-soaped and best-dressed, mouthed religious texts and were rewarded with inscribed cards. After this they would be marched to the Molyneux Church in Upper Leeson Street to fidget interminably round the altar rails. 'To sit motionless and speechless in your best suit in a dark stuffy church on a morning that is fine outside the building, with your young limbs aching with unnatural quiet . . . is enough to lead any sensitive youth to resolve that when he grows up and can do as he likes, the first use he will make of his liberty will be to stay away from church.'

Such respectable habits had been largely ridiculed by Bessie's dissolute brother Walter Gurly, a ship's surgeon who visited them between transatlantic voyages. 'He was a most exhilarating person,' G.B.S. remembered, '. . . always in high spirits, and full of a humor that was barbarous in its blasphemous indecency, but Shakespearian in the elaboration and fantasy of its literary expression . . . He was full of the Bible, which became in his hands a masterpiece of comic literature; and he quoted the sayings of Jesus as models of facetious repartee.'

G.B.S. uses the entertaining figure of Uncle Walter as a comet, shimmering across the skies, to distract our attention from a more significant feature in the religious firmament of the Shaws. There was nothing in Walter Gurly's irreverent jokes that quarrelled with the tradition of Protestant gentry. Irish Protestantism, Shaw explains, 'was not then a religion: it was a side in political faction, a class prejudice, a conviction that Roman Catholics are socially inferior persons who will go to hell when they die and leave Heaven in the exclusive possession of Protestant ladies and gentlemen'.

It is evident from what he wrote that G.B.S. knew that Lee was a Catholic. But he prevaricated. To Stephen Winsten he proclaimed that 'music was the only religion he [Lee] ever professed'; to Frank Harris he wrote: 'The Method was my mother's religion. It was the bond between her and Lee. A bond of sex could not have lasted a year'; to Demetrius O'Bolger he revealed that Lee was 'sceptical' about religion, and added, 'the religion of our house was the religion of singing the right way'. By such means he directed his biographers where he wanted. For although he claimed to be 'in intense reaction against the Shaw snobbery', his own snob-tragedy was to be G.B.S.'s disappointment with Sonny for having felt ashamed among his school friends at sharing a house with someone no Shaw should rightly know.

The only person for whom there seemed no special advantages at Hatch Street was George Carr Shaw. He became 'full of self-reproaches and humiliations when he was not full of secret jokes, and was either biting his moustache and whispering deep-drawn Damns, or shaking with paroxysms of laughter'. In a private note, written for a medical friend in 1879, Shaw described the pattern of his father's drinking:

'In society he drank porter, champagne, whisky, anything he could get, sometimes swallowing stout enough to make him sick . . . Although he was never sober, he was seldom utterly drunk. He made efforts to reform himself, and on one occasion succeeded in abstaining for sixteen months; but these efforts always ended in a relapse. On one or two occasions he disappeared for a few days and returned with his watch broken, clothes damaged and every symptom of uncontrolled excess; but ordinarily he came home in the evening fuddled, eat [*sic*] his dinner, had a nap, and then kept going out for drams until he went to bed. He never drank or kept drink in the house . . . I have seen him when drunk, seize a small article on the mantelpiece and dash it upon the hearthstone, or kick a newspaper into the air; but though he was very irritable, he never used the slightest violence to any person . . . his timidity probably made forbearance habitual to him.'

After his father was dead, G.B.S. eliminated much of this sordidness by giving to his published descriptions of it a hilarious Shavian gloss.

'A boy who has seen "the governor", with an imperfectly wrapped-up goose under one arm and a ham in the same condition under the other (both purchased under heaven knows what delusion of festivity), butting at the garden wall of our Dalkey Cottage in the belief that he was pushing open the gate, and transforming his tall hat to a concertina in the process, and who, instead of being overwhelmed with shame and anxiety at the spectacle, has been so disabled by merriment (uproariously shared by the maternal uncle) that he has hardly been able to rush to the rescue of the hat and pilot its wearer to safety, is clearly not a boy who will make tragedies of trifles instead of making trifles of tragedies.'

After two or three years at Hatch Street, George Carr Shaw was felled on the doorstep by a fit. Shortly afterwards he became so rigid a teetotaller that those who knew him found it 'difficult to realize what he formerly was'.

In a letter to a prospective biographer, G.B.S. wrote: 'You ask whether my father liked Lee. He certainly did not, and would not have tolerated the arrangement if he could have afforded a decent house without it, or if he could have asserted himself against my mother, who probably never consulted him in the matter. There was never any quarrelling in the house: my mother went her own way, which happened to be the musical way of Lee, just as Lee went his; and my father could only look on helplessly.'

It was this impotence that appears to have driven George Carr Shaw to greater drinking excesses. 'When his children had grown too big for him to play with, and the suspense as to whether he would come home drunk or sober never ceased,' G.B.S. told a cousin, 'he got practically no comfortable society from them. His relatives did not want to see him; and my mother did not want to see his relatives: she was interested only in people who could sing, and they were mostly Catholics, not proper company for the Protestant caste of Shaw.'

Before his marriage, and during its early years, George Carr Shaw had been on visiting terms with his smart Protestant relatives. By the 1860s their doors were shut to him and his family. 'My immediate family and the Shaw clan,' G.B.S. recalled, '. . . were barely on speaking terms when we met which we did only accidentally, never intentionally.' Social conditions, which had helped to drive his father to drink, would also one day pervert Lee, and both men disappointed his mother. So Society became the dragon against which the fabulous G.B.S. would lead his campaign of lifelong knight-errantry.

6

THE SHAME OF EDUCATION

> If I had not returned to the house, I don't think they would, any of them, have missed me.
>
> Preface to *London Music* (1937)

At Synge Street Sonny and his sisters had been provided with a day governess. Caroline Hill was an impoverished gentlewoman who puzzled the children by her attempts to teach them the alphabet and mathematical tables. She would punish her pupils when their laughter grew too outrageous by 'little strokes with her fingers that would not have discomposed a fly'.

At the beginning of the summer term of 1865, when he was almost ten, Sonny was sent to his first school, the Wesleyan Connexional, less than half a mile away at 79 St Stephen's Green. He hated this school. 'I have not a good word to say for it,' he wrote. '. . . A more futile boy prison could not be imagined. I was a day-boy: what a boarder's life was like I shudder to conjecture.' The chief reason for his dislike of school appears to have been that it took him further away from his mother. This, he came to believe, had been its real purpose – that of 'preventing my being a nuisance to my mother at home for at least half the day'.

The Wesleyan Connexional School occupied an old private house next door to the mansion of Sir Benjamin Lee Guinness. Its big schoolroom stood at the end of a yard at the rear where the stables had been and which by the 1860s served as a playground. It was the cheapest of those Dublin schools patronized by Protestants. The sanitation was primitive and the lessons meagre. 'In the large classes,' Shaw recalled, 'the utmost examination possible in the lessons meant one question for each boy in alphabetical order, or at most two. If you could answer the questions or do the sums, or construe the few lines that fell to your lot, you passed unscathed: if not, or if you talked in class or misbehaved, you were marked in your judgement book for caning by the headmaster.'

The headmaster when Sonny first went there was Robert Cook, a young Methodist minister who would prepare boys for flogging with spasms of weeping. He was eventually succeeded by a man named Parker who conducted his classes with a ferocious cane in hand.

'When Parker appeared armed with a long lithe chestnut colored oriental cane, which had evidently cost much more than a penny, and slashed our hand with it mercilessly, he established an unprecedented terrorism. He was young (really too young), darkly handsome: apparently a perfect Murdstone. But he soon found that he was carrying his youthful terroristic logic too far . . . he had what no schoolmaster should allow himself to indulge: a dislike of stupid boys as such.'

To his biographers, G.B.S. represented Sonny at school as 'rampant, voluble, impudent . . . a most obstreperous player of rough games . . . [who] avoided his school tasks . . . and was soon given up as incorrigible'. That was how he had felt: it was not how he appeared to others. He was remembered as a quiet boy and on two occasions was awarded good conduct certificates. The other boys liked him for his comic stories about a character called Lobjort borrowed from *Household Words*, but otherwise his remote personality, designed to protect him from unhappiness at home, did not make him popular. His command of long words gave him an air of maturity that appealed more to adults than to children. He seemed unfitted for boy society. 'I think my treatment as an adult at home (like the Micawbers' treatment of David Copperfield) made school very difficult for me.'

The roll books at Wesley show that after only three months in 1865 he was taken away and did not return there until August 1867. After another three months he left again, then came back in February 1868 for nine months. During one or more of these intervals he attended a preparatory school at 23–24 Sandycove Road, Glasthule, near Dalkey.

'My parents,' Shaw wrote, ' . . . acted as if . . . I would come out as an educated gentleman if I wore the usual clothes, ate the usual food, and went to the same school or other every day.' But by the end of 1868 he had fallen so far behind that he was withdrawn altogether from the Wesleyan Connexional.

It was Lee, rather than Sonny's parents, who took the initiative. He had got to know the drawing-master at the Central Model Boys' School in Marlborough Street, Joseph Smeeth, who persuaded him that the teaching there was better than at any other of the cheaper genteel schools in Dublin. By the beginning of February 1869, Sonny was sent to Marlborough Street, where he remained a little over seven months. He was to focus on this school almost all the unhappiness of his boyhood. The Central Model Boys' School, he wrote, was 'undenominational and classless in theory but in fact Roman Catholic . . . It was an enormous place, with huge unscaleable railings and gates on which for me might well have been inscribed "All hope abandon, ye who enter here"; for that the son of a Protestant merchant-gentleman and feudal downstart should pass those bars or associate in any way with its hosts of lower middle class Catholic children, sons of petty shopkeepers and tradesmen, was inconceivable from the Shaw point of view . . . I lost caste outside it and became a boy with whom no Protestant young gentleman would speak or play.'

The enrolment books of the Central Model show that Sonny's form contained eight members of the Established Protestant Church, only five Roman Catholics and one 'Other Denomination'. Fathers' occupations included a hotel porter, two carpenters, a farmer, butcher, solicitor, bricklayer, shopkeeper, hatter, sergeant and gaol warder. It was, in fact as well as theoretically, what Shaw denied it to have been: a non-sectarian experimental school for persons of modest means. What Shaw did, many years afterwards, was to transfer to this place the 'shame and wounded snobbery' arising from his Catholic-infested home at Hatch Street.

When Sonny asked to be taken away from school, George Carr Shaw, relishing perhaps the defeat of Lee's programme, supported him. Sonny left the Central Model on 11 September 1869 and was transferred to the last of his boy prisons. The Dublin English Scientific and Commercial Day School was a large building with broad staircases and stately rooms on the corner of Aungier and Whitefriars Streets, sponsored by the Incorporated Society for Promoting English Protestant Schools in Ireland. Sonny remained here almost two years and became joint head boy. But his repugnance for all schools was implacable.

*

Sonny made one friend at the Dublin Commercial School. Matthew Edward McNulty, later to become a novelist, bank manager and playwright, was 'a corpulent youth with curly black hair'. His first sight of Sonny, at the age of thirteen, was of 'a tallish, slender youngster with straw-colored hair, light greyish-blue eyes, a skin like that of a baby and lips like those of a beautiful girl. There was a faint smile over his face as he listened to his companions and looked around the strange class room . . . We were, in fact, friends at first glance.'

McNulty was the only person with whom Sonny could share his dreams and ideas. When apart they entered into a tremendous correspondence, full of drawings and dramas.

Sonny dreamed of being a great man, probably a great artist like Michelangelo. He borrowed Duchesne's outlines of the Old Masters, bought the Bohn translation of Vasari, prowled for hours through Dublin's deserted National Gallery dragging McNulty with him – two schoolboys, one short and dark, the other tall and fair, going from picture to picture, full of argument, until they knew every work there. They also enrolled together for late afternoon courses at the Royal Dublin Society's School of Art and passed examinations in perspective, practical geometry and freehand drawing. But Sonny was not satisfied and, taking McNulty back to his room in Hatch Street, he announced a bolder plan. 'I was to be his naked model,' McNulty remembered, 'and, in return, he was to be mine . . . but I was adamant and Shaw's long-cherished dream of an inexpensive model was rudely shattered. I was very sorry for him at the time but I would have been more sorry for myself if I had had another attack of bronchitis.'

Sonny eventually renounced the artist's life because 'I could not draw'. He had decided instead, he told McNulty, to found a new religion.

At an early age Sonny had tried to build a fanciful world in which to forget the miseries of the real one – 'a sort of pale blue satin place,' as Broadbent describes it at the end of *John Bull's Other Island*. This dream of heaven presented itself as a small square apartment in which he was sitting with his ankles dangling, poorly dressed and filled with fears because

'I knew that I should presently be brought up for judgment by the recording angel before some awful person in the next room; and I had good private reasons for anticipating that my career would not be found up to the mark . . . on the only occasion on which I ever dreamt myself in heaven, I was glad when I woke. I also dreamt once that I was in hell; but I remember nothing about that except that two of my uncles were there and that it did not hurt. In my waking hours I thought of heaven as a part of the sky where people were dressed in white, had golden harps, did not eat or drink or learn lessons, and were wholly preoccupied in being intensely good.'

When very young he had used the Lord's Prayer as a spell against thunderstorms. But one evening on Torca Hill 'I suddenly asked myself why I went on repeating my prayer every night when, as I put it, I did not believe in it. Being thus brought to book by my intellectual conscience

I felt obliged in common honesty to refrain from superstitious practices.' By the third night, he tells us, his discomfiture vanished 'as completely as if I had been born a heathen . . . this sacrifice of the grace of God, as I had been taught it, to intellectual integrity synchronized with the dawning of moral passion in me which I have described in the first act of *Man and Superman*.'

What Sonny had done was to transfer his religious energy from day-dreaming to his actual life. He had come to recognize that, as an unlovable boy, he could expect nothing from other people. His 'moral passion' was a means of producing, independently of other people, the self-respect he lacked. Though he might not make himself into the sort of person his mother loved, he could become the sort of person she was: insensible to public opinion and a Bohemian without Bohemian vices. Before this 'I was such a ridiculously sensitive child,' he wrote, 'that almost any sort of rebuff that did not enrage me hurt my feelings and made me cry'. This new-found Stoicism reached its heretical peak in 1875 with a letter he wrote to *Public Opinion* attacking the Moody and Sankey revivalist meetings then being celebrated in Dublin. He ridiculed the vanity of their 'awakenings' which created 'highly objectionable members of society', and announced that he had given up religion.

He was by this time a committed Shelleyan. Shelley, who was to make Shaw into a momentary anarchist and lifetime vegetarian, cleared away the refuse of supernatural religions and prepared him for the planting of Creative Evolution. Sonny was a voluminous reader. Before he was ten he was saturated in Shakespeare and the Bible. But he had no access to a library and no money with which to buy books. Nobody at Hatch Street read. Lee, who made a habit of falling asleep at night over Tyndall on Sound, had been perplexed at hearing that Carlyle was an author and not Dublin's Lord Lieutenant, the Earl of Carlisle, and was puzzled by his failure to find, even in the large-print edition of Shakespeare, *The School for Scandal*. But his pupils often presented him with books – anything from Byron's works to Lord Derby's translation of Homer's *Iliad* – and to these were added pirated editions of novels brought back from America by Walter Gurly.

Sonny read all of these. He relished *The Arabian Nights*, *The Pilgrim's Progress*, *The Ancient Mariner*, *John Gilpin*, and fled from his own life into the adventures of Scott and Dumas. 'The falsifications of romance are absolutely necessary to enable people to bear or even to apprehend the terrors of life. Only the very strongest characters can look the facts of life in the face.' But he was determined to become one of this band of 'strongest characters' and started choosing his books accordingly. 'At twelve or thereabouts,' he remembered, 'I began to disapprove of highwaymen on moral grounds and to read Macaulay, George Eliot, Shakespeare, Dickens and so on in the ordinary sophisticated attitude.' He went through John Stuart Mill's autobiography, studied Lewes's *Life of Goethe* and every translation of *Faust* he could lay his hands on. 'No child should be shielded from mischief and danger, either physical or moral, in the library or out of it. Such protection leaves them incapable of resistance when they are exposed, as they finally must be, to all the mischief and danger of the world.'

Shaw's ingenious form of self-protection is best seen in his use of Dickens and Shakespeare. Beginning as a Dickensian disciple, he went on to convert Dickens, as the unconscious prophet of revolution, into an early attempt by the Life Force to produce an authentic Shavian. This sympathetic feeling sprang from the comparison he made between their early unhappiness, and the theatrical methods by which they later superimposed success upon unhappiness. Shaw wrote of his time at the Central Model School as being equivalent to 'what the blacking warehouse was to Dickens'; and his description of Dickens's outward life as 'a feat of acting from beginning to end' is a variation of his self-portrait: 'the real Shaw is the actor, the imaginary Shaw the real one.' By converting his schooldays into a Dickensian episode he gave them a sense of drama and a context in which they could be treated with humorous detachment. This was the power of comedy.

For a time he replaced his own life with the fictions of Dickens and Shakespeare. He knew some of Shakespeare's plays by heart. 'Hamlet and Falstaff were more alive to me than any living politician or even any relative.' In the reading of Shakespeare there was all life except the actual presence of the body from which, as a vehicle of emotion, Sonny had become alienated. In separating the word-music from the meaning he was to become, like Ulysses, tied to the mast and listening to the sirens. For Shaw's prejudice was optimism. To expose yourself to feel what wretches feel could lead to the 'barren pessimism' that Shakespeare himself might survive, but Shaw could not. Shakespeare's celebration of the splendours and miseries of sexual love paralysed Shaw who described it as 'folly gone mad erotically', and used all his wit and critical intelligence to reduce it to 'platitudinous fudge'. He could allow himself to respond to the passionate language only by insisting that it swept literature 'to a plane on which sense is drowned in sound'. So Sonny listened and was comforted by these sounds that filled the place of his captivity.

7

MUSIC IN DUBLIN

Without music we shall surely perish of drink, morphia, and all sorts of artificial exaggerations of the cruder delights of the senses.

'The Religion of the Pianoforte', *Fortnightly Review* (February 1894)

'My university has three colleges,' Shaw used to say. They were Dalkey Hill, the National Gallery, and Lee's Amateur Musical Society. Hatch Street was full of music. 'I was within earshot of a string of musical masterpieces,' Shaw wrote, 'which were rehearsed in our house right up to the point of the full choral & orchestral rehearsals.' Before he was fifteen he knew Beethoven's Mass in C, Mendelssohn's *Athalie*, Handel's *Messiah*, Verdi's *Trovatore*, Donizetti's *Lucrezia* and above all Mozart's *Don Giovanni* from cover to cover. After seeing Gounod's *Faust*, he decorated the walls of his room at Dalkey with watercolour heads of Mephistopheles. 'We made of Mephistopheles a familiar, almost living character,' McNulty recalled.

In music Sonny's senses came alive. He felt he was experiencing all manner of impossible emotions: the 'candour and gallant impulse of the hero, the grace and trouble of the heroine, and the extracted quintessence of their love'. But he could neither play nor read a note of music, for 'nobody dreamt of teaching me anything'. When an amateur player named Phipps offered to teach him the oboe, George Carr Shaw objected that the price of an oboe and tuition fees put it out of the question. Sonny did what he could. Presented by one of his uncles with an ancient cornet-à-piston ('absolutely the very worst and oldest cornet then in existence'), he took lessons twice a week from an English guardsman, walking to his house in Mount Pleasant Street with the obsolete instrument wrapped up in brown paper under his arm.

'My elder sister had a beautiful voice,' Shaw wrote. ' . . . it cost her no effort to sing or play anything she had once heard, or to read any music at sight.' This contrast to himself irked Shaw. Lucy sang, he wrote, 'without the slightest effort and without the slightest point, and was all the more desperately vapid because she suggested artistic gifts wasting in complacent abeyance'.

Although it was Agnes of the hazel eyes and gorgeous curtain of red hair who received most attention within Hatch Street, Lucy was the star. Her expression charmed and interested people, and she had a faint resemblance to Ellen Terry to which she drew attention by wearing

Lyceum-style clothes and feather hats. One of her admirers was Sonny's friend McNulty who later 'asked her to marry me: but she refused on the grounds that she was five years older: and that when I was forty-five she would be "a white haired old woman of fifty". So, that little romance faded.' Away from home, she was 'everybody's darling,' Shaw wrote: 'she broke many hearts, but never her own.' She longed not for a lover, but for a mother and father: a family. Not finding one, she affected a defensively low opinion of men. 'Brothers don't matter to their sisters,' Shaw commented; 'at least I didn't matter to mine: it is the stranger who is loved. The natural dislike for near relatives is ordained to save frightful complications. So presto vivace . . . and away with melancholy!'

Italian opera seemed what Lucy was heading for even before she sang Amina in Lee's production, at the Theatre Royal, Dublin, of Bellini's *La Sonnambula*. Lee had begun to organize musical evenings in the Antient Concert Room at 42½ Great Brunswick Street. These were often in aid of hospitals and would include a popular overture, some ballads and choruses, and the strengthening contribution from a regimental band. For the Shakespeare Tercentenary of 1864, having worked up a programme of Purcell and Schubert, Lee emerged at the head of his Amateur Musical Society as an orchestral conductor. He had no scholarship but, conducting from a first violin or vocal score, gave the right time to the band. 'There was practically no music in Dublin except the music he manufactured,' Shaw wrote.

'He kept giving concerts . . . and he had to provide all the singers for them. If he heard a flute mourning or a fiddle scraping in a house as he walked along the street, he knocked at the door & said "You come along & play in my orchestra." If a respectable citizen came for twelve lessons to entertain small tea parties, he presently had that amazed gentleman, scandalous in tights & tunic, singing as "il rio di Luna" to my mother's Azucena, or Alfonso to her Lucrezia, as the case might be. He coached them into doing things utterly beyond their natural powers.'

'This favourite Society,' reported the *Irish Times* on 30 May 1865, ' . . . includes many of the most distinguished amateur vocalists in the city . . . On few occasions has the Ancient Concert's Music Hall contained a larger and more fashionable attendance . . . and the concert was in every respect most judiciously carried out.' This was typical of the notices that the Amateur Musical Society received in the late 1860s. But Lee wanted to conduct oratorio festivals and operas; and his ambitions were set upon London.

*

It was probably in 1869 that Lee first began to dream of a conquest of London. He appears to have taken Bessie Shaw into his confidence. On 30 October that year Bessie and her brother made an agreement with their father whereby the son received £2,500 (equivalent to £97,500 in 1997) and Bessie £1,500 paid to her at the rate of £100 a year 'for her own sole and separate use and free from the debts control or engagements of her husband'. This was in addition to £400 settled on Agnes either through the estate of Ellen Whitcroft or Mrs Shaw's own trust of 1852. Bessie now had the maximum financial independence it was in her power to command.

Six weeks later, Lee published a book entitled *The Voice: Its Artistic Production, Development, and Preservation*. Encased between heavy dark green boards elaborately stamped in gold, with a woodcut on its cover from Maclise's *Origins of the Harp*, this volume of 130 pages of 'agreeably tinted' paper represented Lee's passport to a larger musical world. It had been ghosted, Shaw tells us, 'by a scamp of a derelict doctor whom he entertained for that purpose' – probably Malachi J. Kilgarriff, Demonstrator at the Ledwich School of Anatomy, a Catholic and one-time neighbour of Lee's in Harrington Street.

Not long after this, while still thirteen, Sonny was sent off to be interviewed by a firm of cloth merchants, Scott, Spain & Rooney, on one of Dublin's quays. His employment in the warehouse loading bales was on the point of being settled when the senior partner walked in and declared that 'I was too young, and that the work was not suitable to me. He evidently considered that my introducer, my parents, and his young partner, had been inconsiderate . . . I have not forgotten his sympathy.'

Unable to convert him from an expenditure at school to a source of income in the warehouse, they had failed to get him off their hands. He returned for another year to the Dublin English and Scientific Commercial Day School. Then, through the influence of his Uncle Frederick he was found employment as office boy in a 'leading and terribly respectable' firm of land agents, Uniacke Townshend & Co. He started work there on 26 October 1871 with an annual salary of £18 (equivalent to £875 in 1997). He was no longer Sonny to his family, but the name he most loathed: George.

Six weeks later an odd, apparently insignificant thing happened: Lee changed his name. In all press notices and legal documents he had been George J. Lee, the J. sometimes appearing as John. After 2 December 1871 the J. is replaced by a V. often lengthened to Vandeleur. This flowering of his name coincided with a fresh thrust to his musical ambitions. Since the publication of *The Voice*, Lee had been extending his Society beyond the giving of charitable concerts for the poor – increasing his advertisements in the press together with the number and glory of his patrons which, by 1871, included His Excellency the Lord Lieutenant. He had by now begun producing Italian Opera (mixed into the menu with burlesque and miscellaneous band music) at the Theatre Royal and the newly opened Gaiety Theatre – taking these productions on tour to Limerick and Cork, and making a reconnaissance himself to London.

The opposition to Lee was led by Sir Robert Prescott Stewart, an ambitious academic who had won many prizes for his glees and rose to become the most highly regarded Irish musician of his day. Stewart made his first move in the summer of 1871 – persuading the more eminent members of Lee's committee to resign. At a meeting on 11 November, following the congratulations on increased membership and money, the *Irish Times* reported that 'some misunderstanding has arisen as to members of the Society performing in English or other operas at the theatre [the Theatre Royal], and in consequence of which a considerable number of the committee refused to offer themselves for re-election'.

Lee acted immediately. He reconstituted his Society into the Amateur Musical, Operatic and Dramatic Society, replaced the various Lords and Generals with a sixteen-man Committee that included a Colonel, two Majors and ten Captains, and announced: A GRAND MILITARY, DRAMATIC AND OPERATIC PERFORMANCE WILL BE GIVEN AT THE NEW GAIETY THEATRE.

In January 1872, Lee transformed his amateurs into the New Philharmonic Society – a title that signalled his ambition to replace the almost fifty-year-old Philharmonic – and, under one title or another, led them indefatigably through concerts, oratorio festivals and truncated operas. Bessie, as his musical adjutant, was indispensable to him, arranging orchestral accompaniments, copying out band parts, composing songs ('The Parting Hour', 'The Night is Closing Round, Mother') under the *nom de plume* 'Hilda' and singing with what the *Irish Times* described as 'artistic grace and expression'. Her voice, which 'never expressed eroticism', was particularly thrilling in the interpretation of songs about bereaved lovers seeking reunion in the next world.

So successful had Lee become that on 19 September he bought the lease of Torca Cottage (which up to then he had merely rented). Though many of his concerts were advertised as being in aid of charity, only what was termed 'the Surplus' found its way to various hospitals. This usually amounted to about £25 – whereas Lee himself, so John O'Donovan has calculated, 'would have pocketed a sum not far off £200 for each concert'.

Early in 1873 Lee fulfilled one of his major ambitions by conducting the Dublin Musical Festival. 'The crowds of persons who besieged each portion of the hall soon filled to its utmost capacity, every particle of available space obtainable . . . the large doors leading into the building at the end of the Hall had to be thrown open and numbers were content to obtain standing room in the outer galleries,' reported the *Irish Times*. After congratulating Lee on his splendid results, the reviewer predicted that with patience he would surely 'reap the rewards his energies and abilities deserve'.

Eager for these rewards, Lee prominently advertised two benefit concerts of 'Amateur Italian Opera' for himself and the leader of his orchestra, the violinist R. M. Levey, in late March or early April. But Robert Prescott Stewart was already at work; with his encouragement the debenture holders availed themselves of their right to one free ticket and crowded the theatre. On 5 April, Lee and Levey published a sarcastic announcement in the *Irish Times* in which they begged 'to return their grateful thanks (?) to the many debenture holders who honoured their BENEFIT . . . by making use of their FREE admissions'.

The deciding battle was fought over the 1873 Exhibition the following month. In his opening concert, Lee, having assembled a combined chorus and orchestra of over five hundred, gave a performance of Mendelssohn's *Athalie*. Three thousand or more people attended the Concert Hall and the *Irish Times* reported that 'the five hundred voices blended most harmoniously'. Stewart was in the audience and next day in the *Daily Express* he published a scathing criticism of the performance, anonymously. Although Mr Lee had been 'heartily applauded' by his own chorus, Stewart concluded: 'Indiscriminate praise is worthless, and e'er long, heartily despised, even by those who are the objects of it.' In private Stewart was more outspoken. On page 50 of his copy of *The Annals of the Theatre Royal, Dublin*, he noted in the margin next to Lee's name: 'an impostor, who traded successfully on the vanity of amateur singers: he had a few aliases; now Mr Geo. Lee; again Mr Geo. J. Lee: and also J. Vandeleur Lee; at last he was Vandeleur Lee simply'. In a letter to Joseph Robinson, he admitted: 'I did in my time one good work in Dublin. I unmasked one arrant impostor and drove him away.'

The details of this 'unmasking' are unknown. On 26 May Lee gave his last concert in Dublin. The attendance was disappointing. At the beginning of June, having abruptly cancelled another concert, he left Dublin for ever and his place as conductor of the New Philharmonic was taken by Sir Robert Prescott Stewart.

Lee had gone to London. A few days later, on 17 June, her twenty-first wedding anniversary, Bessie Shaw followed him, taking Agnes on the boat with her, and at Hatch Street 'all musical activity ceased'.

8

MARKING TIME

> The worst sin towards our fellow creatures is not to hate them, but to be indifferent to them; thats the essence of inhumanity.
>
> *The Devil's Disciple*

'We did not realize, nor did she, that she was never coming back.' But there was much that the young George must have realized, and the later Shaw misremembered. The only suggestion that he had known of Lee's losing battle with Stewart is an acknowledgement in the 1935 Preface to *London Music* that 'Lee became the enemy of every teacher of singing in Dublin; and they reciprocated heartily'. But he gave as the reason for Lee's departure from Ireland his having reached the Dublin limit of excellence: 'Dublin in those days seemed a hopeless place for an artist; for no success counted except a London success.'

In the Shavian version, therefore, 'Lee did not depart suddenly from Dublin . . . there was nothing whatever sudden or unexpected about it.' George obviously knew that his mother had left within a fortnight of Lee but in answer to one of his biographers Shaw wrote: 'As to your question whether Lee's move to London and my mother's were simultaneous, they could not have been. Lee had to make his position in London before he could provide the musical setting for my mother and sister. But the break-up of the family was an economic necessity anyhow, because without Lee we could not afford to keep up the house.' It was towards this 'economic necessity' Shaw pointed his biographers.

'My father's business was not prospering: it was slowly dying. Then there was my eldest sister Lucy . . . She seemed to have a future as a prima donna; and this was about the only future that presented itself as an alternative to a relapse into squalid poverty, and the abandonment of the musical activity which had come to be my mother's whole life.

There was only one solution possible, granting that my mother and father could be quite as happy apart as together, to say the least. Lee was soon able to report a success: all the West End clamoring for lessons at a guinea, and his house in Park Lane a fashionable musical centre. This was clearly the opening for Lucy. It did not take very long for my mother to make up her mind. She sold up Hatch St., after a reconnaissance in London; settled my father and myself in furnished lodgings; and took a house for herself and her two daughters in Victoria Grove, Fulham Road . . . a couple of miles from Park Lane.'

As to George Carr Shaw: 'I should think it was the happiest time of his life.'

When Lee arrived in London he put up in lodgings at Ebury Street where he remained a year. A mile away, at 13 Victoria Grove, Bessie and Agnes were presently joined by Lucy. Though Bessie continued to sing and work for Lee, who was in and out of Victoria Grove very much in the old fashion, it was probably important that they lived apart. According to McNulty, George Carr Shaw initiated court proceedings citing Lee 'not as a criminal offender against the sacredness of Holy Matrimony but rather as an object of jealousy to the Petitioner'. Their 'reconnaissance', as Shaw calls it, lasted nine months during which time they were paying the rent for two separate premises in addition to the rent at Hatch Street which must partly invalidate the argument of 'economic necessity'. It was not until the beginning of March 1874 that Bessie returned to Dublin to sell up the furniture in Hatch Street, raise what money she could, and move her husband and son into rooms at 61 Harcourt Street. Then for the last time she left Dublin with her two daughters and returned to London. Perhaps because of some out-of-court arrangement with George Carr Shaw who agreed to pay her one pound a week, she did not live at the same address as Lee. In April he was to cut his last connection with Ireland by selling the lease of Torca Cottage to a musical colleague, Julian Marshall, from whom he afterwards rented 13 Park Lane in London.

The departure of his mother and Lee was a tragedy for young George. From the pictures in the National Gallery, the hills and bays of Dalkey and Killiney, the music that filled Hatch Street he had woven 'a sort of heaven which made the material squalor of my existence as nothing'. Shaw represents this daydream world as having been extinguished when he was ten, but the evidence suggests that, especially in his ambitions to be an artist or musician, they persisted until his mother finally left him at the age of sixteen. Instead of an artist, he was a clerk; he would enjoy no more summers at Torca; and 'I heard no more music'.

But his mother had not sold the piano. So he bought a technical handbook and taught himself the alphabet of musical notation. He learnt the keyboard from a diagram; then he got out his mother's vocal score of *Don Giovanni* and arranged his fingers on the notes of the first chord. This took ten minutes, 'but when it sounded right at last, it was worth all the trouble it cost'. What he suffered, 'what everybody in the house suffered, whilst I struggled on . . . will never be told'. But he acquired what he wanted: 'the power to take a vocal score and learn its contents as if I had heard it rehearsed by my mother and her colleagues'. From this practice and his reading of textbooks, he also mastered the technical knowledge he would need to become a music critic in London. It was a wonderful example of the advantages of deprivation.

His desk and cash box at the 'highly exclusive gentlemanly estate office' gave him 'the habit of daily work'. For fifteen months, during which his salary was increased from £18 to £24, he filed and manufactured copies of the firm's business letters, kept a postage account, bought penny rolls for the staff's lunch and combined the duties of office with errand boy. In February 1873, after the cashier absconded, George was employed as a substitute. The work gave him no difficulty. 'I, who never knew how much money I had of my own (except when the figure was zero), proved a model of accuracy as to the money of others.' His salary doubled to £48. He bought himself a tailed coat, remodelled his sloped and straggled handwriting into an imitation of his predecessor's compact script and 'in short, I made good in spite of myself'.

He became accustomed to handling large sums of money, and to collecting weekly rents by tram each Tuesday, tiny sums from slum dwellers in Terenure – an experience he had not forgotten when he came to write *Widowers' Houses.* But 'my heart was not in the thing'. He was never uncivil, never happy. He felt orphaned. Thirty-five years later he poured out his bitterness through the nameless clerk in *Misalliance* who seeks to avenge his mother's shame of bearing him out of wedlock:

'I spend my days from nine to six – nine hours of daylight and fresh air – in a stuffy little den counting another man's money . . . I enter and enter, and add and add, and take money and give change, and fill cheques and stamp receipts; and not a penny of that money is my own: not one of those transactions has the smallest interest for me . . . Of all the damnable waste of human life that ever was invented, clerking is the very worst.'

Uniacke Townshend 'was saturated with class feeling which I loathed'. The office was overstaffed with gentleman apprentices, mostly university men, who had paid large premiums for the privilege of learning a genteel profession and who were called Mister while George was plain Shaw. It was his involuntary feeling of inferiority among these colleagues that drove him to excel.

Art was the great solvent of bigotries and snobberies. George found he was most popular with the apprentices in his role as *maestro di cappella.* In his imagination he had become a Lee-like presence, replacing Townshend, and providing the young men there with operatic tuition as value for their premiums. 'I recall one occasion,' he wrote, 'when an apprentice, perched on the washstand with his face shewing above the screen . . . sang *Ah, che la morte* so passionately that he was unconscious of the sudden entry of the senior partner, Charles Uniacke Townshend, who stared stupended at the bleating countenance above the screen, and finally fled upstairs, completely beaten by the situation.' This represented a victory for George over Townshend whom, McNulty recalled, he disliked 'chiefly because he put an "H" in his name, flagrant evidence, in Shaw's opinion, of middle class snobbery'. Townshend was 'a pillar of the Church, of the Royal Dublin Society, and of everything else pillarable in Dublin'.

In his need for someone to look up to and learn from he had fastened at Harcourt Street on another Superman. Chichester Bell took the place of Lee in George's life. He was a far more sophisticated man: physician, chemist, amateur boxer and accomplished pianist. Where other boys collected stamps or trailed girls, George lusted after information. With Bell, who was responsible for converting him to Wagner, George studied everything from physics to pathology, universal alphabets and 'Visible Speech', and completed his education in Ireland.

He saw almost no one else, for he was intensely shy. 'I had no love affairs,' he confessed to Frank Harris. Late in 1877 Shaw came across a letter he had written to Agnes, describing what he was to call 'The Calypso Infatuation', and referring to a girl he had met in 1871. He does not seem to have fallen in love with her until the beginning of May 1875 when he was almost nineteen. A retrospective diary note he made under the heading 'The Lxxx [Love] Episode', in which he records burning his letter to Agnes two days after finding it, ends with 'The Catastrophe, or the indiscretion of No. 2', and is dated at 'about the beginning of August'. He celebrated this aborted romance with a hymn to stupidity. The 'indiscretion of No. 2' may have been her scheme to engage him to a sister after her own marriage to another man, for the poem tells that 'she succumbed to the cruel old fashion' and went to live with her husband not far from Torca Cottage. The poem ends with a tribute to the spell she had laid on him.

> I thought her of women the rarest
>   With strange power to seduce and alarm
> One beside whose black tresses the fairest
>   Seemed barren of charm . . .
> Then farewell, oh bewitching Calypso
>   Thou didst shake my philosophy well
> But believe me, the next time I trip so
>   No poem shall tell.

He felt most when he was rejected, because that was the only love he knew. But he recoiled from searching for happiness in others because their rejection of him carried behind it the annihilating force of his mother's initial rejection.

Work became his mistress. He kept no other company. McNulty, who was employed by a bank, had been sent to Newry. 'Shaw wrote to me every day. Otherwise I was absolutely alone.' The written word was threaded into their friendship. At school some of their favourite reading had been a boys' paper called *Young Men of Great Britain*. McNulty recalled that 'it was meat and drink to us and almost as vital to our existence as the air. We awaited each weekly instalment with feverish impatience.' Here Shaw sent a dramatic short story, involving piracy and highway robbery, that had as its main character a wicked baritone with a gun. He also wrote, in September 1868, asking a question, to which the answer was: 'Write to Mr Lacey, theatrical publisher, Strand, London W. C.' A neighbour remembered him sitting alone 'absorbed in the construction of a toy theatre'. He had a play (perhaps part of *Henry VI*) for this theatre about the fifteenth-century Irish rebel Jack Cade, for which he would cut out scenes and characters bought at a shop opposite the Queen's Theatre. Among his own early works was a gory verse drama, 'Strawberrinos: or, the Haunted Winebin', full of extravagant adventures in which our hero Strawberrinos is constantly bested by a Mephistophelean demon.

At the Theatre Royal in Dublin he had been used to seeing pantomimes, farces and melodramas involving villainous disguises and the convolutions of dense intrigue. In 1870 the great touring actor, Barry Sullivan, had arrived. George joined the crowds, emerging from the theatre with 'all my front buttons down the middle of my back'. Of all the travelling stars, Sullivan seemed to him incomparably the grandest. A man of gigantic personality, he was the last in a dynasty of rhetorical and hyperbolical actors that had begun with Burbage.

'His stage fights in Richard III and Macbeth appealed irresistibly to a boy spectator like myself: I remember one delightful evening when two inches of Macbeth's sword, a special fighting sword carried in that scene only, broke off and whizzed over the heads of the cowering pit (there were no stalls then) to bury itself deep in the front of the dress circle after giving those who sat near its trajectory more of a thrill than they had bargained for. Barry Sullivan was a tall powerful man with a cultivated resonant voice: his stage walk was the perfection of grace and dignity; and his lightning swiftness of action, as when in the last scene of Hamlet he shot up the stage and stabbed the king four times before you could wink, all provided a physical exhibition which attracted audiences quite independently of the play . . .'

This was not a spectacle to George, but an experience. He could feel his blood quickening during the performance, his mind beating, hurrying. This was vicarious living at its most vigorous, where 'existence touches you delicately to the very heart, and where mysteriously thrilling people, secretly known to you in dreams of your childhood, enact a life in which terrors are as fascinating as delights; so that ghosts and death, agony and sin, became, like love and victory, phases of an unaccountable ecstasy'. He forgot loneliness in this palace of dreams. When he came to write plays himself, he instinctively went back to the grand manner and heroic stage business he had seen from the pit of the Theatre Royal.

In 1874 George spent his summer holidays at Newry with his friend McNulty. McNulty had developed what he called 'a morbid condition of nerves'. He was so sensitive to the earth's rotation that he could not trust himself to lie down on a sofa without falling off. 'I fancied I could see the sap circulating in plants and trees,' he wrote. George's scepticism, though not always comfortable, helped to reduce this tension. On their second day the two of them had their photographs taken and they talked of the inevitability of fame. Every evening they would write something different – 'a short story, a comedy, a tragedy, a burlesque and so forth,' McNulty remembered, 'and the real joy of the event lay in reading and forcefully criticizing each other's work. This series we called: "The Newry Nights' Entertainment".'

The following year McNulty was transferred back to Dublin and the two of them saw a good deal of each other. McNulty would call round at Harcourt Street to stagger through duets on the grand piano. George, he observed, 'took little or no notice of his father who still spent his evenings poring miserably over his account books'. Otherwise, his glasses low on his nose, his head tilted back, he browsed before a newspaper or smoked his one clay pipe a day, breaking it when he had finished and throwing the fragments in the grate: 'a lonely, sad little man,' McNulty concluded.

George had resolved never to allow the diffidence he shared with his father to cripple him. He looked to his father as a warning; otherwise, like Lee, he looked to London.

His opportunity came early in 1876. Agnes, suffering from consumption, had been taken down to Balmoral House, a sanatorium on the Isle of Wight. Though he was now getting £84 a year at Uniacke Townshend, George felt more than ever unsatisfied there. One of his colleagues, an old book-keeper, had confided that he 'suffered so much from cold feet that his life was miserable,' Shaw recorded. 'I, full of the fantastic mischievousness of youth, told him that if he would keep his feet in ice-cold water every morning when he got up for two or three minutes, he would be completely cured.' Shortly afterwards the man died. To his horror George was then offered his job. Charles Townshend wanted to install a relative as cashier and boot George upstairs to make room for him. But George refused and had to be moved, with an increased salary, to the position of general clerk. On 29 February 1876 he gave a month's notice. 'My reason is, that I object to receive a salary for which I give no adequate value,' he wrote. 'Not having enough to do, it follows that the little I have is not well done. When I ceased to act as Cashier I anticipated this, and have since become satisfied that I was right.'

This letter shows the paradoxical device of his new authority. It has the regretful air of an employer dismissing an employee. Its succinct superiority must have been galling. But anxious not to offend George's Uncle Frederick at the Valuation Office, Charles Townshend offered him his job back as cashier. George thanked him – however 'I prefer to discontinue my services'.

In retrospect G.B.S. applied a blinding Shavian polish to his arrival in England. Armed with the English language he proposed to advance on London and become 'a professional man of genius'. 'When I left Dublin I left (a few private friendships apart) no society that did not disgust me,' he wrote. 'To this day my sentimental regard for Ireland does not include the capital. I am not enamored of failure, of poverty, of obscurity, and of the ostracism and contempt which these imply; and these were all that Dublin offered to the enormity of my unconscious ambition.'

'Like Hamlet I lack ambition and its push,' he wrote. Yet it was not ambition he lacked: it was (like Hamlet) advancement. He insisted that he never struggled, but was pushed slowly up by the force of his ability. 'It is not possible to escape from the inexorable obligation to succeed on your own merits,' he confessed. He did not cross the Irish Sea for love of the English. 'Emigration was practically compulsory,' he told St John Ervine.

Agnes died of phthisis on 27 March. Between the two opportunities offered by her death and that of the book-keeper, George had never hesitated. Looking back on his twenty years in Ireland he summed up: 'My home in Dublin was a torture and my school was a prison and I had to go through a treadmill of an office.'

He packed a carpet bag, boarded the North Wall boat and arrived in London. It was a fine spring day and he solemnly drove in a 'growler' from Euston to Victoria Grove. Shortly afterwards he travelled down to Ventnor on the Isle of Wight following Agnes's funeral there. The family selected a headstone and an epitaph to be cut on it: 'TO BE WITH CHRIST WHICH IS FAR BETTER' – from a passage in Paul's Epistle to the Philippians where Paul compares the folly of living with the wisdom of dying. Nearly sixty years later Shaw was to write to Margaret Mackail, exposing what he felt about his own childhood: 'as the world is not at present fit for children to live in why not give the little invalids a gorgeous party, and when they have eaten and danced themselves to sleep, turn on the gas and let them all wake up in heaven?'

TWO

I

THE GHOSTING OF VANDELEUR LEE

> I am afraid you will find London a drearily slow place to make a beginning in. Every opening is an accident; and waiting for accidents is rather discouraging.
>
> Shaw to Rhoda Halkett (14 August 1894)

'Unoccupied': this was the word Shaw used to describe his first summer in London. He gave everyone to understand that 'on no account will I enter an office again'. But by September, he was submitting to a crammer's course for admission to the Civil Service. His mother and Lucy breathed out with relief – then in with alarm as, less than two months later, he gave up this 'tutelage of a grinder' and accepted the occupation of Lee's amanuensis.

Lee's credit with the Shaws had fallen dramatically since they came to London. It appears that, having grown so infatuated that 'he wanted to marry her', Lee was bullying Lucy into acting as the principal singer in a musical society he had started called the Troubadours. Lucy intensely disliked working under Lee's direction, and had written to her brother telling him of a huge rumpus. George, at his most paternal, replied: 'As to Lee, I would decline to listen to him. We all know what his tirades are worth, and I think his coming to Victoria Grove and launching out at you as he did, simply outrageous.' Matters between the pair deteriorated and, before George arrived in London, Lucy wrote to explain that 'Lee and I are bitter enemies now; we are frostily civil to each other's faces, and horribly abusive behind backs'.

Lee was no writer, 'and when he was offered an appointment as musical critic to a paper called *The Hornet* . . . in consideration of his praising the neighbourhood in the newspapers, I had the job of writing the criticisms and the articles,' Shaw explained. 'It was to some extent on my account that he undertook such pretences of authorship.'

Shaw provided *The Hornet* with careful criticism and careful jokes that do not carry the generosity of the mature G.B.S. The concert hall becomes a blackboard on which he scrupulously chalks up his remarks. If his writing is a little priggish, it still achieves wonderful confidence for someone aged twenty-one. Carl Rosa's first violin is accused of having played flat 'from beginning to end'; Herr Behrens is spotted frequently substituting 'semiquaver passages for the triplets' and betraying his ignorance of English by selecting the middle of a phrase as a suitable opportunity to take breath. Shaw castigates the timidity of other music critics twice or three times his age who 'can only judge one performance by reference to another'.

Although there is only a hint of G.B.S. in these apprentice buzzings, some Shavian notes are starting to sound towards the end of his *Hornet* life. Signor Rota is complimented as 'a master of the art of shouting'; and Madame Goddard is recorded as fascinating her hearers 'with a strikingly unpleasant imitation of a bagpipes'. In place of military drum and cymbals, Shaw advises the management of Her Majesty's 'to employ a stage carpenter to bang the orchestra door at a pre-arranged signal'. And after a performance of Donizetti's *Lucia* he deplored the Master of Ravenswood's habit of flinging his cloak and hat on the ground as 'ridiculous in the first act, impolite in the second, and only justified by the prospect of suicide in the third'.

Shaw would hand Lee these criticisms and Lee would hand him the fees, 'contenting himself with the consciousness of doing generously by a young and forlorn literary adventurer, and with the honor and glory accruing from the reputed authorship of my articles'. In later years G.B.S. exaggerated the 'vulgarities, follies, and ineptitudes' of these pieces for *The Hornet*. 'I did not know even enough to understand that what was torturing me was the guilt and shame which attend ignorance and incompetence.' But his shame proceeded less from their demerits than from the deception of ghost writing. He had arrived in London determined never to act on second-hand principles or submit to external circumstances. But in his first encounter he found himself in a conspiracy that formed part of the polite fraud he was attempting to demolish. It felt like a step back into cowardice.

By May 1877 the editor of *The Hornet* believed he had uncovered the truth. 'I have frequently rec'd "copy" palpably not your style,' he complained to Lee, 'but that in composition, idea and writing of a Lady.' By September, all was over. 'I must tell you candidly that *our* agreement is not being kept by you,' the editor told Lee. 'I stipulated for *your* production and not that of a Substitute. I can't insert the class of writing I have rec'd the last 2 weeks . . . Please send word to your man to send no more copy.' Shaw's last sting was delivered on 26 September 1877 when Lee was in Scotland. Two years later he reviewed the episode that had made him so miserable: 'I threw up my studies, and set to work to reform the musical profession. At the end of a year my friend [Lee] was one of the most unpopular men in London, the paper was getting into difficulties, and complications were arising from the proprietor's doubts as to a critic who was not only very severe, but capable of being in two places at the same time.'

*

Lee's faltering career, Shaw believed, 'disguised as it was by a few years of fashionable success, was due wholly to the social conditions which compelled him to be a humbug or to starve'. In order to keep going, he advertised himself as being able to make fashionable ladies sing like Patti in twelve lessons. To Bessie, Lee had been 'the sole apostle of The Method: the only true and perfect method of singing: the method that had made her a singer and preserved the purity of her voice in defiance of time'. She knew that the Method required two years of patient practice. The 'moment she found that he had abandoned "the method",' Shaw wrote, ' . . . she gave him up'.

Shaw gave as the particular cause for breaking with Lee, a sexual sentimentality which, ripening in London, had turned towards Lucy. 'My sister, to whom this new attitude was as odious as it was surprising, immediately dropped him completely . . . He came no more to our house; and as far as I can recollect neither my mother nor my sister ever saw him again.'

To G.B.S., this sexual sentimentality and the economic perversion of his musical talent were symptoms of the same disease. He invented a new Lee, an English Hyde who emerged from the Irish Jekyll. Lee was, he tells us, 'no longer the same man'. He was unrecognizable. 'G. J. Lee, with the black whiskers and the clean shaven resolute lip and chin, became Vandeleur Lee, whiskerless, but with a waxed and pointed moustache and an obsequious attitude.' So the Dublin genius collapses into a London humbug. Lee is the victim of a pantomime with Capitalism its bad fairy.

Lucy quickly escaped. She turned professional in 1879 and five years later joined the Carl Rosa Opera Company. For her mother, now nearing fifty, it was less easy. Though she 'despised' Lee, it is impossible to know in what measure her contempt was emotional, financial or moral. Her son makes it exclusively a matter of musical principle. But the language he uses carries other suggestions. 'The result was almost a worse disillusion than her marriage . . . that Lee should be unfaithful! unfaithful to the Method! . . . with all the virtue gone out of him: this was the end of all things; and she never forgave it.'

A symbol of Lee's days of vanity in London was his smart Park Lane house. Number 13 Park Lane lay at the less fashionable end of a street 'sacred to peers and millionaires'. It was half a house (part of number 14) and, because of a murder committed there two years before Lee moved in, less expensive than Shaw imagined. Here, Lee organized a few charity concerts and performances of amateur opera, and it was at one of these that the *Punch* cartoonist George du Maurier, making some sketches of the Shaws and what G.B.S. was to describe as their 'damaged Svengali', conceived his idea for *Trilby*. When, in 1895, du Maurier's novel was adapted for the stage, Shaw was to write:

'Svengali is *not* a villain, but only a poor egotistical wretch who provokes people to pull his nose . . . Imagine, above all, Svengali taken seriously at his own foolish valuation, blazed upon with limelights, spreading himself intolerably over the whole play with nothing fresh to add to the first five minutes of him – Svengali defying heaven, declaring that henceforth he is his own God, and then tumbling down in a paroxysm of heart disease (the blasphemer rebuked, you see), and having to be revived by draughts of brandy . . . surely even the public would just as soon – nay, rather – have the original Svengali, the luckless artist-cad (a very deplorable type of cad, whom Mr du Maurier has hit off to the life).'

Shaw was to try his own hand at creating such a figure in *The Doctor's Dilemma*.

By the time Shaw finished with *The Hornet*, his mother had left Park Lane and, appropriating 'the Method' (much as Eliza Doolittle threatens to make off with Professor Higgins's speech methods), set herself up as a private singing teacher. But Shaw 'remained on friendly terms' with Lee, playing the piano at some of his rehearsals and saving him the cost of a professional accompanist. Once or twice he even sang. Those smart people who had taken Lee up on his arrival in London had moved on to newer sensations, and his later recruits were less exalted. Shaw, who had begun by playing Mozart, ended by rehearsing the Solicitor in Gilbert and Sullivan's *Patience*.

Lee continued living with 'the young lady who had rescued him from entire loneliness', renting his rooms to bachelors and the music chamber for dubious supper parties. He kept in touch with Shaw, offering him odd jobs as *répétiteur* for the occasional lady who wished 'to try over her songs' and asking him to draw up a Prospectus on 'How to Cure Clergyman's Sore Throat'. On the evening of 27 November 1886, while putting his arm through the sleeve of his nightshirt, he dropped dead.

On the morning of the inquest, three days later, one of Lee's musical group told Lucy the news and she passed it on to her brother. Next day, 1 December, he called at 13 Park Lane to verify the report. 'Heard from servant,' he noted in his diary, 'that he was found dead of heart disease on Sunday morning. Went back home to tell Mother . . .' At the inquest on

30 November the jury returned a verdict of death by natural causes. Shaw, who had not gone to this inquest, adds that it 'revealed the fact that his brain was diseased and had been so for a long time'. Neither the newspaper reports nor the death certificate ('Angina Pectoris. Found dead on floor') corroborate this statement which nevertheless enabled Shaw to comfort himself that the mischief converting Lee from Jekyll to Hyde had begun its work years before. 'I was glad to learn that his decay was pathological as well as ecological,' he concluded, 'and that the old efficient and honest Lee had been real after all.'

2

EXPERIMENTS WITH THE NOVEL

> What inexpensive pleasure can be greater than that of strolling through London of an evening, and reconstructing it in imagination? . . . you make Notting Hill low and exalt Maida-vale by carting the one to the other . . . you extend the embankment from Blackfriars to the Tower as an eligible nocturnal promenade . . . you build an underground London in the bowels of the metropolis, and an overhead London piercing the fog curtain above on viaducts, with another and another atop of these, until you have piled up, six cities deep, to Alpine altitudes with a different climate at each level . . . For purposes of transit you will devise a system of pneumatic tubes, through which passengers, previously treated by experienced dentists with nitrous oxide, can be blown from Kensington to Mile-end in a breath . . . What a London that would be!
>
> 'Ideal London', *Pall Mall Gazette* (5 October 1886)

Having escaped from Dublin, Shaw expected to find things ordered differently in London. Oscar Wilde who, though he had visited London before, came to live there two years later, was to inhale an air 'full of the heavy odour of roses . . . the heavy scent of the lilac, or the more delectable perfume of the pink flowering thorn'. The parks and gardens, squares and palisades sprouted their green between the seasoned brick and wedding-cake stucco of the West End where Wilde sauntered. But Wilde had come from respectable Merrion Square via Oxford to Mayfair and did not see the ill-smelling London Shaw was getting to know – a London of primitive streets with clinging red mud, miserably treated animals, and a sullen population storming the pubs at nightfall. Below the prim pattern of bourgeois life that Wilde was so delightfully to shock lay a vast reservoir of squalor and brutality. Drury Lane, the charming ambience of *Pygma-*

lion, was a derelict area until 1900, the territory of men and women in tatters, who crawled the streets like animals.

'Shelley . . . described Hell as "a city much like London". Dickens, who knew London, depicted it as full of strange monsters, Merdles, Veneerings, Finches of the Grove, Barnacles, Marshalseas indigenous to the Borough but cropping up sporadically among the monuments of Rome and Venice: all dreadfully answering to things that we know to be there, and yet cannot believe in without confusion and terror. How pleasant it is to shrink back to the genial Thackeray, who knew comparatively nothing about London, but just saw the fun of the little sets of ideas current in Russell and Bryanston-squares, Pall-mall, Fleet-street, and the art academies in Newman-street.'

The economics of London were to turn Shaw into a socialist. No new planning, he believed, could be achieved without a change of attitude in the country. 'The problem, unfortunately, is not one of realignment and patent dwellings,' he wrote in 1886:

'It is one of the development of individual greed into civic spirit; of the extension of the *laissez-faire* principle to public as well as private enterprise; of bringing all the citizens to a common date in civilization instead of maintaining a savage class, a mediaeval class, a renaissance class, and an Augustan class, with a few nineteenth-century superior persons to fix high-water mark . . . we must be content with the . . . periodical washing of the Albert Memorial . . . until London belongs to, and is governed by, the people who use it.'

*

Number 13 Victoria Grove stood on the east side of a cul-de-sac off the Brompton Road. The houses were semi-detached, with tiny gardens, and they occupied, along with those in a number of parallel groves, a countrified area, still with plenty of orchard and market garden, between Fulham and Putney. Here, for two years after *The Hornet*, Shaw did little but write short stories, literary reviews, articles, essays. It was 'mere brute practice with the pen . . . as a laborer digs or a carpenter planes'.

By February 1878 he was at work on a profane Passion Play in blank verse 'with the mother of the hero represented as a termagant'. Judas and Jesus in this play represent two sides of Shaw. Judas is

a man unblinded
And trained to shun the snare of self delusion

who sees in his corrupt surroundings a 'beastly world'. Jesus, who looks towards an invisible future, embodies hope. In the combination of the two, Shaw argues, the observer and the man of imagination, we reach reality. Judas's advice to the young Jesus is the lesson Shaw himself was endeavouring to master:

> Then must thou
> Learn to stand absolutely by thyself,
> Leaning on nothing, satisfied that thou
> Can'st nothing know, responsible to nothing,
> Fearing no power and being within thyself
> A little independent universe.

After forty-nine pages – 1,260 lines – the play breaks off in the second scene of Act II. Across one abandoned passage he wrote: 'Vile Stuff.' Fifty-five years later, in his Preface to *On the Rocks*, he explained that a modern Passion Play was impossible because 'the trial of a dumb prisoner, at which the judge who puts the crucial question to him remains unanswered, cannot be dramatized unless the judge is to be the hero of the play . . . If ever there was a full dress debate for the forensic championship to be looked forward to with excited confidence by the disciples of the challenged expert it was his trial of Christ. Yet their champion put up no fight.'

Also finished in February 1878 was *My Dear Dorothea*, a didactic pamphlet modelled on George Augustus Sala's squib *Lady Chesterfield's Letters to Her Daughter*, which Shaw had read the previous year. He subtitled his work: 'A Practical System of Moral Education for Females Embodied in a Letter to a Young Person of that Sex'. Much of the advice (including a warning against taking advice) would later become familiar furniture of Shavian philosophy: never be peevishly self-sacrificing; arm yourself with politeness which is a mark of superiority over unpleasant people; cultivate hypocrisy with others for kindness' sake, but never with yourself; read anything except what bores you; leave religion alone until you've grown up; get into mischief, but do not look for pity. Finally: 'Always strive to find out what to do by thinking, without asking anybody.'

The most closely autobiographical passages refer to Dorothea's mother:

'If your mother is always kind to you, love her more than you love anything except your doll . . . If you had indeed such a mother, my dear Dorothea, you would not need my advice at all. But I must not forget how seldom little girls have such guardians; and I will therefore take it for granted that your mother . . . thinks of you only as a troublesome and inquisitive little creature . . .

For such a parent, you must be particularly careful not to form any warm affection. Be very friendly with her, because you are in the same house as she, and it is unpleasant to live with one whom you dislike. If you have any griefs, do not tell her of them. Keep them to yourself if possible . . . You will soon be sent to school, and so get rid of her.'

Shaw's advice was a prescription against suffering. 'It is a most illuminating and sorrowful self-portrait,' Stevie Smith was to write, ' . . . because it shows that Shaw was as proud as the devil and put pride in the place of love. And why should a bright creature of such mercurial wits and fighting frenzies so limit himself if not for fear? . . . every now and then the heart limps in, but he is ashamed of it and begins to bluster.'

In March 1879 he began a novel called, 'with merciless fitness', *Immaturity.* 'As I could not afford a typewriter nor a secretary, I had to write directly and legibly for the printer with my own hand.' Five novels and part of a sixth he got through in this way. His handwriting, neat and spindly, sloping slightly backwards, is that of the chief cashier of Uniacke Townshend. He condemned himself to a daily reckoning of five pages – and so scrupulously that if his fifth page ended in the middle of a sentence he did not finish it until the next day. 'I have drudged year after year until I have very little patience left for anything but work,' says one of the characters, ' . . . it is the holding on day after day only a hair's breadth from failure.'

Immaturity was his 'first attempt at a big book'. The character of Robert Smith is Shaw himself at twenty with 'the culture that is given by loneliness and literature'. Unable to make contact with other people, Smith polishes his isolation to a virtue. His infatuation with a ballet dancer, releasing energy to be used for work, illustrates Shaw's susceptibility to women and his determination not to let them occupy his mind. Mlle Bernadina de Sangallo, as she is called in this first draft, takes her dream-like existence from Ermina Pertoldi, a dancer whom Shaw used to see at the Alhambra and who filled his night thoughts.

Like Smith, Shaw sometimes 'relapsed into that painful yearning which men cherish gloomily at eighteen, and systematically stave off as a nuisance . . . in later years'. Work, with which Shaw began to stave off this nuisance, becomes the hero of *Immaturity.* 'What is there to live for but work?' asks Cyril Scott, an artist modelled on the landscape painter Cyril Lawson. 'Everything else ends in disappointment. It's the only thing that you never get tired of, and that always comes to good.'

Shaw allows another worthy end: marriage. 'There is no gratification which a woman can afford you, that will not be sweeter when that woman is not your wife, except the possession of boys and girls to continue the record when you are in your coffin. Therefore marry the woman who will bring you the finest children, and who will be the best mother to them; and you will never find out that you might have done better elsewhere.'

Since hereditary factors are incalculable, Shaw places his bet on sexual instinct. In the debate he sets up between common sense and romance, it is common sense that is seen to lack courage, and romance, arguing against 'the folly of prudent marriages', that triumphs. 'The chief objection to fictitious romance,' he writes elsewhere in *Immaturity*, 'is that it is seldom so romantic as the truth.'

Smith is repeatedly accused, as Shaw was to be, of matter-of-factness. 'You are really very matter-of-fact, Mr Smith. You rub the gloss off everything.' It is this artificial gloss, reflected by the fashionable poet Hawkshaw (a sort of Shaw gone wrong who owes something to Oscar Wilde) that he dislikes. 'Matter-of-fact people are a great nuisance,' Smith concedes, 'and always will be, so long as they are in the minority.' The implication is that the days of Hawkshaw are numbered. He has not strength enough to resist the applause of a society that is, below its glossy surface, uncaring and uncomprehending. It is society that is the villain of the novel.

In this 'book of a raw youth', there is the outline of a Shaw who existed before his conversion into the fantastic personality of G.B.S. Like Hawkshaw, he was to take on a public gloss. But whereas Hawkshaw acquired his gloss from the caressing of society, the brilliant Shavian creature that emerged and flew away from the chrysalis of Smith wanted to outshine society and lead us to another place ruled over by 'one of my most successful fictions'. Like the 'Vandeleur Lee' who developed from G. J. Lee, 'G.B.S.' was a manufactured identity: not a victim of capitalist society – a weapon to be used against it.

*

Shaw finished *Immaturity* on 28 September 1879 and completed his revisions six weeks later. It was now a question, in the words of his father, of 'thrusting it down the throats of some of the publishers and so getting it into the hands of the mob'. On 7 November Shaw called on Hurst & Blackett and the following day sent them the manuscript. Next week they declined it.

Of his disappointment he showed nothing. At Victoria Grove he was reproached with laziness – his father in Dublin adding to the chorus and, to George's exasperation, obtaining a testimonial from Uniacke Townshend. Now and then he had gone half-heartedly out to look for work –

for example, after an introduction by the poet Richard Hengist Horne, to the Imperial Bank at South Kensington. 'Your son must *not* talk about religion or give his views thereon,' Horne warned Mrs Shaw, '& he must make up his mind to work & do what he is told – if not there is no use his calling.' In such circumstances it was not difficult to avoid employment. But as the pressure from his family tightened he was driven to more elaborate means of escape, and eventually these failed him. From his cousin Mrs Cashel Hoey he had received an introduction to the manager of the Edison Telephone Company, Arnold White, to whom on 5 October 1879, while still revising *Immaturity*, he wrote the sort of devastatingly honest letter he could usually rely on to extricate himself:

'In the last two years I have not filled any post, nor have I been doing anything specially calculated to qualify me for a business one . . .

My only reason for seeking commercial employment is a pecuniary one. I know how to wait for success in literature, but I do not know how to live on air in the interim. My family are in difficulties . . . However, I should be loth to press you for a place in which I might not be the right man.'

Arnold White, who liked Shaw, was not put off by this letter and offered him employment in the Way-Leave Department of the Edison Telephone Company. Shaw began working there on 14 November, immediately following the rejection of *Immaturity*. After six weeks he had earned two shillings and sixpence, and forfeited by way of expenses two guineas, having agreed to be paid on a commission basis. His job was to persuade people in the East End of London to allow insulators, poles and derricks to bristle about their roofs and gardens. 'I liked the exploration involved,' he remembered, 'but my shyness made the business of calling on strangers frightfully uncongenial . . . the impatient rebuffs I had to endure [were] . . . ridiculously painful to me.'

The truth appeared to be that he could not afford regular employment: 'I am under an absolute necessity to discontinue my services forthwith,' he told the head of his department. As a result of this threatened resignation he was given a basic wage of £48 (equivalent to £2,080 in 1997) a year and, two months later, promoted at a salary of £80, to be head of the department and 'organize the work of more thick-skinned adventurers instead of doing it myself'. He was now stationed in one of the basement offices of a building in Queen Victoria Street, loud with Americans who all adored Mr Edison, execrated his rival Mr Bell, worked with a terrible energy out of all proportion to the results achieved, and dreamed emotionally of telephone transmitters patented to their own formula.

Shaw waited patiently for his novel to rescue him. But *Immaturity* was rejected by every British and American publisher to whom he sent it. Sampson Low begged to be spared the pleasure of reading it. 'No,' wrote George Meredith for Chapman & Hall; 'unattractive', decided John Morley at Macmillan. *Immaturity* was 'a museum specimen of the Victorian novel,' Shaw later decided, which had been written at the wrong time.

'The Education Act of 1871 was producing readers who had never before bought books . . . and publishers were finding that these people wanted not George Eliot and the excessively literary novice Bernard Shaw, but such crude tales of impossible adventures published in penny numbers only for schoolboys. The success of Stevenson's *Treasure Island* and Jekyll and Hyde fairy tale, forced this change on the attention of the publishers; and I, as a belated intellectual, went under completely . . . Had I understood this situation at the time I should have been a happier novice instead of an apparently hopeless failure.'

3

SOME FURTHER EXPERIMENTS

> The progress of the world depends on the people who refuse to accept facts and insist on the satisfaction of their instincts.
>
> *Back to Methuselah*

Something was wrong with the Edison telephone: it 'bellowed your most private communications all over the house instead of whispering them with some sort of discretion,' Shaw wrote. 'This was not what the British stockbroker wanted . . .' On 5 June 1880 the Company amalgamated with the Bell Telephone Company and gave its employees one month's notice. Shaw, turning down an invitation to apply for a job with the new United Telephone Company of London, re-entered the literary world.

Immaturity was to lie 'dumb and forgotten' for fifty years; the *Passion Play* and *My Dear Dorothea* remained unpublished during Shaw's life. Of more than a dozen other stories and articles he had written in 1879 on 'subjects ranging from orchestral conducting to oakum picking' most were rejected, some were lost. The two that were eventually published earned him fifteen shillings. In the summer of 1880 he approached John Morley, the new editor of the *Pall Mall Gazette*, enclosing some examples of his work and asking whether he might make a music or theatre critic. 'I cannot hesitate to say,' Morley answered, 'that in my opinion you would do well to get out of journalism.' Describing this period later on, G.B.S. wrote:

'I did not throw myself into the struggle for life: I threw my mother into it. I was not a staff to my father's old age: I hung on to his coat tails . . . People wondered at my heartlessness . . . My mother worked for my living instead of preaching that it was my duty to work for hers: therefore take off your hat to her, and blush.'

Despite the failure of *Immaturity*, a career in novels seemed the only one open to him. Everyone wrote novels in the 1880s. Drama, economics, philosophy were unsaleable. He began to teach himself shorthand; he studied harmony and counterpoint; he persuaded his mother to train his voice by 'the Method' until he could sing 'as well as a man without twopennorth of physical endowment can be made to sing'; he persisted in playing the piano; he read greedily and, worst of all, he wrote.

He started on his second novel that summer, marching through it at the rate of a thousand words each day. 'The only test of competence is acceptance for publication,' he later wrote: 'friendly opinions are of no use.' But every opinion seemed unfriendly. His father was constantly fretting at him to find 'something to do to earn some money. It is much wanted by all of us.' Mrs Shaw unsuccessfully sought interviews for him; and Lucy, having failed to get their mother to turn George out of the house, had persuaded McNulty (as the only person likely to have influence) to write imploring him to take a job. Though sweet on Lucy, McNulty felt uneasy over this commission which put an end to their correspondence for nine months.

Shaw deafened himself to everything, wrote steadily, using some of his experiences at the Edison Telephone Company and some retaliatory observations of Lucy, and finished the novel which he called *The Irrational Knot* on 1 December 1880.

The inventor-engineer hero of this book, Ned Conolly, is not a self-portrait in the sense that Smith had been, but he embodies much that Shaw had learnt to admire since coming to London, and expresses many of his newest ideas. As a workman, a man of talent and integrity, Conolly opposes the perpetual falsehood of London society. 'You seem to see everything reversed,' one character tells him; and another, a clergyman, describes his opinions as being 'exactly upside down'. In sympathy with this upside-down view, Shaw inverts the conventional plot of the Victorian novel by having his heroine marry Conolly near the start and lose him at the end of the book.

Conolly is one of Nature's gentlemen, recognizing excellence by achievement, never by rank. The story throws up almost every situation that could shock society, from illegitimacy and alcoholic marriages to adultery and death. Aiming his attack on the 'villainous institution' of marriage, Shaw later described *The Irrational Knot* as having been 'an early attempt . . . to write *A Doll's House* in English'. In a deceitfully conducted world, it is the half-dead who flourish: men like tailors' dummies, and women like dolls to be gaped at in glass cages. Conolly will not accept such fashionable deception even if it means giving up a woman who sexually attracts him.

Shaw spent a fortnight revising the 641 'prodigiously long' pages of the novel. On 15 December 1880 he sent the manuscript to Macmillan whose reader reported that it was 'a novel of the most disagreeable kind . . . There is nothing conventional either about the structure or the style . . . the thought of the book is all wrong; the whole idea of it is odd, perverse and crude . . . So far as your publication is concerned, it is out of the question. There is too much of adultery and the like matters.'

'The better I wrote,' Shaw concluded, 'the less chance I had.' As an extreme measure, Shaw eventually sent *The Irrational Knot* to an American publisher 'who refused it on the ground of its immorality'. British publishers took a more sophisticated line. Smith Elder regretted that a book 'possessing considerable literary merit' was 'too conversational'; William Heinemann not only declined to publish it but advised the author not to submit it to anyone else: 'the hero is a machine like working man without any attractive qualities – an absolutely impossible person too.' Shaw agreed, in his fashion. Reviewing his novels himself in 1892 – a need arising 'through the extreme difficulty of finding anyone else who has read them' – he wrote of *The Irrational Knot*: 'This was really an extraordinary book for a youth of twenty-four to write; but, from the point of view of the people who think that an author has nothing better to do than to amuse them, it was a failure . . .'

4

RESPECTABLE HABITS

> What people call health – appetite, weight, beefiness – is a mistake. Fragility is the only endurable condition.
>
> Shaw to Charlotte Payne-Townshend (4 April 1898)

On 23 December 1880, a week after *The Irrational Knot* had been sent to Macmillan, the Shaws moved out of Victoria Grove to an unfurnished apartment on the second floor of 37 Fitzroy Street.

The advantage for George was its proximity to the British Museum. He had recently started to use the Reading Room, and now began going there regularly. Here, in what Gissing called 'the Valley of the Shadow of Books', he found a home. It became his club, his university, a refuge, and the centre of his life. He felt closer to strangers in this place than to his own family. He worked here daily for some eight years, applying for more than three hundred books each year, advancing through the *Encyclopaedia Britannica*, medical and municipal statistics for future articles, writing lectures and letters to the press, adding to his musical knowledge and completing his long literary apprenticeship. 'My debt to that great institution . . . is inestimable.'

It was partly as a result of his reading that in January 1881 he became a vegetarian. Shelley had first 'opened my eyes to the savagery of my diet,' he recorded.

> Never again may blood of bird or beast
> Stain with its venomous stream a human feast!

While investigating the art of eating out cheaply, Shaw came across a number of the inexpensive vegetarian restaurants that had recently opened. During his first five years in London he had grown 'tired of beef and mutton, the steam and grease, the waiter looking as though he had been caught in a shower of gravy and not properly dried, the beer, the prevailing redness of nose, and the reek of the slaughter-house that convicted us all of being beasts of prey. I fled to the purer air of the vegetarian restaurant.'

Shaw hoped that vegetarian food might relieve the severe headaches that had started to attack him each month. In one sense, vegetarianism came easily to him. A symptom of his neglect in Ireland had been the poor diet; the only food he had liked was the stoneground bread which his mother had occasionally buttered for him. To reject all this – the evidence of his own rejection – was no hardship. 'I am no gourmet,' he wrote: 'eating is not a pleasure to me, only a troublesome necessity, like dressing or undressing.' He looked forward to a time when people would subsist on an ecstatic diet of air and water. This was Shaw's ambrosia, and the food of his gods.

'If I were to eat it [meat], my evacuations would stink; and I should give myself up for dead,' he wrote in the last year of his life. Too little, he felt, was made of the fact that a frightened animal, terrified by smelling blood and seeing other animals killed in the slaughterhouse, stank. The flesh of such an animal, Shaw suggested, was tainted with poison and to eat it involved abusing the adaptiveness of the digestive system.

The sense of being a living grave for murdered animals filled him with repugnance. Part of this horror arose from the kinship he felt for animals – a fellow-feeling reinforced by the argument of Darwin and other naturalists establishing man's connection with animals. After which the practice of meat-eating became 'cannibalism with its heroic dish omitted'.

Having found from his experiments in the side-street restaurants round Bloomsbury that he could make a financial saving from putting his principles into practice, he went on to recommend vegetarianism as a means of world economy. 'My objection to meat is that it costs too much,' he wrote many years later, 'and involves the slavery of men and women to edible animals that is undesirable.' His campaign was to be an example of his dialectical skill.

Abstinence from dead bodies did not necessarily produce longevity, he argued, but affected the quality of living. He reminded those Englishmen in whom the superstition persisted that 'by eating a beefsteak he can acquire the strength and courage of the bull', that the bull (like an elephant) was vegetarian. He was sensitive to a need for scotching the popular myth that vegetarians were effeminate. Abstention from meat eating 'seems to produce a peculiar ferocity,' he noted. ' . . . And it is the worst form of ferocity: that is, virtuous indignation.' All his life he promoted vegetarians as the most pugnacious of people: 'Hitler, they say, was a vegetarian; and I can well believe it.'

G.B.S. had an air of knowing what was best for people. He calculated that, when the unappetizing truth was coated with Shavian sauce, it would go down a treat. So we often get from him fewer statements of truth than statements designed to hoodwink us into the truth. In private he could write: 'I am a vegetarian purely on humanitarian and mystical grounds; and I have never killed a flea or a mouse vindictively or without remorse.' This was the essential Shaw. But G.B.S. became the most unsentimental of vegetarians. 'He has no objection to the slaughter of animals as such,' his printed card on Vegetarian Diet reads. 'He knows that if we do not kill animals they will kill us . . . But he urges humane killing and does not enjoy it as a sport.'

From the nitrogenous point of view, and in line with Swift's modest proposal for the Irish, he saw no objection to a diet of tender babies, carefully selected, cleanly killed and gently roasted. Eaten with sugar, or a little beer, such a dish would, he estimated, leave nothing to be desired in the way of carbon, but: 'I prefer bread and butter.' If eating people was wrong, so was eating pigs. Bringing millions of disagreeable animals into existence expressly to kill, scorch and ingest their bodies was a monstrous practice which made our children callous to butchery and bloodshed.

Shaw needed courage to insist on his new diet in these early years. Usually it was wiser not to tell anyone he was vegetarian; otherwise he would be confronted with alarming quantities of breadcrumb preparations. At home he ate those vegetables the others took with their fish or meat. Some mornings a housemaid deposited among his books and papers a bowl of glue-like porridge and this often remained there for days while Shaw occasionally spooned a sticky mouthful or two. When travelling, he liked to carry lunch with him, diving his hands into his pockets and coming up with a fistful of almonds and raisins. He enjoyed advising vegetarians to avoid as much as possible all vegetables – particularly asparagus which gave one's urine a disagreeable smell – but it was impossible in England to do without potatoes and brussels sprouts. The vegetarian foods, with names ending in -ose, which were variously disguised forms of oil cake, revolted him; but he liked cheese and fruit, tolerated omelettes for many years, and developed an increasingly sweet tooth for chocolate biscuits, fruit cake, honey, even heaped spoonfuls of sugar.

He drank water, soda water, barley water, an innocent beverage named Instant Postum, ginger beer, milk, cocoa, and 'I dont refuse chocolate in the afternoon when I can get it'. But no tea, 'however mediocre', very little coffee and never alcohol. He had been watching the effect of alcohol with the eye of an expert. 'My father drank too much. I have worked too much.' It was probably as much a weakness in his character, he later acknowledged, as a strength that compelled him to be such a strenuous teetotaller. But that was not the point. Reviewing his first nine years in London – 'years of unbroken failure and rebuff, with crises of broken boots and desperate clothes . . . penniless, loveless, and hard as nails' – he concluded that 'I am quite certain that if I had drunk as much as a single glass of beer a day . . . my powers of endurance would have been enormously diminished'.

Characteristically, he was to ridicule prohibition, assert that 'tea does more harm in the world than beer', buy shares in a municipal public house and eventually advocate the Russian method of piping vodka ('a comparatively mild poison') into society under efficient government control.

Shaw's attitude to drink recalls Dr Johnson's dictum that 'Life is a pill which none of us can bear to swallow without gilding.' In his copy of Bunyan's *The Life and Death of Mr Badman*, Shaw wrote: 'Living is so painful for the poor that it cannot be endured without an anaesthetic.' He saw drunkenness as a symptom of the malignant disease called poverty. To his mind alcohol was a trick, a depressant in the disguise of a stimulant, falsely associated (like corpse-eating) with virility. Drink seldom propelled us into melodramatic ruin and madness; it was a chloroform that lowered our self-criticism and self-respect.

Shaw needed self-respect to withstand the low esteem in which he was held among publishers and at home. Perhaps the new diet he shared with saints and sages would help to change him into a different person. 'The odd thing about being a vegetarian is, not that the things that happen to other people don't happen to me – they all do – but that they happen differently: pain is different, pleasure different, fever different, cold different, even love different.'

5

ON GROWING A BEARD

> Think of my circumstances and prospects getting worse and worse until they culminated in smallpox next year (81) when I forced 'Love Among the Artists' out of myself.
>
> Shaw to Charlotte Payne-Townshend (1 April 1898)

Each day he read at the British Museum and as an extra form of language tuition sang in French three nights a week with a *basso profundo* called Richard Deck in his single room off the Camden Road. He felt peculiarly fond of Deck and, following his death in the autumn of 1882, remembered him as 'a remarkable man, offering me advice concerning pronunciation, directing my attention to the aim of gymnastics . . . and introducing me to the ideas of Proudhon'.

On 19 May he started a new novel. He had been at work on this for about a week when he began to feel ill. In the belief that he was spending too much time indoors, he prescribed for himself a number of rides round

London on the top of omnibuses. A few days later he discovered he had smallpox.

Smallpox was then one of the most dreaded diseases in Western Europe partly because 'the bad cases were so disfiguring, and partly because the increase of population produced by the industrial revolution, and the insanitary conditions in which the new proletariat lived, had made it much commoner and more virulent'. In 1853 Parliament had made compulsory the vaccination of every child in Britain within three months of birth. Sonny had been vaccinated in infancy and the vaccination had taken well. This form of vaccination (which in 1898 was to be banned) meant the injection of cowpox matter from the pustule of a diseased cow or the diseased substance from the inflamed arm of a recently vaccinated person. Shaw makes little reference to his illness except to say that he emerged from it a convinced anti-vaccinationist.

Once, when his mother had been seriously ill in Dublin, Shaw recounts, Lee had taken 'her case in hand unhesitatingly and at the end of a week or so gave my trembling father leave to call in a leading Dublin doctor, who simply said "My work is done" and took his hat'. From this Shaw learnt a lesson he continued to apply. Lee's prescription had been fresh air, extreme cleanliness and a good diet, and these became for him the ingredients of political good health: 'it is now as plain as the sun in the heavens,' he wrote towards the end of his life, 'that pathogenic microbes are products of the zymotic diseases; and that these diseases are products of ugliness, dirt and stink offending every aesthetic instinct . . . that dirt and squalor and ugliness are products of poverty; and that . . . zymotic diseases can be abolished by abolishing poverty, the practical problem being one of economic distribution.'

'You have been vaccinated in your infancy,' a friend wrote, 'so ought if the doctors are to be believed, to have nothing to fear.' But were they to be believed? Or were they to be feared? It was less his helplessness as a smallpox patient that Shaw hated than the unpleasantness of the disease itself into which, he felt, he had been medically tricked.

Shaw externalized Evil. In his world there were no evil men and women except the insane; but there were evil circumstances which he could identify, attack and eliminate. Vaccination let the enemy in and allowed evil to circulate within the body. The method of inoculating children with casual dirt moistened with an undefined pathogenic substance obtained from calves impressed Shaw as being morally insane. His sense of contamination became part of his socialist dogma and a warning against substituting faith in an experimental prophylaxis for a full-scale sanitation programme ensuring good conditions of public health.

After three weeks confined to his room in Fitzroy Street, he went down to recuperate at Leyton in Essex with his uncle Walter Gurly who, having married an English widow during one of his trips to the United States, was living a life of precarious respectability as a country physician near Epping Forest.

Shaw was left with a scar on his right cheek. Whether the disfigurement was slight or he merely made light of it, he felt extremely sensitive. 'I was sorry to hear of your illness,' Aileen Bell wrote to him, 'and the idea of your telling Mrs Horne not to describe your personal appearance – as if I should like you the less . . .'

'I have a rather remarkable chin and would like to let the public see it; but I never had time to shave.' This joke, and several others on similar lines, covered up the initial motive for the beard which was to hide his sensitivity. It became exactly the right beard – a good red socialist affair and vastly conspicuous. Few people who had their attention arrested by this irrepressible flag waving at the head of the Shavian talking-machine, would have known that G.B.S. was publicly concealing something.

Shaw represented himself as the passive partner to his beard: he simply followed it wherever it went. So bewitched had he been with the figure of Mephistopheles that 'when Nature completed my countenance in 1880 or thereabouts . . . I found myself equipped with the upgrowing moustaches and eyebrows, and the sarcastic nostrils of the operatic fiend whose airs (by Gounod) I had sung as a child, and whose attitudes I had affected in my boyhood'. There could be few better examples of G.B.S.'s beard doing the talking.

'Like a Victorian matron I experimented with my brushes and comb.' The face that he designed for himself was startling. 'It is the face of an outlaw,' wrote one woman; 'it is full of protest: wild and determined, a very brigand of a face.' Another woman, observing him among the socialists at William Morris's converted coach-house in Hammersmith, noted:

'His face came out very distinctly in the unshaded light of the stable-room, and as he listened it seemed to me to be lit up not only by that outside light but also, and in a particular way, by some inner lamp, as if Morris's words had lighted a candle of great and incandescent power within him. Shaw's face that night burned itself in on me; I have never seen any face like it since . . . His pale skin, his hair that the light above it turned to gold, and his strong, gleaming teeth, made a picture that no one, I think, could ever forget.'

His taut body seemed wound up with energy, and his movements were rapid. He walked with long springy strides on the front of his feet. When seated he seemed to relax all over, huddling and stretching, sticking out his long legs then pulling them up to his chest as if embracing himself. In this position he chattered and swayed with laughter. Then he stood up, thin, erect, well-pleased with himself it appeared, the head upraised, body tilted back, beard pointed. The impression of this figure, combative and audacious, was often invaded by comedy. It was his comic spirit that, for all the Satanic twirls and flourishes, encouraged a friend to describe his face as an 'unskilfully poached egg', and enabled Shaw himself to write: 'My own beard is so like a tuft of blanched grass that pet animals have nibbled at it.'

The private face shows itself in the novel, *Love Among the Artists*, he forced out of himself while at Leyton. Love among artists is different from love among other people, for artists love their work more than they love other people. Shaw's novel plots social against artistic values. 'I am in a worldly sense an unfortunate man,' says Owen Jack, the hero-composer of the book, 'though in my real life, heaven knows, a most happy and fortunate one.' Jack defines worldly success as 'the compensation of the man who has no genius'. Some men, he says, 'begin by aiming high, and they have to wait till the world comes up to their level'. With such *obiter dicta* Shaw, giving a backward look at Lee's failure, kept his confidence afloat.

Jack (who Shaw asks us to believe was based partly on Beethoven but who reflects something of Richard Deck and something of Vandeleur Lee), and the pianist Aurelie Szczymplica, are the two geniuses of *Love Among the Artists*, and they inhabit the classless world of music in which Shaw felt happiest.

Since marriage 'kills the heart and keeps it dead', it is better, Jack concludes, to 'starve the heart than overfeed it. Better still to feed it on fine food, like music.' Another character, Mrs Herbert, who owes something to Shaw's mother, wonders if there is 'any use in caring for one's children? I really dont believe there is.' The effect of such a mother on her children is described by her son (the blissfully unhappy husband of Aurelie Szczymplica) in a speech that reflects Shaw's feelings about himself and Lucinda Elizabeth:

'Can you understand that a mother and a son may be so different in their dispositions that neither can sympathize with the other? It is my great misfortune to be such a son . . . She is a clever woman, impatient of sentiment, and fond in her own way. My father, like myself, was too diffident to push himself arrogantly through the world; and she despised him for it, thinking him a fool. When she saw that I was like him, she concluded that I, too, was a fool, and that she must arrange my life for me in some easy, lucrative, genteel, brainless conventional way . . . She did not know how much her indifference tortured me, because she had no idea of any keener sensitiveness than her own . . . She taught me to do without her consideration; and I learned the lesson.'

Shaw came to believe that *Love Among the Artists* marked 'a crisis in my progress as a thinker'. He had 'come to the end of my Rationalism and Materialism'. This conversion has an air of paradox. The discovery of knowledge did not emerge at the end of reasoning and as a result of it, but occurred by instalments in the form of fiction, hypotheses or jokes – after which we set about finding reasons for it.

'A man has his beliefs: his arguments are only his excuses for them. Granted that we both want to get to Waterloo Station: the question whether we shall drive across Westminster Bridge or Waterloo, or whether we shall walk across the Hungerford foot bridge, is a matter for our logic; but the destination is dogmatic. The province of reason is the discovery of the means to fulfil our wills; but our wills are beyond reason: we all will to live . . . we only see what we look at: our attention to our temperamental convictions produces complete oversight as to all the facts that tell against us.'

Shaw had returned to 37 Fitzroy Street in October and finished *Love Among the Artists* on 10 January 1882. 'I have a much higher opinion of this work than is as yet generally entertained,' he admitted. The eminent publisher's reader, Edward Garnett, in a report for Fisher Unwin, advised against publishing the book if they could 'get something else from the author'. *Love Among the Artists*, he wrote, *deserved* publication, but would probably fall flat with the general reader. 'The literary art is sound, the people in it are real people, and the fresh unconventionality is pleasing after the ordinary work of the common novelist: but all the same – *few people would understand it, & few papers would praise it*.' Garnett contrasted the novel with W. B. Yeats's first book of verse, *The Wanderings of Oisin*, 'which with certain faults shows a sense of *colour* & *softness* that betrays the artistic mind,' he concluded. 'There is a little genius in Yeats: there is an individuality of mind in Shaw's work, but neither are likely to command much attention.'

While at Leyton, Shaw had finally taught himself Pitman's Shorthand. This, 'probably the worst system of shorthand ever invented', suited him best, he decided, because Greg's was known only in America and Sweet's Current Shorthand had been made 'illegible by anyone except himself'. Pitman himself was everything a man should be – a teetotaller and vegetarian, a radical well-whiskered man of business.

Shorthand enabled Shaw to intensify his programme of self-education at the British Museum and to write at a speed that kept pace with his thoughts. It also raised the family's hopes of his employment. While *Love Among the Artists* was being returned to him by the London publishers, Shaw proposed himself for the job of preparing the work of another unpublished novelist, Ethel Southam, who had advertised for a copyist. From Shaw she received many hundreds of words of advice about punctuation, the use of prepositions, and avoidance of adjectives – after which the partnership collapsed and G.B.S. was deprived of the amusement of pointing to a ghost-written collaboration as his first book.

Pressed again by his family, he read the advertisement columns and applied for employment as secretary to the Smoke Abatement Institute and as secretary to the Thames Subway Committee. He was careful not to conceal his politics ('those of an atheistic radical'), his lack of university education, mathematical and linguistic inabilities ('no German whatsoever'), and experience as secretary or shorthand clerk ('I can write longhand rapidly – in fact more rapidly than I can yet write shorthand').

On 12 April 1882 he began his fourth novel.

6

COURTING MISS LOCKETT

> Which yet my soul seeketh, but I find not: one man in a thousand have I found; but a woman among all these have I not found.
>
> Ecclesiastes vii.28

In a notebook he kept during his first six or seven years in London, Shaw copied down this passage. He described himself at this period as 'a complete outsider'. During his convalescence from smallpox, he had even thought of emigrating to the United States where his friend Chichester Bell was going. The bleakness of these years grew so unbearable that he afterwards translated it into a hatred of his novels.

Though the place was full of culture, London society contrived to get along on an intellectual diet of sport, party politics, fashion and travel. It seemed as if a mighty harvest had left the soil sterile. In Dublin the professions had formed the aristocracy, and without any great income and no experience of horses or guns, one could enjoy the best company without the taint of social inferiority. In London there were different rules and far greater importance was attached to money. 'The real superiority of the English to the Irish,' Shaw was to write, 'lies in the fact that an Englishman will do anything for money and an Irishman will do nothing for it.' But this was a later discovery to which, since for the time being he had no money, 'I had to blind myself'. There were times when he longed for people to blind themselves to him. He was a scarecrow catapulting himself along the streets with a professional habit of cheerfulness, but in broken boots, a tall hat so limp he wore it back to front to avoid doubling the brim when raising it, cuffs whose margins had been refined with his mother's scissors, trousers whose holes were hidden by a tailed coat fading from black to green. He was an example of poverty. 'It is my practice to make a suit of clothes last me six years,' he explained. 'The result is that my clothes acquire individuality, and become characteristic of me. The sleeves and legs cease to be mere tailor-made tubes; they take human shape with knees and elbows recognizably mine. When my friends catch sight of one of my suits hanging on a nail, they pull out their penknives and rush forward, exclaiming, "Good Heavens! he has done it at last."'

His plight was so glaring that people hinted they were good for loans. But he never borrowed, having no reason for believing he could repay them. He was conscious of the charm of his conversation if it never led to a request for five shillings. 'When you borrow money, you sell a friend,' he wrote.

He went to the National Gallery on its free days and, when he had a shilling in his pocket, to the theatre. Almost the only social gatherings in which he was included had been Lee's *soirées musicales*. But by the 1880s, largely through his sister Lucy, he also began to receive invitations to the 'At Homes' of Lady Wilde and of Elizabeth Lawson, mother of the landscape painter Cecil Lawson on whom he had modelled the artist Cyril Scott in *Immaturity*. They were the sort of engagements that make a man long for death. To equip himself for such ordeals he sought out from the catalogue at the British Museum volumes on polite behaviour.

He liked the Lawsons, and the artistic atmosphere of their house in Cheyne Walk was congenial, but he had not mastered the art of pleasing, could not dance, spoke hesitantly though usually to disagree, and occasionally made a jarring exhibition of himself. 'I sometimes walked up and down the Embankment for twenty minutes or more before venturing to knock at the door,' he remembered. ' . . . The worst of it was that when I appeared in the Lawsons' drawingroom I did not appeal to the good-nature of the company as a pardonably and even becomingly bashful novice. I had not then tuned the Shavian note to any sort of harmony.'

He saw very little of anyone with whom he did not work. Politics was to provide him with new colleagues. Otherwise he had few companionships.

Among these were the writer and adventurer Richard Hengist Horne and his wife Sophie; a person of mild exterior, Edwin Habgood, from the Edison Telephone Company; James Lecky, an exchequer clerk from Ireland interested in phonetics, keyboard temperament and Gaelic, who was also a big noise in the English Spelling Reform Association (signing himself 'jeemz leki'), who was to introduce him to the philologists Alexander John Ellis and Henry Sweet; and J. Kingston Barton, a doctor with whom Shaw passed many of his Saturday evenings. On Sundays he saw the Beattys.

Pakenham Beatty – Irish playboy, amateur pugilist, minor poet – was a moustachioed perpetual boy of a man. Born in Brazil, he had spent part of his childhood in Dalkey, been educated somewhere between Harrow and Bonn, and got to know Shaw as a fellow-exile in London. He belonged to a breed of troubadour-entertainers that was to include Frank Harris and Gabriel Pascal, for whom Shaw had a special fondness. Beatty enabled him to enter a life very different from his own. He was not 'sensible' about money. He spent it in the Irish manner, generously, spontaneously, without thought, until everything was gone and he was left with nothing but the settled habit of spending. His source of money was a small inheritance that, before it ran dry, allowed him to flirt with fine art. At the end of 1878, he published a volume of verse entitled *To My Lady and Other Poems.* One of his ladies, Edith Dowling, married him early the following year and became known as 'Ida' Beatty. They had two daughters and a son christened Pakenham William Albert Hengist Mazzini Beatty whom Shaw nicknamed 'Bismarck'.

In this company Shaw became a figure of attention and authority. He had no money but he spent all his advice on them, nuggets of information laboriously quarried out at the British Museum about the children's books, boots, careers, clothing, diet, education, illnesses, pianos and so on; and later, when he was earning money, he gave it to them in sums ranging between £10 and £200 and underwrote a good part of the children's schooling. 'Old grandfather Shaw', as Ida Beatty called him, was a father and a friend to them all.

Shaw made his appearance among them as a practical man, a part invested by his imagination with much glamour. He judged them to be *hopeless*, in which condition they *needed* him. But he also had need of them, since, for all their hopelessness, they had something almost entirely lacking in the Shaws: an atmosphere of family affection. Pakenham Beatty was extravagantly fond of his two sisters-in-law and even went on to shower his attentions jointly on Shaw's sister Lucy and a friend of their mother, Jane Patterson. But Shaw refused to be shocked. One afternoon he came across his friend recovering from delirium tremens and surrounded by whispering relatives who, having bullied him into making a will, were assembled as if for a funeral. 'I dispersed them with roars of laughter and inquiries after pink snakes &c, an exhibition of bad taste which at last converted the poor devil's wandering apprehensive look into a settled grin . . . Tomorrow he goes to a retreat at Rickmansworth, to be reformed.'

Shaw was a rock in this Bohemian whirlpool, splashed, invigorated and unchanged. The Beattys added to his education outside the British Museum. He loved Beatty for his bad verses ('something too awful') and for presenting such an atrocious advertisement for the romantic life. He re-christened him 'Paquito', a name that would serve as an alias for the eponymous hero of *Captain Brassbound's Conversion*. 'My plays are full of your jokes,' he told him.

Paquito's letters to Shaw were mostly in high-flown and facetious verse. His non-poetic intervals were devoured by the ambition to be an amateur light-weight champion. 'I am about to take boxing lessons from the scientific Ned Donnelly, a very amiable though powerful person in appearance . . . If you wish,' he invited Shaw, 'these lessons which I learn from Donnelly I will teach unto you.' Shaw couldn't resist. The comedy of all this was serious business for Shaw. He did his initial training at the British Museum, battling with Pierce Egan's *Boxiana* and other expositions. Paquito had presented him with a copy of Donnelly's *Self-Defence* ('the best book of its kind ever published') and 'insisted on my accompanying him to all the boxing exhibitions'. In consequence Shaw was to gain among his political acquaintances the reputation as 'a tall man with a straight left' whose knowledge of pugilism might prove valuable if it came to revolution.

There were times when Shaw himself seemed to accept such fantasies. He showed up at a school-of-arms in Panton Street called the London Athletic Club where he obtained tuition from Ned Donnelly himself who, as Professor of Boxing, had instructed the most brilliant light-weight of his day, Jack Burke, on whom Shaw based the hero of the novel he was writing. A month after finishing this book, on 17 March 1883, he entered the Queensberry Amateur Boxing Championships on the turf at Lillie Bridge. At a weight of ten stone (140 lbs) he applied to take part in both Middle and Heavyweight Classes, and was given a place for both categories in the programme, but not in the ring. It was the climax of his prize-fighting career, a paper apotheosis, after which he found he 'had exhausted the comedy of the subject'.

Shaw's long affair with boxing was to worry some of his admirers. How could this champion of the vegetable world involve himself in brute pugilism? 'Paradoxing is a useful rhyme to boxing,' he once thanked a journalist. 'I will make a note of it.' He saw at once the great publicity in pugilism. Newspapers, he believed, were 'fearfully mischievous', yet they were creators of public opinion. So what could be more natural than to marry one such brute profession to another? Since the public were more interested in sport than serious politics, Shaw was to spread his political views through the sports pages as he would the music and art columns. Under his treatment boxing was to become an allegory of capitalism, the prize-ring a place where he could exhibit Shavian theories on distribution of income and award a points decision to socialism.

Shaw's knowledge of boxing formed part of an armoury that, by the end of the 1880s, was to make him, in Max Beerbohm's opinion, 'the most brilliant and remarkable journalist in London'. Unlike bicycling, it didn't get you anywhere, and it was not as pleasant as swimming which, with its cleansing effect and the sensation of rendering the body weightless, almost non-existent, became 'the only exercise I have ever taken for its own sake'. But his shadow boxing, even before it was converted into words, was the essence of Shavianism.

For almost six years he visited the Beattys most Sundays, sparred several platonic rounds with Paquito the poet, then sat at the feet of his wife Ida, practising French. This was the first of numerous triangular relationships in which he re-created his mesmeric but chaste version of Vandeleur Lee with Lucinda and George Carr Shaw, and kept those ghosts at peace. 'Dont talk to me of romances: I was sent into the world expressly to dance on them with thick boots – to shatter, stab, and murder them,' he challenged Ida. 'I defy you to be romantic about me . . . and if you attempt it, I will go straight to Paquito; tell him you are being drawn into the whirlpool of fascination which has engulfed all the brunettes I know.' This was shadow boxing from which Shaw emerged very much in control of a situation that did not really exist. He could not exclude dreams of more orthodox affairs, but 'all these foolish fancies only want daylight and fresh air to scatter them,' he instructed Ida, as if the fancies had been hers and not his.

Shaw made himself attractive to women by informing them he was attractive – then warning them against this damnable attractiveness. He converted the neglected Sonny into a besieged G.B.S., who would have fainted with surprise 'if a woman came up to me in the street and said "I DONT adore you"'.

Being in love with Shaw could be a bewildering business. 'You are very contradictory,' Aileen Bell complained. ' . . . What am I to do?' He teased and tested; he loved you and he loved you not. He achieved an air of confidence by taking away your own confidence. 'When we did fight in the old days,' Aileen Bell wrote to him, 'I used to go upstairs afterwards, &

stamp about my room & abuse you, saying "I hate George Shaw".' His talent was to disconcert. He charmed you, then made you too angry for words and (since the affair was one of words) impotent. On paper, where he held absolute authority, he was promiscuous. He attributed to others the romantic daydreams he suppressed in himself, and encircled them in fantastical webs of jealousies and misunderstandings.

Shaw's relations with women during his first four or five years in London are cryptically recorded in his diary notebooks. At the end of 1876, he noted: 'Inauguration during the year of the Terpsichore episode. Also La Carbonaja.' Terpsichore was his codename for Ermina Pertoldi, the ballerina of the Alhambra Theatre and a character in *Immaturity.* La Carbonaja was the daughter of a London hostess who gave him a medal of the Virgin Mary, hoping to convert him to Catholicism. The following year La Carbonaja is 'in the ascendant' and in 1879 'La C flickers until 11th [January] When the star of Leonora gains the ascendant (Terpsichore evaporated) . . . Made the acquaintance of the Lawson family on 5th [January], and met Leonora on the 11th.' From 'Leonora' he preserved a pressed flower together with an odd note: 'These flowers were plucked from the garden of a millionaire by one of his would-be brides as a memento of a sweet prelude to a "might have been".'

Unable to come to terms with women except in make-believe, Shaw conducted his most successful affairs from the galleries of theatres or his gymnasium in the British Museum, and worked himself eventually to sleep at night. Confusion began when this make-believe came in contact with the actual world. Between 1878 and 1894 he kept a correspondence in play with Elinor Huddart, author of *My Heart and I* and other novels that would have won her notoriety 'if I could have persuaded her to . . . use the same pen name, instead of changing it for every book'. She had been impressed by his kindness and good sense. 'How you manage to pick my work to pieces from end to end,' she wrote to him on 16 September 1878, 'and yet never hurt me (and I am rather easily hurt) I cannot conceive.' One reason she was not hurt was that Shaw had invented an Elinor of his own, possessed by his spirit and made into a new creature. 'You are the only man friend I have ever made,' she told him. ' . . . I am content to be your friend and no man's wife.' For someone who appeared so frivolous it was astonishing how persistent he could be. He beat down on her like a sun, warming her, blistering her, trying to blow a new climate round her and imbue her with fresh life as a writer. But 'I can put forth no new leaves,' she objected. 'I am not a beech tree . . . Leave my ashes in peace, they can do you no good.' But he would not leave her. He wanted to pour his will-power into women so that their achievements became the children of the union.

In his exertions to work his will vicariously through women his flirtations became those of a schoolmaster. 'I beg of you,' Aileen Bell once wrote to him, 'not to lecture quite so much.' However much he did lecture, urge, flatter, coax, he could not make the worlds of fantasy and actuality coalesce.

Shaw's love eliminated many things to which women were accustomed. In his plays he was to create a stereotype, Woman-the-Huntress, whom he sent into battle against the Victorian Woman-on-a-pedestal. Debarred by his childhood from forming close emotional attachments, he gave his allegiance to ideas – but saw women as vehicles for those ideas. Shaw took the body away from women and addressed their minds. His own mind was astonishingly fast, but emotionally he was lame. The result was that women found themselves continually out of step with him. When Shaw looked at a woman, he appeared to turn his back on her and raise a mirror. It was a disconcerting stare, positive, remote, and appearing so bold while actually in retreat.

*

Sonny had wanted love; G.B.S. soared wittily above it; and Shaw was pulled between the two. The tug-of-war moved critically backwards and forwards over his first serious girl friend, Alice Lockett. In February 1882 he returned to Leyton and, while recuperating from scarlet fever, was introduced to her. She was twenty-three and robustly good-looking. He fell violently in love – which is to say, he was strongly attracted to her. After his convalescence he managed to return to Leyton by the uncharacteristic means of getting temporary employment there, earning six guineas in as many days counting votes during the election of Poor Law guardians. He saw her, walked in the moonlight, talked, flirted. By 17 April, he felt able to report to Elinor Huddart that 'Alice thinks I am in love with her'. The honeymoon was almost over and the contest between them ready to begin.

Alice and her sister Jane had been conventionally brought up and educated at a Victorian ladies' college. In 1879 their father had died and the next year their elder brother also died. Their mother suffered a paralytic stroke, and her two daughters, transferred to the care of their grandmother, prepared to take up professions. Jane, who was experimenting with a novel called *Yeast* (exorbitantly condemned by Shaw), studied for a career in education; Alice, who enrolled in a nursing course at St Mary's Hospital in Paddington, was taking singing lessons from Mrs Shaw.

The affair was carried on between the railway station and piano stool ('Oh the infinite mischief that a woman may do by stooping forward to turn over a sheet of music!'). Alice felt she had been relegated in the social order by her family misfortunes, and nursed dreams of a dramatic ascent up the ladder of society; Shaw was determined to kick that ladder away. Alice sensed a power in Shaw, but one which he was often misusing. In place of manly leadership, he presented her with exhibitions of clever indecisiveness. Quarrelling between them was inevitable. 'I hate people to hesitate,' she chided him.

In one of his early notebooks Shaw had jotted down his observations on the typical society woman. 'Clever, frivolous, vain, egocentric,' he wrote. 'Pretty & knows it. Sits silent and affects the scornful. Also a morbid sensitiveness and a consequent pleasure in inflicting hurts on others. Effect of this type of egotist in making others seem intolerably egotistical . . .'

It was to save Alice from becoming this woman that Shaw exerted all his powers. He re-created her as a figure from his novels and she became someone through whom he attacked the London society that had lured Lee and Lucinda away from him and, when he followed, rejected him.

Shaw divided Alice into two people. Miss Lockett had been stiffened by the starch of society and was full of protective scorn and attempted sarcasm. Towards men she bore herself tyrannically, having no notion that any interest of men in women might exist apart from a desire to marry. But sometimes Miss Lockett forgot to be offended, scornful, pretentious – and Alice emerged. Alice was the child in her, sympathetic, unspoilt, spontaneously generous, someone capable of considering her own instinctive judgement a safer guide than the formulated rules of society. Alice was capable too of Shavian improvement; the proud and foolish Miss Lockett had gone too far down the hackneyed road of her own dignity to be brought back. Between these two beings Shaw enacted a perpetual drama. Miss Lockett 'is the dragon that preys upon Alice,' he told her, 'and I will rescue Alice from her'.

Shaw dramatized in Miss Alice Lockett a division he knew to exist within himself. In one corner there was G.B.S., 'resolved . . . to walk with the ears of his conscience strained on the alert, to do everything as perfectly as it could be done, and – oh – monstrous! – to improve all those with whom he came in contact'. In the opposite corner stood Sonny, the Irish contender, who was not afraid to become 'as a little child again and was not ashamed to fall in love with Alice'.

But the voice that lectured Miss Lockett on the importance of becoming Alice was that of G.B.S., not Sonny who could seldom 'snatch a few moments from his withering power'. G.B.S. worked day and night; he was seldom out of love with his work – in which condition he accused

Alice of taking advantage 'of the weakest side of my character', and warned her to believe nothing that Sonny whispered to her.

The crisis in Shaw was real. Before a caress with Alice had time to cool, he longed to return to his ascetic life, to his books, his developing socialism. But then the memory of her beauty could prevent him going to bed in peace, and gave him a thrill that could last 'through a political meeting and four hours of private debate on dry questions of economy'. Shaw's appeals to Alice were often the means by which he tried to offend her so as to save himself from falling in love. But sometimes he did not have the heart to succeed – and then Sonny would whisper things that G.B.S. would have to shatter with his laughter.

Shaw had hit on the device of pretending to be what he was – but with a comic exaggeration that prompted disbelief. He pretended to be 'in love' with Alice and she, congratulating herself on not being taken in, accused him of insincerity. Sometimes it seemed as if she were only speaking the lines he had prepared for her. It was oddly unreal. 'We are too cautious, too calculating, too selfish, too heartless, to venture head over heels in love,' he wrote to her. 'And yet there is something – ' Both tried to limit their vulnerability to the other. But Alice did not understand where her power lay – she never realized into what extraordinary suspense her beauty put him. In attempting to hurt him with deliberate cruelty, she merely became the stubborn and timid Miss Lockett of his hostile imagination, squaring up to her impregnable enemy G.B.S.

'George Shaw, I consider you an object to be pitied – but the truth is I might just as well speak to a stone. Nothing affects you . . . Now your book has failed – for which I am truly sorry for your sake, although it is perhaps better for other people. I suppose you mean to begin another and be another year dependent on your mother. Why on earth don't you work?'

Alice had been in the marriage market since leaving school and looked on 'love-making' as the most serious business in life. It was because Shaw believed that Sonny was incapable of inspiring love in women that he invented G.B.S. Alice tried to understand him – but he took care that she should not. In serious moments he could make her see with his eyes, flattering her ('Must I eternally flatter flatter flatter flatter flatter?') by his apparent conviction – which she shared – that she was capable of a higher life. But his political dreams had no meaning for her so 'it is my small troubles that I go to you with,' he told her.

Alice Lockett's challenge to Shaw had been to make him feel his loneliness most painfully. At moments his self-command wavered. 'Write to me,' he asked her, 'and I will make love to you – to relieve the enormous solitude which I carry about with me. I do not like myself, and sometimes I do not like you; but there are moments when our two unfortunate souls seem to cling to the same spar in a gleam of sunshine, free of the other wreckage for a moment.'

Miss Lockett's social ambitions would not allow her to be stranded in this way; she wanted to travel first class. As for Shaw, it was Sonny who was left senseless and G.B.S. who appeared 'too strong for you. I snap your chains like Samson.'

On two occasions they returned each other's letters; several times they decided never to see each other. The affair lasted until 1885 when all love had gone out of it and they drifted apart. In 1890 Alice married a former house-surgeon at St Mary's, William Salisbury Sharpe. Obliged during the Great War to borrow some money from Shaw, she lived on to witness the halo of world renown encircle G.B.S. But in many criticisms of his books and plays she would have been able to read of an absent quality – and to have recognized in this absence the departure of Sonny over which she had helplessly watched.

7

DEATH AND A RENEWAL

It was lonely to be myself; but not to be myself was death in life.

Cashel Byron's Profession

On 22 April 1882, ten days after starting his fourth novel, Shaw moved with his mother to 36 Osnaburgh Street, on the east side of Regent's Park. This was an improvement on the insalubrious rooms in Fitzroy Street where he had often been ill.

They saw little of Lucy. From the Carl Rosa Opera Company she transferred to a D'Oyly Carte group and in 1884 went off with them on tour.

Lucinda Elizabeth Shaw continued methodically to give private tuition in singing. In 1885 she suddenly struck a new vein of work as music instructor at Clapham High School, and the following year became choir-mistress and teacher of class singing at the North London Collegiate School for Ladies where she remained until her retirement in 1906.

Shaw went his own way – to the British Museum – and finished his fourth novel on 6 February 1883. *Cashel Byron's Profession*, as he called it, is a fairy-tale about power. Its hero, Cashel Byron, a prize-fighter as clever with his fists as Shaw was with words, embodies Shaw's fantasy about action. To him is given the first Shavian speech (which goes the distance of three thousand words) on the superiority of 'executive power' over 'good example'. It is a dialectic on the philosophy of winning, and a hymn to skill and science over incoherent strength.

Taking a profession that society officially repudiated, Shaw uses it as a metaphor for the way people unofficially live their lives – a formula he was to try again in *Mrs Warren's Profession* and *Major Barbara* (which he thought of calling 'Andrew Undershaft's Profession'). His make-believe leads the hero and heroine from love at first sight through all supposed social barriers to marriage in the last chapter. The Lady is Cashel's prize – in a way that Ida Beatty or any of the other women with whose husbands G.B.S. sparred would never be Shaw's. In the book, romance won by a knock-out and 'my self-respect took alarm'.

'The lower I go, the better I seem to please,' Shaw wrote hopefully to the publisher Richard Bentley. But though in later years *Cashel Byron's Profession* was so much enjoyed by R. L. Stevenson, W. E. Henley and others that Shaw marvelled at his escape from becoming a popular novelist, it was turned down by the London publishing houses. 'It flies too decidedly in the face of people's prejudices to make it likely that it will be a popular book,' advised the reader for Macmillan. ' . . . well and brightly written, but the subject is not likely to commend itself to any considerable public.'

Reviewing the book himself, Shaw pointed out that one of the fights in the novel was a restaging of the wrestling match in *As You Like It*, and hints at the effort he made to write a book as the public liked it. His reaction to what he called his 'shilling shocker' became studded with the glittering contradictions which formed part of his insulation against failure. In 1886, following at least seven rejections, he recommended it as 'one of the cleverest books I know'. But in 1888, when welcoming another publisher's rejection of it, he burst out: 'I hate the book from my soul.' He hated the conditions in which he had written it and the London publishers for whom he had written it: he hated the person who had written it; he hated failure. He had sailed as near compromise as he dared – too near and to no effect. Next time (for he was not ready to give up) there should be no compromise.

He called his fifth novel *The Heartless Man* – later changing the title to *An Unsocial Socialist*. As with the two previous novels he drafted most of it in shorthand at the British Museum, and then transcribed it in longhand. The plot revolves round Sidney Trefusis, the heartless socialist of both titles. At the beginning of the book, Trefusis shocks everyone by running away from his newly married wife. By accepted standards it has been a brilliant match, full of money and romance. But accepted standards have made women into a class of person fit only for the company of children and flowers. With a man like Trefusis they can have no connection, except sex. Unfortunately the sexual attraction between them was so strong, Trefusis gravely complains to his wife Henrietta, that 'When you are with me I can do nothing but make love to you. You bewitch me.'

As Shaw's mouthpiece for Socialism, Trefusis recognizes the natural inequality of human beings but condemns England's social inequality for exploiting it. This artificial inequality will vanish, he claims, once 'England is made the property of its inhabitants collectively'. The choice is 'Socialism or Smash'.

Most people preferred Smash because it looked safer. To open their eyes, British socialists needed to study feminism, for it was women who, by giving Socialism respectability, could make it grow. Shaw's women are sympathetically drawn but, as custodians of Society's standards, they embellish the capitalist philosophy of Smash. Trefusis's aim, whether through sermonizing or seduction, is to head them off from this course. It is the old struggle to release natural vitality from an unnatural system of morality. The most attractive of these girls, for whose socialist souls he wrestles, is Gertrude Lindsay, Shaw's portrait of Alice Lockett. It is a hostile portrait, done in the colours of revenge, of a discontented girl who counts 'the proposals of marriage she received as a Red Indian counts the scalps he takes', and who treats her dog (a St Bernard) with more kindness than 'any human being'.

It is not Gertrude who becomes Trefusis's second wife, but Agatha Wylie – a Shavian Becky Sharp who was inspired by a glimpse of 'a young lady with an attractive and arresting expression, bold, vivid, and very clever, working at one of the desks' in the British Museum Reading Room. She is a symbol of the future.

By separating his socialist hero into two people, Shaw reflected the division he felt existed in his own character. Some of the most entertaining pages of the novel are those where Trefusis, reluctant heir to a fortune, takes on the role of a talkative labourer – a Dickensian character called Smilash (a compound of the words smile and eyelash). In this partnership, Shaw the comedian and Shaw the reformer are brought together for the same ends. The character of Smilash appeals to the 'vagabond impulse' in Trefusis, and the actor in Shaw. 'I am just mad enough to be a mountebank,' Trefusis explains. 'If I were a little madder, I should perhaps really believe myself Smilash instead of merely acting him.'

Trefusis is the great man who had lain asleep in Smith, the tentative hero of *Immaturity*, and who wakes up by the light of Marxist economics.

Shaw's novels had been experiments to find a political framework in which to develop his thought and personality. Conolly, the engineer of *The Irrational Knot*, had been 'a monster of the mind' embodying rationalism; Owen Jack, the composer from *Love Among the Artists*, was 'a monster of the body' representing unconscious instinct; in *Cashel Byron's Profession* Shaw had toyed with a romantic fusion of mind and body in the marriage of his prize-fighter and educated lady. In *An Unsocial Socialist* the union takes place not between two people but within one. Trefusis is Shaw's first socialist hero and Don Juan figure in whom he attempts to reconcile his sexual and political attitudes. The novel foreshadows *Man and Superman*, with Trefusis a prototype of Tanner.

It was an extraordinary book to have produced in the early 1880s – 'the first English novel written under the influence of Karl Marx with a hero whose character and opinions forecast those of Lenin,' Shaw later declared. He finished his revisions on 15 December 1883. 'We are afraid that the subscribers to the circulating libraries are not much interested in Socialism,' wrote Smith Elder & Co. David Douglas of Edinburgh and Chatto & Windus in London excused themselves from looking at it. For Macmillan, John Morley (not realizing that he had previously advised the author to give up writing) reported that 'the author knows how to write; he is pointed, rapid, forcible, sometimes witty, often powerful and occasionally eloquent'. But, Morley concluded, the socialistic irony would not be attractive to many readers and 'they would not know whether the writer was serious or was laughing at them'. In refusing the book, Macmillan wrote that they would be glad to look at anything else he might write 'of a more substantial kind' – a request that, Shaw replied, 'takes my breath away'. In his correspondence with Macmillan, he came as near making an exasperated appeal for sympathy as he could.

'All my readers, as far as I know them, like the book; but they tell me that although they relish it they dont think the general public would. Which is the more discouraging, as this tendency of each man to consider himself unique is one of the main themes of the novel. Surely out of thirty millions of copyright persons (so to speak) there must be a few thousand who would keep me in bread and cheese for the sake of my story-telling, if you would only let me get at them.'

His new political friends were to give Shaw his chance of getting at the public. *An Unsocial Socialist*, he claimed, 'finished me with the publishers'. Instead of adding it to the pile of rejects, Shaw sent it off to J. L. Joynes, one of the editors of *To-Day*, a new 'Monthly Magazine of Scientific Socialism'. Joynes recommended the serialization of the novel to his fellow-editor, the philosopher E. Belfort Bax, who replied: 'Go on and prosper with Shaw . . .'

An Unsocial Socialist appeared in serial form between March and December 1884. Shaw was not paid, but for the first time he had an audience. 'William Morris spotted it and made my acquaintance on account of it. That took me into print and started me.' Between April 1885 and March 1886 *Cashel Byron's Profession* was also serialized, due largely to the enthusiasm of the magazine's printer, H. H. Champion, a clever, epileptic man who was later to become Shaw's dramatic agent in Australia. Champion stereotyped the pages from *To-Day* and published them in a misshapen 'Modern Press' edition of 2,500 copies in March 1886. This was Shaw's first published book, costing a shilling and carrying a royalty of one penny a copy. Two of his other novels, *The Irrational Knot* (April 1885–February 1887) and *Love Among the Artists* (November 1887–December 1888), were to be published serially in Annie Besant's *Our Corner*.

Shaw's political interests soon devoured his ambitions as a novelist. In 1887 he abandoned an attempt at a sixth novel because 'I could not stand the form: it is too clumsy and unreal. Sometimes I write dialogues; and these are working up to a certain end.' His disenchantment with the novel is apparent in *An Unsocial Socialist*. In the appendix to this book, which takes the form of a letter to the author from Trefusis, Shaw writes: 'I cannot help feeling that, in presenting the facts in the guise of fiction, you have, in spite of yourself, shewn them in a false light. Actions described in novels are judged by a romantic system of morals as fictitious as the actions themselves.' This opinion he shared with Defoe who, in *Serious Reflections*, had described the 'supplying of a story by invention' as 'a sort of lying that makes a great hole in the heart, at which by degrees, a habit of lying enters in'. Like Defoe, Shaw resolved to make his fiction as much like fact as possible.

Now that it was too late, publishers were urging him to go on. His books would reach a good circulation, Swan Sonnenschein encouraged him, providing he 'stick to novels, or go in for plays (which are even more suited to you, in my opinion) . . .' Shaw acknowledged that he might 'descend as low as that one day', but five failures had been 'enough to satisfy my appetite for enterprise in fiction'.

Since he could not marry his story-telling to his socialism, Shaw relinquished story-telling. From his socialist philosophy he was to harvest optimism, while the novels, representing his first nine years in London, remained like dead fruit on the bough. Over fifty years later he wrote that his 'failure to find a publisher for any of them was for me a hardening process from which I have never quite recovered'. Although they carry many ideas that were to be developed in his plays, these novels seemed to Shaw to have been written by someone else – someone with his roots in Ireland who once dreamed of a grand literary conquest in London. That Shaw was almost dead.

*

One final tie with his past was cut when on 19 April 1885 George Carr Shaw died. They had had little communication over the last five years. 'I have nothing else to say that you would care about,' his father had written on 2 September 1880; and again, on 4 December 1882: 'I have nothing else particular to say.' Of his son's published works he read only *An Unsocial Socialist*, liked it, but warned him: 'dont get yourself into Holloway Jail.' Though he often asked for letters, 'whether you have anything to say or not', he seldom heard from George who he felt did not 'have anything sentimental left in you'. Years later, Shaw wrote: 'When I recall certain occasions on which I was inconsiderate to him I understood how Dr Johnson stood in the rain in Lichfield to expiate the same remorse.' But he had never fought his father, so all the battles of his adult life would seem bloodless.

George Carr Shaw died suddenly of congestion of the lungs while recovering from pneumonia in a bed-and-breakfast lodging house in Leeson Park Avenue. 'I hastened there, and was ushered upstairs into a bedroom,' McNulty recorded. '. . . He had died in his sleep: and his lips wore a smile.' He had not been wanted, dead or alive, and he was not missed. Lucy was in Ireland at the time, but she did not go to the funeral. When the news reached Shaw, he sent a note, with two staves of music headed 'Grave', to his friend Kingston Barton:

'Telegram just received to say that the governor has left the universe on rather particular business and set me up as
An Orphan.'

From the insurance on his father's life, Shaw was able to buy that summer his first new clothes for years – an all-wool Jaeger suit, a black coat, vest, collar, cravat and pants, all for £11 1s. 'In short, I had become, for better for worse, a different man.'

THREE

I

IN SEARCH OF A FAMILY

I was a man with some business in the world . . . my main business was Socialism.

Shaw to Archibald Henderson (3 January 1905)

The London in which Shaw had been living was like a City of Revelation. From anarchists and atheists; dress- and diet-reformers; from economists, feminists, philanthropists, was the socialist revival of the late nineteenth century to be drawn. This was the last age of the religious and political tract. One, by a clergyman of the Established Church, proved that Jehovah was a small red venomous snake; a second, by a German, replaced this snake with a fish; yet a third, by a Methodist professor, abolished both snake and fish, explaining that Jehovah was a widower. Such scholarly confusion was intensified by the crumbling of known structures. Science, like a great steam engine, having crashed through the infallibility of the Bible, was being garlanded with the dogmas and symbols of mythology and made the Idol of a new religion.

A fresh urgency entered the progressive movement. New clubs and societies sprang up in London, catering for all talents and temperaments. Many working-class socialists joined the street parades of the Social Democratic Federation; anarchical socialists with a taste for sexual radicalism were attracted to the glamorous Socialist League; while the Fabian Society was filled by middle-class intellectuals who wanted to rewrite the economy and rearrange the social patterns of the country without a shot fired. All were agreed that there was a crisis in the land. Thirty per cent of the population of London – the richest city in the world – were living in poverty. Such was the magnitude of capitalism's failure.

Shaw felt relief at entering this turmoil. His personal need coincided with the need of the age. The 'power to stand alone', which Smith had acquired in *Immaturity*, 'at the expense of much sorrowful solitude', was no longer necessary. G.B.S. stood shoulder to shoulder.

The man who, in 1885, could admit that 'I hate all fraternity mongering just as heartily as any other variety of cant' and go on to declare himself the 'member of an individualist state, and therefore nobody's comrade', had decided at the beginning of 1887 that 'it is time for us to abandon the principle of Individualism, and to substitute that of Socialism, on pain of national decay'. By 1891 he had reconciled his instinct with his practice by discovering that 'the way to Communism lies through the most resolute and uncompromising Individualism' – 'pragmatic' individualism, but not *laissez-faire* 'economic' individualism. So he could still reassure a friend: 'Believe me, I always was, & am, an intense Individualist.'

His first manoeuvres towards shedding his neglected self aimed at replacing his family with a community of his own choosing. 'I haunted public meetings,' he remembered, 'like an officer afflicted with cowardice, who takes every opportunity of going under fire.' Towards the end of 1880 he had joined the Zetetical Society, which met weekly in the rooms of the Women's Protective & Provident League in Long Acre. Though 'nervous & self-conscious to a heartbreaking degree . . . I could not hold my tongue. I started up and said something in the debate, and then felt that I had made such a fool of myself . . . I vowed I would . . . become a speaker or perish in the attempt . . . I suffered agonies that no one suspected . . . my heart used to beat as painfully as a recruit's, going under fire for the first time. I could not use notes: when I looked at the paper in my hand I could not collect myself enough to decipher a word.'

The Zetetical Society was a junior copy of the London Dialectical Society which Shaw joined in 1881, reading his first paper there (on the virtues of Capital Punishment over Life Imprisonment) early the following year. Women took an important part in the debates of both societies and helped to insist upon uncensored speech. From the practice of examining each speaker with questions at the conclusion of his paper (heckling was also part of the menu), Shaw began to sense his formidable debating powers.

He also experimented with some literary groups, passing calm evenings with the New Shakespere Society, and more breezy ones with the Browning Society. In 1886 he acted as press officer for the Shelley Society's private production of *The Cenci*. This five-act blank-verse tragedy was, Shaw wrote, 'a strenuous but futile and never-to-be-repeated attempt to bottle the new wine in the old skins'.

He was surprised to find that the Shelley Society presented the poet 'as a Church of England country gentleman whose pastime was writing sermons in verse'. When he announced to the Society that 'I am a Socialist, an Atheist and a Vegetarian', two members resigned. Having begun to submerge his self-consciousness into a social conscience, he wanted, like Shelley, to pierce the illusions that made the present order seem eternal, and show the world its future. He wanted 'a cause and a creed to live for'.

He found them on the evening of 5 September 1882 at the nonconformist Memorial Hall in Farringdon Street where the American economist, Henry George, was speaking on Land Nationalization. George spoke with an appealing American intonation. He was simple, he was sentimental; and, like the best avant-garde Americans, he was fifty years behind the times in most of Europe. But he gave to politics the powerful orchestration of religion.

George's *Progress and Poverty*, which Shaw bought that evening for sixpence, offered an explanation as to why increasing economic progress brought increasing poverty. The ownership of land had always been a precondition of power in Britain. These few landowners monopolized the birthright of the people, but the nationalization of this land would give the people back their birthright.

For the first time it flashed on Shaw that all this controversy between Science and Religion, Darwin and the Bible, was barren ground. 'The importance of the economic basis dawned on me.' George's book helped Shaw come to terms with his own past. He had been betrayed into his one exhibition of feeling (seizing and kissing his mother's hand) over the possession of Torca Cottage – and that had led to disillusion. Now he could find an impersonal reason, bleached of grievance, for his loveless home and miserable years in the estate office of Uniacke Townshend. All had been part of an inhumane system of property-owning.

Henry George was to reduce Land Nationalization to a single tax on land - a casting back to the *impôt unique* of Honoré Mirabeau. His Single Tax was a stepping stone to socialism, and socialists stepping over it did not take it with them. They were converted by George, but not to him. Shaw, who played Voltaire to George's Mirabeau, had no sooner read *Progress and Poverty* than he went on to Karl Marx, and finally 'devoted about four years to the study of abstract economics so as to get my foundations sound for my work as a socialist in devising practicable methods of industrial and political reconstruction'.

He spoke at clubs; he read in the British Museum. He searched among new organizations for a political headquarters. He tried out his voice at the Bedford Debating Society organized by an Irish Unitarian preacher, Stopford Brooke (on whom Shaw partly modelled the Reverend James Morrell in *Candida*); he joined two discussion groups in Hampstead, and he went to meetings of the Democratic Federation, the first political organization of socialists in Britain.

The Federation was led by H. M. Hyndman who saw himself, in his immaculate frock-coat, fine gloves and silk hat, leading his rough proletarian army to a revolutionary dawn. But it was ballet rather than revolution. His drilling of the unemployed and parading of the working class in the streets appeared to be rehearsals for the Apocalypse which was fixed for 1889, the anniversary of the French Revolution. With his high-chested carriage, he already looked like a prime minister. Hyndman had known Marx and, when leaving his house one day, put on his hat by mistake and found that it fitted. In 1881 he had published a book, *England for All*, that, while introducing Marxist doctrines to English readers, did so without mentioning Marx's name – except (a point that failed to satisfy Marx) in a Preface. But it was Hyndman's connection with Henry George that had attracted Shaw to what became known as the Social Democratic Federation. At his first meeting, he mentioned George and was told to go off and read Marx. There was no English version available so he studied the first volume of *Das Kapital* in Deville's French translation, working during the autumn of 1883 at the British Museum. 'That was the turning point in my career,' he told Hesketh Pearson. 'Marx was a revelation . . . He opened my eyes to the facts of history and civilization, gave me an entirely fresh conception of the universe, provided me with a purpose and a mission in life.' *Das Kapital*, he wrote, 'achieved the greatest feat of which a book is capable – that of changing the minds of the people who read it'.

But when, brimming with Marxism, he returned to the SDF, he found that Hyndman's lieutenants had not read him themselves. He was now a 'candidate member' of the SDF, but for two reasons decided not to join. The first was Hyndman's own incapacity for teamwork. His famous temper was responsible for driving away many socialists – Edward Aveling, Belfort Bax, Walter Crane, Eleanor Marx and William Morris, who formed themselves into an anti-parliamentary group called the Socialist League, soon to be infiltrated by the anarchists.

But there was a second reason why Shaw turned his back on Hyndman. 'I wanted to work with men of my own mental training.' It was then that he came across the first tract, *Why are the Many Poor?*, of the newly formed Fabian Society. Here was an educated body appealing to the middle-class intelligentsia: 'my own class in fact.' From this tract he discovered the Society's address and on 16 May 1884 turned up for its next meeting.

*

The nominal founder of the Fabian Society had been Thomas Davidson, the illegitimate son of a Scottish shepherd. Davidson was an inspired talker and very strong on immortality. In 1881 he had blazed through London, inflaming miscellaneous agitators and idealists with what William James called his 'inward glory'. On his next visit two years later some of these acolytes formed 'a sort of club'. Members were of two conditions: those whose impulse was primarily religious; and others, more politically minded, who wished to reconstruct society. Soon the club split up into two branches – 'The Fellowship of the New Life' attracting the former and the Fabian Society the socialists.

'What does the name mean? Why Fabian?' asked Edward Pease, the first secretary of the Society. The Fabian Society's motto was printed as an epigraph to the Fabian Tract that Shaw read in the spring of 1884.

'For the right moment you must wait, as Fabius did, most patiently, when warring against Hannibal, though many censured his delays; but when the time comes you must strike hard, as Fabius did, or your waiting will be vain and fruitless.'

When critics asked the name of the history from which this quotation came, Pease answered gleefully that the work of the Fabian Society was not to repeat history, but to make it. Since the instincts of the early Fabians were literary as well as political, their business – chiefly under Shaw's influence – was to alter history by rewriting it.

The Minutes of the meeting of 16 May had a famous mauve-ink side-note in unmistakably Shavian hand and style – the careful signature with its incongruous flourish of defiance: 'This meeting was made memorable by the first appearance of Bernard Shaw.' On 5 September he formally enrolled and before the end of the year had published an unsigned two-page leaflet entitled *A Manifesto*, listed as Fabian Tract No. 2. Never again was Shaw so succinct. His seventeen propositions have a trenchancy and wit giving it a different tone from other socialist documents. Under present circumstances, he wrote, 'wealth cannot be enjoyed without dis-honour or foregone without misery'; the result of nineteenth-century capitalism in Britain had been to divide society 'into hostile classes, with large appetites and no dinners at one extreme and large dinners and no appetites at the other'; under *laissez-faire*, competition 'has the effect of rendering adulteration, dishonest dealing and inhumanity compulsory'; instead of leaving National Industry to organize itself, the State should compete 'with all its might in every department of production'; and there should be equal political rights for the sexes, since 'Men no longer need special political privileges to protect them against Women'. The Manifesto ended with the proposition: That we had 'rather face a Civil War than such another century of suffering as the present one has been'.

By the beginning of 1885 two things had been achieved. The Fabians had found a programme – and Shaw a platform.

2

HEROES AND FRIENDS

> I found that I had only to say with perfect simplicity what I seriously meant just as it struck me, to make everybody laugh. My method is to take the utmost trouble to find the right thing to say, and then say it with the utmost levity. And all the time the real joke is that I am in earnest.

During 1884 and 1885, Shaw had taken on two gruelling jobs. Between November and April he edited for H. H. Champion's Modern Press an edition of Lawrence Gronland's *The Cooperative Commonwealth*, an exposition of socialism that had recently appeared in the United States. 'By God, I never read [such] English!' he exclaimed to Champion. Shaw's editing gave the book a sparkling tone. He polished it with optimism. His payment for this editing was to be £5, 'if the book ever produces anything over the costs & advts' – a figure that became more remote once Gronland, repudiating Shaw's version, published his American 'authorized' edition, with a preface addressed 'To the British Reader'.

Even less profitable was a commission Shaw had accepted as early as January 1884 to provide a glossary and index for the Hunterian Club's edition of Thomas Lodge's Works. 'I wasted the year deplorably,' he noted in his diary. At intervals over the following year he would receive imploring letters from the Club, and these would result in desperate resolutions to buy an alarm clock. In July 1885 he transferred the commission to Thomas Tyler, a 'rectangular, waistless, neckless, ankleless . . . man of letters of an uncommercial kind' who had previously made a translation of Ecclesiastes. Tyler completed the job but not long afterwards died, 'sinking unnoted like a stone in the sea' – though remaining for the grateful Shaw 'a vivid spot of memory in the void of my forgetfulness'.

During 1885 Shaw 'slipped into paid journalism'. This had come about through his friendship with William Archer who, two months younger than Shaw, had already made his name with a charming series of articles on theatre in the *London Figaro*. Working at the British Museum Reading Room in 1883, Archer's attention had been drawn to what appeared as an undelivered brown paper parcel on the next seat. This was Shaw. 'There I used to sit day by day,' Archer recalled, 'beside a pallid young man with red hair and beard, dressed in Jaeger all-wool clothing which rather harmonized with his complexion. My interest was excited . . . by the literature to which he devoted himself day after day. It consisted of Karl Marx's *Das Kapital* in French, and a full orchestral score of Wagner's

Tristan und Isolde.' Before long they were introduced. 'We had many interests in common,' Archer recalled, 'and soon became intimate friends.'

Shaw loved Archer and Archer reciprocated this love. They shared an intimacy of humour, and neither mistook the other's emotional reticence for lack of feeling. When emotional, Archer grew so wooden that, on the point of tears, he looked like a piece of mahogany. Shaw admired him for his unpretentiousness and integrity. They teased and chided and fathered monstrous advice on each other freely. The candour of their exchanges was a relief to them both, for they inflicted no malice and received no wounds. Under the device of open disagreement they made a secret code of their affection.

They disagreed most on whatever interested them most. As dual champions of Ibsen they each regretted that the other was not an Ibsenite. Each wanted the other to succeed – and felt that he alone knew how this quality of success was to be come by. Archer might not be able to combat his high cheek-bones or the outline of his jaw, but he could unbutton the collar that gave 'his head the appearance of being wedged by the neck into a jampot' – and, in doing so, Shaw counselled, 'consent to make an ass of yourself publicly'. Shaw had to do the opposite thing: quell all that reckless extravaganza, grow up, and cease from making an ass of himself in public. 'He loses influence by being such an incorrigible jester,' Archer lamented, 'by wearing the cap and bells in and out of season.'

Both had made one awful error: Shaw in writing plays, and Archer in not writing plays. 'Why the devil dont you write a play instead of perpetually talking about it?' Shaw demanded. Goaded by the perpetual stings, when just short of his sixty-fifth birthday, Archer woke up one morning from a dream of a Rajah in the depths of the Himalayas accompanied by his valet – obviously a 'complete scheme for a romantic melodrama,' he revealed to Shaw, 'which only needs your co-operation to be infallibly THE PLAY OF THE CENTURY.' But Shaw collaborated only to the extent of helping him to transform the dream into a lurid plot 'about an Asiatic Rajah made cynical by a western education, and a Green Goddess who had to be propitiated by blood sacrifices'. *The Green Goddess* became a melodramatic success because, Shaw felt, 'collaboration between us was impossible'. He had learned this when, in the late summer of 1884, he set to work on an earlier theatrical notion of Archer's.

With our knowledge of Shaw's success in the theatre, it is easy to ridicule Archer's cordial discouragement. But Shaw's plays were *not* plays. Archer had no trouble in spotting this. His friend had dispensed with plot, with character, with drama and the red corpuscles of life, to demonstrate that argument squeezed into a well-built dramatic machine was as good as any play. So: 'Let us be grateful for him as he is, and . . . enjoy and applaud him. He is not, and he never will be, a great dramatist; but he is something rarer, if not better – a philosophic humorist, with the art of expressing himself in dramatic form.'

Archer's criticism, presented as friendly and despairing advice, required Shaw to change into someone else (or to reverse the change into G.B.S.). 'I doubt whether there has ever been a more extraordinary and fascinating combination of gifts in one single human brain,' he acknowledged. He saw through Shaw's optimism; he did not see Shaw's need for optimism. It was the urgency of this need that was driving Shaw to hammer together, like a magical raft, his philosophy and float lightly upon it over the sea around him. Archer wanted him to abandon this whimsical craft and plunge into the water. But Shaw's nourishment came not from reality as Archer witnessed and experienced it, but from a fantasy that, for all its hard businesslike style, slid along a slice of invisible air. His word-addiction kept him incredibly suspended, and he seldom allowed himself to fall victim to events. But Archer believed this limited his appeal. He would never get a ducking. His audiences might not be able to ignore him but, resenting his superiority, they were resolved never to take him seriously.

Archer would occasionally slip along to Shaw's little room on the second floor of 36 Osnaburgh Street. Troubled by what he saw, he 'took my affairs in hand,' Shaw recorded, planting him among the reviewing staff of the *Pall Mall Gazette*, where he contributed book reviews from May 1885 to December 1888. He also procured him a place on the *Magazine of Music*, which applied to Shaw for articles pretty regularly during the later months of 1884; and he introduced him to an Irishman named Edwin Palmer who, in February 1885, started the *Dramatic Review* and employed Shaw as his music critic.

But Shaw was not an easy man to help. 'I am making more money than I have any present need for, and shall always be glad to help you to keep going until one or other of your argosies comes home,' Archer wrote to him. Such help, which Shaw was frequently to offer others in a similar manner, he could never receive himself. Archer, however, had hit on a more delicate ruse. He had been prevailed upon by Edmund Yates, editor of *The World*, through whose columns he had recently begun what Shaw called 'his victorious career' as theatre critic, to double as a critic of art. Knowing nothing about pictures, yet knowing Shaw, Archer invited his friend to accompany him round the galleries. Shaw agreed and, as Archer had expected, poured forth a stream of comment and suggestion. Archer listened, then wrote the article and forwarded to Shaw a cheque for £1 6s. 8d., being half his fee. But Shaw, recommending more exercise and earlier hours, sent it back. Archer, exasperated by his friend's stubbornness, told him he was a 'damned fool not to accept the money,' adding,

'I certainly should in your position.' Since Archer's incorruptibility was notorious this should have served as a telling argument when he sent the cheque back to Shaw: 'If you took the trouble to read what I do write you would see that every second idea is yours . . . So be a good fellow and stow your logic.'

But Shaw was proof against this plea. He re-returned the cheque, 'and if you re-re-return it,' he warned, 'I will re-re-re-return it'. He then treated Archer to an outpouring of Shavian economics that, by way of Ricardo's Law of rent and Lassalle's Law of wages, concluded that it paid him famously to go without remuneration: 'I have the advantage of seeing the galleries for nothing without the drudgery of writing the articles.' Archer was adding to his schooling in the National Gallery of Ireland, with a free education and: 'we all grow stupid and mad to just the extent to which we have not been artistically educated.'

Archer had no way of telling that the arrangement he was proposing reproduced for Shaw those ghost-writing days with Lee on *The Hornet*. It was as if Shaw was being given an opportunity to scrub away that tainted year when he had submitted to polite fraud. It was particularly ingenious that he should be tempted by his closest and most honourable friend, and from the worthiest motives. As an admirer of *The Pilgrim's Progress*, Shaw would not have had it differently. It was a soft and amiable corruption to which he was being beckoned, and the first major test of whether his socialism was making a new man of him. Archer, the innocent implement of this trial, is a siren voice: everything he says is reasonable, well-intentioned and brimful of sense. But Shaw steadfastly refuses. He is impoverished and free.

Archer, however, was not free. For some weeks he continued to work laboriously as art critic for *The World* 'until my conscience could endure it no longer'. He then persuaded Shaw to do a specimen article which he sent to Yates and which secured him the post. In Shavian language, Archer had 'rescued me by a stratagem', having deliberately planned to resign his post as soon as Shaw got a firm hold on it. This, so Archer held, was a lovely essay in *a priori* Shavianism, where true belief becomes a matter of will over chronology.

*

Shaw held the post of art critic on *The World* from the spring of 1886 to the autumn of 1889. He had in June 1885 started to contribute an 'Art Corner' (covering all the arts) to *Our Corner*, having met its editor Annie Besant at the Dialectical Society that January, and he continued this column until September 1886. 'On art I am prepared to dogmatize; on traffic, ask a policeman,' he wrote. It was his comic dogmatism that made these catalogues of pictures so entertaining to readers of *Our Corner* and *The World*:

'Concerning Mr Poynter's "Difference of Opinion", with its expanse of closely-clipped grass glittering in the sun, one can only suggest, not disrespectfully, that it would make a capital advertisement for a lawn-mower . . .'

'Mr Phil Morris's "Storm on Albion's Coast" contains a raging ocean made of what I think is called "tulle" . . . Mr Kennedy has spent much careful work to doubtful advantage on something resembling an East End starveling stuffed into the tail of a stale salmon, and called a mermaid. Miss Dorothy Tennant is reviving the traditional "brown tree" with a vengeance, as a background to her dainty little nude figures. The humorous picture of the year is Mr C. Shannon's "Will he come in?" a group of primeval men in a pond, where they have taken refuge from a red-haired mammoth . . .'

' "Disaster" is the title given by Mr Walter Langley to his scene in a Cornish fishing-village; and, on the whole, I agree . . . The tiger in "Alert" is sitting for its portrait with immense self-satisfaction . . .'

'The President's [Walter Crane's] design, in which Mr Gladstone axe in hand, cuts down a serpent a thousand feet high, is allegory reduced to the desperation of mixed metaphor . . .'

Shaw's two gods in matters of art were Ruskin and Morris. Of Ruskin, 'a really great artist-philosopher,' he was to write: 'He begins as a painter, a lover of music, a poet and rhetorician, and presently becomes an economist and sociologist, finally developing sociology and economics . . . to an almost divine condition.' Even in a small way Shaw considered himself as carrying on Ruskin's business. 'In a society in which we are all striving after the thief's ideal of living well and doing nothing,' he said, ' . . . and in which the only people who can afford to buy valuable pictures are those who have attained to this ideal, a great artist with anything short of compulsory powers of attraction must either be a hypocrite . . . or starve.' We looked for no valuable advance in art, he argued, 'until we redistribute our immense Wealth and our immense Leisure so as to secure to every honest man his due share of both in return for his share of the national labour'.

Shaw enjoyed affronting picture-gallery conventions. He advised artists to sell their paintings 'by the foot'. 'Did they never teach you that the frame is the most important part of the picture, and a good "trade finish" (like Van Eyck's) its most indispensable quality?' he innocently asked Austin Spare.

Shaw followed Ruskin's taste as well as his example. 'I went into the National Gallery and spent more than an hour over the Turner drawings in the basement with deep pleasure in them,' he noted in his diary. But he claimed to be as much a politician at the press-view as a Member of Parliament on the hustings: 'I am always electioneering.' Recalling his work as art critic half a dozen years later, he wrote: 'Certain reforms in painting which I desired were advocated by the Impressionist party, and resisted by the Academic party. Until these reforms had been effectually wrought I fought for the Impressionists . . . [and] did everything I could to make the public conscious of the ugly unreality of studio-lit landscape and the inanity of second-hand classicism.'

Shaw criticized the 'insistently mundane' exhibitions at Burlington House and championed the Society of British Artists led by Whistler who 'must be at least as well satisfied as any propagandist in London,' he commented. 'The defeat of his opponents at the [1887] winter exhibitions is decisive.' This was an example of Shavian electioneering by a critic who privately believed Whistler to be a gentleman painter clever enough to make a merit of his limited ability. Yet his work was preferable to that of the future President of the Royal Academy, Sir Frederick Leighton, who specialized in 'the arts of the toilet as practised by rich ladies'.

Shaw was ideologically committed to progress and sensed that the notations of Whistler's 'symphonies' and 'harmonies', dashed off in an hour or two, were shorthand messages from the future. At the same time Whistler was Ruskin's enemy, and had declared in his famous *Ten O'Clock* lecture that art was 'selfishly preoccupied with her own perfection only . . . having no desire to teach'. Shaw's art criticism is impressive in its political dexterity: he treats Whistler more as a campaigner-artist than an artist-philosopher. Closer to his natural taste were the Pre-Raphaelites. The prize painter of the Brotherhood was Burne-Jones, who 'has the power to change the character of an entire exhibition by contributing or withholding his work'.

At least three times a week Shaw would abscond from literature and art, go down among the Fabians and, like a man bathing himself, 'talk seriously on serious subjects to serious people. For this reason . . . I never once lost touch with the real world.' The real world without art was deeply unsatisfying to Shaw, but the art world without reality seemed worse. As a compromise he supported the Arts and Crafts movement:

'It has been for a long time past evident that the first step towards making our picture-galleries endurable is to get rid of the pictures – the detestable pictures – the silly British pictures, the vicious foreign pictures, the venal popular pictures, the pigheaded academic pictures, signboards all of them of the wasted talent and perverted ambition of men who might have been passably useful as architects, engineers, potters, cabinet-makers, smiths, or bookbinders. But there comes an end to all things; and perhaps the beginning of the end of the easel-picture despotism is the appearance in the New Gallery of the handicraftsman with his pots and pans, textiles and fictiles, and things in general that have some other use than to hang on a nail and collect bacteria. Here, for instance, is Mr Cobden Sanderson, a gentleman of artistic instincts. Does Mr Cobden Sanderson paint wooden portraits of his female-relatives, and label them Juliet or Ophelia, according to the colour of their hair? No: he binds books, and makes them pleasant to look at, pleasant to handle, pleasant to open and shut, pleasant to possess, and as much of a delight as the outside of a book can be.'

Shaw promoted artists as people who, while apparently providing something that few people wanted, anticipated a demand. Whether it preached or argued, exposed, assured, revealed, consoled, art was a magic and, like Prospero's Ariel, it commanded kings. Through new combinations of sound, new bridges of feeling and rhythms of colour, people absorbed information that, presented merely as information, they would reject from prejudice or boredom. This was the penetrating power of art, and when Shaw spoke of it he turned naturally to music. 'And great artists, in order to get a hearing, have to fascinate their hearers; they have to provide a garment of almost supernatural beauty for the message they have to deliver. Therefore, when a man has a message to deliver in literature, with great effort and toil he masters words until he can turn them into music.'

This formed part of Shaw's case against Whistler's concept of art. We must not limit art, he argued, to the satisfaction of our desire for beauty. People cannot endure beauty any more than they can endure love. The paradoxical triumph of romanticism was to have drugged us into believing that we worshipped love and beauty even as we struggled to avoid their demands. Self-respect curdled into self-love, in Shaw's prescription, unless preserved by seriousness: the dilettante was *always* narcissistic. Oscar Wilde appeared the pre-eminent dilettante; the best example of the serious man was William Morris. His love of the medieval world sprang from a longing to regain those happy years 'when I was a little chap'. He summoned up a vision of the long past, a garden of happiness where nature, in the pattern of leaves and flowers, invaded the rooms: 'it was a positive satisfaction to be in his houses,' Shaw remembered. Morris had set his heart on founding a brotherhood that, by seeking medieval cures for the malaise of capitalism, would crusade against industrial squalor and replace it with a regenerated Britain – a green-tree land of gardens, fields and forests. His revolutionary politics followed a revolution in his own life to which Shaw's attitude is revealing.

Like Shaw, Morris had an extreme fear of emotional suffering; like Shaw, he identified schools as prisons, locking him out of Eden. But he returned to Eden when, in 1859, he married 'an apparition of fearful and wonderful beauty', Janey Burden, the daughter of a groom. For her, as for Augustus John's Dorelia, beauty had been a means of emancipation. She looked like a 'figure cut out of a missal,' Henry James said, and had been raised from her simple working-class life to be Queen of the Pre-Raphaelite kingdom, a Blessed Damozel, tragic, imposing, silent. Morris's developing interest in the working class seemed to threaten her with a return to the mean conditions of her past. Shaw observed no unhappiness. 'Their harmony seemed to me to be perfect. In his set, beauty in women was a cult.' When Morris, in old age, covered the forests of his wallpapers with whitewash, Shaw recognized not the extinction of something essential but an advance in 'his need for the clean, the wholesome, & the sensible'.

To Shaw, it was as if Morris had woken up from an impossible dream of fair women, opened his eyes on a Ruskinian landscape and strode out to reach the communism that 'was part of his commonsense'. He had transferred his hopes from an individual to a collective sphere, achieving fulfilment through the integration of politics and art. No matter that he had little natural aptitude for politics. Shaw acknowledged his position as head of the Socialist League to be 'absurdly false', recommending that he be treated with marked consideration as 'a privileged eccentric and in no way an authority as to socialist policy' – almost exactly in the same manner as the Labour Party was later to regard G.B.S. himself.

Morris was the clearest example of a hero in the Shavian iconoclastic world. Shaw felt wonderfully at home at his house on Hammersmith Terrace where he met many kindred spirits – men such as Sydney Cockerell and Walter Crane. In place of Wilde's aesthetics for the élite stood a man who worked with others on behalf of everyone – a man who wanted to bring applied arts and the perspective of beauty into all life. The 'idle singer of an empty day' had grown into the busy singer of a bursting day. Shaw believed that the artist's wares had to be marketed in the knowledge that most customers hated beauty because, as a reflection of love, it could hurt them. Though his capacity for loving was undeveloped, Shaw did not lack emotion. Cunningly fenced off behind some of the most brilliantly unsentimental prose in the language, is plenty of feeling. His faith in the employment of the arts is expressed in a puritan encyclical:

'The claim of art to our respect must stand or fall with the validity of its pretension to cultivate and refine our senses and faculties until seeing, hearing, feeling, smelling and tasting become highly conscious and critical acts with us . . . The worthy artist or craftsman is he who serves the physical and moral senses by feeding them with pictures, musical compositions, pleasant houses and gardens, good clothes and fine implements, poems, fictions, essays and dramas which call the heightened senses and ennobled faculties into pleasurable activity. The great artist is he who goes a step beyond the demand, and, by supplying works of a higher beauty and a higher interest than have yet been perceived, succeeds after a brief struggle with its strangeness, in adding this fresh extension of sense to the heritage of the race.'

3

THE PROSPECTIVE LOVER

> People who are much admired often get wheedled or persecuted into love affairs with persons whom they would have let alone if they themselves had been let alone.

These words appear in a short story, 'Don Giovanni Explains', that Shaw wrote in the summer of 1887. He makes use in this story of his experiences with women over the past three years to find the best truth available to him. Like Shaw, Don Giovanni had been born a shy man.

'On rare occasions, some woman would strike my young fancy; and I would worship her at a distance for a long time, never venturing to seek her acquaintance . . . At last a widow lady at whose house I sometimes visited, and of whose sentiments towards me I had not the least suspicion, grew desperate at my stupidity, and one evening threw herself into my arms and confessed her passion for me. The surprise, the flattery, my inexperience, and her pretty distress, overwhelmed me. I was incapable of the brutality of repulsing her; and indeed for nearly a month I enjoyed without scruple the pleasure she gave me, and sought her company whenever I could find nothing better to do. It was my first consummated love affair; and though for nearly two years the lady had no reason to complain of my fidelity, I found the romantic side of our intercourse, which seemed never to pall on her, tedious, unreasonable, and even forced and insincere except at rare moments, when the power of love made her beautiful, body and soul.'

There were three categories of relationship in Shaw's life: flirtations with single women, usually at this time young Fabian girls; philanderings with the wives of friends, usually socialist colleagues; and a consummated love affair with a divorced or separated lady. With Alice Lockett he had tried to combine all his emotional needs in one person, and concluded that it could not be done. On 29 September 1888, more than three years after they had parted, Alice spent the day with Shaw in London. 'I sang some of the old *Figaro* bits with Alice, who presently went home,' he noted in his diary, 'overcome, I think, by old associations.'

There was no chance of Shaw being overcome: he overcame. He had plumed himself into a dazzling lecturer, enthralling audiences with his vitality and wit. He was marvellously adroit too in debate, catching his opponents' sallies in mid-air like a conjuror and returning them with amazing speed. The expectations he raised are beautifully caught by a young Fabian called Grace Black. 'People are so exceedingly miserable in every class, that I should lose hope if I did not know there are many who devote themselves entirely to trying to make things better,' she wrote to him.

' . . . you have a greater power of seeing truth than most people: you can do more than most. It is impossible to help expecting a great deal from you and now is the point – don't fail – please don't. For one thing I don't know how I could bear it – but that is not the point. What I fear is that you do not care for nor believe in people sufficiently . . . do care more for people for that is where you seem to fail.'

Shaw recognized at once a case of Fabian love. He could diagnose love as efficiently as a doctor identifying death. His objection to it was part of his hatred of private property. People said that all the world loved a lover: the truth was that a lover loved all the world, and therein lay his crime. Providing we were in love, the world was a fine place, and we condoned its awfulness. That we needed to love, he knew. But he represented the *partiality* of romantic love as a perversion of our deepest desire. For it was not to this person, then to that person, but to the whole world that we owed the comprehension of love. The world, however, was not ready for love. To renounce the indulgence of loving was in itself an act of love – the act of deferred love we call faith.

Grace Black had asked for no answer – 'if you sent me one, you might make me unhappy,' she told him. But Shaw could not let this alone. He sent his first letter to her by return of post. Her reply was a rebuke:

'I guessed you would think I was in love with you. So I am, but that has nothing to do with my letter and it is a pity if that thought has clouded my meaning. My personal happiness is certainly connected with your success as a teacher of socialism, & in a less degree by that of Hyndman & Morris, because I care very much for what is implied to me by socialism. But apart from that I do love you, & why do you wish to dissuade me from that and from believing in you? . . . There is nothing in my attitude of humility, dependence or expectancy which would give reason for irritation . . . But it is true that I wish that love were an easier simpler thing than it is now; but that is to wish for heaven . . . You are not much older than me, but all experience is to the bad. I am serious.'

Shaw's experience of love had been 'to the bad', and from Grace Black's feelings he took care to protect himself. His description of Grace's announcement in 1889 of her marriage is a good example of inverted Shavian romanticism: she 'sent me a note to say what she was going to do,' he wrote, 'adding, by way of apology for throwing me over, that she could never marry a man she loved'. The letter he actually received read as follows:

'You know that the reason I began to love you was because I believed you cared more for truth and would do more to help socialism than any other man . . . Long ago I saw that my love for you was a waste of force, because you were so different to me: but it is only lately I have been able to love anyone else. I do now, and am engaged to marry Edwin Human a Socialist . . . You have a place deep in my heart: my feelings have run through all the personal currents in respect of you & can't go back but have ended as they began in something quite impersonal, rather painful but in a way sacred.'

Meeting Grace some years after her marriage, he records: 'She looked extraordinarily youthful; she has children; her marriage is obviously as happy as it is possible for a marriage to be; her husband no more grudges her her adorations than he grudges her a motor car.' In casting himself as a piece of extra-marital machinery, Shaw re-creates what he hoped were the circumstances of his own Dublin household.

One family to have benefited from Shaw's interference had been the Beattys. Among others by now were the Avelings and the Blands. At the head of all three families was a husband notorious for his illicit love-affairs. Shaw, who was to place Edward Aveling on the stage as Louis Dubedat in *The Doctor's Dilemma*, described him as the man who 'seduced every woman he met and borrowed from every man', and yet would have 'gone to the stake bravely rather than admit that Marx was not infallible or that God existed'. As his interest in politics deepened he turned his attention to Karl Marx's youngest daughter, Eleanor. Shaw used to see this clever dark-haired girl at the British Museum, working for eighteen pence an hour as a literary hack. In June 1884 she decided to go and live with Aveling on the understanding that they would marry if his wife died. For Shaw, who regarded himself as unattractive, here was a revelation. 'Though no woman seemed able to resist him,' he wrote of Aveling, 'he was short, with the face and eyes of a lizard, and no physical charm except a voice like a euphonium.' Like Wilkes, he was only a quarter of an hour behind the handsomest man in Europe. Shaw seemed determined to pursue this mystery. Aveling worked on the staff of the *Dramatic Review* and Shaw often called at his home, but his diary reveals that it was Eleanor (or 'Mrs Aveling') he came to see. She was not sure what to make of him. 'If you are mad,' she wrote, 'there is marvellous method in your madness & penetration that sanity wd gambol from . . . oh, most amiable and sympathetic of cynics.' She would appeal to him to save her 'from a long day and evening of tête-à-tête with myself', and he responded.

17 February Called on the Avelings . . . Talked with Mrs A between 17 and 18 (A went out shortly after I came in).
28 February Mrs Aveling asked me to call in the afternoon and have a chat. Went at 17 and stayed until 20 nearly. Aveling absent at Crystal Palace concert. Urged her to go on the stage. Chatted about this, death, sex, and a lot of things.
28 March Went to Mrs Aveling and discussed *Love Among the Artists* with her.
14 April Called on the Avelings – A[veling] at Ventnor: Eleanor at home: stayed with her from 17 to 19.45.
20 June After meeting on musical pitch called on Mrs Aveling. Aveling came in later on. Went home and played all the evening.
24 August Rumour of split between the Avelings mentioned by [J.M.] Robertson.

Shaw recoiled at the news that the Avelings might separate. His instinct whispered retreat. The Avelings' later history exposed everything he most feared about sexual passion. In 1897, following the death of his wife, Aveling secretly married Eva Frye, and following an anonymous letter telling her of this marriage, Eleanor poisoned herself. 'My last word to you,' she wrote in her suicide note, 'is the same as I have said during all these long, sad years – love.' But Shaw could not endure the agony of such love. In his tight little note on her death, he referred to 'the news of Eleanor Marx's suicide in consequence of Aveling having spent all her money'.

As he began easing out of the Avelings' home, so he started to infiltrate the marriage of the Blands. Hubert Bland had been a founder of the Fabian Society, and its first treasurer. He was a man of Norman exterior, imperialist instincts, and huge physical strength, though to Shaw he seemed 'an affectionate, imaginative sort of person'. Like Hyndman, he wore Tory clothes and 'never was seen without an irreproachable frock coat, tall hat, and a single eyeglass which infuriated everybody'.

'Hubert was not a restful husband,' Shaw conceded. He had married his wife, Edith Nesbit, in 1880, when she was twenty-one and seven months pregnant, and subsequently had children by two other women. The first of these women Edith befriended; the second, Alice Hoatson, already was her friend and a part of the Bland household, where her daughter Rosamund was brought up by Edith as her own child. The Blands' home was a disorganized ménage and the conglomeration of parties, charades, music and children formed a refreshing contrast to sterner Fabian entertainments. Shaw would slip on boxing-gloves and dance round the short-sighted Bland who was incapable of deliberately hurting anyone. 'I was taller by a couple of inches and with longer reach,' Shaw calculated. And Edith watched.

According to Edward Pease, Edith was acknowledged as 'the most attractive and vivacious woman of our circle', though burdened with spectacular fainting fits and, at supreme moments of Fabian drama, the habit of calling sensationally for glasses of water. She abstained from corsets (a false method of 'girding the loins'), rolled her cigarettes which she smoked from a long holder, and looked every inch an advanced woman. 'On the other hand,' Shaw believed, 'she is excessively conventional; and her ideas are not a woman's ideas, but the ideas which men have foisted, in their own interest, on women.'

She was soon confiding her ideas to Shaw. Sometimes she would invite him to tea, but more often she met him at the British Museum, and they would go for long striding walks. By the summer of 1886 these meetings had grown longer and more intricate. 'On the whole the day was devoted to Mrs Bland,' Shaw wrote on 26 June 1886. 'We dined together, had tea together, and I went out to Lee with her and played and sang there until Bland came in from his volunteer work. A memorable evening!'

Edith, who was to become famous as a writer of stories for children, appealed to Shaw partly because she retained so much of the child in her. In the 1880s she wrote poetry. 'The faults of the poems are so directly and intimately the faults of the woman,' Shaw wrote in a review of her *Lays and Legends* (1886), '. . . there is too much of the luxury of unreal grief, of getting into the vein by imagining churchyards and jiltings and the like.' Shaw composed music for some of these verses, among which were love poems to himself.

She called him 'the grossest flatterer (of men women and children impartially) I ever met'. He 'repeats everything he hears, and does not always stick to the truth, and is *very plain* . . . and yet is one of the most fascinating men I ever met'. She would pursue him to his lair in the British Museum, and he would hurry her out to pretty scenes on the river and in the park; give her tea in the Wheatsheaf; see her on to buses and trains. On their way to Baker Street Station one day, they called in at Shaw's home. From then on it became a struggle for her to get into his house, and for him to keep her walking in the open air. If, on their way to some bus stop or railway station, he needed to leave his books at home, she accompanied him inside and beckoned him upstairs; at other times he went on grimly walking through all weathers, hour after hour, till she dropped exhausted and veered off home. It was an exercising business.

It became increasingly difficult to detect in Bland the overflowing gratitude Shaw claimed such husbands lavished on him. He hoped, by everything short of a sexual relationship, to give Edith compensation for her husband's infidelities. But she protested to him: 'You had no right to write the Preface if you were not going to write the book.' He had made her determined to bring matters to a climax. On 11 May 1887, finding him hunched over More's *Utopia* in the Reading Room, she marched him out to tea at the Austrian Café and insisted on leading him off to his home. Believing his mother to be there, he agreed. His mother was out. There followed 'an unpleasant scene caused by my telling her that I wished her to go, as I was afraid that a visit to me alone would compromise her'. She went: but the friendship survived and the marriage endured. For Shaw, in his fashion, was a true friend of this marriage, rather than the ally of one partner. In 1914, when Bland was dying and felt troubled as to whether there would be enough money for the education of one of his sons, he told his daughter: 'If there is not enough, ask Shaw' – and indeed it was Shaw who paid for John Bland to go to Cambridge.

'I was, in fact, a born philanderer,' he later told Frank Harris. In his play *The Philanderer* he was to portray himself in the part of Leonard Charteris, whom he described as 'the real Don Juan'. With married women and Fabian girls, Shaw philandered. But Mrs Jane Patterson was to make a Don Juan out of him.

*

'Jenny' Patterson was a particular friend of Shaw's mother – indeed she was closer in age to Mrs Shaw than to her son and may have known the family in Ireland where she had been married to a well-to-do country gentleman. After his death, she moved to London and by 1885 was living in Brompton Square. Coming home from the British Museum, Shaw would find the two women together. Sometimes he joined them singing, sometimes he escorted Mrs Patterson to her bus home; but there seems to have been no romantic interest on his part until after his father's death on 19 April 1885. Almost at once their relationship changed. On 20 April, finding Mrs Patterson at home when he returned, he 'wasted all the evening' with her – the first entry of this sort in his diary. Seven days later occurs a note of his visiting her alone in Brompton Square: 'Went to Richter concert in the evening, but instead of waiting for the symphony went on to Mrs Patterson. Found her alone, and chatted until past midnight.' Up to the time he was twenty-nine, he told Ellen Terry, 'I was too shabby for any woman to tolerate me . . . Then I got a job to do & bought a suit of clothes with the proceeds. A lady immediately invited me to tea, threw her arms round me, and said she adored me . . . Never having regarded myself as an attractive man, I was surprised; but I kept up appearances successfully.'

The clothes with which Shaw tells his story, while fashioning an outline of the truth, also conceal something. At the beginning of his 1885 diary he had written: 'Took to the woollen clothing system, and gave up using sheets in bed.' He had been persuaded to 'rational dress' by a friend of William Morris, Andreas Scheu, an advocate of Dr Gustave Jaeger's sanatory system. Jaeger expected to regenerate the world by wool. He claimed to have tried out his wool-theories on himself and to have been restored by them from a sick creature – 'fat and scant of breath' with haemorrhoids and tendencies to indigestion – to a man who everywhere inspired affection. Shaw, who recognized in Jaeger another Vandeleur Lee, was enthusiastically converted.

He ordered his first Jaeger outfit on 19 June 1885 – 'the first new garments I have had for years'. They were 'paid for out of the insurance on my father's life,' he noted in his diary. The reddish-brown Jaeger suit was to become part of his physical personality – 'as if it were a sort of reddish brown fur,' G. K. Chesterton observed. The uniform was finished off with correct knee-breeches and stockings after a formula devised by Dr Jaeger to replace the insalubrious tubes of trousers. This was the Shavian equivalent to Oscar Wilde's aesthetic costumes.

Many of Jaeger's most faithful 'Woolleners', as they were called, came from among the Fabians who paid fastidious attention to diet and clothes, eating vegetables and wearing animals. Shaw advertised his brown combination as being 'the plumes and tunic of Don Juan' and so irresistible to women that almost anyone could knit himself into popularity. In fact it seems to have been less a matter of women regarding him so favourably in wool as of the woollen Shaw looking at women more confidently.

On 30 June, he 'got clothes from Jaeger's and put them on'. Next day he caught a cold but by 4 July was sufficiently recovered to call on Mrs Patterson and stayed with her till one o'clock. 'Vein of conversation decidedly gallant,' he logged in his diary. Over the next three weeks he visited her constantly. She provoked him, taunted him, half-defying and half-inviting him to advance, and he seemed spellbound. 'Supper, music and curious conversation,' he noted on 10 July after another evening in Brompton Square, 'and a declaration of passion. Left at 3. *Virgo intacta* still.' But only just. For these evenings were unlike his visits into other people's love lives. There he had been Vandeleur Lee, the chaste wizard; here, dressed in the clothes from his father's life insurance and with his mother's closest friend, he could re-enact and improve on the romance of George Carr Shaw and Lucinda Elizabeth. On 18 July he bought some contraceptives ('French letters 5/–') which, on examination, 'extraordinarily revolted me' – so much that in the evening at Jenny's there were 'forced caresses' instead of love-making. Much of this must have been known to Lucinda Shaw. She and Jenny had spent most of 25 July together. In the evening, Shaw came across them walking along the Brompton Road 'looking for a bus, but they were all full,' he noted. 'So, on the corner of Montpelier St. Mother went on by herself, and I returned to the Square with JP, and stayed there until 3 o'clock on my 29th birthday which I celebrated by a new experience. Was watched by an old woman next door, whose evil interpretation of the lateness of my departure greatly alarmed us.'

He had been starved of sex. 'I was an absolute novice,' he wrote in his diary. 'I did not take the initiative in the matter.' During his 'teens and twenties he was 'perfectly continent except for the involuntary incontinences of dreamland'. All these years he exercised his imagination in daydreams about women, but not until Jenny Patterson broke through his celibacy did he know the power of sex. Sometimes he resented this power she had over him. 'The spell of your happiness has been potent.' But when the spell evaporated, he was filled with mortification. Love un-Shavianized him, robbed him of his authority and the hard discipline of work through which he was trying to re-create himself. In retrospect his embraces with Jenny became part of a wrestling match between her possessiveness and his independence. His diary entries over the next weeks indicate the ambivalence of his feelings.

27 July No work done. Went to Museum and wrote a letter to JP . . .
3 August Wrote full circumstantial account of affair with JP to E.

McN[ulty] . . . Spent the evening with Sidney Webb at Colonial Office. He told me about his love affair and disappointment. Wrote a rather fierce letter to JP on my return.
4 August Did nothing practically. Called on Eleanor Aveling in the afternoon. Resolved to begin new *Pilgrim's Progress* at once . . . Wrote JP in reply to her answer to yesterday's explosion.
5 August Wrote the beginning of *Pilgrim's Progress* . . . to JP to eat and make love until 1.20.
10 August . . . JP came. To dinner at 16 then to Jaeger's where I ordered a knitted woollen suit. Mother and JP at Jaeger's too. After tea went home with JP & stayed until five minutes before midnight.'

He saw her every week, ending the day with her at Brompton Square and walking back home in the early hours. There would be intervals when she went out of town, usually to her cottage in Broadstairs, but when she returned, the entries in Shaw's diary would start up again: 'Called on JP'; 'Went to JP in the evening'; 'JP here when I came home. Walked to Brompton Square with her.' He turned up whenever he could not stay away – she hardly knew when it might be. Sometimes he came when she would have preferred him not to: 'You will not believe me I know,' she was to write to him, 'but it is absolutely true that often my body has been an unwilling minister to you.' At other times he would arrive so late that she was asleep and he would stand in the square looking up at the unlit windows.

In the shorthand diaries where he listed his expenditure on food and travel, he also noted in code the number of times he and Jenny made love: once on the 2 and 10 August; twice on 16 and 22 August – and so on. 'Sexual experience seemed a natural appetite,' G.B.S. wrote forty years later, 'and its satisfaction a completion of human experience necessary for fully qualified authorship.' The author learned about the demands and excitements of loving; and the wiles of self-protection. 'Only by intercourse with men and women,' he reasoned, could we learn humanity. 'This involves an active life, not a contemplative one . . . you must . . . give and receive hate, love, and friendship with all sorts of people before you can acquire the sense of humanity.'

'I wanted to love,' he wrote, 'but not to be appropriated.' He wanted Jenny to take the edge off his lust so that he was unassailable in his Fabian flirtations and with those wives into whose marriages he had introduced himself as the favourite son. Whenever he felt restless, he looked to her to settle him; but 'I was never duped by sex as a basis for permanent relations, nor dreamt of marriage in connection with it,' he insisted. 'I put everything else before it, and never refused or broke an engagement to speak on Socialism to pass a gallant evening.' But once the Fabian meetings were over, he would find himself, like a sleepwalker, back at her house. 'Went to JP's,' he wrote in his diary on 9 January 1886. 'Revulsion.' But three days later he was there making love to her again. 'Went to JP in the evening and there met T. Tighe Hopkins. He was bent on seduction, and we tried which should outstay the other. Eventually he had to go for his train . . . To bed late.'

'What a fascinating & charming lady your friend Mrs Patterson is!' May Morris told Shaw. 'I wonder why you professed to be reluctant to introduce me to her.' He *was* reluctant – but not to talk about her. 'Are you not a rather disloyal friend?' May questioned him. 'I confess I should hate to be scoffed at behind my back as you profess to scoff at Mrs Patterson.' But Shaw admitted to betraying everybody's confidences in the most exaggerated way. It was a sample, he explained, of Irish tact. Everyone branded him a mischief-maker but thought no worse of the people gossiped over.

Shaw's natural tendency to put Jenny Patterson in a compartment was strengthened by her jealousy. She accuses him of having 'kissed & mauled about' other women. She assails him with her need for reassurance. 'Are you thinking of me? Wanting me? . . . I wish you were here now! Good-night my darling love – when shall I see you?' Then came apologies for her 'awful' rages – 'You know how hard it is to master oneself and it is doubly hard for one like myself who has never been educated or controlled – in fact a savage.' She woos him back to Brompton Square with fresh grapes, honey, cocoa, brown bread, strawberries and the promise that they could both be fast asleep by 2 a.m. 'You are absolutely free to do as you please,' she instructs him. But not for long. 'You will run many dangers from my abandoned sex. You will be hardly safe without me . . . don't fall in love with anyone but me . . .'

Early in 1886 Shaw made an effort to end their relationship. 'Do you wish never to see me again?' she asks him, and adds, with truth: 'I could never make you see me if you did not want to . . . You have done me no harm. Nor have I harmed you.' But Shaw felt he had harmed her; he had used her body and only he knew what he felt when he did so. His urge to make a confession to McNulty and to start a 'new Pilgrim's Progress' were symptoms of his dissatisfaction. 'Be happy,' he had written to her in the first week of their affair, 'for I have not the fortitude enough to bear your misfortunes.' 'Let me be happy,' she wrote back to him. 'I love you.' But the currency of their love was different, and there could be no exchange between them that seemed fair. He could not make her happy for long. 'When a woman does what I have done & expects either consider-ation or love from her lover she is a fool. I am one for I believed in you &

loved you. I alas love you too much now . . . You are the one man in all the world to me & this I feel I know after nearly ten months of intimacy.' This letter was written on 8 May and preceded a 'violent scene' between them at Brompton Square the following day. When Shaw got home that night he wrote to tell her that 'our future intercourse must be platonic'. In this letter, which made Jenny 'unutterably unhappy', Shaw tried to explain his own guilt: 'I see plainly that I have played a very poor part for some time past . . . I have sacrificed you and am so far the better for it – but you are the worse . . . I had nothing to lose – but I had something to gain and therein lies the rascality of it.'

Jenny was unhappy, but by no means 'unutterably' so. In page after page over the next two days she went through her fears and regrets: 'You make me suffer tortures. Have pity on me. I have some little right to ask it of you. I write in despair . . . oh my love, my love, be good to me . . . do not abandon me . . . I said leave me but you would not. The parting then would have been less hard for me . . . You tell me to take other lovers as if I took them as easily as a new pair of gloves . . . I deeply deplore Sunday's work – but I am the sufferer. I couldn't help it. My grief is for your loss to me.'

She feared to open his letters, writing to ask whether they were unkind – and not daring to open the answers. He filled the backs of her envelopes with notes for political speeches. But what he wrote to her was not unkind. 'I do not mean to abandon or desert you – I will not change – but in one thing [sex]. All shall be as before – but that.' Knowing she still had some physical influence over him, Jenny decided to go and see him. 'JP called here in the morning distracted about my letter,' Shaw jotted in his diary on 13 May. 'There was a scene and much pathetic petting and kissing, after which she went away comparatively happy', and Shaw, with intense relief, settled down to the economic study of Jevonian curves of indifference. A few days later she wrote to him accepting 'all you offer. It will be for you to prove that it [sex] was not "the" one thing that brought you here, that nothing is altered betwixt us really except the thing you hold so cheap.' But, she added, 'I do know that you are outraging nature.'

He continued visiting her, but less often; and he left earlier. This had been one of the difficulties between them: whether he should stay the night and neglect his work, or return home at night and neglect her. Fearing that they would drift apart she promised to be 'as good as I possibly can if you will come, not even try to kiss you – unless you wish it'. So he began seeing more of her, sometimes walking her to the door of her house, sometimes going in. Seven Sundays after their platonic intercourse had begun they made love – twice – and things were calmer. 'My Friend & Lover,' she wrote to him at the end of July 1886, 'I am content that there are no barriers betwixt us – that you have taken me back. I will try to make you content with me.' But over the next eighteen months they made each other deeply discontented. When she went off to her cottage at Broadstairs, he felt 'much indisposed for her society'; when she returned to London he found himself 'much out of humour with her and things in general'. On 16 December, their relationship exploded in a quarrel that lasted till one o'clock in the morning.

'I am so happy when I am with you. Be as platonic as you will,' she had written to him. ' . . . I can care for you without any sensuality.' What he apparently wanted was a platonic experiment with full sexual intercourse. The uncertainty of her position swept Jenny into a variety of distracted moods. She would demand that he 'sacrifice something or someone for me'; plead with him: 'Where are you? . . . its a million years since I have been in your arms'; cross-examine him: 'Have you been faithful? Absolutely faithful??' The thought of his unfaithfulness made her ill. 'I am consumed by all sorts of fancies about you.' During platonic intervals, Shaw would drop in on her to change his clothes, plunge into a bath or dash off letters to other women. Once, after she caught him writing to Annie Besant, she followed the two of them next day in the street and was soon plastering him with reproaches. 'You belong to me,' she insisted.

*

At the beginning of his diary for 1886 Shaw recorded that 'my work at the Fabian brought me much into contact with Mrs Besant, and towards the end of the year this intimacy became of a very close and personal sort, without, however, going further than a friendship'.

Annie Besant was nine years older than Shaw. Though separated from her husband she was still legally tied to him and, better still, 'had absolutely no sex appeal'. Like Shaw, she had endured a loveless childhood, but at the age of twenty propelled herself into a painful marriage with a clergyman, Frank Besant, by whom she had two children, and from which she emerged with a fascination for celibacy and a devotion to atheism. Expelled from their home, she set out on an extraordinary pilgrimage, moving from one cause to another, each embodied by a man. The first had been the great secularist saint, Charles Bradlaugh, with whom she had 'fought all England in the cause of liberty of conscience'. Then she veered towards the insidious Aveling, but he had left her for Eleanor Marx. She had then persuaded a dependable young Scottish secularist, John Mackinnon Robertson, to take Aveling's place on Bradlaugh's *National Reformer* as well as her own new journal *Our Corner.*

She and Shaw met formally in January 1885 at the Dialectical Society near Oxford Circus where Shaw was to deliver a socialist address. It was rumoured that Annie, as the most redoubtable champion of individualist free-thought, had come down to 'destroy me,' Shaw recalled, 'and that from the moment she rose to speak my cause was lost'. Public meetings were the elixir of life to her. From the platform her voice, low and thrilling, seemed neither that of a woman nor of a man, but godlike and of irresistible authority. To Shaw's mind she was the greatest orator in England. Everyone waited for her that night to lead the opposition against Shaw, but she did not rise and the opposition was taken up by another member. 'After he had finished, Annie Besant, to the amazement of the meeting, got up and utterly demolished him,' Shaw remembered. ' . . . At the end she asked me to nominate her to the Fabian Society and invited me to dine with her.' She was, he concluded, 'a woman of swift decisions'. And she was an 'incorrigible benefactress'. She arranged the serialization of *The Irrational Knot* and *Love Among the Artists* in *Our Corner*; and it was she who launched him there as an art critic. But she found, as Archer had previously done, that Shaw was extremely difficult to help. He had 'a perfect genius for "aggravating" her'. When he declared, after her death, that she had had no sex appeal, he meant that she was without a sense of humour. 'Comedy was not her clue to life,' he admitted:

' . . . no truth came to her first as a joke. Injustice, waste, and the defeat of noble aspirations did not revolt her by way of irony and paradox: they stirred her to direct and powerful indignation and to active resistance . . . the apparently heartless levity with which I spoke and acted in matters which seemed deeply serious . . . must have made it very hard for her to work with me at times.'

At the beginning of his diary for 1887 he noted that their intimacy had reached 'a point at which it threatened to become a vulgar intrigue, chiefly through my fault. But I roused myself in time and avoided this.' Such Shavian rousing was signalled from his side by the despatch of his photograph, and from hers by the composition of a number of fevered poems which, her sympathetic biographer Arthur H. Nethercot comments, 'perhaps fortunately, have not survived'. They orchestrated their incompatibilities over a series of piano duets on Monday nights. 'Shaw always came in, sat down at the piano, and plunged ahead,' Nethercot records, 'but Mrs Besant whenever possible practised for hours to perfect her parts in advance. The neighbourhood resounded with their efforts to keep in time.'

Annie Besant seemed to borrow everything from other people, adding nothing except the wonder of her voice. Beatrice Webb, who disliked her, nevertheless felt that she was 'the most wonderful woman of her century'. To Shaw also she was wonderful, but as someone on stage. 'Like all great public speakers she was a born actress,' he wrote. He tried to make her a good Fabian. 'I ought to have done much more for her,' he concluded, 'and she much less for me, than we did.' Annie, too, had hoped for more. In August 1887 she wrote in the *National Reformer*: 'Life had nothing fairer for its favourites than friendship kissed into the passion of love.' Shaw's love had two qualities – extreme levity and extreme tenacity. In December 1887 she presented him with a contract setting forth the terms on which they were to live together. When he refused to sign it ('I had rather be legally married to you ten times over,' he cautiously fulminated) she produced a casket in which she kept all his letters and handed it to him. Next day, 24 December, he returned her side of the correspondence, and on reaching home found that Jenny Patterson had been to his room 'and had read my letters to Mrs B. which I had incautiously left on my table'. Some of these letters mentioning herself she had taken with her. 'I make no excuse for taking the letters,' she wrote.

'You have taken advantage of . . . my belief & trust in you . . . I am ill & numb . . . & [my] loneliness is almost unbearable. I try to think what it is I have done to deserve this evil . . . I have a thousand memories of you that I can't forget . . . I feel ashamed beyond telling when I try to imagine what she must think of me. You have humbled me in the dust.'

On the morning of Christmas Day, Shaw was woken by a hammering at the door. It was Jenny Patterson, bristling with letters. They argued about it all, and then 'I at last got those she had taken and destroyed them'. The following evening they passed together, and so far mended matters that a few days later they saw in the New Year by making love.

Jenny still engaged his body as Annie Besant faded to a luminous voice in his memory. She flung herself violently into street socialism and then surrendered to the masculine charm of Madame Blavatsky, 'one of the most accomplished impostors in history'. 'Gone to Theosophy,' Pease noted on his Fabian list, and crossed out her name.

As for Shaw: 'Reading over my letters before destroying them rather disgusted me with the trifling of the last 2 years with women.'

4

INTRODUCING SIDNEY WEBB

> The Fabian lecturers are famous throughout the world. Their women are beautiful; their men brave. Their executive council challenges the universe for quality . . . Say to the horseleech, 'I have joined the Fabian,' and he will drop off as though you have overwhelmed him with salt.
>
> Shaw to Pakenham Beatty (27 May 1887)

'Whatever Society I joined,' Shaw wrote, 'I was immediately placed on the executive committee.' The Fabians had elected him to their executive on 2 January 1885, and Hyndman came to accept that he was lost for ever to the Social Democratic Federation. In selecting a political partner for himself, Shaw was guided by the need to discover someone as unlike Hyndman as possible, someone vividly unheroic and unfrockcoated, who would never play at soldiers in the street. He had already spotted the man: a crushingly plain clerk from the Colonial Office, his bulky head set on a dumpy body, graceless in movement, and as a public speaker inaudible. According to his future wife, he looked something between a London tradesman and a German professor. 'This was the ablest man in England,' Shaw decided: 'Sidney Webb. Quite the wisest thing I ever did was to force my friendship on him and to keep it.'

He had first met Webb in October 1880 at the Zetetical Society. 'He knew all about the subject of debate,' Shaw recalled; 'knew more than the lecturer; knew more than anybody present; had read everything that had ever been written; and remembered all the facts that bore on the subject. He used notes, read them, ticked them off one by one, threw them away, and finished with a coolness and clearness that seemed to me miraculous.' Though Webb was to laugh away this recollection, he acknowledged fifty years later that their meeting led to a friendship 'which has been most fruitful to me. I look back on it with wonder at the advantage, and indeed, the beauty of [it] . . . Apart from marriage, it has certainly been the biggest thing in my life.' And Shaw, in his ninetieth year, wrote in a letter to Webb that 'I never met a man who combined your extraordinary ability with your unique simplicity and integrity of character . . . you knew everything that I didn't know and I knew everything that you didn't know. We had everything to learn from one another and brains enough to do it.'

Webb was indefatigably packed with information. But in Shaw's opinion, his simplicity of character was a political disadvantage. He was not mean, he had no envy, he was never a Party man. He had little humour, was impatient with people less clever than himself, and incapable of dramatizing himself or his subject. 'I did all that for him,' Shaw told Kingsley Martin, and in a letter to Lady Londonderry he explained: 'All I could do for Webb was to beat the big drum in front of his booth, as he would not master that useful instrument himself.' The description he gave of Webb as one who 'never posed, never acted . . . and was never in danger of becoming a humbug and a living fiction, not to say a living lie', points to the disgust felt by the fastidious Shaw at the gyrations G.B.S. went through to gain public attention. He produced a fountain of sparkling illustrations to make the dullest subject entertaining. And people listened. For the first time Webb's arguments began to command an audience. Shaw had become his loudspeaker. From the other side of a Fabian screen that hid his physical defects, Webb planned to get his ideas implanted in the smart, the powerful, rich and successful figures of the world. People who felt chilled by Webb's programme of national efficiency adored Shaw's jokes, his acting, and gift for addressing two boys, a woman and a baby in the rain as if they were the greatest demonstration in the world. And behind him, invisible to the public, Webb was whispering the researched facts. But who had really 'permeated' the other was more difficult to know.

According to Webb, the Fabians always expressed Shaw's 'political views and work'. According to Shaw, Webb was 'the real inventor of Fabian Socialism'. Each was a wonder to the other. Writing in the third person for his biographer Archibald Henderson, Shaw declared that 'they valued and even over-valued one another'. But in overvaluing each other they overlooked one quality, essential in politics, that neither of them possessed: the ability to take action. Neither of them wanted to go directly into national politics, and it was this side-stepping that gave the Fabians their peculiar obliqueness.

Webb, the man of numbers, gave the Fabians their policy; Shaw, the man of letters, their tactics; and the two of them created the Fabian legend. From Webb came the distinguished Fabian tradition of research and education. In Shaw, they had a propagandist of brilliance. Everything he touched was given a bewilderingly cheerful coherence. Under their joint management, the Fabian Society became a club, a debating chamber, an ideas factory for the Labour movement in Britain, a focus for sociological research and literary-political propaganda. In place of the old revolutionary notion of attracting recruits until they were numerous enough to defeat capitalism at the barricades, the Fabians substituted the novelty that socialists should join other groups and permeate them with socialist ideas. They took socialism off the streets and sat it down in the drawing-room. They made it respectable by dealing it out as a series of parliamentary measures designed to merge political radicalism with economic collectivism. Shaw offered revolution without tears – you would hardly know it had happened. 'A party informed at all points by men of gentle habits and trained reasoning powers may achieve a complete Revolution without a single act of violence,' he stated.

Fabianism came to mean 'permeation'. In the political vocabulary it was the Fabians who patented the word. This policy gradually gave the Society its identity. Shaw and Webb believed in argument on paper. Other leading Fabians were also men of paper, for example Graham Wallas, a schoolmaster and political scientist who eventually lost his capacity for agreeable companionship in the grind of public service. A more attractive figure was Sydney Olivier. 'He was handsome and strongly sexed,' wrote Shaw, 'looking like a Spanish grandee . . . I believe he could have carried a cottage piano upstairs; but it would have cracked in his grip.' Shaw recognized in Olivier the powerful man needed by the Fabians.

Olivier joined the Fabians with Webb in May 1885, and Wallas enrolled the following year. They became known among Fabians as 'the Three Musketeers', with Shaw taking the role of d'Artagnan. This small group directed the affairs of the Society. The 'fifth wheel' on the Musketeers' coach was Annie Besant: 'a sort of expeditionary force,' in Shaw's words, 'always to the front when there was trouble and danger . . . founding branches for us throughout the country, dashing into the great strikes and free-speech agitations of that time . . . generally leaving the routine to us and taking the fighting on herself.'

With the support of Hubert Bland, Annie Besant urged the Fabians to advance boldly into front-line politics. But Shaw resisted this appeal and persuaded her that society must be reformed 'by a slow process of evolution, not by revolution and bloodshed'. This was a preliminary to Webb's famous phrase, first uttered in 1923: 'the Inevitability of Gradualness' – a philosophy that, by emphasizing the practical nature of their socialism, surrounded the Fabians with the glow of constitutional power and postponed for many years Shaw's disillusion with parliamentary politics in Britain.

*

Shaw calculated that if the Fabian Society was to become the centre of British socialism then its independence from other groups must be established not only in tone and tactics, but also in the dismal matter of economic theory.

The job of shifting the Fabians out of the shadow of Marx had begun late in 1884. Marx's value theory defined the value of a commodity as being determined by the labour involved in producing it. But Philip

Wicksteed, a Unitarian minister devoted to the works of Ibsen and the study of economics, had argued that Marxist economists failed to account for the obvious dependence of prices on supply and demand and concluded that value depended on the utility of the commodity to the consumer. From 1885 to 1889, Shaw went to the meetings of a group which, under Wicksteed's leadership, later grew into the British Economic Association. It was composed mainly of professional economists and members of the faculty of University College, London, and 'was the closest Shaw had ever come to a university education'. A controversy with Wicksteed 'ended in my education and conversion by my opponent,' Shaw later concluded, 'and the disappearance of the Marxian theory of value from the articles of faith of British Socialism'.

This was the first step for Shaw in getting rid of Marx's inevitable class war. Marx, he insisted, had been a foreigner who, though he could analyse capitalist policy like a god, did not understand the British social system. As someone outside that system, he had lusted after its violent destruction. Those who swallowed Marxism whole were possessed by a need for war. Shaw's need was for peace – to an extent where he made war (in *Arms and the Man*, for example, or in his journalism on boxing) unreal by mockery. Instead of a Marxist class war, he saw a conflict of interest between producers and the privileged unemployed – those who earned money and those who lived off rent. Such lines of battle did not run neatly between social classes, he pointed out, but through them. A continual civil war (as to some extent envisaged by Marx) could only come about if the Trade Unions and Employers' Federations were determined to play the capitalist game of labourer versus employer, particularly through free collective bargaining.

On alternate weeks, Shaw attended another group, later known as the Hampstead Historic Society, that met at Wildwood Farm, a house on the northern edge of Hampstead Heath belonging to a stockbroker, Arthur Wilson. At the centre of this group was his wife Charlotte Wilson, a firebrand bluestocking from Merton Hall, Cambridge.

The Hampstead Historic Society became the chief policy-making forum of the Fabian cabinet. They would stride up to Hampstead and argue between themselves so forcefully that other socialists could not believe they would remain friends. For Shaw, the elimination of the traditional class war took the political initiative from the socialist body and gave it to the socialist head – a transference from the proletariat to the intellectual. If Shaw's and Webb's analyses of capitalism were right, then such men as they were to have the power in the twentieth century. The sense of this power gives Shaw's Fabian writings their tone of authority, and Webb's social investigations their extraordinary persistence.

But as Shaw admitted: 'The fact is, 1886 and 1887 were not favorable years for drawing-room Socialism and scientific politics.' These were the years in which the Tories, under Lord Salisbury, swept back to power, replacing Gladstone's promise of Home Rule with the continuation of British dominance over Ireland, and replacing Chamberlain's programme of land and housing reform financed by higher taxes on the rich with a policy of expanding the Empire abroad and protecting property at home. The new order was without authority in Parliament. The trade depression of these years had thrown many out of work. 'They were years of great distress among the working-classes,' Shaw wrote. In many large towns throughout the country stones were thrown, railings uprooted, windows smashed, shops looted. The times seemed to belong to the militants – in particular to Hyndman, who had created in the SDF 'a machine that could mobilize up to twenty thousand demonstrators'. Compared with that, what was this stage army of Fabians – sixty-seven strong in 1886 and with an income of £35 19s.? The Fabian voice, insisting that true socialism was a matter of justice to the poor and not envy of the rich, was drowned. For the unemployed had begun to march and the Fabians, protesting their respectability, had no choice but to tag along behind them.

In the autumn of 1885 a police attempt to shut down a traditional 'speakers' corner' had led to a socialist demonstration in which Shaw, as one of the volunteer speakers, had pledged himself to be imprisoned. 'The prospect is anything but agreeable.' But no arrests were made and the battle for free speech was won. The following February, the SDF paraded in Trafalgar Square and there was a 'monstrous riot,' as Queen Victoria described it, '. . . a momentary triumph for socialism and a disgrace to the capital'. London seemed open to a 'French Revolution'.

The SDF planned the largest demonstration of all to take place once more in Trafalgar Square, on Sunday 13 November 1887 – a week after Sir Charles Warren, the new chief of the Metropolitan Police, had closed it for further meetings. Originally a protest against the Government's Irish policy, it became another trial of strength over free speech. Every radical, socialist and anarchist body united to confront the forces of public order.

That day groups from all over London attempted to force their way into the square and were met by 1,500 police, 200 mounted Life Guards and a detachment of Grenadier Guards. Shaw, having studied the Act under which Warren had closed Trafalgar Square and decided that it was being illegally applied, joined the group at Clerkenwell Green. After speeches from William Morris, Annie Besant and Shaw himself, exhorting the people to be orderly and to press on in their irresistible numbers if attacked, the drums rattled, banners nodded, and they set off.

Shaw's various descriptions of what became known as 'Bloody Sunday' are exultant. In every avenue leading to Trafalgar Square, the forces of Labour were broken up by squads of police. At High Holborn, Shaw and Annie Besant were swept aside by the front ranks of their own procession in counter-revolutionary retreat. 'Running hardly expresses our collective action,' he reported. 'We *skedaddled* . . . On the whole, I think it was the most abjectly disgraceful defeat ever suffered by a band of heroes outnumbering their foes a thousand to one.'

The scene at Trafalgar Square was a débâcle. The red-haired adventurer Cunninghame Graham, rising like a Scottish Mephistopheles from the sulphurous smoke of Charing Cross Underground, was truncheoned to the ground and, along with the engineer John Burns, arrested and imprisoned. Annie Besant rushed everywhere trying to organize a defence line of carts and wagons against the Foot Guards. The mild-mannered Edward Carpenter was manhandled, he furiously wrote, 'by that crawling thing a policeman'. Stuart Glennie, a Scottish philosophic historian whose special period was 6000 BC, charged the thin red line of Grenadiers with his raised umbrella as they were fixing bayonets. Shaw arrived unostentatiously with his vegetarian friend Henry Salt who, discovering his watch had been stolen, realized he could not complain to the police since he was there to complain against them. Shaw consulted his own watch and, deciding it was tea-time, walked home. After tea, he went with Annie Besant to Farringdon Hall where she chaired his evening lecture on 'Practical Socialism'.

There were many lessons to be derived from Bloody Sunday. William Morris withdrew from outdoor militancy to the converted stable of his house on the Thames and the gatherings of his Hammersmith Socialist Society. For Hyndman it was the beginning of the end, as popular support hesitated, and veered elsewhere. To Shaw and Webb the retreat seemed a victory, not for capitalism over socialism, but for Fabian tactics over those of their socialist rivals. Once the Local Government Act of 1888 was passed, they set about turning defeat into success by working in municipal politics – a programme Hyndman called 'gas and water socialism'. But two people, Annie Besant and John Burns, learnt another lesson for the twentieth century.

Amid all the vengeful growlings over their rout it was Annie Besant who acted most constructively, collecting funds, organizing newspaper support, arranging for the bail and legal defence of prisoners, storming the courts, contradicting witnesses, browbeating the police and overawing magistrates. She was all for returning the following Sunday to the Square, and made an impassioned appeal to the Fabians to do so. But Shaw, speaking in opposition, carried a reluctant meeting with him. 'I object to a defiant policy altogether at present,' he explained to William Morris. 'If we persist in it, we shall be eaten bit by bit like an artichoke. They will provoke; we will defy; they will punish. I do not see the wisdom of that.'

Annie Besant was left with a conviction that success would have to depend on efficient planning and precisely calculated aims, on influencing public opinion through newspapers and the power of organization through the unions. Her leadership of the match-girls' strike in 1888, which ended with improvements in working conditions and pay and led to the formation of a Matchworkers' Union, was recognized as a triumph for these new orderly tactics.

Of the many strikes of 1889, the greatest, beginning on 14 August, was the London Dock Strike led by John Burns, which was won with the aid of funds from Australian unions and London demonstrations planned in consultation with the police. Burns emerged from the Dock Strike victory as a potential leader of British socialism. The future belonged to such people – a working-class man who represented Battersea on the London County Council, went into Parliament in 1892 and became the 'first artisan to reach cabinet rank'.

The great Fabian success of these years was the publication, in December 1889, of *Fabian Essays in Socialism*. Shaw had been appointed editor and given the job of preparing the book from a number of Fabian lectures. Having been told by the publishers that the book was 'commercially unproducible', the Fabians decided to bring out a subscription edition themselves – a thousand copies at six shillings. It had decorations in dark green by Walter Crane on the front and by May Morris on the spine, and was distributed from Pease's flat. The preface and two of the eight essays were supplied by Shaw, who also compiled the index, chose the paper and type, and drafted a handbill announcement. Within a month the entire edition was sold out – 'it went off like smoke'. A year later, over 20,000 had gone and it was still selling at the rate of 400 copies a week. By becoming a best-seller, socialism was made respectable in capitalist terms.

Fabian Essays became a socialist bible. Suddenly Fabianism was famous. In 1891, 335,000 tracts were distributed; by 1893, the membership, which included many influential figures (Keir Hardie, Ramsay MacDonald, Emmeline Pankhurst), rose to over five hundred and, in addition to the metropolitan groups, seventy local societies had sprung up.

One of the reviewers of *Fabian Essays* was William Morris. He regretted that such lucid economic analysis and exposition of socialist principles was no longer at the service of the revolutionary movement. Instead the Fabians advocated 'the fantastic and unreal tactic' of permeation which 'could not be carried out in practice; and which, if it could be, would still leave us in a position from which we should have to begin our attack on capitalism over again'. Morris blamed Webb for this 'somewhat disastrous move'. Webb had falsified the class struggle, substituted pieties about state regulation and reduced socialism to the mechanism of a system of property-holding. For Morris himself, socialism remained a 'complete theory of human life, founded indeed on the visible necessities of animal life [which] . . . will not indeed enable us to get rid of the tragedy of life . . . but will enable us to meet it without fear and without shame'. He wrote warmly, if regretfully, of Shaw. 'If he could only forget the Sidney-Webbian permeation tactic . . . what an advantage it would be to us all!'

Morris and Webb were Shaw's political mentors. Morris was a great man and Webb a great brain; Morris a hero for all time and Webb a man of the times. Shaw wanted to unite the applied arts with the social sciences and use Webb's logic to circumvent Morris's sense of history. But they remained two heralds beckoning Shaw in different directions. So he continued speaking of the Fabians with two voices. His most persistent voice aggrandized the Fabian achievement. The other voice sounded his despair that they had not achieved more. He insisted that 'Webb made no mistake'. But he was also to acknowledge by the 1930s the possibility that 'Morris was right after all'. He turned to one and then to the other: and eventually he turned to Soviet Russia.

FOUR

I

THE PERFECT IBSENITE

> I attack the current morality because it has come to mean a system of strict observance of certain fixed rules of conduct . . . intensified by the addition to the ten commandments of sentimental obligations to act up to ideal standards of heroism. Now what Ibsen has done is to call attention to the fact that the moment we begin to worship these commandments and ideals for their own sakes, we actually place them in opposition to the very purpose they were instituted to serve, i.e. human happiness.
>
> Shaw to Jules Magny (16 December 1890)

On 7 February 1887, their landlord having gone bankrupt, the Shaws had received notice to leave their flat at 36 Osnaburgh Street. 'Looking for lodgings in Marylebone and Gray's Inn,' Shaw noted in his diary on 26 February, 'where my feelings were somewhat hurt by the brusqueness with which the steward received my question as to whether ladies were permitted to reside within the precincts.'

Towards the end of March he joined his mother on the third and fourth floors of 29 Fitzroy Square. A big room overlooking the square became his bedroom, and he turned one of the rooms on the top floor into a study. Here, in grand disorder he was to write his first seven plays, his literary, music and theatre criticism, and carry on his most active political campaigning.

Number 29 Fitzroy Square had a handsome façade, but was in poor condition. Shaw, who later bought the lease for his mother, described it as 'a most repulsive house'. There was no bathroom and 'the sanitary arrangements had had no place in the original plans,' he discovered. 'In impressive architecture it is the outside that matters most; and the servants do not matter at all.' It was a fine place for the flowering of his socialism. After a series of humiliating interviews, he established himself as being not his mother's lodger but head of the household, so that in November 1888 he was able to register 'the first vote I ever gave in my life at an election, though I am over 32 years of age'.

Wherever he spoke his words were 'straight as a ray of light,' wrote H. M. Tomlinson, 'such as we get once or twice in a few centuries, as the result of a passionate morality that happens to be gifted with the complete control of full expression'. Many who heard this 'tall, thin man with a very pale and gentle face' speaking with deadly playfulness, and denouncing as robbers those usually regarded as the ornaments of society, were convinced that here was the leader of 'a revolutionary rising which would upset many of our conventions and bring a new dispensation, political and economic, into the London world'.

In 1887 he delivered sixty-six public lectures; by the end of ten years he had given nearly a thousand. Every Sunday he spoke, sometimes against the blaring of brass bands, often at workmen's clubs and coffee houses, arguing from squalid platforms in dens full of tobacco smoke, to a little knot of members whom he had pulled away from their beer and billiards. The 'ubiquitous Mr Shaw', as *The Star* called him, was soon well known: 'a strange and rather startling figure', erect and agile in his serviceable suit of tweed, red scarf, wide-brimmed felt hat and jauntily swinging umbrella – 'a tall, lean, icy man,' reported the *Workman's Times*, 'white-faced, with a hard, clear, fleshless voice, restless grey-blue eyes, neatly-parted fair hair, big feet, and a reddish, untamed beard'.

He preferred speaking in the open air – under lamp-posts, at dock gates, in parks, squares, market places – and in all sorts of weather. He never wrote or read his speeches. By the late 1880s he had laboriously perfected his technique 'until I could put a candle out with a consonant'.

Whether it was 'Capitalism' at the Wolverhampton Trades and Labour Council, 'Communism' at the Dulwich Working Men's Club, 'Socialism' at Plumstead, or 'Food, Death and Civilization' at the headquarters of the London Vegetarian League, he spoke, stretching his long fingers to reach out to his audience, as if all their lives depended upon it. He packed the halls with crowds of people; he made them listen, made them laugh. It is clear from the text of those lectures he later wrote up for publication that Shaw was passionately serious.

'Your authorised system of medicine is nothing but a debased survival of witchcraft. Your schools are machines for forcing a spurious literary culture on children in order that your universities may stamp them as educated men when they have fairly got hold of the wrong end of every stick in the faggot of knowledge. The tall silk hats and starched linen fronts which you force me to wear, and without which I cannot successfully practise as a physician, clergyman, schoolmaster, lawyer or merchant, are inconvenient, insanitary, ugly, pompous and offensive . . . your popular forms of worship are . . . only redeemed from gross superstition by their obvious insincerity . . . Under color of protecting my person you forcibly take my money to support an armed force for the execution of barbarous and detestable laws; for the urging of wars I abhor . . . Your tyranny makes my very individuality a hindrance to me: I am outdone and outbred by the mediocre, the docile, the time-serving. Evolution under such conditions means degeneracy.'

This was the voice of a man who had raised the torch of revolution. No wonder there was sometimes violence – and he had to escape through a window or back door.

'Your slaves are beyond caring for your cries . . . In the midst of the riches which their labor piles up for you, their misery rises up too and stifles you. You withdraw in disgust to the other end of the town from them; you appoint special carriages on your railways and special seats in your churches and theatres for them; you set your life apart from theirs by every class barrier you can devise; and yet they swarm about you still . . . they poison your life as remorselessly as you have sacrificed theirs heartlessly . . . Then comes the terror of their revolting; the drilling and arming of bodies of them to keep down the rest; the prison, the hospital, paroxysms of frantic coercion, followed by paroxysms of frantic charity. And in the meantime, the population continues to increase!'

Henry Sidgwick, Professor of Moral Philosophy at Cambridge, who heard him speak at Bath, noted in his diary that the speaker was 'a live Socialist, redhot "from the Streets"' who

'sketched in a really brilliant address the rapid series of steps by which modern society is to pass peacefully into social democracy . . . It is now *urban* ground-rent that the municipal governments will have to seize, to meet the ever-growing necessity of providing work and wages for the unemployed . . . There was a peroration rhetorically effective as well as daring, in which he explained that the bliss of perfected socialism would only come by slow degrees, with lingering step and long delays, and claimed our sympathy for the noble-hearted men whose ardent philanthropy had led them to cut these delays short by immediate revolution . . . Altogether a noteworthy performance: – the man's name is *Bernard Shaw*.'

Shaw's oratory was like a spur to insurrection, and if he stopped short of calling for the bombardment of the London slums by the new dynamite, it seemed only with reluctance. Gradualness might be inevitable, but it was not welcome: 'if we feel relieved that the change is to be slow enough to avert personal risk to ourselves; if we feel anything less than acute disappointment and bitter humiliation at the discovery that there is yet between us and the promised land a wilderness in which many must perish miserably of want and despair: then I submit to you that our institutions have corrupted us to the most dastardly degree of selfishness.'

For his thousand lectures over these years Shaw received no payment. 'He gives up willingly time, labour, the opportunities of self-advancement,' reported *The Star*. 'To such men we can forgive much.' At the election of 1892, while Shaw was speaking at the Town Hall in Dover, a man rose and warned his audience not to be taken in by someone whose opinions were purchased: 'I immediately offered to sell him my emoluments for £5,' Shaw recalled. 'He hesitated; and I came down to £4. I offered to make it five shillings – half-a-crown – a shilling – sixpence. When he would not deal even at a penny I claimed that he must know perfectly well that I was there at my own expense. If I had not been able to do this, the meeting, which was a difficult and hostile one . . . would probably have broken up.'

The art of public speaking answered his need for attention, though much of it was 'terrible tongue work'. He never admired this need in himself. The development of his public manner had forced brashness on to a nature that was ordinarily sensitive. 'Oratory is a vice,' he complained to the actress Lena Ashwell. He could not delude himself: the applause that rose through his meetings was an empty sound. 'My career as a public speaker was not only futile politically,' he later concluded: 'It was sometimes disgraceful and degrading . . . I suffered agonies of disgust at the whole business and shame for my part in it.'

The success of *Fabian Essays* in 1889 soon led to a train of provincial lectures, particularly in the north of England, and Shaw's flame-coloured beard and illuminated white face were seen in places that had never before borne witness to socialism. He worked eighteen hours a day and on the seventh day he worked. 'My hours that make my days, my days that make my years,' he wrote, 'follow one another pell mell into the maw of Socialism.'

*

He had hoped to convert some of this lecture-work into book-work: 'It is quite possible to get into a volume of 200 pages an adequate and bright explanation of the law of rent and the law of value, which really cover the laws of production and of exchange, and so, in a fair sense, cover the whole field of economics,' he explained to Havelock Ellis. ' . . . I could produce such a book before the middle of next year.' But early in 1889 he wrote to Ellis: 'I see about as much prospect of having "Production & Exchange" ready by June as of establishing the millennium . . . I have to keep up my lectures (five this week); and I have to keep myself alive by journalism all the time. This is not "Production & Exchange".'

In the summer of 1890, the Fabians found themselves committed to a programme of addresses under the heading 'Socialism in Contemporary Literature'. Between May and July Shaw worked on a paper about Ibsen which he delivered on 18 July at the St James's Restaurant. The minutes record that 'the effect on the packed audience was overwhelming'. But not all the Fabians were happy. 'It is very clever,' Sidney Webb wrote, 'and not so bad as I feared . . . But his glorification of the Individual Will distresses me.'

It was probably the Parnell case that decided Shaw to expand his lecture into a book. This *cause célèbre* had resulted in November 1891 in Captain O'Shea being granted a decree nisi against his wife, naming Charles Stewart Parnell, leader of the Irish Party in the House of Commons, as co-respondent. Both in private letters and letters to *The Star*, Shaw had defended Parnell against the outcry 'Parnell Must GO!' following this flouting of domestic ideals by a public figure. On the same day, 16 December, that he wrote to Sydney Olivier, criticizing the opposition to Parnell from within the Fabian Society, he decided to publish *The Quintessence of Ibsenism*.

The book was a product of Shaw's friendship with Archer through whom he had first got to know Ibsen's work. Meeting Ibsen in Denmark in 1887, Archer had observed that he 'is essentially a kindred spirit with Shaw – a paradoxist, a sort of Devil's Advocate, who goes about picking holes in every "well-known fact"'. It was this similarity that helped to give Shaw such an instinctive insight into Ibsen's plays. These plays had the power to move Shaw more than the work of any other living dramatist. Of a performance of *The Wild Duck*, he was to write:

'To sit there getting deeper and deeper in that Ekdal home, and getting deeper and deeper into your own life all the time, until you forget you are in a theatre; to look on with horror and pity at a profound tragedy, shaking with laughter all the time at an irresistible comedy; to go out, not from a diversion, but from an experience deeper than real life ever brings to most men, or often brings to any man: that is what The Wild Duck was like last Monday at the Globe.'

The joy of his *Quintessence* is that of feeling Shaw's agile and ingenious mind working with such vitality on material so sympathetic to him. He prefaced the book with the warning that he is not concerned here with Ibsen as a dramatist, but as a teacher; that this is not literary criticism but analysis of the philosophy of which Ibsen was an exponent. In seeking a symbolic leader who would unite the contradictory impulses within himself, Shaw leads him into battle against those conventional ideals that he felt formed the chief obstacle to progress.

By the early 1890s, following productions of *A Doll's House* and *Ghosts*, the name of Ibsen (who was sixty-three when the *Quintessence* appeared) had emerged from obscurity into huge contention in Britain as the playwright who was forcing a whole generation to re-evaluate its ideas. Shaw assumed the generalship of the British campaign.

As a model for his argument Shaw had adapted Matthew Arnold and used a threefold division of mankind into philistine, idealist and (pending the word superman) realist. He proposes a hypothetical community of one thousand people in which seven hundred are easygoing philistines, two hundred and ninety-nine dangerous idealists ('the idealist is a more dangerous animal than the philistine just as a man is a more dangerous animal than a sheep'), and there is one realistic pioneer essential to the evolution of the species. The philistine, substituting 'custom for conscience', is satisfied with the social system as it is. The irony of his position is that, though he sees any interference with the social machinery as highly dangerous, the real danger comes from allowing that machinery to grow outdated. The philistine employs the idealist to think for him and to 'idealize' his lack of thought. The idealist, though higher in the ascent of human evolution than the philistine, is a moral coward coerced by the majority into conformity. Ideals, in Shavian terminology, are therefore illusions which have their origin in fear; idealism is life by the rule of precedent, and the idealist a pedlar of fancy pictures which advertise this rule. Shaw likens these pictures to beautiful masks which the idealist puts for us on the unbearable faces of truth: the poetic mask of immortality on that king of terrors, death; the mask of romantic happiness, within the prison-house of marriage, on the sex instinct.

But the realist, bolder than the rest, believing in the 'unflinching recognition of facts, and the abandonment of the conspiracy to ignore such of them as do not bolster up the ideals', lays hold of a mask that we have not dared to discard and reveals the disagreeable truth. So he helps to relieve us from sacrifice to the tyranny of ideals: for 'the destroyer of ideals, though denounced as an enemy to society, is in fact sweeping the world clear of lies'. This was the Ibsen-impulse: 'to get away from idolatry and get to the truth regardless of shattered ideals'; and it became Shaw's philosophy of democratic élitism.

In a number of passages added to the 1913 edition Shaw makes clear that he is enshrining individual will only when it works in harmony with the world-will (or Life Force as it would become known). Although society needs to be shocked pretty often, he argues that the 'need for freedom of evolution is the sole basis of toleration, the valid argument against Inquisitions and Censorships, the sole reason for not burning heretics and sending every eccentric person to the madhouse'. So the heretic of today (Galileo, Darwin, Marx and perhaps Shaw himself), striving to realize future possibilities, becomes the pillar of the community tomorrow. But pillars of the community are idealists. So realism has constantly to be kept up to date.

Some of the confusion surrounding the *Quintessence* arose from Shaw's choice of one word. In the same way as 'superman', with its Nietzschean associations, was to suggest not a symbol of synthesis but an immature dictatorship, so the word 'Will', with its Schopenhauerian associations, indicated not 'our old friend the soul or spirit' but an assertion of power. In neither case did Shaw originally intend this, but the ambiguity of these words points to an impulse that was gradually to gain possession of him.

'Life is an adventure, not the compounding of a prescription.' Human conduct must 'justify itself by its effect on happiness'. By 'happiness' Shaw meant human welfare and for the 1913 edition he changed 'happiness' to 'life'. In the interval between the first publication and his preparation of the 1913 edition, though he maintained the same apparatus of argument, Shaw's attitude shifted. In 1891 he had used the word 'idealist' pejoratively to cover all those who inhabited too exclusively the world of ideas, whether they were blinded by illusions or held a fixed vision of a better life. Such people, by preferring fantasy to the actual world, risked being made prisoners of abstractions, he argued, since morality was relative and must be continually tested by experience. But his experience as a Fabian would drive him, as a source for optimism, to a metaphysical creed depending on the ideal formula of equality of income.

The 1891 *Quintessence*, which aims its ingenious attack at the man he was to become, is a paradoxically prophetic work – and nowhere more so than in the pages about *Emperor and Galilean*, where Shaw begins to explore the synthesis of relations that Ibsen's Maximus called 'the third empire' – 'the empire of Man asserting the eternal validity of his own will,' Shaw wrote.

'He who can see that not on Olympus, not nailed to the cross, but in himself is God: he is the man to build Brand's bridge between the flesh and the spirit, establishing this third empire in which the spirit shall not be unknown, nor the flesh starved, nor the will tortured and baffled.'

Within *Emperor and Galilean* Shaw was to find the theme and dialectical pattern of his middle plays. Yet the habit of segregation persisted like a hereditary trait, and finally established itself in the flesh-starved Ancients at the end of *Back to Methuselah*. In these almost bodiless fantasies the author of the original *Quintessence* might have seen a dramatic example of the failure of an idealist to accept man as he is.

2

A CRUST FOR THE CRITICS

> Some time in the eighties . . . the New Journalism was introduced. Lawless young men began to write and print the living English language of their own day . . . Musical critics, instead of reading books about their business and elegantly regurgitating their erudition, began to listen to music and distinguish between sounds . . . The interview, the illustration and the cross-heading, hitherto looked on as American vulgarities impossible to English literary gentlemen, invaded all our papers.
>
> 'Van Amburgh Revived', *Saturday Review* (7 May 1898)

The Quintessence of Ibsenism was the most sustained and sophisticated work Shaw wrote before the age of thirty-five. His care in guarding the book against being 'swept into an eddy of mere literary criticism' reflects his own experience of criticism up to this time. It was 'literary criticism' in the form of readers' reports that had put a stop to his novels; it was 'literary criticism' – over a hundred anonymous notices for the *Pall Mall Gazette* – on which he had become financially dependent from the spring of 1885 to Christmas 1888.

The *Pall Mall Gazette* was the centre of what Matthew Arnold called 'the New Journalism'. It was edited by W. T. Stead who altered the character of daily journalism in Britain during the mid-1880s. Papers became simpler – as he wished the world to be. He popularized interviews, added illustrations, invented picturesque headlines, pursued virtuous crusades.

Shaw was a contributor to the *Pall Mall* under Stead's editorship, 'but as my department was literature and art, and he was an utter Philistine, no contacts between us were possible'. Yet the paper had Oscar Wilde, George Moore and William Archer writing on the arts pages, and it was a sign of Stead's journalistic flair that he should also employ there this 'satirical contributor with a turn for prophecy'.

Shaw insisted that literature and the arts must not be segregated from politics. He deplored the editorial habit of the literary department of giving 'a page and a half of vapid comment to a book destined to be forgotten without having influenced the conduct or opinions of a single human being; whilst pamphlets that circulate by thousands, dealing with vital questions of national economy and private morals, are tossed aside into the waste-paper basket . . .' But the publication of the truth about anything or anyone 'is attended with considerable risk in English society,' Shaw explained.

'We have agreed to keep up a national pretence that the black spots in human nature are white; and we enforce the convention by treating any person who even betrays his consciousness of them . . . as a prurient person and an enemy of public morals . . . the convention rigorously exacts – under pretence of not speaking evilly of the dead – that biographers should exhibit great men, not as they were, but as ideal figures . . . That the very worst sort of evil speaking, whether of the living or the dead, is the telling of lies about them . . . is not taken into account in judging biography . . . The censors will tolerate no offence against hypocrisy, because . . . an offence against hypocrisy is an offence against decency, and is punishable as such.'

Shaw's prescription for biography looks forward to the biographical revolution of Lytton Strachey thirty-five years later, and is most ironically expressed in his review of a Jubilee chronicle of Queen Victoria:

'With her merits we are familiar . . . We know that she has been of all wives the best, of all mothers the fondest, of all widows the most faithful. We have often seen her, despite her lofty station, moved by famines, colliery explosions, shipwrecks, and railway accidents; thereby teaching us that a heart beats in her Royal breast as in the humblest of her subjects. She has proved that she can, when she chooses, put off her state and play the pianoforte, write books, and illustrate them like any common lady novelist. We all remember how she repealed the corn laws, invented the steam locomotive, and introduced railways; devised the penny post, developed telegraphy, and laid the Atlantic cable . . . in short, went through such a programme as no previous potentate ever dreamed of. What we need now is a book entitled "Queen Victoria: by a Personal Acquaintance who dislikes her".'

But it was through the world of the Victorian novel that his route mainly lay. 'The most dangerous public house in London is at the corner of Oxford St,' Shaw told one of his audiences, 'and is kept by a gentleman named Mudie.' The books in Mudie's Library were uniform, and by recommending any novel as 'very popular at Mudie's' Shaw meant that it was another mammoth romance. 'Such books,' he concluded, 'are not fair game for the reviewer: they are addressed to children of all ages who are willing to shut their eyes and open their mouths.' Second-rate fiction, he concluded, might be good enough for some adults but 'first rate fiction is needed for children themselves'.

'Many of our worst habits are acquired in an imaginary world,' Shaw warned.

'... we have got the nation corrupting fiction, and fiction reacting on the nation to make it more corrupt ... Hence springs up a false morality which seeks to establish dignity, refinement, education, social importance, wealth, power and magnificence, on a hidden foundation of idleness, dishonesty, sensuality, hypocrisy, tyranny, rapacity, cruelty, and scorn. When the novelist comes to build his imaginary castle, he builds on the same foundation, but adds heroism, beauty, romance, and above all, possibility of exquisite happiness to the superstructure, thereby making it more beautiful to the ignorant, and more monstrous to the initiated.'

Looking out from Shaw's imprisonment in this castle, we may catch a splendid view of popular late Victorian fiction. What journeys its characters make! Their route lay encumbered by avalanches, attacks of consumption, unmuzzled dogs, ghosts, lunatics, Chinese executions, runaway trains, fire engines, daggers and gunpowder. Outside towers a background of crag and fortress, cloud and sea, with green walls of pine and a mountain torrent. Within, aged hounds lie stretched on the carpet, curtains are continually tweaked aside by jewelled fingers and ropes of roses adorn the staircases ascending to the boudoirs. These strongholds, which in the last chapter are all burnt to matchwood, are inhabited by a throng of murderers, bigamists, coquettes and so on. Nearly everything takes place at night (to the cry of owls, nightingales and cat-birds), except for a little cockfighting perhaps and the regular afternoon calls which usually carry on the business of the second volume. There are a few old people past love-making, but they have all had prehistoric turns at it and each carries a sorrow to the grave. The villains, who break out under stress into uncouth scraps of French, are consumed by earthquakes or engulfed in shipwrecks carrying many innocuous travellers down with them. The hero is easily recognized by his faculty for alighting on haystacks when flung from continental expresses, for inheriting fortunes, and for tracking diamond smugglers to their doom. A composite photograph of the heroines at Mudie's would have shown golden tresses, a pair of blue eyes occasionally changing under degrees of emotion to green or hazel, and a plain white dress with a flower at the throat. For three volumes intransigent relatives and designing reprobates block her way to the altar, only to be arbitrarily removed in the last pages by violent Acts of God or the Devil, the sympathetic reader breathing more and more freely as the slaughter proceeds.

With such caricatures of the love he had once longed for himself, Shaw spent many hours, months, years of his time, first as a book reviewer and subsequently as a theatre critic. In this world of reviewing he needed to fasten his talent to a stimulating purpose: the creation, by use of irresistible ridicule, of a revolution in the habits of the book-reading, theatre-going public in Britain. The bookshop or theatre should no longer be an oubliette with its trap-door sealed against reality. 'Whilst the slums exist and the sewers are out of order, it is better to force them on the attention even of the polite classes than to engage in the manufacture of eau-de-cologne for sprinkling purposes.'

Shaw's voice in the columns of the *Pall Mall Gazette* was one of exasperated geniality, below which moved a current of resentment at being obliged to spend his time reading trivial books brought out by publishers who had rejected all his own novels. It was particularly galling to see that the other Irishmen on the paper were given major writers to review: George Moore wrote on Huysmans and Zola; Oscar Wilde on Dostoevsky, William Morris, Tolstoy and Turgenev. Occasionally Shaw was allowed a minor work by an interesting writer: J. M. Barrie's *Better Dead*; Wilkie Collins's *The Evil Genius*; and *A Mere Accident* by George Moore, whose 'commendable reticence' in evading the realities of a rape 'might have been taken further, even to the point of not writing the book'.

Shaw's long sojourn in this world of reviewing later enlivened his picture of hell in *Man and Superman*. He used the stock-in-trade of the novelist and playwright as a block against which to sharpen his prose style. 'A true original style is never achieved for its own sake,' he wrote. 'Effectiveness of assertion is the Alpha and Omega of style. He who has nothing to assert has no style and can have none: he who has something to assert will go as far in power of style as its momentousness and his conviction will carry him.' What he gave up in texture, he gained in pace and authority. His writing is luminous with conviction and humour. He seldom weeds out the clichés: when in love, his heart is as 'hard as nails'; his longer plays are inevitably 'cut to the bone'. 'The more familiar the word, the better,' he told his translator, Sobieniowski. Elsewhere he announced: 'I also am a journalist, proud of it, deliberately cutting out of my works all that is not journalism, convinced that nothing that is not journalism will live long as literature, or be of any use whilst it does live.' This was part of a cleansing exercise against his long immersion in pretentious literature.

It was a bright smiling instrument, his typewriter, a marvellously efficient machine for turning all the difficulties and despairs of life into an argument – not a bad-tempered argument, but an exchange of point and counterpoint that beats down relentlessly until the rough places are made plane. In his diaries, where Shaw is unprotected by the brilliant shell of this style, we see him several times accidentally coming close to some dreadful event and feeling the shock waves: 'In Wigmore [Street] we saw a young rough beating a girl and I disturbed myself for the rest of the evening by flying at him.' 'Was much upset by having to interfere in an altercation between a young couple and a private watchman who was apparently trying to blackmail them.' Though he attacked the substitution of literature for life, his own battery of words, eliminating suffering, was in some sense a replacement for action. 'A writer,' he advised Norman Clark, 'must have a gift of intimacy, which is dangerous and offensive without good manners or tact.' Shaw had outrageously good manners, but in place of intimacy he gives us a whirling informality. The effect of his prose is like alcohol upon the nerves: we are exhilarated, intoxicated, breathless and, before the end, exhausted – and still the talkative spirit, the ascending wit, drive on. For it is a style that is always in top gear: emphatic, industrious, omniscient, studded with surprises, and better-trained for shorter distances than discursiveness.

Shaw's columns in the *Pall Mall Gazette*, though without a byline, were soon making his name notorious in the trade. Two or three times an exceptional book fell his way: the *Rural Rides* of William Cobbett ('probably more dangerous to corrupt Governments than any single man known to English history, excepting only Jonathan Swift'); *A Handbook of the History of Philosophy* by Belfort Bax, and Samuel Butler's *Luck or Cunning*, both of which (as he indicates in his Preface to *Major Barbara*) influenced his thought. But for the most part, he was kept to heart-throb fiction. He seemed to fill his reviews from a magic well that never ran dry or lost its sparkle provided he pumped hard enough. But he chafed against the restriction. In the summer of 1887 he sent Stead a long letter in which he tried to palm a socialist programme on to him. Stead read it, kept it, and did nothing: its campaign for social reform was too bleak for him. Besides, as an instrument of persuasion, there was a quality in Shaw's letter that was to mar so much of his dazzling propaganda: it was too knowing – everything it said was correct and calculated to be flattering to Stead, but the calculations showed. To act on Shaw's advice so often meant parading one's inferiority to him. His tact was like a brilliant varnish: one saw straight through it.

However much he wrote, since he could not get what he wanted, he still searched for opportunities elsewhere. Letters editors of *To-Day*, *Justice*, *The Echo*, *St James's Gazette*, *Truth*, were harried with correspondence from George Bunnerd, Shendar Bwra, A. Donis, Redbarn Wash, G. B. S. Larking, Amelia Mackintosh, Horatia Ribbonson and the Reverend C. W. Stiggins Jnr, as well as from the 'milkman', an 'English mistress', 'Inveterate Gambler' and 'A Novelist'. Under one name or another, or no name at all, he was everywhere, pleading for the retention of the split infinitive and the abolition of Christmas, protesting against the Russian use of Siberian exile for dissidents and the prosecution of Henry Vizetelly for publishing an English translation of Zola's *La Terre*. As G. Bernard Shaw he wrote of Jack the Ripper as an 'independent genius' who by 'private enterprise' had succeeded where socialism failed in getting the press to take some sympathetic interest in the conditions of London's East End.

The power Shaw felt within him seemed everywhere to be blocked. In the summer of 1888, he accepted a proposal from H. W. Massingham, deputy editor of *The Star*, that he cover occasional musical events which 'Musigena', the paper's regular music critic E. Belfort Bax, could not attend. Towards Massingham Shaw felt lifelong gratitude and respect – he was 'the perfect master journalist,' he wrote. When Bax went on holiday in August, Shaw acted as his substitute; after which he carried on as the anonymous second-string critic until, Bax resigning in February 1889, Shaw took his place at two guineas per week.

Later that year, 'I did a thing that has been in my mind for some time,' he noted in his diary, ' – wrote to Edmund Yates asking him to give the art-criticship of *The World* to Lady Colin Campbell, as it is no longer worth my while to do so much work for so little satisfaction, not to mention money.' Yates replied admitting that Shaw had been 'cavalierly treated', but concluding: 'I have no idea of loosening my hold on you.'

But Shaw had made up his mind to give himself the sack as a reviewer of pictures for *The World*. Preparing to bow out of the galleries, he told his readers on 23 October 1889: 'I cannot guarantee my very favourable impression of the Hanover Gallery, as I only saw it by gaslight. This was the fault of Sarasate, who played the Ancient Mariner with me. He fixed me with his violin on my way to Bond Street, and though, like the wedding guest, I tried my best, I could not choose but to hear.'

3

MYSTICAL BETROTHAL

> The pleasure of the senses I can sympathise with and share; but the substitution of sensuous ecstasy for intellectual activity and honesty is the very devil.
>
> Preface to *Three Plays for Puritans*

Money was one measurement of success. In 1885, his first full year in journalism, Shaw had earned £112. At the end of each year he would note in his diary what he had made from contributions to papers: £150 in 1888; £197 6s. 10d. in 1889; £252 13s. 2d. in 1890; £281 16s. 10d. for 1891. Much of this money he would hand to his mother, 'asking her for a pound when my pockets were empty'. Ten years later he was earning almost £800 (equivalent to £43,000 in 1997). He trained hard, buying coloured spectacles, a pair of dumb-bells and a pendulum alarm clock. He took regular cold baths; he went on spectacular walks. At night he opened his windows so wide that cats and birds sailed through, interrupting his sleep. He dieted, logged his weight, kept himself at about ten stone ten pounds. To his shelves he added volumes on algebra, Danish and German; on his desk he stood a modern typewriter bought from H. W. Massingham for £13 and, 'as our rent was reduced and our earnings rather enlarged, we got a new piano on the hire system, and began to live a very little more freely'.

Behind this programme of self-improvement lay a history of backsliding. He sleeps through the alarm clock, or if it wakes him, takes a nap in the British Museum. Despite his diet, he cannot resist a heap of cherries, a few overripe bananas, some indiscreet mushrooms, and sweetmeats from a machine, to which are attributed fits of indigestion, plagues of gumboils and terrific nightmares. However icy his baths he breaks out in sweats and spells of influenza. He increases his walks, but trips and falls; he starts off again, but ends up lame; he bellows out songs 'rather violently' at the piano, 'for the sake of my lungs', and loses his voice; he covers page after page and sees them all swoop and vanish under the wheels of a train. Despite the grimmest of attempts, he learns no languages, no algebra. His letters to the press are returned, his private correspondence placed in the wrong envelopes. He develops a tendency of 'clean forgetting' to turn up at rallies where he is principal speaker and at meetings where he is chairman; of arriving at theatres without his tickets, mistaking matinées for evening performances, and presenting himself at the Steinway Hall instead of the Princes Hall and vice versa; he believes it to be Thursday when it isn't; he calls on people who by arrangement are calling on him and attends At Homes where everyone is abroad. He recklessly gives away money to drunkards and minor poets, crossing-sweepers and 'Street Arabs'. Outdoors he watches a squirrel playing in a tree and a huge spider making a web, indoors he dawdles over the piano harmonizing the *Marseillaise* – all when he should have been forming a committee for the municipalization of land. Suddenly unable 'to face more political cackle', he rushes off from an important conference to a performance of *Cymbeline* – 'and enjoyed it much more than I should have enjoyed the meeting'.

More unShavian still are the adventures with his typewriter. Within a month he has mastered the brute and declares himself 'much pleased' with it. Yet his expertise is oddly hypothetical, having come to him (as with bicycling and photography) by way of accidents. Despite everything, the machine won't 'settle'. At last 'to my great annoyance' he is obliged to ask for professional advice, but when he tries to put this advice into practice the typewriter breaks down altogether and he is 'furious over it'.

The diaries become strewn with Johnsonian lamentations over 'my inveterate laziness and procrastination'. 'Not up till 10 (curse this laziness),' he writes and chides himself for doing nothing except utter good resolutions. 'Very tired and greatly disposed to curse my fate,' he notes. For Shaw to be off his work has all the pathos of a domestic animal not eating. He loses strength; he loses authority over himself. 'For weeks now I have been going to bed at 2 and not getting up until 11,' he admits. Often he starts towards his desk, only to find himself seated at the piano. 'Restless and full of work in the morning,' he writes for 9 October 1889; 'but only sat down at the piano after all and played *Parsifal* with a very deep sense of it all.' He is disgusted with this waste of time but goes on playing and singing nonetheless. When he shakes off this idleness and works strictly to timetable, he is overcome by fits of giddiness. Even his mother notices how his hands shake and his nerves are stretched. Is his diet insufficiently austere? he wonders. Perhaps his teeth are at fault. Finally, he admits: 'Am driving myself too hard,' and tries, unsuccessfully, to take it easy by means of more exercise.

Anything in the style of a holiday unnerved him. Early in 1888, he experimented with a Sunday on the Surrey Hills.

'The uneven, ankle-twisting roads; the dusty hedges; the ditch with its dead dogs, rank weeds, and swarms of poisonous flies; the groups of children torturing something; the dull, toil-broken, prematurely old agricultural laborer; the savage tramp; the manure heaps with their horrible odor; the chain of mile-stones from inn to inn, from cemetery to cemetery . . . From the village street into the railway station is a leap across five centuries from the brutalizing torpor of Nature's tyranny over Man into the order and alertness of Man's organized dominion over Nature.'

The following year he went on his first trip to the Continent: a week in April to the Netherlands, reporting on an opera for *The Star*. 'My worst forebodings have been realized,' he assured William Archer. Antwerp was 'exactly like Limerick, only duller'; and, like the Liffey in Dublin, the 'smell of the canal disgusted me with the Hague'. On the way back he sat on deck all night and was ingloriously sick. 'Nature conspires with you in vain to palm off the Continent on me as a success,' he wrote to Archer.

Three months later *The Star*'s music critic was sick *en route* for Bayreuth. 'Carried out my program successfully,' he noted in his diary – four articles on Wagner, and such vigorous sight-seeing through Germany that he split his mackintosh 'like a trick coat in a farce'. Returning from a six-day ordeal in Paris the following spring, Shaw's admission of having been 'Very sick crossing . . . thoroughly wet and cold' was turned by the music critic into a plea for the Channel Tunnel, but for the want of which *The Star* 'would be as great a musical power in Europe as it is in England'.

In August 1890 he attempted a summer holiday with Sidney Webb, the one man whose dislike of all holidaymaking exceeded his own. Their destination was the Passion Play at Oberammergau where, in a downpour of rain, Shaw bounded up the mountainside leaving Webb, seated among trees at its base, apparently 'writing an article on municipal death duties . . .'

Though he gradually grew bolder, he quickly regretted it. From Italy, where he went on a tour organized by the Art Workers' Guild in the autumn of 1891, he wrote complaining to William Morris of 'the fearful solitude created by these 27 men, most of whom have taken up art as the last refuge of general incompetence'. This was an untypical rebuke from Shaw, indicating the extent of his irritation at having to travel as a devout Catholic in order to obtain vegetarian meals. 'On reflection,' he added, 'I doubt if this remark will bear examination: I suppose it is in the nature of such an expedition that we should all appear fools to one another.'

If there was anything Shaw learnt, it was how travel narrowed the mind. His one weapon, language, broke in his hand and he concluded that the only country you could learn about by going abroad was your own. He also came to recognize how much closer you could feel to those whom you had left behind. There was an increasing number of people for him to feel close to in this way: for example, Grace Gilchrist. 'I have no doubt

Miss Gilchrist fell in love with you,' another Fabian, Marjorie Davidson, assured him.

It seemed impossible for a young man and woman to have a friendship in Victorian Britain that was not tainted by assumptions of marriage. Shaw's attentions to Grace Gilchrist were much whispered over. He singled her out for long talks; he addressed letters to her and noted each sighting in his diary; he wrote music to Browning's 'I go to find my soul' for her. But by 1888 they were joined, not in marriage, but in a bond of misunderstanding. On Easter Day, Grace's friend the novelist Emma Brooke called on Shaw and 'heaped abuse on me'. It was like a plot from one of his novels: Shaw embodying the new morality; Grace, struggling unhappily through socialism to escape the marriage market; and Miss Brooke valuing her friend's happiness above Shaw's principles. 'Write no more letters,' Emma Brooke instructed him after he had tried to explain himself. 'In letters we do not seem able to touch any point of mutual comprehension.' Eventually she infuriated Shaw by returning his letters unopened. But by then, he had come to realize that there was 'Great Gossip about Grace Gilchrist' and even her family had counted on their marriage. It was exasperating.

On Hampstead Heath nine months later, Grace and Shaw hurried past each other without a word. Both felt that injustice had been done, Grace to her genuine feelings, Shaw to his good intentions, and no words had been able to reconcile such feelings and intentions. If Shaw treated Grace's unhappiness rather easily, this was partly because, compared with the awful poverty which was the chief concern of the Fabians, her romantic disappointment seemed almost an indulgence. He had enjoyed Grace's company and he seems to have found her good-looking. But he had never proposed marriage; he had never compromised her sexually; and if he had compromised her socially then it was due to absurd mores which she should have been too intelligent to accept.

'Someday a pair of dark eyes, a fierce temperament and a woman will obtain your body and soul,' Elinor Huddart had written to him. If he was on the lookout for such a creature, it was in order to avoid her. Even before the Gilchrist excitement was over, Shaw was gazing at 'a pretty girl named Geraldine Spooner'. He neither pursued the 'fair and fluffy' Miss Spooner nor ignored her but, after two years doing neither, decided that he was 'rather in love with Geraldine' – after which he saw a good deal less of her. He seemed to her 'a strange and very wonderful looking man, tall, and thin as a whipping post'. He had walked her to railway stations and they had eaten lunches at an Aerated Bread Shop. Each seemed to be presenting the other with opportunities for taking the initiative and neither of them took it – until, Shaw's lack of initiative growing excessive, Geraldine married the philosopher Herbert Wildon Carr. As soon as it was too late Shaw plunged into action, advancing on 'my old love Geraldine', in spite of the desperate fact of her now living in Surrey.

If I could truly now declare
I love but you alone . . .

But he couldn't. The visit had been in the nature of a reconnaissance – to learn whether the Carrs might grow into another of those families where he could act the Sunday husband. When Geraldine drove him off to the station in the horse cart, he made straight for the Salts where his Sunday husbandship was by now well-established.

Shaw was a lifelong admirer of Henry Salt. They shared many tastes – Ruskin and Shelley, vegetarianism and anti-vivisection. But though Shaw described his Old Etonian socialist colleague as 'a born revolutionist' he seemed more of a born naturalist, armed only with binoculars and eventually 'working all day at my profession which is looking for, and at wildflowers'. Salt, who was 'the mildest-mannered man that ever defied society', made a centre for his reforming spirit in the Humanitarian League of which he was a co-founder and whose journals, dedicated to the abolition of blood sports, corporal punishment, the death penalty and the commercial vulgarization of the countryside, he edited for a quarter of a century.

At the Salts Shaw bathed, rode on a tandem tricycle, made friends with Cosy, 'a cat of fearful passions', put into practice his special theories of bed-making and washing-up, cheated outrageously at an exhibition of table turning, gossiped, sang and played a great quantity of piano duets with Mrs Salt – and that was all he did. There was no need for 'gallantries' with Kate Salt since she only fell in love with other women. She treated Shaw as a confidant but she felt an idealized love for Edward Carpenter who was homosexual. This preference sometimes riled Shaw. 'Attacked Carpenter rather strongly over his lecture – perhaps too strongly,' he confessed in his diary. In Shaw's opinion, Carpenter exalted Kate's lesbianism into a cult (she called herself an *Urning*, one of the chosen race). Her problems would vanish when she had two or three children to look after. Kate hated this chilling cheeriness of Shaw's. 'Mrs Salt complained considerably of me,' he revealed after a breezy visit in 1896:

' . . . said she believed I had been practising scales (an unheard-of accusation); said I was in a destructively electrical condition and made her feel that she wanted to cry; said that if I undressed in the dark when going to bed, sparks would come out of me; and generally made me conscious of a grinding, destroying energy, and a heart transmuted to adamant . . . I am really only fit for intercourse with sensitive souls when I am broken and weary.'

*

Shaw counted his friendship with the Salts as one of the most successful of his triangular liaisons. More questionable were the appearances he was making in the family life of William Morris's daughter, May.

For years he had enveloped May Morris in a romantic haze that emanated from his feelings for what she called 'the father'. 'Great men are fabulous monsters, like unicorns, griffins, dragons, and heraldic lions,' Shaw was to write. ' . . . William Morris was great not only among little men but among great ones.' He still saw Morris as a crusader, struggling to make nasty people nice and ugly places beautiful. To go from the barren places of the Fabians to the 'Morris paradise' at their house in Hammersmith was wonderfully refreshing. Shaw went there often and sometimes, he owned, 'to see May Morris'. In what was to become a famous passage Shaw tells of a particular incident between them that took place in 1886.

'One Sunday evening after lecturing and supping, I was on the threshold of the Hammersmith house when I turned to make my farewell, and at this moment she came from the diningroom into the hall. I looked at her, rejoicing in her lovely dress and lovely self; and she looked at me very carefully and quite deliberately made a gesture of assent with her eyes. I was immediately conscious that a Mystic Betrothal was registered in heaven, to be fulfilled when all the material obstacles should melt away, and my own position rescued from the squalors of my poverty and unsuccess . . . I made no sign at all: I had no doubt that the thing was written on the skies for both of us.'

Characteristically, this metaphysical episode contains and conceals the truth. When Shaw submitted it fifty years later as part of his Introduction to the second volume of May's book on her father, she allowed its publication. 'People who don't count will view it as an amusing romance in the Shaw manner, and those who count – so few left – will read it understandingly.'

The Shaw manner suggests that he treated May as an ornament in her father's Pre-Raphaelite world. She was a picture, not real; something to look at and never touch. But she had never occupied the jewelled place he ascribed to her in the William Morris world. 'Yes, well, of course I'm a remarkable woman,' she later told him, ' – always was, though none of you seemed to think so.' The affair was one of suppers, songs, socialism. He wooed her politically, tried to seduce her from the Socialist League to the Fabians: 'I shall have to overcome my shyness of the Fabians – they are all so gruesomely respectable,' she protested. It was Shaw's respectability that made her shy. It was like a strait-jacket and he an inspired lunatic, tied hand and foot. Sometimes he made her laugh so much she felt enfeebled the next day; and it was beautiful to hear him lecture so passionately. 'I don't know if you are aware that our audiences love you very much,' she told him; 'their faces broaden with pleasure when we promise them that if they are good Bernard Shaw shall be their next teacher.' Did he love her? It seemed impossible to tell. 'You have succeeded in perplexing *me*. I don't believe I know you a bit better now than when we were first acquainted,' she wrote to him, after they had known each other for more than a year. 'Inscrutable man! I suppose this is *your* form of vanity.'

He seems to have been terrified of the unhappiness he would risk if she became real. Instinctively he countered fear with fear, making her feel that, although she wanted to be close to him, 'you keep me in a constant state of terror by your fantastic sarcasms, so I suppose it is impossible'. Sometimes, in her frustration, she was short-tempered: 'I do not know what possesses me to be always so rude when you are invariably kind and courteous to me,' she apologized. In another letter she referred to 'our harmless personal relations'. After a year or more of harmlessness, she turned elsewhere. Early in April 1886, Shaw wrote in his diary: 'Came back with Sparling, who told me of the love affair between him and May Morris.' Henry Halliday Sparling was a socialist colleague, 'a tall slim immature man,' Shaw decided, 'with a long thin neck on champagne bottle shoulders'.

Shortly afterwards May wrote Shaw a letter accepting, as it were, his mystic rejection of her the previous year. 'Your resolution when we became acquainted not to make love was most judicious and worthy of all praise, having, as you say, the most entirely satisfying results. I dont think our intercourse could have caused you more pleasure than it has me.'

Her irony was well-merited. By treating May Morris as a woman-on-a-pedestal, Shaw exhibited all the sentimental idealism he later attacked so vividly in *The Quintessence of Ibsenism*. The insignificance of Sparling amounted almost to an invitation for Shaw to supplant him. But still he could not escape the strait-jacket. 'So nothing happened,' he wrote, 'except that the round of Socialist agitation went on and brought us together from time to time.' They spent almost a week together at Kelmscott

Manor in August 1888, Shaw rowing and sailing on the river, playing hide and seek, shooting bows and arrows, guessing 'animal, vegetable or mineral' with various children, and feeling very happy. But on 14 June 1890, May married Sparling.

'This was perfectly natural, and entirely my own fault for taking the Mystical Betrothal for granted; but . . . [Sparling] was even less eligible than I was; for he was no better off financially; and, though he could not be expected to know this, his possibilities of future eminence were more limited.'

Yet Shaw, who had accepted the love affair, could not accept the marriage. In fantasy, he saw May as belonging to her father: William Morris was her man. By marrying her, Sparling had violated the idyllic union between father and daughter that Shaw in 'my limitless imagination' had dreamed into existence, with himself understudying the great William Morris.

He continued seeing the Sparlings, playing the piano with May sometimes till past midnight, as if nothing had happened. One evening, in the summer of 1891, after leaving Hammersmith for Jenny Patterson's house in Brompton Square, he noted: 'May only appeared as I was leaving . . . Gloomy evening. Sorry I left Hammersmith.' But was there any need to leave? That autumn he began staying at Hammersmith odd nights; and then having, as it were, placed one foot in the door, he felt obligated to call on the other foot to follow. Fitzroy Square seemed 'unbearable' when, late in 1892, the building was being redecorated. To escape the smell of paint, and of the drains, he moved to Hammersmith Terrace for part of November, December and January 1893. This was the nearest he came to impersonating Vandeleur Lee and reproducing the Dublin *ménage à trois*. His description of these months, though revealing the satisfaction this arrangement gave him (he even borrowed 'a change of clothes from Sparling'), is skilfully disingenuous. The 'young couple . . . invited me to stay with them awhile. I accepted, and so found myself most blessedly resting and content in their house . . .

'Everything went well for a time in that *ménage-à-trois* . . . It was probably the happiest passage in our three lives.

But the violated Betrothal was avenging itself. It made me from the first the centre of the household; and when I had quite recovered and there was no longer any excuse for staying unless I proposed to do so permanently and parasitically, her legal marriage had dissolved as all illusions do; and the mystic marriage asserted itself irresistibly. I had to consummate it or vanish.'

Reader, he vanished.

Like George Carr Shaw, Sparling had been reduced to nullity in the house. Shaw's explanation for what happened went naturally back to his childhood. 'My mother was enabled to bear a disappointing marriage by the addition to our household of a musician of genius,' he wrote. '. . . I had therefore, to my own great advantage, been brought up in a *ménage à trois*, and knew that it might be a quite innocent and beneficial arrangement.' In Shaw's scheme, the music critic of the 1890s must do nothing that the musician of genius had not done in the 1860s. 'I was perfectly content to leave all that to Sparling and go on Platonically,' he added, 'but May was not.' So there was no alternative but to leave.

But Shaw left less convincingly than Sparling. For having gone, he often returned to Hammersmith, admiring her embroidery, reading poetry and 'playing all the evening with May'. Soon she started calling for tea at Fitzroy Square – 'the worst of it was she always wore her heart on her sleeve,' Lucy Shaw remembered, 'and everyone knew about her madness for G[eorge]'. They seemed to go everywhere together – to concerts, theatres; on long walks in the park; for skating and sculling along the river together between Chiswick and Barnes ('and got abominably blistered').

Shaw's conviction that this *ménage à trois* 'was probably the happiest passage in our three lives' has the same Panglossian ring as his description of George Carr Shaw's last years in Dublin after Bessie and the children had left: 'the happiest time of his life'. Sparling apparently believed that Shaw and May had slept together. In the summer of 1893 they had even gone to Zurich – with sixty other members of the British delegation to the International Socialist Workers' Congress. In any event, Shaw captivated May who 'might have been an iceberg so far as her future relations with her husband went'. Sparling finally went to live in Paris. 'The *ménage* which had prospered so pleasantly as a *ménage-à-trois* proved intolerable as a *ménage-à-deux*,' Shaw wrote. 'Of the particulars of the rupture I know nothing; but in the upshot he fled to the Continent and eventually submitted chivalrously to being divorced as the guilty party, though the alternative was technically arranged for him.'

Shaw made Sparling into a Hardyesque figure pursued by the remorseless Fates, while he himself is an observer of this retribution. But it is difficult to credit that he knew 'nothing' of the particulars of the rupture he had caused. How, for example, did he know that Sparling had legal grounds for obtaining a divorce against May – the 'alternative' that had been 'technically arranged for him' – unless perhaps that technicality had been arranged on one of the nights he slept at her house? But by the time Sparling left, Shaw had entered a new triangular liaison. In his imagination, May had returned to the immortal William Morris and her predestined place for all time. Even Morris's death in 1896 could not alter this: 'You can lose a man like that by your own death,' Shaw wrote, 'but not by his.' May's divorce (decree nisi) from Sparling became law on 18 July 1898. 'May and I discontent one another extremely,' Shaw admitted, 'carefully avoiding the subject we are both thinking of. I mount my bike and fly.'

May reverted to her maiden name, and never remarried. 'I made a mess of things then,' she wrote, 'and always, and [have] only myself to blame for a waste of life.' But thirty years later she could accept Shaw's re-creation of their relationship because by then it was 'a story out of another world', as it always had been for him.

4

CORNO DI BASSETTO

Only a musician's appreciation has any gratification for me.

Shaw to Neville Cardus (6 January 1939)

The first duty for '*The Star*'s Own Captious Critic' was to invent a resounding pseudonym: Corno di Bassetto.

The basset horn had been used by Mozart in his Requiem because of its 'peculiar watery melancholy'; Shaw's musical journalism was designed to drive melancholy away, as music itself had driven melancholy from his Dublin home. Lee's music had not unified Shaw's mother and father, but under its spell Sonny had been able to forget the divisions in the house. If there was love during those years, it was love conveyed by the play of musical instruments and the coming together of voices. The miraculous world of opera became a necessity in Shaw's life. What others found in loving relationships, Shaw believed he experienced in music. The years of self-tuition from mastering the classics in piano transcription in Dublin to the study of musical treatises in the British Museum, the lessons in harmony and counterpoint, and the long variety of piano duets with everyone's wife, amounted to an unsentimental labour of love. For him words were the 'counters of thinking, not of feeling', and music 'the sublimest of the arts'.

Between February 1885 and February 1889 he had written some ninety thousand words of music criticism for the *Dramatic Review*, the *Magazine of Music*, the *Pall Mall Gazette*. In these papers the spirit of 'Corno di Bassetto' was conceived. The readership of *The Star* was 'the bicycle clubs and the polytechnics', not 'the Royal Society of Literature or the Musical Association'. The collaboration he now started between *Star*-writer and *Star*-reader, and the changes he imposed on himself to make this collaboration effective, were part of the human engineering behind his development into a public man. What had begun with almost-an-apology was to become almost-a-boast. In a letter to the conductor August Manns two months before the birth of Bassetto, he had written: 'The writer who ventures to criticize you in a public newspaper is . . . a person of no consequence whatever . . . and he was never more astonished and flattered in his life than when he learned that his irresponsible sallies had attracted your attention.'

This, the voice of Shaw's father, appeared to be drowned in later years by a clamour of self-approval, and was only heard again when he confronted people such as Rodin or Einstein, who had not made the sort of public compromise at which G.B.S. excelled. His attitude to this compromise sometimes betrays the self-disgust that was one side of his nature. 'I daresay these articles would seem shabby, vulgar, cheap, silly, vapid enough if they were dug up and exposed to the twentieth century light,' he wrote of his Bassetto pieces in 1906. In his Preface, written in 1935, to the publication of *London Music in 1888–89 As Heard by Corno di Bassetto*, Shaw's tone has shifted: 'Vulgarity is a necessary part of a complete author's equipment; and the clown is sometimes the best part of the circus . . . I purposely vulgarized musical criticism, which was then refined and academic to the point of being unreadable and often nonsensical.'

To perform his job of making 'deaf stockbrokers read my two pages on music' it was vital to convince everyone that he knew nothing.

'When people hand me a sheet of instrumental music, and ask my opinion of it, I carefully hold it upside down, and pretend to study it in that position with the eye of an expert. When they invite me to try their new grand piano, I attempt to open it at the wrong end; and when the young lady of the house informs me that she is practising the 'cello, I innocently ask her whether the mouthpiece did not cut her lips dreadfully at first.'

This is the voice of the irresistible G.B.S./Bassetto – and Shaw means us not to resist, but to laugh and swallow his words and then discover that what we have assimilated is his burning sense of undervaluation and the resentment he felt at having to overcome it with such imposture. Bassetto's business 'is not to be funny, but to be accurate'; he explains that 'seriousness is only a small man's affectation of bigness', but that 'there is nothing so serious as great humor'. Though spoken of as severe,

Bassetto speaks of himself as 'lenient, almost foolishly goodnatured'. He never indulges in the cruel practice of giving misleading flattery. He has his passions: he hates the banjo ('If it be true that the Prince of Wales banjoizes, then I protest against his succession to the throne'); he hates the interruptions of encores and the habit of bouquet-throwing (the poor artists having to take the same vast bouquet to performance after performance to have it spontaneously hurled at them); he hates the old (Mendelssohn) when used as an obstacle to the new (Wagner); and he hates audiences, especially the practised coughers who should be removed to Piccadilly where their ailment can be treated 'by gently passing a warm steam-roller over their chests'. More annoying still were the men who beat time – one actually did it by shooting his ears up and down. 'Imagine the sensation of looking at a man with his ears pulsating 116 times per minute in a quick movement from one of Verdi's operas.'

But his chief objection to aristocracy-ridden London audiences was their imposition on music of artificial social standards. A wastefully competitive system obliged managers to convert opera houses and concert halls into fashionable post-prandial resorts. Intervals, which for many were the main events of the evening, were extended so that part of the audience was still chattering at full blast while the music was being played. Bassetto did not lack for a solution. The soldiers at present placed for show purposes in the vestibule should be moved into the stalls where they could turn their rifles on anyone who disturbed a performance. He urged the use of convict labour for the chorus and scene-shifting, and the taxing of private box-holders at twenty shillings in the pound to finance a Public Entertainments Trust under the chairmanship of Corno di Bassetto. After which they could get rid of the sham classical performances that had made the British into a race of cultural humbugs. 'The hypocrisy of culture, like other cast-off fashions, finds its last asylum among the poor,' he wrote.

Shaw calculated that the sort of social criticism that the editor T. P. O'Connor had found unendurable on the political pages of *The Star* would be acceptable when paraded through its musical columns. His objections to the tyranny of evening dress were famous. Bassetto disliked wearing the uniform of an idealist 'class of gentlemen to which I do not belong, and should be ashamed to belong'. In his eyes, it acted as a false passport. 'Next season, I shall purchase a stall for the most important evening I can select,' Shaw threatened Augustus Harris, the cautious manager of Covent Garden Opera House. 'I shall dress in white flannels.

'I shall then hire for the evening the most repulsive waiter I can find in the lowest oyster shop in London. I shall rub him with bacon crackling, smooth his hair with fried sausages, shower stale gravy upon him, season him with Worcester sauce, and give him just enough drink to make him self-assertive without making him actually drunk. With him I shall present myself at the stalls; explain that he is my brother; and that we have arranged that I am to see the opera unless evening dress is indispensable, in which case my brother, being in evening dress, will take my place.'

Shaw admitted the easy advantages of a compulsory costume that was cheap, simple, durable. It 'prevents rivalry and extravagance on the part of the male leaders of fashion,' he wrote, 'annihilates class distinctions, and gives men who are poor and doubtful of their social position (that is, the majority of men) a sense of security and satisfaction'. Such arguments applied equally to women's clothes: yet they were free to pursue private enterprise with horrible consequences:

'At 9 o'clock (the Opera began at 8) a lady came in and sat down very conspicuously in my line of sight. She remained there until the beginning of the last act. I do not complain of her coming late and going early: on the contrary, I wish she had come later and gone earlier. For this lady, who had very black hair, had stuck over her right ear the pitiable corpse of a large white bird, which looked exactly as if someone had killed it by stamping on its breast and then nailed it to the lady's temple, which was presumably of sufficient solidity to bear the operation . . . I presume that if I had presented myself at the doors with a dead snake round my neck, a collection of blackbeetles pinned to my shirtfront, and a grouse in my hair, I should have been refused admission. Why, then, is a woman to be allowed to commit such a public outrage? . . . I suggest to the Covent Garden authorities that, if they feel bound to protect their subscribers against the danger of my shocking them with a blue tie, they are at least equally bound to protect me against the danger of a woman shocking me with a dead bird.'

Bassetto's 'Musical Mems' were a continual protest against distractions from good musical performance. The worse the music, the more Bassetto diversified. Readers liked to hear of the voice trainer who hit his pupils, declaring that it was the only method to make them produce the vowel *o*; they liked to discover Bassetto himself, after a visit to the ballet, at dawn the next day with a policeman, a postman and a milkman ('who unfortunately broke his leg') attempting *pirouettes* and *entrechats* in Fitzroy Square; they liked, as part of a teetotal campaign, his plea for dancing in church, which just stopped short of converting Westminster Abbey into a ballroom; they even accepted his rank socialism: 'What we want is not music for the people, but bread for the people, rest for the people, immunity from robbery and scorn for the people, hope for them, enjoyment, equal respect and consideration, life and aspiration, instead of drudgery and despair. When we get that I imagine the people will make tolerable music for themselves.'

Almost the only person not to be diverted was T. P. O'Connor. Bassetto had fabricated for the public a very pretty relationship between critic and editor. But the reality was unpleasant. 'I find it impossible to continue as I have been doing lately,' Shaw told Massingham early in 1890. 'This week I have had to attend five concerts; have advanced fourteen shillings from my exhausted exchequer; and have written the Bassetto column, all for two guineas.' But T. P. O'Connor refused to increase Bassetto's salary. He wanted to be rid of him and of his attempts to turn his Liberal paper into a Socialist one. But to do so would make him one of the most unpopular editors in London. So he starved him out. Bassetto had sometimes made fun of his own resignation – 'this threat never fails to bring Stonecutter Street to its knees,' he told readers; 'though, lest too frequent repetition should blunt it, I am careful not to employ it more than three times in any one week.' In private, Shaw was driven by destitution to walk to and from many of the concerts and to wait a year for the repayment of some of his expenses.

By the early summer of 1890 their relationship had grown so strained that 'we came to the very grave point of having to exchange assurances that we esteemed one another beyond all created mortals'. The day O'Connor had been looking forward to arrived in the middle of May 1890, when Bassetto of *The Star* became G.B.S. of *The World*. It was William Archer who persuaded Yates to re-employ Shaw. 'Arranged to take the musical criticship of *The World*,' Shaw wrote in his diary on 14 May, 'if T. P. O'Connor has nothing to say to the contrary.' In his own style, O'Connor had everything to say in its favour. 'I am extremely glad to hear you have got the excellent offer of *The World*,' he congratulated Shaw the next day. '. . . Take the offer by all means.' Above Corno di Bassetto's last column which appeared on 16 May, O'Connor stuck a discordant adieu: 'The larger salary of a weekly organ of the classes has proved too much for the virtue even of a Fabian.' 'After the malediction, the valediction,' Bassetto countered, and went on to show how all grievance (though not forgotten) could be submerged in humour:

'A man who, like myself, has to rise regularly at eleven o'clock every morning cannot sit up night after night writing opera notices . . . I ask some indulgence for my successor, handicapped as he will be for a time by the inevitable comparison . . . I hope he will never suffer the musical department of the Star to lose that pre-eminence which has distinguished it throughout the administration of "Corno di Bassetto".'

*

The character adopted by G.B.S. in *The World* was less dramatic than Bassetto. Anyone who made him laugh melted most of the criticism out of him. By offering the most far-fetched comparisons and analogies as stepping stones to his conclusions – the training of circus horses to compose dance music or the installation on the site of the prompter's box of a steam crane to hoist despairing critics out of their seats and drop them at the refreshment bar – G.B.S. amused the deaf stockbrokers, but also encouraged them to overlook what lay behind these fantasies, and to dismiss his serious recommendations as more absurdity. For the first time in his writing a note of exasperated despair sounds over the misreading of his careful statements. 'It has taken me nearly twenty years of studied self-restraint, aided by the natural decay of my faculties, to make myself dull enough to be accepted as a serious person by the British public; and I am not sure that I am not still regarded as a suspicious character in some quarters.'

Shaw's method of judging music, he once stated, was to do with his ears what he did with his eyes when he stared. Some critics imposed on the public by displays of 'scientific analysis'. G.B.S. resented this fashion for 'silly little musical parsing exercises to impress the laity'. In one of his most effective debunking feats, he parodied this scholarly pretentiousness with a comparable 'analysis' of Hamlet's soliloquy on death:

'Shakespear, dispensing with the customary exordium, announces his subject at once in the infinitive, in which mood it is presently repeated after a short connecting passage in which, brief as it is, we recognize the alternative and negative forms on which so much of the significance of repetition depends. Here we reach a colon; and a pointed desitory phrase, in which the accent falls decisively on the relative pronoun, brings us to the first full stop.'

Academic preconceptions, G.B.S. argued, had encouraged a ruck of 'barren professors of the art of doing what has been done before and need not be done again'. He detected a gentlemanly gang at work in the musical world, and it was with outcast irony that he asked: 'who am I that I should be believed, to the disparagement of eminent musicians?' Commenting on Professor Stanford's *Eden*, he continued:

'If you doubt that Eden is a masterpiece, ask Dr Parry and Dr Mackenzie, and they will applaud it to the skies. Surely Dr Mackenzie's opinion is conclusive: for is he not the composer of Veni Creator, guaranteed as excellent music by Professor Stanford and Dr Parry? You want to know who Dr Parry is? Why, the composer of Blest Pair of Sirens, as to the merits of which you have only to consult Dr Mackenzie and Professor Stanford.'

As early as 1885 Shaw made out his historical case against the persisting influence of these composers. 'Our really serious music is no longer recognized as religious,' he wrote, 'whilst our professedly religious music . . . is only remarkable as *naïve* blasphemy, wonderfully elaborated, and convinced of its own piety.

'It was Mendelssohn who popularized the pious romancing which is now called sacred music; in other words, the Bible with the thought left out. M. Gounod proved his capacity in this direction by giving us Faust with all Goethe's thought left out, the result having been so successful (and, it must be confessed, so irresistibly charming), it is natural that he should turn his attention to the Bible, which is worshipped in England so devoutly by people who never open it, that a composer has but to pick a subject, or even a name, from it, to ensure a half-gagged criticism and the gravest attention for his work, however trivial.'

G.B.S. was merciless on the 'flagrant pedantry . . . and waste of musical funds' which the oratorio market produced for English festivals. 'I do not know how it is possible to listen to these works without indignation, especially in circumstances implying a parallel between them and the genuine epic stuff of Handel.' Had oratorio been invented in Dante's time, 'the seventh circle in his Inferno would have been simply a magnified Albert Hall, with millions of British choristers stolidly singing, All that hath life and breath, sing to the Lord, in the galleries, and the condemned, kept awake by demons, in the arena, clothed in evening dress'.

He was obliged to listen to a good deal of work by contemporary composers: Sir Frederick Cowen, Sir Alexander Mackenzie, Sir Hubert Parry, Sir Charles Stanford, Sir Arthur Sullivan, and other knights and bachelors of music, most of whose works he would happily have committed 'to the nearest County Council "destructor"'. Sullivan, a musician of care and refinement, who had spent over twenty years composing for the drawing-room and the Church, achieved success through a burlesque of the classics he revered. 'They trained him to make Europe yawn; and he took advantage of their teaching to make London and New York laugh and whistle.' In Stanford, G.B.S. detected a similar division exposed by the 'somewhat scandalous' success of his Irish Symphony, into which Shaw read 'a record of fearful conflict between the aboriginal Celt and the Professor'.

Here was a beginning in his quest for a formula that, with its symbol of a reconciled England and Ireland, would integrate inherited factors in such deep conflict that they had forced his parents to occupy separate countries and were eventually to neutralize himself as a man without nationality. For who was Shaw to censure Stanford for not displaying his emotions in public? Yet it is partly as self-censure, self-analysis and self-encouragement that we should read such passages:

'When Professor Stanford is genteel, cultured, classic, pious, and experimentally mixolydian, he is dull beyond belief. His dullness is all the harder to bear because it is the restless, ingenious, trifling, flippant dullness of the Irishman, instead of the stupid, bovine, sleepable-through dullness of the Englishman . . . Far from being a respectable oratorio-manufacturing talent, it is, when it gets loose, eccentric, violent, romantic, patriotic, and held in check only by a mortal fear of being found deficient in what are called "the manners and tone of good society". This fear, too, is Irish: it is, possibly, the racial consciousness of having missed that four hundred years of Roman civilization which gave England a sort of university education when Ireland was in the hedge school.

In those periods when nobody questions the superiority of the university to the hedge school, the Irishman, lamed by a sense of inferiority, blusters most intolerably . . . Then the fashion changes; Ruskin leads young Oxford out into the hedge school to dig roads; there is general disparagement in advanced circles of civilization, the university, respectability, law and order . . . This reaction is the opportunity of the Irishman in England to rehabilitate his self-respect, since it gives him a standpoint from which he can value himself as a hedge-school man . . . If he seizes the opportunity, he may end in founding a race of cultivated Irishmen whose mission in England will be to teach Englishmen to play with their brains as well as with their bodies; for it is all work and no play in the brain department that makes John Bull such an uncommonly dull boy.'

His few aberrations in judgement usually arise from treating music historically, that is, with the type of academic measuring-rod he scorns. He placed Hermann Goetz 'above all other German composers of the last hundred years, save only Mozart and Beethoven, Weber and Wagner', partly because his Symphony in F was technically and intellectually more symphonic in form that any by Schumann or Schubert. He undervalued Schubert and considered him overplayed because 'I could not see that

Schubert added anything to Mozart & Beethoven except sugar: and though the sugar was extraordinarily rich and sweet, I rather jumped over him to Mendelssohn'. Music composed out of the dramatic instinct (such as Goetz's *Taming of the Shrew*) attracted him far more than anything intimate. He was sometimes a poor judge of chamber music because it tended to conflict with his commitment to twenty-four-hours-a-day cheerfulness.

He sniped at Brahms, insisting that with all his great powers of utterance he had nothing to say ('Brahms' enormous gift of music is paralleled by nothing on earth but Mr Gladstone's gift of words'). Shaw's hostility to Brahms focused on his Requiem ('patiently borne only by the corpse'). In 1947 he explained that 'the first performances of Brahms's Requiem in London were dreadfully and insincerely mock-solemn and dull. Now that I know the work, its fugal bits and march music amuse me; and its one Mendelssohnic chorus is a favourite of mine.' But this explanation cannot conceal Shaw's antipathy to all near-contemporary religious music, especially when connected with death. He empties these works of poetry and makes them colossal monuments to boredom. He literally cannot listen to them.

But when he listens to other music it is with acute attentiveness. Whenever possible before a performance he studied the score and would expose cuts, interpolations and other textual deviations, as well as derivations from the work of other composers. His descriptions of performers have an exactness that enables us to differentiate one from another precisely: the exuberant hammer-play of Paderewski, the cool muscular strength of another musical gymnast, Slivinski, a prodigiously rapid pianist of the Leschetizky school, and the hugely energetic Rubinstein, a player of marvellous manual dexterity limited by his narrowness of intellectual sympathy. Among violinists he discriminates so finely between the judgement of Reményi, the sensitive hand of Sarasate, Joachim's peculiarly thoughtful style and the self-assertiveness of Ysaÿe that we can almost hear their playing. He analyses the varying styles of the conductors from Richard Wagner and Richter to Henschel's London Symphony Orchestra, Charles Hallé's Manchester concerts, and the Saturday concerts led by August Manns at the Crystal Palace. He brings in reports from music halls and from amateur events in the country such as the brass band of shoemakers playing on a racecourse at Northampton – the sort of place where the music of the country was kept alive. He argues that public opera houses are as essential to people as public museums and public galleries, and a powerful competition to public houses. He wants to transform this brainless country 'where you cannot have even a cheap piano provided for the children to march to in a Board School without some mean millionaire or other crying out that the rates will ruin him'. Among his targets for criticism are charity concerts that promoted bad music for well-meaning ends, as if a good orchestra was not as 'important to a town as a good hospital'.

The critic who amused stockbrokers in the 1880s and 1890s was to become one of our best guides to the history of music performed in England during the late nineteenth century. He had perfected the Shavian note – assertive, audacious, fantastic, expertly wrapped round with the illusion of intimacy – until he became his own description of the confident journalist-critic: 'magnificently endowed with the superb quality which we dishonor by the ignoble name of Cheek – a quality which has enabled men from time immemorial to fly without wings, and to live sumptuously without incomes'.

'The critic who is modest is lost,' Shaw wrote. But he also knew the damage that could be done to those who, to gain the popular ear, force 'vulgarity upon a talent that is naturally quiet and sympathetic'.

5

EXITS AND ENTRANCES

Very few people in the world have ever had a love affair.

'Beethoven's "Unsterbliche Geliebte" ', *The World* (1 November 1893)

Florence Farr was 'an *amiable* woman, with semicircular eyebrows' whom Shaw describes in his portrait of Grace Tranfield from *The Philanderer*: 'slight of build, delicate of feature, and sensitive in expression . . . but her well closed mouth, proudly set brows, firm chin, and elegant carriage shew plenty of determination and self-respect'. She was four years younger than Shaw and unlike any woman he had met. She seemed to resemble some of the New Women he had optimistically invented in his novels. It was partly her feminism that had brought her to William Morris's house in Hammersmith where she was learning embroidery with May through whom, in about 1890, she met Shaw.

He had seen her act in John Todhunter's *A Sicilian Idyll*, remarking on her 'striking and appropriate good looks'. Then, on 4 October 1890, he 'had a long talk' with her at the private view of an Arts and Crafts exhibition, after which they went 'gadding about' to plays and recitals together, to the Pine Apple and Orange Grove restaurants and, for long teas, to ABC shops where he 'chatted and chatted' and she 'laughed and laughed'. He would turn up out of the night at her lodgings in 123

Dalling Road, only half a mile from May Morris, play a little, sing a little, and take her for walks round Ravenscourt Park. 'First really intimate conversation,' Shaw recorded after an evening with her on 15 November. As the daughter of a sanitary reformer who had tried to persuade his countrymen that England was dying of dirt, her Shavian provenance was impeccable. She had been schooled in Shakespeare and tap-dancing, then married a handsome actor, Edward Emery, who spent much of his time resting. Florence was not an observant woman: it was almost four years later, in 1888, that she noticed that Edward was no longer there. He had gone to America, leaving her an independent married woman.

Like Jenny Patterson Florence took the initiative over Shaw. 'As she was clever, goodnatured, and very goodlooking, all her men friends fell in love with her,' he recalled. Before the end of the year they had become lovers. Shaw made no secret of his love for Florence. 'Went over to FE in the evening,' he wrote in his diary on 30 December 1890: and added uncharacteristically, ' – a happy evening.' He told his friends he was in love with her; he told Florence herself she was 'my other self – no, not my other self, but my very self', and 'the happiest of all my great happinesses, the deepest and restfullest of all my tranquillities, the very inmost of all my loves'.

Whenever he felt incapable of further work and craved for exercise, he would leap away from his desk and usually find himself six miles off at Florence's lodgings, where he 'let time slip and lost my train back'. One night he arrived to 'find the place in darkness'. He 'wandered about disappointed for a time', then returned to Fitzroy Square, put down the feelings released in him by her absence, and sent them to her as a letter: 'I have fallen in with my boyhood's mistress, Solitude, and wandered aimlessly with her once more . . . reminding me of the days when disappointment seemed my inevitable & constant lot.'

Florence promised him a future he had believed to be impossible. 'Women tend to regard love as a fusion of body, spirit and mind,' he later told one of his biographers. 'It has never been so with me.' Yet for a time, perhaps a year, it seemed as if it could be so. Florence had, according to W. B. Yeats, 'three great gifts, a tranquil beauty . . . an incomparable sense of rhythm and a beautiful voice'. For Shaw, her attractiveness lay partly in her beauty and partly in her attitude. Though unpuritanical she was fastidious, 'claimed 14 lovers', but retained her independence. 'When a man begins to make love to me,' she admitted, 'I instantly see it as a stage performance.'

Almost before they knew themselves that they were in love, Jenny Patterson knew it. Towards the end of 1890 she had gone abroad, and for almost four months Shaw and Florence saw each other freely. But then, on 27 April 1891, Shaw 'went in to JP's. Fearful scene about FE, this being our first meeting since her return from the East. Did not get home until about 3.' These scenes grew fiercer, but each time she won a battle she won less. 'Not for forty thousand such relations will I forgo one forty thousandth part of my relation with you,' Shaw promised Florence. '. . . The silly triumph with which she [Jenny Patterson] takes, with the air of a conqueror, that which I have torn out of my own entrails for her, almost brings the lightning down on her . . . Damnation! triple damnation! You must give me back my peace.'

Once Jenny Patterson too had given him peace, but it had been a peace of the body only, as she well understood: 'Any other woman would have brough[t] you the sleep I did.' After the Annie Besant rumpus, she expected their sexual relationship to go on as before: and to some extent it had. Shaw was neglectful, long-suffering, and passionate by turns. 'You are beginning again the old games,' she had warned him in January 1888. But the next month she wrote: 'Be as ardent as you were last week, it is your place to be so – I adore to be made love to like that. It takes my breath away . . .'

Yet she could not conceal from herself that his feelings for her were not what they had been 'when I was dear Mrs Patterson & worth seeing . . . oh les beaux jours'. Her expectations of him seemed to fade. 'How my lover is becoming less my lover every month . . . just thinking of me as a sucking baby does of its mar when it is hungry!' she had complained on 20 October 1888. 'Adieu most disappointing of men.' She could say goodbye, she could not leave him; and the next month she is begging him to 'write me again so that I may have something to live on until I see you'.

But their relationship had become stale to Shaw. He tried not to hurt her – 'You are gentle and good nearly always to me,' she allowed – but increasingly recoiled from the physical centre of their liaison. Nevertheless, though he flirted with Fabian girls and other men's wives he had made love only to Mrs Patterson and perhaps May Morris until he fell in love with Florence. His love affair with Jenny Patterson had separated sex from other interests. She repeatedly writes of it as if it were a commodity like some bargain at a shop. 'My boy you got all for nothing – it was not to be bought at any price.' Sex was everything she had to bargain with, and through it she gave her whole self. She loved him in a way he could not love her. Hers is a small world and her feeling for him so fills it that there is no place for interests or enthusiasms beyond her infatuation. 'You are my love, my life & all the world to me,' she writes.

This love was Shaw's small private hell. Jenny may have been going through the change of life. She weeps, rages, flings a book at his head, provokes quarrels over imaginary offences, breaks off their relationship, arranges a luxurious reconciliation. In his chapter called 'The Womanly Woman' from *The Quintessence of Ibsenism*, Shaw was obviously using his experiences with Jenny Patterson when he describes 'the infatuation of passionate sexual desire'.

'Everyone who becomes the object of that infatuation shrinks from it instinctively. Love loses its charm when it is not free . . . it becomes valueless and even abhorrent, like the caresses of a maniac. The desire to give inspires no affection unless there is also the power to withhold; and the successful wooer, in both sexes alike, is the one who can stand out for honorable conditions, and, failing them, go without.'

Only with his New Woman could he achieve these honourable conditions. Shaw never explained that Florence was infertile. This may help to account for her list of lovers, and why Shaw entered his name on it so prominently. By implication it may also elucidate a mysterious passage from a letter he wrote in 1930 to Frank Harris and later published in *Sixteen Self Sketches*: 'If you have any doubts as to my normal virility, dismiss them from your mind. I was not impotent; I was not sterile; I was not homosexual; and I was extremely susceptible, though not promiscuously.' How then did he know that he was not sterile? The evidence, though meagre, suggests that in the first half of 1886 Jenny Patterson may have had a miscarriage. She had gone to see Shaw's medical friend Kingston Barton early in February. 'I have seen "the" Barton,' she told him and followed this with an enigmatic row of dots. On 10 May, in the first of her desperate pleas to him not to abandon her, she writes of having to hide her predicament from 'Lucy's sharp eyes' and play at being her 'old self' to Shaw's mother: 'I dread being ill it will all come out I fear then.' But it is clear from Shaw's diary that his mother and sister knew of Mrs Patterson's attachment to him. So there must have been something more to come out. During the spring Jenny Patterson had complained of illness, and her letter of 11 May contains a definite allusion to pregnancy. 'You cant help wronging me. I trusted you entirely. Had there been results I should have had to bear that also alone.' So by the second week of May two things were established: that there was now no pregnancy and that they would henceforward experiment with a platonic relationship. The fear of pregnancy and the revulsion caused by a miscarriage could only have been extra brakes to Shaw enjoying sexual intercourse with other women until he met one who was herself sterile. It would also deepen the sexual guilt with which, despite all his freethinking morality, Jenny Patterson had encircled him.

With Florence there was no tyranny or guilt; and from his gratitude arose a dazzling overestimation of 'the magnetic Miss Farr'. There were times when she could make him feel 'more deeply moved than I could have imagined'. But she also brought him something deeper than the 'revulsion' he had noted against Jenny Patterson's name, and this, as he put in his diary, was 'Disillusion'.

After her husband's disappearance Florence had turned simultaneously towards two writers: W. B. Yeats and Shaw.

> Great minds have sought you – lacking someone else
> You have been second always . . .

Ezra Pound assured her:

> You are a person of some interest, one comes to you
> And takes strange gain away:
> Trophies fished up: some curious suggestion;
> Fact that leads nowhere: and a tale or two,
> Pregnant with mandrakes, or with something else
> That might prove useful and yet never proves . . .
> No! there is nothing! In the whole and all,
> Nothing that's quite your own.
> Yet this is you.

Both Shaw and Yeats fashioned castles in the air with Florence, their amiable Princess, waving airily from them. While Shaw beckoned her towards a bright future, Yeats serenaded her back to the magical past. To Yeats she could 'tell everything'; from Shaw she heard everything. Like him she had sent herself to school in the Reading Room of the British Museum, and absorbed a fine store of facts that led nowhere. 'It is impossible to mention anything she does not know,' Shaw exclaimed in astonishment. He felt a tremendous challenge to discover some purpose within the debris of her knowledge. She had flirted professionally with the stage before her marriage, and was now preparing to float back to it by way of Ibsen's *The Lady from the Sea*. But Shaw 'delivered to her so powerful a discourse on *Rosmersholm* that she presently told me that she was resolved to create Rebecca or die'.

Shaw's fascination with the stage had been intensifying during his fifteen years in London. He had taken part in the copyright performances of one or two plays, acted in various amateur theatricals produced by the Socialist League and a '3rd rate comedy' with May Morris. He had been able to express his feelings for May more accurately on the stage than in real life: 'I do not love her – I have too much sense for such follies; but I hate and envy the detestable villain who plays her lover with all my soul.'

The stage appealed to Shaw as a place where actions were governed by words. His interest in Florence rapidly concentrated on her acting. 'I have an extraordinary desire to make the most of you – to make effective & visible *all* your artistic potentialities,' he told her. During February 1891 they went through *Rosmersholm* and from Shaw's diary come whispers of their excitement.

6 February Went over *Rosmersholm* (first few scenes) with FE. Found it hard to leave . . .
11 February . . . to FE's. She gave up her intention of going out to dinner and I stayed all the evening. We were playing, singing, trying on *Rosmersholm* dresses, going over the part etc.

The success of *Rosmersholm* was moderate and Shaw redoubled his efforts to make Florence's originality blaze forth. He became her tutor, calling round at Dalling Road to 'work on her dramatic elocution' and prepare her during the summer of 1892 for playing Beatrice in *The Cenci*. The scenes where Owen Jack coaches Madge Brailsford for the stage in *Love Among the Artists* had invaded life and were to return to fiction in *Pygmalion* (later Shaw was to advise Florence to study phonetics with Beerbohm Tree, the first Professor Higgins, at his school of drama). The name Doolittle irresistibly suggests Florence. She did not lack intelligence or feeling or beauty; she did not lack voice. But there seemed a 'frightful vacuity' at the centre of her life. Shaw strove to plant in this void the seeds of a vigorous and improving energy. She needed will-power, and it was his role to supply this power vicariously from the batteries of his own will.

During rehearsals at the Bedford Park Club on 30 June, Florence fainted but stood up bravely at the opening a fortnight later when 'the white robe and striking beauty of Beatrice' were favourably noticed by the anonymous critic of the *Daily Chronicle*, G. Bernard Shaw. But there were still Himalayas to cross before she could pass as an important leading lady. Behind the beating of Shaw's optimism emerges a bathos whenever he insists too much on the success of their collaboration: 'She actually realized greater possibilities than she had (what a sentence!).'

At the same time he had prudently invested his hopes in another actress. 'Interesting young woman,' he observed on 16 June 1889, after sitting next to Janet Achurch at a dinner in the Novelty Theatre celebrating the English première of *A Doll's House*. Shaw's mother, who accompanied him to this production, had also been struck by Janet, remarking with conviction: 'That one's a *divil.*' But Shaw found himself 'suddenly magnetized, irradiated, transported, fired, rejuvenated, bewitched', and sat up till 2 a.m. the following night writing to his 'wild and glorious young woman'.

Janet was married to another actor, Charles Charrington Martin. Together they had played in a company managed by F. R. Benson, a splendidly incomprehensible actor whose mission to spread Shakespeare through the country was aided by the widespread belief that he was related to the Archbishop of Canterbury.

There was no conventional prettiness to Janet. She was Amazonian. Shaw could never think of her noble outline 'without imagining myself lost at sea in the night, and turning for refuge toward a distant lighthouse, which, somehow, is you'. Others contemplating her voluptuous appearance thought of Helen and Guinevere and 'those Northern beauties who strangled the souls and bodies of heroes in the meshes of their golden tresses'.

She and Charles Charrington had signed an agreement to tour Australia and New Zealand for two years. It was with money borrowed in advance of their salary that they had financed one week's performance of *A Doll's House* at the Novelty Theatre.

That Janet was to leave for the other side of the world in less than three weeks stirred Shaw's feeling magnificently. He saw *A Doll's House* five times, and sent her two of his novels. On the morning of 5 July he went to Charing Cross to see them both off on their Australian tour. He had pledged himself to work in Janet's absence but would find himself wasting time with a long letter to her. She sent him her photograph and asked for his news. He replied, telling her of all the 'nibblings at Ibsen' in London and of his own *Quintessence*. William Archer's criticism was gaining wonderfully in its recklessness, he added, while 'I am getting middle-aged and uninteresting. Political drudgery has swamped my literary career altogether. Still, as all the follies of love and ambition fall off from me, my soul burns with a brighter flame.' Then there was the music criticism: Corno di Bassetto of *The Star* was dead – long live (on five pounds a week) G.B.S. of *The World*! 'Since I began to write for the World, revising my work with great labor and going to great numbers of performances, I have become more and more a slave to art, and can by no means be satisfied with intellectual interest,' he divulged.

'. . . Consequently, my last word tonight shall be said to you, with whom I have no ignoble or unlovely associations . . . I see you quite distinctly – on the stage of the Novelty . . . Take courage then; for if you can cast these magic spells on a man thousands of miles away, after years – centuries – of absence, what can you not do to those only separated from you by a row of footlights, with Ibsen to help you?'

The music, his preoccupation with Ibsen and the spell exercised on his imagination by Janet Achurch and Florence Farr, were combining to move him towards the theatre. But when 'the fearsome Charringtons', as Henry James called them, returned to England early in 1892 and revived *A Doll's House* at the Avenue Theatre, something had changed. Janet exploded into fortissimo and tightened her lower lip 'like an India rubber band'. But 'my admiration is in nowise abated,' G.B.S. reassured her. Admiration was the form Shaw's love for Janet was now taking. 'I am actually less enamoured than before,' he wrote, 'because my admiration elbows out the commoner sentiment. I speak as a critic, not merely as a miserable two legged man.'

To move his emotions on to the stage was a new experiment for Shaw. But in 1893, turning down an opportunity of producing *Rosmersholm*, Janet and Charrington mounted their own season of plays in London: Richard Voss's *Alexandra*; Brandon Thomas's *Clever Alice*; and Scribe and Legouvé's *Adrienne Lecouvreur*. Shaw was appalled. 'Those old stalking horses are no use: the better you do them the more hopeless do they appear,' he reprimanded them.

Part of the trouble had to be Charrington. As Helmer in *A Doll's House* his failure had been complete. But he was more dangerous off the stage where, in addition to being Janet's husband, he played the more serious role – one obviously intended for Shaw – of her business manager. A man with a considerable knowledge of pawnbrokers, he developed a talent for converting other people's investments into thin air. Shaw, who often insisted that he was 'not fit to be trusted with money', handed him a good deal of his own over the years.

Charrington's debt-collecting was obviously an 'incurable neurosis'; Janet's neurosis took Shaw longer to identify. On their long way back from Australia she had fallen ill, getting through her parts only with the help of morphia which the doctors had prescribed after she nearly died in childbirth. Previously she had had a tendency to alcoholism; now she added an addiction to morphia. As her condition became clear to Shaw, a method of driving out her disabling addiction by means of a more ingenious drug, distilled upon the stage, began to form in his mind.

The Charringtons appealed to his instinct for turning failure into success. Janet's happy prior attachment obliged Shaw to direct almost all his emotional energy towards her stage life. 'I had to be sensible about Janet,' he explained.

'I have two sorts of feeling for you . . . one is an ordinary man-and-woman hankering after you . . . you are very handsome and clever, and rich in a fine sort of passionate ardor which I enjoy, in an entirely selfish way, like any other man. But I have another feeling for you. As an artist and trained critic, I have a very strong sense of artistic faculty and its value. I have as you know, a high opinion of your power as an actress; and just as I want to have my own powers in action and to preserve them from waste or coarsening, so I have sympathetically a strong desire to see your powers in action . . . This is the side on which you may find me useful.'

Charrington's impracticalities opened the way for Shaw's most romantic role – that of the expert businessman, crackling with exasperated energy. 'Mind you do exactly what I tell you,' he instructed Charrington. But the Charringtons, while valuing his financial help, tested his instinct for success to its limits. 'Why were you ever born?' he burst out. 'Why did you get married?' And, echoing his mother: 'Oh Charles and Janet, what a devil of a pair you are!'

The Charringtons did not rest at dissipating Janet's genius: they conspired to tip the frailer talent of Florence Farr over the precipice, having persuaded her to play the Princess in their production of *Adrienne Lecouvreur*. 'The unspeakable absurdity of that performance is only surpassed by the unparalleled blastedness of the play,' Shaw admonished.

At the same time Shaw felt committed to Florence and still hoped to produce from that commitment a miraculous transformation. His loyalty to her was intensified by his final break with Jenny Patterson. Between the spring of 1891 and of 1893 the scenes with Jenny had grown worse until both of them looked like caricatures of themselves – he stonily refusing to 'sentimentalize' while Jenny, pretending to open none of his letters to her, scrutinized as many of other people's letters to him as she could put her hands on. In the intervals of remorse they behaved with studied kindness to each other. They got on best while she was away in Australia, Egypt and Ireland – and Shaw could spend more evenings with Florence. 'We read a lot of Walt Whitman and were very happy,' he noted simply in his diary on 26 January 1893. But when Jenny came back all her jealousy revived. She besieged him in his room so that he had to make his way out by physical force, take up asylum in the British Museum and telegraph his mother to clear the house before he returned. But 'the scene upset me,' he admitted.

Jenny's hounding of him at Fitzroy Square had probably been an inducement for Shaw to go and stay with the Sparlings, so near to Florence's lodgings. Nevertheless her emotional influence over him was waning. Something spectacular was needed.

Something spectacular happened on 4 February 1893. 'In the evening,' Shaw wrote in his diary:

'I went to FE; and JP burst in on us very late in the evening. There was a most shocking scene, JP being violent and using atrocious language. At last I sent FE out of the room, having to restrain JP by force from attacking her. I was two hours getting her out of the house and I did not get her home to Brompton Square until near 1, nor could I get away myself until 3. I was horribly tired and shocked and upset; but I kept patience and did not behave badly nor ungently. Did not get to bed until 4; and had but a disturbed night of it. I made JP write a letter to me expressing her regret and promising not to annoy FE again. This was sent to FE to reassure her.'

Next day he wrote letters to both Florence (which he got May Morris to deliver) and to Jenny. There was an embattled pause. Then on 22 February 'Got a letter from JP, which I burnt at the first glance. Wrote to tell her so, feeling the uselessness of doing anything else.' It was the end. Jenny never forgave him; and he never forgot her – he even remembered her in his will by leaving her one hundred pounds, though she successfully avoided this by dying first.

They corresponded once more – in *The Star* about the case of a police constable condemned to be hanged for the murder of his mistress. This tragedy 'will recur tomorrow or the next day with some other pair,' Shaw predicted. 'We shall never be rid of these butcheries until we make up our minds as to what a woman's claims exactly are upon a man who, having formerly loved her, now wishes to get free from her society. If we find that she has some claims, let us enforce them and protect the man from any molestation that goes beyond them.' In a letter signed E four days later, Jenny Patterson replied: 'I know too well the feeling when a girl knows she is no more loved by the one she has given her all to, but is only a thing to be cast aside like a toy which has been tired of.' Shaw concluded the correspondence by describing this as showing precisely the 'unreason that has got the woman killed and the man hanged. At the bottom of all the unreason, however, will be found the old theory that an act of sexual intercourse gives the parties a lifelong claim on one another for better or worse.'

FIVE

I

THE COURTSHIP OF THE WEBBS

In politics, all facts are selected facts . . . To put it another way, the very honestest man has an unfair mind.

'Why a Labor Year Book?', *The Labour Party Year Book* (1916)

While Shaw had been leaping up the mountains at Oberammergau, in the heather down below Webb had not after all been writing on municipal death duties, but pouring out love letters to a woman called Beatrice Potter. 'I do not see how I can go on without you,' he implored. Shaw, he added, 'does not suspect my feeling for you'. Later on G.B.S. would claim to have sleuthed out the facts from Webb's complexion ('Sidney used to come out in spots when he fell in love').

Beatrice was then in her early thirties. Handsome, with huge black eyes, sweeping brown hair tortured into a knot at the back of her head, a wide rather sensuous mouth, she had what was known as a 'beautiful carriage'. Her origins, Beatrice admitted, 'lie in my sensual nature'. But she had sought to quell this nature, feeling it wicked to crave from men the love and attention she had missed as a child. 'My childhood was not on the whole a happy one,' she wrote. She was scrupulously ignored by her mother who had wanted a son instead of her eighth daughter, and who considered her 'the only one of my children who is below the average in intelligence'. As she grew up, Beatrice turned to the informal warmth of the servants' quarters, curling up among the sheets and tablecloths in the laundry or sitting on the ironing board and confiding to the maids her intention of becoming a nun. 'I must pour my poor crooked thoughts into somebody's heart,' she wrote, aged fifteen at the beginning of her diary, 'even if it be my own.'

To one man she did give her heart – Joseph Chamberlain. He was 'intensely attractive to me,' she confessed, yet she could not overlook his 'personal ambition and desire to dominate'. Sexual passion and the attraction of power divided her – it seemed impossible to reconcile her sensual with her intellectual needs. 'I don't know how it will end,' she wrote. 'Certainly not in *my happiness*.' Chamberlain's rejection drove her into suicidal depression. 'If Death comes it will be welcome,' she wrote. ' . . . It is curious this feeling of life being ended.'

Another life came to her through social work which moved her emotional energies into politics. She brooded over statistics, went on a study of Sweating in the tailoring trade, kept company with trade unionists. 'At last I am a Socialist,' she exulted in January 1890.

That month she had met Sidney Webb – 'a London retail tradesman,' as she described him, 'with the aims of a Napoleon'. Though she liked to claim that she was without a sense of beauty, she had an almost voluptuous appreciation of ugliness. 'His tiny tadpole body, unhealthy skin, lack of manner, Cockney pronunciation, poverty, are all against him,' she noted. He strutted round the room with an expression of inexhaustible conceit. But despite his 'bad habits' she liked him. Beneath the bourgeois black coat, inside the bulky head, lurked an improbable monster of romance who wanted to marry a beauty and to see his ideas command the lives of Cabinet Ministers such as Joseph Chamberlain. 'You have it in your hands to make me, in the noblest sense, great,' he informed her. And Beatrice responded. 'One grasp of the hand,' she recorded, 'and we were soon in a warm discussion on some question of Economics.' He wooed her with charts and equations. As he lay in bed at night, a vision of her face flashed before him 'in the guise of a co-worker . . . between the lines of the despatches'. She had devised a concordat to hoist their 'camaraderie' from 'the predominance of lower feeling' to the pinnacles of high-mindedness. 'The agony is unendurable,' he assured her. She urged him to consider his clothes, and the string to his pince-nez. 'Take care of your voice pronunciation,' she commanded: 'it is the chief instrument of influence.' Her heart seemed imprisoned by its past attachment to Chamberlain. 'I am not capable of loving,' she insisted.

The courtship grew so desperate as to bewilder them both. 'The question is,' Beatrice urgently demanded, 'what is the present position?' Whatever it was, suddenly it changed and she began to brood on matrimony. One day, after Sidney had finally given up all hope, she failed to withdraw her hand from his. 'I am still a little in a dream,' he owned.

Marriage, they were agreed, was the waste-paper basket of the emotions. Optimistically he sent her his full-length portrait, but: 'No dear,' she chided him, 'I do not even look at your photograph. It is too hideous . . . it is the head only that I am marrying.' 'You have made a splendid beginning,' he responded. Their engagement was cemented, in Sidney's phrase, over the death of Beatrice's father, and on 23 July 1892, in 'a prosaic, almost sordid ceremony', they were married at St Pancras vestry hall, spending their honeymoon in Dublin investigating Irish trade unionism. 'We are very very happy – far too happy to be reasonable.'

'If all marriages were as happy,' Shaw concluded, 'England, and indeed the civilized world, would be a Fabian paradise.'

*

Beatrice initially disliked Shaw. 'We embarrass each other frightfully when we are alone together,' he observed, 'without some subject of keen and immediate interest to discuss.' His philanderings riled her. 'His stupid gallantries bar out from him the friendship of women who are either too sensible, too puritanical or too much "otherwise engaged" to care to bandy personal flatteries with him,' she noted contemptuously in her diary. 'One large section of women, comprising some, at any rate, of the finest types, remains hidden from him.' 'Nothing annoyed her so much,' Shaw recognized, 'as being suspected of any sensual attachment to me.' Nor could he resist playing on this until she found a way of neutralizing him. 'You cannot fall in love with a *sprite*: and Shaw is a sprite in such matters, not a real person,' she explained. And Shaw himself agreed: 'It is certainly true.'

They came to understand each other well because of the Fabian 'dry goods' they shared. 'We are committed for life to Socialism,' Shaw acknowledged. It was after her that Shaw created Vivie Warren in *Mrs Warren's Profession* – an 'attractive . . . sensible . . . self-possessed' woman in whom William Archer (not knowing Beatrice) could see nothing 'but a Shaw in petticoats'. It was Shaw's 'most serious play,' Beatrice decided.

Each summer the Webbs would take a house in the country for three months – first an enlarged Jacobean mansion called Argoed, at Penallt in the Wye Valley; subsequently a rectory in Suffolk or a farm in Surrey – and here they would invite Sidney's friends on the Fabian executive. 'The Fabian old gang can only afford a country house for a holiday,' Shaw bluntly put it, 'because one of us has a wife with a thousand a year.' They passed their mornings, each in separate rooms, writing; stopped for a ravenous plain meal ('we do not have butter for Sidney's breakfast'); strode off on crushing walks during the afternoon and spent the evenings arguing violently over politics. By the mid-1890s they had changed from walkers into bicyclists.

'My new toy is my bicycle,' Shaw proclaimed in 1895. That spring, to the convulsions of the coastguards, he started learning to ride this new hobby horse with the Webbs on Beachy Head: 'I will do twenty yards and a destructive fall against any professional in England,' he told Janet Achurch. 'My God, the stiffness, the blisters, the bruises, the pains in every twisted muscle, the crashes against the chalk road that I have endured – and at my age [39] too. But I shall come like gold from the furnace: I will not be beaten by that hellish machine.' Beatrice, who scudded into a wasps' nest but managed to cure herself with whisky, calculated that 'One's "byke" is a great addition to the pleasure of life.'

And Shaw, lying exhausted in a deep ditch near Argoed, the moonlight filtering onto him through the revolving spokes of the wheels and the laced thorn twigs of a briar, reflected: 'Bicycling's a capital thing for a literary man.' On wheels, the Fabians appeared to become schoolboys and girls again. Beatrice (until Sidney had one smash too many) rigorously prescribed it during the long Fabian summer afternoons; and Shaw hygienically explained: 'Unless I seize every opportunity of bicycling off into the country, if only for a couple of hours, I get beaten by the evil atmosphere in which I have to pass so much of my time.'

For a dozen years, until 1908 when he took dangerously to cars, the bicycle was a prime article of Shavian equipment. Its effect was enormous, he reasoned, since the bicyclist could extend a day's travel from the pedestrian's few miles to the region of a hundred miles. So, by increasing the efficiency of existence, the bicycle which was popularly attacked as the terror of horses and a temptation to women, became a symbol of modernity. As such it was wheeled by way of metaphor and analogy into many Shavian arguments.

By 1896 he had enrolled as the 621st member of the Cyclist Touring Club whose Annual General Meeting he considerably lengthened by a plea against improving the tone of the Club's *Gazette* (where fiction, he thought, should be found only among the advertisements). To actresses, parents, schoolboys, he poured out information about the varieties of crack machines. 'Do not expect to improve with practice,' he recommended. 'You wont. The change from hopeless failure to complete success is instantaneous and miraculous.' One miracle was staying alive, though 'if you keep on bicycling long enough,' he promised, 'you will break your leg'.

For someone physically timid, Shaw's experiments by bicycle were extraordinary. He would raise his feet to the handlebars and simply *toboggan* down the steep places. Many of his falls, from which he would prance away crying 'I am not hurt', with black eyes, violet lips and a red face, acted as trials for his optimism. The surgery afterwards was an education in itself. Each toss he took was a point scored for one or more of his fads. After one appalling smash (hills, clouds and farmhouses tumbling around drunkenly), he wrote: 'Still I am not thoroughly convinced yet that I was not killed. Anybody but a vegetarian would have been. Nobody but a teetotaller would have faced a bicycle again for six months.' After four years of intrepid pedalling, he could claim: 'If I had taken to the ring I should, on the whole, have suffered less than I have, physically.'

*

He saw a good deal of the Webbs during the first half-dozen years of their marriage. The income that Beatrice inherited from her father enabled Sidney to retire from the Colonial Office; and together they planned to give unpaid service to society in return for this unearned income. Beatrice immediately put Sidney to work, writing their books on trade unionism, industrial democracy and English local government. This work established the Fabian tradition of research. It was complemented by their 'permeation' policy of infiltration and persuasion. Under Beatrice's direction, this was to take a more social turn. She was not a good hostess. Like Shaw, her achievement was built on the repression of the body. She grew addicted to fasting, weighing herself regularly at Charing Cross Station and gloating over each little loss of weight. Her bare lunches and dinners, though feasts of intellect, never added an atmosphere of seduction to the manipulating activity of permeation.

Beatrice was to be the *salonnière* of the Fabian Society, with Shaw its instant historian. What his audiences heard from him on the platform, what they read by him in their newspapers, kept morale sparkling with the sense that political events were going their way. It also enabled them the more easily to accept decisions in their name that had been made exclusively by the Webbs and Shaw.

Only one Socialist, Keir Hardie, had been returned to Parliament at the General Election of 1892. The Fabians generally supported the Liberals on whom, by means of what was called the Newcastle programme, they believed that they had imposed a detailed plan for constructive social reform. At the beginning of 1893, the future of a Labour Party in Parliament was remote; but implementation by Gladstone's Liberal Government of the Fabian-inspired Newcastle Programme, involving new factory legislation, the extension of free education, municipal reform, payment of MPs and the 'mending or ending' of the House of Lords, seemed imminent. Six months later, it had become clear that Gladstone had abandoned almost all radical reforms and handed Parliament's time over to an Irish Home Rule Bill. To the Fabians, this was a waste of time (literally so, since the House of Lords halted the Home Rule Bill), and a betrayal of election promises. 'We must,' Shaw wrote to a hesitant Graham Wallas, ' . . . satisfy the legitimate aspirations of the ardent spirits by getting out a furious attack on the Government.'

This furious attack, written by Shaw with Webb's assistance and signed 'By the Fabian Society', appeared in the November *Fortnightly Review* using the Biblical call to revolt, 'To Your Tents, Oh Israel!' Acknowledging that legislative reforms might have been limited by the small Liberal majority, Shaw's manifesto examined each of the departments of State and showed what administrative reforms, not subject to this limitation, might have been effected so that individual ministers could redeem some of their Government's pledges. 'Had the will existed,' the manifesto concluded, 'there would have been no difficulty about the way.' This was a triumphant piece of political journalism, which Shaw elaborated in January 1894 into Fabian Tract No. 49, *A Plan of Campaign for Labor*, which called for the trade unions to raise 'a parliamentary fund of at least £30,000, and the running of fifty *independent* Labor candidates at the next general election'. But this manifesto produced two reactions: it alienated the Liberal Party and all those Fabians who still saw in Liberalism a means of introducing a progressive programme into Parliament; and it came too late to kindle sympathy with men such as Keir Hardie, who was to lose his seat in the 1895 General Election, and who described the Fabians as 'the worst enemies of the social revolution'. For though *A Plan of Campaign for Labor* proposed similar measures to those of the Independent Labour Party, Shaw feared that any amalgamation would lead to the extinction of his Fabian family. Already by the spring of 1894 the Society, which Shaw was to urge not to 'waste another five minutes on permeation', was drifting back to the idea of grafting collectivism on to Rosebery who had then succeeded Gladstone as Liberal Prime Minister. At the 1895 General Election, 'sitting with their hands in their laps', the Fabians neutrally committed themselves to the principle of a Collectivist Party, distinct from Liberals, Conservatives and the ILP. The large Conservative victory that summer seemed to mark an end to the socialist resurgence in Britain. The trade-union movement had faltered, the ILP had done badly, and the Fabians had done nothing at all.

Fabian strategy during the 1890s exemplified Shaw's dogma of adaptability. He excelled at seizing the initiative in retrospect. In whichever direction history plunged, there was the Fabian waiting to guide and explain. To some extent these twists and weavings were the natural trials and errors of Shaw's political education. He felt strongly convinced that the humane and reasoned voice of the intellectual must not be lost amid the struggle of party politicians and the rough and tumble of popular democracy. To be heard, seen, and valued as advocates of progress with safeguards against revolution, the Fabians needed someone to play these political games and command popular appeal – while leaving the central concept of egalitarian English socialism uncontaminated. It was on such an understanding that Shaw was exploiting his dialectical skills.

2

PLAYS UNPLEASANT

> Widowers' Houses seemed to me better worth printing than burning . . . I am not burning it: I am just finishing another play . . . Then I shall write another; and I have no doubt that when I have written ten or eleven more or less simple and crude plays I shall be able to write a complex and perhaps powerful one.
>
> Shaw to Karl Pearson (20 June 1893)

He had been hovering on the edge of writing plays for a long time. This fascination with the stage, deriving from those visits in Dublin to the Theatre Royal and the new Gaiety Theatre, had hidden itself in his novels, for he was (so he confessed to readers of the *Pall Mall Gazette*), 'a sufferer from that strange brain disease which drives its victims to write long stories that are not true, and to delight in them more than in any other literature'.

In 1884 he had begun his first serious attempt to write a full-length play in collaboration with Archer. The plan was for Archer to borrow a plot from a domestic 'cup-and-saucer comedy' by Emile Augier called *Ceinture Dorée*, Archer doing it into English scene by scene and ladling it out to Shaw who would set about reconciling it, in sparkling dialogue, with his Marxist passion for political economy. It was to be called *The Way to a Woman's Heart*, though they soon began calling it *Rheingold* (later anglicized to *Rhinegold*). Shaw started on 18 August and by 12 September completed the first act. A month later, the second act was also completed; but in mid-November, after writing twenty-three lines of Act III, he stopped, with the explanation that he had exhausted all Archer's plot. In fact he was able to find use for all too little of it. His difficulty lay in matching this contrived Parisian structure to an analysis of contemporary slum landlordism. Increasingly he was driven away from Augier's story to plunder other sources – *Little Dorrit*, some scenes from his own last novel, *An Unsocial Socialist*, and a penny pamphlet called *The Bitter Cry of Outcast London* that was to lead to a Royal Commission. But eventually he 'gave up fiction and took to Socialism,' as he explained to Janet Achurch.

There were occasions over the next two or three years when, coming across his notebooks, Shaw would copy out some pages of *Rhinegold* in the hope of regaining his momentum. But the play still lacked direction. 'Wrote no new fiction,' Shaw noted at the beginning of his 1886 diary. He felt the lack of creative writing, and by 14 April 1887 observed himself to be 'hovering on the confines of beginning a novel'. A month later he registered in his diary that he 'began a new novel and sat up till 3 at it. Hooray!' But after two months there is no further mention of it. Having put aside the novel he again picked up his play. Early that autumn he made a fair copy in longhand of the first two acts which he left with Archer on 4 October. 'They are not supposed to be complete,' he told him, 'but they present a series of consecutive dialogues in which your idea is prepared and developed . . . but I have no idea of how it is to proceed.'

Two days later Shaw read Archer the first act of their unfinished drama. A long argument followed, and when Shaw began reading the second act, Archer closed his eyes. 'I softly put the manuscript away,' Shaw wrote, 'and let him have his sleep out.'

Archer believed that realism represented 'the hope of the dramatic future'. Ibsen had told him that there was always a stage when his writing might as 'easily turn into an essay as a drama'. What his playwriting experiment taught Archer was that his own future lay in writing realistic essays. There was not even money to be made from a collaboration with Shaw who was a fantasist rather than a realist. So he closed his eyes on a playwriting dream.

Archer's opinion was important to Shaw. Though he had trained himself to do without encouragement, he needed the support of this man who had given him so much of his theatrical education. Not receiving it, he was lost.

The following year he tried something new. 'Worked at the plan of the play which has come into my head,' he noted in his diary on 29 June 1889. The idea of this play had been stimulated by an incident involving Janet Achurch and the Archers. Frances Archer had apparently objected to Shaw having declared his love for Janet, a married woman. Shaw replied that conventional marriage stifled the imagination. He even told Archer that his wife was spoiling him and that he would be 'a lost man' unless he broke free. Archer replied that Shaw must not visit their home while he held views so disparaging to his wife.

But the notion that marriage had meant 'checkmate' to Archer as a playwright 'for years to come' persisted in Shaw. Why else had Archer let him down over *Rhinegold*? The idea began to infiltrate a new work. At odd moments, in parks and restaurants, on trains and political platforms – even during the intervals of other people's plays – he would write passages of dialogue for what was turning out to be a comedy of intrigue, called *The Cassone*, with characters based on the Archers, the Charringtons and himself. It was a revenge for *Rhinegold* and a precursor to *Candida*, a battle of the artistic versus the domestic instinct. But his life was so pell-mell with politics and journalism he had no opportunity to complete *The Cassone*.

After the failure of his collaboration with Archer, Shaw had despaired of writing an actable play. 'I wish I could write you a real play myself,' he told the actress Alma Murray, 'but unfortunately I have not the faculty.' But he did not completely give up. 'I was surprised one day when he told me that he had been trying his hand at a new sort of stuff, some of which he showed me, written lengthwise in a reporter's note-book in his exquisite handwriting, unaffected by the vibration of railway travelling, and which I realized was a dramatic dialogue,' Sydney Olivier remembered.

'. . . I was surprised, because the quality of British play-wrighting, and the deadly artificiality and narrow conventions of native contemporary British Drama were at that time so repellent to me that I could not imagine any man of the intelligence of Shaw . . . conceiving that there was any possibility . . . for expressing himself in that medium.'

What nerved Shaw to continue was the example of Ibsen who had demonstrated how serious business (such as the working out of a new system of social values) could be conducted from the stage. After seeing Archer's translation of *A Doll's House* acted by the Charringtons, he had written:

'I find people enjoying themselves there who have been practically driven from the other theatres by the intolerable emptiness of the ordinary performances. I miss the conventional lies of the stage there; and I do not droop, wither, and protest I am being poisoned for want of them . . . [I] see a vital truth searched out and held up in a light intense enough to dispel all the mists and shadows that obscure it in actual life. I see people silent, attentive, thoughtful, startled – struck to the heart, some of them.'

From the affinity he felt with Ibsen, Shaw emerged with new confidence. 'But not only has the comedy to be made, but the actors, the manager, the theatre, the audience. Somebody must do these things,' he wrote.

It was a Dutchman, J. T. Grein, who did this thing by starting what Shaw called 'the most important theatrical enterprise of its time'. Hiring a cheap hall ('the nearest thing to a barn left in Tottenham Court Road'), Grein announced a performance of Ibsen's *Ghosts* in 1891 to inaugurate 'The Independent Theatre', with Thomas Hardy, Henry Arthur Jones, Meredith, George Moore and Pinero among its members. 'Result – barn too small; performance transferred gloriously' to the Royalty Theatre, and Grein, suddenly the most famous theatrical entrepreneur in Britain.

It was Grein who, the following year, struck the spark of encouragement Shaw needed. While the two of them were walking one autumn night from Hammersmith, Grein mentioned his disappointment at the absence of new British playwrights for his theatre; and Shaw replied that he had written a new British play 'that you'll never have the courage to produce'. Grein answered the challenge by asking for the manuscript. It came, a few days later, 'written partly in a large notebook and for the rest on loose sheets,' Grein recalled, 'and I spent a long and attentive evening in sorting and deciphering it. I had never had a doubt as to my acceptance . . . But I could very well understand how little chance that play would have had [with] . . . the average theatre manager.'

The two acts of *Rhinegold* had lain among Shaw's discarded manuscripts for over four and a half years until, on 29 July 1892, while attempting to set his papers in order, he came across them. Next day he had 'set to work to finish the comedy'. On 31 July he was 'still amusing myself finishing the comedy', and by 2 August he 'began to revise the comedy'. That he was now to solve the problem that had baffled him in the 1880s was due to his education by Ibsen. The hero of the play, Harry Trench, proposes to Blanche Sartorius and is accepted by her in Act I. But in Act II, finding that her money comes from slum properties, he breaks off their engagement. How then was Shaw to bring the lovers together without violating his own and his hero's principles? His solution, by the summer of 1892, was to make the hero less 'heroic', and by showing the slum landlord Sartorius to be not a villain but the symptom of a social system in which everyone was implicated.

'I think, by the bye, that the title Rheingold ought to be saved for a romantic play,' he had suggested when leaving the first two acts with Archer. 'This is realism.' On 20 October 1892, while working at a new scene near the end of Act II, he decided on the 'far-fetched Scriptural title', *Widowers' Houses*. From its conception over seven years earlier the play had changed so fundamentally as to make Archer a collaborator only in the sense of having set Shaw's imagination to work.

The ramshackle rehearsals, scheduled for 14 November, started punctually the following day at a public house, 'the Mona Hotel'. Sometimes there were not enough actors to carry through a rehearsal at all. When they did turn up they vied anxiously with one another to avoid various parts – in particular Lickcheese, the Dickensian rent collector, who was played by James Welch after entering the pub for a drink. Shaw was there, he was everywhere, until begged to stay away so that the actors could get their words.

Widowers' Houses opened at the Royalty Theatre in Dean Street, Soho, on 9 December, the most obvious vocal part that evening being the prompter's. It was a curious example, commented Archer in *The World*, 'of what can be done in art by sheer brainpower'. At the end of the performance, Shaw hurried before the curtain to make a speech and was acclaimed with hisses. At the second and final performance, a matinée on 13 December, he again climbed on to the stage and, there being no critics present, was applauded.

If it had not achieved success, it had 'made a sensation,' Shaw contended. After more than eight years, he squeezed out the stimulus he needed. *Widowers' Houses* had been born: its job now was to give birth to him as a professional dramatist.

*

The novelty of *Widowers' Houses* lay in the anti-romantic use to which Shaw put theatrical cliché. When the father discovers his daughter in the arms of a stranger, he omits to horsewhip him, but pitches into negotiations over the marriage – and these negotiations reveal a naked money-for-social-position bargain. It is the young girl, not the young man, who takes the initiative in the love scenes, and when her fiancé initially refuses to accept his father-in-law's dowry because it has been acquired from appalling exploitation of the poor, she does not forsake all for love – in fact, she does the opposite. Unlike Augier's hero, who tips his tainted gold into the Rhine, Shaw's hero comes to accept it ('We're all in the same boat it appears'); and the final happy ending is a lustful surrender to corruption. In relation to the Victorian theatre, this 'was a prodigious feat,' wrote the critic Eric Bentley some fifty years later; 'it remains the most revolutionary act in modern English drama.'

Standing on stage that first night in his dazzling Jaeger wool, Shaw welcomed the turbulent hooting by agreeing that, 'yes', it was a disgraceful state of affairs they had just witnessed, a true picture of things then going on in middle-class society that he hoped would soon become unintelligible to London audiences. Later on, Shaw would instruct producers that Lickcheese, the reptilian rent-collector, should be played with pathos and sincerity, even geniality. 'There should be absolutely no unpleasantness at all about him . . . The audience should delight in him in a thoroughly friendly way: and he should wallow in their friendliness.' Shaw's point was that Lickcheese, the other characters, and the audience itself, were all incapable of being better than the world around them: it is a cast of philistines, with Sartorius the idealist at their head.

But 'friendly', in the Shavian vocabulary, is a dangerous word. What gives *Widowers' Houses* its power is Shaw's anger. He was writing here from personal experience, as the young man who had 'collected slum rentals weekly with these hands' in Dublin, and who in London was immersing himself in municipal politics. Shaw wanted to make his audience 'thoroughly uncomfortable whilst entertaining them artistically'. This philistine audience retaliated through its idealist critics by calling the play 'not a play' and the playwright 'no playwright'. He was, they allowed, a fine speaker and would have done well in comic opera or the Church. So began Shaw's lifelong battle with the critics for whom he was (in the words of A. B. Walkley), 'a detestable dramatist', having started his career with 'a singularly bad piece of work'.

Widowers' Houses contains the stereotype figures (heavy father, low comedian, *femme fatale*), but displaced by Shaw from their familiar roles. Lickcheese was to develop into Doolittle; the slum landlord Sartorius into the armaments manufacturer, Undershaft; Blanche Sartorius into Ann Whitefield. But they present themselves more crudely here, and without self-mockery or Shavian guile. In a sense this is Shaw's most human play. Nowhere else is his dislike of the world as it exists more plainly felt. The perfect embodiment of this world is Blanche Sartorius, over whom the pact between aristocratic respectability and financial exploitation is made. 'I see I have made a real lady of you, Blanche,' says her father a little wistfully. She is an enslaving woman, a landlady of the emotions who betrays, more clearly than anywhere else in Shaw's work, the results of Jenny Patterson's rigorous devotion. Here, on paper, was his revenge; and given on the stage an ironic twist by the casting of Florence Farr in the part. The predatory Blanche, with her terrifying temper, prompted Oscar Wilde to congratulate Shaw: 'I admire the horrible flesh and blood of your creatures.'

Though *Widowers' Houses* presents a socialist view of life, there is no socialist in it. Trench is an innocent Conservative who decides that he is not called upon to remake the world at his own expense. But his adaptability to facts becomes merely an acquiescence to corruption and his innocence is lost. To what extent socialism made compromise honourable was a question that was to be tested on Shaw with his next play.

*

With the press-cuttings crammed into his bag, Shaw caught a train to join William Morris's Christmas house party at Kelmscott Manor, in Oxfordshire. Over the holiday he began pondering his first Preface and dreaming of his second play. He would do such things . . . He would sail, all guns smoking, into the topical storm that was engulfing the New Woman; demolish the marriage and divorce laws, expose the evil of vivisection, violently assault modern doctors for reducing human beings to chemical machines. It was to be a grand cleaning-up operation. In his exhilaration he opened a wider window, cracked thicker ice, that winter.

For Easter 1893 he went to Oxted to stay with the Salts. His travelling companion on the train was Sydney Olivier who, it seemed, was also writing a play – which was surprising in view of the dismay he had shown over Shaw's writing of *Widowers' Houses.* Olivier read part of his play to the Salts one day, and was generally 'very full' of it, Shaw observed. Here was the pacemaker he needed to get going. His diary entry for the next day, 29 March, reads: 'After breakfast went up to the Common by Rickfield Rd and selected a spot on the West Heath, near the orphanage, where I lay down and got to work on the new play which I have resolved to call *The Philanderer.*'

Much of the play was written on trains to and from his various lectures and speeches, and (sometimes under an umbrella) in Hyde Park and Regent's Park, on the Embankment and on the top of Primrose Hill – whenever he could snatch an hour or two. Then he suddenly got stuck. On 23 May, he wrote in his diary: 'After dinner I went out to Putney and walked by way of Roehampton to Richmond Park, where I tried to get to work on the third act of the play, but could not think of a subject for it.'

The following day he went to William Archer's house to hear the reading of Olivier's play. Afterwards, on a bus to Shepherd's Bush, 'I hit on the third act of my new play.' The idea he had hit on was the marriage and divorce question. He continued intermittently working on this act and discussing it with Janet Achurch.

On the afternoon of 17 June he read a revised text to Lady Colin Campbell. What then happened changed the content of the play and the course Shaw's work was to follow. Lady Colin Campbell, he explained, 'pointed out to me that the third act at which I have been working ought to be put into the fire. This opened my eyes for the first time to the fact that I have started on quite a new trail and must reserve this act for the beginning of a new play.' A few days later, on 22 June, 'I went up to the top of Primrose Hill and there wrote a new scene for the beginning of the new third act of the play, as suggested by Lady Colin.'

Lady Colin Campbell was a formidable woman. She rode, she swam, she wrote books on etiquette and was Shaw's successor as art critic on *The World.* She was also Irish. But she was best known for having obtained, in a sensational series of court actions, a judicial separation from her husband, the youngest son of the eighth Duke of Argyll. She was a practical woman and a sensitive judge of public opinion. What she told Shaw was that no audience in the early 1890s would accept the last act as he had written it. He was in his thirty-seventh year. After that tiny taste of success with *Widowers' Houses*, he hungered to have his play produced. But by substituting her suggestion for his original inspiration he was going against much that he claimed for himself as a dramatist.

This may help to explain the revulsion that sometimes overtook him with this play.

In the original third act there is one extra character, a comic butler called Spedding. It takes place at the house of Dr Paramore on his third wedding anniversary to Julia Craven (the character based on Jenny Patterson). Only a man with the name Paramore and the inventor of a non-existent illness, 'Paramore's Disease', would marry Julia. But now he is a changed man, as tired of his wife as she is of him, and in love with Grace Tranfield (the character based on Florence Farr). He is – and this gives a nice symmetry to the play – in very much the same position as the philanderer Charteris in Act I: that is, on with the new love before he is off with the old, but with the additional complication of being married. It is this subject of marriage and divorce that occupies this act, during which they decide to go to South Dakota where the divorce laws have been better adapted to human nature.

The plot is carried forward by means of conversation. It is, in fact, Shaw's first discussion drama. There is an interweaving of ideas, an elegance of argument pushed to the point of comic exasperation, and a dissolving of action into talk – all innovations in the theatre that were not actually to reach the stage for more than another ten years.

By the end of June, *The Philanderer* (with Lady Colin Campbell's last act) was finished and early the following month Shaw had his chessmen out and was experimenting with the stage positions of his characters. As the second of what he was to call his 'unpleasant' plays, *The Philanderer* dealt with sex – with the power game of sex that was played in the society of the 1890s. Charteris, we are meant to understand, has had sexual intercourse with Julia Craven and Grace Tranfield. He is 'making love' to Grace on a sofa before Julia arrives early in Act I. In a letter to his Swedish translator, Shaw explained:

'A philanderer is a man who is strongly attracted by women. He flirts with them, falls half in love with them, makes them fall in love with him, but will not commit himself to any permanent relation with them, and often retreats at the last moment if his suit is successful – loves them but loves himself more – is too cautious, too fastidious, ever to give himself away.'

The Philanderer was an unlucky play. Shaw had wanted to include 'everything that is supposed to be hopelessly undramatic, and make them the most amusing part of the piece,' he told Charles Charrington. 'It will be unspeakably improper: so I expect it will only see the light at the Independent Theatre. Grein is already after it eagerly.' But Grein was unimpressed. 'Shaw was probably much amused at our lack of appreciation, and took his manuscript away.'

That Grein suspected him to have been 'amused' at this rejection shows how well Shaw could conceal his feelings. At the last moment he had compromised – and his compromise had led nowhere. He had told Archer that *The Philanderer* was to be 'a step nearer to something'. It was true that 'the ideas and atmosphere of it belonged to a new world as yet undiscovered at the West End Theatres', but at the last moment he had taken a pace back.

*

After his failure with *The Philanderer*, Shaw returned to the vein he had worked in *Widowers' Houses*, writing a problem play that was to reveal the corruption produced by compromising too readily with society. Once again the theme is one of social inheritance and the profit motive; once again he shadows his audience with guilt.

'Do you think you are guiltless in the matter? Take care . . . The wages of prostitution are stitched into your button-holes and into your blouse, pasted into your matchboxes and your boxes of pins, stuffed into your mattress, mixed with the paint on your walls and stuck between the joints of your water-pipes . . . you will not cheat the Recording Angel into putting down your debts to the wrong account.'

Writing in 1901 a Note for the end of *Cashel Byron's Profession*, he was to explain that 'the word prostitution should either not be used at all, or else applied impartially to all persons who do things for money that they would not do if they had other assured means of livelihood'. In his play, which he called *Mrs Warren's Profession*, he used the same formula as in *Cashel Byron's Profession*, that of taking 'a profession which society officially repudiates as a metaphor for the way in which that larger society is really conducted'.

Ever since the licensing of continental brothels in the 1870s and the subsequent discovery that British girls were being exported to Brussels and Vienna (where Mrs Warren conducted her business), 'The Great Social Evil', as the Victorians called prostitution, had begun to exceed slum-landlordism as the most controversial topic for the press. In 1885, W. T. Stead launched his sensational series, 'The Maiden Tribute of Modern Babylon' in the *Pall Mall Gazette*, his first article revealing how Mrs Armstrong had sold her daughter for £3. 'I am quite willing to take as many quires of the paper as I can carry and sell them (for a penny) in any thoroughfare in London,' Shaw wrote to Stead. On discovering that

Stead had doctored his facts, Shaw felt that he had been betrayed: 'he [Stead] was so stupendously ignorant that he never played the game.' Stead's game had been to force the Criminal Law Amendment Bill (the chief provision of which was to raise the age of consent from thirteen to sixteen) through Parliament.

The immense press coverage gave Shaw an insight into the nineteenth century's attitude towards its 'unfortunates'. Victorian domestic virtues were represented by the middle-class family with its many children and dominating paterfamilias. The wife-and-mother, guardian of the hearth, who ran the household and bore the children, was a sexless being whose gentility (physicians were agreed) was outward proof of the absence of a female orgasm. For sexual satisfaction, the husband-and-father had to explore the lesser breeds, such as working-class women earning a shilling a day in the sweatshop, for whom prostitution could bring a vital addition to their income. London was honeycombed with houses of assignation illegally maintained through police bribery; but only on the Continent had the brothel become an established social institution. The more superior of these brothels were run as clubs and they offered businessmen, such as Mrs Warren's Sir George Crofts, opportunities of forming profitable syndicates. These syndicates, which would purchase premises, secure licences and supply girls, provided investments similar to those made in the eighteenth century by city merchant houses in the slave trade.

In representing prostitution as an economic phenomenon ('Prostitution is not a question of sex: it is a question of money') Shaw was writing from the point of view of women; but he also wrote as a socialist ('Every increase in women's wages produces a decrease in prostitution') who prescribed as his remedy a living wage for women ('a Minimum Wage law and . . . proper provision for the unemployed'); and finally he wrote as a man struggling to supplant the sex instinct in himself.

It was Janet Achurch who fired the starting gun by telling Shaw the story of a play she was then writing called *Mrs Daintree's Daughter* based on Maupassant's *Yvette.* On 30 August 1893 he announced to Archer: 'I have finished the first act of my new play, in which I have skilfully blended the plot of The Second Mrs Tanqueray with that of The Cenci. It will be just the thing for the I[ndependent] T[heatre].'

Beatrice Webb suggested that he 'should put on the stage a real modern lady of the governing class – not the sort of thing that theatrical and critical authorities imagine such a lady to be'. To which Shaw added: 'I did so: and the result was Miss Vivie Warren.' Reporting his progress on 4 September, he wrote to the woman he hoped would play Vivie, Janet Achurch:

'The play progresses bravely; but it has left the original lines. I have made the daughter the heroine, and the mother a most deplorable old rip (saving your presence). The great scene will be the crushing of the mother by the daughter. I retain the old roué, but keep him restrained by a continual doubt as to whether the heroine may not be his daughter. The young lover's father, an outrageous clergyman, is in the same perplexity, he also being an old flame of the mother's. The lover is an agreeable young spark, wholly good-for-nothing. The girl is a quite original character. The mother, uncertain who the girl's father is, keeps all the old men at bay by telling each one that he is the parent.'

He continued working on it between visits to the Jaeger Wool Shop and the British Museum. He set out for walks with the play in his pocket, camping from time to time on wayside seats to write up the speeches. He called on his friends and, for purposes of revision and casting, delivered his lines. By the time he had finished all four acts on 2 November, he had tried it out on Archer, the Charringtons, Florence Farr, Sydney Olivier, the Salts, the Webbs and Mrs Theodore Wright, who being London's first Mrs Alving in Ibsen's *Ghosts* would, Shaw hoped, take the title role. He also read it to Lady Colin Campbell who, ironically, was going into collaboration with Janet Achurch over her version which, though licensed the following year, was never professionally performed. After all this preparation *Mrs Warren's Profession* was ready for the Independent Theatre by the second week of December.

Unlike Maupassant's *Yvette*, Vivie Warren neither attempts to kill herself nor becomes a courtesan like her mother; unlike Pinero's Mrs Tanqueray, Mrs Warren declines to step into the next room and commit suicide. She is 'a counter-portrait to the general image of the romantic, sentimentally attractive courtesan of the stage'. The cast is largely made up of prostitutes like Mrs Warren herself, and their clients: Sir George Crofts the big-time client; the old vicar who has sold himself for his benefice and turned from rake into sanctimonious humbug; and his son Frank, the nearest to an authorial presence in the play, who almost sells himself in marriage to Vivie. Below the talking surface of the play move mysterious undercurrents of incest.

This theme of incest (deriving from *The Cenci* as well as from Ibsen's *Ghosts* and *Rosmersholm*), was muted after Shaw's corrections to the first draft. Originally Frank and Vivie were established as half-brother and sister, and Vivie welcomes this fact as saving her from 'the sort of relation my mother's life had tainted for ever for me'. She returns to the moonlight illusion of being 'babes in the wood . . . covered up with leaves'; but as the curtain descends at the end of Act III she 'lifts her face & presses his lips on hers'. The confusing remnants from such incestuous moments suggest that Shaw felt all sex to be tainted for Vivie. 'I am like you,' Vivie tells her mother. But by focusing his play on the daughter and not (like Pinero and Maupassant) on the mother, Shaw seeks to convert sexual destiny into work destiny. 'There's no alternative,' says Madame Obardi, the prostitute mother, to Yvette who is shown as unable to avoid her fate in the 'world of gilded prostitution'. But for Vivie Warren there is an alternative: 'my work is not your work,' she tells her mother, 'and my way is not your way.' She gains integrity through sexual isolation – 'away from it all – away from the sentiment of the tie I formed under the spell of that ghastly moonlight, away from the very air breathed by my mother and that man, away from the world they are part of'. These words of Vivie's Shaw dropped from the published version: but they still lie between the lines and provide an uneasy sub-text to the play.

Shaw's case is that there are two ways of preventing the present from repeating the errors of the past: love and work. In love we forget, are reborn, speak like infants. Then the good moment goes, for the world is not lovable. But if what we call love also supplies the future generations, it is work that decides what sort of life those generations will follow. Instinct tells us whether we should love, and what work we should do; and will-power gives us the vitality to carry through this work.

Shaw places his emphasis on the gospel of work and against the religion of love. When Frank sees Vivie with her arm round her mother's waist, he is revolted: 'Dont it make your flesh creep.' But when he appeals to the love-instinct in Vivie ('Come and be covered up with leaves again') she gives a 'cry of disgust' and tells him: 'You make my flesh creep.' Is this because of the revelation that she is Frank's half-sister as well as the revelation of how her mother's money is made? That Frank's father had gone through some sexual involvement with Vivie's mother seems probable; but in such an atmosphere of consanguinity (like the atmosphere of Sonny's home), uncertainty prevails. Arising from Shaw's doubts about his parenthood and ambiguous feelings for his mother, incest is made to cover us all, like the leaves. Something of Mrs Shaw can been seen in Mrs Warren, and this may help to account for the uncertainty and aggression of the play. 'I can't stand *anybody* as Mrs Warren, because I can't stand the play itself,' he told Gertrude Kingston in 1925. ' . . . Ugh!'

When Vivie Warren 'buries herself luxuriously in her actuarial calculations as the curtain falls we are conscious that she has experienced horror and a sense of contamination'. This was the reaction, too, of G.B.S. who tried to turn himself from his mother's son into an immaculate speaking and writing machine. There is autobiographical passion and pathos in the final stage directions:

[*Mrs Warren goes out, slamming the door behind her. The strain on Vivie's face relaxes; her grave expression breaks up into one of joyous content; her breath goes out in a half sob, half laugh of intense relief. She goes buoyantly to her place at the writing table; pushes the electric lamp out of the way; pulls over a great sheaf of papers . . . Then she goes at her work with a plunge, and soon becomes absorbed in its figures.*]

'I do not think there is the least chance of the play being licensed,' Shaw wrote cheerfully to Grein. He had not foreseen that Grein would feel that *Mrs Warren's Profession* was unfit 'for women's ears' and that, since it might lead even strong men to 'insanity and suicide', he could not allow a private production. 'I am at my wits end about this unlucky play of mine,' Shaw told the actress Elizabeth Robins.

Mrs Warren's Profession had to wait until 1902 for the first of two private performances by the Stage Society and until 1925 for its first public production in Britain: 'too late,' Shaw remarked. He failed to get a copyright performance in Ireland, and after its world première in the United States in 1905, it was prosecuted in the courts. Even as late as 1955 the play was banned as 'amoral' from the Salle Luxembourg in Paris by the selection committee of the Comédie Française.

Shaw had taken immense trouble to tailor his play to the conventions of the stage. The difficulties preventing its performance thrust him deep into a vigorous campaign against theatre censorship; and it changed his orientation as a dramatist. Slum-landlordism, the marriage laws and prostitution had all proved 'unspeakable' subjects on the Victorian stage, and Shaw made the decision to write no more plays with a social purpose, and to become a writer of plays with no purpose 'except the purpose of all poets and dramatists' – that is 'plays of life, character and human destiny'. In order to get his words spoken on the stage he moved the emphasis 'from the public institution to the private imagination'; set out to make his audiences laugh rather than feel uncomfortable (though sometimes to laugh at themselves); and resolved to 'sport with human follies, not with crimes'. Having put aside *Mrs Warren's Profession*, he went back to the beginning and started again – this time with a nursery play. His diary entry for 26 November 1893 reads: 'spent the evening beginning a new play – a romantic one – for F[lorence] E[mery].'

3

ARMS AND THE MAN

> I greatly regret that my play, 'Arms and the Man', has wounded the susceptibilities of Bulgarian students in Berlin and Vienna. But I ask them to remember that it is the business of the writer of a comedy to wound the susceptibilities of his audience. The classical definition of his function is 'the chastening of morals by ridicule' . . . When the Bulgarian students, with my sincerely friendly assistance, have developed a sense of humor there will be no more trouble.
>
> *The World Wide News Service Inc.* (16 November 1924)

By the mid-1890s, despite all his reverses, Shaw had become thoroughly well known. Scurrilous attacks, disguised as interviews, were regularly made on him by the press. Extra-special reporters, athletic rather than intellectual, would force their way into his room apparently for no purpose other than to bully and insult him. Shaw would defend himself in heart-rending tones. 'I have kept my temper for eighteen years, and have never been uncivil to an interviewer,' he explained. Many readers felt that here was an astonishing example of Christian forbearance. Only a few realized that the interviews had been written by himself.

'I presume, Mr Shaw,' one imaginary reporter asked before the opening of his new play, 'that when the eventful night comes, the most enjoyable part of it will be your speech after —.' Stepping out before the curtain after the first performance of *Arms and the Man*, Shaw addressed his short speech to the solitary man who in a cheering audience had uttered a loud 'Boo!' 'My dear fellow,' he exclaimed, 'I quite agree with you, but what are we against so many?'

In this Wildean *mot* Shaw placed his true feelings. Writing to his fellow-playwright, Henry Arthur Jones, some eight months later, he explained: 'Like you, I write plays because I like it, and because I cannot remember any period in my life when I could help inventing people and scenes.' But, he went on:

> 'I am not a storyteller: things occur to me as scenes, with action and dialogue – as moments, developing themselves out of their own vitality . . . my quarrel with the conventional drama is that it is doctrinaire to the uttermost extreme of dogmatism . . . clever people predominate in a first night audience; and, accordingly, in 'Arms & the Man', I had the curious experience of witnessing an apparently insane success . . . and of going

before the curtain to tremendous applause, the only person in the theatre who knew that the whole affair was a ghastly failure.'

Part of the 'intelligent misunderstanding' of Shaw's plays arose from his method of dressing himself in the strait-jacket of theatrical conventions and performing tricks of elastic unconventionality. But it came too from the discrepancy between a sophisticated intellect and emotions that still responded to the adult world from the doorway of the nursery. Of the horrors of war *Arms and the Man* conveyed as little as *Mrs Warren's Profession* did the pleasures of sexual intercourse. 'I do not yet feel grown up,' he wrote when almost fifty.

Mrs Warren's Profession had derived from Janet Achurch: *Arms and the Man* revolved round Florence Farr, who had received a sum of money via an occult society to promote a theatrical season at the Avenue Theatre in London. Her backer, whose identity was kept secret from Shaw for another dozen years (it came to him, he would claim, in a dream), was Annie Horniman. Thin and medieval in appearance (she wore a huge jewelled dragon in oxidized silver round her neck), Annie Horniman smoked cigarettes and bicycled in slacks (she had a black eye when Shaw finally met her). 'She was wonderful about the money really,' Florence Farr later told Shaw, '& just gave it me to do anything I liked with in the way of advertising myself.'

Florence asked both Yeats and Shaw to write plays for her. 'I have made a desperate attempt to begin a real romantic play for F.F. in the style of Victor Hugo,' Shaw reported to Janet Achurch. 'The first act is nearly finished; and it is quite the funniest attempt at that style of composition ever made.' But he was too dilatory for Florence. By way of encouragement she would read to him from her own novel, *The Dancing Faun* (at the end of which her Shavian cad, George Travers, is most satisfactorily shot by his titled mistress); and she invited him to Dalling Road to hear Yeats read his verse play, *The Land of Heart's Desire*, in which a wife escapes domestic drudgery, through death, into fairyland. Following these goadings, Shaw would surge onwards.

In its first version, tentatively entitled *Alps and Balkans* (Salt had suggested *Battlefields and Boudoirs*), he had given the play no geography – 'nothing but a war with a machine gun in it' – the names of the places being left blank and the characters simply called the Father, the Daughter, the Heroic Lover, the Stranger and so on. He then went to Sidney Webb and asked him to find a good war for his purpose. Webb 'spent about two minutes in a rapid survey of every war that has ever been waged and then told me that the Servo-Bulgarian was what I wanted,' Shaw remembered. 'I then read the account of the war in the *Annual Register* with a modern railway map of the Balkan peninsula before me, and filled in my blanks, making all the action take place in Servia, in the house of a Servian family.' He also got a good deal of information from Admiral Serebryekov, who had commanded the Danube flotilla for the Bulgarians, as a result of which the 'play proved impossible from beginning to end,' Shaw told Charles Charrington. 'I have had to shift the scene from Servia to Bulgaria, and to make the most absurd alterations in detail for the sake of local color,' which, Shaw added, would convince people that 'I have actually been in Bulgaria'.

All this research and rewriting meant that the play, now called *Arms and the Man* from the first line of Dryden's heroic verse translation of Virgil's *Aeneid* ('*Arma virumque cano*'), was not ready for the opening of Florence Farr's season. Instead, using Yeats's *The Land of Heart's Desire* as a *lever de rideau*, she produced *A Comedy of Sighs* by the Irish pastoral playwright, John Todhunter. Shaw, who attended the first night on 29 March, noted that 'the play at the Avenue Theatre failed rather badly'. Yeats was to describe the fiasco more voluminously. 'For two hours and a half, pit and gallery drowned the voices of the players with boos and jeers that were meant to be bitter to the author who sat visible to all in his box surrounded by his family, and to the actress struggling bravely through her weary part,' he remembered. Todhunter sat on 'listening to the howling of his enemies, while his friends slipped out one by one, till one saw everywhere their empty seats'. Archer described Florence's performance as 'panic-stricken' – and this was the most excruciating part of the evening for Shaw: 'have you ever seen so horrible a portent on the stage as this transformation of an amiable, clever sort of woman into a nightmare, a Medusa, a cold, loathly, terrifying, grey, callous, sexless devil?' he asked Elizabeth Robins.

'What madness led Todhunter to write her a part like that? – what idiocy has led me to do virtually the same thing in the play which I have written to help her in this hellish enterprise? . . . Had she been able to give full effect to herself, the audience would have torn her to pieces. I lay under harrows of red hot steel.'

The next day Shaw received a telegram summoning him to the theatre where he found Florence with *Widowers' Houses* open before her, contemplating its production in despair. Dissuading her from this he took 'my new play out on to the Embankment Gardens and there and then put the last touches to it before leaving it to be typewritten'.

Arms and the Man went into rehearsal on 11 April, three days before Todhunter's play was withdrawn. Among the audience on the first night were Archer, Henry Arthur Jones, H. W. Massingham, George Moore, Oscar Wilde and W. B. Yeats, whose little play was again used as a curtain raiser. Sidney Webb, who 'might possibly bring a cabinet minister if he has a box', was joined by fellow-Fabians Sydney Olivier and Graham Wallas. The Charringtons came, Janet being specially seated 'where her beauty will not be lost'. Edith Bland, too, Shaw estimated, 'will be worth a thousand posters in Blackheath'. 'Chuckers out' were hired, and the only group Shaw forgot to invite was his family.

Shaw himself arrived towards the end of Yeats's play. His chocolate cream soldier forced his way into Raina's bedroom some twenty minutes later, in what seemed to be the start of a stereotype military melodrama. 'The whole pit and gallery, except certain members of the Fabian Society, started to laugh at the author and then, discovering that they themselves were being laughed at, sat there not converted – their hatred was too bitter for that – but dumbfounded, while the rest of the house cheered and laughed,' Yeats later recalled. ' . . . I listened to *Arms and the Man* with admiration and hatred. It seemed to me inorganic, logical straightness and not the crooked road of life, yet I stood aghast before its energy as to-day before that of the Stone Drill by Mr Epstein or of some design by Mr Wyndham Lewis . . . Presently I had a nightmare that I was haunted by a sewing machine, that clicked and shone, but the incredible thing was that the machine smiled, smiled perpetually.'

No one forgot this opening performance. 'It was applauded,' wrote G. K. Chesterton, 'by that indescribable element in all of us which rejoices to see the genuine thing prevail against the plausible.' Yeats described this venture as 'the first contest between the old commercial school of theatrical folk and the new artistic school'. The Prince of Wales (later Edward VII) came and kept repeating: 'The man is mad, the man is mad.'

Arms and the Man presents the adult world of warfare through the eyes of a child. Shaw contrasted the child's simplicity with the farcical sophistication of parents trying to escape the consequences of their own childhood. *Arms and the Man* is a 'play' in the sense of it being a childish activity. Every stage trick in its clockwork machinery 'suggests a puppet play for human actors, or a moving toy shop,' writes Margery Morgan. ' . . . The ease with which Shaw regressed to childishness can be regarded as a sign of psychological weakness and emotional immaturity . . . [but] released within the frame of the play, it is this childishness that constitutes Shaw's genius. He used it as a means of attacking insidiously and openly every form of humbug and pretentiousness, including the unnaturalness of moral virtue that children . . . instinctively detect.'

Shaw was particularly exasperated when his deconstruction of heroism – professional soldiers who carry chocolates instead of cartridges and weep when scolded; battles waged mostly by paperwork and won through ludicrously lucky errors – was treated not in the tradition of Cervantes but as Gilbertian cynicism. Gilbert was the child who mimicked the adult world; Shaw was the child who saw through it. In a letter to Archer, Shaw explained what he felt was the difference:

'Gilbert is simply a paradoxically humorous cynic. He accepts the conventional ideals implicitly, but observes that people do not really live up to them. This he regards as a failure on their part at which he mocks bitterly. This position is precisely that of Sergius in the play . . . I do not accept the conventional ideals . . . and no longer use them even for dramatic effect. Sergius is ridiculous through the breakdown of his ideals, not odious from his falling short of them. As Gilbert sees, they dont work; but what Gilbert does not see is that there is something else that does work, and that in that something else there is a completely satisfactory asylum for the affections.'

'On my honor it was a serious play,' Shaw protested. But the 'tragedy' with which he insisted he had replaced Gilbertian 'heartlessness' was a petit tragedy – though a delightful comedy. The attempt to show pragmatism and instinct in triumphant league against idealism and rationalism was ingeniously outflanked by the public's instinctive, and the critics' reasoned, misunderstanding. Shaw changed the subtitle from 'A Romantic Comedy' to 'An Anti-Romantic Comedy', but the joyous misapprehension continued to swell, finally exploding in Oscar Straus's comic opera *The Chocolate Soldier* ('that degradation of a decent comedy into a dirty farce,' as Shaw called it).

Arms and the Man ran for fifty performances between 21 April and 7 July, and was followed by a provincial tour and a production in the United States. But Shaw had doubts over the play. In the contest between 'the old commercial school of theatrical folk and the new artistic school', G.B.S. the new artist suspected he had borrowed too much from the armoury of the old commercial school. It was not quite the masterpiece he needed.

His royalties from *Arms and the Man* at the end of 1894 came to £341 15s. 2d. (equivalent to £17,000 in 1997). That autumn, after seven years of continuous musical criticism, he dropped his column in *The World*. 'I had not before realized the severity of the strain on the attention involved by musical criticism,' he noted in his diary. It seemed as if, in entering his thirty-ninth year, he had at last achieved popularity. 'When you take a theatre of your own,' he told the manager of the Avenue Theatre, 'just bring me pen and ink, a ream of paper, a bottle of ginger beer, and a few beans, and you shall have the most brilliant play of the century to open with.' But privately he knew the quicksand on which he was advancing. 'I have taken the very serious step,' he confided to McNulty, 'of cutting off my income by privately arranging to drop the World business at the end of the season; and now, if I cannot make something out of the theatre, I am a ruined man.'

4

THE PLAYWRIGHT AND THE ACTRESS

> I hereby warn mankind to beware of women with large eyes . . . and a love of miracles and moonshees. I warn them against all who like intellectual pastimes; who prefer liberty, happiness and irresponsibility to care, suffering and life . . . who reject the deep universal material of human relationship and select only the luxuries of love, friendship, and amusing conversation.
>
> Shaw to Florence Farr (14 October 1896)

Florence Farr's performance in Todhunter's play had been shocking, and Shaw's relegation of her from the part of Raina, the romantic lead, to that of Louka, her maidservant, in *Arms and the Man* represented a fall in his estimation, almost from grace. Florence was aware of this. Walking back from the Avenue Theatre in the evenings with Yeats, they would often discuss Shaw. What feelings lived under his bright surface and, among all that rattle of words, what poetry? For all his knowledge, his vitality, his busy politics, there seemed (except for its impenetrable absence) no mystery, no beating of a religious pulse. Florence, like Yeats, had been caught up in the stream of occultism flowing over traditional Western religion. She had looked into Egyptology and Babylonish lore, hovered over astral projections, investigated alchemy, covered the walls at Dalling Road with Oriental drapery, practised the hermetic arts; and she was about to be promoted to Praemonstratrix in the ineffable Order of the Golden Dawn. The chasm separating her aspirations from her abilities, starkly illuminated by the footlights, vanished amid these mysteries.

Shaw had been pressing Florence to get herself divorced from the ever-absent Edward Emery; and eventually in 1894 she agreed. The procedure, which involved an accusation of adultery, was unpleasant but by February the following year the decree was made absolute. Shaw used the technicality of her freedom to chide Janet Achurch: 'There will be a mail in tomorrow, I suppose: and if I hear nothing then, F.F. shall be Mrs Bernard

Shaw at the earliest date thereafter permitted by statute.' But to Florence, as to May Morris, he said nothing. Two days after this divorce, it was not Shaw but Yeats who travelled to Dalling Road. He came bearing esoteric apparatus and escorted by a mediumistic chemist's assistant. Together they drew the curtains and unwrapped their miracles. It was a relief to turn from the hectic Shavian vocabulary to the less demanding presence of Yeats. Florence's consonants withered, her phonetics fell away and the athletic articulation drilled into her by Shaw sighed to a stop. Yeats provided for her a single twanging instrument. She plucked interesting discords, meditated on colours, muttered verse invocations that intensified 'ordinary twaddling,' Shaw protested, 'into a nerve destroying crooning like the maunderings of an idiot-banshee'.

It was now Yeats's turn to see Florence as a 'great success'. Her tranquillity dazzled him. She was a fairy child and would make his poetry a garden for magical thought, and the Chanted Word. 'Cats do the same thing when they are serenading one another,' advised Shaw; and even Yeats spoke of her giving 'the worst performance on the psaltery I have ever heard' – adding: 'There are times when she makes me despair of the whole thing.'

In time Florence dismissed both her Irish champions as 'half-baked'. 'And now you think to undo the work of all these years by a phrase & a shilling's work of exoteric Egyptology,' Shaw had railed at her.

'Now a great horror & weariness comes on me. I cannot help anyone except by taking help from them; and you cannot help me. You have brains and imagination – the means of deceiving yourself, without faith, honor, heart, holiness – the means of saving yourself. I have the greatest regard for you; but now to be with you is to be in hell: you make me frightfully unhappy . . . Forgive me; but you have driven me to utter desperation.'

What had gone wrong? When he called on her he found 'her windows were dark [and] I did not go in'. He began sleeping badly – and waking late. In November 1894 they ceased being lovers. Fabian and Occult forces had pulled them apart. They were still friends. Strolling pleasantly through Richmond Park in the spring of 1895, they chatted about bicycling and literature, but kept what they really cared for to themselves. She lured him with a casual reference to the quarter of a million pounds that Annie Horniman might give her for another theatrical enterprise; but her heart was not in it, and he was not seriously tempted. Their excitement in each other's company had evaporated, leaving vacancy. His sense of loss was painful. He had so little heart, he told another actress, 'that when it kindles for ten minutes once a year I hasten to cry out what I feel, lest I should die without having once done anything to save life from emptiness'.

They continued to see or correspond with each other, amiably but with longer intervals almost until 1912, when Florence travelled to Ceylon and, at the request of Sir Pannamballam Ramanathan, was appointed the first principal at his College for Girls. There she died in 1917; and thirty years later, after reading her story in the *Ceylon Daily News*, Shaw (then in his nineties) confessed himself astonished. 'I thought that Yeats and I knew her through and through, as far as there was anything to know,' he wrote. 'I now see that we did not know her at all.' To Yeats she had appeared to move 'upwards out of life' to her 'unnoticed end'. But Shaw suspected that Pannamballam Ramanathan had 'opened her mind and developed the real woman. I should have said that she was the last woman on earth to become the authoritative head of a college, or to break her way out of the little cliques in which she figured in London, and find a spiritual home in philosophic India. I was wrong. I was the wrong man for her, and I am deeply glad that she found the right one after I had passed out of her life.'

5

CANDIDAMANIA

> It is only the people who have the courage and independence to let themselves go without scruple who discover what a terrifically powerful instinct chastity is.
>
> Shaw to Barbara Low (17 September 1917)

In leaving Jenny Patterson for Florence, Shaw had renounced a love that was exclusively sexual; in turning from Florence to Janet Achurch in the mid-1890s he was replacing sex and planting his words in the woman he loved so that she could bring his plays to life. Florence had been sterile – but sterile on the stage. 'I renounce spiritual intercourse with you,' he told her. But it was sexual intercourse he was renouncing and spiritual intercourse with Janet he was taking up. 'I have become a sort of sublime monster,' he wrote to Janet early in 1896.

'. . . Do you know who will buy for twopence a body for which I no longer have any use? I have made tolerable love with it in my time; but now I have found nobler instruments – the imagination of a poet, the heart of a child, all discovered through the necessity – the not-to-be denied inmost necessity – of making my way to an innocent love for Janet.'

*

There had been a moment when, quailing before the challenge of Janet with her interfering husband, her heavy drinking, her drugs, Shaw turned to 'a destroying angel in a bonnet', the Ibsen actress Elizabeth Robins. Elizabeth was an enigma. For two years she had been married to an American actor, George Parks, who one midnight (wearing a suit of stage armour) had stepped into the Charles River in Boston, and drowned. Dressed in black, Elizabeth had sailed to England. Wonderfully impressed by Janet Achurch in *A Doll's House*, she had gone in 1891 with her chaperon to see William Archer about a translation of *Hedda Gabler*. Her performance as Hedda that April at the Vaudeville Theatre was described by Archer, reviewing it in *The World*, as 'the finest piece of modern tragedy within my recollection. Sarah Bernhardt could not have done it better.' The anti-Ibsenites had been equally re-assured. 'It was like a visit to the Morgue,' declared Clement Scott in the *Daily Telegraph*. Shaw, who saw the production two or three times, assured Elizabeth Robins that 'you may safely accept all the compliments you get about the play and the part. I never had a more tremendous sensation in a theatre.'

In the battle over Ibsen, Shaw knew where his loyalties lay. But Elizabeth was Archer's protégée and therefore a rival to Shaw's Janet. Both Archer and Shaw were attracted to Elizabeth. She was a hardworking actress, ambitious and businesslike; and, now in her late twenties, she was dramatically beautiful, with hypnotic blue eyes, chestnut hair and an erotic southern American voice. But she seemed nervous of men and fearful of male sexuality. She was to make an exception of Archer for whom she became the love of a lifetime. But Shaw's flattery-and-effrontery alarmed her. He implied that Archer was not unaware of her sex appeal; he begged her not to mind his Irish suggestiveness; he boasted that her 'lustrous eyes' would never turn his head; he even called informally at her apartment, before her production of *The Master Builder* in 1893, for the purpose of interviewing her – and she was obliged to threaten him with a revolver.

Shaw promised to play no more pranks on her. But he suspected that she and Archer were lovers, and he could not resist interfering. Both of them were used to suppressing their sexual instincts, and they sealed their relationship from him. Someone who had dramatized his own love affairs in *The Philanderer* might play havoc with their lives.

Elizabeth had glorified the brother-and-sister relationship, and Shaw dreamed of supplanting a wife with a mother. Both wanted to free one sex from the power of the other. But the only way Shaw could overcome his vulnerability to women who interested him was to envelop their bodies with his words, and then fall in love with his own verbal clothing. What attracted him to Elizabeth was that, like his mother, she was at best indifferent to him. It was difficult for an actress to make a successful career in the theatre, but she did not believe Shaw would ever succeed as a playwright and when he offered to write a leading part 'especially designed for you & all the other parts about six lines long', she heard only the voice of the seducer. Her apprehensions were confirmed when he sent her *Mrs Warren's Profession*, a play about prostitution. 'It was black ingratitude to try and let you in for this villainous play which is quite unworthy of you,' Shaw admitted. Yet, granted that she could not endure him, could they not for stage purposes use each other? 'What has frightened you?' he asked. What had frightened him? This fear was what they shared, and it prevented them from becoming what Ibsen would have called an 'episode' in each other's lives.

*

While Shaw was still involving himself with Florence and hazardously experimenting with Elizabeth Robins, the Charringtons had been sinking. A quintuple bill they presented at Terry's Theatre in 1893 including, besides plays by J. M. Barrie, Conan Doyle and Thomas Hardy, a farce by Lady Colin Campbell, had prompted some critical acclaim; and closed after a week. 'Then smash!' Charrington explained; cheaper lodgings, unsuccessful scripts, smaller parts, shifty deals.

Unlike Nora in *A Doll's House* (after whom she had christened her daughter), Janet could not slam the door on her husband – though he would ruin her if she continued to trust in him. But from the practical consequences of his own advice Shaw instinctively shrank. He was obsessively replaying the old triangular liaison. Until the autumn of 1894 he could find no way of dissolving his sexual attraction for Janet into his admiration for her talent. Then, on 2 October, following another visit to Italy with the Art Workers' Guild, he began *Candida*, his 'modern pre-Raphaelite play'. 'Titian's Virgin of the Assumption in the Accademia in Venice, and Correggio's in the dome of the cathedral in Parma,' he afterwards remembered, 'boiled down into Cockney Candida.'

It was to be their play, his and Janet's. It was to be their salvation. Candida derived from his mother who was to be replaced by Janet. 'I have been no saint myself – have hunted after one form of happiness occasionally,' he confided. 'Janet *recreates* me with an emotion which lifts me high out of that.' *Candida* had been conceived as a spiritual orgasm.

Janet would re-create herself by playing the 'clean dry, strong and straight heroine', the 'true Virgin Mother' Candida, and feel no further need for the stimulants prescribed by Charrington.

The Reverend James Mavor Morell, the cocksure Christian Socialist clergyman, is Shaw's pre-Raphaelite; his Raphaelite is Marchbanks, the shy, aristocratic, unconvincing poet. Shaw claimed to have based Marchbanks on De Quincey, though Shelley and Yeats were also to be mentioned as models. 'I certainly never thought of myself as a model,' he objected. Nevertheless, Marchbanks was the vehicle for Shavian beliefs and a silhouette of the almost twenty-year-old Sonny. The rivalry between Marchbanks and Morell over Morell's wife Candida carries echoes from several of Shaw's three-cornered affairs, in particular that of May Morris and Sparling, but was intended as an interpretation of the current drama between himself and the Charringtons. The writing and production of *Candida* was to be a spell, no less magical than the spells of Yeats and Florence Farr, through which Shaw would manifest his will. He had designed the play as *A Doll's House* in reverse, showing the household doll to be the husband. In Candida herself he had written a part at which Janet would excel. Its success, he hoped, would nerve her to separate her interests from Charrington's, emerging from domesticity as an independent actress of genius. That, at any rate, was the play he intended to write; what he actually wrote was something else. 'Candida does not change, as Shaw believed Janet must,' Margot Peters has written.

'She is at the end of the play what she was at the beginning, the mother-sister-nurse-wife of her boy husband Morell, trapped by the very altruism that Shaw was trying to root out of Janet so that she could put herself and her art first. It is Eugene Marchbanks who experiences the metamorphosis from sensuality to spirituality and artistic dedication . . . he concludes that domesticity, security, and love are inferior ends compared with the sublime and lonely renunciation of the artist. Shaw thus washed his hands of Janet.'

The 'pure' (as her white name indicates) and patronizing Candida is not Janet: she was 'entirely imagined'. But she shares with Janet a sexual charm that she can use to get her own way – and from which Marchbanks disengages himself. But his escape is not a sublimation of lust into admiration; it is rejection, an optimistic re-writing of Lucinda Shaw's rejection of Sonny.

The crisis between Candida and Marchbanks comes early in the third act when Candida offers herself ('Do you want anything more?') to Marchbanks. We have been prepared for this and told how to interpret it in her conversation with Morell in the previous act – and the words and situation were as much as the Examiner of Plays would allow. The poker that Candida holds 'upright in her hand . . . looking intently at the point of it' until it 'must have hypnotised me', is converted from an obvious phallic image into an emblem of knightly chastity: 'a flaming sword that turned every way, so that I couldnt go in; for I saw that that was really the gate of Hell'. The affinity between them is that of mother and son, and the weapon that guards them from Hell is the taboo of incest. It is because the Virgin Mother outlaws sex that she is Shaw's ideal. Candida reduces all men to children by emotional castration. In providing other explanations Shaw falls into the error that he himself had defined so brilliantly in *The Quintessence of Ibsenism*. He idealizes. It is the minor characters who provide the corrective, in particular the secretary, 'a brisk little woman of about 30', Miss Proserpine Garnett, nicknamed Prossy. She, as her classical name suggests, represents amorousness unanswered. She is secretly – though it is an open secret – in love with Morell, and her only expression of love is to make herself his idolizing slave. Others, with whom she is not in love, she can see clearly.

Shaw romanticized Marchbanks's chastity. He has not blown away illusions but transferred them from people to work. *Candida* was a prophecy rather than a catalyst in Janet Achurch's life; and that prophecy was to find its proof in the negotiations over the play's production.

*

Candida is the most tightly constructed and economical of Shaw's plays. Driven on by the Charringtons' debts, he finished writing it on 7 December 1894, and before the end of the year had tried it out on two leading actor-managers. Wiping his eyes at the end of the final scene, Charles Wyndham, the most accomplished performer of light comedy parts at the Criterion Theatre, told him that, dear God, it would be a quarter of a century before the London stage was ready for such matter. Shaw also took it to George Alexander, whose St James's Theatre, as the most fashionable playhouse in London, specialized in dramas featuring peers of the realm. One of the handsomest men in England, who had recently caused a sensation with Mrs Patrick Campbell in Pinero's *The Second Mrs Tanqueray*, Alexander offered to play the eighteen-year-old aristocratic Marchbanks if Shaw, to combine an easier disguise with a larger claim for sympathy, would render the poet blind.

By reserving the part of Candida for Janet, Shaw had created an extra obstacle for the London actor-managers. But he would not be moved on this, and in February 1895 he decided instead to try the play in the United States.

There were good reasons for his decision. *Arms and the Man* had been taken the previous year to the United States by the actor-manager Richard Mansfield. Mansfield was an Englishman two years older than Shaw who had appeared on the London stage between 1877 and 1882 before emigrating to New York. He was a man who spoke plainly. He believed that life was for living, and plays were for playing; and he was seldom afraid to say so. He had slipped one evening into the Avenue Theatre to see *Arms and the Man* and decided to put it on. Shaw was summoned to see him at the Langham Hotel and an invigorating antipathy sprang up between them. Each knew better than the other about everything; but each valued the other as a property. A contract, drafted by Shaw, was signed on 9 June 1894 and, some three months later, *Arms and the Man* opened at the Herald Square Theatre in New York where, after sixteen performances, it 'produced reputation, discussion, advertisement', and put Shaw 'to the inconvenience of having a bank account'. By retaining the play in his repertory for the rest of the season and sending it on tour, Mansfield gave Shaw a new theatrical experience: 'It was not an absolute failure.'

It was to Mansfield, on 22 February 1895, that Shaw sent a tantalizing letter about *Candida*. 'Now let me ask you whether you can play a boy of eighteen – a strange creature – a poet – a bundle of nerves – a genius – and a rattling good part,' he wrote.

Shaw challenged him to sail over to London, play the poet for half a dozen matinées opposite Janet's Candida, and, having set all London buzzing, 'disappear in a flash of blue fire'. There was need for haste. Already Janet was growing obstreperous; she had made a drunken scene when he took her to the theatre, had brazenly dyed her hair a heartbreaking yellow and was smoking cigarettes. Shaw warned her that 'you will grow fatter; and your flesh instead of being braced and healthy will be slack and open to chills; and you will have heavy sensual eyelids and swimming eyes instead of a clear, open, divine brow'. There was nothing for it, until Janet was reborn in *Candida*, but to wag his finger in this way. His lectures offended her and were a terror to himself lest they ended their relationship.

It was Richard Mansfield who, barely in time, thundered to their rescue. He had been intrigued by Shaw's description of *Candida* ('I still play youths of 18. The only trouble is I look too young for the part'). In the first week of March he cabled his acceptance to Shaw.

'WILL PLAY CANDIDA WILL ENGAGE JANET WILL COME TO LONDON CONTRACT JANET NOT LESS THAN THREE SEASONS . . . ALL MUST COME NEW YORK QUICK – MANSFIELD'

Shaw had promised the Charringtons that he would get his plays performed; and now 'it is all settled and our fortunes are made'. The next ten days were hectic. Despite a swirling Fabian programme of lectures and articles on other people's plays, Shaw finished his minutely detailed plan of the stage action ('the full score of Candida and the band parts'), arranged for the prompt copies to be typed and corrected, and had everything ready for the boat on Saturday 16 March. At the station, Janet was so overcome as to take an affectionate farewell of Mansfield's brother Felix (who was travelling with her) under the impression he was her husband Charrington; and Shaw tottered back shakily to his bed like an exhausted dog.

Janet was now on her own: 'the time for pupilage is past.' Yet wherever she went Shaw's voice went with her. He seemed unable to leave his pupil alone. He prescribed distilled water, oatmeal bannocks, walnuts, honey and peaches. 'I urge you to go to church once a day at least to tranquillise your nerves . . . Read the gospel of St John and the lives of the saints: they will do everything for you that morphia only pretends to do.' She must not seek bold type; she must not purr or smoke; she must not place New York at her feet; she must not be fringy or fluffy. He recommended she part her hair in the middle – better still, send for a barber and 'have your hair shaved absolutely bald. Then get a brown wig.' She would become like the Madonna by Antonio Rossellino he had seen at Santa Croce in Florence.

Having told her what way to go, he told Mansfield to let her go her own way. 'She comes from Manchester,' he explained, 'she will grab everything you try to keep from her . . . Give her everything she dares ask . . . I hereby authorize you to announce her as the authoress of the play, if that will please her.'

Having condescended to everyone's follies, Shaw awaited the results. They came swiftly: a cablegram from Janet telling him and Charrington that *Candida* had been withdrawn. It seemed that she and Mansfield, far from being transformed by Shaw's words, had never been more themselves. In Mansfield's opinion there were two things wrong: Shaw's play and Shaw's actress. Mansfield could see too that Shaw had put a lot of himself into the play, and there, perhaps, lay the fault. Now, as Mansfield knew, the world was tired of all this morbid philosophy and womanish whatnot – a bustling, striving, pushing, stirring American audience wouldn't stand for it or sit through it, and Mansfield wholeheartedly agreed with them. 'All the world is crying out for deeds – for action!' he informed Shaw.

On the subject of Janet, too, Mansfield was obligingly frank. 'I couldn't have made love to your Candida (Miss Janet Achurch) if I had taken ether,' he began.

'I detest an aroma of stale tobacco and gin. I detest intrigue and slyness and sham ambitions. I don't like women who sit on the floor – or kneel by your side and have designs on your shirt-bosom – I don't like women who comb their tawny locks with their fingers, and claw their necks and scratch the air with their chins.'

Mansfield represented everything that Shaw was to pit his strength against over the next three years. But his success in the theatre, begun with *Arms and the Man* and soon to be established with *The Devil's Disciple*, was to be achieved by a man with whom he could not remain on speaking terms.

He did not show Mansfield's letter to Charrington who, his face swelling alarmingly, was fingering Atlantic time-tables and rehearsing the strangulation of Mansfield in New York. Shaw envied Charrington in that moment. 'Charrington is right because he *is* a fool . . . hating what he doesn't like and loving what he likes, fighting the one and grudging it its crust, backing up the other in the teeth of all justice.'

But over *Candida* Shaw conceded defeat. 'I have played my last card, and am beaten, as far as I can see, without remedy,' he told Janet. For once his equanimity seemed to falter. Mansfield produced an unusual effect on him. 'He drives me out of my senses.' Since this often prevented them from addressing each other, Shaw conducted much of his business with Mrs Mansfield, 'which is much pleasanter'. The rivalry that Shaw neutralized with this stratagem had begun to show itself in the two men's struggle over Janet. Mansfield offered to produce *Candida* with her in the leading role 'if I need not appear'. But Shaw, believing that Mansfield was looking to put on the play with a bad cast so as to establish its failure 'and prevent Janet from making a success in New York', forbade him from producing it 'on any terms whatever'. Despite his dislike of Janet, Mansfield invited her to join his company knowing how hard Shaw would be hit if she accepted. But Shaw's influence persisting, she refused and, surrounded by many exciting rumours of her plans, she sailed in the second week of June back to London.

SIX

I

LIVING WITH THE *SATURDAY*

> We all swore by the *Saturday* . . . Life was not worth living without it; it gave us the latest news from the front. And we craned our necks nightly over the gallery rails to see Shaw our champion take his seat among the well-groomed critics in their 'glad rags'. Shaw played up well to us in the gallery.
>
> Dan Rider, *Adventures with Bernard Shaw* (1929)

'The first man I wrote to was George Bernard Shaw,' wrote Frank Harris.

Harris had been editor of the Conservative *Evening News* in direct competition with W. T. Stead's *Pall Mall Gazette*. He had quadrupled its circulation by sending his New Journalists to the police courts, and startling his readers with alluring headlines: 'Extraordinary Charge Against a Clergyman'; 'Gross Outrage on a Female'. It was Harris who had reported in scabrous detail the divorce case of Lady Colin Campbell, receiving an indictment for obscene libel that assisted the paper's Tory proprietor in dismissing him in 1886. From this crisis he quickly recovered, replacing John Morley as editor of the *Fortnightly Review*, a sober literary magazine that (as its title somehow fails to suggest) appeared once a month. The sensationalism of the *Evening News* was unknown to the editor of the *Fortnightly*. 'Every month the review appears regularly,' complained Whistler, 'just what one looks for, a work of high-class English mediocrity: lamentable . . .' Yet from time to time Harris would pluck aside the skirts of respectability by printing Verlaine's poems, or Wilde's *The Soul of Man Under Socialism*, or his own short story about the adulterous passion of a Baptist minister for one of his deacons' wives.

It was at this period that Harris first asked Shaw to write for him: 'Is there no subject on which you would like to unbosom yourself in the Fortnightly?' Intermittently during the early 1890s, Shaw would hand him contributions on subjects ranging from Home Rule to 'The Religion of the Pianoforte' and including early drafts of Fabian tracts such as *Socialism and Superior Brains*. None of these could have pleased Frederick Chapman of Chapman & Hall, the proprietor-publisher of the *Fortnightly*, to whom 'Bernard Shaw was anathema'. Worse still were Harris's flirtations with anarchism, reflected in an article that praised two bomb-throwers, 'the sweetest and noblest of men', and led, in the autumn of 1894, to Harris being fired. But in next to no time he was back in London and had taken over the editorship of the *Saturday Review*, a moribund magazine that, at £560, was being hawked around for the price of one pound per reader.

While editor of the sensational *Evening News* he had been torridly in love with 'Laura', the obsessive passion of his life. As editor of the dignified *Fortnightly* he lived smartly in Park Lane as the husband of a woman of 'high position', often entertaining the Duke of Cambridge. But in 1895 the new editor of the *Saturday Review* was a single man, who had turned his back on advancement through marriage and decided to become immortal through his genius as a man of letters. He wished to raise the *Saturday Review*, then known as the *Saturday Reviler*, from a finder of faults to a finder of stars. But the stars he gathered round him were irresistible fault-finders. Shaw's theatre criticism ('Happy is the nation that has no history, and happy the play that has no criticism in this column'), led to some managements withdrawing their free seats; and several of the book reviewers were so severe that publishers cancelled their advertisements, obliging Harris to fill the spaces with publicity for pneumatic tyres and South African mining companies.

Shaw had been summoned to the *Saturday Review* office in Southampton Street during the late afternoon of 4 December 1894. He was, Harris observed, 'thin as a rail, with a long, bony, bearded face. His untrimmed beard was reddish, though his hair was fairer. He was dressed carelessly in tweeds with the inevitable Jaeger collar. His entrance into the room, his abrupt movements – as jerky as the ever-changing mind – his perfect unconstraint, his devilish look, all showed a man very conscious of his ability, very direct, very sharply decisive.' They were as ill-matched as Don Quixote and Sancho Panza. And yet, Shaw decided, Harris was 'the very man for me, and I the very man for him'.

Although he had been happy to resign as *The World*'s music critic, Shaw was soon missing the bustle and involvement of weekly journalism. Harris's offer came at exactly the right time (as he was finishing *Candida*) and guaranteed him a salary of £6 a week – £1 more than Edmund Yates had given him: 'not bad pay in those days'. He would end up 'a ruined man,' he had predicted to McNulty, 'if I cannot make something out of the theatre'. It was as theatre critic rather than playwright that he was to make his basic income over the next three and a half years.

He had long wanted to have a regular theatre column. 'I wish for the sake of Ibsen that I could get a turn at dramatic criticism,' he had told Janet Achurch when still employed by *The World*. There was one qualm that delayed his acceptance of the job: the question of whether a playwright should also play dramatic critic.

'The cardinal guarantee for a critic's integrity is simply the force of the critical instinct itself. To try to prevent me from criticizing by pointing out to me the superior pecuniary advantages of puffing is like trying to keep a young Irving from going on the stage by pointing out the superior pecuniary advantages of stockbroking. If my own father were an actor manager, and his life depended on his getting favorable notices of his performance, I should orphan myself without an instant's hesitation if he acted badly . . . So stubborn is the critic within me, that with every disposition to be as goodnatured and as popular an authority as the worst enemy of art could desire, I am to all intents and purposes incorruptible.'

On New Year's Day 1895, he went to the Garrick Theatre to see *Slaves of the Ring* by Sydney Grundy. Next week, readers of the *Saturday Review* were able to share the experience with him.

'It is not a work of art at all: it is a mere contrivance for filling a theatre bill . . . Mr Grundy somehow managed to plunge me into the densest confusion as to who was who, a confusion which almost touched aberration when I saw a double leading lady walk on to the stage, both of her in full wedding dress . . . The spectacular effect alone of so much white silk was sufficiently unhingeing. But when the two brides proceeded solemnly to marry one another with a wedding ring, I really did feel for a moment a horrible misgiving that I had at last broken through that "thin partition" which divides great wits from madness.'

2

SOME DRAMATIC OPINIONS

> The whole world is ruled by theatrical illusion . . . The great critics are those who penetrate and understand the illusion: the great men are those who, as dramatists planning the development of nations, or as actors carrying out the drama, are behind the scenes of the world instead of gaping and gushing in the auditorium after paying their taxes at the door.
>
> 'Toujours Shakespeare', *Saturday Review* (5 December 1896)

'I enjoy a first night,' Shaw wrote, 'as a surgeon enjoys an operation.' Sometimes the evening would open with a curtain raiser, 'to keep the gallery amused whilst waiting for the plutocracy to finish their dinners and get down to their reserved seats'. Then came the main play – a never-ending melodrama or all-conquering farce. Melodramas were equipped with 'French windows' and misdirected bottles of poison, and kept going with soliloquies (accompanied by harps, horns and violins writhing 'like a heap of trodden worms' in its pit). The action was waged immaculately off-stage, being announced to the audience by telegrams or reported by characters staring wildly through the wings. What the melodrama lacked in reality it tried to make up in verisimilitude. Real water cascaded; a couple of horses were led on for the race or polo match; and some actual guns for the battle in the fourth act. Why not, Shaw eagerly enquired, a mad bull to exercise the hero? Real babies, ostentatiously dandled, were popular; and no drawing-room dared reveal itself without an elaborate display of spirit stands, siphons and decanters, combining 'the charms of the private and the public house'. The gentleman-hero, husky with emotion, would have his knuckles imprinted with the kisses of kneeling ladies and his back resoundingly thumped by manly men. The villain, with his accomplice the comic Jew, knew he was performing well if the theatre filled with hisses whenever he presented himself before his arrest in the ballroom at the final curtain. Farces were not so different from melodramas, though the humour usually depended on the underclothing of the ladies, such 'abject little naughtinesses furtively slipped in under cover of the tamest propriety'.

Upright and silent in the stalls sat Shaw, isolated in his boredom from the starched and sweating audience; acutely conscious of the bad smells, bad music, humbug and snobbery playing round him; his spirits sinking as the hour grew late until 'at such moments I pull out handfuls of my hair, and sit contemplating them vacantly, asking myself what I am doing in such an absurd place as the British theatre'.

The real question that Shaw was asking himself was how, without abandoning all hope, could such idiocy be explained. Money-making in the theatre was founded on the assumption that it was 'impossible to underrate the taste and intelligence of the British public'. To enter a theatre was to go back two hundred years. Theatrical art had become an exploitation of the public - what was called giving the public what pleased it. But audiences did not want to be pleased.

'They want to be excited, and upset, and made miserable, to have their flesh set creeping, to gloat and quake over scenes of misfortune, injustice, violence, and cruelty, with the discomforture and punishment of somebody to make the ending "happy". The only sort of horror they dislike is the horror that they cannot fasten on some individual whom they can hate, dread, and finally torture after revelling in his crimes.'

In a number of devastating passages Shaw's anger brings forth the misery and disgust he feels with his fellow human beings. This is not sexual disgust – he strongly attacks the secretary of the National Vigilance Association for that form of misanthropy ('Human nature and the human body are to him nasty things. Sex is a scourge. Woman is a walking temptation which should be covered up'). Shaw's horror derives from people's brutality and silliness exploited for profit by theatre managers. He used all his ingenuity to escape the Shakespearian pessimism to which these reflections naturally led. The British public could not stand being given what it wanted for long. The indiscriminate bawling and booing, hissing and hooting of the audiences ('like dogs who had been purposely run over'), the riots and uproars lasting up to half an hour were all evidence of their dissatisfaction.

The monopoly of the star system, Shaw argued, was being broken and only progress was safe. 'Let their flatterer slip, as he always does sooner or later, and they are at his throat mercilessly before he can recover himself,' he gloatingly warned. As with critics so with dramatists: 'there is nothing the public despises so much as an attempt to please it.' Obsequiousness never created beauty, it aped fashion, did not produce drama, but a fuss. 'No great play,' he declared, 'can ever be written by a man who will allow the public to dictate to him.' He assured his readers that the business of the playwright, as of the politician, was 'to strive incessantly with the public; to insist on earnest relations with it, and not merely voluptuous ones; to lead it, nerve it, withstand its constant tendency to relapse into carelessness and vulgar familiarity; in short, to attain to public esteem, authority, and needfulness to the national welfare (things undreamt of in the relations between the theatrical profession and the public today), instead of to the camp-follower's refuge of mere popularity'.

This was Shaw bringing the philosophy of his *Quintessence of Ibsenism* to the practical matters of stage business. He tried to persuade theatre managers that there was money in Ibsen and the German playwright Hermann Sudermann; he urged British dramatists to raise their courage in the face of that legendary dragon, the great British donkey of the public. He waved his pen and the philistine brute disappeared. The way was clear for masterpieces – and yet it was not clear after all. One man stood obstructing: the Lord Chamberlain in the person of his Examiner of Plays. 'He is the Tsar of the theatres, able to do things that no prime minister dare do,' Shaw explained. Early in 1895 the holder of this office, E. F. Smyth Pigott, died, and the press teemed with tributes to his 'admirable discretion', his 'kindly blue pencil'. To these plaudits, Shaw added his own citation in the *Saturday Review*:

'The late Mr Pigott is declared on all hands to have been the best reader of plays we have ever had; and yet he was a walking compendium of vulgar insular prejudice . . . He had French immorality on the brain; he had American indecency on the brain; he had the womanly woman on the brain; he had the Divorce Court on the brain; he had "not before a mixed audience" on the brain; his official career in relation to the higher drama was one long folly and panic . . . It is a frightful thing to see the greatest thinkers, poets, and authors of modern Europe – men like Ibsen, Wagner, Tolstoi, and the leaders of our own literature – delivered helpless into the vulgar hands of such a noodle as this amiable old gentleman – this despised and incapable old official – most notoriously was.'

This is quintessentially Shavian – and oddly courageous since, while attracting the charge of being 'a cowardly attack on a dead man', it risked a good deal of unpopularity from among the living. Shaw insists that the late censor, a 'stupendously incompetent' man, uttering bushels of 'immoral balderdash', was invincibly well-intentioned, that his 'personal character' was never in question – indeed that he was 'as excellent a man for all private purposes as Charles I'.

It was Pigott who had told the Royal Commission in 1892 that all the characters in Ibsen's plays were 'morally deranged' and that William Archer's praise of Ibsen had been a device to make money out of him. Pigott it was who had banned the centenary performance of *The Cenci*. Shaw's 'obituary' was a plea for the appointment of a censor prepared to take responsibility for licensing those plays on which the growth and vitality of the theatre depended. It made an excellent impression on Frank Harris – and none at all on the Lord Chamberlain. Pigott's successor as his Examiner of Plays was G. A. Redford, an ex-bank manager, who, during his sixteen years in the post, refused licences to *Mrs Warren's Profession*, *The Shewing-up of Blanco Posnet* and the original version of *Press Cuttings*.

Several battles in Shaw's long war against this 'Malvolio of St James's Palace' were fought out in the *Saturday Review*. It was clear to Shaw that if his post were abolished, the theatre would revert to being the social and political power it had been before Walpole instituted censorship, and stopped Fielding's stage exposure of parliamentary corruption. From the 'idealistic' point of view, which regarded new opinions as dangerous, almost everything written by Shaw, whose instinct was 'to attack every idea which has been full grown for ten years', strengthened the case for censorship. So he continued firing off brilliant salvoes at the enemy – though with the suspicion that he was armed with chocolates rather than real ammunition.

*

The censor became a symbolic figure in Shaw's imagination. When in 1886 a licence had been refused for *The Cenci*, the Shelley Society had taken over the Grand Theatre in Islington to give a 'private' performance for its members, headed by Robert Browning. Technically, since no money was taken at the door, no licence was needed for what was in law a meeting of a society rather than the public representation of a play. But the censor was not to be so easily cheated. When the annual licence of the Grand Theatre came to be renewed, the lessee found himself obliged to accept a new clause forbidding performances of unlicensed plays on the premises. This warning had been well understood by other managers. After that, the blockade had been run chiefly by the Independent Theatre, which was technically 'private' like the Shelley Society and which operated mainly by using various halls for its theatrical 'At Homes'.

In addition to Grein's Independent Theatre Shaw reported on such academic-revolutionary bodies as the New Century Theatre, started in 1897 by an aspiring combination of enthusiasts – Archer and Massingham, Alfred Sutro and Elizabeth Robins. These painfully evolved little organs were free both from actor-managership and censorship. Indifferent to public demand, yet wishing to create a taste for the work of those playwrights who seemed to be the most advanced of the time, these enterprises functioned like laboratories where experiments could be tried out on a particular audience. 'The real history of the drama for the last ten years,' Shaw wrote, 'is not the history of the prosperous enterprises of Mr Hare, Mr Irving, and the established West-end theatres, but of the forlorn hopes led by Mr Vernon, Mr Charrington, Mr Grein, Messrs Henley and Stevenson, Miss Achurch, Miss Robins and Miss Lea, Miss Farr, and the rest of the Impossibilists.'

Shaw argued for the infiltration of the experimental stage repertory into the repertory of the fashionable theatres. It was useless to appeal to Augustin Daly or Henry Irving, who seemed 'fit for nothing but to be stuffed and mounted under glass to adorn the staircase of the Garrick Club'; but if more imaginative actor-managers – George Alexander, for instance, or Herbert Tree at the magnificent new Her Majesty's Theatre – were to insert a series of matinées of serious plays into their popular farce-and-melodrama seasons, they might lay the foundations of a genuine classic theatre. It was in the context of this need for artistic and financial co-operation that he fashioned his own plays and judged the work of contemporary dramatists.

Shaw the dramatist continued to make use of the rickety mechanisms he ridiculed as a critic: *Widowers' Houses* had derived from *Ceinture Dorée*; for *Mrs Warren's Profession* he had borrowed the plot of Pinero's *The Second Mrs Tanqueray*; the mechanics of *Arms and the Man* were Gilbertian; *The Man of Destiny*, which he wrote during his first summer as dramatic critic, was 'an old-fashioned play, as completely pre-Ibsen as Sardou or Scribe'; while *You Never Can Tell* he described as 'a frightful example of the result of trying to write for the *théâtre de nos jours*'. What Shaw objected to were the limitations imposed by these theatrical constructions, but he reluctantly accepted some of this machinery as being unavoidable for those who wanted their plays produced commercially. He valued such work by how skilfully it permeated the commercial theatre with social and artistic truth.

This method of evaluation is most lucidly seen in his comparative criticism of Pinero and Henry Arthur Jones. It was Pinero's 'aptitude for doing what other people have done before that makes him a reactionary force in English dramatic literature,' Shaw asserted. To destroy the legend of his mastery of stagecraft Shaw devastatingly analysed the structure of *The Second Mrs Tanqueray*, concluding that it amounted to little more than 'recklessness in the substitution of dead machinery and lay figures for vital action and real characters'. The purpose of much of his criticism of Pinero was to combat the popular belief that he embodied a new spirit in the theatre. This popularity derived from his subtle powers of flattery – he was 'simply an adroit describer of people as the ordinary man sees and judges them' – and a bogus reputation for courage: 'he has had no idea beyond that of doing something daring,' commented Shaw of *The Notorious Mrs Ebbsmith*, 'and bringing down the house by running away from the consequences.' Only for *The Benefit of the Doubt* did Shaw praise Pinero's honesty of perception: 'Consciously or unconsciously, he has this time seen his world as it really is.'

Pinero was a darling of the drawing-room world, while Henry Arthur Jones merely had one foot in its door – and principally for that reason, Shaw affirmed, 'I unhesitatingly class Mr Jones as first, and eminently first, among the surviving fittest of his own generation.' He saw in Jones's plays, which were regularly produced in the West End, the best available chance of beginning the reformation of that fashionable theatre and making it a force for change. Jones, he wrote, was the only popular dramatist whose sense of real life 'has been deep enough to bring him into serious conflict with the limitations and levities of our theatre'.

Shaw's support of Jones involved much special pleading. Shaw knew that Jones's heroines were apt to die of 'nothing but the need for making the audience cry'; he recognized the tendency of his last scenes to collapse, and his characters to act as if hypnotized by public opinion. But there was a detachment in Jones – 'he describes Mayfair as an English traveller describes the pygmies' – that Shaw laboured to encourage. Yet sometimes he would feel a revulsion from all this special pleading.

'Those safe old hands Pinero, Grundy, and Jones, cautiously playing the new game according to the safe old rules, fail to retrieve the situation . . . the public are getting tired of the old-fashioned plays faster than the actors are learning to make the new ones effective . . . The managers do not seem to me yet to grasp this feature of the situation. If they did, they would only meddle with the strongest specimens of the new drama, instead of timidly going to the old firms and ordering moderate plays cut in the new style.'

This complaint was written in the same month, July 1895, that he made an abortive attempt, with *You Never Can Tell*, to fashion a moderate play for the West End, cut in its new style. After the experience of having his first five plays turned down by every commercial theatre in London, he had gone to these theatres as a dramatic critic and seen productions of awful plays. Humiliation and grievance had fuelled his criticisms; he had mocked, goaded, tiraded in the *Saturday Review*. As a dramatic critic he was revolutionary; and as a dramatic critic he had represented himself as a revolutionary dramatist. 'Some plays are written to please the author,' he wrote; 'some to please the actor-manager (these are the worst); some to please the public; and some – my own, for instance – to please nobody.'

Yet between the author of *Widowers' Houses* and *The Devil's Disciple* (written in 1897), some compromise had begun to take place. In an article published in *The Humanitarian* in May 1895, Shaw argued that, at periods when political institutions lagged too far behind cultural changes, it was natural for the imagination of dramatists to be set in action on behalf of social reform. But despite this, 'the greatest dramatists shew a preference for the non-political drama . . . for subjects in which the conflict is between man and his apparently inevitable and eternal rather than his political and temporal circumstances'. In writing this, Shaw may have had in mind his own move from 'unpleasant' to 'pleasant' plays. But Pinero also wrote pleasant plays. How then must the critic differentiate between great drama and merely professional plays? In a passage from the *Saturday Review*, Shaw gave his answer.

'Vital art work comes always from a cross between art and life: art being one sex only, and quite sterile by itself. Such a cross is always possible; for though the artist may not have the capacity to bring his art into contact with the higher life of his time, fermenting in its religion, its philosophy, its science, and its statesmanship . . . he can at least bring it into contact with the obvious life and common passions of the streets.'

As a critic Shaw had banished the bogey of public opinion and invented a new audience to whom he addressed his plays. For this mythical public – and bypassing so far as he could the requirements of the censor – he adapted the artificial conventions of nineteenth-century theatre, eventually permeating the old traditions of the theatre with curious new sounds. 'The present transition from romantic to sincerely human drama is a revolutionary one,' he announced, but then added: 'those who make half-revolutions dig their own graves.' In the *Saturday Review* between 1895 and 1898 there are many passages in which the critic seems to be warning the playwright about the possible dangers of his work: 'Let us have the new ideas in the new style, or the old tricks in the old style; but the new ideas combined with the old tricks in no style at all cannot be borne.'

Shaw's dramatic criticism lies in the classic tradition of Hazlitt and G. H. Lewes. Shaw himself believed that 'Lewes in some respects anticipated me'. He pointed to Lewes's flexibility, fun and particularly 'his free use of vulgarity and impudence whenever they happened to be the proper tools for his job.

'He had a rare gift of integrity as a critic. When he was at his business, he seldom remembered that he was a gentleman or a scholar. In this he shewed himself a true craftsman, intent on making the measurements and analyses of his criticism as accurate, and their expression as clear and vivid, as possible, instead of allowing himself to be distracted by the vanity of playing the elegant man of letters, or writing with perfect good taste, or hinting in every line that he was above his work.'

Shaw had established a model for himself in Lewes whose 'combination of a laborious criticism with a recklessly flippant manner' reminded him of a certain Corno di Bassetto. Then, almost as an afterthought, he threw in one further trait: Lewes, he added, 'wrote plays of the kind which, as a critic, he particularly disliked'.

3

TILTING WITH HENRY IRVING

I shall never be able to begin a new play until I fall in love with somebody else.

Shaw to Janet Achurch (30 March 1895)

The Fabian social critic; the anonymous literary critic of the *Pall Mall Gazette*; the art critic of *Our Corner* and *The World*; the variously named musical critics of the *Dramatic Review*, *The Star* and *The World*: all were given a voice in the dramatic opinions of the *Saturday Review*. It was the Fabian who called for the establishment both of a National Theatre and of local theatres supported by local government, claiming for the drama 'as high a place in the collectivist program as municipal gas, water and tramways'. It was the Fabian, too, who campaigned for better wages for supporting actors and actresses, and who proposed a Royal College of the Drama 'with scholarships, and a library scantily furnished with memoirs and reminiscences, and liberally furnished with technical works, including theatrical instruction and stage mechanism'.

Shaw the art critic felt able to recommend George Alexander to dye his upholstery and curtains green (a more restful colour than crimson for entertainments lasting four hours); to review *King Arthur* as if it were an occasion for enjoying Burne-Jones's sets; or suddenly to surrender almost all the theatre page to the paintings of Watts and Ford Madox Brown.

But more persistent than any of these is the voice of Corno di Bassetto. As a dramatist Shaw was to claim that 'my method, my system, my tradition, is founded upon music'. He went back to nineteenth-century opera, which contained its counterpoint of spoken sequences, and concluded that operatic music was essentially a drama of the passions. 'Drama can do little to delight the senses: all the apparent instances to the contrary are instances of the personal fascination of the performers. The drama of pure feeling is no longer in the hands of the playwright: it has been conquered by the musician, after whose enchantments all the verbal arts seem cold and tame . . . there is, flatly, no future now for any drama without music except the drama of thought.'

As a critic Shaw was primarily a listener rather than a watcher. He was not imposed upon by Beerbohm Tree's profusion of stage pageantry, preferring the careful readings of William Poel's Elizabethan Stage Society, assisted by the authentic pipe and tabor of Arnold Dolmetsch, which could do for sixteenth-century blank verse, he believed, what conductors such as Richter and Mottl had successfully done for Beethoven and Wagner. It was to the orchestration of words, 'a rhetorical notation based on musical pitch and dynamics', that he was particularly attentive.

Shaw's dramatic criticism is itself dramatic writing, supplying cries from the audience and giving contrasting transcriptions of the comedian's technique – for example, between Coquelin and John Hare in Sydney Grundy's *Mamma*, where the hero discovers that his elaborate labours to murder his mother-in-law have been in vain.

'Coquelin clowned it, even to the length of bounding into the air and throwing forward his arms and legs as if to frighten off some dangerous animal. But he did not produce the electric effect of Mr Hare's white, tense face and appalled stare, conveying somehow a mad speed of emotion and a frightful suspense of action never to be forgotten by any playgoer with the true dramatic memory.'

But Shaw's imagination was most vividly awakened on the stage by women. He mocked himself for this susceptibility. 'Woman's greatest art is to lie low, and let the imagination of the male endow her with depths,' he warned. He had transferred into the theatre his struggle to be master of himself in the company of women. For Shaw the greatest actress was Eleanora Duse.

Duse had no obvious sex-appeal. She was a plain little woman, with genius: 'a most laborious artist hard at work, and not a pretty woman making an exhibition of herself', was how Shaw described her. He refers to her 'exquisite intelligence', and represents her as the finest exponent of the new drama, where emotion existed 'to make thought live and move us'. He uses her acting against which to measure the performances of other actresses – most famously in the beautiful passages comparing her playing of Sudermann's *Magda* with Sarah Bernhardt's. The two crucial words Shaw uses to explain Duse's 'vigilant sense of beauty of thought, feeling and action' were 'integrity' and 'integration'. She did not trade in flattery, solicit applause, manufacture a sham appeal for journalists. Most good actresses created themselves, Shaw believed, but were incapable of superimposing another character on top of that creation. 'Duse's greatest work is Duse,' he wrote, 'but that does not prevent Césarine, Santuzza, and Camille from being three totally different women, none of them Duses, though Duse is all of them.' And in *Magda*, her face shadowed and lined ('they are the credentials of her humanity'), it seemed to him that she spoke and acted for every woman 'as they are hardly ever able to speak and act for themselves'.

In contrast to Duse stood Mrs Patrick Campbell, a magnificent animal of a woman, perilously bewitching, whose talent depended upon her 'irresistible physical gifts'. It was away from the excitement of Mrs Pat and towards the non-sexual appeal of Duse that Shaw was trying to move Janet Achurch 'whose playing of Alexandra, in Voss's play,' he wrote, 'came nearer to Duse's work in subtlety, continuity and variety of detail, and in beauty of execution, than anything I have seen on the English stage.

'But Duse has been helped to her supremacy by the fortunate sternness of Nature in giving her nothing but her genius . . . Miss Terry or Miss Achurch, if they had no more skill than can be acquired by any person of ordinary capacity in the course of a few years' experience, would always find a certain degree of favor as pretty leading ladies.'

This was not the first time that Shaw had slipped Ellen Terry's name in next to Janet's. News of Mansfield's withdrawal of *Candida* reached him in April 1895. The following month, while Janet still lingered in America, he began to write a new play for Ellen Terry.

*

He thought her unique. Her voice, slightly veiled, seemed to enfold herself and those to whom she spoke in a glow of happiness. Shaw described her as 'heartwise', meaning perhaps a little cautious since, nearing fifty, she knew where her tender heart might still lead her. He admired her for her charm and beauty, but most of all for her refusal to trade on them with the public. Her acting 'reminds me of my imaginary violin-playing,' he wrote; 'she seems utterly innocent of it, and yet there it is, all happening infallibly and delightfully.'

Ellen Terry was over nine years older than Shaw and had been brought up 'healthy, happy and wise – theatre-wise at any rate'. At the age of sixteen she had abruptly left the theatre to marry the middle-aged painter G. F. Watts. The marriage had failed and she returned to the stage but absconded again two years later to live with the man she loved, the architect Edward William Godwin, by whom she had two children, Gordon and Edy Craig. The need for money had taken her back into the theatre after six years; and in 1877, largely to give her children legal status, she married Charles Wardell, 'a manly bulldog sort of man', who had walked in from soldiering on to the boards. Making him her leading man, she had scored a huge success with *New Men and Old Acres* at the Court Theatre in 1878. Shaw, who was in the stalls, dismissed the play as 'piffling'. But Ellen Terry had enthralled him: 'I was completely conquered.'

The public too was conquered and granted her a place, as its popular darling, set apart from Victorian standards of morality. For her emotional life had become increasingly unconventional. Before the end of 1878 she had joined Henry Irving at the Lyceum; then her marriage to Wardell began to deteriorate and in 1881 they separated. 'I should have died had I lived one more month with him,' she later told Shaw.

With Irving, Ellen Terry had tried to unite 'the great happiness of occupation' with the great excitement of romance – 'I doted on his looks,' she said. She helped to manage the Lyceum cast as if they were a family of children, acting as Irving's hostess at public banquets, touring with him, and leaving the theatre with him at night. But though he bought a house and made it ready, they never lived together: and eventually the house was sold. 'We were terribly in love for awhile,' she said. 'Then, later on, when it didn't matter so much to me, he wanted us to go on, and so I did, because I was very very fond of him and he said he needed me.'

In one of his early notices for the *Saturday Review*, Shaw wrote indignantly of Ellen Terry as 'a born actress of real women's parts condemned to figure as a mere artist's model in costume plays which, from the woman's point of view, are foolish flatteries written by gentlemen for gentlemen'. She 'OUGHT to have played in the Lady from the Sea,' he claimed, though at the same time acknowledging that she 'was never called an advanced woman' – perhaps forgetting that he had himself described her in the *Saturday Review* as 'the only real New Woman'. In their *Correspondence*, while parading his feminist credentials ('no male writer born in the nineteenth century outside Norway and Sweden did more to knock Woman off her pedestal and plant her on the solid earth than I'), he called her 'goddesslike' and raised her onto a stage pedestal, explaining: 'I was steeped in the tendency against which I was reacting.'

In Shaw's mind such contradictions reflected two Ellen Terrys, one inside the other. *His* Ellen of the 'ultra-modern talent' was waiting to be released from Henry Irving's leading actress. For almost twenty years she had lain locked in the ancient dungeons of the Lyceum Theatre, guarded by an ogre called 'His Immensity'. Up to this castle, in the year 1895, Shaw pranced in his Ibsenite armour, and flung over the battlements a strange challenge: *The Man of Destiny.*

*

They had sent each other a few letters haphazardly, but it was not until near the end of 1895, when he revealed his 'beautiful little one act play for Napoleon and a strange lady', that their flirtatious correspondence really opened. She demanded to be given the play ('Lord, how attractively tingling it sounds'), and on 28 November he despatched it to her.

'I really do love Ellen,' he was to write. He loved her for helping to move his romantic feelings from a bruising world on to the stage, from the body to the page. She gave him love without physical life and therefore without threat of death. They *acted* love. She drew his imagination out into 'a thousand wild stories and extravagances and adorations' while he sat solitary at his desk 'blarneying audacities'. They protected each other and were safe – but: 'Only the second rate are safe.'

In *The Man of Destiny* Shaw had written of 'one universal passion: fear'. It was this fear that confined them to an island of enchantment where there was no pain or regret and no growing old. They knew about such things and, when the atmosphere of charm lifted a little, could spy them far off; then go back to their play-acting together.

'Let those who may complain that it was all on paper,' Shaw later cautioned, 'remember that only on paper has humanity yet achieved glory, beauty, truth, knowledge, virtue, and abiding love.' Like soldiers, these strong and rather beautiful words guarded his frightened soul, concealing the truth that we may not put more courage, virtue, love into our words than we practise in our life. It was for this reason that he could not write for Ellen 'one of my great plays', but offered her instead this trifle, *The Man of Destiny*, 'a perfectly idiotic play' that itself revolved around a piece of paper, a supposed love letter.

The Man of Destiny was a token, plucked from his involvement with Janet Achurch and handed over to Ellen Terry as a symbol of his new engagement. 'If I make money out of my new play I will produce *Candida* at my own expense,' he told her, 'and you & Janet shall play it on alternate nights.' When turning down *Candida*, Richard Mansfield had taken the trouble to instruct Shaw that the stage was for romance. 'You'll have to write a play that a *man* can play and about a woman that heroes fought for and a bit of ribbon that a knight tied to his lance.' *The Man of Destiny*, which Shaw began less than a month after receiving Mansfield's letter, is this bit of ribbon – 'a harlequinade,' he told Janet Achurch, 'in which Napoleon and a strange lady play harlequin & columbine'.

The contest between Napoleon and the Strange Lady – a tactical duel between the man of action and a woman of words – was to be parodied by a duel of actor-manager versus playwright. 'Just read your play. Delicious,' Ellen telegraphed. She loved Shaw's shrewdly inserted description of herself as the Strange Lady:

' . . . extraordinarily graceful, with a delicately intelligent, apprehensive, questioning face: perception in the brow, sensitiveness in the nostrils, character in the chin: all keen, refined, and original . . . very feminine, but by no means weak: the lithe tender figure is hung on a strong frame . . .

She enters with the self-possession of a woman accustomed to the privileges of rank and beauty.'

The Strange Lady had Ellen's appearance; but did she have her character? In the play she succeeds in persuading the twenty-seven-year-old general to let her burn unread a letter that might compromise Josephine and the Director Barras. Ellen Terry's task, to persuade Irving to read and produce *The Man of Destiny* at the Lyceum with the two of them in its star roles, was hardly less daunting.

She began well. Irving read it and, despite the difficulty of fitting a one-act play into the Lyceum bill, positively did not turn it down. 'H.I. quite loves it,' Ellen translated, 'and will do it finely.' But Shaw was suspicious. A production at the Lyceum 'would of course be quite the best thing that could happen to it'. But did he dare hope for this? 'As long as I remain a dramatic critic,' he asked Ellen to tell Irving, 'I can neither sell plays nor take advances. I must depend altogether on royalties and percentages on actual performances. Otherwise, you see, I should simply be bribed right and left.' This followed his familiar tactic of moving to high moral ground from which to cross swords. He was fighting two battles: first to get his 'opera bouffe' produced; and secondly to win Ellen's allegiance from Irving. Behind these battles lay the warfare he was conducting against the late Victorian theatre.

*

Shaw had first seen Irving on stage at the Theatre Royal, Dublin, in *The Two Roses*, and 'at once picked him out as the actor for me'. Irving seemed 'born to play ultra-modern parts' – that is to bring to life 'the Shavian drama incipient in me'. Then he saw Ellen Terry in the first glory of her talent and beauty – and 'there I had my leading couple'.

Beside Sonny's hero, the splendid Barry Sullivan, Irving seemed a meagre presence with spindly legs, a shambling dance for a walk and 'a voice made resonant in his nose which became a whinny when he tried to rant'. Yet he had triumphed over these limitations to become the unchallengeable leader of the British stage.

Ever since arriving in London, Shaw had been studying Irving's performances. Between April and July 1879, he had seen him as Hamlet, as Claude Melnotte in *Lady of Lyons*, as Cardinal Richelieu and Charles I. 'Richelieu had been incessantly excruciating: Hamlet had only moments of violent ineptitude separated by lengths of dullness,' Shaw reported.

'... Before Claude Melnotte had moved his wrist and chin twice, I saw that he had mastered the rhetorical style at last. His virtuosity of execution soon became extraordinary. His Charles I, for instance, became a miracle of the most elaborate class of this sort of acting. It was a hard-earned and well-deserved triumph; and by it his destiny was accomplished.'

A man of two destinies, Irving had harnessed his new style of acting to no new dramatist of talent. He had returned to the much older rhetorical art that, while not itself false, was given over to acting versions that were falsifications of old plays, particularly spurious Shakespeare. Had he persisted in producing studies of modern life and character, 'we should have had the ablest manager of the day driven by life-or-death necessity to extract from contemporary literature the proper food for the modern side of his talent, and thus to create a new drama instead of galvanizing an old one and cutting himself off from all contact with the dramatic vitality of his time'.

By the 1890s the 'great possibilities' of Ellen Terry, that Shaw accused Irving of sacrificing, seemed little more than a gallant Shavian hypothesis. The symbolic choice with which Shaw apparently presented Irving – either Sardou's Napoleon, 'the jealous husband of a thousand fashionable dramas', or his own 'baby comediatta' – was never a real one. Shaw claimed to bear Irving 'an ancient grudge which I never quite forgave him . . . So I was never really fair to him . . . for, scrupulously judicial as my criticisms were . . . you can smell a certain grudge in them.' His real grudge lay against Irving's power based partly on something that Shaw himself lacked: money. Money was freedom of action and the power to limit other people's freedom. Money was a substitute for generosity, even for affection. Money was false romance.

'It was part of H.I.'s mixture of policy with sardonic humor to buy everybody. He liked to see them selling themselves, and bought them partly to gratify that taste. He knew he was being robbed; but would not sack the robbers because it put them in his power and at his command. He tried to buy me, and believed I had come to sell myself. But he did not always buy the right people.'

*

What Shaw interpreted as Irving's attempt to 'buy me in the market like a rabbit', took place between the summer of 1896 and late spring the following year. For over seven months *The Man of Destiny* had lain at the Lyceum: and nothing had happened. Yet Ellen Terry refused to let up and in the first week of July 1896 Irving wilted, indicating that he would 'agree to produce The Man of Destiny next year, or forfeit rights, if that must be an imperative condition,' Ellen reported to Shaw. 'He wants the play very much (and so do I want him to have it), and he would like to buy it.'

Shaw communicated the following week with Irving, regretting that his play was 'so trivial an affair; but when I wrote it I had no idea it would be so fortunate'. Even now he felt it could be little more than 'a fancy of Miss T's', in which case 'a performance or two on some special occasion' would meet the case. 'I should of course be delighted to license any such without any question of terms.'

Irving countered this with his standard payment of £50 (equivalent to £2,700 in 1997) for a year's exclusive option – a proposal Shaw politely described as 'reasonable' but which, he repeated, 'raises a lot of difficulties for me . . . it is impossible for a critic to take money except for actual performances without placing both himself and the manager in a false position.' He therefore suggested that a few performances be given in 1897 without any guarantee as to fees, adding as an apparent 'concession' that 'If you produce a play by Ibsen . . . then I will not only consent to a postponement of "The Man of Destiny" but will hand over the rights for all the world to you absolutely to do as you like with until your retirement without fee or condition of any kind.'

With Ellen Terry looking on laughing, there was nothing much Irving could do but (with the deletion of Ibsen) appear to accept the Shavian counter-proposal. Shaw had won a paper victory.

Irving could not have taken kindly to being lectured *de haut en bas* on financial ethics. Yet he could not afford to look mean, so he grandly did nothing for a further two months. Then, with Shaw in the audience, he announced from the stage that the Lyceum would be producing Sardou's Napoleon show, *Madame Sans-Gêne*, in the spring of 1897. This, the actor's riposte to the writer, was a wonderful provocation to Shaw, who sent an over-polite enquiry as to whether he was 'for the first time' free to submit *The Man of Destiny* elsewhere. Irving's response was to invite him to the Lyceum.

So, at half-past twelve on 26 September 1896, the two men met in Irving's office. There was no one with a more imposing presence than Irving; no one bolder with words than Shaw. Both had been provoked. That morning the *Saturday Review* published Shaw's ferocious analysis of Irving's *Cymbeline*. 'In the true republic of art Sir Henry Irving would ere this have expiated his acting versions on the scaffold,' Shaw had written.

'He does not merely cut plays; he disembowels them . . . This curious want of connoisseurship in literature would disable Sir Henry Irving seriously if he were an interpretative actor. But it is, happily, the fault of a great quality – the creative quality . . . The truth is that he has never in his life conceived or interpreted the characters of any author except himself.'

Like royalty, Irving rose above Shaw's journalism, knew nothing about it, extinguished it. Though Shaw was able to hold to his principle of not accepting money, Irving was magnanimous here too. He tolerated Shaw's eccentricities. Fifty pounds was nothing to him. Of course he would stage *The Man of Destiny* – notwithstanding Sardou's play – sometime. The man whom Shaw had that day accused in public of having no literary judgement was pleased to think highly of *The Man of Destiny*. So the interview, which Shaw was never to describe, ended with what seemed an uneasy truce; and a stage victory for Irving.

*

The two men had met, but the man and the woman, even after a year of letter writing, had not. Ellen came to the door where Shaw and Irving were talking, heard their voices, and skedaddled. 'I think I'd rather never meet you -- in the flesh,' she had written to him, and he had replied: 'Very well, you shant meet me in the flesh if you'd rather not. There is something deeply touching in that.' It was lack of confidence that kept them apart. She felt old. Her body ached, sometimes even disgusted her. She could regain her attractiveness only through an illusion. 'They love me, you know!' she wrote. 'Not for what I am, but for what they imagine I am . . . I never *feel* like myself when I am acting, but some one else, so nice, and so young and so happy, and always in-the-air, light, and bodyless.' She felt he understood. And he confirmed this understanding: 'Our brains evidently work in the same way.' For he too felt better bodyless. In body he was 'a disagreeably cruel looking middle aged Irishman with a red beard' who, in the *Saturday Review*, turned into a magic Shaw. So they sent out their imaginary selves to meet each other, she so schoolgirlish, he so cocksure. He entertained her, made her 'fly out laughing', and sometimes strengthened her stage confidence. 'You have become a habit with me,' she acknowledged. She gave him 'that lost feeling of unfulfilment'. He thought he had found someone like himself, vulnerable yet determined to be self-sufficient: 'you are a fully self-possessed woman and therefore not really the slave of love.' Each enabled the other to keep these illusions, and each was aware of this conspiracy. 'I, too, fear to break the spell,' he wrote, 'remorses, presentiments, all sorts of tendernesses wring my heart at the thought of materialising this beautiful friendship of ours by a meeting.' It was the same for her: 'I love you more every minute,' she owned. 'I cant help it, and I guessed it would be like that! And so we wont meet.'

What he called 'silly longings . . . waves of tenderness' almost broke the spell. He slipped the words 'I love you' into one of his letters, and she admitted not being able to 'cure' herself of him. Sometimes, in bed at night, she felt the need 'to touch you, to put my hand on your arm'. Then he too would grow impatient at the row of footlights separating them and want to hold her in his arms: 'Don't let us break the spell, *do* let us break the spell – don't, do, don't, do, don't, do, don't – ' And the spell did not break.

In place of their bodies they put their work. 'I *must* attach myself to you somehow,' he had written: 'Let me therefore do it as a matter of business.' And she agreed: 'I'm not going to write any more 'cept on business.' His business was to make her 'the greatest actress in the world'.

Much of his correspondence is an attempt to undermine Ellen's faith in Irving. 'Has he ever loved you for the millionth fraction of a moment?' he wondered. Such questions worried Ellen. She had always been in awe of Irving – his beauty, his distinction – but felt frustrated in the patriarchy of the Lyceum. Irving was so crafty. 'I wish he were more ingenuous and more direct,' she confided in her diary. ' . . . I think it is not quite right in him that he does not care for anybody much.' But to Shaw she wrote: 'I wish you were friends – that *you knew each other* . . . I think everything of him (is that "love"?). He can do everything – except be fond of *people* . . . but that's his great misfortune . . . Love him & be sorry for him.'

*

Irving's magisterial 'Governor' at the Lyceum was an equivalent self-production to Shaw's phenomenal G.B.S. of the *Saturday Review*. 'I really care deeply for nothing but *fine work*,' Shaw had insisted, and the same was true of Irving. Since their work stood opposed they appeared implacable enemies. It is hard not to feel sympathy for Irving. 'The artist sacrifices everything to his art, beginning with himself,' Shaw had written of Irving. 'But his art *is* himself; and when the art is the art of acting, the self is both body and soul.' It was Irving's body and soul that Shaw held up to ridicule in the *Saturday Review*. 'Mr Irving must remember that we now applaud him, not critically, but affectionately,' he reminded him.

'. . . We indulge him, every evening at the Lyceum, with a broadsword combat the solemn absurdity of which quite baffles my powers of description. If we treat his orations as lectures, do we not also treat Mr Gladstone's tree-felling exploits as acts of statesmanship? No one can say that we are not indulgent to our favorites.'

What could have exasperated Irving more than the Shavian endorsement of his knighthood conferred on him, *Saturday Review* readers understood, 'by his own peremptory demand, which no mere gentleman would have dared to make lest he should have offended the court and made himself ridiculous'. It was a battle of author versus actor, dramatist against theatrical manager. Who should rule the theatre?

'The history of the Lyceum, with its twenty years' steady cultivation of the actor as a personal force, and its utter neglect of the drama, is the history of the English stage during that period. Those twenty years have raised the social status of the theatrical profession, and culminated in the official recognition of our chief actor as the peer of the President of the Royal Academy, and the figure-heads of the other arts. And now I, being a dramatist and not an actor, want to know when the drama is to have its turn. I do not suggest that G.B.S. should condescend to become K.C.B.; but I do confidently affirm that if the actors think they can do without the drama, they are most prodigiously mistaken.'

In the *Saturday Review* Shaw dramatizes the ghastly struggle between Irving and Shakespeare, urging his readers to bear in mind the venerable actor's deep sincerity in preferring his own treasons 'to the unmutilated masterpieces of the genius' on whom he had 'lavished lip-honor'. For these treasons Shaw recommended a small penalty: 'my regard for Sir Henry Irving cannot blind me to the fact that it would have been better for us twenty-five years ago to have tied him up in a sack with every existing copy of the works of Shakespeare, and dropped him into the crater of the nearest volcano.' By such tricks did Shaw hope to arrange for Irving's entrances on stage to be greeted with bursts of laughter – a fitting penalty for the actor who (in one sense or another) had played the dramatist off the stage, and become 'the despair of all authors and true Shakespeareans'.

Shaw is here classing himself among the true Shakespeareans. He had kept up to date with new textual criticism of Shakespeare, and his attack on the Lyceum's mutilated versions complemented the philological and photographic facsimile scholarship of F. J. Furnival (whom he had met at the New Shakespere Society), and the austere Elizabethan production methods of William Poel (which he had studied as a dramatic critic). As Sonny, he had lived in Shakespeare's world more vividly than his own, and to the extent that something of Sonny persisted in Shaw, to that extent there lived on in him a legacy of love for Shakespeare. But when Sonny had turned to Dickens, he had taken his first step into the theatricality of the stage where G.B.S. now enshrined Ellen Terry. His emotional instincts tended to despair; but his mind needed optimism as the oxygen with which to go on breathing. The Shavian theatre became a factory for the manufacture of this life-supporting tonic.

At their best Shaw's tirades against 'the poor foolish old Swan' were part of theatre politics, and an attempt to cleanse the Victorian theatre of its snobbish bardolatry. But at their worst they dissolve into a stream of puerilities as irrelevant to Shakespeare's work as anything performed at the Lyceum by Henry Irving; and as self-advertising: 'With the single exception of Homer, there is no eminent writer, not even Sir Walter Scott, whom I can despise so entirely as I despise Shakespeare when I measure my mind against his.' Irving had reduced Shakespeare to a pantomime pet; Shaw fashioned him into a journalistic Aunt Sally whose politics 'would hardly impress the Thames Conservancy Board'. Whenever this rain of abuse against Shakespeare's 'economics' abates, Shaw's scrupulous knowledge of the poetry gleams through. 'It is as though he resented his own susceptibility,' Hilary Spurling was to observe, as though he had to punish him before he could 'admit how deeply he has been moved – overpowered is his own word – by the beauties of the play in question'.

Shaw's attitude to Shakespeare and Irving reflect his attitudes to sex and power. As there are two Shakespeares in Shaw's world, so there were two Irvings: the dictatorial actor-manager and the man with humours parallel to Shaw's own.

'All attempts to sustain our conduct at a higher level than is natural to us produce violent reactions . . . I remember years ago going into the Lyceum Theatre under the impression that I was about to witness a performance of Richard III. After one act of that tragedy, however, Mr Irving relapsed into an impersonation of Alfred Jingle. He concealed piles of sandwiches in his hat; so that when he afterwards raised it to introduce himself as "Alfred Jingle, Esq., of No Hall, Nowhere," a rain of ham and bread descended on him . . . He was simply taking his revenge on Shakespear and himself for months of sustained dignity . . . I am the last person in the world to object; for I, too, have something of that aboriginal need for an occasional carnival in me.'

Through absurdity we become human. It was this humanity that Shaw warmed to whenever he could change their positions and make Irving the clown or outsider. 'Does H.I. really say that you are in love with me?' he asked Ellen. 'For that be all his sins forgiven him! . . . I am also touched by his refusing to believe that we have never met.'

*

Shaw's article on Irving's *Richard III* had appeared in December 1896, and like a time-bomb exploded four months later under *The Man of Destiny.* The play had seemed fated to bring Shaw and Ellen Terry together. But in April 1897 the Lyceum decided after all not to stage his play.

It was almost a relief. 'I hate failure,' Shaw had once confided to Ellen. So did Irving. It seemed important to each man that he should be judged by Ellen to have acted the better. She was their referee, and in her reaction was success to be sought. For many Saturdays Shaw had been prodding out his dramatic opinions and trying to goad his opponent into committing some moral foul. For eighteen months they had circled each other while Ellen, believing it actually was a dance and not a fight, looked on.

Irving's sudden action took Ellen by surprise. At first he gave Shaw no reason, allowing the great paradoxer to make a conventional deduction. 'I am in ecstasies. I have been spoiling for a row,' Shaw told Ellen. But Ellen felt irritated. Why were these men quarrelling? They were like schoolboys. 'My dear, this vexes me very much,' she reproved Shaw. 'My friends to fight! And I love both of them, and want each to win.

'Henry has been much vexed lately (I only learned this last evening) by what he calls "your attacks" upon him in the Saturday Review, the Olivia article especially annoying him . . . I said I believed he had another reason . . . I believe he was ashamed and I felt strangely powerfully sorry for him . . . he and I are going for a long drive this afternoon, and he shall tell me all then.'

Shaw did not wait to be told more. 'Of course I knew all about it,' he answered:

'a good surgeon knows when his knife touches a nerve; a good critic knows the same with his pen. There was a terrible thing in that "Olivia" notice . . . if he is clever enough to tell you on that afternoon drive – as I should in his place – that he is giving up the play because he is jealous of me about you, take his part and console him: it is when a man is too much hurt to do the perfectly magnanimous thing that he most needs standing by.'

Shaw then proceeded to what he assumed must be a quick magnanimous victory. He informed Irving's manager that if the Lyceum broke its pledge on no other grounds than that his *Saturday Review* criticism had been impolite, then the only conclusion to be made was that Irving had used *The Man of Destiny* to purchase good notices. 'I am not likely to put myself in the wrong,' he assured Ellen, 'with you standing between us.'

By the time she read this Ellen realized it was to be a more complicated business. On their drive that Sunday, Irving indicated that Shaw's article on *Richard III* was an accusation of drunkenness on stage. With someone who used his journalistic position for such a libel no gentleman's agreement was binding.

Shaw's criticism in the *Saturday Review* contains too many oblique references to drunkenness to be accidental.

'He [Irving] was not, as it seemed to me, answering his helm satisfactorily; and he was occasionally a little out of temper with his own nervous condition. He made some odd slips in the text . . . Once he inadvertently electrified the house by very unexpectedly asking Miss Milton to get further up the stage in the blank verse and penetrating tones of Richard. Finally, the worry of playing against the vein tired him. In the tent and battle scenes his exhaustion was too genuine to be quite acceptable as part of the play. The fight was, perhaps, a relief to his feelings . . . If Kean were to return to life and do the combat for us, we should very likely find it as absurd as his habit of lying down on a sofa when he was too tired or too drunk to keep his feet during the final scenes.'

On 10 April Sardou's Napoleon play had opened at the Lyceum, where the box-office manager, making a half-hearted attempt to refuse admission to Shaw, was brushed aside. Shaw's notice, treating *Madame Sans Gêne* almost as a rehearsal for *The Man of Destiny*, had come out on the same day as he received the Lyceum's rejection. It had been nicely timed. *The Era* suggested that previous reports of the Lyceum having accepted the play were false; the *Glasgow Herald* announced that Irving, having found Shaw's Napoleon unsuited to him, 'has thought it best to return the manuscript to the author with, it is understood, a handsome compliment and a present'. Suddenly Shaw found himself in a flurried situation where his own moral supremacy seemed unclear. It was, he told a friendly journalist, 'enough to make a saint swear'.

'For the first time in all my long long life I am most frightfully dispirited,' Ellen wrote to him. 'Oh God, how frightful it is . . . Dont quarrel with H[enry]. That would add to my unhappiness.' 'This is at heart a tragic business,' Shaw admitted. ' . . . Dont be anxious: I'll behave nicely and nothing particular will happen.' By behaving nicely Shaw meant that instead of going to the press he would try to settle matters privately with Irving. On 29 April he wrote to him in brisk and embattled fashion. There had been no imputation of drunkenness, he stated: 'I never dreamt of such a thing.' Irving's reply was unaccommodating. 'I had not the privilege of reading your criticism – as you call it – of Richard. I never read a criticism of yours in my life. I have read lots of your droll, amusing, irrelevant and sometimes impertinent pages, but criticism containing judgement and sympathy I have never seen by your pen.'

With journalists clamouring for some riposte, it was becoming increasingly difficult for Shaw to remain silent. But for Ellen's sake he decided to make one more appeal to Irving. Either the Lyceum must announce the production of *The Man of Destiny* later that year; or they must concoct together an explanation, highly creditable to them both, for the abandonment of the play. For this second course Shaw had ready a scenario involving Mrs Patrick Campbell and Johnston Forbes-Robertson as an alternative cast. 'If you can think of anything better than this, let me know,' he offered. But for Irving anything was better – even nothing was better. To accept such a plan would reduce him to a Shavian puppet. So he simply arranged for his manager to send back the manuscript of Shaw's play with a brief note of rejection, followed by a more indignant expostulation drafted by his secretary.

Ellen had begged Shaw not to quarrel with Irving. Quarrel he would not; but a 'mild tussle,' he advised, would clear the blood. To Ellen it appeared that Irving was behaving much the worse. She had not seen his first performance in *Richard III*, and could find nothing wrong with Shaw's notice of it in the *Saturday Review*. His rudeness to her friend and lack of consideration for herself made her feel 'tired and sad and hopeless'. After all those years together, she still could not penetrate the elegant-grotesque veneer of his personality. Sometimes she found herself hating him – and immediately hated herself for doing so. 'H and I are out! A little bit,' she confided to Shaw. For the first time she began to criticize one man to the other. 'I've spoiled him! I was born meek. (Ugh) . . . I do assure you it is *I* all along who wished so hard for the play. He never wishes for anything much outside his own individual effort. I admire him for it, and I hate him for it, that he appreciates NOTHING and NOBODY . . . He wants a good slapping, but *you* must not do that, and *I* wont.'

The men had had their tussle and Shaw, by not going to the newspapers, would win her tribute. But as she turned to him, so he turned to his public.

The Lyceum door had been slammed in his face for all to see. Ellen, after all, did not seem to be his Strange Lady; Irving, when not acting (like Napoleon when not soldiering), was nobody – and in respect of Shaw's plays would remain nobody. 'Forgive me; but your Henry is not a hero off the stage,' he wrote to Ellen. He was almost forty-two and he had written eight plays. *The Man of Destiny* had been one more battle lost. He needed two things as his spoils of defeat: to revenge himself on Irving through Ellen; and to rewrite the whole history of the event through the press.

He felt safe in attacking Irving because Ellen had already begun to criticize him herself. '*You* must not take his part now: I declare him unworthy of my Ellen,' he wrote to her.

'Your career has been sacrificed to the egotism of a fool: he has warmed his wretched hands callously at the embers of nearly twenty of your priceless years; and now they will flame up, scorch his eyes, burn off his rumbathed hair, and finally consume him . . . He tries to hide himself from himself with a rampart of lies; and he got behind it to hide himself from me. That was why he became an actor – to escape from himself.'

This was sent to Ellen on 13 May, by which day he had already drafted a long interview with himself for the *Daily Mail*. It was characteristic of Shaw to make this the occasion for helping a young office clerk in his ambition to become a journalist; and that this man, Reginald Golding Bright (later to become Shaw's London theatrical agent), should turn out to have been that solitary member of the audience who had heckled *Arms and the Man*. 'Vengeance I leave to Destiny,' Shaw announced to Ellen. What better evidence of this superiority to vengeance could there now be than his helping hand to Golding Bright? Their 'interview' in the *Daily Mail* contained no obvious malice at all, though by describing Irving as 'still obstinately under the spell of my genius' he converts him to a comic Shavian invention.

But Ellen wasn't fooled. She could tell from Irving's furtive expression how much he was affected. His last letter to Shaw was in effect a cry of 'For God's sake, leave me alone!' How much more human this seemed than all Shaw's acrobatics. 'My poor Henry!' she exclaimed. Why hadn't Shaw been able to leave him alone – for her sake? 'Well, you are quite stupid after all and *not* so unlike other people. You should have given in and said, "Take the play and do it when you can . . ." I'm angry with you.'

Shaw had told Ellen that sometimes on Sundays he used to see her and Irving driving along Richmond Terrace 'like two children in a gigantic perambulator, and [I] have longed to seize him, throw him out, get up, take his place, and calmly tell the coachman to proceed'. What Ellen had learnt from this quarrel was that Shaw wanted to let her proceed alone. 'And NOW – well go your ways,' she decided. They were self-centred impractical men, and jealous.

She could not always remember her lines; she was on the verge of breaking down – and yet at a sound or a touch, she could still feel a throb of her heart. 'I fly from "throbs" in these days. It is not becoming. It's absurd.' She flew to her work, which was another sort of love. 'Work hardens and alerts me,' she confirmed in Shavian style. But the discipline of work without a little bit of real love became mechanical. Neither Irving nor Shaw could give her real love; neither would touch her, produce that throb.

From the wreckage of those hopes they had placed in each other, kindness persisted. And from that kindness came an honesty; and from honesty a muted revival of hope. Shaw's letters to Ellen tell of his childhood, of his dilemma of loving and the escape from incest into fantasy.

'I have only one thing to say to you . . . wanting to sleep, and yet to sleep with you. Only, do you know what the consequences would be? Well, about tomorrow at noon when the sun would be warm & the birds in full song, you would feel an irresistible impulse to fly into the woods. And there, to your great astonishment & scandal, you would be *confined* of a baby that would immediately spread a pair of wings and fly, and before you could rise to catch it it would be followed by another & another and another – hundreds of them, and they would finally catch you up & fly away with you to some heavenly country where they would grow into strong sweetheart sons with whom, in defiance of the prayerbook, you would found a divine race. Would you not like to be the mother of your own grandchildren? If you were my mother, I am sure I should carry you away to the tribe in Central America where – but I have a lot of things to say . . .'

In such passages, and without ever stating openly that the need he felt for his mother's love had set a pattern for his relationships with women, Shaw tried to indicate why he had supplanted the physical act of love with 'a lot of things to say'. In his fashion he loved Ellen; at any rate he wanted to love Ellen; but he could more easily hurt than touch her and felt he must 'get beyond love'. However much of this Ellen understood, she recognized the integrity and limitation of his feeling for her: 'You are a dear old kind fellow, as well as everything else.'

So they laid the preparations for a second chapter of their love, in another place than the Lyceum. For he had promised her: 'Nevertheless you shall play for me yet; but not with him, not with him, not with him.'

4

CANDIDA REFINISHED

> Here am I, the god who *has* been happy, among people who say 'I want to be happy just once'. The result, though, is alarming – desiring nothing further, I have become a sublime monster, to whose disembodied heart the consummation of ordinary lives is a mere anti-climax.
>
> Shaw to Janet Achurch (29 January 1896)

Four months after her return from New York, Janet Achurch stepped onto the stage of the Metropole in Camberwell in the revival of Wilkie Collins's *The New Magdalen*. It was a fashionably sentimental drama of the sort that had once provoked Shaw's 'unpleasant plays'. But he was in the mood to be generous. Describing her as 'the only tragic actress of genius we now possess,' he wrote that 'Miss Achurch [has] taken this innocent old figment of Wilkie Collins's benevolent and chivalrous imagination, and played into it a grim truth that it was never meant to bear . . . so that the curious atmosphere of reluctance and remonstrance from which Calvé use to wring the applause of the huge audiences at Covent Garden when the curtain fell on her Carmen, arose more than once when Miss Achurch disturbed and appalled us.'

Shaw had designed his notice so as to help re-establish Janet's career. While she was abroad he had kept her name before the public by linking it to Ellen Terry's. Ellen and Janet held twin attractions for him. Under their spell he was like a child playing at mothers-and-fathers. About business affairs they needed a stream of fatherly advice; and while he handed them this advice they encircled him with such powerful maternal appeal that, by 1896, he was imagining them performing on alternate nights in *Candida* which he described as 'THE Mother Play'.

Janet had talent but, as Ellen Terry noticed, she would '*overdo* it'. She had barely grasped her words from the prompter than she fell ill. On 10 November Shaw's medical friend Kingston Barton diagnosed typhoid fever. Her illness 'occupied me a good deal during the last two months of the year [1895],' Shaw noted in his diary, 'partly because of its bearing on all possible plans for the production of *Candida*, and partly because I have come into relations of intimate friendship with the Charringtons'.

He was under tremendous strain. The money he earned from his journalism was absorbed by his family, but whatever small change he could squeeze out he handed over to Charrington; and whatever time he could scratch together, often from his hours of sleep, he spent with Janet at Onslow Square. The atmosphere in the house was appalling. But Shaw, though suffering from terrible headaches, refused to admit pessimism – even when Charrington, rousing himself with a bout of hostility, objected to his closeness to Janet in her bedroom. A nurse was installed, but Janet grew worse until, her death appearing possible, Shaw was denied her room altogether.

But Janet did not die: and with her recovery Shaw's hopes took off again. Perhaps she might play his Strange Lady. From her illness had come health; but after her convalescence she began to slip back into 'your brandy and soda self, your fabling, pretending, promising, company promoting, heavy eyelidded, morphia injecting self,' he admonished her.

With Shaw's help, Charrington had succeeded J. T. Grein as managing director of the Independent Theatre. It was a calculated gamble, aimed at helping Charrington's chances of achieving a stage career separate from his wife, whom Shaw had once more exhorted to 'live out your own life in your own way, and leave him [Charrington] to do the same'. This was Shaw's way of forbidding Janet's bedroom to her husband. But his confidence in Janet was diminishing as his interest, denied access to Elizabeth Robins, mounted in Ellen Terry. The plot of *Candida* was being enacted in his own life. In a letter he wrote to Janet while Charrington was away in April 1896 can be heard again the accents of Marchbanks at the end of the play. 'The step up to the plains of heaven was made on your bosom, I know; and it was a higher step than those I had previously taken on other bosoms,' he warned her.

'But he who mounts does not take the stairs with him . . . I have left the lower stairs behind me and must in turn leave you unless you too mount along with me.'

What Shaw had achieved for himself through will-power, he wanted to achieve for Janet vicariously. He wanted to become her guide and the source of her power; he wanted to replace her ordinary husband-and-wife liaison with Charrington by a motherly communion with himself.

Janet gave Shaw her answer the following month by revealing that she had been faithless to his principles 'to the extent of making "Candida" impossible until after next February [1897], when she expects to become once more a mother'. Watching Janet, seeing her beauty (her eyes like moons in a wet fog), Shaw understood what physical joy she took in her pregnancy. It was for her, as it had been for Ellen Terry, a voluptuous confinement. But Ellen was not pregnant and never would be again; while Janet's pregnancy moved the plot of their lives back from the stage into life. In short: she could not act in 'THE Mother Play' because she was to be a mother. 'I daren't be devoted now,' he told her in a moment of rare pathos. 'The appeal of your present experience to my sympathy is too strong to be indulged. So don't be angry with Shaw, Limited.'

*

Late in 1896 Janet seems to have had a miscarriage. 'Poor Janet,' Ellen Terry commiserated to Shaw. 'But tell her to wait. One gets everything if one will only wait, and she can. She is young and clever.' Early the next year, 1897, in her home town of Manchester, she enjoyed a 'glorious rampage', playing Cleopatra opposite Louis Calvert's 'inexcusably fat' Antony. But Shaw could not share her enjoyment. She had abandoned the experimental drama for which members of the Independent paid their subscriptions and replaced it with a thirty-year-old acting version of Shakespeare that might be seen any evening at the Lyceum. For the first time Janet was made an object for the hilarious sarcasm Irving knew so well:

'She is determined that Cleopatra shall have rings on her fingers and bells on her toes, and that she shall have music wherever she goes . . . The lacerating discord of her wailings is in my tormented ears as I write, reconciling me to the grave . . . I am a broken man . . . I begin to have hopes of a great metropolitan vogue for that lady now, since she has at last done something that is thoroughly wrong from beginning to end.'

What did he do to these women? He had laughed at Archer's susceptibility to Elizabeth Robins and its effect on his criticism in *The World*, but what of his own *Saturday Review* writings on Janet?

That May, Janet put on *The Doll's House* again, enabling Shaw to compare her performance with the one that had so hypnotized him eight years before. She had lost, he thought, her naturalness – a loss comparable to that of Alice in Miss Lockett, and matching the disappearance of Sonny within G.B.S. Their story was ending with a curious reversal. 'At last I am beginning to understand anti-Ibsenism,' Shaw told his *Saturday Review* readers:

'I no longer dwell on the awakening of the woman, which was once the central point of the drama. Why should I? The play solves that problem just as it is being solved in real life. The woman's eyes are opened; and instantly her doll's dress is thrown off and her husband left staring at her, helpless, bound thenceforth either to do without her (an alternative which makes short work of his independence) or else treat her as a human being like himself, fully recognizing that he is not a creature of one superior species, Man, living with a creature of another and inferior species, Woman, but that Mankind is male and female . . . We see a fellow-creature blindly wrecking his happiness and losing his "love-life", and are touched dramatically.'

The sympathy he feels for Helmer reflects a new sympathy for Janet's husband, and his rising fear of being imprisoned himself within a secure and happy marriage. The Independent Theatre's next production, *The Wild Duck*, did not feature Janet, and gave him the opportunity to declare that it had been Charrington who struck the decisive blow for Ibsen in England.

'Mr Charrington, like Mr Kendal and Mr Bancroft, has a wife; and the difference made by Miss Janet Achurch's acting has always been more obvious than that made by her husband's management to a public which has lost all tradition of what stage management really is, apart from lavish expenditure on scenery and furniture . . . Now, however, we have him at last with Miss Janet Achurch out of the bill. The result is conclusive . . . there is not a moment of bewilderment during the development . . . The dialogue, which in any other hands would have been cut to ribbons, is given without the slightest regard to the clock . . . That is a real triumph of management. It may be said that it is a triumph of Ibsen's genius; but of what use is Ibsen's genius if the manager has not the genius to believe in it.'

Shaw still believed that Janet and Charrington ought to part – but now it was for his sake more than hers. During 1897 Shaw used his *Saturday Review* column to persuade his readers that Charrington was 'the only stage-manager of genius the new movement has produced . . . [an] adventurer who explores the new territory at his own risk and is superseded by commercial enterprise the moment he is seen to pick up anything'. Here was a handsome apology to Charrington, transformed in Shaw's public imagination from the friend of pawnbrokers, who only cared for 'a pipe, a glass of whisky, a caress from a respectable woman', into a dedicated man-of-the-theatre crippled by obsessive love for his wife.

So when, having achieved success nowhere else, Shaw finally consented in the summer of 1897 to let the Independent Theatre produce *Candida*, it was into the 'capable hands' of Charrington, not to Janet, that he gave it. Ellen would not act for him: but why should her daughter, Edy

Craig, not play Prossy in the production? 'Would she go, do you think?' Shaw asked Ellen. '. . . she might pick up something from Charrington; and Janet would keep her in gossip for a twelve-month to come.' So Shaw proposed; Ellen consented; and Edy was signed up for £20 a week.

Ellen felt tantalized by Shaw's friendship with her daughter. She had sent him a picture of both her children; Shaw had responded with one of himself – but with his eyes averted. So the photograph had not looked at her. But some evenings when Ellen was at the Lyceum, he would call at her home in Barkston Gardens and read his latest play to Edy and her friend Sally Fairchild. By the time Ellen returned, he was gone. They still had not met. He was, it seemed, 'the vainest flirt'. 'He'd coquet with a piece of string,' Sally Fairchild volunteered. But they had seen the dreadful fatigue behind his teasing.

'Oh, I'd love to have a baby every year,' Ellen had written to Shaw. Of course it was a fantasy: all men were babies to her. But to her own children she was not a good mother, spoiling her son, dominating her daughter. She had rejected Edy's suitors, and she welcomed this tour. Her daughter's watching eyes, that cool voice, unsettled her.

Candida was first presented to the public for one performance on 30 July 1897 in Aberdeen. The *Aberdeen Daily Journal* called it a 'risky business', though the drunken scene had been 'much appreciated'. 'I don't think we'll be much troubled with Mr Shaw's comedy,' predicted the *Northern Figaro*. 'I am sorry for Miss Achurch, she had such an uncongenial part to play, she certainly did her best with it, but I don't think she will ever say that "Candida" is her favourite part.'

When the Charringtons' tour reached Eastbourne, Ellen went to see it. 'It comes out on the stage even better than when one reads it. It is absorbingly interesting every second . . . Even the audience understood it all.' As for Janet, Ellen would write to her 'about one or two trifling things in her acting, suggestions which she may care, or not care, to try over'.

But 'I daren't face it,' Shaw told Janet. He was out of love with the theatre, with theatrical people, and with Janet. She had tried to borrow money from Ellen Terry and, worse still, from Edy. She had even tried to take advantage of a new friend of Shaw's, a 'public spirited Irish Lady' called Charlotte Payne-Townshend. Once he had retreated before the 'moral vacuity' of Florence Farr; now he backed away from Janet, accusing her of being 'a moral void – a vacuum'.

Eventually he saw his 'unhappy play' when the Charringtons did a London performance for the Stage Society in the summer of 1900. Edy 'pulled off the typist successfully,' he assured Ellen. But Janet, he decided, 'wasnt the right woman for it at all'.

She still had power to charm him. Calling round one evening at the end of 1897 he had found her as adorable as ever. But soon she grew loud and, after dinner, fuddled – reminding Shaw of his father. He knew then what he must do. He must walk out into the night.

'I held up a mirror in which Janet was beautiful as long as I could, in private and in print: now I've held it up with Janet inarticulate and rowdy. Avoid me now as you would the devil . . . it's sufficient that I loved you when I was young. Now I can do nothing but harm unless I say farewell, farewell, farewell, farewell, farewell, farewell, farewell, farewell.'

5

A FIRST PLAY FOR PURITANS

> My reputation as a dramatist grows with every play of mine that is *not* performed.
>
> 'The Man of Destiny', *Daily Mail* (15 May 1897)

Between the end of 1895 and the beginning of 1897 Shaw gave the West End stage two more chances of discovering him. *You Never Can Tell* was a farce, and *The Devil's Disciple* a melodrama. Both were conventional as to form but extraordinary in style. 'When I got to the end,' wrote George Alexander, returning the text of *You Never Can Tell*, 'I had no more idea what you meant by it than a tom-cat.'

In his Preface to *Plays Pleasant* Shaw described *You Never Can Tell* as an attempt to answer the many requests of managers in search of fashionable comedies for West End theatres. 'I had no difficulty in complying,' he explained,

'as I have always cast my plays in the ordinary practical comedy form in use at all the theatres; and far from taking an unsympathetic view of the popular preference for fun, fashionable dresses, a little music, and even an exhibition of eating and drinking by people with an expensive air, attended by an if-possible-comic waiter, I was more than willing to shew that the drama can humanize these things as easily as they, in the wrong hands, can dehumanize the drama.'

You Never Can Tell has all the extravagant materials of farce: lost parents, antiphonal twins, outrageous coincidences, transparent disguises and the crowning emblem of a comic waiter. With dentistry as his metaphor, Shaw used laughing gas (specifically identified in the original manuscript version) to 'pluck from the memory a rooted sorrow', and refill theatrical comedy with new material.

In his Preface to *The Shewing-up of Blanco Posnet* he was to liken the nation's morals to its teeth ('the more decayed they are the more it hurts to touch them'), and he once wrote to a dentist comparing their professions. 'I spend my life cutting out carious material from people's minds and replacing it with such gold as I possess. It is a painful process and you hear them screaming all through the press. I cannot give anaesthetics, but I do it as amusingly as I can.'

You Never Can Tell was his attempt to write for, without succumbing to, the theatre of Oscar Wilde's *The Importance of Being Earnest*. He had criticized Wilde's comedy for the *Saturday Review* at the end of February 1895 and begun his first attempt at *You Never Can Tell* some four months later.

'I cannot say that I greatly cared for The Importance of Being Earnest. It amused me, of course; but unless comedy touches me as well as amuses me, it leaves me with a sense of having wasted my evening . . . though I laugh as much as anybody at a farcical comedy, I am out of spirits before the end of the second act, and out of temper before the end of the third, my miserable mechanical laughter intensifying these symptoms at every outburst.'

This reaction is so singular that some critics have attributed it to envy. But *The Importance of Being Earnest* seems to have pressed on a concealed bruise that unsettled Shaw.

One morning, before Sonny's first birthday, his father had gone down to the railway station to see his wife as she went through on the train. But 'there you were with your head stuck down into a Book and of course you did not pretend to see me,' he complained. ' . . . there is a queer feel over me today, I did not mind it yesterday but I feel so forlorn, forsaken, alone.' Wilde's comedy, involving the identity of a handbagged baby in the cloakroom at Victoria Station, seemed to stir in Shaw the same 'queer feel' experienced by his father, against which G.B.S. had hardened his adult mind. There are echoes in *You Never Can Tell* of *The Importance of Being Earnest*. The recommendation of Valentine, the five-shilling dentist, to his patients, the young Clandons, to acquire 'a father alive or dead' for social respectability, is close to Lady Bracknell's recommendation to Jack Worthing to 'produce at any rate one parent, of either sex, before the season is quite over'.

Both plays use the theatrical device of the chance reunion of a separated family. The long-lost father in *You Never Can Tell* appears to have stepped out of a standard Victorian farce. But his drinking and outbursts of temper are seen as deriving from marriage to a woman who did not love him; and he has most to gain from the affectionate pantomime atmosphere Shaw works up at the end. This dance from grimness into gaiety represents the humanity Shaw found lacking in Wilde's play.

The autobiographical interest in *You Never Can Tell* is never literal, but is part of the reshaping of facts Shaw made while hammering out his philosophy of optimism. In the first version the play was set not in Devon but the Isle of Wight, where he had gone with Lucy and his mother after his sister Agnes had died there. The cast included improved versions of his father and mother, Lucy, Agnes ('Yuppy') and himself: they are Fergus Crampton, the abandoned father with 'an atrociously obstinate ill-tempered grasping mouth, and a dogmatic voice'; his wife, now calling herself Mrs Clandon who rules out 'all attempt at sex attraction'; and the three children she has brought up by herself: Gloria, 'the incarnation of haughty high-mindedness', and the twins, a 'darling little creature', Dolly, who is spoilt by her mother, and the 'handsome man in miniature', Philip, whose self-consciousness would be 'insufferable in a less prepossessing youth'. All of them are transferred from their Shaw family background into the landscape of Shakespearian romantic comedy, while the imposing Finch McComas, who twenty years before fired the imagination of Mrs Clandon, occupies the place of Vandeleur Lee, but is now made an agent for the reunion of the family.

On stage his family is in Shaw's power. He can dress them up, make them move to his music, manhandle them into pleasant reconciliation. His characters all carry the germs of real suffering. Bohun, the lawyer, speaks for everyone when he says: 'It's unwise to be born; it's unwise to be married; it's unwise to live; and it's wise to die.' And his father, the waiter, gives Shaw's answer: 'so much the worse for wisdom!'

But in an unwise world what can human beings do? First, Shaw suggests, they can use their intelligence. Bohun, even in a false nose and goggles, represents the 'terrifying power' of the trained mind, and demonstrates how tragedies may be avoided *in advance* by using intelligence freely; the encouraging presence of the waiter shows how we can avoid giving pain *at the time* by exercising tact and the spirit of acceptance recommended by Shakespeare's *As You Like It* and *What You Will* (*Twelfth Night*); and in Valentine the dentist we are given an example of how to deal with pain *in retrospect*, extracting it with magical ease. He is the only character without a surname and therefore a character without a past.

You Never Can Tell is Shaw's attempt to enact Valentine's philosophy.

Mr Crampton acknowledges '*in sudden dread*' that feeling is 'the only thing that can help us'. But the emotions are dangerous. 'Stop. Youre going to tell me about your feelings, Mr Crampton. Dont,' Bohun interrupts. And Gloria too interrupts Valentine: 'Oh, stop telling me what you feel: I can't bear it.' The sea ('You can imagine that the waves are its breathing, and that it is troubled and stirred to its great depths by some emotion that cannot be described') was used by Shaw to indicate the unconscious feelings and is a remnant from the imagery in *The Lady from the Sea*. But he eliminated much of this imagery from the published version of his play and presents us for the most part with a happy seaside spectacle. And for this, he implies, our response should echo the first two words with which Dolly opens the play after her successful operation in the dentist's chair: 'Thank you.' The dentist's anaesthetic at 'five shillings extra' is Shaw's own numbing of emotion ('I have never felt anything since').

The title, with its Shakespearian associations, summed up most people's reactions to the play. They couldn't tell: and Shaw, perhaps because he flinched from this violation of his own past, was politely unhelpful. There was always hope. 'Cheer up, sir, cheer up . . . You never can tell, sir: you never can tell.'

By 18 May 1896 it was officially finished, though three months later he was still toiling 'to get it ready for the stage'. This stage was the Haymarket Theatre whose 'exceptionally brilliant' management, he told Ellen Terry, 'appear to be making up their minds to ruin themselves with it'. He had designed it for the West End; and the West End had apparently accepted it. On 26 February 1897 a memorandum of agreement was finally signed with Frederick Harrison and the actor-manager Cyril Maude who was to play the waiter in the Haymarket production.

The rehearsals started badly and grew worse. Shaw prowled the theatre getting on everyone's nerves. He was particularly disliked by Alan Aynesworth, a young man who had played Algy in *The Importance of Being Earnest*, and to whom Cyril Maude was anxious to give the lead. Shaw had suspected that the Life Force love scene at the end of Act II was beyond Aynesworth, and now found his suspicions confirmed. At one moment of exasperation Aynesworth turned on Shaw and demanded: 'Let us see you play it yourself.' Shaw sprang up on to the stage and delivered his lines. 'But that,' protested the actor, 'is comedy!' Why had no one told him they were in a comedy? Both of them turned to Cyril Maude who seemed affably paralysed.

After a fortnight Shaw went to Frederick Harrison, the manager of the Haymarket, telling him he must come to the next rehearsal. 'After the rehearsal,' Shaw later recounted, 'Harrison joined us with such a long face that Maude saw it was all up.

'It was a miserable moment: they had been a thoroughly happy family; and my confounded play was going to break it up . . . I rescued them by saying that "we" had better withdraw the play and wait for another opportunity. They were enormously relieved.'

'I don't know how to express my appreciation of the way in which you met us over the withdrawal of your play,' Frederick Harrison wrote to him. Shaw was adept at concealing disappointment. His behaviour was impeccable. But a fear had been planted in him as to whether his plays were unactable. Could any actor play Valentine? 'There is no difficulty about You Never Can Tell,' he told Mrs Mansfield eighteen months later, 'except the difficulty of getting it acted. The end of the second act requires a consummate comedian; and that comedian has never been available.' Only occasionally did he reveal the keenness of his disappointment. 'It maddens me,' he burst out to Ellen Terry. 'I'll have my revenge in the preface by offering it as a frightful example of the result of trying to write for the *théâtre de nos jours.*'

You Never Can Tell was not presented in public for another three years when it was staged at the Strand Theatre. Once again 'the rehearsals lacerated my very soul', and he refused to let it proceed beyond six matinées. He had believed *You Never Can Tell* to be what he later called 'a champion money-maker'. But for eight years it made him almost nothing.

In one respect he was successful. When in 1903 Cyril Maude was writing his history of the Haymarket Theatre, he sent Shaw the chapter dealing with this period and Shaw replied with his own version, written as if from Maude's point of view, which was tipped into the book as Chapter XVI, under the transparent guise of it having been composed by Maude. The narrative describes how Svengali-Shaw hypnotized Aynesworth into confusion over the end of Act II; how he almost caused a divorce between Mr and Mrs Maude; how, using 'a certain superficial reasonableness', he took over the whole business of stage-managership: and then surveyed the wreckage he had created 'with that perfidious air of making the best of everything which never deserted him'. Finally, having unnerved them all, he entered the theatre *in a new suit of clothes* bought in anticipation of the play's royalties.

The burlesque into which he turned his disappointment was a counterpart of the pantomime at the end of the play, and proof that he could dissolve bitterness and grievance into 'lightness of heart'. But it was also evidence of how he excelled at overcoming rather than confronting truth. For the truth was devastating. 'I sincerely hope that you will bring us another comedy presently,' Frederick Harrison had written to him, 'which we can carry to a successful issue.' But for Shaw, now in his early forties, the time for comedy seemed over. He had finished with the stage.

*

You Never Can Tell, the last of Shaw's pleasant plays, advocated lightness of heart; *The Devil's Disciple*, the first of his plays for Puritans, advocated seriousness of instinct. The Life Force which appears in *You Never Can Tell* as a biological current moving mainly through women, changes its course in *The Devil's Disciple* and works politically through the men.

The form of melodrama was suggested by William Terriss, a member of Irving's company who had moved to the Adelphi Theatre, which, by the 1890s, had reached the summit of its glory as the home of melodrama. Terriss himself, now in his fiftieth year, invariably played the hero; his mistress, Jessie Millward, was the heroine; and comic relief came from Harry Nichols. On the afternoon of 7 February 1896, Shaw went to the Adelphi where Terriss informed him that he intended to make a world tour and would like to add to his repertoire a play that should contain 'every "surefire" melodramatic situation' – a series of hair-raising adventures with (between the acts) miraculously unexplained escapes. These would culminate in a hanging that, to preserve the happy ending, turned out to be the nightmare of a sleeping bridegroom shortly before his marriage – the tolling death bell at the hero's execution developing as he woke into a brilliant peal of wedding bells. From Terriss's cupboard of ingredients, why should Shaw not cook up a masterpiece?

Shaw judged the scenario to be not quite 'in my line'. In a letter the following morning, he explained that what Terriss needed for a world tour was not another Adelphi melodrama but 'something like Hamlet – on popular lines'.

That autumn Shaw agreed to have his portrait painted by a Slade School artist, Nellie Heath, and turned the sittings to account by scrawling his play in a series of pocket notebooks. 'The play progresses,' he told Ellen Terry on 16 October 1896, ' . . . such a melodrama! I sit in a little hole of a room off Euston Road on the corner of a table with an easel propped before me so that I can write and be painted at the same time.' It was more than melodrama; it was all the plots of all the melodramas he had ever sat through for the *Saturday Review*. 'The whole character of the piece must be allegorical, idealistic, full of generalisations and moral lessons,' he had written, describing the ideal Adelphi production; 'and it must represent conduct as producing swiftly and certainly on the individual the results which in actual life it only produces on the race in the course of many centuries.' It was in this last concept that Shaw believed there was room for original ideas. The danger was that, attempting simultaneously to exploit and subvert the stage melodrama, he would get trapped within its conventions. 'I finished my play today,' he wrote to Ellen Terry on 30 November, '... but I want your opinion; for I have never tried melodrama before; and this thing, with ... its sobbings & speeches & declamations, may possibly be the most monstrous piece of farcical absurdity that ever made an audience shriek with laughter.'

He had written it round the scene of Dick Dudgeon's arrest 'which had always been floating in my head as a situation for a play' and which had probably floated in from Sydney Carton's heroic sacrifice at the end of *A Tale of Two Cities*. Dickens's novel was regularly dramatized for the Victorian stage which, though it never dared exhibit sexual love, always alleged that love was the motive behind noble action. Like all theatrical heroes, Sydney Carton went to the gallows for the sake of the heroine. Shaw took this situation and gave it another motive. Judith Anderson, who embodies the love motive, concludes that Dick Dudgeon has taken the place of her husband and let himself be arrested 'for my sake'. But Dick Dudgeon, like Hamlet, is a 'tragic figure in black'. He has 'no motive and no interest', and denies acting out of love. Everyone, he tells Judith from prison, could 'rise to some sort of goodness and kindness when they were in love [*the word love comes from him with true Puritan scorn*]. That has taught me to set very little store by the goodness that only comes out red hot. What I did last night, I did in cold blood, caring not half so much for your husband, or [*ruthlessly*] for you [*she droops, stricken*] as I do for myself ... I have been brought up standing by the law of my own nature; and I may not go against it, gallows or no gallows.'

Like Shaw, Dick appears a mountebank, mixing instinctive good manners with the desire to shock by acting *impersonally*. That Shaw recognized himself in Dick can be shown by comparing Dick's prison speech to Judith with a letter Shaw himself wrote over ten years later: 'The only aim that is at all peculiar to me is my disregard of *warm* feelings. They are quite well able to take care of themselves. What I want is a race of men who can be kind in cold blood. Anybody can be kind in emotional moments.'

He placed the action during the American Revolution, and he fixed the date in October 1777 with the surrender of General Burgoyne at Saratoga. This, he implied, like the distant background of Madeira in *You Never Can Tell*, was culturally equivalent to modern Ireland. Shaw's Burgoyne is a fabricated figure through whom the Shavian comedy works best and who, making his entrance in the last act, often steals the show. In *The*

Devil's Disciple (as in his next play, *Caesar and Cleopatra*) Shaw rewrote history and set it on course for the future he wanted. 'What will History say?' Major Swindon asks Burgoyne as he contemplates the defeat of Britain by the Americans. 'History, sir, will tell lies as usual,' Burgoyne assures him. For these schoolroom lies Shaw substitutes a dramatic narrative that eliminates evil and identifies the real enemy of human progress as 'Jobbery and snobbery, incompetence and Red Tape'. The America of 1777 is a man's world full of crude notions that women can see through but do not have the legal or political status to alter.

'The Devil's Disciple has, in truth, a genuine novelty in it,' Shaw later wrote. But he was careful not to let this novelty spoil the story. It is, in that sense, one of the least Shavian of his plays. He took it to Terriss even before it was completely finished. But Terriss's dreams of a world tour had failed and he had no recollection of his arrangement with Shaw. The reading took place at Jessie Millward's flat and was probably, Shaw believed, at her insistence. His account of what happened in some respects resembles his story of reading *Widowers' Houses* to Archer. Terriss 'composed himself dismally' as if Jessie Millward 'had taken him to church', listening in deep perplexity as Shaw plunged into his play. At the climax of the first act, he suddenly interrupted to ask whether 'this is an interior?' Then, a short way into the second act, he again apologetically broke in: 'I beg your pardon: but *is* this an interior?' Shaw's answer, he declared, had set him 'completely at rest'. This seemed to be true, for a few minutes later he uttered a long drawn snore.

After that nothing seemed to go right for *The Devil's Disciple*. 'I think I shall die lonely,' Shaw wrote to Ellen Terry, 'as far as my third acts are concerned.' He still believed that Terriss would be the best person to do it, but on 16 December 1897 Terriss was motivelessly assassinated on the steps of the Adelphi and died in Jessie Millward's arms. So he became 'only a name and a batch of lies in the newspapers', while the history of *The Devil's Disciple*, Shaw told Charrington, 'has given me such practice in hardening my heart that I have lost all human sympathy'.

*

He was not to start another play for fifteen months, when he gave up his drama criticism for the *Saturday Review*. 'What is the matter with the theatre, that a strong man can die of it?' he was to enquire in his Preface to *Three Plays for Puritans*. He had been attracted to the stage by the opportunities it seemed to offer him of overriding his private life with a public career. He wanted to be reborn through his work and use the theatrical world to develop his new identity, fulfilling what he called 'my instinct . . . to turn failure into success'. His rejection by the West End hit the same spot made sensitive by all his early neglect – though this was now a well-bandaged wound. He had looked to the stage for another existence but as Terriss's assassination suggested, the insidious illusion of the theatre flowed out and contaminated ordinary life. 'When we want to read of the deeds that are done for love, whither do we turn? To the murder column: and there we are rarely disappointed.'

There is anger and disgust in Shaw's condemnation. He had entered a paradise of fools where the actor-manager was enthroned as god, the actress as star: and the author was merely its word-carpenter. Everyone, even his friend Archer, insisted that he could not write plays. Yet he persisted. 'Here am I, after 20 years drudging away, at last venturing to tell myself that if I *begin* writing for the stage, I will master the business by the time I am fifty or so,' he wrote to Janet Achurch in the spring of 1896. But the rejection of his last two plays seemed to have cracked this confidence. He had risked prostituting his talent. His thought was far more subtle than his orchestration of it for trumpet and big drum suggests. The rhetoric, the overstatement, the ear-catching tricks, jokes to the gallery, all proceeded from his need to be heard; but they masked what he wanted to say and enabled the public, whose ear he eventually caught, to hear only the voice of an Irish paradoxer who did not mean half of what he said.

Even his sentimental loyalties, it seemed to Shaw, had played him false. He had failed to liberate Ellen Terry from the hypnotic rule of Irving; he had failed to separate Janet Achurch from Charrington or to free her from the dominance of alcohol and morphia; he had failed to make an actress of Florence Farr. In all these endeavours he had sent his plays out to do his work, but the scarcity and poor quality of their performances gave life no chance to imitate the Shavian drama. 'Give up *wanting* to have the plays produced,' he advised another dramatist, 'if you value your happiness as a man and your dignity as an artist.' Early in 1897 he took this advice himself. On being elected a member of the St Pancras Vestry he plunged into local politics, recognizing 'that there is better work to be done in the Vestry than in the theatre'. At about the same time, in another essay at turning failure into success, he decided to publish his plays.

It was not an easy decision. Only two categories of drama were commonly published as books: non-dramatic plays by poets such as Browning and Tennyson; and acting editions, using a good deal of technical stage business.

Towards the end of 1896, one of W. T. Stead's young men, Grant Richards, having set up a new publishing company, offered to become 'publisher in ordinary and publisher extraordinary' of his dramatic works. Shaw replied categorically that 'the public does not read plays'. But

Richards was not put off: 'I went after G.B.S.' He caught up with him after a theatrical first night and together they walked back, Shaw in a baggy Jaeger suit, Richards in evening dress, to Fitzroy Square.

Shaw had been longing for someone to take no notice of him. All his sensible arguments had been taken from others. Richards had borrowed £700 (equivalent to £37,500 in 1997) from his uncle, Grant Allen, and another £700 from his bank, and was now presenting himself to various authors he admired: Wells, Bennett, Chesterton, Masefield, Housman. He was blatantly monocled, had a taste for Monte Carlo, and a charm that reconciled friends to his lack of scruples. Shaw's threats of the Bankruptcy Court left him amiably unruffled. The struggle between them went on through the winter, Shaw resisting, Richards never tiring; and in the spring of 1897 Shaw suddenly succumbed. 'I am being pressed to publish my plays,' he wrote to Ellen Terry. 'I think I will, and give up troubling the theatre.' The decision in some ways reflected his disenchantment with the stage as a place on which to conduct his love affairs. Fifteen months earlier, in a letter to Janet Achurch, he had predicted that if he could not find beautiful women to play his roles, 'then I will do what I am often tempted to do – publish my plays and appeal to the imaginations of those who are capable of reading them without wasting myself on trying to have them performed without utter profanation'. That time had now come.

Richards and Shaw combined well. 'You are the most incompetent publisher I ever heard of,' Shaw told him. And Richards replied: 'You are just about as businesslike a man as I have ever met in my short life.' Shaw seemed to recognize in Richards the sort of 'young villain' that Sonny might have turned into had he remained in Ireland. He had 'allowed himself to fall in Love with Literature', which was tragic in a publisher.

Shaw, Richards acknowledged, was 'the born man of affairs'. In fact it was like an affair of love for Shaw; while for Richards it was an education. 'Make yourself pleasant, no matter what provocation you may get,' Shaw later recommended him, 'and you will not only be doing what you do best usually, but you will be pursuing the only possible policy under the circumstances.' This was roughly how their partnership worked. Shaw ordered him to 'sit tight' and 'trust my judgment'; and Richards complied.

So G.B.S. got to work. He issued injunctions on punctuation (which often indicates where the actor shall breathe), demanded narrow margins, made proposals on pagination, introduced experiments with the title page. He employed lower-case italics in square brackets for stage directions, abolished apostrophes from contracted words and substituted spaced letters for italic in underlined words. He selected a green binding and went in search of the blackest printing ink. He let it be known that a single misprint upset him more than the deaths of his father and his sister 'with whom I was on excellent terms'. He threatened proof corrections on the scale of Balzac and Carlyle ('you may charge me for all corrections over and above 95% of the total cost of production'), and prescribed the price and print run. In short, he enjoyed himself extravagantly.

Shaw's ideas on book design derived from William Morris. He looked at a page as a picture and at a book as an ornament that could be admired by a man who could not read a word of it, 'as a XII century chalice or loving cup may be cherished by a heathen or a teetotaller'. By the end of August 1897, Shaw reported to Richards that he had sent three plays to the printer 'transmogrified beyond recognition, made more thrilling than any novel'. In re-forming these plays for the press Shaw treated the pen and the *viva vox* as different instruments, the one producing a literary language for the eye, the other sounds mainly intelligible to the ear, and each needing separate scoring to blend into an unbroken narrative. To attract the novel-reading public he made it a rule with his stage directions never to mention the stage, proscenium or spectators; to discard all technical expressions and insert plenty of descriptive matter; to give sufficient guidance to the theatre management and information to the actor of *what* but not *how* to act – without spoiling anything for the reader.

Shaw took a further step away from the stage with his Prefaces, which 'have practically nothing to do with the plays'. The Shavian Preface was to be a treatise on the social problems with which the plays were connected. 'Every play, every preface I wrote conveys a message,' he told an interviewer. 'I am the messenger boy of the new age.'

By adding the publication of his plays to his Fabian activities and theatre reviewing, Shaw filled up each day with sixteen hours of work 'that nobody should ever touch after lunch'. He felt exhausted even in the morning. 'I get out of bed so tired that I am in despair until I have braced myself with tubbing,' he told Ellen Terry. 'When I sit down my back gets tired: when I jump up, I get giddy & have to catch hold of something to save myself from falling.' The plays crept through the press with Shaw scanning every item in the proofs.

He had decided to divide the plays into two books, 'Pleasant' and 'Unpleasant'. He began the Unpleasant Plays (*Widowers' Houses*, *The Philanderer* and *Mrs Warren's Profession*) with a Preface, 'Mainly About Myself', which he continued without further title at the beginning of the Pleasant Plays (*Arms and the Man*, *Candida*, *The Man of Destiny* and *You Never Can Tell*). Only *The Devil's Disciple* was laid aside for another volume, *Three Plays for Puritans*.

These first two books were to inaugurate a long series of Shaw's plays in the same format, and change the fashion in play publishing. 'I was as proud as Punch,' declared Grant Richards. 'The look and feel of it gave me intense pleasure. But it did not make me rich.'

Plays Pleasant and Unpleasant were published in April 1898. Archer, in the *Daily Chronicle*, called *Candida* a work of genius, *Mrs Warren's Profession* a masterpiece, *Widowers' Houses* a crude 'prentice work, and *The Philanderer* 'an outrage upon art and decency, for which even my indignation cannot find a printable term of contumely'. Henry Arthur Jones, whose plays Shaw had consistently overpraised in the *Saturday Review*, wrote that 'much of them is not dramatic and would never be interesting in any circumstances to any possible audience'. But the most devastating response came from Shaw's *Saturday Review*:

'The men are all disputative machines, ingeniously constructed, and the women, who, almost without exception, belong to the strange cult of the fountain-pen, are, if anything, rather more self-conscious than the men . . . Mr Shaw is not, as the truly serious dramatist must be, one who loves to study and depict men and women for their own sake, with or without moral purpose. When Mr Shaw is not morally purposeful, he is fantastic and frivolous, and it is then that his plays are good . . . his serious characters are just so many skeletons, which do but dance and grin and rattle their bones. I can hardly wonder that Mr Shaw has so often hesitated about allowing this or that theatrical manager to produce one of his serious plays. To produce one of them really well would be almost impossible at any ordinary theatre.'

This criticism had been composed by Max Beerbohm, and appeared in the same issue of the *Saturday Review* (21 May 1898) in which Shaw, writing his valedictory as the paper's theatre critic, welcomed his successor 'the incomparable Max'. It was a characteristic example of Frank Harris's editing: lazy but provocative. His booming voice awed his staff, from whom he excited the loyalty due to a sea-rover, but by 1898 the 'little old pirate ship', Max Beerbohm wrote to Shaw, was already 'going down into the waves, with you (Admiral of the Moral Fleet) suddenly perceived standing, in full uniform, with folded arms and steadfast eyes, on the bridge; and with me and other respectable people clinging to the rigging'.

Harris was bought out of the *Saturday Review* six months after Shaw left. There had been a number of libel cases and rumours of blackmail – later put down by Shaw to Harris's innocence of English business methods. But though Shaw was to take this mitigating stance, his description of Harris as 'neither first-rate, nor second-rate, nor tenth-rate . . . just his horrible unique self', indicates how much he disliked sharing his professional life with him. His work for the *Saturday Review* had seriously reduced his health and offered little 'to the enormity of my unconscious ambition'. His valedictory shows at what exorbitant human cost he had overcome the poverty, obscurity, ostracism and contempt that infected his Dublin years. 'I have been the slave of the theatre,' he wrote.

'It has tethered me to the mile radius of foul and sooty air which has its centre in the Strand, as a goat is tethered in the little circle of cropped and trampled grass that makes the meadow ashamed. Every week it clamors for its tale of written words; so that I am like a man fighting a windmill: I have hardly time to stagger to my feet from the knock-down blow of one sail, when the next strikes me down . . . Do I receive any spontaneous recognition for the prodigies of skill and industry I lavish on an unworthy institution and a stupid public? Not a bit of it: half my time is spent in telling people what a clever man I am. It is no use merely doing clever things in England . . .

Unfortunately, the building process has been a most painful one to me, because I am congenitally an extremely modest man. Shyness is the form my vanity and self-consciousness take by nature. It is humiliating, too, after making the most dazzling displays of professional ability, to have to tell people how capital it all is. Besides, they get so tired of it, that finally . . . they begin to detest it.

. . . I can never justify to myself the spending of four years on dramatic criticism. I have sworn an oath to endure no more of it. Never again will I cross the threshold of a theatre. The subject is exhausted; and so am I.'

'Now the playwrights may sleep in peace,' observed the actor-manager of the Criterion, Charles Wyndham, 'and the actor may take his forty winks without anxiety.'

SEVEN

I

ST PANCRAS VESTRYMAN

> People think of me as a theatrical man, but I am really proud of having served six years as a municipal councillor.
>
> *New York Times* (24 March 1933)

Fabian progress through the north of England after the success of *Fabian Essays* had been helped by an elderly supporter, Henry Hunt Hutchinson. Crusty and querulous, exuberantly describing his marriage as a penal servitude, he reminded Shaw of Samuel Butler. 'I liked the man,' he decided. But 'Old Hutch' did not much like Shaw. He would alternate with his cheques to the Fabians cantankerous letters complaining of Shaw's rudeness. The Fabian executive, banking the cheques and applauding Old Hutch's public spirit, would deplore his advancing age and infirmity. What would happen, they wondered, to Fabian finances when he died?

In the summer of 1894 they had their answer when Old Hutch shot himself. The Webbs were staying in the Surrey hills, with Shaw and Wallas, when Sidney received a letter informing him that he had been appointed one of Hutchinson's trustees. Old Hutch had been a solicitor and had made a will that was almost certainly invalid. To his wife he bequeathed £100; his two sons and two daughters received smaller bequests; and Fabianism was to benefit, over a period of ten years, by almost £10,000. This money had been left to trustees (of whom Sidney became first Chairman), to be used for 'the propaganda and other purposes' of the Fabian Society 'and its Socialism', and for promoting Fabian goals 'in any way' that the trustees thought 'advisable'. At breakfast the next morning, the Webbs told Shaw and Wallas of their decision to found in London a School of Economics and Political Science, similar to the Massachusetts Institute of Technology or the Ecole Libre des Sciences Politiques, where experts could be specially trained for the purpose of reforming society. Shaw, who believed that Hutchinson had 'left his money for Red propaganda by Red vans', would have preferred using it to enliven Fabian campaigns. Yet it was he who acted as Webb's spokesman and cleverly avoided antagonizing Olivier and Bland, both of whom objected to Webb's plans.

Sidney had to placate the Hutchinson family and the Fabian executive.

He had to win support both from the London County Council and from businessmen by representing his school as an institution with commercial courses, though dedicated (despite its socialist propaganda) to disinterested research. Knowing that disinterested research inevitably led to socialist conclusions, Sidney detected no discrepancy in this – especially since small amounts of the Hutchinson money were to be segregated for the promotion of Fabian lectures and an increase in the secretary's salary. But it was too paradoxical for Shaw. Always scrupulous in financial affairs, he warned Beatrice that Sidney was antagonizing the Fabian executive by what looked like a plan to bribe them in return for permission 'to commit an atrocious malversation of the rest of the bequest'.

As Webb had once frowned on Shaw's individualism, so Shaw now worried over Webb's idealism, fearing that his love for this new invention could cause a break-up in the Fabian family. Nevertheless, for reasons of unity, Shaw reluctantly supported his friend's dream of a centre for sociological research.

So, by means of a suspect will, at variance with anything Old Hutch could have envisaged, and amid a good deal of Fabian grumbling, one of Webb's lasting achievements was begun. 'It is honestly scientific,' Beatrice pronounced after the school had opened in the summer of 1895. And Shaw later admitted that 'Sidney Webb performed miracles with his money which I should never have done'.

*

The London School of Economics became another instrument for long-term permeation (particularly valuable since Lord Salisbury's Tory Government was elected), and for the introduction of collectivism by educationists rather than political partisans. Before their marriage, Beatrice had revealed her doubts as to whether Sidney was 'a really big man' like Chamberlain, but assured him that he might be capable of doing 'first-rate work on the London County Council'. After their marriage she supported his refusal to go into Parliament, partly because she believed that 'the finest part of his mind and character' would be unemployed in the House of Commons, and partly because she recognized in a parliamentary career the 'enemy of domesticity'. They had moved at the end of 1893 to an austere ten-room house at 41 Grosvenor Road on the Embankment. It was a short distance from Spring Gardens, where the London County Council held its meetings, and from Adelphi Terrace, where in 1896 the London School of Economics moved. After his meetings and lectures Sidney would return in the evening to Beatrice's simple meat suppers with cigarettes.

At first sight Shaw's maverick figure does not find a part in the undramatic plans Webb had made for revolution through research. He had refused in 1889 to stand for the London County Council in Deptford – the seat Webb was to win from the Tories three years later. But his experiences in the theatre over the next eight years made him see that it was no longer a grand choice between Parliament and the West End, but a means of combining a limited commitment to municipal politics with a limited success in provincial theatres. Early in 1894 he had refused an invitation to put himself up as the parliamentary candidate for Chelsea; but he stood in the School Board elections at the end of that year for the St Pancras Vestry – and was handsomely defeated. Then, letting his name go forward as a Progressive candidate at an uncontested election in May 1897, he was appointed to the Vestry Committee of Ward 7 of St Pancras, together with an architect, barrister, builder and tea-dealer.

London local government in the 1890s was an 'archaic patchwork' of vestries. The St Pancras Vestry, stretching from Islington to Marylebone and from Holborn to Hampstead and Hornsey, contained almost two hundred thousand inhabitants. Their culture 'may be inferred from the fact that there was not a single bookshop in the entire borough,' Shaw recorded. But it clustered with 'houses of ill-fame', especially in the side streets off Tottenham Court Road (one of which was named Warren Street). And there were slums often owned by landlords like Sartorius and managed by rent-collectors such as Lickcheese.

On behalf of their constituents the vestrymen looked after an elastic range of matters from manure receptacles (maintenance of), horns (blowing of), graves (purchase of) and noxious literature (sale of), to the management of ice cream notices, street cries, the sampling of milk-in-transit and all business involving public baths, lighting, tramways. The strength of local government was planted, Shaw believed, in its independence from Parliament. The St Pancras Vestry had a Chairman and 116 vestrymen. They did not operate under the party system. 'Every member can vote as he thinks best without the slightest risk of throwing his party out of power and bringing on a General Election,' Shaw explained. 'If a motion is defeated, nobody resigns: if it is carried, nobody's position is changed.' Reviewing his six years as a vestryman and borough councillor at the age of eighty, he recalled that 'I never had to vote on any question otherwise than on its specific merits . . .

'in Parliament I should have been a back row chorus man, allowed to amuse the House with a speech occasionally . . . [the] perversion of parliament has produced all the modern dictatorships . . . The little socialism we have is gas and water Socialism. And it is by extension of Gas & Water Socialism that industry will be socialized.'

Shaw's first meeting took place at the Vestry Hall, Pancras Road, on 26 May 1897. He was soon joined by a young Methodist minister named Ensor Walters;

'the vestry, as far as it knew anything about me, classed me as a Socialist and therefore an atheist, sure to differ with the Methodist minister on every question. What actually happened was that he and I immediately formed a party two strong all to ourselves. And we troubled ourselves about no other party . . . He was out to make a little corner for the Kingdom of God in St Pancras; and nothing could have suited me better.'

Shaw served on the Health Committee of which Ensor Walters became Chairman, on the Officers Committee and the Committee for Electricity and Public Lighting. These were three of ten sub-committees which met separately and 'set forth their conclusions as to what the Council ought to do in their departments in a series of resolutions. When the whole Council meets, these strings of resolutions are brought up as the reports of the Committees, and are confirmed or rejected or amended by the general vote.'

This system impressed Shaw as being so sensible that he wondered why parliamentary business should not be conducted on similar lines. He discovered local government, however, to be undermined by two factors: the inadequacy of the men who were elected and the paralysing poverty of the municipalities. His fellow-vestrymen were well-intentioned people but 'absurdly unequal to the magnitude of our task.

'Our ablest leaders were a greengrocer and a bootmaker, both of them much more capable than most members of Parliament; for it needs considerable character and ability to succeed as a shopkeeper, especially as a publican, whereas persons with unearned money enough can easily get into Parliament without having ever succeeded in anything. I found them excellent company, and liked and respected them for their personal qualities . . . but in the effective lump we were as ignorantly helpless politically as the mob of ratepayers who elected us, and who would never have elected me had they had the faintest suspicion of my ultimate political views.'

By their policy of under-rating, these men had by 1900 put the St Pancras Vestry in debt to the bank by £17,000. It was this insolvency that weakened the local authority. A weak vestry, Shaw argued, was at the mercy of its officials and of parliamentary rule. 'He saw in municipal government a valuable decentralizing balance and counter-check to Parliamentary government,' wrote H. M. Geduld. 'It existed to ensure that local necessities were not sacrificed to national interests . . . Unfortunately, Parliamentary government frequently forces its inefficient decisions upon weak municipalities.'

The vestrymen deliberately kept the rates down because they themselves, and the people who had voted for them, could not afford a rating figure that would ensure municipal solvency. Shaw strove unsuccessfully to alter the rating system so as to relieve ordinary ratepayers and arrest reckless overdrawing on the bank. 'There is only one remedy,' he wrote, 'and that is to take the burden off the shoulders of the men who do the work & conduct the business of London, & throw it on to those who take enormous sums in rent and interest out of our business to squander in idleness.' He proposed to do this by the taxation of ground values ('or, as I want it, taxation of unearned incomes'), with a rating exemption limit and a series of abatement limits as in the case of income tax.

The London Government Act of 1899 replaced the forty-two vestries with twenty-eight Metropolitan Boroughs each with a Mayor and Council. Wards 7 and 8 of the old Vestry were amalgamated into the Southern Division of the new St Pancras Borough and ten candidates stood for the six available seats at the election on 1 November 1900. For Shaw (who with 704 votes came second only to a clergyman, beating a bootmaker, removal contractor and store proprietor), this was the one successfully contested political election of his career. He campaigned hard, armed himself against failure ('the relief will be enormous'), and described his success as 'a sentence of hard labor'.

He had opposed the London Government Act in that it disqualified women, who had been part of the vestries, from sitting on the Borough Councils, and he attempted to give publicity to the need for women on public bodies, but *The Times* declined to publish a letter he wrote that threw off 'the customary polite assumption that women are angels'.

'English decency is a . . . string of taboos. You must not mention this: you must not appear conscious of that . . . everything that must not be mentioned in public is mentioned in private as a naughty joke. One day, at a meeting of the Health Committee of the Borough Council of which I was a member, a doctor rose to bring a case before the Committee. It was the case of a woman. The gravity of the case depended on the fact that the woman was pregnant. No sooner had the doctor mentioned this than the whole Committee burst into a roar of laughter, as if the speaker had made a scandalous but irresistible joke. And please bear in mind that we were not schoolboys. We were grave, mostly elderly men, fathers of families . . . There is only one absolutely certain and final preventive for such indecency, and that is the presence of women. If there were no other argument for giving women the vote, I would support it myself on no other ground than that men will not behave themselves when women are not present.'

In the Borough of St Pancras women had two unmentionable grievances: first, there were few public lavatories for them; secondly, where these had been provided they necessarily consisted not of urinals but separate closets, entrance to which traditionally cost one penny – 'an absolutely prohibitive charge for a poor woman'. The grotesque struggle for free lavatories raged for years, and with particular heat round a site in Camden High Road. Some councillors objected that persons who so far 'forgot their sex' did not deserve a lavatory; one suggested that the water supply would be used by flower girls to wash the violets that he occasionally purchased for his buttonhole. The site was also assailed as a terror to traffic and a feature so gross as to contaminate the value of all property in the neighbourhood.

It is not easy to chronicle Shaw's work as a vestryman and borough councillor. Fearing that his own proposals might not be listened to seriously, he often filtered them through other councillors. Nevertheless, a pattern to his municipal work can be picked out. He voted in favour of more free time for workers employed by the Council (every other Sunday off instead of every third Sunday for lavatory attendants) and for trams against underground railways in the interests of shopkeepers; and he introduced a motion to raise the salaries of the Council's clerical staff by means of promotion through independent tests of their qualifications. After St Pancras became a metropolitan borough, the Chairman of the Vestry was translated into a Mayor. The Vestry Chairman had been unpaid, and the first Mayor of St Pancras, Alderman Barnes, proposed continuing this magnanimous tradition. Shaw objected, warning the Council against making a new precedent:

'It was, of course, very handsome of Mr Barnes to say he would not accept any salary, but at the same time a definite sum of money ought to be placed at his disposal . . . He [Shaw] moved that this question of the paying of the Mayor be adjourned for further consideration, because it would not be a proper or democratic thing to pass a resolution that might prevent a poor man accepting the office of Mayor.'

Shaw's motion was defeated, but when in 1903 the Council appointed as their second mayor W. H. Matthews, a greengrocer (and the model for Bill Collins in *Getting Married*), the matter of a salary was again discussed,

£200 a year being proposed. Shaw made a strong speech, emphasizing that 'it was quite legal to pay the Mayor, and no other method would place every man there on a footing of absolute equality.

'But 200 pounds a year was a ridiculous sum; he would multiply it by five. There was no sounder democratic principle than that a man should be paid for public services. At present in that Council when they wanted a man to be Mayor they had first to find out if he could afford it.'

But he was again outvoted and the office of Mayor continued unsalaried.

Shaw annoyed his fellow-councillors by a persistent campaign against badges of office, regalia and robes that converted the St Pancras aldermen into 'animated pillar boxes'. Were not such grandiose uniforms an obvious misuse of public money? Even on issues he supported Shaw looked carefully at expenditure. When the Mayor proposed spending £40 to send a delegation of councillors rambling into the countryside to report on the public installation of a crematorium in St Pancras, Shaw intervened to say that he

'sometimes spent his week-ends near Woking, and if they would lend him a councillor for the purposes of cremation (much laughter) he would bring up a report of all that happened (laughter) without cost to anyone (laughter)'.

Shaw's advocacy of cremation was part of a campaign for public hygiene he pursued on the Health Committee. He urged that 'if earth-to-earth burial was to be continued, the depth below the surface ought not to be more than a couple of inches, and the coffin of the flimsiest material it was possible to have'. As a member of this committee he visited work-houses, hospitals, sweatshops and the homes of the poor, and saw the destitution and disease. Many of the tenements were lice-ridden; there were epidemics of smallpox, and occasional cases of typhoid fever, and even bubonic plague. Houses were disinfected with sulphur candles, on the fumes of which pathogenic bacilli actually multiplied. On asking the Medical Officer of Health why ratepayers' money was spent on a useless fumigant, Shaw was told that, though the real disinfectants were soap, water and sunshine, no stripper or cleaner would dare enter an infected house unless it was filled with the superstitious stink of sulphur.

Shaw accepted sulphur but not vaccination which, he believed, was seen as a cheap prophylactic and employed as an alternative to a decent housing programme. During the spread of smallpox in 1901 Shaw battled with the medical advisers in St Pancras, who were urging on the Council a compulsory vaccination scheme. But he found limited support from the Borough Medical Officer, Dr Sykes. The difference was one of private practice versus socialized medicine. The Council paid half a crown for each revaccination. 'No doubt the doctors were honestly convinced that vaccination is harmless and prevents smallpox; but the half-crown had more to do with that honest conviction than an unbiased scientific study of the subject.'

Dr Sykes's position was dependent on the good health of the district – it was what Shaw called 'the position that one wants Socialism to place all doctors in'. He could be dismissed only by the Local Government Board which judged his efficiency by the health statistics.

'Dr Sykes's income did not get larger when the district got sick. The private practitioners' did . . . you could see the private practitioners getting new ties and new hats. When the death-rate went up they always looked better off and happier. That was not the case with the medical officer of health: he looked more worried: it was a bad time for him.'

What he heard passed in Council convinced Shaw that medical opinion was often little more than a conspiracy to exploit public credulity. Over two years, in a series of what were called 'curious pathological effusions' to *The Times*, the *British Medical Journal*, the *Saturday Review* and *Vaccination Inquirer*, he pressed for an independent re-examination of statistics, and for a socialized health service as a replacement to the money motive in medicine.

Shaw treated the press as a democratic instrument through which he poured information and advice to the public and from which he hoped to get instructions formed by that advice. The principles by which he tried to reach a workmanlike relationship with voters are revealed by some remarks he made to vestrymen and borough councillors. 'Never do anything for the public that the public would do for themselves,' he told them. And: 'Give the public not what they want but what they ought to want and dont.' It was the responsibility of councillors and Members of Parliament to persuade the public to want what was best in the long term.

What Shaw wanted was to command political action without the horror of submerging himself in political life. The need to earn money from his other work made it impossible for him to attend all meetings. Of the possible 321 council and sub-committee meetings he was eligible to attend between November 1900 and September 1903, he turned up at 192.

In public, Shaw's attitude to his municipal duties was one of undisguised optimism – which is to say, disguised pessimism: 'I love the reality of the

Vestry,' he told Ellen Terry, ' . . . after the silly visionary fashion-ridden theatres.' But that had been at the start of his vestry duties. An almanac Shaw kept in the early spring of 1898 shows under what strain this municipal work, with its hours of talk (no less fashion-ridden than the theatre) 'about our dignity & respectability', was beginning to place him. 'Vestry beyond all endurance,' he recorded on 30 March.

Shaw was to use his experience in local politics as raw material for his plays. Of *Man and Superman* he wrote: 'The mornings I gave to it were followed by afternoons & evenings spent in the committee rooms of a London Borough Council, fighting questions of drainage, paving, lighting, rates, clerk's salaries.' Such occupation, he maintained, had enabled him to create realistic dramas so unrecognized in the fashionable London theatre that critics believed them to be fantastical – in fact not plays at all. But what are the picturesque tramps of the Sierra Nevada doing at the opening of 'Don Juan in Hell' but holding a St Pancras Vestry meeting? Who are the municipal characters in *Getting Married* but the aldermen and borough councillors with whom Shaw had sat those long unventilated hours? And where do the conflicting opinions of the medical specialists in *The Doctor's Dilemma* come from but the Health Sub-Committee? All this he took from St Pancras; and if he gave back no dramatic triumphs of municipal legislation, he presented it with a theatre of entertainment.

After half a dozen years, Shaw concluded that the theatre, after all, was a vehicle for social and cultural change better suited to his abilities. Shortly before his fiftieth year, he 'faded out of vestrydom having,' he wrote, 'more important work'.

In a speech supporting Alderman Matthews as Mayor of St Pancras, Shaw gave an oblique notice of his retirement from local politics, in the parentheses of which we may hear that 'universal laughter' drowning Tanner's words at the end of *Man and Superman*.

'Councillor G. Bernard Shaw was glad, speaking from the Progressive part of the chamber, to support the nomination of Alderman Matthews, although it was difficult for them to realize the extent of his (the speaker's) self-sacrifice in taking that course (laughter) . . . He regarded him as a respectable gentleman (laughter), with little to say and with no political opinions whatever (much laughter). He never was more astonished than when Mr Matthews was out of the chair, because then he found him an active politician with a great deal to say for himself (laughter). In the chair he was most admirable and orderly, out of it he was the most disorderly man he had ever met (laughter). His (the speaker's) self-sacrifice he told them was very great, because he wanted to be the man for Mayor (laughter). He had looked forward to the time very fondly when he would find his life crowned by becoming Mayor of St Pancras (laughter). He had carefully calculated the number of years it would take him to get it, and came to the conclusion that when all the Aldermen of the present Council, all the chairmen of the old Vestry, and some of the more prominent Councillors, had their turn, that the number of years would be 22 (laughter). That was the prospect before him (laughter), and thus it would come to pass that in the year 1924 an old man, with white hair, dim of sight, and hard of hearing, would be elected Mayor of St Pancras and would pass up the Council chamber to the chair amid encouraging cries of 'Good old Shaw!' and sympathetic murmurs of 'Poor old chap!' (laughter). Having said that, he had now to say that nobody supported the nomination of Alderman Matthews more heartily than himself (applause) . . . He (the speaker) had spent the greater part of the preceding day with Sir James Hoyle, the Lord Mayor of Manchester, who like their out-going Mayor, Councillor Barnes, had become a distinguished public man in connection with education. They had a technical school in connection with the City Council of Manchester . . . on the school was spent 30,000 pounds a year out of the rates. The population was not more than twice as large as St Pancras, where they had not the courage to make sufficient rates to cover their liabilities. As time went on he hoped their ideals would expand, and instead of trying to resist the County Council they should enter into competition with it, and try as far as they could to take this part of London off their hands. In the name of the Progressives he supported the nomination from that intellectual part of the Council chamber (laughter and applause).'

2

COURTSHIP DANCES

> His sensuality has all drifted into sexual vanity – delight in being the candle to the moths – with a dash of intellectual curiosity to give flavour to his tickled vanity. And he is mistaken if he thinks that it does not affect his artistic work. His incompleteness as a thinker, his shallow and vulgar view of many human relationships . . . all these defects come largely from the flippant and worthless self-complacency brought about by the worship of rather second-rate women . . . Whether I like him, admire him or despise him most I do not know.
>
> *The Diary of Beatrice Webb* (8 May 1897)

If Shaw could settle down to marriage as she and Sidney had done,

Beatrice Webb felt certain she would come to like him better. Already, almost in spite of himself, she was beginning to see 'a sort of affectionateness' beneath his layer of vanity. He was so extraordinarily good-natured, spending days over Sidney's and her *Industrial Democracy* and *Problems of Modern Industry*. His method, which turned everything inside out to see whether the other side wouldn't do as well, was genuinely interesting. 'If only he would concentrate his really brilliant intellect on some consecutive thought.'

Shaw was seeing a good deal of the Webbs in the mid-1890s. But this was different from his previous triangular relationships. He could not flirt with Beatrice and retain his friendship with Sidney; and so he could not flirt. He felt painfully excluded watching them petting each other as if, he noted, they were still honeymooning. 'I – I, George Bernard Shaw – have actually suffered from something which in anyone else I should call unhappiness.' His body ached for 'a moment of really sacred intimacy'. He was physically attracted to Beatrice and sensed that she found him attractive, in much the same hostile way as Judith Anderson in *The Devil's Disciple* is unconsciously drawn to Dick Dudgeon. Feeling her embarrassment, her antipathy, he also felt the strain of all that was unspoken between them rising to 'a perfectly devilish intensity'.

What he was witnessing in the Webbs' marriage was the merging of passion into a shared obsession for work. That was a marriage he could understand. But could he ever make such a partnership for himself? Beatrice decided to find out.

Bertha Newcombe looked a good candidate. That she was Fabian was essential; that she was 'lady-like' no disadvantage; and that she was 'not wholly inartistic' an unlooked-for bonus. She was in her thirties and, despite her aquiline features, thin lips and a figure that put Beatrice in mind of a wizened child, not perhaps lacking absolutely in all attraction. At least she was quite smartly turned out, *petite* and dark, with neat, heavily fringed black hair. And she was devoted to Shaw.

He had sat to Bertha for his portrait as early as 1892. She had painted him as the platform spellbinder, full-length, hand-on-hip, his mouth slightly open as if uttering one of his formidable ripostes, his red-gold hair and Irish blue eyes adding to the impression of easy confidence – 'a powerful picture,' Beatrice decided, 'in which the love of the woman had given genius to the artist'.

She had painted him as a spellbinder, then fallen under his spell. Later, while he was writing *The Man of Destiny*, lying in a field with his fountain pen and a notebook, she painted him again: *A Snake in the Grass*. He had not deceived her, but he had bewitched her. He was so easy, delightful; almost intimate, though not quite. Not understanding him, she complained that he did not understand her, and doubted whether he had the gift of sympathetic penetration into any woman's nature.

He seems to have liked her, but was protected from deeper involvement by her obvious obsession with him. It was an obsession he helped to rouse. He had told her of his adoration for Ellen Terry and introduced her to Janet Achurch – 'the wonderful woman who absorbed Shaw's leisure to an extent of which I was only half-conscious'. He also joked about Beatrice Webb's zeal to see him married. Though he felt the power and pleasure of love, he was determined never to repeat his experiences with Jenny Patterson.

Bertha sensed the latent passion that Jenny Patterson had aroused in him, but she could not reach it herself. Her love awoke his apprehensions. 'The sight of a woman deeply in love with him annoyed him,' Bertha commented.

'Unfortunately on my side there was a deep feeling most injudiciously displayed . . . I realize how exasperating it must have been to him. He had decided I think on a line of honourable conduct – honourable to his thinking. He kept strictly to the letter of it while allowing himself every opportunity of transgressing the spirit. Frequent talking, talking, talking of the pros and cons of marriage, even to my prospects of money or the want of it, his dislike of the sexual relation & so on, would create an atmosphere of love-making without any need for caresses and endearments.'

What she did not see was that his talk was a method of testing her strength. Everyone was recommending him to marry Bertha. But were they really well-matched? If he married it must be to someone whose love was threaded with shared interests. Bertha and he could never be useful partners like the Webbs. 'She ought to marry someone else,' he told Janet.

'She is only wasting her affections on me. I give her nothing; and I do not even take everything – in fact I dont take anything, which makes her most miserable . . . she would like to tie me like a pet dog to the leg of her easel & have me always to make love to her when she is tired of painting . . . I wish somebody could come along & marry her before she worries herself into a state of brokenheartedness.'

Shaw's campaign to steer Bertha away from 'this lunacy of hers' employed every means except one: he could not absent himself from her infelicity. 'Heavens! I had forgotten you – totally forgotten you,' he reminded her. He would not let her alone. In desperation she wrote to

Beatrice who, on Shaw's instructions, had stopped inviting them together to the Fabian countryside. For five years Bertha had been loyally devoted to Shaw. She had endured rumours of flirtations, largely because she knew that Beatrice was counselling him to marry her. Now she was dismayed to hear that Beatrice was encouraging him to marry someone else. Why?

Beatrice came to the dark wainscoted studio in Cheyne Walk to give her answer. So long as there had seemed a chance of marriage she had welcomed her as Shaw's prospective wife. But now she realized he would never marry her she had backed out of the affair. As Beatrice proceeded with her explanation, Bertha's small face seemed to shrink; and, remembering perhaps her own pain over Chamberlain, Beatrice suddenly raged against Shaw. 'You are well out of it, Miss Newcombe,' she said. '... You know my opinion of him – as a friend and a colleague, as a critic and literary worker, there are few men for whom I have so warm a liking – but in his relations with women he is vulgar – if not worse.'

'It is so horribly lonely,' Bertha answered. 'I daresay it is more peaceful than being kept on the rack – but it is like the peace of death.'

Partly because of the inconclusive nature of their romance, Bertha was never at peace over Shaw. She remained at Cheyne Walk and never married. By 1909, having taken the post of Honorary Secretary of the Civic and Dramatic Guild, she found herself responsible for the private production of his *Press Cuttings*. They met; he read her this 'ghastly absurdity', then went home to write her a letter.

'I expected to find a broken hearted, prematurely aged woman: I found an exceedingly smart lady, not an hour older, noting with a triumphant gleam in her eye my white hairs and lined face. When I think that I allowed those brutal letters to hurt me – ME – Bernard Shaw!! Are you not ashamed?'

But Shaw's teasing, even when intended to be supportive, never amused Bertha. The following month they were quarrelling and she was calling him a 'villain'.

'It is far better that I should again efface myself for another 11 years. Possibly we may all die before then ... Do you still continue to think of yourself as an idol for adoring women? That idol was shattered for me years ago – – – Inadvertently when you mention the care that has been taken of you, you touch upon the lasting grievance.'

And her grievance did last. A World War came and went. Bertha was approaching sixty, approaching seventy; and still it lasted. 'B[ertha] *wont* accept the situation,' Shaw protested to Charrington, who had taken the part of go-between, '... [it] is beyond human patience.' He tried to present himself as unappealing, but could not resist the paradoxical flourish, the shattering joke – then would recover himself, too late. 'I am still the same writing speaking machine you know of old,' he assured her in 1922.

'I am in my 66th year; my hair is white, and I am as heartless a brute as ever ... women adore me more, and are less ashamed of it than when you painted The Snake in the Grass. Hearts can be heard breaking in all directions like china in the hands of a clumsy housemaid ... You have my books – the best of me.'

It was not enough, the shattered idol and the broken china. From such debris it had once seemed possible to piece together something valuable. But their correspondence, reviving past expectations, tormented Bertha with these ruined images, and much of it she destroyed. 'Your memories terrify me,' Shaw wrote to her in 1925. 'Thank God there will be no letters.'

That was their future.

So Beatrice Webb rose to go. 'Come and see me,' she told Bertha, ' – someday.' There seemed nothing else to say. She kissed her on the forehead and escaped downstairs. 'I doubt,' she confided in her diary, 'whether Bernard Shaw could be induced to marry.'

*

But it was Beatrice who had inadvertently put an end to Shaw's interest in Bertha. At a luncheon party in the early autumn of 1895 she and Sidney had met an Irish lady named Charlotte Payne-Townshend, 'a large graceful woman with masses of chocolate brown hair,' Beatrice later described her. 'She dresses well, in flowing white evening robes she approaches beauty. At moments she is plain.

'By temperament she is an anarchist, feeling any regulation or rule intolerable, a tendency which has been exaggerated by her irresponsible wealth. She is romantic but thinks herself cynical. She is a Socialist and a Radical, not because she understands the Collectivist standpoint, but because she is by nature a rebel ... She is fond of men and impatient of most women, bitterly resents her enforced celibacy but thinks she could not tolerate the matter-of-fact side of marriage. Sweet tempered, sympathetic and

1 Vandeleur Lee, with Shaw's mother on his right and Shaw's father behind on his left

2 Lucinda Elizabeth ('Bessie') Shaw

3 George Carr Shaw

4 Bernard Shaw, aged nineteen, c. 1875

5 Jenny Patterson

6 Alice Lockett

7 Shaw, 1891

8 Charlotte Payne-Townsend, shortly before her marriage, 1898

9 Elizabeth Robins,
aged twenty-nine, 1891

10 William Archer, c. 1900

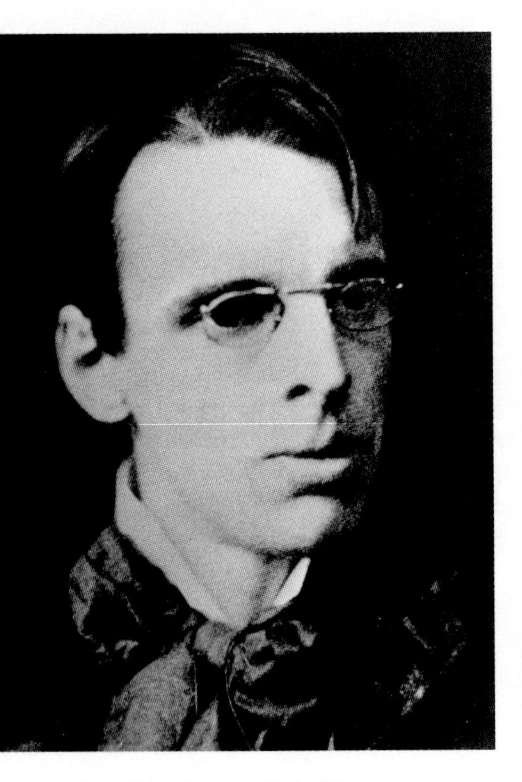

11 W. B. Yeats, mid 1890s

12 Florence Farr, 1890

genuinely anxious to increase the world's enjoyment and diminish the world's pain.'

Beatrice interested Charlotte in the London School of Economics, and was rewarded with a subscription of £1,000 for the library and the endowment of a woman's scholarship. Charlotte also agreed, at a rent and service charge of £300 a year, to take rooms on the two upper floors above the School when, in October 1896, it moved to 10 Adelphi Terrace. Beatrice soon began to absorb her 'into our little set of comrades', nominating her for the Fabian Society, with a note to the secretary that the amount of her cheque testified to the degree of her convictions.

Shaw was introduced to her on 29 January 1896. She noted the event without comment; and he did not go two months later to her At Home at LSE. But he was apparently 'prepared to take my part' in a plan Beatrice had formed to marry Charlotte off to Graham Wallas. In the late summer of 1896 the Webbs rented a Spartan rectory at the village of Stratford St Andrew in Suffolk; and Wallas and Charlotte were invited. Shaw was there as a matter of course. Everything seemed in train for a satisfactory Fabian match.

But Wallas, who left early, arrived four days late; and in those four days the pantomime ostrich spread before Charlotte his most brilliant plumage. They were constant companions, pedaling round the country all day, sitting up late at night talking. 'They are, I gather from him, on very confidential terms,' Beatrice noted in her diary, 'and have "explained" their relative positions . . . I am somewhat uneasy.'

*

'I had a perfectly hellish childhood and youth . . .' There was much in what Charlotte said about herself to interest Shaw. She was six months younger than he and her family came from County Cork; at least her father's did. Horace Townsend had been 'a marvel of patience'. Charlotte, who 'was always attracted to men of action', longed for him to assert himself. It was astonishing how his gentleness provoked everyone – especially his wife, a domineering English lady fretted by social ambitions. She got hold of him, hyphenated and then aspirated his name, dug him up from Rosscarbery. If only he had quelled her. But she 'could not bear opposition; if it was offered she either became quite violent or she cried.'

Early in February 1885 Horace decided to die. There was nothing much wrong with him and he was comparatively young. But his patience had given out, and for a polite man there was nothing else to do.

His wife was incredulous, but Charlotte understood. She understood that her mother had killed him – not legally, of course, but in fact. By everything she now did she sought to avenge his death. Her mother had one ambition left: to see her two daughters brilliantly married. Charlotte refused to give her mother that satisfaction. 'Even in my earliest years I had determined I would never marry.'

Mother and daughter were determined women. In a furious dance they struggled across Europe, always in 'the best circles' and seldom anywhere for more than a week. Inevitably Charlotte blundered into offers of marriage. J. S. Black proposed in 'as few words as I can' in a note from his club; Count Sponnek declared himself in South Kensington and, being rebuffed, rushed off in an emotional state to St Petersburg; Finch Hutton sent her the skin of a bear shot in Wyoming and twelve dressed beaver skins: but 'I cannot marry you,' Charlotte replied; Herbert Oakley, a barrister, died before completing his case; the wife of Arthur Smith-Barry also died, leaving Arthur Smith-Barry wondering whether Charlotte would take her place. She didn't. And there were others. Majors and Generals and Major-Generals. Mrs Payne-Townshend watched them all, her hopes pumping up and down. The hatred between the two women was by now 'almost a tangible thing'. For the first time in her life Mrs Payne-Townshend was not going to get her own way. She felt ill. A doctor was called but he could find nothing wrong with her except 'nerves'. A few days later she died. 'It is really awful to think how glad I was,' Charlotte admitted.

She was thirty-four and at last free. For the first time in her life she allowed herself to fall in love. Dr Axel Munthe, hypnotist and story-teller, caught her in the immense web of his vanity and left her there. Extricating herself had been painful, and it was then that she had flown into the Webbs' parlour.

Graham Wallas arrived, bored Charlotte, then left. Shaw and she resumed their companionship.

'If the walls of this simple-minded rectory could only describe the games they have witnessed, the parson would move, horror-stricken, to another house,' he wrote to Janet Achurch.

'We have made many bicycling expeditions together *à deux*. Also, instead of going to bed at ten, we go out and stroll about among the trees for a while. She, being also Irish, does not succumb to my arts as the unsuspecting and literal Englishwoman does; but we get on together all the better, repairing bicycles, talking philosophy and religion and Shaw table talk, or, when we are in a mischievous or sentimental humor, philandering shamelessly and outrageously. Such is life at Stratford St Andrew.'

The loneliness and irritation Shaw had felt at watching the Webbs caressing each other evaporated. Falling out of love with actresses, he was suddenly able to make them an audience for his own romantic play-acting opposite this 'Irish lady with the light green eyes and the million of money'. 'I am going to refresh my heart by falling in love with her,' he announced to Ellen Terry, ' . . . but, mind, only with her, not with the million; so someone else must marry her if she can stand him after me.' It *was* play-acting. What else could it be? They were genuinely fond of each other, but Charlotte was no slave to romance and 'she doesnt really *love* me'. Kissing in the evening among the trees was very pleasant, but 'She knows the value of her unencumbered independence, having suffered a good deal from family bonds & conventionality before the death of her mother & the marriage of her sister left her free,' Shaw confided to Ellen Terry. 'The idea of tying herself up again by a marriage before she knows anything – before she has exploited her freedom & money power to the utmost – seems to her intellect to be unbearably foolish.'

He liked her honesty; he liked her involvement with the political side of his life; and he liked her independence. 'You don't love me the least bit in the world,' he informed her. 'But I am all the more grateful.'

Watching them uneasily over these weeks at Stratford St Andrew, Beatrice reached a different conclusion. 'These warmhearted unmarried women of a certain age are audacious and almost childishly reckless of consequences.'

*

On 17 September, Shaw and Charlotte, Sidney and Beatrice, ascended their machines and wheeled off back to London, which they reached in pouring rain four days later. Shaw was immediately engulfed in business. There was time for only the most tantalizing note to Charlotte who missed him and rather miserably told him so. 'You look as if you had returned to your old amusement of eating your heart,' he reproved her, remembering Axel Munthe. ' . . . you must get something to do: I have a mind to go upstairs & shake you, only then I should lose my train.'

He was determined that she must remain strong. 'Don't fall in love: be your own, not mine or anyone else's.

'From the moment that you can't do without me, you're lost, like Bertha. Never fear: if we want one another we shall find it out. All I know is that you made the autumn very happy, and that I shall always be fond of you for that. About the future . . . let us do what lies to our hands & wait for events. My dearest!'

Fearing that she was falling in love with him, Charlotte suddenly left for Ireland. Shaw felt nonplussed: he was unused to people taking his advice. The kick of his disappointment took him aback. She had surpassed his expectations. He began by welcoming her journey ('I had rather you were well a thousand miles away than ill in my wretched arms'), then complained of her removal ('oh for ten minutes peace in the moonlight at Stratford! . . . keep me deep in your heart . . . I wish I were with you among those hills'). But his eloquence and even his teasing seemed to lose itself in her absence.

On the day before Charlotte's return from Ireland, he sent her an exactly truthful letter. 'I will contrive to see you somehow, at all hazards,' he wrote: 'I *must*; and that "must" which "rather alarms" you, TERRIFIES me.

'If it were possible to run away – if it would do any good – I'd do it; so mortally afraid am I that my trifling & lying and ingrained treachery and levity with women are going to make you miserable when my whole sane desire is to make you hap – I mean strong and self possessed and tranquil. However, we must talk about it . . . let's meet, meet, meet, meet, meet: bless me! how I should like to see you again for pure *liking*; for there is something between us . . .'

He saw her the night she returned. For hours beforehand he had felt curiously agitated. Then they were together and 'I really was happy . . . I am satisfied, satisfied, satisfied deep in my heart.' He had found with Charlotte a real friendliness mixed with some sexual interest. But that sexual interest put a faint shadow over his happiness. 'I wish there was nothing to look forward to,' he wrote to her later that night, 'nothing to covet, nothing to gain.' What he actually feared was that there was something to lose. Charlotte, he had told Ellen Terry, 'knows that what she lacks is physical experience, and that without it she will be in ten years time an old maid'. But he could not stay away from Adelphi Terrace. He came – 'and now, dear Ellen,' he confided, 'she sleeps like a child, and her arms will be plump, and she is a free woman, and it has not cost her half a farthing, and she has fancied herself in love, and known secretly that she was only taking a prescription, and been relieved to find the lover at last laughing at her & reading her thoughts and confessing himself a mere bottle of nerve medicine, and riding gaily off'.

Often before Shaw had implored women to *use* him. 'All my love affairs end tragically because the women *can't* use me.' Charlotte had used him and 'in the blackest depths' he felt robbed of 'that most blessed of things – unsatisfied desire'. From this desire he conceived the make-believe of his plays. Now, he told Charlotte, 'I have squandered on you all the material out of which my illusions are made'. Once again Charlotte had confounded his expectations. Prim and socially self-effacing, she could take off her inhibitions once she selected a man for intimacy. It was one of those 'volcanic tendencies' Beatrice had detected in her.

Charlotte had an apprehension of sexual intercourse, deriving from what Shaw later described as 'a morbid horror of maternity'. She was in her fortieth year and 'there was never any question of breeding'. Over the next eighteen months they seem to have found together a habit of careful sexual experience, reducing for her the risk of conception and preserving for him his subliminal illusions. To such muted sexuality Shaw could give assent. 'ALL CLEAR NOW YES A THOUSAND TIMES,' he had cabled Charlotte in October. That autumn too he started to terminate his relationship with Bertha Newcombe; blow away Ellen Terry's daydreams of becoming his mother-in-law; renounce retrospectively 'spiritual intercourse' with Florence Farr; and tell Janet Achurch that her maternity had made her 'stark raving mad'. Then, turning back to Charlotte he resumed his intrepid *doubles entendres*: 'Cold much worse – fatal consummation highly probable. Shall see you tonight . . . What an exacting woman you are! Is this freedom?'

*

Charlotte soon made herself almost indispensable to Shaw. She learnt to read his shorthand and to type, took dictation and helped him prepare his plays for the press. Her flat above the London School of Economics became 'very convenient for me' – more convenient than Fitzroy Square. There was no question of turning up there at any time in the casual way he had dropped in on Jenny Patterson, Janet Achurch, Florence Farr and others. He would invite her to theatres and picture galleries; and she invited him to lunch or dinner, seeing to it that her cook became expert in vegetarian dishes. There were interruptions: his migraines, her neuralgia; his work, her journeys. And there was a momentary crisis when she threatened to buy a poodle – which drew from him the panicky suggestion that she 'have (or hire) a baby' instead. In a spirit of compromise she attended lectures at the School of Medicine for Women.

Between April and June 1897 Charlotte shared with Sidney and Beatrice the expenses of a pretty cottage called Lotus on the North Downs, near Dorking. Shaw went down as frequently as he could. But he had less time than at Stratford the previous year – 'tired and careworn' he described himself. But the Webbs were in excellent working form. The sun streamed through the dancing leaves and they revelled, almost childlike with excitement, in the economic characteristics of Trade Unionism; while Charlotte sat upstairs miserably typewriting *Plays Unpleasant*, and the playwright himself strode the garden forming his Dramatic Opinions. Beatrice watched with concern. It was obvious that Charlotte was deeply attached to Shaw, but 'I see no sign on his side of the growth of any genuine and steadfast affection,' she noted.

Though she found everything 'very interesting', Charlotte could take only a modest part in what Shaw called 'our eternal political shop'. On Sundays they enlisted a stream of visitors – young radicals, mostly: William Pember Reeves and his wife Maud; Bertrand and Alys Russell; Herbert Samuel; Charles Trevelyan; Graham Wallas – and Charlotte sometimes felt excluded. She hung on, but her face showed at times 'a blank haggard look'. Beatrice felt that Shaw must share her own irritation at Charlotte's lack of purpose. 'If she would set to – and do even the smallest and least considerable task of intellectual work – I believe she could retain his interest and perhaps develop his feeling for her.'

Charlotte struggled to make an occupation out of Shaw's work. On Sundays in London she had made her way to the dock gates and street corners to hear him speak. But these experiences mortified her. She hated the roughness of the crowds. 'It appears that my demagogic denunciations of the idle rich – my demands for taxation of unearned incomes – lacerate her conscience; for she has great possessions. What am I to do: she won't stay away; and I can't talk Primrose League. Was there ever such a situation?'

Although the author of *The Philanderer* believed it was better for 'two people who do not mean to devote themselves to a regular domestic, nursery career to maintain a clandestine connection than to run the risks of marriage', Charlotte was surprised to find that his advice to women was to 'insist on marriage, and refuse to compromise themselves with any man on cheaper terms'. He considered the status of a married woman as 'almost indispensable under existing circumstances to a woman's fullest possible freedom.

'In short, I prescribed marriage for women, and refused it for myself. I upset her ideas in many directions; for she was prepared for conventional unconventionality, but not for a criticism of it as severe as its own criticism of conventionality.'

Within this argument seems to lie the biological politics that were to vitalize *Man and Superman*. In fact the philosophy of this play was one of the 'illusions' that Shaw substituted for actual experience. For Charlotte did not want marriage in order to have children; she was beginning to want it as a partnership that, though different from the Webbs', would be no less satisfactory. At that level Shaw had little to say. Eventually she began to run out of patience with him.

Charlotte had surprised Shaw before by taking his advice. Now, she attempted to do so again. If it was her job to marry, he would not object to her making the proposal. This it seems is what she attempted to do in the second week of July 1897. Shaw described the scene as 'a sort of earthquake'. He received the golden moment, he told Ellen Terry, 'with shuddering horror & wildly asked the fare to Australia'. This description, given a fortnight after the event, is a good example of the replacement of 'Shaw Limited' by 'G.B.S.'. Pain, regret, tenderness are dissolved in the triumphant playing of a Shavian scherzo. 'I have an iron ring round my chest, which tightens and grips my heart when I remember that you are perhaps still tormented,' he wrote to her the day after the proposal.

'Loosen it, oh ever dear to me, by a word to say that you slept well and have never been better than today. Or else lend me my fare to Australia, to Siberia, to the mountains of the moon, to any place where I can torment nobody but myself. I am sorry – not vainly sorry; for I have done a good morning's work, but painfully, wistfully, affectionately sorry that you were hurt; but if you had seen my mind you would not have been hurt . . . Write me something happy, but only a few words, and don't sit down to *think* over them.'

She was rich, he was poor. Marriage for property, he had written, was prostitution; to marry her would be the act of an adventurer. This financial scruple had the advantage of being kindly; it was not a *personal* rejection. Yet it was a prevarication, and did not protect Charlotte from being 'inexpressibly taken aback'. It was absurd for him to turn his back on a richer woman simply because people might regard him as a fortune-hunter.

Politically, Shaw had put his faith in the power of words to inspire action. But in his personal life he employed words to avoid taking action. His letters to Ellen Terry and others had developed into an oblique device for this avoidance. He talked himself out of emotional danger. Advancing to the front of the stage he put his case mockingly to the audience:

'I will put an end to it all by marrying. Do you know a reasonably healthy woman of about sixty, accustomed to plain vegetarian cookery, and able to read & write enough to forward letters when her husband is away, but otherwise uneducated? Must be plain featured, and of an easy, unjealous temperament. No relatives, if possible. Must not be a lady. One who has never been in a theatre preferred. Separate rooms.'

Such a monologue, though it floods the auditorium with amusement, does not advance the event-plot of the play. And does it convince? At least one member of his audience with a shrewd knowledge of such performances thought not. 'Well,' Ellen Terry responded, 'you two will marry.'

*

Superficially the rupture between Shaw and Charlotte healed quickly. But added pressure was now being placed on him to marry. Webb had uncharacteristically given him a talking to; and then, at the end of July, Graham Wallas unexpectedly announced his own engagement to a high-principled short-story writer, Ada Radford. With this 'desertion' Shaw was to become the only unmarried member of the Fabian Old Gang.

That August he had arranged to stay at Argoed with Charlotte and the Webbs. He was more deeply exhausted than ever – too tired to fix up the hammocks Charlotte had brought, too tired to draw rein from writing even for a day. The days flew past, 'like the telegraph poles on a railway journey', and he worked on. But 'I am in the most disagreeable humor possible,' he complained to Florence Farr. His 'victory' over Charlotte had disappointed him. They lived an irreproachable life, the writing machine and the typist, in the bosom of the Webb family. It was apparently everything he had wanted. Yet a dialogue began to develop between G.B.S. and Shaw Limited in his correspondence.

'I am fond of women (one in a thousand, say); but I am in earnest about quite other things. To most women one man and one lifetime make a world. I require whole populations and historical epochs to engage my interests seriously . . . love is only diversion and recreation to me.'

Shaw Limited sees G.B.S. as a bragging emotional bankrupt playing timidly with the serious things of life and dealing seriously with the plays. His appeal to the audience carries a far-off echo of Sonny's voice:

'It is not the small things that women miss in me, but the big things. My pockets are always full of the small change of love-making; but it is magic money, not real money.'

For his mother's elopement with Vandeleur Lee, G.B.S. had substituted an economic for the emotional necessity; and he had used a financial argument to trick himself out of marrying Charlotte. So now Shaw Limited brings a money metaphor to expose the unreality of G.B.S. If only Charlotte had had the confidence to tear up that ridiculous Shavian balance sheet. Instead, unknown to Shaw, she had committed herself to him on the very terms by which he had rejected her, making a will that (barring a bequest to a cousin) left him her entire fortune.

But after their return to London at the end of August, Charlotte's behaviour changed. Suddenly she seemed less anxious to be with Shaw. Early in October she absconded to Leicester to visit her sister, Mary Cholmondeley who, Shaw knew, disliked him. 'Where am I to spend my evenings?' he complained. Charlotte returned, but suddenly veered off again back to her sister. 'It is most inconvenient having Adelphi Terrace shut up,' he pointed out. 'I have nowhere to go, nobody to talk to.' When Charlotte returned again, she was curiously unavailable. When he called one afternoon he was told by the maid that Charlotte was out. She always seemed to be 'out'. But three days later, on his way to dine at the Metropole, he suddenly found 'to my astonishment my legs walked off with me through the railway arches to Adelphi Terrace', where he saw the lights on in Charlotte's bedroom, signalling (he assumed) *her* unhappiness; but hardly had he written triumphantly to tell her so than she had disappeared to Paris. 'I miss you in lots of ways,' he wrote. ' . . . I wish you could stay in Paris & that I could get there in quarter of an hour. I feel that you are much better & brighter there; but it is damnably inconvenient to have you out of my reach.'

Charlotte came back early in November – but not to London. Instead she went straight to Hertfordshire to stay with some rich Fabian friends, Robert and 'Lion' Phillimore. This was too much for Shaw who pursued her on his bicycle and, travelling back at night, took one of his formidable tosses down a hill. He put the accident to instant use in an article for the *Saturday Review*, 'On Pleasure Bent'. All the same, Charlotte did not return at once.

When she did get back to London, he was almost cumbersomely tactful. 'I shall not intrude on my secretary tomorrow. If she desires to resume her duties, doubtless she will come to me.' A week later the tone was brisker: 'Secretary required tomorrow, not later than eleven.' But, for Charlotte, typing and shorthand had been a means to an end that seemed to be fading. She was not amused by his evasive joking. 'Charlotte can not only resist jokes, but dislikes them,' Shaw later explained to Pinero. 'Hence she was not seduced, as you would have been, by my humorous aberrations.' He made ready for Charlotte's arrival next morning to continue her secretarial work. He swept the hearth and made the fire; he laid out Charlotte's shawl and footwarmer; and then he waited – and she did not come. She had gone to Dieppe! 'What do you mean by this inconceivable conduct?' he demanded. 'Do you forsake *all* your duties . . . Must I also go back to writing my own articles, and wasting half hours between the sentences with long trains of reflection? Not a word: not a sign! . . . Are there no stamps? has the post been abolished? have all the channel steamers foundered?'

He was genuinely put out. So, after making fun of himself, he turned on Charlotte and accused her of everything she would most dislike. 'Go, then, ungrateful wretch,' he wrote, 'have your heart's desire:

'find a Master – one who will spend your money, and rule in your house, and order your servants about, and forbid you to ride in hansoms because it's unladylike, and remind you that the honor of his name is in your keeping, and . . . consummate his marriage in the church lest the housemaid should regard his proceedings as clandestine. Protect yourself for ever from freedom, independence, love, unfettered communion with the choice spirits of your day . . . But at least tell me when youre *not* coming; and say whether I am to get a new secretary or not.

G.B.S.'

This letter points to one of Charlotte's hidden attractions for Shaw: she was a member of the same family as the 'terribly respectable' land agents, Uniacke Townshend, that had employed him as an office boy twenty-five years ago in Dublin. His attitude seems divided: the socialist responding ironically, the Irishman romantically to this fact. He knew that, though the Irish might grudgingly admit him to be (in Edith Somerville's words) 'distinctly somebody in a literary way', it was assumed that socially 'he can't be a gentleman'. Marriage to Charlotte would shock some of those who had looked down on the office boy and who (if he ever returned to Ireland) would have to open their doors to him. Such things would of course never influence him; but it was pleasant to speculate on them.

Though he repeatedly insisted on the independence of women, Shaw continued to make them dependent on him. He excited interest: then ran. But Charlotte, who had money and the habit of travel, ran first and ran further. She was emotionally dependent but financially independent. Such manoeuvres gave Shaw the appearance of pursuing her.

The New Year bristled with good intentions. Charlotte was particularly attentive, rubbing vaseline on his bicycle wounds and encouraging him to use Adelphi Terrace as office and convalescent station. Shaw struggled to be reasonable.

That March 1898, the Webbs planned to be off on a tour round America and the Antipodes, 'seeing Anglo-Saxon democracy', and they invited Charlotte to go with them. 'If she does,' Shaw told Ellen Terry, 'she will be away for about a year, just time enough for a new love affair.'

Perhaps because she felt the danger of this herself, Charlotte did not take up the Webbs' invitation, but accepted instead an offer from Lion Phillimore to go for seven weeks to Rome. 'Charlotte deserts me at 11,' Shaw noted in his almanac. He felt 'quite desperate' and put it down to 'lack of exercise'. His friend Wallas was away with his new wife; Sydney Olivier had decided to go to the United States; his audience of actresses had dispersed and he was alone.

3

A TERRIBLE ADVENTURE

> By the way, would you advise me to get married?
>
> Shaw to Henry Arthur Jones (20 May 1898)

'Sisterless men are always afraid of women,' Shaw was to write; yet his own fears proceeded from the women in his family. He had seen their contempt for men – for his father and himself, even for Vandeleur Lee once his usefulness was exhausted.

On 25 November 1886 his sister Lucy had brought home a young man called Harry Butterfield to meet her mother. The purpose of this introduction was to announce her engagement – to Harry's brother, Charles, who may have been unavailable that evening because he was having an affair with another woman.

Besides his couple of 'wives', Charles had two names. As 'Cecil Burt' he travelled with a band of wanderers called 'Leslie's No. 1', performing as a cherubic tenor. 'He sang with difficulty,' Shaw remembered. He and Lucy Shaw sang together in Alfred Cellier's popular comedy-opera *Dorothy*, which had opened in London late in 1886. Shaw missed the first night; he also missed their wedding ('did not get to the church until the ceremony was over') and the small wedding party at Fitzroy Square a year later. But (as Corno di Bassetto) he caught up with them at Morton's Theatre, Greenwich, in the autumn of 1889 for the 789th performance of *Dorothy*'s provincial tour. His brother-in-law, Shaw observed, 'originally, I have no doubt, a fine young man . . . was evidently counting the days until death should release him from the part'.

Into the description of *Dorothy* he poured his long-standing resentment at having to submit to Lucy's alleged superiority. He knew her mind was commonplace, her talent little more than a trick of facility, her attractions superficial. It had been Lucy whom Bessie had taken with her to London;

and Lucy whom Lee had favoured; and Lucy who had been welcome at some of the London salons where George felt so *gauche*; and again Lucy whom people thought so lovable and entertaining. Great things had been expected of her; great things by the age of thirty-six had led to *Dorothy* at Morton's Theatre, Greenwich.

'She will apparently spend her life in artistic self-murder by induced Dorothitis without a pang of remorse, provided she be praised and paid regularly. Dorothy herself, a beauteous young lady of distinguished mien, with an immense variety of accents ranging from the finest Tunbridge Wells English (for genteel comedy) to the broadest Irish (for repartee and low comedy), sang without the slightest effort and without the slightest point, and was all the more desperately vapid because she suggested artistic gifts wasting in complacent abeyance.'

The impulse behind what Lucy called this 'typically fraternal – Irish fraternal – act' was part of the Shaw family feeling from which Lucy wanted to escape. 'She was more popular outside the family than inside it,' her cousin Judy Gillmore explained, 'and . . . she preferred people who would look up to her to those who would stand up to her.' Like her brother, Lucy had largely substituted theatre for home life; like him too she tried to replace her own family with another. Shaw had made use of the Fabians; Lucy used her husband's relatives. It was these relatives she had married. That was the significance of announcing her engagement in the presence of her future brother-in-law. Both George and Lucy, having grown up in a matriarchal family, instinctively cast about for a mother elsewhere.

Charles Butterfield was not an immediately attractive man. But he had an exceptional mother who knitted Lucy into the pattern of the Butterfield family with its comforting social world in the suburbs of Denmark Hill. But after Mrs Butterfield died, Lucy had drifted back to Fitzroy Square. 'LOVE,' she wrote, ' . . . is dead sea fruit, whether it is parental, fraternal or marital, and anyone who sacrifices their all on its altar plays a game that is lost before it is begun . . . it's a damnable world.' She seemed little more now than a figure of derision to her mother. Much of the money Shaw squeezed out from journalism went towards the maintenance of this unhappy household, which included Bessie's hunchback sister, Kate Gurly (whose 'state of unparalleled inclination' preceded her final plunge into Roman Catholicism), and from time to time her brother Walter Gurly, who would arrive at Fitzroy Square paralytically drunk, threatening to leave his nephew his heavily mortgaged Carlow property.

From this 'damnable world', with planchette and ouija, Shaw's mother had ridden away to parlay with the dead. She found them more congenial company than the living. First there was her favourite child Yuppy; and even her husband and her father seemed faintly less intolerable since their deaths. But on the whole she preferred chatting with people she had never known, the more remote the better, eventually settling for intercourse with a sage who had visited the earth in 6000 BC.

Bessie's spiritualism was an embarrassment to her son: '[I] held my tongue because I did not like to say anything that could worry my mother.' In his diary he had privately dismissed spiritualism as a 'paltry fraud'. At a session of spirit-rapping and table-turning with Belfort Bax and H. W. Massingham, he had cheated from the first and 'caused the spirits to rap out long stories, lift the table into the air, and finally drink tumblers of whisky and water, to the complete bewilderment of Bax . . . I have not laughed so much for years.' He released some of this laughter anonymously into the *Pall Mall Gazette*.

'Every Englishman believes that he is entitled to a ghost after death to compensate him for the loss of his body, and to enable him to haunt anybody that may have murdered or otherwise ill-used him in the days when he was solid.'

Bessie's wishful writings appeared like a non-malignant growth in an otherwise healthy body. But the escapist illusions of spiritualism raised in his mind the whole question of the morality of fiction. 'A person who describes events that never happened and persons that never existed is generally classed as a liar – possibly a genial and entertaining liar,' he wrote. 'And what is the business of a novelist if not to describe events that never happened and to repeat conversations that never took place.' To such an uncomfortable conclusion had his failure as a novelist driven him; and his comparative failure as a dramatist was persuading him to look on his plays too as methods of extending his self-deception.

'When we are young our inordinate fondness for theatrical and novel-writing leads us to simulate and describe emotions which we do not feel. Later, when the struggle for existence becomes too serious for such follies, real emotions come to us in battalions; but we take as much trouble to conceal them as we formerly did to affect them . . . [and] Life comes to mean finance.'

He had kept up the appearance of a realist; but who could say whether he too had not been misled by illusions? Asking himself why his mother had chosen to practise such an apparently senseless activity as spirit writings, he added another question: 'Why was I doing essentially the same as a playwright?' And answered: 'I do not know. We both got some satisfaction from it or we would not have done it.'

Lucy had made a brief escape from Fitzroy Square to the United States in 1897, playing in Villiers Stanford's *Shamus O'Brien*. This, the last small success of her career, merged with the first large success of her brother. *The Devil's Disciple* had opened at the Fifth Avenue Theatre on 4 October 1897, running to full houses for sixty-four performances until, early in 1898, Richard Mansfield took it off on a popular Mid-West tour. From this production of *The Devil's Disciple* Shaw earned £2,000 (equivalent to over £100,000 in 1997) and came to be recognized 'as a possible winner in the box office gamble'. It was a turning point of his career. For more than twenty years he had lived from hand to mouth. By the time Charlotte was preparing to return from Rome, he was suddenly in easy circumstances and 'with every reason to believe that things would improve'.

One result of this affluence had been his decision to give up drama criticism. Another result was his decision to write plays again. He chose Shakespeare's birthday, 23 April, on which to compose a Puritan prelude to *Antony and Cleopatra*. 'Snatch up my note book & make a start at last on "Caesar & Cleopatra",' he wrote. 'Lifelike scene in the courtyard of the palace at Alexandria among the bodyguard of Cleopatra. Screamingly amusing . . . [it] is going to save my life.'

Something was needed to save his life, for he was now in his own words 'a fearful wreck'.

*

During Charlotte's absence Shaw had struggled to maintain his self-sufficiency, working until 'I got into a sort of superhuman trance'. He had engaged Henry Salt's wife, Kate, to do his typing and dictation. Now that he was alone, he claimed to be 'no longer unhappy, and no longer happy: I am myself.' Mrs Salt would arrive, carrying a brown paper parcel containing a three-legged stool, some bananas and biscuits. 'We achieve a phenomenal performance with the arrears of correspondence,' Shaw wrote to Charlotte. ' . . . Your memory is totally obliterated . . . This is indeed a secretary.' But it was 'frightful not to be able to kiss your secretary'.

The longer Charlotte remained in Italy, the more unstable Shaw grew. He felt he was growing old and breaking up. 'I want a woman & a sound sleep,' he exclaimed. ' . . . Oh Charlotte, Charlotte: is this a time to be gadding about in Rome!'

He dared not trust his feelings. He missed her; but felt relieved that she was gone, as if a crisis had receded. So there must be two Charlottes, as there had been two Alice Locketts. In her absence, he could plant her neatly in his fantasy world. 'You count that I have lost only one Charlotte,' he wrote to her; 'but I have lost two; and one of the losses is a prodigious relief.

'. . . the terrible Charlotte, the lier-in-wait, the soul hypochondriac, always watching and dragging me into bondage, always planning nice, sensible, comfortable, selfish destruction for me, wincing at every accent of freedom in my voice, so that at last I get the trick of hiding myself from her, hating me & longing for me with the absorbing passion of the spider for the fly. Now that she is gone, I realize for the first time the infernal tyranny of the past year, which left me the licence of the rebel, not the freedom of the man who stands alone. I will have no more of it . . . *That's* the Charlotte I want to see married . . . yet I have her in my dreamland, and sometimes doubt whether the other devil ever had anything to do with her.'

This letter shows the extent to which Shaw had been unable to absorb Charlotte into his private mythology. So solid, yet elusive, she occupied his dreamland but threatened him with everyday experience. His letter seems deliberately hurtful, as if he is provoking her to break it off. But she would not.

To marry, or not to marry: that was the question: and he answered it differently each hour. 'I probably will marry the lady,' he told the Pakenham Beattys that April. But to the mathematician and biologist Karl Pearson he maintained that he was 'as firmly set against such a step as ever I was in my most inveterate youth and bachelordom'. Walking through the park, bicycling into the country: doing anything that awakened him from the oblivion of his work-addiction, exacerbated the dilemma. Charlotte still lingered in Rome, but her companion Lion Phillimore had returned in April and she and her husband invited Shaw to their home for Easter. Once there they started to bully him for his stupidity in not marrying Charlotte. One of the chief delights of married life, they told him, was the avoidance of the pre-nuptial obligation to be constantly paying amorous attentions to one another. Against such a Shavian device, 'I was totally incapable of self-defence'.

The length of Charlotte's Italian visit and the infrequency of her letters to him was not due, as Shaw suggested, to 'some Italian doctor'. Though Dr Axel Munthe was then in Rome, Charlotte had avoided seeing him. She was busy, in Fabian fashion, with a study of the municipal services of the city and could not return to London until she had properly collated her notes. Shaw, who had so often complained about her incapacity for work, could not now complain over the reason for her extended absence. It was as if everyone had learnt the Shavian game, and was playing it against him.

In the middle of April, while lacing one of his shoes too tightly, Shaw pinched his left instep. A week later, when riding his bicycle to see the Beattys, the foot expanded 'to the size of a leg of mutton'. He felt confident of curing it 'with hot water', and had just succeeded when, under stress of theatre reviewing in the evenings and vestry meetings during the day, the foot swelled up 'to the size of a church bell'. Some of his friends suggested 'vegetarian gout'. Walking soon became so excruciating that 'I now simply hop,' he wrote to Charlotte, 'my left foot being no longer of any use'. On 23 April he called in Dr Salisbury Sharpe, Alice Lockett's husband, who told him that his two toe joints had slipped over each other and become inflamed. 'My medical skill is completely vindicated: I have been doing exactly the right thing,' Shaw congratulated himself after the doctor had left. The hot water treatments continued and these were of great benefit to *Caesar and Cleopatra*. 'Finished whole scene of Cleopatra,' he noted in the almanac he was keeping each day and sending to Charlotte, ' . . . quintessence of everything that has most revolted the chivalrous critics Ha! Ha! Julius Caesar as the psychological woman tamer.'

Shaw, as woman tamer, had been letting Charlotte have almost daily reports on his foot with the result that she came 'back from Italy to nurse me'. She left Rome at the end of April. She was due to arrive in London on the evening of 1 May. Shaw limped down Tottenham Court Road, descended at Charing Cross, and went on slowly to Adelphi Terrace. 'With a long gasp of relief, I lay my two-months burden down & ring the bell.' Martha, the parlourmaid, answered the door. Charlotte was not there! He could do nothing but leave her a note of protest and hobble all the way back to Fitzroy Square. 'Wretch, devil, fiend ! . . . Satan's own daughter would have telegraphed.'

Travelling from Naples by sea, Charlotte arrived later that night and replied next day on the back of Shaw's note:

'Yes, I *might* have telegraphed: it was horrid of me. I am a wreck, mental and physical. Such a journey as it was! I don't believe I shall ever get over it.

My dear – and your foot? Shall I go up to you or will you come here and when? Only tell me what you would prefer. Of course I am quite free.

Charlotte'

*

'Come when it is most convenient to you . . . the sooner the better (for the first moment at least).'

She went at once to Fitzroy Square and was appalled. His room was a shipwreck. Correspondence and miscellaneous manuscripts, agitated by his perpetually open window, lay fluttering among the solid debris of cutlery, saucepans, apples, cups of trembling cocoa, plates of half-finished hardening porridge and a drifting surface of smuts and dust. Charlotte could only squeeze in sideways. Unshoe'd, his mobility had 'contracted itself to within hopping distance of my chair'. He could no longer look after himself and no one else there had any interest in him. For over twenty years mother and son had lived under the same roof in London, seldom communicating, and in such conditions that Charlotte's horror turned at once to a hatred of his mother and sister.

Something needed to be done. Charlotte demanded back the post as his secretary – and he refused. Kate Salt, he said, was looking after his secretarial needs very well; she was excellent at dictation and eminently bullyable. He did not want to bully Charlotte. He wanted her to bully him. He did not want a replacement for Mrs Salt but for Mrs Shaw. Charlotte retired to consider how best she might deal with his predicament. His foot looked terrible, and he appeared haggard with strain. Ellen Terry had sent them tickets for a new play at the Lyceum on 5 May, and he 'nearly killed myself' getting in a review on time.

The day after the Lyceum Charlotte suddenly took the initiative, calling at Fitzroy Square and taking Shaw back to Adelphi Terrace for a long talk. There is little record of what they said to each other. Three days later he underwent an operation on his left foot. An anaesthetist arrived at Fitzroy Square at half-past eight in the evening together with nurse Alice Lockett and her physician husband. After coming round from the chloroform, Shaw was told by Dr Sharpe that an abscess had formed on his foot. An attempt had been made to scrape the necrosed bone clean, but until it healed he would be on crutches.

He made this the subject of his penultimate article, 'G.B.S. Vivisected', for the *Saturday Review*. 'A few weeks ago one of my feet, which had borne me without complaining for forty years, struck work,' he wrote.

'The foot got into such a condition that it literally had to be looked into . . . My doctor's investigation of my interior has disclosed the fact that for many years I have been converting the entire stock of my energy extractable from my food (which I regret to say he disparages) into pure genius. Expecting to find bone and tissue, he has been almost wholly disappointed . . . He has therefore put it bluntly to me that I am already almost an angel and that it rests with myself to complete the process summarily by writing any more articles before I have recovered . . . It is also essential, in order to keep up the sympathy which rages at my bedside, to make the very worst of my exhausted condition.'

This notice of his operation in the theatre pages of the *Saturday Review* was part of the relentless Shavianizing of these strange weeks. Having planted his injured foot in the middle of Frank Harris's paper, he made it the ludicrous substitute for a broken heart. There was nothing pedestrian about Shaw's foot. It was part of the theatrical traffic in what reads like the scenario for a miracle play, helping prepare the public for the extraordinary happening of his marriage.

'For the first time in my life I tasted the bliss of having no morals to restrain me from lying, and no sense of reality to restrain me from romancing. I overflowed with what people call "heart". I acted and lied in the most touchingly sympathetic fashion . . . I carefully composed effective little ravings, and repeated them, and then started again and let my voice die away, without an atom of shame. I called everybody by their Christian names . . .

At last they quietly extinguished the lights, and stole out of the chamber of the sweet invalid who was now sleeping like a child, but who, noticing that the last person to leave the room was a lady, softly breathed that lady's name in his dreams. Then the effect of the anaesthetic passed away more and more; and in less than an hour I was an honest taxpayer again, with my heart perfectly well in hand. And now comes the great question, Was that a gain or a loss?'

This question invites us to see his marriage to Charlotte (which he refers to elsewhere as 'the second operation he has undergone lately') being performed under ether. The starting point was the reversal of a cliché: that marriage is a fate worse than death. 'I found myself without the slightest objection to death, and stranger still, with the smallest objection to marriage.' Nevertheless 'death did not come; but . . . Marriage did,' he told the economist Philip Wicksteed. The following year, in a letter to another of his correspondents, Richard Mansfield's wife Beatrice, he presented the story epigrammatically. 'I proposed to make her [Charlotte] my widow.' The Shavian paradox appears with the fact that the union produces not a mother of children but the father of plays.

Some eighteen years later Shaw was still insisting that he had considered the situation, 'from the point of view of a dying man'. In fact he had considered it as a method of prolonging active life. Work was his life; as he lived so he must write. But if he persisted working and writing in Fitzroy Square, 'nailed by one foot to the floor like a doomed Strasburg goose', he would become an invalid – that was Charlotte's verdict, and there can be little doubt that she put it to him strongly that day at Adelphi Terrace. The moment for a decision had come; she took it and he acceded. It was agreed between them that he was starved, if not of red meat, then of fresh air and rest. Charlotte proposed renting a house in the country, hiring two nurses and a staff of servants, and superintending his recovery however long that might take.

Charlotte's sister, Mary Cholmondeley – or 'Mrs Chumly' as Shaw liked to write her name ('I forget the full spelling') – refused to meet her future brother-in-law and, 'as a last kindness to me', requested Charlotte to secure her money. Lucinda Elizabeth Shaw seemed less interested in their news, making no comment beyond saying that it would be difficult to call Miss Payne-Townshend 'Charlotte' since she looked more like a 'Carlotta' – the mockingly glamorous name by which Lucinda and Lucy Shaw were always to know her.

Charlotte had spoken that day in Adelphi Terrace of Shaw's health and they must have spoken too of her money. The success of Mansfield's American production of *The Devil's Disciple* had removed Shaw's financial scruple against marriage. 'It did not make me as rich as my wife; but it placed me beyond all suspicion of being a fortune hunter or a parasite.' In 1896 he had earned £589 5s. 1d. (equivalent to £31,000 in 1997); in 1897 his income had risen to £1098 4s. 0d. of which £674 8s. 3d. had come from the opening weeks of *The Devil's Disciple*. One of the financial matters they seem to have discussed was a marriage settlement to enable 'my mother, if I died, to end her days without having to beg from my widow or from anyone else'. In fact Shaw safeguarded Lucinda, who was now in her sixty-ninth year, by means of an annuity and a private understanding with Charlotte that, if he were unable to meet the payments, she would make them without revealing herself as the source. In May 1899 Charlotte's solicitors drew up a settlement that guaranteed the income from two trust funds (administered by Sidney Webb and a clerk in the Bank of England and founder of the Stage Society, Frederick Whelen) to Shaw himself – these funds reverting to Charlotte in the event of his predeceasing her. Two years later, on 1 July 1901, Shaw was to make a will, appointing Charlotte as his sole executrix and trustee, bequeathing her his literary manuscripts and copyrights and all the estate not otherwise disposed of. Among his specific bequests was an annuity of

£600 to be paid to Lucinda Elizabeth Shaw, and, in the event of her death, an alternative annuity of £300 for his sister Lucy.

Between themselves they agreed to share basic expenses, but to keep their unequal incomes mainly apart. 'Her property is a separate property,' Shaw later notified the Special Commissioners of Income Tax, to whom he refused to file a joint income-tax return. 'She keeps a separate banking account at a separate bank.'

Besides health and money what else was there – except the crucial question of a marriage proposal? This was slipped into the agenda by Shaw as an item of social etiquette and accepted by Charlotte 'without comment'. It has the air of 'any other business'.

By presenting his marriage contract as a document of social intercourse, Shaw underlined the fact that it was not primarily a sexual arrangement he had entered into with Charlotte. Only with this proposal, he told Beatrice Webb, had the relation between them 'completely lost its inevitable preliminary character of a love affair'. Now, as patient and nurse, they were nearer to being parent and child, and with the possibility of beginning a new life.

Shaw continued to screen their feelings behind a rattling extravaganza. 'My disabled condition has driven Miss Payne Townshend into the most humiliating experiences,' he exulted in a letter to Graham Wallas. 'I sent in for the man next door to marry us; but he said he only did births and deaths.

'Miss Payne Townshend then found a place in Henrietta Street, where she had to explain to a boy that she wanted to get married. The boy sent the news up a tube through which shrieks of merriment were exchanged . . . Miss Payne Townshend then had to suffer the final humiliation of buying a ring . . . at last she succeeded, and returned with the symbol of slavery . . . of such portentous weight and thickness, that it is impossible for anyone but a professional pianist to wear it; so my mother has presented her with my grandfather's wedding ring for general use.'

He had asked Graham Wallas to act as one of the witnesses and, following a refusal from Kate Salt ('who violently objects to the whole proceeding'), invited as his second witness her husband Henry Salt. 'CAN YOU MEET US AT FIFTEEN HENRIETTA STREET COVENT GARDEN AT ELEVEN THIRTY TOMORROW WEDNESDAY TO WITNESS A CONTRACT.'

Shaw arrived on crutches and in an old jacket with armpits patched with leather that the crutches had badly frayed, and was taken by the registrar for 'the inevitable beggar who completes all wedding processions.

'Wallas, who is considerably over six feet high, seemed to him the hero of the occasion, and he was proceeding to marry him calmly to my betrothed, when Wallas, thinking the formula rather strong for a mere witness, hesitated at the last moment and left the prize to me.'

They were married in the afternoon of 1 June 1898. A week before Shaw had written that if 'ever I get married, it will have to be done very secretly'. In fact the newspapers pounced on the event 'as eagerly as the death of Gladstone' – largely because of a report in *The Star* drafted by G.B.S. himself.

'As a lady and gentleman were out driving in Henrietta-st., Covent-garden yesterday, a heavy shower drove them to take shelter in the office of the Superintendent Registrar there, and in the confusion of the moment he married them. The lady was an Irish lady named Miss Payne-Townshend, and the gentleman was George Bernard Shaw.

. . . Startling as was the liberty undertaken by the Henrietta-st. official, it turns out well. Miss Payne-Townshend is . . . deeply interested in the London School of Economics, and that is the common ground on which the brilliant couple met. Years of married bliss to them.'

With these Shavian flourishes, G.B.S. started on the 'terrible adventure' that was to turn him into 'a respectable married man'.

EIGHT

I

THE HAPPY ACCIDENTS OF MARRIAGE

Every busy man should go to bed for a year when he is forty.
Shaw to Hesketh Pearson (25 October 1918)

The adventure began between Haslemere and Hindhead. After reconnoitring several places in Surrey, Charlotte had taken Pitfold, a rather 'small, stuffy house' on the south slope of Hindhead. The air was so fine that 'our troubles seemed to be over,' Shaw told Beatrice Webb. Charlotte and Shaw had different ideas about air. It was a convalescent substance, soporific, supportive – that was Charlotte's opinion. But on Shaw it appeared to act as an intoxicant. Air went to his head. He had emerged from the London smoke into the ventilation of the country on 10 June 1898 and, despite his invalidism, set fiercely to work on his metaphysical study of the *Ring* cycle, *The Perfect Wagnerite*. Then, on the morning of 17 June, hurrying downstairs on his crutches, he fell into the hall, breaking his left arm and making 'a hopeless mess of the Wagner book'. Charlotte rushed forward with some butter pats, fastened them into splints and called the doctor.

This was the first of several accidents over the next eighteen months that were to keep Shaw largely convalescent. On 27 July an illustrious surgeon named Anthony Bowlby, attended by three doctors, came down to perform a double operation. He dug out most of the bad bone from the instep, charged Shaw 60 guineas and instructed him he would be healed in three weeks. Then he went away: but – *he had forgot the arm*. 'I am so unspeakably tickled by this triumph over the profession that I cannot resist the temptation to impart it to you,' Shaw wrote the next day to his vegetarian friend Henry Salt. Charlotte added a postscript: 'He is doing very well – but must be kept absolutely quiet.'

Shaw was discovering that his wife had a genius for worrying. Her mind ran largely on sickness and travel, diagnosing one, prescribing the other. Shaw represents these smashes as keeping her 'in a state of exhausting devotion'. His prolonged disablement seemed to emphasize certain elements in their marriage. He felt 'as helpless as a baby'. Sex was postponed until its absence became part of the habit of their lives. But having scarcely possessed him sexually, Charlotte felt peculiarly insecure.

She dreaded having to *act* an effusive friendship with his theatrical friends, and wanted to assert her predominance over his past. After a visit in the spring of 1900, Beatrice Webb noted that 'Charlotte Shaw did not want to have us. Perhaps this is a morbid impression. But it is clear that now that she is happily married we must not presume on her impulsive hospitality and kindly acquiescence in our proposals.'

Work was another subject about which Shaw and Charlotte could not agree. She took dictation and prepared copy for his typist (Ethel Dickens, a granddaughter of the novelist). But, as she later admitted to Nancy Astor, 'I don't really like work.' G.B.S. liked nothing better – especially the sort of 'creative work,' Charlotte complained, 'that pulls him to pieces'. Unfortunately 'it is the only occupation he really cares for'.

Shaw's illnesses gave Charlotte an occupation that seemed to unite his needs with her wishes. He did not underrate what she had done: she 'brought me back to life,' he told Beatrice Mansfield. But it was dismaying for her to see how tenuously her husband was attached to life. 'She has an instinctive sense that there is a certain way in which I do not care for myself,' Shaw wrote to Sidney Webb, 'and that it follows that I do not care, *in* that way, for anybody else either; and she is quite right.' He was going through a change of life, he believed, a little death. Whether it actually killed him, or helped to fortify him for another forty years, 'I do not greatly care,' he told Sidney Webb; 'I am satisfied that, on the whole, I have used myself economically and fired my whole broadside.'

The independence he had fixed upon before marriage had been shattered by his accidents. His income during the first year of marriage came to only £473 and by 1902 it had shrunk to £90 (equivalent to £24,000 and £4,400 in 1997). He lived almost entirely from Charlotte's money. To safeguard himself from going 'soft with domesticity and luxury', he began to separate his work from the experience of his life. These early years of his marriage were marked by a burst of creativity. 'I no longer sleep: I dream, dream, dream,' he told Charrington. Once he had confided to Ellen Terry that his childhood had been 'rich only in dreams, frightful and loveless in realities'. Now he began to manufacture from his dreams another world locked deep in himself and fortified against the encircling love and invalidism of his marriage. This was another reason for Charlotte's opposition to his work: it gave him a legitimate escape from her loving custody. She always knew where he was, but not what he was thinking. As his existence grew more comfortable, his work became oddly anarchical. 'He still writes,' Beatrice Webb noted after a visit to Hindhead, 'but his work seems to be getting unreal: he leads a hothouse life, he cannot walk or get among his equals.'

After six months, Shaw's foot was no better – indeed it seemed to

Charlotte decidedly worse. At the beginning of November, they went up to London to consult Bowlby, the specialist who that previous summer had predicted a three weeks' cure. He examined the foot and recommended a further period of disuse – about three weeks. To Charlotte's horror, Shaw decided that he would prefer to have his toe amputated than to endure a longer spell of inactivity. At the end of the month he returned to Bowlby and demanded an immediate removal of the whole bone and toe. To his surprise, Bowlby observed that if it were his toe, he would stick to it. 'He declares that my health is improving visibly; that I am pulling up from a breakdown . . . So I am waiting.'

While Shaw waited and worked, Charlotte acted, moving them both from Pitfold to Blen-Cathra, a larger house with 'lofty, airy rooms,' she told Beatrice Webb, on the main Portsmouth–London road between Hindhead and Haslemere. 'This place beats Pitfold all to fits,' Shaw told Henry Arthur Jones. 'I am a new man since I came here.' A week later, on 9 December, he completed *Caesar and Cleopatra*.

Shaw's health improved throughout 1899. By 23 March he reported himself in a doubly accurate phrase as being 'fed up' to eleven stone, a gain of five pounds. On 12 April he announced that 'the vegetables have triumphed over their traducers', an X-ray having shown a 'perfectly mended solid bone'. He began in May and completed in July *Captain Brassbound's Conversion* – after which Charlotte insisted on an unmitigated holiday.

In the middle of August they arrived at a rented house in Ruan Minor. 'I am down here, wallowing in the sea twice a day,' Shaw wrote, 'swimming being the only exercise I ever take for its own sake.' Not liking him to float off too far, Charlotte allowed Shaw to teach her to swim 'with nothing between her and death but a firm grip of my neck'. His publisher Grant Richards came down and Shaw, with his recently broken arm and sprained ankle, swam him out to sea and brought him back in terror of drowning.

So beneficial was the sea air that Charlotte felt justified in having ordered a recuperative cruise round the Mediterranean in an Orient steamer, the SS *Lusitania*. 'Anything better calculated to destroy me, body & soul, than a Mediterranean cruise on a pleasure steamer in October & Sept (the sirocco months) it would be hard to devise,' Shaw told Beatrice Mansfield. Like Lady Cicely in *Captain Brassbound's Conversion*, Charlotte was in her element coping with these pleasures. She tackled the rigorous sightseeing, digested the rich food, paid their bills and calculated the gratuities in complicated currencies. Trapped on this 'floating pleasure machine' as it moved through a sickly sea, the band striking up perpetual polkas and skirt dances, Shaw came to feel that every condition of a healthy life was being violated. He was at the plutocratic centre of capitalism. 'It is a guzzling, lounging, gambling, dog's life,' he cried. Passing through the Greek archipelago he was violently sick; in the overwhelming damp heat between Crete and Malta he sat at sunset in his overcoat, shivering, with the mercury as high as seventy-five Fahrenheit. 'I wake up in the morning like one in prison,' he wrote, 'realizing where I am with a pang.'

They arrived back in London at the end of October. At the time of their marriage they had agreed to retain their separate addresses in town, and Shaw openly speculated as to whether he would 'revert to my old state of mind & my bachelor existence'. Now, at the beginning of November 1899, he moved some of his belongings at 29 Fitzroy Square into Charlotte's double-decker apartment at the south corner of Adelphi Terrace. It seemed a pleasant place to live, overlooking the river and Embankment Gardens and, except for the occasional hooting of the boats, undisturbed. Shaw slept in a converted box-room off Charlotte's bedroom. 'The dining-room and large drawing-room were on the second floor, with the bedrooms, a study for G.B.S., and the kitchen on the third floor. There was no bathroom; the maids took cans of hot water into the bedrooms and filled a hip bath.' On the staircase Shaw installed a huge wicker gate with a bell-push on the gatepost, marking the Shavian frontier and reinforced by a hedge of pointed steel spikes attached to the balustrade, making the place, he claimed, look like a private madhouse. He worked in a small plain oblong room, above the river, his desk planted near the window which, summer and winter, remained open. There was a little Bechstein piano; an etching by Whistler, drawings by Sargent and Rothenstein, stuck like stamps on the flowered Morris paper which covered the ceiling as well as the walls, giving the impression of an inside-out box. The drawing-room mantelpiece had been designed by the Adam brothers: over the fireplace was cut the sixteenth-century inscription *Thay say. Quhat say thay? Lat Thame say* – the morality of which Shaw reckoned to be 'very questionable'. He was to live here almost thirty years 'before I realised how uncomfortable I was'. For £150 a year he leased Fitzroy Street for his mother who was joined there by her half-sister Arabella Gillmore and her half-niece Georgina ('Judy') Gillmore.

Shaw's foot was now completely mended following treatment of the sinus by pipe water in place of idoform gauze, and he was 'diabolically busy'. The new century seemed full of promise and activity. He had two new plays on his hands, a preface to write and text to revise for his second collection; he was beginning to involve himself with the newly formed Stage Society ('a sort of Sunday night Independent Theatre') which had chosen *You Never Can Tell* for its opening performance. The Boer War had started, forcing the Fabian Society 'to a new birth pang with a foreign policy' and Shaw to act as midwife with a manifesto, speeches and letters.

The honeymoon was over. 'I spent eighteen months on crutches, unable to put my foot to the ground,' he summed up. Within that period he had produced *The Perfect Wagnerite*, *Caesar and Cleopatra* and *Captain Brassbound's Conversion*: and, though he had not married for happiness, 'I cannot remember that I was in the least less happy than at other times'.

2

ON HEROINES AND HERO-WORSHIP

> Charlotte and Shaw have settled down into the most devoted married couple, she gentle and refined with happiness added thereto, and he showing no sign of breaking loose from her dominion . . . It is interesting to watch his fitful struggles.
>
> *The Diary of Beatrice Webb* (30 October 1899)

When William Archer first noticed Shaw in the Reading Room of the British Museum, he had observed how the young Dubliner was balancing Deville's French translation of *Das Kapital* against the orchestral score of *Tristan und Isolde*. Shavianizing Marx had been a matter of pulling politics off the barricades and into the tract. But Shaw also wanted to pull Wagner out of his antiquated heavens and place him in the contemporary socialist scene. *The Perfect Wagnerite* is an extraordinarily lucid exposition that uses Wagner as he had previously used Ibsen to work out his own philosophical position.

During the seven years that separated *The Quintessence of Ibsenism* from *The Perfect Wagnerite*, Shaw had begun to revise his political philosophy. In the earlier work he had divided human beings into three classes: philistines, idealists and those realists on whom progress depended. In the sequel he again makes a threefold division, representing the Wagnerian dwarfs, giants and gods as 'dramatizations of the three main orders of men: to wit, the instinctive, predatory, lustful, greedy people; the patient, toiling, stupid, respectful, money-worshipping people; and the intellectual, moral, talented people who devise and administer States and Churches'.

This change (subdividing the philistines into dwarfs and giants) reflects a shift towards a deeper pessimism arising from his greater experience of national and local politics. He had begun to feel that progress by instalments through the permeation tactics of the Fabians was too slow. A more romantic figure than that of the civil servant and political researcher was needed to fire the imagination of the philistine. The quietist should dress himself in a loud coat – a magical garment, its pockets rattling with the fool's gold of those idealistic illusions Shaw had derided in *The Quintessence of Ibsenism*. For most people had to be paid in such coin. Change the appearance of things and you were a long way to changing the reality. Acknowledging this, Shaw appears to accommodate a fourth class of human being into his philosophy: 'History shews us,' he writes, 'only one order higher than the highest of these: namely, the order of Heros.'

In fact Shaw's heroes are his realists from the *Quintessence* in disguise; they are Wagner's blond warriors, raised out of recognition into a higher organization of man ready to do their work in the twentieth century. Wagner's cycle of music dramas had told a story of love lost and regained; Shaw's commentary is a retelling of the story as love lost and replaced by something else. His 'frightful & loveless' childhood, followed by his years of poverty and social unacceptability in London, made him immediately sympathetic to Wagner's view of human history. There is no mistaking his personal involvement. Man, he writes, 'may be an ugly, ungracious, unamiable person, whose affections may seem merely ludicrous and despicable to you.

'In that case you may repulse him, and most bitterly humiliate and disappoint him. What is left to him then but to curse the love he can never win, and turn remorselessly to the gold?'

From Shaw's reading of the *Ring* we see human beings in loveless desperation as giant philistines succumbing to the corrupt millions of the Rhinegold. He also portrays them as dwarf philistines exploiting the malign systems of capitalism. These systems displace the need for human love with a love for the machinery of power. They establish their dominion over the world through the majesty and superstition of the Church, and guard them with the terrifying powers of the law. Only one quality can defeat this tyranny of religion and law, and that is the quality of fearlessness. The redemption of mankind therefore depends upon the appearance in the world of a hero or the spirit of heroism.

Wagner's Siegfried is a symbol of love, the original deprivation of which had been the genesis of man's tragic story. For Shaw, love was not a romantic solution to social difficulties because it could have little place in the down-to-earth conflict between humanity and its gods and governments. Love belonged to heaven where Wagner transported us once the *Ring* changed with *Götterdämmerung* from music drama into opera – which Shaw regarded as a decline, almost a betrayal. Shaw does not seek to lead us from earth to heaven, but to conduct a marriage of heaven and earth, religion and politics. He was to supplant Siegfried as a dramatic symbol with a succession of eccentrically inspired common-sense figures from

Julius Caesar to St Joan and to experiment with ways of substituting the Shavian Life Force for Wagnerian resurrection. 'The only faith which any reasonable disciple can gain from The Ring is not in love,' he wrote, 'but in life itself as a tireless power which is continually driving onward and upward.' From this faith emerged the creed of Creative Evolution Shaw was to explore in the dream sequence of *Man and Superman*. It is a moral commitment to progress through the Will, answering the need for optimism in someone whose observation of the world was growing more Pessimistic.

Concurrently with *The Perfect Wagnerite* he had been creating his own Puritan hero. His Caesar was more directly descended from Parsifal than Siegfried, a protagonist conventionally seen less as a hero than a fool: 'one who, instead of exulting in the slaughter of a dragon, was ashamed of having shot a swan. The change in the conception of the Deliverer could hardly be more complete.'

*

Shaw's Caesar was born from his longing that such men should exist and be thought great; and that in our better liking of them might lie a seed for our advancement. Caesar is a man of words – an author rather given to preaching – a politician, financier and administrator who, in middle age, has turned his hand to 'this tedious, brutal life of action' because public expectation has made it necessary. His battles are like Christ's miracles: 'advertisements for an eminence that would never have become popular without them'. At fifty-four he is 'old and rather thin and stringy' to Cleopatra's eyes. But his victories (particularly his paradoxical knack of turning defeat into victory) have given a sheen of heroic idealism to his pragmatic nature. He is plainly dressed, drinks barley water, works hard ('I always work') and rules 'without punishment. Without revenge. Without judgment.' He is rather vain, wears an oak wreath to conceal his baldness and is 'easily deceived by women'. Yet he 'loves no one . . . has no hatred in him . . . makes friends with everyone as he does with dogs and children'. This indiscriminate kindness is part of his avuncular superiority – what Shaw called his 'immense social talents and moral gifts'. Such was the man whom Shaw believed might initiate evolutionary progress for mankind.

He had come initially from Mommsen's *History of Rome*, from the fifth volume of which Shaw made extensive notes. 'I stuck nearly as closely to him,' he wrote, 'as Shakespeare did to Plutarch or Holinshed.' Shakespeare was a contributory influence in the shaping of the play. In his appraisal of *Julius Caesar* for the *Saturday Review* Shaw had expressed his indignation 'at this travestying of a great man as a silly braggart'. Lifting

Caesar from Plutarch, Shakespeare had added the qualities of vacillation and conceit from his general knowledge of dictators and his particular observation of Queen Elizabeth. Shaw replaced this Elizabethan stage tyrant by adding to Mommsen's Caesar something of Christ – a paraphrase, for example, at the climax of the play of the Sermon on the Mount.

The play was composed for Forbes-Robertson, 'the only actor on the English stage capable of playing a classical part in the grand manner without losing the charm and lightness of heart of an accomplished comedian'. What he looked for, and eventually received from Forbes-Robertson, Shaw was to set out in an article written at the time of the play's first presentation in London. *Caesar and Cleopatra* was 'an attempt of mine to pay an instalment on the debt that all dramatists owe to the art of heroic acting. . .

'We want credible heroes. The old demand for the incredible, the impossible, the superhuman, which was supplied by bombast, inflation, and the piling of crimes on catastrophes and factitious raptures on artificial agonies, has fallen off; and the demand now is for heroes in whom we can recognise our own humanity, and who, instead of walking, talking, eating, drinking, sleeping, making love and fighting single combats in a monotonous ecstasy of continuous heroism, are heroic in the true human fashion: that is, touching the summits only at rare moments, and finding the proper level on all occasions.'

Shaw was engaging the best Shakespearian actor of the time to help him make obsolete Shakespeare's *Julius Caesar* and undermine *Antony and Cleopatra*. His Caesar is a hero for the realists: Shakespeare's Antony is the idealistic hero created for the philistines. 'You are a bad hand at a bargain, mistress,' Rufio tells Cleopatra at the end of the play, 'if you will swop Caesar for Antony.'

Between the attractions of love and power Antony seems perpetually divided. Caesar is subject to no such struggle. By reducing Cleopatra's age from twenty-one to sixteen and ignoring Caesarion, the legendary child of Caesar and Cleopatra, Shaw is able to write off the threat of sex. 'It is extremely important that Cleopatra's charm should be that of a beautiful child, *not of sex*,' he wrote years later. 'The whole play would be disgusting if Caesar were an old man seducing a child.' Shakespeare's Cleopatra was a physically mature woman drawn from life, a dramatic portrait of the 'black' mistress of the Sonnets from whom he created a role so consummate, Shaw judged, 'that the part reduced the best actress to absurdity'. Shaw's Cleopatra is based on his observation of 'an actress of extraordinary witchery', Mrs Patrick Campbell. It is a part conceived from the stalls, yet with some faint foreknowledge perhaps of their emotional involvement to come. That involvement, which was to impair the Shavian Will in his mid-fifties, offers an ironic comment on Caesar's untroubled control of his sexual susceptibility.

Whatever was taken from Mommsen, anticipated as Christ, or dressed up as Johnston Forbes-Robertson, Caesar is Shaw: a figure to promote his way of life and dramatize his philosophy. Caesar is as fearless in life as Shaw was on the page, and becomes a fantasy image of Shaw himself upon the Fabian stage and in the theatre of politics.

The ancient Briton of the play, Britannus, Julius Caesar's loyal secretary, is like a modern Englishman. Shaw never wrote costume drama for its own sake: his plays were always addressed to the present. The figure of Britannus keeps the audience imaginatively half in the present (which was one of the ways Shaw became a model for Brecht). Since there had been such little progress through generations of sexual reproduction we are left with example as the stimulus for improvement. But Caesar's example is not followed by anyone in the play and will lead, we know, to 'his assassination by a conspiracy of moralists'. His schoolmastering of Cleopatra is easily defeated by her egocentricity ('But me! me!! me!!! what is to become of me?'). At the beginning she is a child full of fear ('*She moans with fear . . . shivering with dread . . . almost beside herself with apprehension*'). 'You must feel no fear,' Caesar instructs her. But when he leaves her at the end she is, he acknowledges, 'as much a child as ever'. All she has added to herself is the trick of imitating Caesar and this trick (unlike a similar trick learned by Eliza Doolittle) has not altered her.

Caesar is as alone at the end as when, at the beginning of Act I, he confronted the Sphinx:

'I have wandered in many lands, seeking the lost regions from which my birth into this world exiled me, and the company of creatures such as myself. I have found . . . no other Caesar, no air native to me, no man kindred to me, none who can do my day's deed, and think my night's thought . . . Sphinx, you and I, strangers to the race of men, are no strangers to one another.'

This is Shaw's own isolation. Caesar's address to the Sphinx anticipates a passage from the Preface to *Immaturity*, written over twenty years later, in which Shaw tells of a 'strangeness which has made me all my life a sojourner on this planet rather than a native of it'. That strangeness seemed intensified by his life with Charlotte. For, as his next play would continue to protest, he was unfitted for the institution of marriage.

*

Lady Cicely Waynflete is the female equivalent in Shaw's world of Caesar. 'If you can frighten Lady Cicely,' her brother-in-law Sir Howard Hallam tells Captain Brassbound, 'you will confer a great obligation on her family. If she had any sense of danger, perhaps she would keep out of it.'

Lady Cicely has walked across Africa with nothing but a little dog and put up with six cannibal chiefs who everyone insisted would kill her. In fact: 'The kings always wanted to marry me.' Her power lies partly in the authority of a mother over her children: 'all men,' she insists, 'are children in the nursery.' Her far-sightedness and tact being so much more effective than their conventional logic, she constantly runs rings round these men. 'Strong people are always so gentle,' she announces, but her own air of gentleness is an obvious imposture. Like Caesar she is surrounded by bullies whom she must constantly outwit. She re-educates them by a mixture of shrewdness and an attraction that does not depend on the erotic use of sex. She is Shaw's ideal of womanhood.

The interest of *Captain Brassbound's Conversion* focuses upon the character and performance of Lady Cicely. She is the only woman in the play. Her adventures give Shaw the opportunity of making a statement about the policy of British Imperialism that was increasingly occupying the Fabian Society at this time. Captain Brassbound had served under General Gordon before he was killed by the Mahdi. Britain had then re-annexed the Sudan from the Mahdi and was about to annex the two Boer Republics. It was for this reason that Shaw set his play in Morocco, 'the very place where Imperialism is most believed to be necessary'.

Shaw wanted to contrast travellers with conquerors, to show Europe's *mission civilisatrice* carried forward by the 'good tempered, sympathetic woman' who rules by natural authority against 'physically strong, violent, dangerous, domineering armed men' who shoot and bully in the name of Imperialism. In a letter to Ellen Terry, he spelled out this opposition between the male and female principles in human nature, telling her to read two books: H. M. Stanley's *In Darkest Africa* and Mary Kingsley's *Travels in West Africa*. 'Compare the brave woman, with her common-sense and good will, with the wild-beast man, with his elephant rifle, and his atmosphere of dread and murder, breaking his way by mad selfish assassination out of the difficulties created by his own cowardice.'

Lady Cicely's historical model was Mary Kingsley; her literary model Shelley's 'The Witch of Atlas'; her actress model Ellen Terry; and her model from life Charlotte whose passion for tourism had persuaded Shaw to read a number of travel books and to pick up, after completing *Captain Brassbound's Conversion*, his only first-hand knowledge of Morocco: 'a morning's walk through Tangier, and a cursory observation of the coast through a binocular from the deck of an Orient steamer'.

It was to Ellen, he let it be known, that the play owed its existence. Lady Cicely is not a portrait of Ellen Terry but a vehicle that incorporates something of her manner and magnifies it hugely. This is how he wanted her to be; this is how he believed she might become if she grew into the part. For the motive behind *Captain Brassbound's Conversion* was similar to that behind *The Man of Destiny*: to make one last effort to infiltrate the Lyceum with Shavian drama or, in failing, to detach Ellen Terry from Henry Irving.

The Lyceum had in 1898 been turned into a limited liability company. It was a step that, though designed to ease Irving's financial burdens, precipitated the end by making it more difficult for him to obtain credit. Early in 1899 Shaw approached Max Hecht, the principal investor in the new 'Lyceum Ltd' ('which I understand to be a benevolent society for the relief of distressed authors & actors'), and made the 'entirely interested suggestion' that the newly managed theatre should put on his 'recklessly expensive play' *Caesar and Cleopatra*, with Forbes-Robertson and Mrs Patrick Campbell in the title roles. 'On the whole, Forbes Robertson & Mrs Pat look more like the heir & heiress apparent to Irving & Ellen Terry than any other pair,' he wrote.

The copyright performance of *Caesar and Cleopatra* had taken place on 15 March 1899 at the Theatre Royal in Newcastle with Mrs Pat reading Cleopatra. But she 'was not attracted by her part' and did not accept Shaw's invitation to 'bring Caesar down to lunch' at Hindhead. Forbes-Robertson by himself could not risk such a production and Shaw's scheme for entering the Lyceum by the back door while Irving was abroad stuck. It was at this moment that he started 'Ellen's play'.

For years Ellen had supported Irving's romantic one-man dramas; now Shaw was presenting her with a non-romantic drama for one woman. 'I dont think that Play of yours will do for me at all!' she answered. Yet it was just the sort of thing she had consistently been helping Irving to produce. There was, in her abasement to him, a curious sense of superiority. She felt he depended on her far more than he could acknowledge; and she had come to rely on his dependence. After she had complicated their relationship by introducing Shaw with his Napoleon play showing how a real Man of Destiny rises above jealousy, Irving had begun to turn to Mrs Aria. He said nothing to Ellen. 'But who is Mrs A?' she had asked Shaw.

Eliza Aria was a social journalist and *salonnière* who had contrived to make herself the perfect companion. Attractive in appearance, generous with her praise, she was able to give Irving an encouraging reflection of himself. Ellen could see how Irving was renewed by Mrs Aria – and she determined to feel pleased for him. She did feel pleased: but she also felt betrayed. For she had the power to help him more than anyone, if only he would let her. But Irving was almost impossible to help – a presence that cocooned itself in silence. She wondered how his other friends and lovers felt. 'I have contempt and affection and admiration. What a mixture!' He was curiously tortured: 'a silly Ass,' Ellen called him. Sometimes she was frankly impertinent like this: at other times in awe. He still had the power to wound her. Appearing 'stouter, very grey, sly-looking, and more cautious than ever', he had informed her early in 1899 that he was ruined. He intended to mend his fortunes by touring the provinces with a small company. As for Ellen she could 'for the present' do as she liked. Ellen was furious. She had contemplated leaving him: 'I simply must do something else.' But she did not leave.

This was why she wanted something special from Shaw, something to bring back the glorious days of the old Lyceum. She had first wanted *Caesar and Cleopatra*: Irving, she was convinced, 'could have done *wonders* with that Play'. But Shaw had not seen her as his Cleopatra: 'She is an animal – a bad lot. Yours is a beneficent personality.' Also Irving made it clear that he would never produce a play by Shaw – in which case, Shaw retaliated, the only feasible alternative would be to produce his next play at the Lyceum when Irving was away.

He sent Ellen *Captain Brassbound's Conversion* at the end of July 1899 and she read it with disappointment. 'I couldnt do this one,' she told him, ' . . . it is surely for Mrs Pat.' He was dismayed. *Captain Brassbound's Conversion* had been conjured out of the last four years of their letter-writing love-affair: and she had not recognized it. 'Alas! dear Ellen, is it really so?' he wrote back. 'Then I can do nothing for you.

'I honestly thought that Lady Cicely would fit you like a glove . . . I wont suggest it to Mrs Pat, because I am now quite convinced that she would consider herself born to play it, just as you want to play Cleopatra . . . And so farewell our project – all fancy, like most projects.'

It was almost the end, a divorce between her acting and his playwriting skills. But he would not let them separate without a protest. 'Of course you never *really* meant Lady Cicely for me,' she had written to him. 'Oh you lie, Ellen,' he answered, 'you lie:

'never was there a part so deeply written for a woman as this for you . . . Here then is your portrait painted on a map of the world – and you . . . want to get back to Cleopatra! . . . do you think I regard you as a person needing to be arranged with sphinxes & limelights to be relished by a luxurious public? Oh Ellen, Ellen, Ellen, Ellen, Ellen. This is the end of everything.'

How much of this impassioned letter could Ellen afford to understand? In her autobiography she was to advise her readers that 'it doesn't answer to take Bernard Shaw seriously. He is not a man of convictions.' Here certainly were the methods of Lady Cicely Waynflete, but used for the opposite ends: to keep out the truth. Yet Shaw's letter unsettled her. She *did* know what he meant: 'the horridness of it all is, that all the time I think exactly as you do!' But to convert his words into her actions would mean emerging from the womb of the Lyceum and becoming independent – and it was too late. 'Of course I know it's *me* all the while . . . What is the good of words to me?' But words were all Shaw had to give her: the power of words to change our lives. And she could not change. All Shaw had done was to force her to recognize this fact.

So *Captain Brassbound's Conversion* went back on the shelf. As a consolation, Irving allowed Ellen to go through the copyright ceremony with the Lyceum company at the Court Theatre in Liverpool before they sailed for the United States in the autumn of 1899. But nobody liked Lady Cicely. 'It's because I read it wrong,' Ellen reasoned. But her daughter Edy, sitting out in front, remarked that she couldn't have read the lines differently, and that it seemed Shaw had thought his Lady Cicely one sort of woman but had written another.

The other woman was Charlotte. When she commanded him to go travelling, he went as obediently and unwillingly as Sir Howard Hallam and Captain Brassbound and his crew followed Lady Cicely into the Atlas Mountains. Robbed of his Old Testament religion of revenge for what he imagined had been done to his mother, the idealistic Brassbound proposes to fill this emptiness with love. 'I want to take service under you,' he tells Lady Cicely. 'And theres no way in which that can be done except marrying you. Will you let me do it?' But love is rejected as the solution as it had been earlier by Caesar and by Shaw himself in *The Perfect Wagnerite*. It is not Ellen Terry or Charlotte or any other woman who gives Lady Cicely's answer to Brassbound: 'I have never been in love with any real person; and I never shall. How could I manage people if I had that mad little bit of self left in me? Thats my secret.' By forestalling their marriage with warning gunfire ('Rescue for you – safety, freedom!'), Shaw is asserting his own 'mad little bit of self', and his intellectual isolation from Charlotte.

In Brassbound's saturnine features, grimly set mouth, dark eyebrows, his wordless but significant presence, we may also see something of Henry

Irving – and the imaginary conversion of Irving to Shavianism. Ellen had pretty well decided to leave Irving – but not quite. She was frightened of poverty – and then Henry could always weaken her resolve when she was most determined to go by appealing for her help. 'I appear to be of strange *use* to H, and I have always thought to be *useful*, *really* useful to any one person *is* rather fine and satisfactory.' So Shaw was persuaded to give up the struggle.

'Now for one of my celebrated *volte-faces*. I hold on pretty hard until the stars declare themselves against me, and then I always give up and try something else . . . now I recognize that you and I can never be associated as author and player – that you will remain Olivia, and that Lady Cicely is some young creature in short skirts at a High School at this moment. I have pitched so many dreams out of the window that one more or less makes little difference – in fact, by this time I take a certain Satanic delight in doing it and noting how little it hurts me. So out of the window you go, my dear Ellen; and off goes my play to my agents as in the market for the highest bidder.'

This letter reveals in what depth of disappointment Shaw lit his candle of optimism and converted its spectral shadows into a world of solid reality. In the open market only Charrington's Stage Society was interested in presenting his play with (the final shuddering irony) Ellen's role given to Janet Achurch. Ellen had had to choose: and she had chosen Henry. Was it loyalty or lack of courage? 'Ah, I feel so certain Henry just hates me!' she wrote to Shaw.

Here was Shaw's consolation. Into his love for Ellen had been poured a hatred of Irving. Like two stage monsters, Dracula and Svengali, they had fought with all their magical powers over the leading lady, both claiming victory at the final curtain. 'Of course he hates you when you talk to him about me,' Shaw burst out. 'Talk to him about himself: then he will love you – to your great alarm.'

Captain Brassbound's Conversion was first presented by the Stage Society at the Strand Theatre on 16 December 1900. Ellen came, and after the performance, on her way to the dressing-room of Laurence Irving (who played Brassbound), passing under the stage, she spoke to Shaw for the first time. They had been corresponding with each other for more than five years, and had feared that a meeting would rub the bloom off their romance. And now, having met briefly and parted, they apparently did not send each other a loving letter for almost a year and a half. 'They say you could not bear me, when we met, that one time, under the stage,' Ellen went on to explain in December 1902. Her self-esteem, undermined and exploited (with her own co-operation) by Irving, had to be fed by the persistent reassurance of her usefulness. What Shaw had said that could have reached her in this form and who carried such words to her is unknown. But it is difficult not to suspect that her daughter Edy was involved: Edy who had watched their long-running romance while two of her own had been ended by Ellen; Edy whose jealous gossip (Ellen went on to warn Shaw that same December) needed a 'little salt'.

It was at the end of this silent period that Ellen began to separate from Irving. 'She broke loose from the Ogre's castle,' Shaw wrote, '. . . only to find that she had waited too long for his sake, and that her withdrawal was rather a last service to him than a first to herself.'

Ellen's last service to Shaw was to play Lady Cicely at the Royal Court Theatre in 1906, eighteen months after Irving's death. 'Sooner or later I know I'll play Lady C.,' she had promised him. It had been a hope: and finally it was a fact. She was fifty-eight, could not remember her lines, felt easily demoralized. Shaw made certain that the producer treated her with gentleness and to Ellen herself he wrote: 'Behave as if you were more precious than many plays, which is the truth . . . The only other point of importance is that you look 25; and I love you.'

When the play opened on 20 March, *The Times* drama critic noted that 'Miss Terry is, as always, a little slow, the victim of a treacherous memory'; and Desmond MacCarthy in *The Speaker* observed that 'there was a hesitation in her acting sometimes, which robbed it of effect'. She recognized this herself. 'You try to keep up your illusions about me,' she wrote to Shaw, 'about my acting, altho' you know all the while – ' But Shaw refused to know. He had no time for this 'saintly humility'. The marriage of her acting with his playwriting had at last taken place and its beauty was manifest. 'She is immense, though she is 58, and cant remember half my words,' he wrote. '. . . now that she has at last actually *become* Lady C, and *lives* the part, saying just what comes into her head without bothering about my lines, she is very successful.'

The following year Ellen took *Captain Brassbound's Conversion* on her farewell tour of the United States. On 22 March, in Pittsburgh 'of all places in the world' she married James Carew, the American actor who played Captain Kearney in the play. Though Dame Ellen would never become Lady Cicely, 'her history has become your history,' Shaw acknowledged. '. . . Why could you not have been content with my adoration?' But most people preferred conventional romance to Shavian adoration and would attempt to infiltrate it into his plays. When in 1912 Gertrude Kingston acted the role of Lady Cicely, she replaced in rehearsal Shaw's final line – 'How glorious! And what an escape!' – with her own: 'How glorious! And what a disappointment!' But the disappointment, brilliantly concealed, was Shaw's. 'Lady Cecilys [*sic*] no longer exist,' he conceded in a letter to Gertrude Kingston, ' – if they ever did.'

*

Shaw was developing into an ingenious 'Ladies' Tailor'. But what was the use of this if no lady would wear his clothes? The late Victorian theatre was so different from any living world, that he could see 'no real women in the plays except heavily caricatured low comedy ones,' he later wrote to Edy Craig; 'and what the leading actresses had to do was to provide an embodiment of romantic charm . . . without having a single touch of nature in the lines and gestures dictated by the author's script . . . unless they could smuggle in something of their own between the lines.'

Shaw had been at this smuggling game now for ten plays and was almost always caught, either by the Lord Chamberlain's office, or by the male actor-manager's régime of the West End. Together, they policed a theatre-going public that was not yet ready for the New Drama as a vehicle for the New Woman. Shaw's huntresses and persons 'exactly like myself' peopled the army he had called up to invade the *fin de siècle* theatre, topple the womanly women from their stage pedestals, then march down from the boards to the stalls and out into the world. But finding the doors of the theatre heavily barricaded, his regiment veered off instead to the offices of Grant Richards. Having failed as a novelist and, it seemed, also as a dramatist, from these two failures Shaw proposed to manufacture success with a literary genre composed of essay, play and novel.

By November 1900 *Three Plays for Puritans* had been passed for the press and in January 1901 an edition of 2,500 copies was published. 'The effort has almost slain me,' Shaw admitted. He had not done it for money; he had not worked sixteen hours a day with Charlotte's approval; and he had gone directly against the advice of William Archer who predicted popularity for at least one of these plays leading to an inevitable Shaw boom if he would give it 'a chance, by waiting at least two years for somebody to produce it before publishing it'. Why then had he done this?

Shaw was acutely aware of the continuous current of sex in the Victorian theatre because, like the sex in his own life, it was suppressed. He argued that the sensuous conventionality of Victorian stage sex was pornographic in that it was not frank. This lack of frankness, he added, had been what 'finally disgusted me'. With such passages – and there are many of them in his Preface – he disclaims being a prude and identifies himself as a proponent of the realistic treatment of sex in contemporary drama. But for Shaw realistic sex meant less sex. He passes in his preface almost unnoticeably from demolishing the genteel assumptions of the sex instinct as shown on the stage, to a demolition of the sex instinct itself.

Before marriage, in his three-cornered affairs with women, Shaw's part had been an impersonation of George Vandeleur Lee, the interloper in his parents' marriage. In marriage he had taken on a double role, that of George Carr Shaw and George Vandeleur Lee together. He was legitimately married but it was a *mariage blanc*. The dominant role was that of Lee whose 'potency' arose from his public life – as did Shaw's. Casting off the ambiguous skin of 'George', Shaw had literally 'made a name for himself' as a writer, the magnificently impersonal G.B.S. (his equivalent of Lee's 'Vandeleur'). His frustration at not getting the work of G.B.S. performed manifested itself as an impotence. From this impotence came his impatience – his inability to take Archer's advice to wait – and his confusing paradoxes in the Preface between celibacy and pornography. He had already waited too long. His only channel for reaching the public was the book world. But this outlet was unsatisfactory since he could not put his potent words into the mouths of actresses, could not direct them on a stage, could not witness their effect on audiences, could only, with the aid of his written narrative, transport them into his imagination. It gave him only temporary relief.

'No: it is clear that I have nothing to do with the theatre of today,' he had written to Ellen Terry. To create a family of plays for future generations was still Shaw's ultimate aim. In the short term, however, there was another theatre where he could perform: the theatre of politics. 'It is time to do something more in Shaw-philosophy, in politics & sociology. Your author, dear Ellen, must be more than a common dramatist.'

3

BOER WAR MANOEUVRES

If I were not a politician I would be a Fabian.

R. B. Haldane to Bernard Shaw (15 October 1900)

Shaw was with Charlotte on board the 'floating pleasure machine' SS *Lusitania* when on 11 October 1899 the war in the Transvaal broke out. When he arrived back in England he found the country in a state of civil war over South Africa. The prosperity of the Empire, the longevity of the widowed Queen herself, seemed to have sunk Britain in the doldrums of peace and the public was more than ready to take off for some foreign adventuring. The novels of Trollope, with their solid domestic themes, were beginning to lose popularity and being replaced in the public imagination by Kipling's Indian stories, the adventures of R. L. Stevenson and the historical romances of Conan Doyle. Doyle shared with thousands of 'men in the street' an attitude that converted warfare into sport. 'If ever England gets into a hole,' he had declared, 'you may depend on it that her sporting men will pull her out of it.'

Shaw had wanted to have nothing to do with it. But the eruption of hostilities was of such violence, shifting the landscape of British politics, that non-involvement became impossible. The atmosphere in Britain of conflicting imperialist and pro-Boer passions, gathering up the vague discontents of years, was considerably less sportsmanlike than on the smoke-filled battlefields of South Africa. John Burns, 'the Man with the Red Flag' who ten years earlier had led the Dock Strike, was obliged to take up his cricket bat one night to defend himself against a crowd attempting to break into his home.

The Conservative Party, saw Englishmen riding 'the white steed of destiny' all over South Africa. Most socialists joined in opposition to the war – Keir Hardie, for example, picturing the Boers as pure-living, God-fearing farmers grazing peacefully under the Christ-like guardianship of President Kruger. Between the romanticism of the right and the sentimentality of the left floundered the Liberal Party with its cautious new leader Campbell-Bannerman. It was the middle ground of British politics that was torn apart by the South African war; and since the Fabian Society, with its policy of permeation, had been cultivating this middle ground, it now found itself at the centre of a crisis.

The Webbs' attitude to South Africa was simple. They did their best to ignore it. Beatrice, who described the war as an 'underbred business', was determined that the Fabians should be 'so far removed from political influence that it is not necessary for Sidney to express any opinion'.

It was Sidney's lack of interest in foreign politics – despite his years at the Colonial Office – that had dictated the Fabian silence over Imperialism. But since it was impossible any longer to smother things in silence, he handed over the 'show' to the Fabian literary expert. Shaw's brief was complicated. He had to discover some honourable method by which, while the war issue dominated British politics, the Fabians could legitimately continue to produce tracts on municipal bakeries, fire insurance and the milk supply.

His attitude had begun to change over this year until, with the publication of *Fabianism and the Empire*, it seemed to invert the traditional socialist standpoint, supporting pacifist permeation tactics at home while tolerating a good deal of bloodshed overseas. He urged all Fabians to stick together. No party or society could entirely discharge the soul's message of every member; and no member, he added, 'can find a Society 800 strong which is an extension of his own self – even the society of 2 called marriage is a failure from that point of view'.

Shaw tried to suffocate the moral issue of the war by spreading over it his theory of pragmatism. In its most negative phase Shaw's pragmatism meant that socialism should not touch any problem that it did not have a reasonable chance of solving; more positively it meant in this case waiting for the inevitable annexation of the Transvaal, and then introducing there the social organization on which the Fabians had been working. In a letter to Ramsay MacDonald he explained, 'I have done my best to avert the fight for which the democratic spirit and the large grasp of human ideas is always spoiling, and for which the jingo spirit is no doubt equally ready. If you wont take my way, and wont find a better way, then punch one another's heads and be damned.'

Of what use, he asked, were ethics that were taken out of the cupboard from time to time and that led to conclusions no one could act on? 'I am a revolutionist in ethics as much as in economics,' he told Walter Crane;

> 'and the moment you demand virtuous indignation from me, I give you up . . . the Fabian ought to be warproof; and yet Capitalism has only to fire a gun, and split a great shaving off us.'

In fact Shaw was extraordinarily successful in keeping the Fabian peace. By the time the Treaty of Vereeniging was signed in 1902 (leaving the enfranchisement of the native population to be settled in due course) 22,000 British soldiers had been killed and £223,000,000 spent – but no great shaving had been split off the Fabian Society. In steering them out of war-range, Shaw had removed the Fabians from the rest of the socialist fleet, taken them, it seemed, out of politics and stranded them on the high ground of political philosophy. He had also plucked from politics the 'heroic' quality he had so recently inserted into his plays.

Shaw hated war; he hated the human beings who were attracted by war; and he felt that every human being, whatever his moral stance, was implicated. His revulsion at the Boer War, and the policy he formed based on this revulsion, is most succinctly expressed in a letter to a fellow-Fabian, George Samuel. 'The Boer and the Britisher are both fighting animals, like all animals who live in a chronic panic of death and defeat,' he wrote.

> '. . . Do you expect me solemnly to inform a listening nation that the solution of the South African problem is that the lion shall lie down with highly-armed lamb in mutual raptures of quakerism, vegetarianism, and teetotalism? . . . Let us face the facts. Two hordes of predatory animals

are fighting, after their manner, for the possession of South Africa, where neither of them has, or ever had, any business to be from the abstractly-moral, virtuously indignant Radical, or (probably) the native point of view . . . The moral position of the Boers and the British is precisely identical in every respect; that is, it does not exist. Two dogs are fighting for a bone thrown before them by Mrs Nature, an old-established butcher with a branch establishment in South Africa. The Socialist has only to consider which dog to back; that is, which dog will do most for Socialism if it wins.'

Fabianism and the Empire was produced as a Fabian foreign policy document, one hundred pages long, published at one shilling by Grant Richards and directed at the 'Khaki' election in the autumn of 1900. The first draft, which took Shaw three months to complete, was sent to every member of the Fabian Society, 134 of whom returned comments which, with extraordinary ingenuity, he attempted to stitch into his text. The final version was such a 'masterpiece' of literary craft that no more than fourteen Fabians voted against its publication. 'By this time the controversy over the war had reached an intensity which those who cannot recollect it will find difficult to believe,' Pease remembered, 'and nobody but the author could have written an effective document on the war so skilfully as to satisfy the great majority of the supporters of both parties in the Society.'

He recommends reforms for the army, the Consular Service and the administration and social justice of Imperialism, drafting what Beatrice Webb called 'the most prescient and permanently instructive public document of its date'. But on the General Election, the Treaty of Vereeniging and the subsequent social conditions in South Africa, *Fabianism and the Empire* had no influence at all, and 1,500 copies were remaindered the following year.

In the new Parliament the Tories had won 402 seats, the Liberals 186 and the Nationalists 82. Keir Hardie was the only independent Labour politician to survive the election, but it was not through him that the Fabians sought to operate. As Beatrice noted, 'a Conservative Government is as good for us as a Liberal Government'. The Fabians were ascending in society, becoming friendly with Bishops and Tory Cabinet Ministers, while among the Liberals they chose Lord Rosebery as their man – partly on account of his admiration for Shaw's manifesto. '*Our* policy is clearly to back him for all we are worth,' Shaw urged Beatrice who noted in her diary: 'We have succumbed to his flattery.' A few weeks later, in the autumn of 1901, Sidney published 'Lord Rosebery's Escape from Houndsditch' – an invitation for him to lead the progressive Liberals in their campaign to raise each department of national life to its maximum efficiency.

NINE

I

SOME UNEXPECTED CHARACTERS

> I stand just now at a point where a failure would put me quite out of court, and a success would 'chair me ever'.
>
> Shaw to William Archer (26 March 1902)

After six years' 'Borough Councilling', Shaw concluded in 1903, 'I am convinced that the Borough Councils must be abolished'. His method of quitting local politics was characteristically 'Shavian'. In the spring of 1904 he stood as a Progressive candidate for one of the two London County Council seats in South St Pancras. 'The Shaws have been good friends to us,' Beatrice wrote in her diary, 'and we would not like them to have a humiliating defeat.' The party organizers however had long ago given up the seat as lost and even Beatrice admitted 'he is not likely to get in'. But this was not good enough for G.B.S. He needed, while campaigning with tremendous gusto and geniality, to make *absolutely certain* of not getting in. Every day of the campaign he showed himself as 'hopelessly intractable' – except to his enemies, to whom he was 'the most accommodating candidate that was ever known'. He insisted that he was an atheist; that, though a teetotaller, he would 'force every citizen to imbibe a quartern of rum to cure any tendency to intoxication . . . chaffed the Catholics about transubstantiation; abused the Liberals, and contemptuously patronized the Conservatives – until every section was equally disgruntled'. As a result, he was triumphantly beaten into third place. And so, with honour high, Shaw paraded out of party politics. 'We are not wholly grieved,' Beatrice wrote. 'His . . . quixotic chivalry to his opponents and cold drawn truth, ruthlessly administered, to possible supporters, are magnificent but not war.'

Shaw's election defeat was probably more disappointing to Charlotte than to the Webbs. She wanted to find him a respectable career in politics. Though she believed in his gifts as a playwright she could not blink the facts. In the summer of 1903, he was in his forty-eighth year and still almost wholly unknown to British audiences. From such facts and her conflicting reactions to them, Charlotte hit on a curious programme of nudging him into professional politics at home while furthering his reputation as a dramatist abroad.

Her opportunity to help Shaw's plays on to the European stage came with a visit early in 1902 of a young Austrian writer, Siegfried Trebitsch. Trebitsch was a sentimentalist of wonderful persistence – the sort of person Shaw had been sent into the world to quell but who in practice so often got the better of him. 'I held forth for quite a while about his plays,' Trebitsch remembered.

'What do you mean to do with me?' Shaw interrupted.

Trebitsch knew the answer to this. He meant to become Shaw's 'apostle in Central Europe' and conquer the German stage for him. In short he allowed himself to 'speake straight forward' and give his 'dear adored Shaw' what he called 'a peace of my mind'. The result was that Shaw jumped up and ran out of the room, crying out for Charlotte to 'try to calm' this 'young lunatic'.

Obediently Charlotte appeared and Trebitsch 'expounded my intentions to her'. The grandeur of these intentions, contrasted with the inadequacy of the language in which they were expressed, did not strike Charlotte as funny. She summoned her husband back into the room and Shaw spoke forbiddingly about the 'extremely important matter of copyright' of which Trebitsch knew nothing. Trebitsch left soon afterwards and a few days later received a letter from Charlotte inviting him to lunch. It became clear to him during this meal that, though she took no part in the conversation, Charlotte approved of him and that this approval had been responsible for a change in her husband's manner.

For Trebitsch to translate his plays into German involved Shaw in mastering the German language – or at least buying 'a devil of a big dictionary, also a grammar'. He teased and tutored Trebitsch terrifically. His translation of *Caesar and Cleopatra* was stuffed with misunderstandings; *Arms and the Man* 'full of hideous and devastating errors'; and *Candida*, Trebitsch's favourite, was worst of all. 'You didnt understand the play: you only wallowed in it . . . I tore out large handfuls of my hair and uttered screams of rage . . . I plucked up my beard by the roots and threw it after my hair.'

From such comments, over several years, Trebitsch began to sense that something was not quite right. 'I have just met the most beautiful Shavian I have ever seen,' Trebitsch deciphered at the end of one of Shaw's letters to him. 'She is the wife of one of our diplomatic staff, who is joining the British Embassy in Vienna very soon. I think I will ask her to correct your translations: you can make mistakes on purpose.' What could this mean? 'You must learn to laugh,' Shaw suggested. Was it all some joke? Perhaps not, since Shaw had also advised him: 'I have no objection to being taken seriously. What ruins me in England is that people think I am always joking.'

To be the perfect translator of Shaw's plays Trebitsch needed to be resolved into a German edition of G.B.S. Shaw spelled out the prescription minutely. Trebitsch must use the same menu as Shaw himself. 'Never eat meat or drink tea, coffee, or wine again as long as you live,' he warned. '... If you are very very very bad, become religious, and go ... round all the Stations of the Cross on your knees, and pray incessantly. When you begin to feel sceptical you will be getting well.'

It was agreed that Trebitsch should translate three plays and hold exclusive rights in them for one year. He chose *The Devil's Disciple*, *Candida* and *Arms and the Man*, and kept them 'ceaselessly circulating among publishers, theatrical people, producers'. The proprietor of the Entsch theatrical publishing firm in Berlin refused 'to have anything to do with this crazy Irishman' whom he described as 'a lost cause'. Trebitsch was advised to 'stop being so obstinate' or he would endanger his own career. 'I was somewhat desperate,' he wrote. 'But I did not lose heart.' He continued working 'feverishly, usually the whole day, and often half the night as well, for, after all, I had a time limit'.

Within the year Trebitsch began to accomplish what Shaw had been failing to achieve in Britain over more than a decade. He persuaded the director of the Raimund Theatre in Vienna to stage *The Devil's Disciple* in February 1903, and the Stuttgart publishers Cotta to bring out all three plays, *Drei Dramen*, in the same year. In 1904 the Deutsches Volkstheater produced *Candida* and *Arms and the Man*; and within the next three years there were productions by leading directors of *You Never Can Tell*, *Mrs Warren's Profession* and *Man and Superman*, all in Trebitsch's translations. Germany came to recognize Shaw's 'importance to the modern stage,' Thomas Mann wrote, 'indeed to modern intellectual life as a whole, earlier than the English-speaking world.

'His fame actually reached England only by way of Germany, just as Ibsen and Hamsun conquered Norway, and Strindberg Sweden, by the same roundabout route, for London's independent theatre fell short of doing for Shaw's reputation – soon to grow to world-wide dimensions – what men like Otto Brahm and Max Reinhardt ... were able to accomplish, for the simple reason that at that time the German stage was ahead of its British counterpart.'

Trebitsch recorded that it 'made a very great impression on Shaw that I had kept my word and accomplished what I set out to do'. What Shaw felt for Trebitsch was naked gratitude – the emotion he usually denied and invariably distrusted. Trebitsch in his autobiography presents a chronicle of unchecked success. The first night of *The Devil's Disciple* 'was one of the most remarkable I have ever experienced,' he writes. *Mrs Warren's Profession* 'was the greatest success of the season'. The production of *Candida* 'turned out to be a sensation' and so on. The stream of Shaw's letters along this triumphant passage form a curious undercurrent. Over a period of two and a half years, he writes:

'Give up all anxiety about those plays . . . let this experience cure you of your excessive sensitiveness to reviews . . . If I bothered about such things I should go mad three times a week, and die on the alternate dates . . . you must not lie awake and get neuralgia . . . As to the play being ruined for all German stages, do not trouble about that. When you have been ruined as often as I have, you will find your reputation growing with every successive catastrophe. Never ruin yourself less than twice a year, or the public will forget about you . . . Dismiss it from your mind now: there is no use bothering about a commercial failure . . . we can say that it is the public that failed . . . let us laugh and try again . . . nothing succeeds like failure . . . We shall be hissed into celebrity if this goes on.'

Shaw developed a paternal tenderness for Trebitsch. For many years Trebitsch was violently attacked in Germany for knowing neither German nor English. He never learned what Shaw called 'the grand style of fighting', falling upon your opponent and clubbing him dead with the weapons of generosity and politeness. In spite of Shaw's work with the dictionary, many misunderstandings persisted, the most notorious being Trebitsch's interpretation of the Waiter's remark in *You Never Can Tell*: 'I really must draw the line at sitting down' – after which, following Trebitsch's stage directions, he goes to the window and, before taking his seat, draws the curtains. Shaw knew all about these howlers. 'Never join in attacks on translators,' he advised one of his biographers. His loyalty to Trebitsch took the form of claiming for these 'so-called translations' the status of 'excellent original plays'. Had they been the least like his own, he explained, they could never have succeeded so well.

Shaw's experiences with Trebitsch influenced his arrangements with other translators. 'I calculated that the only way to make the job really worth doing was to catch some man in each country who would undertake *all* my work, and thus get something like an income out of half the fees,' he wrote to Henry Arthur Jones in 1908. 'At last I succeeded everywhere except in Portugal . . . Sometimes I picked a man who had never dreamt of the job and hypnotised and subsidised him into it. Whenever possible, I got a man with an English or American wife . . . The results have been very varied.'

He chose his translators because they charmed him, touched his sense of humour or presented impeccable political credentials. His most extreme translators were Augustin and Henriette Hamon. He was a socialist and an anarchist of 'terrific intellectual integrity . . . whose main means of subsistence has always been borrowing money'; she knew some English, which was helpful. Hamon did what he could to wriggle away. He was not a literary man, had never written a play and knew little of the theatre. It was true that he had published a number of works on hygiene and sociology. It was also true that he was the radical editor of *L'Humanité Nouvelle*, a periodical frequently visited by the police. Yet Shaw seemed determined to prove Hamon 'a born homme de théâtre'. That Hamon was an individual bicyclist and a revolutionary with exemplary collectivist principles pleased him. As evidence of his good choice, Shaw pointed to the 'dramatic liveliness' of Hamon's reports on various socialist congresses.

So Shaw bought a Larousse dictionary and set about becoming a co-translator of his plays into the French language. He enjoyed firing off letters in a French that was so 'extremely Britannic' that it 'must be positively painful' to any man of literary sensibility to read them. ' "Hard as nails" – "dure comme un clou" – is an expression which ought,' he judged, 'to enrich the French language.' The Hamons were able, he discovered, to concentrate into ten amazing lines of their translated text 'all the errors which I spend my life in combating'. Hamon had no notion that he might be translating comedies, and was once seen rushing from the theatre when the audience began to laugh, crying to his wife, '*Mon Dieu! On rit. Tout est perdu.*'

All Shaw's schooling could not make these translations good. They were caustically attacked in France as forming a permanent barrier to the acceptance of Shaw's plays by the French public. Hamon never fathomed 'the utter illiteracy of the playgoing public', to prepare for which, Shaw reminded him, Molière used to read his plays aloud to his cook. The great failing of the Frenchman, Shaw maintained, was his academicism. 'Every Frenchman is a born pedant,' he advised Hamon. 'He thinks it a crime to repeat a word – the crime of tautology.'

Despite the pleas of many eminent translators, Hamon went on to translate almost all Shaw's plays. Only seven or eight of these plays were produced in Paris, not at the commercial *théâtres du boulevard* but the small *coterie* theatres. 'I have given up all hope of getting into touch with France,' Shaw conceded in the 1920s, shortly before the success of *Saint Joan*.

'This is all the more annoying as I do not believe for a moment that the French reading public is less accessible to my methods than any other public . . . I still believe that if only I could have secured a pulpit in

France, I could have amused the inhabitants quite as effectively as the Germans.'

In the words of Vicomte Robert d'Humières, Shaw became attached to his translator 'like a criminal is attached to the rope which hanged him'. It was 'a defiant and heroic act', intensely Shavian, that would end in 'suicide on the threshold of our admiration'. To a perpetual gunfire of criticism Hamon dug in for the rest of his life with the work he had never wanted to do. He and his wife remained desperately poor. Feeling perhaps his own part in the Hamons' poverty, Shaw purchased their house in Brittany for them and in the 1930s bought 'an annuity for his own and his wife's life, of £12 a month,' Shaw revealed to Trebitsch. 'And this enables him to live comfortably according to his standard of comfort.'

Trebitsch and Hamon were two principal members of Shaw's family of translators over whom he exercised great power and generosity. The antagonism which their amateur status and exclusive rights brought them in their own countries intensified their loyalty. They became part of a special Shavian clan (their intimacy seldom tested by an actual meeting) through which, like pollen on the wind, Shaw's words were eccentrically spread across the world.

2

HOME LIFE AND HOLIDAYS

> A true dramatist should be interested in everything.
>
> Shaw to Trebitsch (16 August 1903)

Charlotte treated her husband partly as an employer, partly as her child. It was the employer whose correspondence she dealt with, whose manuscripts she took to the typist. She also arranged lunches with people he should meet and protected him from other people who would worry him needlessly. It was on behalf of this employer, too, that she still sat on committees at the London School of Economics and the School of Medicine for Women, and had joined the play-reading committee of the Stage Society.

But it was the child who exercised her talent for anxiety. Some of his young hobbies – photography or the piano – were harmless. She didn't mind him taking her picture in the least (though she hated others doing so) and she grew to like his playing to her in the evening. Bicycles were dangerous; and he did very naughty things in newspapers – writing, for example, after the Queen died to denounce the rapturous lying-in-state as 'insanitary'.

She had given instructions to the servants to vary his diet as much as possible, and from time to time felt half-persuaded to try it herself. Whenever she was unwell she would pick at something of his vegetarian food, washed down with a glass of whisky. 'My wife has at last become a convinced vegetarian,' Shaw reported to Henry Salt in the summer of 1903, '. . . and she now eats nothing but birds & fish, which are not "butcher's meat".'

Charlotte regarded G.B.S.'s lust for publicity as part of the odder equipment of his genius. There was no other respectable way of explaining it. He literally *asked* for what he got sometimes, arriving at Max Beerbohm's house on his bicycle and requesting the cartoonist to do a drawing of him. 'Max was less gratified by this than might have been expected,' Lord David Cecil wrote, '. . . and suspected that Shaw was actuated less by admiration than by a desire for the publicity the cartoon might bring him. Max also found Shaw's appearance unappetizing; his pallid pitted skin and red hair like seaweed. And he was repelled by the back of his neck. "The back of his neck was especially bleak; very long, untenanted, and dead white," he explained.'

Max did over forty caricatures of G.B.S.'s 'temperance beverage face' and, as dramatic critic, reviewed more than twenty of his plays. 'My admiration for his genius has during fifty years and more been marred for me by dissent from almost any view that he holds about anything,' Max was to acknowledge in a letter written for Shaw's ninetieth birthday. And G.B.S. endorsed this: 'Max's blessings are all of them thinly disguised curses.' Max reinforced the disgust Shaw himself felt at the Shavian publicity phenomenon. After a couple of highly successful speeches in Glasgow during the first week of October 1903 he wrote to Trebitsch: 'I have hardly yet quite recovered from the self-loathing which such triumphs produce . . .

'I always suffer torments of remorse when the degrading exhibition is over. However, the thing had to be done; and there was no doing it by halves . . . I am not at all ashamed of what I said: it was excellent sense; but the way I said it – ugh! All that assumption of stupendous earnestness – merely to drive a little common sense into a crowd, like nails into a very tough board – leaves one empty, exhausted, disgusted.'

Max and Charlotte found themselves in agreement over G.B.S. He was never an artist, they said, but a reformer. 'That is what I always tell him,' insisted Charlotte. But in their married life it was she who attempted to reform him. Since it was only on holiday that, as he put it, 'I prefer to leave my public character behind me and to be treated as far as possible as a quite private and unknown individual', she tried to lead him on a succession of long holidays. During April and May 1901 she had him touring through France with her; and in July and August she planted him in Studland Rectory at Corfe Castle in Dorset. 'This is a very enchanting place – to look at,' Shaw informed Beatrice Webb. 'It also has the curious property of reviving every malady, every cramp, every pain, every bone fracture even, from which one has ever suffered.'

Next year Charlotte packed them both off to a safe hotel on the Norfolk coast for the summer. 'The only way to rest and get plenty of work done at the same time is to go to sea,' Shaw later concluded. This was not what Charlotte had in mind. She wanted to take him away from all his work. She wanted to banish the employer and make him wholly, for a time, her child.

In the spring of 1903 she rushed him through Parma, Perugia, Assisi, Orvieto, Siena, Genoa and Milan. 'I am getting old and demoralized,' he confessed to Janet Achurch, 'I have been in Italy for three weeks.' Three months later she placed him in Scotland, and held him there for ten weeks. 'There is no railway, no town, no shops, no society, no music, no entertainments, no beautiful ladies, absolutely nothing but fresh air and eternal rain,' Shaw wrote. 'Our house is primitive; our food is primitive; we do nothing but wander about, cycle against impossible winds, or pull a heavy fisherman's boat about the loch . . .'

For most Christmases Charlotte would board him out with her at a bracing hotel or in one of the houses she had rented. In April 1902 they had given up Piccard's Cottage at Guildford and the following year took instead a country house, Maybury Knoll, in a favourite part of Surrey, near Woking. Here they spent winter weekends and the whole of Christmas at the end of 1903, after which Charlotte was to rent a grander place at the top of a hill overlooking Welwyn which she liked better.

No sooner had Charlotte marched him up to the top of the hill than she marched him down again – and back to Italy. They started out on 1 May 1904 and arrived back in London on 10 June. A week later Shaw began a new play, his thirteenth, to be called *John Bull's Other Island*. Charlotte shuttled him between Adelphi Terrace and Welwyn, and then returned him, protesting, for the summer to Scotland. 'Our expedition has been so far a ruinous failure,' he calculated. 'The place is impossible – no place to write – no place to bathe . . . Oh these holidays, these accursed holidays!'

For fourteen years they were to go through every holiday side by side, despite his belief that married people 'should never travel together: they blame one another for everything that goes wrong.' It was particularly irritating for him to see how she preened herself on toning up his health while really driving him mad; it was exasperating for her to find, however exorbitant their journeys, he never failed to carry his work with him everywhere. But still they manacled themselves, each for the sake of the other. 'I am overacting the part of a respectable married man,' Shaw admitted. 'But I am only rehearsing for my old age: my guiltiest passions are still glowing beneath the surface.'

3

SHAKES VERSUS SHAV

I am not writing popular plays just now.

Shaw to Alma Murray (19 February 1901)

'You know all about "The Admirable Bashville", or at least you would know if you ever read my books,' Trebitsch read in one of Shaw's letters.

The Admirable Bashville or *Constancy Unrewarded* was itself a translation from Shaw's novel, *Cashel Byron's Profession*, into a three-act play in 'the primitive Elizabethan style'. This was Shaw's eleventh play and he had finished it in a week on 2 February 1901. Hearing rumours that there were several pirated stage versions of his novel in the United States, and that one of these productions was coming to Britain, he 'took the opportunity to produce a masterpiece' in order to protect his copyright. He squeezed out of this exercise all the fun he could, using it as another squib against bardolatry and claiming that he had been forced to employ the rigmarole of Shakespearian verse (of which 'I am childishly fond'), occasionally patching in actual lines from Shakespeare and Marlowe, because he did not have the time to write it all in prose. Having plagiarized his own work and parodied Shakespeare's, he produced a caricature of his advertising methods. It was, he assured Trebitsch, 'my greatest play'. But this delight in what was 'my only achievement in pure letters' began to recoil once other playwrights hit on the notion of agreeing with him.

A number of Shaw's 'serious intentions' are planted in the burlesque. He has some fun with phonetics; he airs his expertise on self-defence; he owns up to the loneliness of excellence and devotes some mighty lines to family and filial sentiment. There is a surge of real feeling when Cashel contrasts the presumed barbarities of boxing with the concealed cruelties of polite life.

> . . . this hand
> That many a two days bruise hath ruthless given,
> Hath kept no dungeon locked for twenty years,
> Hath slain no sentient creature for my sport.
> I am too squeamish for your dainty world,
> That cowers behind the gallows and the lash,
> The world that robs the poor, and with their spoil
> Does what its tradesmen tell it. Oh, your ladies!
> Sealskinned and egret-feathered; all defiance
> To Nature; cowering if one say to them
> 'What will the servants think?' Your gentlemen!
> Your tailor-tyrannized visitors of whom
> Flutter of wing and singing in the wood
> Make chickenbutchers. And your medicine men!
> Groping for cures in the tormented entrails
> Of friendly dogs. Pray have you asked all these
> To change their occupations? Find you mine
> So grimly crueller? I cannot breathe
> An air so petty and so poisonous.

Shaw assisted Harley Granville Barker in directing the first professional presentation of the play, put on by the Stage Society on 7 and 8 June 1903 at the Imperial Theatre in London. It was an early instance of the working association between the two men, and laid down the lines for their later collaborative work at the Court Theatre. Barker was (in the modern sense) stage-manager and Shaw arrived fairly late in the preparation of his play. He hunted enthusiastically for bird-whistles, some soft-nosed spears, a white beaver hat, post-horn, one enormous blue handkerchief with white spots, a throne: also 'We shall want a crowd'); and directed it in the Elizabethan stage manner with traverses, and two beefeaters with placards denoting the scenes. He insisted that it should be announced as 'Bernard Shaw's celebrated drama in blank verse with, possibly, an epigraph: "If you have tears, prepare to shed them now." Shakespeare.'

As in his subsequent 'Interlude', *The Dark Lady of the Sonnets*, the humour depends upon the audience's familiarity with Shakespeare. Those with no Shakespearian knowledge would sit bewildered or else, in all earnestness, break into applause. Despite its awkward playing length, the Stage Society production 'went with a roar from beginning to end'. The policeman (played by the cricketer C. Aubrey Smith, later to become famous as a Hollywood film actor) was made up as G.B.S. so effectively that his mother, sitting next to him, was deeply perplexed.

Also performed was the copyright trick of upstaging all American dramatizations of the novel – including one by Stanislas Strange (who was to write the libretto for *The Chocolate Soldier*) and starring, as Cashel Byron, former world heavyweight champion 'Gentleman Jim' Corbett.

The Admirable Bashville was published by Grant Richards in October 1901 as part of a new edition of *Cashel Byron's Profession* that also included Shaw's essay 'A Note on Modern Prizefighting'. The book was reviewed at length, and disconcertingly, by Max Beerbohm.

'As a passage by steam is to a voyage by sail, so is Mr Shaw's fiction to true fiction . . . he wants to impress certain theories on us, to convert us to this or that view. The true creator wishes mainly to illude us with a sense of actual or imaginative reality. To achieve that aim, he must suppress himself and his theories: they kill illusion. He must accept life as it presents itself to his experience or imagination, not use his brain to twist it into the patterns of a purpose. Such self-sacrifice is beyond Mr Shaw.'

Here was the most coherent argument so far raised against the Shavian art. Shaw could not create: his characters were all victims of Shavian theses, all parts of himself differentiated only by quick changes and superficial idiosyncrasies. On another level, as a personality, G.B.S. was immortal. There was no one like him. Seriousness and frivolity were the essence of Shavianism. 'He is not a serious man trying to be frivolous,' Beerbohm explained. 'He is a serious man who cannot help being frivolous, and in him height of spirits is combined with depth of conviction more illustriously than in any of his compatriots.' It did not matter what he wrote. All his writing was filleted with Shavianism – that quality whose deep seriousness served artistically to raise the humour. 'As a teacher, as a propagandist, Mr Shaw is no good at all,' Beerbohm joyfully concluded. It was as a comedian whose frivolity, vampire-like, sucked the seriousness from his work, that he was unique. So when he claimed apropos his next play, *Man and Superman*, that 'the matter isnt really in my hands. I have to say the things that seem to me to want saying', everyone sharing Beerbohm's view of G.B.S. drew in their breath and prepared to greet it with a good laugh.

4

MAN AND SUPERMAN

You must not translate it, as you would get six years in a fortress for the preface alone.

Shaw to Trebitsch (7 July 1902)

The characters had started talking inside Shaw's head over two years before. In May 1900 he began outlining a Parliament in Hell between Don Juan and the Devil. Around the Socratic debate he composed a three-act comedy, completing the scenario between 2 July and 8 October 1901. He worked between accidents and on journeys, in hotels and at home: he worked whenever Charlotte took her eye off him until, in June 1902, this many-layered work, now called *Man and Superman. A Comedy and a Philosophy*, was finished – when the business of revision immediately began. In January 1903 Shaw read it aloud to the Webbs at the Overstrand Hotel at Cromer in Norfolk. 'To me it seems a great work; quite the biggest thing he has done,' Beatrice wrote in her diary. 'He has found his *form*: a play which is not a play; but only a combination of essay, treatise, interlude, lyric – all the different forms illustrating the same central idea.'

Since it was 'useless as an acting play', he explained to Hamon, being 'as long as three Meyerbeer operas and no audience that had not already had a Shaw education could stand it', he had decided to publish *Man and Superman* himself, abandoning Grant Richards and signing an agreement with Archibald Constable to act as distribution agent for his works – an agreement that lasted the remaining forty-seven years of his life.

Man and Superman was published on 11 August 1903. 'I cannot be a bellettrist,' Shaw wrote in his Preface. 'Effectiveness of assertion is the Alpha and Omega of style. He who has nothing to assert has no style and can have none: he who has something to assert will go as far in power of style as its momentousness and his conviction will carry him. Disprove his assertion after it is made, yet its style remains.'

Between style and art and power and reality Shaw crossed the lines of his argument with such dexterity as to bring almost everyone into confusion. Critics were fixed in his net of words – though not Max Beerbohm who seemed to slip between the meshes. Max was to draw a caricature of Shaw bringing a bundle of clothes to the Danish critic, Georg Brandes (who is represented as a pawnbroker), and asking for immortality in exchange for the lot. Brandes protests: 'Come, I've handled these goods before! Coat, Mr Schopenhauer's; waistcoat, Mr Ibsen's; Mr Nietzsche's trousers – .' To which Shaw answers: 'Ah, but look at the patches!' As for style, Max astutely judged his Alpha and Omega to be 'more akin to the art of oral debating than of literary exposition. That is because he trained himself to speak before he trained himself to write.'

For the same reason, Max conceded, Shaw excelled in writing words to be spoken by the human voice. 'In swiftness, tenseness and lucidity of dialogue no living writer can touch the hem of Mr Shaw's garment,' Max wrote. 'In *Man and Superman* every phrase rings and flashes. Here, though Mr Shaw will be angry with me, is perfect art.' For Shaw *used* art 'as a means of making people listen to him . . .

'He is as eager to be a popular dramatist and . . . willing to demean himself in any way that may help him to the goal . . . I hope he will reach the goal. It is only the theatrical managers who stand between him and the off-chance of a real popular success.'

Man and Superman, Max concluded, was Shaw's masterpiece so far. This 'most complete expression of the most distinct personality in current literature' showed G.B.S. able to employ art without becoming an artist and excelling in dialogue without developing into a playwright. From this opinion Max somewhat recanted two years later when he saw *Man and Superman* (in its three-act version) performed on stage. It was not only the humanizing of Shaw's words by living actors that changed his mind. He also appears to have been swayed by Shaw's argument that, as a caricaturist, Max also did not 'see things and men as they are', but that his distortions, far from disqualifying him as an artist, were the essence of his art. The artist creates his own reality and his own epoch: and Britain was about to enter a Shavian epoch. Max sensed this. Shaw was one of those for whom the visible world had largely ceased to exist and was being replaced by a world seen through his mind's eye. That it was a world disliked by Max was partly the reason why he had denied its creator artistic capacity. The production of *John Bull's Other Island* in 1904 was to convince him that Shaw had 'an instinct for the theatre'. And when he saw *Man and Superman* on stage in 1905, he prepared to make way for the coming Shavian revolution in the British theatre:

'Mr Shaw, it is insisted, cannot draw life: he can only distort it. He has no knowledge of human nature: he is but a theorist. All his characters are but so many incarnations of himself. Above all, he cannot write plays. He has no dramatic instinct, no theatrical technique . . .

That theory might have held water in the days before Mr Shaw's plays were acted. Indeed, I was in the habit of propounding it myself . . . When

Man and Superman was published, I . . . said that (even without the philosophic scene in hell) it would be quite unsuited to any stage. When I saw it performed . . . I found that as a piece of theatrical construction it was perfect . . . to deny that he is a dramatist merely because he chooses, for the most part, to get drama out of contrasted types of character and thought, without action, and without appeal to the emotions, seems to me both unjust and absurd. His technique is peculiar because his purpose is peculiar. But it is not the less technique.'

*

Man and Superman is the first in a trilogy of plays in which Shaw's thesis and antithesis of fact and fantasy produced the synthesis of evolutionary progress. Creative evolution had the potential for replacing his lonely sense of being 'a sojourner on this planet rather than a native of it' with the feeling of being part of the collective consciousness 'up to the chin in the life of his own time'. The Life Force was not a rival scientific theory to Darwin's Natural Selection, but a different outlook on life. By making external a division he felt to exist within himself Shaw was able to use an intellectual method – the Hegelian triad which he had picked up from the British socialist philosopher Belfort Bax – of reconciling opposites and bringing harmony to his life. He wished to create the new drama in which, as in a series of parables, he could rewrite history and set it on a new course.

The Hegelian structure became a model for his thought. Reviewing a novel by Moncure Conway early in 1888, he had written of Hegelianism as never having been positively 'adapted and translated into practical English politics'. In the hands of Marx, it had been 'chiefly effective as a scathing but quite negative criticism of industrial individualism'.

It was positive Hegelianism that Shaw wanted to import into English politics. This is made explicit in a letter he sent some fifteen years later to the Labour Member of Parliament Charles Trevelyan. 'A Government . . . if it is really to govern and propagate its species . . . must have a common religion, which nowadays means a philosophy and a science, and it must have an economic policy founded on that religion.

'Well, I contend that such a nexus exists . . . you will find it in Thomas Hardy's poems at one extreme of literature and in the blitherings of Christian Science at the other. But take two expositions that may be known to you: the third act of Man and Superman and Bergson's Creative Evolution. These are totally independent of one another: Bergson and I would have written as we did, word for word, each if the other had never been born. And yet one is a dramatization of the other. Our very catchwords, Life Force and Élan Vital, are translations of one another . . . why not a creative-evolutionist party? . . .

The economic policy of the party is clear enough. Everyone who can see the sun shining at noon can also see that there is only one main problem to be solved, and that is the redistribution of income. Also that it is not only an economic question, but a political and biological one. Here you have a body of doctrine on which a party could be built literally over a whole epoch.'

Towards the third act of his play Shaw felt especially protective. Its long second scene, staged as a dream and held in a chronological paradox 'Beyond Space, Beyond Time', is a science fiction made from Shaw's retrospective longings. It is a contest between his optimism for which the Tanner-surrogate Don Juan speaks, and his pessimism which is represented by Mendoza's counterpart, the Devil. Agreeing on much, they are divided in their debate over the need and practicality of human progress. Both are contemptuous of the morality of pretence which filled the Victorian theatre and reflected the conventions of life outside. But what are the alternatives? The Devil says fantasy and play; Don Juan says the evolution of a higher type of human being.

Heaven and hell are not states of afterlife but metaphors for opposing temperaments, values and philosophies. Juan defines hell as 'the home of the unreal and of the seekers for happiness . . . Here you escape this tyranny of the flesh; for here you are not an animal at all: you are . . . in a word, bodiless . . . here there are no hard facts to contradict you, no ironic contrast of your needs with your pretensions, no human comedy, nothing but a perpetual romance.'

This aspect of Shaw's hell was to become a factor of his theology almost twenty years later in *Back to Methuselah* where the tyranny of the flesh disappears in a whirlpool of pure thought. Here was a three-hundred-year romance by an extremely fastidious man whose disgust with the physical condition of human beings compelled him to eliminate them from his philosophy. 'There are no social questions here, no political questions, no religious questions, best of all, perhaps, no sanitary questions.' Shaw's formula for hell in *Man and Superman* has enough in common with the bodiless Utopia of *Back to Methuselah* to suggest that the Devil may surreptitiously be going to win a good part of his case.

Conventional morals will always succumb to the Devil's attractions. To resist his hell, Juan argues, we need evolutionary morals. If reality is worry, ugliness and age, sadness and tragedy and death, why not, asks the Devil, use your ingenuity to create a life of endless escape from it? For two reasons, answers Juan. Nature has given man a brain; he needs the power of self-awareness and understanding. The direct pursuit of happiness and beauty leads to misery – happiness may only be gained as a by-product of other endeavours. Secondly, life is not composed as the Devil would like us to believe. It is an illusion to think that we can solve our problems. From each problem solved springs some new challenge. So life must forever progress upwards: or end. Man's quest for knowledge has set him off on the great adventure of transforming his environment and understanding the universe. He may not stop the world and go off on a perpetual holiday.

Juan's belief in brains provokes the Devil into his first great counter-attack. 'Have you walked up and down upon the earth lately?' he enquires. What have human brains done but produce more awful weapons of destruction? It is when we become too ambitious on behalf of the human race that we end up destroying ourselves. His monologue amounts to a conservative attack on the illusions of progress and a recommendation of the aristocratic principle of cultivated living.

Don Juan's reply reveals his belief that salvation depends upon the urge to transcend past achievements. It is easily conceivable that the world will blow itself up, or Western civilization peter out, unless this human urge is renewed. But the Devil is no vulgar hedonist. 'I am also on the intellectual plane,' he says. It is the credulous strivers after perfection in the social organization, he insists, who slaughter millions. He, the Devil, stands for moral principles in that he treats people as ends, not means.

The resolution to their debate comes through Doña Ana with her cry at the end of the scene: 'a father for the Superman!' And so, from the two ways of serving the Life Force, the biological and the intellectual, Shaw gives priority in time to the first. Evolutionary progress, he suggests, depends on sexual instinct; on the coming together of opposites to produce through generations a better human combination of mind and body. In *The Quintessence of Ibsenism* and *The Perfect Wagnerite*, the battle had been fought between realist and idealist for the mind of the philistine; in *Man and Superman* the evolutionary need for greater intelligence lies in the sexual conquest of the realist by the philistine. So the dramatic pursuit of the intellectual Tanner by the predatory Ann is not a defeat for intelligence after all. Tanner's dream and disquisition with the Devil is Shaw's attempt, through operatic argument, to achieve the 'drama of thought'. But Don Juan's speeches grow too long and, behind their resolute optimism, reveal Shaw's panic.

There is no doubt that Shaw intended Don Juan to win the debate. Against the common belief in a God who looked at the world and saw that it was good, he postulated a God who looked and saw it could be bettered. 'I tell you that as long as I can conceive something better than myself I cannot be easy unless I am striving to bring it into existence or clearing the way for it,' says Juan. 'That is the law of my life.' That this purpose is Shaw's own is made clear by a parallel passage in the 'Epistle Dedicatory', where he writes: 'This is the true joy in life, the being used for a purpose recognized by yourself as a mighty one.'

Tanner wins all his word-battles. Ann wins the actual battle between them. Shaw's Superman was a symbol for the synthesis between word and deed.

Only the obtuseness of theatre managers, as Beerbohm had said, was able to postpone Shaw's success as a playwright. The younger generation of theatre audiences was waiting for him. Almost two years after publication of the book the three-act play was first performed. This version, full of melancholic autobiographical undertones, has a precise theatrical unity. It is a romantic courtship comedy about the stock subjects of marriage and money, and has all the farcical episodes of the love-chase. The Victorian and Edwardian theatregoer would easily recognize the situations and characters. There is a love-pursuit through Europe, a capture by brigands and a rescue; there is a clandestine marriage, an emotional triangle, the reading of a will, a happy ending; the stage is peopled by standard figures – the romantic artist, the heavy father, the lover and the servant in a long line from Leporello and Sancho Panza to Sam Weller and Jeeves.

Yet nothing is what it seems to be and everywhere romantic expectation is confounded. Shaw replaces the woman-on-a-pedestal with the female huntress; the new woman with the technological man. The play is crowded with paradoxical reversals. His brigands are vestrymen and Fabians, their leader a love-afflicted sentimentalist; the rich and difficult father turns out to be a social eccentric who wants a misalliance for his son and is reconciled to his marriage not by his daughter-in-law's purity and sweetness but her business acumen. A daughter dominates her mother; a servant rules his employer; and the governing action of the play is the woman's pursuit of her lover. Hell is revealed as a sentimentalist's picture of heaven.

In this skill at inverting popular conventions and creating genre antitypes lay the special power of Shaw's 'heretical' plays. He welcomed his audience into a world where everything was familiar to them, then upset all its values and forced it to 'reconsider its morals'.

5

JOHN BULL'S OTHER ISLAND

> The object of the play is to teach Irish people the value of an Englishman as well as to shew the Englishman his own absurdities.
>
> 'Author's Instructions to the Producer', *John Bull's Other Island*

Two years separated the completion of *Man and Superman* from the composition of Shaw's next play. Shortly before the publication of *Man and Superman*, Shaw confided to Yeats that he had it 'quite seriously in my head to write an Irish play (frightfully modern – no banshees or leprechauns)'; but he did nothing further until what seemed a fair chance appeared.

It was Yeats who gave him this chance. Together with Lady Gregory and Edward Martyn, he had founded the Irish Literary Theatre which proposed to create in Dublin 'a Celtic and Irish school of dramatic literature . . . [with] that freedom to experiment which is not found in theatres of England'. They must 'escape the stupefying memory of the theatre of commerce' which clung to London's West End.

There was much that was familiar in this to Shaw and much that appealed to him. Lady Gregory was to his mind 'the greatest living Irishwoman'; Edward Martyn, an owl-blinking misogynist, lover of wine and caviar, and first president of Sinn Fein, was an admirer of Ibsen; and Yeats manoeuvred his theatre colleagues with all the skill Shaw devoted to the Fabians. In 1902 Yeats fell in with the Fay brothers, Frank and Willy, and their little band of Irish actors. From this association, the following year, the Irish National Theatre Society was born with Yeats himself as president, and a new set of colleagues, Maud Gonne, Douglas Hyde and the poet, theosophist and visionary painter George Russell (known as A.E.) its vice-presidents. In the spring of 1904, the Society was invited to play at the Royalty Theatre in London, and Shaw went along to watch them. They played Synge's *In the Shadow of the Glen* and *Riders to the Sea*; Yeats's *The King's Threshold* and *A Pot of Broth*; and Padraic Colum's *Broken Soil*, all showing the influence of Gordon Craig's revolt against the elaborate productions of Irving and Beerbohm Tree. It was then that Shaw opened his eyes to a renaissance in the Irish theatre.

Yet it had been, until this year, a hole-and-corner affair not dissimilar, in its fashion, to the Stage Society. What changed matters was the involvement of Annie Horniman who bought a ninety-nine-year lease on a small music-hall theatre within the Mechanics Institute on the corner of Lower Abbey Street, and adjacent premises in Marlborough Street that 'had served as a bank, the home of a nationalist debating society, a recruiting centre for the Fenian movement, and the City Morgue'. She now offered Yeats, as president of the Society, use of the new theatre cost-free. The Abbey Theatre was to open its doors at the end of 1904, and it was for this opening, 'as a patriotic contribution to the repertory of the Irish Literary Theatre', that Yeats invited Shaw to write his next play.

'Not a word of the play yet on paper,' Shaw promised Lady Gregory on 20 June. In fact he had begun writing it, under the provisional title *Rule Britannia*, in a pocket notebook three days earlier while staying with Charlotte at Hindhead. It continued seething in his mind and filling his notebooks over the next ten weeks.

On 7 September Shaw sent the completed play to Ethel Dickens with instructions to type it out and forward a copy to Yeats. He had been horrified to find that the autograph manuscript, scattered through four pocket notebooks, contained about 32,000 words. Henry Arthur Jones, he recollected, had put 18,000 as the correct length, 'but I am too exhausted to attempt to cut it,' he told Yeats.

In *John Bull's Other Island* Shaw contrasted the twenty years of his upbringing in Dublin with the twenty years of his career in London. At one level, which he later developed in his Preface, the play is about the opposing political histories and national characteristics of the two countries. But Ireland and England are also metaphors for differing philosophies: and Shaw's experiment at reconciling them is the theme of this self-revealing work.

'Live in contact with dreams and you will get something of their charm: live in contact with facts and you will get something of their brutality. I wish I could find a country to live in where the facts were not brutal and the dreams not unreal.' This wish, voiced by Larry Doyle, the exiled Irishman working in England, was the motive-power behind these middle-period plays. Larry Doyle is the vertex of a triangle at one corner of which stands the successful English businessman Tom Broadbent, and at the other Peter Keegan, the unfrocked Irish priest, who meet over Broadbent's plan to form a Land Development Syndicate.

In Broadbent Shaw created, for Irish audiences, the stage-Englishman, having in the first scene chased the stage-Irishman Tim Haffigan off as an impostor. Broadbent represents the world of facts, however brutal; Keegan the world of dreams, however unreal. Broadbent is the perfect philistine, a 'robust, full-blooded, energetic man in the prime of life'. His kingdom is the material world. He feels happy in what Keegan describes as 'very clearly a place of torment and penance'. On the contrary, Broadbent declares, it is 'quite good enough for me: rather a jolly place, in fact'.

The key to Broadbent's success is his narrowness of intelligence and imagination. He simplifies everything for profitable use. 'The only really simple thing is to go straight for what you want and grab it,' says another philistine, Ann Whitefield, in *Man and Superman*. Broadbent is the acquisitive man. Within twenty-four hours of arriving at Rosscullen he has collared the parliamentary seat, taken up Larry's sweetheart Nora Reilly and acquired the land for development. He brings to Ireland a terrible corruption of Shaw's belief in improvement, but he brings it cheerfully. The stage directions picture him as 'always buoyant and irresistible'.

Everything that is absent from Broadbent goes to make the character of Peter Keegan. Broadbent could be played by a Falstaffian performer; Keegan needed 'a poetic actor'. Broadbent is a land speculator interested in the modern technology of motor cars, neat golf links, new hotels. Keegan, who loves the land, speaks with grasshoppers and calls the donkey, the ass and the pig his brothers. In contrast to Father Dempsey, the parochial reality, Keegan is 'an ideal Catholic', the first and most convincing of Shaw's mystical sages, who retreats at the end of the play to the Round Tower and will reappear briefly as Androcles and later as the damaged Captain Shotover in *Heartbreak House*.

Into Keegan's mouth Shaw put his own fastidious sense of horror at Broadbent's world –

'[a] place where the fool flourishes and the good and wise are hated and persecuted, a place where men and women torture one another in the name of love; where children are scourged and enslaved in the name of parental duty and education; where the weak in body are poisoned and mutilated in the name of healing, and the weak in character are put to the horrible torture of imprisonment, not for hours but for years, in the name of justice.'

Broadbent's schemes for the future ('this place may have an industrial future, or it may have a residential future') do not impress Keegan who replies that it 'may have no future at all'.

Broadbent embodies action, Keegan speaks for the emotions and Larry Doyle represents the intellect. Throughout the play there is a bias in favour of action. Larry has had only two ideas: 'to learn to do something; and then to get out of Ireland and have a chance of doing it'. Ireland 'produces two kinds of men in strange perfection: saints and traitors,' we are told. If Keegan is the saint, Larry Doyle is the traitor. He has repressed everything he shares with Keegan: he has rejected Ireland. Shaw's stage directions throughout Larry's long speech on 'the dreaming! the torturing, heart-scalding, never satisfying dreaming, dreaming, dreaming, dreaming!' of Ireland underline the personal feeling he put into these pages: '*With sudden anguish . . . Savagely . . . bitterly, at Broadbent . . . With fierce shivering self-contempt . . . Dropping his voice like a man making some shameful confidence.*'

Not sharing Keegan's self-sufficiency, Larry must borrow his strength from Broadbent's self-confidence. Otherwise, he says, 'I should never have done anything'. It is Broadbent who sees clearly the price Larry has paid. 'He has absolutely no capacity for enjoyment,' Broadbent tells Nora: 'he couldn't make any woman happy. He's as clever as be-blowed; but . . . he doesn't really care for anything or anybody.'

Keegan is the man Sonny might have grown into if he had been able to endure the anguish of living in the Land of Dreams; Larry Doyle, with his 'clever head', his 'suggestion of thinskinnedness and dissatisfaction' and determination to be ruthless, must have been Shaw's nightmare. The syndicate which Keegan and Broadbent have formed (in which Larry owns a 'bit of the stock') is not the synthesis between dreams and facts for which Shaw was looking. It is a business partnership in which Larry's intellectual powers are used to serve Broadbent's philistine aims.

The second partnership in the play, that between Broadbent and Nora, is not a marriage of body and spirit, but a devouring of the spirit by the body. A 'frail figure', she is 'almost sexless' and he, with his 'good broad chest', promises to 'plump out your muscles and make em elastic and set up your figure'. She is his ethereal 'ideal' and he will make her into the housewife of 'a solid four-square home'.

Everyone remains separated in the play and no one is converted. Broadbent takes charge of the world; Keegan retires to his tower; and the conflict within Larry is not reconciled. He has split life into dreams and facts, and chosen facts as reality.

But was the world of facts real? Shaw's insistence that it was is continually interrupted by his subversive humour and a pessimism that undermines much of what he dedicated his career to establishing. 'Every dream is a prophecy: every jest is an earnest in the womb of Time,' says Keegan who explains to Nora that 'my way of joking is to tell the truth'. It is Keegan who sees reality in dreams and strikes an apocalyptic note over Shaw's own Fabian territory of statistics: 'For four wicked centuries the world has dreamed this foolish dream of efficiency; and the end is not yet. But the end will come.'

*

The play was 'a wonderful piece of work' and 'full of good things,' William Fay, the Abbey Theatre manager, reported to Yeats. Synge, too, believed it would 'hold a Dublin audience, and at times move them if even tolerably played'. And Yeats wrote to Shaw: 'I thought in reading the first act that you had forgotten Ireland, but I found in the other acts that it is the only subject on which you are entirely serious . . .

'You have said things in this play which are entirely true about Ireland, things which nobody has ever said before . . . It astonishes me that you should have been so long in London and yet have remembered so much. To some extent this play is unlike anything you have done before. Hitherto you have taken your situations from melodrama, and called up logic to make them ridiculous. Your process here seems to be quite different, you are taking your situations more from life, you are for the first time trying to get the atmosphere of a place . . . a geographical conscience . . . You have laughed at the things that are ripe for laughter, and not where the ear is still green . . . we can play it, and survive to play something else.'

Yet there were difficulties. The company met to discuss these difficulties in the second week of October 1904: the difficulty of length; the difficulty of getting a cast; the difficulty of handling modern appliances such as grasshoppers and hydraulic bridges. These difficulties accumulated as they argued, silencing a more fundamental difficulty: that (to use Shaw's words in the Preface to the 1906 edition) 'it was uncongenial to the whole spirit of the neo-Gaelic movement, which is bent on creating a new Ireland after its own ideal, whereas my play is a very uncompromising presentment of the real old Ireland'. Yeats was to concede when he saw it performed in London that 'it acts very much better than one could have foreseen'. Like Max Beerbohm, he had underrated Shaw's instinct for the theatre partly because 'I don't really like it,' he wrote. 'It is fundamentally ugly and shapeless.'

The shape of the play, loosely constructed round a string of character-turns with the emphasis directed away from the action and focused on a parallel series of discussions that occur at rather unremarkable moments (the after-breakfast pause, the after-tea stroll) makes use of the conventional props of Irish Romance to explode the Irish romantic ideal. Yeats instinctively felt opposed to such extravaganza. Yeats's writing was oblique and Shaw's assertive; and Yeats wrote poetry where Shaw laughed. All they shared were the same enemies. 'If I had gone to the hills nearby to look upon Dublin and to ponder upon myself, I too might have become a poet like Yeats, Synge and the rest of them,' Shaw stated. 'But I prided myself on thinking clearly, and therefore could not stay. Whenever I took a problem or a state of life of which my Irish contemporaries sang sad songs, I always pushed it to its logical conclusions, and then inevitably it resolved itself into comedy.'

Such a passage helps to explain Yeats's description of Shaw as a 'barbarian of the barricades'. When Shaw made Larry Doyle deride Keegan as sentimental, chastise the eternal dreaming in himself, and question the holy ground on which they both stood, he uprooted the Irish legends from which sprang Lady Gregory's and Yeats's plays. His 'queer elephant' of a play seemed antagonistic to everything the Abbey Theatre was to achieve. 'We all admire it,' Yeats wrote: and between them all a polite understanding was kept up that it had merely been too large and difficult a work for the Abbey to handle.

Yeats could recognize the wonderful power of Shaw's pen – its logic, justice, audacity, conviction. But Shaw represented 'the spirit of the press, of hurry, of immediate interests' over what Yeats felt was the slow-burning spirit of literature. He was consuming his own talent with superficial theatricality, the unnerving tic of his wit, rambling vulgarity – anything that seemed to stiffen the purpose of the moment.

6

GRANVILLE BARKER COMES TO COURT

> We shall have to play off the piece as a very advanced and earnest card in the noble game of elevating the British theatre.
>
> Shaw to Granville Barker (24 August 1904)

Looking around for an actor suitable to play Marchbanks for a Sunday performance of *Candida* at the Strand Theatre in the summer of 1900, Charrington had proposed the name of Harley Granville Barker. At the sixth 'meeting' of the Stage Society, Barker played Marchbanks and was 'the success of the piece', Shaw told Archer. This performance of *Candida* completed the Stage Society's first season. The Society was now the principal rallying point for things modern in the theatre. On 16 July 1900 the maximum membership was increased from three to five hundred (each paying a yearly subscription of two guineas) and a decision was taken to add to the private Sunday evening presentation a weekday matinée to which the press (though required to pay) would be admitted. Performances were still described as 'meetings'; no scenery was employed and no salary offered to the actors who all received the same nominal sum – one guinea – for expenses. These rules enabled the Society legally to present new British plays as well as classical and contemporary foreign dramas (for some of which the Censor had refused a licence).

The Stage Society's Sunday evening and Monday afternoon performances gave Barker some experience as a director as well as actor, particularly in the presentation of his own four-act comedy, *The Marrying of Ann Leete*. 'Do you realise that he is a great poet and dramatist,' Shaw asked Henry Arthur Jones. ' . . . His *The Marrying of Ann Leete* is really an exquisite play. I truckle to G.B. in order to conciliate him when he is forty.' Behind this half-frivolous tone was the feeling that he was no longer alone: at last he had a successor in the theatre, someone to share, inherit and modify the Shavian stage experiment. Before *Ann Leete*, Barker had written other plays. Like Shaw's, they had seemed unplayable. But Shaw 'found them fascinating'. At first he had doubted whether Barker's 'delicacy of style' would travel across the footlights. But on seeing *Ann Leete* performed under Barker's own stage management, 'I had to confess that he had succeeded,' Shaw wrote.

'There is a sort of dainty strangeness about it that fits its eighteenth century period and costumes; and the curious way in which it begins in a garden at midnight takes it so effectually out of the Philistine key that its quaint fantastic conversation, consisting mostly of hints and innuendoes, seems to belong to it naturally.'

Here lay the theatre of the future. Shaw felt a special tenderness towards the young man, as if his own blatant qualities, obliterating much that was sensitive in himself, had served to protect him. After all, it had been to bulldoze Irving's execrable Lyceum mutilations off the stage that the phenomenon of G.B.S. had been partly manufactured. That Barker could afford to take no notice of Irving was partly due to G.B.S.; and partly, of course, a matter of age.

Shaw was twenty-one years older than Barker, 'old enough', he wrote, 'to be his father'. This was indeed the peculiar kinship he felt for him. He had grown up in an atmosphere of good speech and drama and with a thorough knowledge of Dickens and Shakespeare. He scored his first stage success in 1899 playing Richard II for William Poel, but was to be no happier as a successful actor than Shaw was as a successful platform speaker. Beatrice Webb observed him to be 'a most attractive person . . . good looking in a charming refined fashion – with a subtle intellectual expression – faculties more analytic than artistic?

' . . . with varied interests, good memory, a sharp observer of human nature and above all a delicate appreciation of music, poetry and art – a medley of talents of which I do not yet see a very definite whole. He has not yet emancipated himself from G.B.S.'s influence or found his own soul.'

Barker's incompleteness fascinated people. What Beatrice thought of as the influence of G.B.S. was probably a similarity of temperament. 'I am an intellectual, but by no means a dramatic disciple of G.B.S.,' Barker declared. 'We have quite different ideas . . .' G.B.S. agreed. 'We were as different as Verdi from Debussy.' Yet there was a natural intimacy between them. They talked much in quotations from Dickens and Shakespeare, using them as a private code. But they seldom discussed their own plays. 'We took them as they came, like facts of nature.' Shaw was able to watch and direct Barker in a number of his roles during the early stages of their friendship: he was Marchbanks, the poet Shaw had repressed in himself; he was Father Keegan, the best self Shaw had sealed up in the Round Tower; he played Jack Tanner made up with a beard to look like a younger G.B.S.; and in Shaw's next play *Major Barbara*, he was to play Adolphus Cusins, the foundling academic who is adopted as his heir by the Shavian father figure of Undershaft, also a foundling. From this succession of sympathetic roles a whisper arose that Barker was Shaw's natural son. The notion appealed to Shaw who observed that most people rejected the hypothesis 'on the ground that I am physically incapable of parentage'.

Barker fulfilled the imaginative role of son to Shaw's father and Charlotte's mother, replacing the natural child they never had. He seemed all things to all people – whatever they wanted most. Charlotte was one of several childless women in whom he prompted a maternal instinct. For G.B.S., Barker became someone to scold and schoolmaster, encourage and idealize; he was the juvenile lead with whom G.B.S. shared the family companionship of work.

In the summer of 1901 Barker and Shaw had joined the management committee of the Stage Society which had decided to put on *Mrs Warren's Profession* towards the end of that year. Because the play had not been granted a licence, however, thirteen theatres, three hotels, two music halls and the Royal Society of British Artists refused to lend their premises. From these difficulties and delays Shaw and Barker drew differing lessons. Shaw felt that the Stage Society was capable of putting on a 'tomfoolery' such as *The Admirable Bashville*; but a performance even of the first act of *Caesar and Cleopatra* was too large an enterprise: the Society could not scrape together 'the price of a sphinx & an old pantomime wardrobe for the Egyptian & Roman soldiers'. It was for this reason that he had turned to the Abbey Theatre.

For Barker, the cap-in-hand, door-to-door experiences over *Mrs Warren's Profession* had emphasized the need for a permanent theatre. His chance came early in 1904 when he was invited to produce *Two Gentlemen of Verona* at the Court Theatre in Sloane Square. The lease of this theatre had recently been bought by J. H. Leigh, a wealthy businessman and amateur actor, to stage a series of 'Shakespearean Representations' featuring his wife Thyrza Norman. The first two productions had been unsatisfactory and Leigh, coming to William Archer for help, was advised to employ Granville Barker for his next play. Leigh struck up an arrangement with Barker that allowed him to give six matinées of *Candida* at the Court. The play was well-received by the critics and actually made a profit.

Three weeks later Barker was producing Gilbert Murray's rhyming translation of Euripides' *Hippolytus* at the Lyric Theatre. 'J. H. Leigh has expressed himself bitten with the idea of doing Greek plays,' Barker confided to Murray. 'Not a word – but let us talk anon.' This talk between Barker, Leigh and the Court Theatre's manager J. E. Vedrenne 'led to the most important development in Barker's career'. He suggested giving regular matinées at the Court on those afternoons when the London West End theatres were closed. The management would then be able to engage first-class professional actors who would not be playing at those hours and, because they were interested in this new work, would be prepared to act for a nominal salary. Vedrenne took charge of the management and, with the backing of small sums of money from friends, they agreed to begin the experiment that autumn.

As the opening performance at the Court Theatre, he repeated the Murray–Euripides *Hippolytus*. The second Court play, after a good deal of negotiation, was *John Bull's Other Island*.

Nominally it was Barker who produced *John Bull's Other Island*; in fact it was Shaw. 'You can imagine the state I am in with rehearsing,' he wrote to the actress Ada Rehan. 'It is great fun; and I have got them all to the point of believing that this is the turning point of their careers, and that something immense is happening.' He had got himself to believe this too.

Shaw had strong opinions as to how all the parts should be played. But these opinions were for the actors to interpret and adapt: 'Dont worry yourself by trying to carry out my suggestions exactly or hampering yourself in any way with them,' he advised J. L. Shine, who was playing Larry Doyle. 'Very likely when you study them over you will be able to improve on them.

'That's all they're for. I think I am probably nearly right as to the best changes and stopping places on the journey; but as to the way of making them, follow your own feeling and make the most of your own skill: turn the whole thing inside out if you like . . . dont hesitate on my account to make the part entirely your own.'

He was full of advice, but also ready to learn; and his tirades, being comic performances themselves, did not shrivel the actors' self-confidence. 'I know very well that it is often the artists who give the author least trouble who get the least acknowledgement and have their virtues taken as a matter of course,' he wrote to Ellen O'Malley, who took the part of Nora. 'This is not so, I hope, with me: I am very sensible of how good you have been in every way, though I have had no opportunity of saying so.'

The reviews, though sometimes niggardly, were good, and the best critics wrote most enthusiastically. Max Beerbohm's notice in the *Saturday Review* was headed 'Mr Shaw at his Best'. Desmond MacCarthy declared the play to be 'an absolute success'; and William Archer in *The World* wrote that Shaw 'has done nothing more original'.

To the fifth matinée, on 10 November, Beatrice Webb brought the Conservative Prime Minister, Arthur Balfour. To her surprise he liked the play so much that he eventually saw it five times, bringing with him two leaders of the Liberal Opposition, Campbell-Bannerman and Asquith. Most people in London saw it as a largely affectionate satire on the Liberal Party's attitude towards Ireland, and Balfour himself praised it for clearing away humbug. His interest led to a special evening performance being given, on 11 March 1905, for King Edward VII. The King laughed so belligerently that he broke the special chair Vedrenne had hired for the evening and, in falling, flung Shaw's dramatic reputation high into the air. Here, a few months short of his fiftieth year, was success. Yet he felt uneasy. What was it worth? What had been the cost? The Prime Minister had told the King, and the King had told his countrymen, and now they were all telling the world that G.B.S. was the funniest of Irishmen. He began to react against the play, and gave his answer to his King's heehawing by adding to the programme of a later production a 'personal appeal' to the audience not to demoralize the actors with shouts of laughter and noisy applause.

'Would you dream of stopping the performance of a piece of music to applaud every bar that happened to please you? and do you not know that an act of a play is intended, just like a piece of music, to be heard without interruption from beginning to end? . . . Have you noticed that people look very nice when they smile or look pleased, but look shockingly ugly when they roar with laughter or shout excitedly or sob loudly? Smiles make no noise.'

Eleven days after the royal command performance of *John Bull's Other Island*, he began a new play. In this, the last of his 'big three', he would challenge his own popularity and present himself as a moral revolutionist. 'The play is wildly impossible,' he told the actress Eleanor Robson. '. . . It would run for a week. But what a week that would be!'

7

CURTAIN UP ON *MAJOR BARBARA*

> It seems to me that what Barbara finds out is that the ancient Greek (whoever he was) who said 'First make sure of an income and then practise virtue' was rightly preaching natural morality.
>
> Shaw to Gilbert Murray (5 September 1941)

Father Keegan had been a saint, 'and now I want to see whether I can make a woman a saint too,' Shaw wrote to Eleanor Robson. 'The heroine is so like you that I see nobody in the wide world who can play her except you.'

Charlotte was not happy with the way her husband corresponded with actresses. But he believed that Eleanor Robson would be striking in the piquant role of his Salvation Army officer. She was little more perhaps than a professional model for the part: the biographical model was Beatrice Webb. Like Barbara, Beatrice was a rich man's daughter and had gone East Ending with the gospel of social salvation. Her violent reaction to the play ('a dance of devils . . . hell tossed on the stage, with no hope of heaven . . . the triumph of the unmoral purpose') registered her involvement in the ruin of Barbara's salvationism.

Barbara, as a prototype of St Joan, is a woman apparently converted from religion to a creed of action. But hers is not really a conversion: it is a growing-up. She is a chip off the old block, her father Undershaft having a genius for action that Barbara inherits. The man who stands between Barbara and Undershaft, Adolphus Cusins, is the real convert. Modelled on the classicist Gilbert Murray, Cusins represents Shaw's own position: that of the fastidious scholar trying to find his place in the political world. He is attracted to Undershaft as the only man who can make him effective through marrying his intellect to power.

There are more false starts, deletions and drastic changes in the holograph manuscript of *Major Barbara* than in any of Shaw's previous plays. In the intervals and 'mostly in Great Northern express trains', he polished off a 'new and original tragedy' early that summer. *Passion Poison and Petrifaction or The Fatal Gazogene* completed a trilogy of 'tomfooleries' done while still at work on his 'big three'. The invitation had come from Cyril Maude on behalf of the Actors' Orphanage which each year commissioned a playwright to compose a burlesque of old-time melodrama to be performed in the Royal Botanical Gardens of Regent's Park during the Theatrical Garden Party. Shaw's idea came from a story he had once told the Archer children about his aunt, who liked making plaster of Paris figures, and her cat which one day mistook the liquid plaster of Paris for milk and, while asleep, turned into a ponderous mass of cement – to be used by the aunt as a doorstop. From the beginning when the cuckoo clock strikes sixteen (signifying eleven o'clock at night) to the moment when Lady Magnesia Fitztollemache's lover is obliged to eat part of the ceiling (containing lime) as an antidote to the jealous husband's poison, we are, as Irving Wardle writes, 'into Ionesco territory'.

This 'brief tragedy for Barns and Booths' by the 'Chelsea Shakespeare' was performed 'for the first time in any tent' at intervals during the afternoon of 14 July. The author, who was absent, described it as a 'colossal success', and arranged for the royalties on all performances for the rest of its copyright life to be paid to the Actors' Orphanage Fund. 'Charities are remorseless,' he explained.

He returned to, but could not finish, *Major Barbara*. At the beginning of July Charlotte took charge. She proposed returning G.B.S. to Ireland. It was twenty-nine years since he had boarded the North Wall boat for London. Like Larry Doyle, he had 'an instinct against going back to Ireland'. Nevertheless, like Larry Doyle, he went. It was not of course on his own initiative. 'I went back to please my wife; and a curious reluctance to retrace my steps made me land in the south and enter Dublin through the backdoor from Meath rather than return as I came, through the front door on the sea.'

They were to stay at Charlotte's father's house three miles out of Rosscarbery, a little market town in County Cork. It was a solid grey stone structure built on rising ground with gardens that sloped down to a lake. From the terrace, facing south, they 'could look out on a great sweep of the bay, with a lighthouse rising like the stub of a pencil on the farthest point of land'. But could he work there? Did the house have a sitting-room well away from the drawing-room? This was vital since they were to be joined by Charlotte's sister, Mary Cholmondeley, and her husband who was a colonel. It was important to be out of earshot.

G.B.S. spent much of the next three months in that sitting-room getting on 'scrap by scrap' with his new play. It progressed very slowly – 'a speech a day or so,' he informed Vedrenne. 'I have not yet finished the play,' he wrote to Eleanor Robson on 21 August; 'and my inspiration, as far as the heroine is concerned, is gone. I shall finish it with my brains alone.' On 11 September he reported that it was 'just finished': but he had been left 'in a condition of sullen desperation concerning it'.

He had turned back from autobiography to politics – from his marriage and the country of his childhood to the economic questions that had first provided the themes of his *Plays Unpleasant*. Over twenty years separated the beginning of *Widowers' Houses* from the completion of *Major Barbara*, and though the living standards of the middle class had risen in this period there were now almost a million people in the country receiving Poor Law relief. In London at the beginning of 1905 the number of paupers had risen to 150,000, of whom 1,500 were 'casual paupers' sleeping in the streets or the casual wards of workhouses and living, according to William Booth, 'below the standard of the London cab-horse'. Booth had founded the Salvation Army in 1878 to make war on poverty. Though Britain was still at the summit of her imperial power, much of her population existed on the edge of destitution. It was this paradox that Shaw investigated in his play using, as a symbol of Imperialist prosperity, the armaments industry.

'One never really makes portraits of people in fiction,' he wrote: 'what happens is that certain people inspire one to invent fictitious characters for them, which is quite another matter.' The millionaire munitions capitalist, Andrew Undershaft, seems to have had a composite inspiration: there was the dramatist Charles McEvoy's father, a benign grey-haired gentleman who, after fighting on the side of the Confederacy in the American Civil War, settled down quietly to establish a torpedo factory; there was Hans Renold, a businessman who came to lecture the Fabian Society on the principles of 'service before self' in the manufacture of high explosives. Another prototype was Alfred Nobel, 'the gentle Bolshevik' who had patented dynamite in 1867 and in 1901 endowed the Nobel Peace Prize which, as the critic Louis Crompton commented, 'challenged the humanitarian liberals among his personal friends to solve the problems his discoveries had created'. William Manchester has argued that Shaw's model was Friedrich Alfred Krupp, the Prussian 'Cannon King' whose paternalistic welfare arrangements for his workers in Essen may have suggested Undershaft's model town. Krupp had died in 1902 and was succeeded by his daughter Bertha. 'In 1906 – the year after the publication of *Major Barbara* – she married Dr Gustav von Bohlen und Halbach,' wrote Maurice Valency, 'who later assumed the name of Krupp, and took over the management of the Krupp combine, thus fulfilling in reality the role of Dr Cusins in Shaw's play.' Shaw himself wrote that Undershaft emerged into the world as Henry Ford. Other critics assumed that he derived from the legendary Basil Zaharoff, chief salesman of Vickers, who 'made wars so that I could sell arms to both sides'.

Such a multiplicity of candidates attests to the rise of arms traffic throughout the world at the turn of the century. Some, like Zaharoff, made no apology for their merchandise. Others, such as Britain's largest arms maker Sir William Armstrong, placed the responsibility for 'legitimate application' of weapons on the buyer and speculated that better armaments might well render war less barbarous. Others again, such as Nobel, argued for the deterrent effect of explosives.

Undershaft expresses all these attitudes. But when he challenges Cusins to 'make war on war' he is deliberately tempting him with the conventional paradox of those times which soon led to German, French and British soldiers being shot down with guns made by their fellow-countrymen in a 'war to end wars'.

The first act of the play is a drawing-room comedy set in the library of Lady Britomart's house in Wilton Crescent which displays the wealth of capitalist society; the second act is a Dickensian melodrama showing capitalism's destitution at the West Ham Shelter of the Salvation Army. Shaw had got as far as Undershaft's arrival at West Ham when he took his manuscript to Ireland. From then on Undershaft begins to take control of the play and in the third act, a political fantasy set in Perivale St Andrews, a futuristic model town, he dominates the stage.

On 8 September Shaw scribbled 'End of the Play' at the conclusion of the third act. But Undershaft's annihilation of everyone else had left him feeling dissatisfied. Why had it happened? He appeared to have let his unconscious Will, with its fantasies of violence, speak through Undershaft. That name itself brings together the wishes of the unconscious and the underground kingdom of the Devil.

In London earlier that year he had blamed the pressure of business for his difficult progress on the play; at Rosscarbery he attributed his difficulties to the moisture of the Irish climate. His aggressive instincts, however, are more likely to have been aroused by 'Mrs Chumly', Charlotte's sister. Mary Cholmondeley's determination never to see her brother-in-law had gradually wavered. She had heard a good deal about him and, pricked by curiosity, allowed Charlotte to persuade her after half a dozen years to meet him. For the first week or two, perhaps feeling her disapproval, G.B.S. stayed working all day in the sitting-room. Charlotte joined him there in the mornings to do secretarial work; and in the afternoons she would visit friends in the neighbourhood with 'Sissy'. Soon G.B.S. was accompanying them on these walks. 'Mrs C and I, in view of our previously rather distant relations, laid ourselves out to conciliate one another, and rather more than succeeded,' he confided to Beatrice Webb.

'I have the important advantage in such matters of not being nearly so disagreeable personally as one would suppose from my writings. I am now completely adopted on the usual lunatic privileged terms in the Cholmondeley household. I have taken several photographs of Mrs C and taught her to swim. The Colonel has presented me with a watch which tells the date and the phases of the moon. I play accompaniments to Mrs C's singing and the past is buried.'

From that past and behind the patina of politeness the sinister figure of Undershaft expanded. So favourable an impression meanwhile was G.B.S. making on the Cholmondeleys that they invited him to go with them on a round of Irish peers in their castles and only accepted his refusal ('the worm turned at last') on the understanding that he would rejoin them the following month at Edstaston, their home in Shropshire.

Shaw arrived back in London alone on 30 September and the next day went down to read his play at Gilbert Murray's house in Oxford. The ostensible reason for his visit was to ensure that those people on whom his characters were modelled would not be offended. He had written to Murray asking whether Murray himself minded being represented as a foundling. Murray replied that the only thing that Shaw did at his peril was to fasten on him the Christian name Adolphus. In Shaw's first draft the professor had been called Dolly Tankerville. But he changed this Wildean surname to Cusins, suggesting the foundling's curious relationship (his own cousin) to himself.

His audience at Oxford that day included Murray and Granville Barker who was shortly to play the part of Cusins. At the end of the second act they were, Murray remembered, 'thrilled with enthusiasm, especially at the Salvation Army scenes. Act 3, in which the idealists surrender to the armaments industries, was a terrible disappointment to us.'

Shaw returned to London and that night wrote to Murray confessing that he felt 'quite desperate about my last act: I think I must simply rewrite it.'

To encourage himself he went next day to the Albert Hall where the Salvation Army was holding a festival to commemorate dead comrades. As the band played

'When the roll is called up yonder
I'LL BE THERE'

he stood in the middle of the centre grand tier box, in the front row, 'and sang it as it has never been sung before,' he told Vedrenne. 'The Times will announce my conversion tomorrow.'

The following afternoon he joined Charlotte and the Cholmondeleys at Edstaston. He had received a letter from Gilbert Murray enclosing some ideas set down in dialogue for the third act. 'What I am driving at, is to get the real dénouement of the play, after Act ii,' Murray explained. '... It makes Cusens come out much stronger, but I think that rather an advantage. Otherwise you get a simple defeat of the Barbara principles by the Undershaft principles.'

The rewriting of his last scene took Shaw eleven days. 'I want to get Cusins beyond the point of wanting power,' he replied to Murray. The Edstaston manuscript was completed on 15 October 1905. It is perhaps the most complex and ambiguous scene Shaw ever wrote. The debate between Undershaft, Barbara and Cusins takes place at many levels. Barbara, who represents evangelical Christianity, has lost her faith by the end of Act II, using Christ's words upon the cross: 'My God: why hast thou forsaken me?' Cusins represents scepticism, a purely negative force by itself; and Undershaft embodies Shaw's concept of the Life Force, a mindless power for good-or-evil depending (like all technology) on what human beings themselves decide to do with it.

Barbara's transfiguration must come through a resurrected faith that involves Cusins and Undershaft – her future husband and her father: three in one and one in three. While she occupies the position of the Son, Cusins is the Holy Ghost and Undershaft God the Father. But Undershaft is also the Devil – 'You may be a devil; but God speaks through you sometimes,' Barbara admits. In the religion of Creative Evolution, life arises from the anonymous concept of energy. It is a force without morality and, as Barbara discovers, 'there is no wicked side: life is all one.'

Cusins recognizes in Undershaft the mysterious spirit of Dionysus, capable of creation and destruction. Human beings therefore 'create' God or the Devil according to the way in which they employ Divine Energy. On the psychological level Barbara is the superego, Cusins the ego and Undershaft the id: three in one and one in three. According to the system laid out in *The Quintessence of Ibsenism*, Barbara is the idealist, Cusins the realist and Undershaft the philistine. In his last scene Shaw attempts to unite all three: Cusins is to be Barbara's husband and, as the foundling inheritor of his father-in-law's munitions factory, will become Andrew Undershaft VIII. He will be able to join his intelligence and Barbara's spiritual passion to his father-in-law's money and material strength.

For all his pragmatism and lack of hypocrisy, Undershaft is a limited man. He writes up UNASHAMED as his motto and is contemptuous of democratic shams. The 'ballot paper that really governs,' he says, 'is the paper that has a bullet wrapped up in it'. But though he exults in his power he is also its prisoner. Armaments are the instruments of revolutionary change and also the means by which authoritarian governments repress change. The will to live must do battle with the tendency to self-destruction.

The ambiguity of the play partly derives from the conflict of Undershaft's motives. By inviting Cusins to be his successor is he tempting him, as Mephistopheles tempted Faust, to his damnation? Or is he an instinctive agent for the Life Force seeking in Cusins a better use of the power he commands? In fact he is doing both: that is how life operates. 'You cannot have power for good without having power for evil, too.'

Cusins believes that he will reject the armourer's faith and 'sell cannons to whom I please and refuse them to whom I please'. To this Undershaft replies: 'From the moment when you become Andrew Undershaft, you will never do as you please again.' This seems to be the percipient voice of the Devil having recruited a partner in his hellish trade. But elsewhere Undershaft appears to challenge Cusins and Barbara to use this power in a fundamentally different way: 'Society cannot be saved,' he says (paraphrasing Plato's *Republic*), 'until either the Professors of Greek take to making gunpowder, or else the makers of gunpowder become Professors of Greek.'

In the earlier manuscript Undershaft had posed a conundrum for Cusins: 'Why is a government a government?' And Cusins answered: 'Because the people are fools.' In the Edstaston manuscript Cusins states his belief in the common man:

'I love the common people. I want to arm them against the lawyer, doctor, the priest, the literary man, the professor, the artist and the politician, who, once in authority, are the most dangerous, disastrous and tyrannical of all the fools, rascals and impostors. I want a democratic power strong enough to force the intellectual oligarchy to use its genius for the general good or else perish.'

Cusins enshrines something of Gilbert Murray's political idealism – it is not surprising that Murray's later work for the League of Nations should be in line with Cusins's decision to 'make war on war'. Shaw and Barker felt the excitement of working in the theatre with this brilliant young Oxford professor. He was, Shaw told Pinero, a 'genuine artistic anarchic character'. Shaw wanted to bring Murray's classical scholarship to bear on twentieth-century politics and he uses Undershaft to give muscle to a man D. H. Lawrence was to call 'all disembodied mind'. The passionate thinking Shaw put into *Major Barbara* was partly the result of this association with Murray; and their friendship became a bonus added to the successful breakthrough of Shaw's plays at the Court. Both these factors helped to make the positive ending to *Major Barbara* – an ending with the 'inconsequence of madness in it'.

This hard-won optimism had survived the initial effects of Shavian irony, but there are signs of rejection to the graft. Beatrice Webb records Shaw as arguing 'earnestly and cleverly, even persuasively, in favour of what he imagines to be his central theme – *the need for preliminary good physical environment before anything could be done to raise the intelligence and morality of the average sensual man*'. But Undershaft's general attitude towards life continued to trouble people.

Of all the play's aphorisms and ideas echoing from Plato, Euripides, Nietzsche, the most significant derive from Shaw's reading of Blake's *Marriage of Heaven and Hell*. What Shaw believed to be the central theme of *Major Barbara* – that 'the way of life lies through the factory of death' – is similar to several proverbs of Blake, with whom Shaw shared a religious faith in Energy. He could expound this faith so well that even Beatrice Webb 'found it difficult to answer him'. Yet, she added, 'he did not convince me.

'. . . the impression left is that Cusins and Barbara are neither of them convinced by Undershaft's argument, but that they are uttering words, like the silly son, to bridge over a betrayal of their own convictions.'

Shaw's genius went into the creation of Undershaft. The armaments manufacturer loves his enemies because they have kept him in business. Like Christ, he comes 'not to send peace but a sword'. Cusins he had constructed 'with my brains alone' – and with Gilbert Murray's. 'But you are driving me against my nature,' Cusins protests to Undershaft. 'I hate war.' Shaw, too, seems to be driven against his nature. He had wanted to move Cusins and Barbara 'beyond the point of wanting power'. But their final permeation of the Undershaft firm lacks conviction on stage. Shaw knew this. He continued tinkering with this last scene up to 1930 when the Standard Edition of the play was published, trying to make Barbara and Cusins 'more prominent' and giving them 'more commanding positions on stage and stronger movement'. But as he told Robert Morley ten years later during the making of the film version of the play: 'That's always been a terrible act. I don't think anyone could do anything with it.'

'You have learnt something,' Undershaft tells Barbara at a genuinely touching moment. 'That always feels at first as if you have lost something.'

Shaw himself seems to have felt this sensation of loss. 'But oh! Eleanor between ourselves, the play, especially in the last act, is a mere ghost, at least so it seems to me . . . It was a fearful job . . . Brainwork comes natural to me; but this time I knew I was working – and now nobody understands.'

This lack of understanding proceeds from the complexity of what Shaw was questioning. Is socialism at odds with human nature? Are the self-destructive impulses of human beings ineradicable? Are there ways of disarming oppressive power that do not betray the cause that uses them? Though the affirmation comes out strongly, getting through to it had been the hardest work the playwright had done. And the chance that he is wrong remains. The Devil's Force of Death speech in *Man and Superman*, with its more efficient engines of destruction ('of sword and gun and poison gas') leads straight to Undershaft's weapons factory with its 'aerial battleships' that eventually will fly over Captain Shotover's villa at the climax of *Heartbreak House*, threatening with its '*terrific explosion*' the end of humankind.

Shaw's optimism was a perilous act of faith focused on the future. He had looked in *John Bull's Other Island* for a country where the 'facts were not brutal and the dreams not unreal'. In Perivale St Andrews nothing is achieved 'by words and dreams': killing is 'the final test of conviction'. It is the nightmare of a man with 'honour and humanity on my side, wit in my head, skill in my hand, and a higher life for my aim', who has a vision of world war to come. In the aftermath of this war, through the fantasy of *Back to Methuselah*, he will refashion humankind in the image of his heart's desire.

*

The Salvation Army lent uniforms for the production at the Court Theatre. The audience for the first performance on 28 November 1905 included a box full of uniformed Salvation Army Commissioners who for the first time in their lives had entered a theatre. Among 'the intelligentsia of London' sat the Prime Minister, Arthur Balfour, in the last week of his Government, with Beatrice Webb, whom five days before he had appointed to the new Royal Commission on the Poor Law. The foyer of the Court was crowded to bursting – hundreds of people had to be turned away – and above the excitement floated a rumour that the play was blasphemous. The curtain rose.

TEN

I

FABIAN BEDFELLOWS

> What a transformation scene from those first years I knew him: the scathing bitter opponent of wealth and leisure, and now! the adored one of the smartest and most cynical set of English Society . . . our good sense preserve us!
>
> *The Diary of Beatrice Webb* (14 October 1905)

'Politics are very topsy-turvy just now,' Beatrice Webb wrote at the end of December 1903, 'and one never knows who may be one's bedfellow!' Many of the Fabians were suspicious of the social glamour with which the Webbs surrounded themselves. Sidney himself warned Beatrice that they should not be 'seen in the houses of great people'. But the Fabian policy of permeation made it obligatory for them to enter the drawing-rooms of Edwardian polite society.

This permeation was taking the Webbs away from the evolution of the Labour Party. They took little notice of the attempts to bring socialism and the trade unions together as a parliamentary Labour Party. As Shaw warned Pease, 'any sort of amalgamation means, for us, extinction'. Power, they believed, still resided with the traditional parties in Parliament and access to power must still lie through persuading them.

Among the Liberals, they had chosen Lord Rosebery, an enigmatic figure who had left the leadership of the party in 1896. The speech he made in Chesterfield at the end of 1901 owed much to 'Lord Rosebery's Escape from Houndsditch', the article that Sidney Webb had written, and Shaw toned up, the previous September. Using this as his brief, Rosebery attacked the record of party politics and called for a 'clean slate' on which to draft a programme of national efficiency.

At the top of this clean slate, the Webbs hoped to chalk up housing and education. But what did Rosebery himself intend? He was grateful to Sidney Webb for giving him something to say, but he had taken off his 'Gladstonian old clothes' and, instead of putting on the new collectivist garments that Sidney Webb handed him, he simply put himself to bed and switched out the light. 'Why are we in this galley?' Beatrice wondered. And Shaw himself was driven to concede the emptiness of their Rosebery campaign.

But permeation did seem to work with the Conservatives. Their Tory bedfellow was Arthur Balfour who succeeded his uncle Lord Salisbury as Prime Minister in the summer of 1902 and 'will I think,' Beatrice predicted, 'make no ripple of change'. Quietly scintillating at the dinner table, he was well-spoken and precise-sounding in the House of Commons, and as a political thinker elegantly indecisive. Like Beatrice, he sometimes felt he would have preferred a contemplative to a public life – in fact it struck Beatrice as 'the oddest fact' that he should be 'mixed up . . . with democratic politics'. Really he had gone into politics to please his mother and then developed the knack of pleasing all sorts of people. He was at home on the golf course, in the concert hall and among the 'gallants and graces' of the fashionable world; popular too with the finer minds of the universities, the pick of the clergy, the flower of the bench: and also with the Webbs.

It seemed to them incredible that a Prime Minister in his mid-fifties should have preserved an open mind on so many political questions. His opinions shifted uneasily between the need for action and the futility of taking it. Unlike Rosebery he was not to be persuaded by what might be popular but by whether he was bored or not. He was easily bored – so much politics was without refinement of thought or sensibility. It was here that the Webbs saw their opportunity. Between 1902 and 1905 they 'slipped into' friendship with him. 'He comes in to dinner whenever we ask him, and talks most agreeably,' Beatrice noted. Balfour responded to these Fabians as a connoisseur might respond to an unusual wine. He believed Shaw to be 'the finest man of letters of to-day' – though he would not read his *Plays Unpleasant* because 'I never read unpleasant things'. He counted on the Fabians painlessly fitting such unpleasant things into the perfect equilibrium of his life, and the Webbs endeavoured to oblige. 'I set myself to amuse and interest him,' Beatrice wrote. And he was so responsive intellectually, so courteous, that 'we found ourselves in accord on most questions'.

But Beatrice distrusted her attraction to Balfour. She had with difficulty walked away from the social world to which her family belonged and dedicated herself to disinterested public service – and now found that this service was leading her back into the milieu she had abandoned. For Balfour belonged to 'the Souls', that exquisite group of intellectuals with artistic and aristocratic tastes who were to find an obituary in *Heartbreak House*.

This immersion in party-giving-and-going seemed justified by what the Fabians achieved over the Education Acts of 1902 and 1903. Sidney's Fabian Tract No. 106, *The Education Muddle and the Way Out*, recommended the abolition of School Boards and the passing of control for education to the local government bodies. The Education Act of 1902 (which did not apply to London) 'followed almost precisely the lines laid down in our tract,' wrote Edward Pease. 'Our support of the Conservative Government in their education policy caused much surprise.'

It caused more than surprise: it caused misgivings at the invasion of education by party politics, and Webb's proposal to give assistance out of public funds to reactionary Church schools fomented outright opposition. It was far from being the 'clean slate' other socialists wanted. Over the Education Act of 1903, which transferred the School Boards' powers to the London County Council, Webb experienced still greater difficulties. To Ramsay MacDonald it seemed that Sidney was collaborating with Balfour in order to get a Government post.

The Fabian success had been achieved at a dismaying price. There was, as Beatrice put it, 'a slump in Webbs' on the political market. After the local elections of 1904 Sidney was voted off the Progressive Party Committee and denied all positions of authority on the London County Council. He had hoped to be brought back into communication with the trade union world through his appointment by Balfour to a new Royal Commission on trade union law. But this became a 'fiasco' when the trade unions boycotted the Commission. Suddenly the Fabians seemed isolated. Through their educational reforms they had lost much of the interest they had spent years nurturing among the Liberals; and by their pronouncements on tariff reform they were to assist in the downfall of their one political ally, Balfour.

*

Webb had conducted the Fabian policy on education; it was Shaw who stage-managed their fiscal policy. The rightfulness of Free Trade had been taken for granted. But following Chamberlain's speech in May 1903, 'Free Trade versus Fair Trade', tariff reform suddenly became a controversial electioneering issue. 'I think we are clearly called upon to oraculate on the present crisis,' Shaw wrote to Pease: and Webb reluctantly agreed. At a Fabian meeting in June 1903 he had given a tentative analysis of the situation, on balance against tariffs, but in effect recommending more Fabian research into the subject.

Shaw's attitude was more dramatic. Following instinct rather than research, he had come out as 'a Protectionist right down to my boots', at one with Ruskin and Carlyle in his belief that 'Free Trade is heart-breaking nonsense'.

Over the last six months of 1903, Fabian opinion had come to lodge halfway between tariff and Free Trade. To give commanding expression to such mixed opinion needed unusual dexterity. Shaw was convinced that the Fabian Society 'must say something that nobody else is saying'. He had wanted to demonstrate that sensible tariff reform involved, as a preliminary step, the introduction of socialism. He proposed an agreement where, in exchange for their support of Chamberlain's protectionist scheme, the workers were guaranteed a minimum wage. He also proposed that Chamberlain be invited to give a pledge that any extra revenue arising from tariffs would be applied to 'public purposes' and not 'to still further reduce the existing shamefully inadequate taxation of unearned incomes'.

Shaw argued that, in principle, there was no objection from a socialist point of view to 'State interference with trade, both to suppress sweating at home and to guide and assist our exporters abroad'. Socialists were therefore necessarily anti-Free Trade as they were anti-Laissez-faire, both systems being historical counterparts of each other and idealizing the exploitation of market forces.

At a Fabian meeting on 22 January 1904 the draft of Shaw's Tract No. 116, *Fabianism and the Fiscal Question*, was fought over page by page. With numerous amendments, it was published on 31 March. 'Though I am the pen man of this Tract, its authorship is genuinely collective,' Shaw explained in a Preface. It was as adept a performance as *Fabianism and the Empire*. Both tracts submerge immediate election questions and extreme Fabian differences in the creed of international collectivism and a lucid exposition of the practical benefits of domestic socialism that might be wrung out of an imperial policy.

Shaw did not believe that the Labour Party would win seats at the next election. He expected Chamberlain to become Prime Minister, and if Chamberlain could be persuaded to accept a minimum wage for workers, the Fabian work on tariff reform would not be in vain.

But in the election following Balfour's resignation on 4 December, the Liberals won an unprecedented majority. Their leader, Sir Henry Campbell-Bannerman, that 'weak, vain man' whom 'nobody will follow', became Prime Minister and various Liberal friends of the Webbs (Asquith, Grey and Haldane), making their peace, accepted office under him. Balfour was never again to lead the party in office; and Joseph Chamberlain (who suffered a stroke not long afterwards) never again held political office.

There was one further surprise at the election: fifty-three seats were captured by Labour men. Of these, twenty-four were trade unionists (mostly textile and mining men) who owed their primary allegiance not to Ramsay MacDonald and Keir Hardie, but to the Liberal Party which had pledged to restore protection of union funds from liability for loss caused through industrial disputes. The complexion of British politics was changing. A successful pact had been made between socialism and trade unionism that gave the Labour movement a parliamentary base in national politics. In *The Clarion* Shaw laid down some 'Fabian Notes' on the election. The Labour members had provided nothing more than 'a nominally independent Trade Unionist and Radical group,' he wrote. '. . . I apologise to the Universe for my connection with such a party.'

2

WELLS JOINS THE CAST

> We have always been misunderstood, mistrusted, and from time to time roundly denounced and vilified not only by the other Socialist Societies but even by a minority of the Fabian Society . . . From William Morris in 1890 to H. G. Wells in 1906, all the able, energetic and impatient spirits have begun by demanding an abandonment of the Fabian policy, and have ended by perceiving that it is the only possible policy under the circumstances.
>
> Discarded section of Shaw's leaflet, *Election of Executive Committee 1907–8* (8 February 1907)

The unease felt by growing numbers of Fabians swelled after the General Election of January 1906 into a tumour of discontent. Their policy of permeation looked like a series of little interferences and minor activities that had wasted resources and produced dubious results. What was the point of Sidney Webb ingratiating himself with Tories and Liberals at the dinner table while Shaw drastically insulted both parties in his tracts? 'I quite understand that you can so define permeation as to cover all forms of Socialist activity,' S. G. Hobson wrote to Shaw. 'But that won't help us.'

Hobson and others felt that the Fabian Society was in danger of counting for very little in politics. During its first twelve years, it had lined up what was potentially a great following in the country. Then it had 'ossified'. The last ten years seemed to be a history of lost opportunities. They had been supplanted by Ramsay MacDonald and Keir Hardie, by the Independent Labour Party and the Labour Representation Committee.

Like Fabius, the Fabians had waited. But when the new century arrived they had not struck hard – they had gone on waiting. Rising numbers of them however were insisting that the waiting game must end. 'Webb has repeatedly told me that he does not believe in the possibility of a Socialist Party,' Hobson told Shaw. 'On the contrary, I think that an organised

Socialist Party which shall include the LRC and the ILP is quite feasible and in every sense desirable.'

Shaw was not unsympathetic to this argument. The Fabian tracts gave the new Labour Party a programme for a decade of electioneering. Shaw argued that the Fabian Society must nevertheless continue with the policy of placing its work at the disposal of 'anybody and everybody, including the established capitalist governments, who can and will carry out any instalment of it'. If, however, socialism precipitated itself into a genuine political party, then the Fabian Society must back it for all it was worth. But if trade unionism and traditional radicalism prevailed, then the next job for the Fabians would be to detach socialists from the Labour Party and 'form a Socialist party in parliament independent of all other parties, but leading the advanced elements in all of them by its ideas and its political science'.

He envisaged the bulk of this new party coming from the middle-class proletariat, and substituting middle-class methods of business and conceptions of democracy for trade union methods – representative government in place of bodies of delegates. Their socialism (what Shaw would later call communism) would work to reverse the policy of capitalism by transferring private property into common wealth. The question was whether such a revolutionary programme could be carried out by Parliament, the municipalities and parish councils.

'Do not let us delude ourselves with any dreams of a peaceful evolution of Capitalism into Socialism, of automatic Liberal Progress . . . The man who is not a Socialist is quite prepared to fight for his private property . . . We must clear our minds from cant and cowardice on this subject. It is true that the old barricade revolutionists were childishly and romantically wrong in their methods; and the Fabians were right in making an end of them and formulating constitutional Socialism. But nothing is so constitutional as fighting.'

Once a true socialist party was born in Britain, the Fabian Society 'would shrink into a little academic body'. Shaw had been on the Fabian executive now for twenty years. He felt loyalty; he felt weariness. He wanted freedom as well as ownership – his child must grow up, become independent and powerful: *his child*. 'We cannot sit there any longer making a mere habit of the thing,' he advised Webb.

He dreamt sometimes of a Fabian party in Parliament. If the thing caught on it would prove the 'right climax of the whole Fabian adventure' – and if it failed what was there to lose? 'This is the psychological moment,' Shaw told Webb late in 1906. He had been convinced of this by a new leader that the Fabians had thrown up – a brilliant intellectual prospector on whom he might unload his political burden, as he hoped one day to hand over the theatrical future to Harley Granville Barker.

*

H. G. Wells was ten years younger than Shaw. He had seen the aggressive Dubliner with his 'thin flame-coloured beard beneath his white illumined face' at Kelmscott House. Like other students, Wells had been converted to socialism under the aesthetic influence of Blake, Carlyle and Ruskin. Late at night, walking back from Hammersmith through the gas-lit streets, or travelling by the sulphurous underground railway, their red ties giving zest to frayed and shabby costumes, he and his fellow-students would speak enthusiastically of Morris and Shaw – how fierce they were in spirit, how sage in method. A revolution seemed to be breaking out around them.

But by the time Wells and Shaw met almost a decade later, this revolution seemed to have become a cultural event. Wells, at the beginning of 1895, was suddenly given the post of theatre critic for the *Pall Mall Gazette*. On 5 January he turned up at the St James's Theatre to see *Guy Domville*, 'an extremely weak drama' by Henry James. There were two audiences in the theatre that night. When the curtain came down 'jeers, hisses, catcalls were followed by great waves of applause . . . The two audiences declared war.'

Wells, in his new evening clothes, had noticed how Shaw 'broke the ranks of the boiled shirts and black and white ties in the stalls, with a modest brown jacket suit, a very white face and very red whiskers'. The new drama critic of the *Pall Mall Gazette* accosted the new drama critic of the *Saturday Review* as a colleague and, as Wells had to pass Fitzroy Square to reach his home near Euston, the two writers walked back together, a lean spring-heeled marcher and a valiant sparrow hopping beside him.

'Fires and civil commotions loosen tongues,' commented Wells, who described Shaw as talking 'like an elder brother to me'. His conversation was a 'contribution to my education,' Wells recalled. But Wells felt out of place in the theatre, whereas Shaw understood that the pandemonium at the St James's, likened by Henry James to a set of savages pouncing on a gold watch, had been a warning of what might happen in Britain if Fabian tactics failed.

After four months on the *Pall Mall Gazette* Wells decided to throw over theatre reviewing. During the next half-dozen years, he created a new genre of scientific fairy-tale with his vivid fantasies, allegories, fables and adventures – *The Time Machine*, *The Island of Dr Moreau*, *The War of the Worlds*, *The First Men in the Moon*. He wrote one book, then another, and then half a dozen more. They came like magic. 'It did not take us long to recognise that here was Genius,' wrote Ford Madox Ford. '. . . And all great London lay prostrate at his feet.'

Shaw too had been impressed. A natural story-teller, with a fertile imagination, Wells spoke directly to the people and was 'our nearest to a twentieth century Dickens'. His romances of time and space stimulated Shaw's optimism. Dickens's world 'becomes a world of great expectations cruelly disappointed,' he wrote. 'The Wells world is a world of greater and greater expectations continually being fulfilled.'

Wells was the modern man who accepted nothing of the past and could hardly wait to experiment with the future. He wanted to write history before it happened. It was after his next book, a 'prospectus' called *Anticipations*, that Shaw asked Graham Wallas (whose sister-in-law was Wells's neighbour at Sandgate) formally to introduce them. 'He [Wells] interests me considerably.'

Wells had also begun to interest the Webbs. Beatrice Webb confided in her diary that *Anticipations* was the 'most remarkable book of the year . . . full of luminous hypotheses and worth careful study by those who are trying to look forward'. She gave the book to Sidney. Wells had imagined a technocratic élite called 'the New Republicans' that could regenerate the nation. I 'find myself in sympathy with many of your feelings and criticisms and suggestions,' Sidney wrote.

The Webbs seemed to stand for the more disciplined, better-informed expression of all that Wells was eager to achieve. 'We discovered each other immensely; for a time it produced a tremendous sense of kindred and co-operation,' he wrote. This was the beginning of a pincer movement by the Webbs and the Shaws to recruit him to the Fabian Society. Wells is 'a good instrument for popularising ideas,' Beatrice noted in her diary, '. . . it is refreshing to talk to a man who has shaken himself loose from so many of the current assumptions, and is looking at life as an explorer of a new world.'

Wells was nervous of the Webbs. Sidney was so excessively devoted to the public service; and the handsome figure of Beatrice alarmed him. But he liked the notion of meeting influential people – Members of Parliament such as Asquith, Haldane and Grey, philosophers such as Bertrand Russell, and Pember Reeves, soon to be made High Commissioner for New Zealand – at their political dinners.

In February 1903 Wells joined the Fabians. The Society 'is always open to new ideas,' Charlotte innocently encouraged him, '& to criticism of its past action.' Sidney Webb had listed Wells's *Anticipations* as one of his favourite books of 1901. Wells had chosen *Three Plays for Puritans*. 'You are, now that Wilde is dead, the one living playwright in my esteem,' he wrote to Shaw. He went to see *John Bull's Other Island* at the Court Theatre, pretended that the figure of Broadbent had been a 'disgusting caricature' of himself ('even my slight tendency to embonpoint was brought in'), and concluded: 'The play has some really gorgeous rhetoric, beautiful effects, much more serious Shaw than ever before & I'd rather see it again than see anyone else's new play.'

But underlying Wells's admiration of Shaw boiled a vast irritation. In the mid-1890s he had been prepared to learn from the older writer as from an elder brother: he was not content to do so ten years later – especially on subjects about which he was educated and G.B.S. was not. 'I was a biologist first and foremost, and Shaw had a physiological disgust at vital activities,' he was to write. ' . . . He detected an element of cruelty, to which I am blind, in sexual matters.' Shaw's main impulse towards other human beings was to establish a dominant relationship over them – something which Wells fiercely resisted. He regretted having fallen in with these Fabians.

A year after joining the Society, Wells attempted to resign. He was working so hard at his new books – *A Modern Utopia* and *Kipps* – he did not have time to attend the Fabian meetings. At once the prevailing influences of the Fabians, the Webbs and the Shaws closed in on him. And Wells capitulated.

He now felt trapped. For he was an escapologist, and this need to escape lay at the centre of his politics, utopias and love affairs. The claustrophobia of marriage was to become endurable for him only after he had set up an alternative household with a mistress and could oscillate between two homes. 'He is a romancer spoilt by romancing,' Beatrice decided in her diary, ' – but in the present stage of sociology he is useful.'

Of the two romances he published in 1905, *Kipps* was an affectionate glance backwards at what had moved him in the past, and *A Modern Utopia* a blue book vision of the future disinfected of pain. His anxiety to escape from the present fitted perfectly with the mood of a country travelling from Victorian traditions into the complex territory of the twentieth century. He had made converts to socialism by translating the Fabian creed of national efficiency into popular fiction. In *A Modern Utopia* he reinvented the 'New Republicans' as a benevolent dictatorship of noblemen called 'the Samurai' who preside as social engineers over the ideal state. 'The chapters on the Samurai will pander to all your worst instincts,' he assured Beatrice Webb. But he had done what the Webbs had wanted. 'He is full of intellectual courage and initiative,' Beatrice observed.

A Modern Utopia made Wells a hero among the more radical Fabians.

'I'm going to turn the Fabian Society inside out,' he promised Ford Madox Ford, 'and then throw it into the dustbin.'

*

Wells's campaign opened on 6 January 1906 with a Fabian lecture, 'This Misery of Boots', using the shoe trade to satirize the condition of England. It was both an illustration of what he wanted from the new Fabians, and an indictment of Shaw and the Webbs, 'who will assure you that some odd little jobbing about municipal gas and water is Socialism, and back-stairs intervention between Conservative and Liberal is the way to the millennium'.

He launched his main attack in a second lecture a month later on 9 February. 'Faults of the Fabian' was Wells at his most comic-destructive. Almost everything in the sphere of thought had changed in the last twenty years – unless it was the Fabian Society. 'I am here to-night to ask it to change.' A great deal of work, 'with a certain lack of charm perhaps', had been invested in permeation. Some of it was gratuitous, some of it unfortunate; and almost all of it was removed from socialism. Their indirect methods were a senile conceit of cunning: 'something like a belief that the world may be manoeuvred into socialism without knowing it; that . . . we shall presently be able to confront the world with a delighted, "But you *are* socialists! We chalked it on your back when you weren't looking . . ."

'The mouse decided to adopt indirect and inconspicuous methods, not to complicate its proceedings by too many associates, to win over and attract the cat by friendly advances rather than frighten her by a sudden attack. It is believed that in the end the mouse did succeed in permeating the cat, but the cat is still living – and the mouse can't be found.'

Wells's next criticism of the Society was its size. It had an air of arrested growth, as if by the effort of taking an office in a cellar in Clement's Inn, it had exhausted its energy. From this cellar, through the burrowings of one secretary and his assistant, the Fabian Society was to shift the industrial basis of civilization. Amid the jungle of politics it looked to Wells like 'a pot-bound plant'.

They were also poor, the Fabians, always in debt. 'You have it from Mr Bernard Shaw that poverty is a crime, and if so, then by the evidence of your balance-sheet ours is a criminal organization.'

Wells spoke on, adding to his catalogue of defects and accusations. The Fabians had evolved into a conservative society, and were collectivist only by definition of their collective inactivity. 'We don't advertise, thank you;

it's not quite our style. We cry socialism as the reduced gentlewoman cried "oranges": "I do so hope nobody will hear me." '

After an hour and a half Wells had nearly concluded his Fabian indictment. He had just one more vice to nail. 'Our society is small; and in relation to its great mission small minded; it is poor; it is collectively, as a society, inactive; it is suspicious of help, and exclusive,' he summarized. And, he added: 'it is afflicted with a giggle.'

Of all the faults of the Fabians, he declared, this juvenile joking was probably the worst. No wonder they were never taken seriously by politicians. The giggling excitement that ran through their meetings 'flows over and obscures all sorts of grave issues, it chills and kills enthusiasm,' he said. 'Its particular victim in this society is Mr Bernard Shaw.

'It pursues him with unrelenting delight, simply because he is not like everybody else, as he rises, before he opens his mouth to speak it begins. Shaw has a habit of vivid statement . . . and he has a natural inclination to paradox. Our accursed giggle lives on these things. Now Bernard Shaw is at bottom an intensely serious man, whatever momentary effect this instant dissolution of sober discussion into mirth may produce on him, he does in the long run, hate this pursuit of laughter . . . you will not suppose that in attacking laughter I am assailing Bernard Shaw. But I do assail the strained attempts to play up to Shaw, the constant endeavour of members devoid of any natural wit or wildness to catch his manner, to ape his egotism, to fall in with an assumed pretence that this grave high business of Socialism, to which it would be a small offering for us to give all our lives, is an idiotic middle-class joke.'

The timing of this attack on the political insidiousness of Shavianism, and the humorous requiem over permeation, was perfect and during the discussion afterwards, and in the weeks that followed, Wells was engulfed by support. 'People in the provinces think H. G. Wells is a great man,' the secretary of a Socialist League branch in a Yorkshire mill town wrote to him, 'and I can assure you they pay great attention to anything you say. Your audience is assured already, let the prophet appear.'

The prophet's chariot took the form of a Special Committee – a squadron of Wells-picked men and women whose mission was to increase the 'scope, influence, income and activity of the Society'. Wells had wanted them to move fast, finishing their work before he left at the end of March for a lecture tour in the United States. But Shaw and the Webbs, word-perfect in gradualism, entangled him with their assistance. The Webbs believed that, lacking the capacity for co-operation, he would not have the stamina to carry through his revisionist programme.

'The more I think of Mr Wells's Fabian Reforms the more do I welcome them & if only everyone will be sensible & broadminded I foresee a new era for Fabianism,' wrote Marjorie Pease. Shaw too believed Wells was vitally important to the future of Fabians. But below his admiration lay resentment, almost envy. He saw Wells as attractive, gifted with intimacy and lovable while he was fated to be unloved. Wells had succeeded at once and (so it seemed to Shaw) without effort. 'He was born cleverer than anybody within hail of him,' Shaw wrote, using his own upbringing as an invisible comparison. 'You can see from his pleasant figure that he was never awkward or uncouth or clumsy-footed or heavy-handed . . .

'He was probably stuffed with sweets and smothered with kisses . . . He won scholarships . . . The world that other men of genius had to struggle with, and which sometimes starved them dead, came to him and licked his boots. He did what he liked; and when he did not like what he had done, he threw it aside and tried something else.'

Shaw knew nothing of the illnesses and insecurities of Wells's early years. He simply saw, in contrast to himself, someone who had 'never missed a meal, never wandered through the streets without a penny in his pocket, never had to wear seedy clothes, never was unemployed'. And now he was being fussed over by the whole family of Fabians.

Wells arrived back from the United States still eager to put 'woosh' into the Fabians. The contrast between the go-ahead Americans and recalcitrant Englishmen had stimulated his radical energies. He wanted to change permeation into propaganda: to make the Society into a bigger, richer, simpler, less centralized organization. He wanted to obliterate Shaw's influence, to fade him out of its past by rewriting the Fabian tracts himself, and by realigning Fabian loyalties with the Labour Party and Keir Hardie who had fought the battle for socialism while Shaw had been making jokes elsewhere. He proposed changing the name of the Society to the British Socialist Party – but this was unanimously rejected by the executive which also rejected (by six votes to five) Wells's redefinition of the purpose of the Society as forwarding the progress of socialism 'by all available means'.

His report was published in November together with a Counter Report and Resolutions on behalf of the executive which had been written by Shaw. To Wells it seemed the most 'mischievous piece of writing I have read for a long time', destined, with its preposterous fables of Fabian foresight, to become 'a classic in the humorous literature of Socialism'.

Most of the issues which divided these two teeming documents were matters of internal reorganization and not difficult to reconcile. But beneath this administrative business lay a hidden agenda. The Fabians were a family, with Wells their rebel son. They had prevented him leaving and he now turned murderously back on them. He wanted to kill off the parents and, in his own image, father a new breed of this family. His fantasy of omnipotence, with its current of sexual energy, attracted crowds of excited Fabians for his dramatic confrontation with G.B.S.

Their first crossing of swords took place on 7 December at Essex Hall. Shaw moved the executive's resolution. His tone was friendly, his argument ominously reasonable.

Then Wells rushed up and began to address the meeting. Until then it had seemed as if, like the magical hero in his story 'The Man Who Could Work Miracles', he might perform anything he wished. But he spoke badly. His proposals for reorganizing the Society degenerated into a list of accusations against Shaw and the Webbs. He moved an amendment calling for the abolition of the executive and its replacement by a larger representative body that would endorse the 'spirit and purport' of his Special Committee's proposals. There had been a swell in favour of his amendment at the start; by the time he ended it had sunk. A second-reading debate was arranged one week later.

During the interval both parties prepared. Wells had described as 'shabby and unwise' the Fabian failure to co-operate with Keir Hardie. What he did not reveal was that he had written to Keir Hardie and been advised by him not to waste time bullying these steady-going Fabians 'who would continue to do their own useful work'. It was 'not quite fair' to the Society. 'Why not leave it to pursue its own way by its own methods,' Keir Hardie suggested, 'and come in and take your part in the political side of the movement as represented by the ILP?'

The answer to this was that Wells wanted to capture the Fabian army from Shaw, lead it over to Keir Hardie, and then go off to do something else. But Keir Hardie had been critical of Shaw too. Had his report been 'more accurate historically and less bombastic,' he wrote to G.B.S., 'the task of averting a menace to the movement wd have been easier.

'That apart what I wd like to see passed wd be a declaration of loyalty to the Labour Party which wd be binding on the Society and on its officials [who] . . . shall not support the candidates of other political parties . . . in this respect members of the Fabian Society are sad sinners.'

Neither Wells nor Shaw mentioned their letters from Keir Hardie when Wells turned up at Adelphi Terrace the day after the Essex Hall encounter. He came with an offer of compromise. 'Why dont you see how entirely I am expressing you in all these things?' he had asked G.B.S. But Shaw had scented victory. He proposed leading this second debate. It would be a peculiarly Shavian exercise – a 'terrific' verbal victory achieved without 'saying anything unkind'. He retreated into the country to gather his superiority. 'All I dread is being in bad form,' he wrote; 'for I am overworked.'

The crowd was even larger for this second contest. At nine o'clock Shaw rose to speak. If Wells's amendment abolishing the executive were passed, he said, the executive would obey it 'by not offering themselves for re-election'. It would be dismissal with dishonour: they would be drummed out. But this amendment, he reminded the audience, had nothing to do with the two reports. Over the serious business of the proposals in these reports, the executive would never resign, even if defeated on every resolution, but would faithfully carry out the decisions of the Society. Above the uproar Wells was heard pledging himself not to resign. 'That is a great relief to my mind,' continued Shaw. 'I can now pitch into Mr Wells without fear of consequences.'

He then offered up Wells for Fabian entertainment. 'During his Committee's deliberations he [Wells] produced a book on America,' Shaw told his audience. 'And a very good book too. But whilst I was drafting our reply I produced a play.' Shaw paused and there was silence. S. G. Hobson in the audience noticed his eyes vacantly glancing round the ceiling. 'It really seemed that he had lost his train of thought,' Hobson remembered. 'When we were all thoroughly uncomfortable, he resumed: "Ladies and gentlemen: I paused there to enable Mr Wells to say: 'And a very good play too!'"'

Wells had paid the penalty for having attacked the Shavian joke. For it was this joke which seemed to dissolve him into sustained laughter. The chairman took it for granted that the amendment was withdrawn by consent: and Wells made no protest. 'Keats was snuffed out by an article,' commented Hobson; 'Wells was squelched by a joke.'

'No part of my career rankles so acutely in my memory with the conviction of bad judgement, gusty impulse and real inexcusable vanity,' Wells afterwards admitted. But: 'I was fundamentally right.' He had reacted with imaginative enthusiasm to the future; and to the past with splenetic irritation. The present had been turned into theatre, which he had never liked or understood. 'Now we shall see whether he will forgive G.B.S.,' commented Beatrice.

This was not how G.B.S. saw it. He had arranged everything so that Wells could 'come up smiling' again among the Fabians. His purpose extended not a frown further. For he recognized that 'Wells is a great man'. He was a glamorously popular figure, particularly among the women of the new Fabian nursery. 'Tell the dear man that it is almost impossible to do anything without him,' Maud Reeves wrote to Wells's wife. Other Fabians, too, begged him not to desert them. To Shaw it seemed that the worse Wells behaved the more he was indulged.

No one knew what Wells would do next. The past still rankled: he felt a grievance. It seemed to him that Shaw's mind had been corrupted by public speaking and destroyed by the committee habit. Nevertheless he told Shaw: 'you are always sound hearted & I am always, through all our disputes & slanging matches, Yours most affectionately, H.G.' And Shaw agreed that Wells had played a 'great game' with 'immense vitality and fun'. There was no excuse for quarrelling – yet it seemed inevitable.

'I'm damnably sorry we're all made so,' wrote Wells.

'To complain of such things is to complain that the leaves are green and the sky blue,' wrote Shaw.

But what good came of it in the end? The issue had been shifted from a comparison of reports and policies to a gladiatorial contest of personalities. To Wells's frankness, his raging desire to discover the truth, Shaw had opposed something polemically formidable and professionally correct, yet somehow dubious. 'I incline to the prophecy that five years will see H. G. Wells out of the Society,' Beatrice Webb wrote. '. . . It will be interesting to watch.'

3

A REVOLUTION AT THE COURT

As a matter of fact, I am overrated as an author: most great men are.

When the curtain came down on 28 November 1905, it was clear that *Major Barbara* was to be Shaw's most controversial success. The critics were impressively divided. Desmond MacCarthy told his readers: 'Mr Shaw has written the first play with religious passion for its theme and has made it real. That is a triumph no criticisms can lessen.' But the anonymous critic of the *Pall Mall Gazette* found that the play betrayed 'an utter want of the religious sense' and that its author was 'destitute of the religious emotion'. In the *Sunday Times*, while acknowledging G.B.S. to be 'the most original English dramatist of the day', J. T. Grein recoiled from Bill Walker's punching of the down-and-out Rummy Mitchens and his assault on the young Salvation Army lass Jenny Hill; this 'double act of brutality literally moved the audience to shudders. It was beyond all bounds of realism in art. It was ugly and revolting.' But Max Beerbohm saw that 'the actor impersonating the ruffian aimed a noticeably gentle blow in the air, at a noticeably great distance from the face of the actress impersonating the lass'. Critics who professed themselves outraged, Beerbohm concluded, 'must have been very hard up for a fair means of attack'.

These critics felt inconvenienced on several counts. The play's 'lack of straightforward intelligible purpose' (*Morning Post*) made it spectacularly difficult for them to calculate its effect on audiences. Collectively they offered the choice between 'an audacious propagandist drama' (*Clarion*), 'one of the most remarkable plays put upon the English stage' (*Speaker*), a work of 'deliberate perversity' (*Morning Post*) or of the 'keenest insight and sense of spiritual beauty' (*Saturday Review*). There was no consensus as to whether G.B.S. was 'ephemeral' (John Galsworthy) or 'a high genius' (Oliver Lodge).

The war that had opened between the two audiences at Henry James's *Guy Domville* was now breaking out between critics and the public. Against all odds Shaw had become a fashionable craze. 'The old order is changing,' calculated one of the *Clarion* writers. Shaw's message to society 'to cast all its obsolete creeds and moral codes to the scrap heap' matched the new order.

Yet Shaw's career was now being blessed by the guardians of a society he was working to destroy. On the first night of *Major Barbara* there were almost as many carriages and motor cars outside the Court 'as there are in the Mall on a Drawing-room day'. Shaw was box office at last. Rupert Brooke, after flying visits to the Court from Rugby and then Cambridge, described *John Bull's Other Island* as 'unspeakably delightful', *Candida* 'the best play in the world' and *Major Barbara* 'highly amusing & interesting, & very brutal'. G.B.S. had been voted 'one of our leaders in the revolutionary movement of our youth,' wrote Leonard Woolf. Though Shaw's dramas did not have the grandeur of Ibsen's, they were played at the Court Theatre with relentless gusto, like a hurricane sweeping into the alley of Victorian morality and scattering the accumulated litter. Shaw, the champion of free speech and free thought, of paradoxical common sense and the ingenious use of reason, had 'a message of tremendous importance to us'. Along with Wells and Arnold Bennett, he had become one of the idols of young intellectuals. Many of the young men and women who attended the Court Theatre entered as *fin de siècle* Bohemians and emerged as twentieth-century radicals. Even A. B. Walkley, the reactionary critic of *The Times*, was obliged to admit that 'there is no such all-round acting in London as is nowadays to be seen at the Court theatre'.

The ensemble playing at the Court handed over the actor-manager's authority to the dramatist-producer. For over two centuries, from Thomas Betterton to Beerbohm Tree, the history of the British theatre had been the history of great actors. The Court Theatre set up a different standard of merit, bringing the acting and production of plays more in line with that of the contemporary Scandinavian and German stage. It changed the public's attitude. They went to see the play rather than an actor; and they had confidence in the all-round excellence of the cast.

Because the actors recognized Barker and Shaw as practical men of the theatre and respected their choice of plays, knowledge of stagecraft and skill at casting, they were willing to work as a team, accepting the smallest parts however successful they had earlier been in major roles. Barker believed that a variety of parts extended an actor's range, and he believed in repertory as a method of sustaining a school of actors.

Barker was a more literary and autocratic producer than Shaw. He liked to question his actors over the past history of their characters. 'You are not, I hope, going to tell me that the fellow drops from the skies, ready-made, at the moment you walk on the stage?' The biographies he provided became green-room legends. 'I want when you enter to give the impression of a man who is steeped in the poetry of Tennyson,' he was reputed to have told Dennis Eadie. For a scene in one of his own plays, he advised an actress that 'from the moment you come in you must make the audience understand that you live in a small town in the provinces and visit a great deal with the local clergy; you make slippers for the curate and go to dreary tea-parties.' Her one line in this scene was: 'How do you do?' Though a target for jokes, Barker was introducing a form of Stanislavsky's method of psychological realism which, he claimed, had been forced on actors by the bare dialogue of Ibsen with so much implicit in it.

Shaw was more matter-of-fact. If the producer, watching rehearsals, noted 'Show influence of Kierkegaard on Ibsen in this scene' or 'the Oedipus complex must be very apparent here. Discuss with the Queen', then 'the sooner he is packed out of the theatre the better'. If he noted 'Ears too red', 'Further up to make room for X', 'He, not Ee', 'This comes too suddenly', then, Shaw concluded, 'the producer knows his job and his place'.

Shaw would read his plays, first to friends, then to the company. Before the first rehearsal, he worked out on a chessboard with chessmen and a boy's box of assorted bricks, every entry, movement, rising or sitting, disposal of tambourine and tennis racket. The first rehearsals at the Court were always choreographic, the actors having their books in hand and the producer on the bare stage with them (the exits marked by a couple of chairs) teaching them their movements. Once these had been mastered, the words learned, and the actors made comfortable with what was going on, the books were discarded and the producer would leave the stage to sit front of house with a notebook and torch. 'From that moment, he should watch the stage as a cat watches a mouse,' Shaw advised, 'but never utter a word or interrupt a scene during its repetition no matter how completely the play goes to pieces, as it must at first when the players are trying to remember their parts and cues so desperately that they are incapable of acting.'

The producer at the Court (whom we would now call director) involved himself in reading plays, choosing casts, inventing the machinery, arranging the lighting, designing scenery and costume, adding incidental music, and co-ordinating everything except finance, which belonged to Vedrenne. Shaw liked to take a week over the stage movements, a fortnight for memorizing, and a final week for the dress rehearsals, when he would come on the stage again, going through passages that needed finishing, and interrupting now whenever he felt like it. Barker liked longer but in the crowded Court schedule this was seldom practicable.

Shaw had come to the theatre with the twin aspirations of giving the British public a political education and creating verbal opera; Barker's aim was to discover, through fractured syntax, crafted inarticulateness, oblique dénouement, the naturalistic dialogue to express a new stage situation. From those different aims as composers of plays arose their different styles of conducting the players.

Barker had never witnessed the heroic acting of old-timers. His taste for low tones, which worked perfectly for his own plays and those of Galsworthy, did not seem to suit Shaw who entreated him to 'leave me the drunken, stagey, brassbowelled barnstormers my plays are written for'. Barker's restrained style 'makes me blush for the comparative blatancy of my own plays,' Shaw conceded.

Shaw was patient and persistent, used a good deal of flattery, and took advice from some of the better actors. Barker was more persistent and less patient. Shaw set a limit of three hours (preferably between breakfast and lunch) and ensured that actors with only a few lines to speak were not kept hanging around all day while the principals rehearsed. Barker was a perfectionist and sometimes refused to leave off rehearsing until, according to Shaw, 'the unfortunate company had lost their last trains and buses and he had tired himself'. He also got alarmingly annoyed. 'His curses are neither loud nor deep: they are atmospheric,' one actor remembered. 'It is what he doesn't say that paralyses one. He *looks*; and having looked, he turns his back to the stage – and you can still see him looking through the back of his head.'

But it was exciting to work for Barker. If he did not spare his actors, he did not spare himself. They had the sense of collaborating at the beginning of a revolution in British stage production. The plays Barker presented had the appearance of being more natural, more lifelike, than anything else being performed in London and gave audiences a sensation of participating in the drama, rather than watching it from the auditorium.

Shaw's fatherly feelings for Barker spilled over on to the whole company at the Court. They felt part of a family, working to restore the English theatre to its rightful place in national life. A vivid example was the career of Lillah McCarthy. Shaw had seen her first in 1895 as a sixteen-year-old Lady Macbeth, 'immature, unskilful, and entirely artificial'. Yet she had gone at it bravely, her instinct and courage helping where her skill failed, and produced an effect that was 'very nearly thrilling'. 'She can hold an audience whilst she is doing everything wrongly,' he wrote in the *Saturday Review*. ' . . . I venture on the responsibility of saying that her Lady Macbeth was a highly promising performance, and that some years of hard work would make her a valuable recruit to the London stage.'

After ten years of hard work she wrote and asked to see Shaw. He was at this time looking for someone to play Ann Whitefield in *Man and Superman*. When she arrived at Adelphi Terrace ('a gorgeously good-looking young lady in a green dress and huge picture hat . . . in which she looked splendid, with the figure and gait of a Diana'), he gave her a broad smile of recognition: 'Why, here's Ann Whitefield.'

As one of the principal players at the Court, Lillah 'created the first generation of Shavian heroines with dazzling success'. Her technique, which combined the manner of 'the grand school with a natural impulse to murder the Victorian womanly woman', fell in perfectly with his stage needs. 'And with that young lady,' he wrote a quarter of a century later, 'I achieved performances of my plays which will probably never be surpassed.'

Working at the Court was a revelation for Lillah. She seemed hypnotized by G.B.S. 'With complete unselfconsciousness he would show us how to draw the full value out of a line,' she wrote. ' . . . With his amazing hands he would illustrate the mood of a line. We used to watch his hands in wonder. I learned as much from his hands, almost, as from his little notes of correction.' During rehearsals they often lunched together at the Queen's Restaurant in Sloane Square – apples, cheese, macaroni and salads with chilly milk and soda. 'I ate it because everything he did seemed right to me,' she remembered.

Lillah worshipped Shaw: but she did not understand his plays. Mrs Pankhurst was to tell her that Ann Whitefield had 'strengthened her purpose and fortified her courage' and many other women told her that Ann had 'brought them to life and that they remodelled themselves upon Ann's pattern'. Lillah played Ann Whitefield at the Court in May and June 1905, and again in October and November, and bore witness that 'she made a new woman of me'. She acted the part of Ann with earnest intensity. Barker, in the role of Tanner, 'carried the thing through remarkably well'. But it was difficult to keep Lillah's feet on the ground. 'Her life was rich in wonderful experiences that had never happened, and in friendships with wonderful people (including myself) who never existed,' Shaw remarked. She pursued Barker across the Court Theatre: and on 24 April 1906, at the West Strand Registry Office, she caught and married him.

The marriage had the air of being a brilliant success. 'She was an admirable hostess; and her enjoyment of the open air and of travelling made her a most healthy companion for him,' Shaw explained. Marriage suited Barker, who was no Bohemian. 'The admirations and adorations the pair excited in the cultured sections of London society could be indulged and gratified in country houses where interesting and brilliant young married couples were welcome.' Why then was Shaw 'instinctively dismayed'? As his Court 'children', their marriage was that of brother and sister. They had no children, and were not well cast for what the other needed: a mother for him, a father for her. 'There were no two people on earth less suited to one another,' Shaw wrote. It was the marriage of actors and actresses, a stepping aside from reality, an escapade.

That summer after their marriage they went to stay with the Webbs. 'I think what he [Barker] lacks is warmth of feeling – he is cold, with little active pity or admiration, or faithful devotion,' Beatrice wrote in her diary. 'A better acquaintance than a friend, a better friend than a husband . . .

'She is a strikingly handsome lady, also hard-working and dutiful – a puritan, I think, by temperament . . . Otherwise, I fear she is . . . commonplace, and he has all the appearance of being bored by her after two months' marriage.'

By the end of October 1906, they were back on stage as Tanner and Ann Whitefield. Next month they stepped into a new Shaw play at the Court: a tragedy in which Barker was an artist dying of consumption, with Lillah his wife – 'the sort of woman I hate', Shaw notified her.

4
CONCERNING *THE DOCTOR'S DILEMMA*

> Here am I, for instance, by class a respectable man, by common sense a hater of waste and disorder, by intellectual constitution legally minded to the verge of pedantry, and by temperament apprehensive and economically disposed to the limit of old-maidishness; yet I am, and have always been, and shall now always be, a revolutionary writer.
>
> Preface to *Major Barbara*

Over the early summer of 1906 Shaw wrote prefaces to *John Bull's Other Island* and *Major Barbara*. The first, discursively favourable to Home Rule, ridiculed nationalism and the military and bureaucratic imagination that supported it. The second, in celebration of social equality, included some powerful invective against the malicious injury of judicial punishments and the social damage resulting from an inequitable distribution of money. Both prefaces were assaults on institutions of power. Then over the late summer, he wrote *The Doctor's Dilemma*, a play aimed at another powerful institution, the medical profession.

It was Charlotte who reminded him of a good dramatic subject he had come across earlier that year at St Mary's Hospital, Paddington. The Principal of the Institute of Pathology there was Almroth Wright who had recently created a scientific sensation by claiming to have found a method of measuring the protective substances in the human blood. Wright 'discovered that the white corpuscles or phagocytes which attack and devour disease germs for us do their work only when we butter the disease germs appetizingly for them with a natural sauce'. The chemical condiments ebbed and flowed like the tide. Wright believed he had invented a means of calculating the periodical climaxes. Vaccine therapy could now proceed, he announced, on a scientific basis.

Shaw was keen to let the London drama critics know that the 'scientific side' of his play was 'correct and up to date'. Sir Colenso Ridgeon, the hero, 'is, serum pathologically, Sir Almroth Wright, knighted last birthday (May [1906]) for his opsonic discovery,' he informed A. B. Walkley. Some of Sir Almroth's friends would drop in to his research institute at St Mary's at night and, among the glass tubes, bottles, powders, plasters, discuss the newest theories of 'Vaccinotherapy'. Shaw was present at one of these late-night tea parties when a discussion arose among the physicians over admitting an extra tuberculosis patient who had arrived that day for experimental treatment. Wright's chief assistant objected: 'We've got too many cases on our hands already.' Shaw then asked: 'What would happen if more people applied to you for help than you could properly look after?' And Wright answered: 'We should have to consider which life was worth saving.'

This weighing of human worth on the scales of life and death is superficially the problem at the centre of Shaw's play. Whose life is of greater value: the unprincipled artist of genius or the honest sixpenny doctor? If there is an air of unreality about this choice it is because, as G. K. Chesterton pointed out, nobody at sea shouts 'Bad citizen overboard!' In real life, the doctor 'doesn't fool himself that the moral value of the characters comes into it,' James Fenton was to write. 'He chooses the people he has the best chance of saving.'

The real dilemma in the play, and the pivot of Colenso Ridgeon's choice, involves the nature of our unconscious motives and the idealizing process of logic by which we justify them to ourselves and represent them to one another. Almroth Wright was a misogynist who had concluded in *The Unexpurgated Case Against Woman Suffrage* that the feminine mind 'accepts the congenial as true, and rejects the uncongenial as false: takes the imaginary which is desired for reality'. In *The Doctor's Dilemma*, Shaw takes Wright's view of the inferior and irrational feminine mind and applies it to his gallery of scientific men. In particular he focuses on the unconscious sexual motives of Sir Colenso Ridgeon, the fashionable physician modelled on Wright who, listing his symptoms, innocently takes medical advice when he is about to fall in love.

Shaw liked Wright and disagreed with him about almost everything. Lord Moran, who heard some of their contests at St Mary's, remembered feeling sorry for Wright once Shaw had finished speaking. 'I felt that he had been pulverized, but at the end of Wright's reply I blushed to think that Shaw, who was after all a guest, had been so mercilessly shown up. The devastating effect of such speech depends on the art of selection. Every single sentence was a direct hit; there was not a single word which did not contribute to the confusion of the enemy.'

Here is a source and echo of the medical crosstalk in *The Doctor's Dilemma*. Shaw's sense of vulnerability to the power of this medical élite, displacing a fear of death, gave his satire its edge; his sparring matches with Wright also enabled him to parody his own habit of presenting himself as morally superior to human frailty and devastatingly up to date with scientific fashion. Unlike Wright, who had won an extraordinary pile of medals, honours and academic prizes, Shaw had never learned anything at school. 'I could not pass an examination and win a certificate in an elementary school to this day.' He was an academic *manqué* and resented his exclusion from university excellence – that nest of singing birds.

Behind these years of controversy with Wright, and the play that derived from their association, there lay a wish to take authority from the orthodoxly educated and give it to outsiders. Like the scholastic profession, the medical freemasonry was a closed circle of privileged people whose mesmeric power over other human beings angered Shaw. 'It is awful how these scientific men wallow in orthodoxy, when they get the chance,' he complained to Gilbert Murray. ' . . . Free thought really depends on the men of letters – and progressive thought, too.'

*

The Doctor's Dilemma shows us a cabal of physicians driven into the position of private tradesmen, abjectly dependent upon their patients' incomes and delusions. Beneath the invented drama of the play with its surface tension of ethics versus aesthetics, lies a theme that confronts the philosophies of science for science's sake with the social usefulness of art, balancing Wright's way of looking at the world against Shaw's. Sir Colenso Ridgeon's choice, which is intended to illustrate the subjective foundations of scientific reasoning, exposes him at the end of the play as having been so emotionally self-deluded as to have 'committed a purely disinterested murder!'

The most effective sections of the play depended on Shaw's instinct rather than his research. He sensed that something was wrong with Wright's reputation. The War Office, wanting to use Wright's anti-typhoid injections, 'first had him knighted and then used his knighthood as evidence of the unassailability of his theories' – a similar process to that of Ridgeon's knighthood in Act I of the play. One reason for the popularity of Wright's treatment seems to have been its novelty. No Harley Street specialist could afford to see his patient leave him for someone more 'up to date'. But looking back from 1970, W. D. Foster concluded in *A History of Medical Bacteriology*: 'It is doubtful if this form of treatment produced any good results and certainly in most instances, it was valueless to the point of fraudulence.'

Shaw said of Wright that it was 'useful to know a man who has discovered the philosopher's stone but does not know the value of gold'. It was a percipient statement. The concept of certain body cells reacting in a measurable way to an invasion by bacteria 'had great importance for the future development of bacteriology and immunology,' wrote Dr Gregory Scott in *British Medicine*. But the significance of this discovery was taken up by Wright's junior at St Mary's, Alexander Fleming. While accidentally finding a drug that would take the place of vaccine therapy, Fleming was financed by money raised from the use of Wright's vaccine, and obliged to pay perpetual lip-service to the man who became nicknamed 'Sir Almost Wright'. The story was to end with the renaming of St Mary's laboratory as the Wright-Fleming Institute and the development of the wonder-drug penicillin by Florey and Chain. Shaw's instinct had alerted him to recurring and timeless patterns within the medical community.

There were several models for the artist Dubedat. Chief among them was Edward Aveling, the basilisk-eyed 'blackguard' whom Eleanor Marx had idolized. When Ridgeon assures Jennifer Dubedat that 'your hero must be preserved to you', he is protecting her from Eleanor Marx's suicidal destiny by ensuring that her illusions survive her husband's death. Shaw also recycled some of his feelings for H. G. Wells and Charles Charrington, used the case histories of Beardsley and Rossetti, as well as a scandal from the career of Sir Alfred Gilbert, sculptor of Eros in Piccadilly Circus, and cast a backward look at Vandeleur Lee.

In the play Dubedat becomes the figure through whom 'the Shavian devil is most active,' writes Margery Morgan. 'For the debate reflects a division that ran deep in the author himself.' Critics have proposed that since Dubedat admits 'I'm a disciple of Bernard Shaw', he represents G.B.S. But he had taken this statement from a court case. A youth called Rankin, sentenced early that year to six months' imprisonment for attempting to blackmail his father, a schoolmaster, had pleaded guilty to being a disciple of Bernard Shaw as the explanation of his crime. In Wormwood Scrubs he refused the ministrations of the chaplain, and asked that G.B.S. be sent for. As Shaw was abroad, Stewart Headlam visited him in gaol. 'It was quite clear that he was under the impression that my teaching was simply an advocacy of reckless and shameless disregard of all social and moral obligations,' Shaw later reported, 'an error which he owes, I should say, not to reading my works unsophisticatedly, but to reading the follies which the press utters about me . . . It was as a reductio-ad-absurdum of this error and partly as a warning against it that I made Dubedat in the play use Rankin's defence.'

Shaw subtitled his play 'A Tragedy'. To peddle self-delusion and advertise it as a happiness-drug was to manufacture human tragedy. Shaw recommended people to 'stop taking any opiates or palliatives if you can endure life without them'; and he used the medical profession as a metaphor for every conspiracy of self-deception that worked against the public interest. The doctors in his play are all amiable men. It is public fear that insists on their omniscience, public superstition that equips them with their hocus-pocus of charms and cures, public ignorance that obliges them to trade in hypochondria. They are the idealists of Shaw's philosophy, who are paid to give the philistines what they want and will be out of a job unless they do so.

Shaw believed that most progress depended on heretics but that most heretics were not vehicles for progress. In Dubedat we are shown a realist infected by poverty and the atmosphere of idealism. Ridgeon, the physician, romantically idealizes Jennifer who romantically idealizes her artist-husband Dubedat who idealizes his work as the murderous doctors idealize theirs.

The embodiment of romanticism is Jennifer. 'Provisionally I have called her Andromeda; but Mrs Andromeda Dubedat is too long,' Shaw wrote to Lillah McCarthy from Cornwall. 'Here in King Arthur's country the name Guinevere survives as Jennifer.' The names reveal Shaw's intention to parody the Greek and Arthurian myths of chivalry. Ridgeon sees himself as a Perseus rescuing his beautiful Andromeda by killing her monster-husband. By calling her Jennifer and preserving the connection with Arthurian legend, Shaw recalls his own 'Mystic Betrothal' to May Morris whose mother Jane had been painted as Guinevere by William Morris. The more recent case of Guineverism, Shaw implies, had been Lillah and Barker.

Shaw wrote his play, he said, in response to a challenge from Archer who had written that G.B.S. was incapable of writing a convincing death scene. 'It is not the glory but the limitation of Mr Shaw's theatre that it is peopled by immortals,' he wrote. Shaw intended *The Doctor's Dilemma* to be a 'tragic comedy, with death conducting the orchestra'. To assist the critics, who had not yet heard of black comedy, Shaw issued a press release in which he prophesied 'it will probably be called a *farce macabre*'; and as an aid for his audiences he added a quotation to the programme: 'Life does not cease to be funny when people die, any more than it ceases to be serious when people laugh.'

The death of Dubedat is usually more interesting to scholars than spectators. The serious artist in Dubedat is already dead and the tragedy over. What remains is an actor performing a death scene for his audience on stage. The long operatic farewell, with its comic chorus, has none of the sordidness of death from tuberculosis.

Shaw was fond of his death scene. He described it as 'none the worse because its climax is "derived" (not to say stolen) from Wagner's End of a Musician in Paris'. The scholarship in which he wrapped the King of Terrors round becomes the weapon for a perfect riposte to charges of bad taste and cheap art.

'The creed of the dying artist, which has been reprobated on all hands as a sally of which only the bad taste of Bernard Shaw could be capable, is openly borrowed with gratitude and admiration by me from one of the best known prose writings of the most famous man of the nineteenth century. In Richard Wagner's well known story, dated 1841 . . . the dying musician begins his creed with the words, "I believe in God, Mozart and

Beethoven". It is a curious instance of the enormous Philistinism of English criticism that this passage should not only be unknown among us, but that a repetition of its thought and imagery 65 years later should still find us with a conception of creative force so narrow that the association of Art with Religion conveys nothing to us but a sense of far fetched impropriety.

I am, Sir, your obedient servant

G. Bernard Shaw.'

5

INVASION OF THE WEST END

Touchstone: Wast ever at the Court, shepherd?
Corin: No, truly.
Touchstone: Then thou art damned.

Shakespeare, *As You Like It*

The materials for his play had accumulated gradually: but the writing was fast. Shaw had begun it on 11 August 1906 at Mevagissey on the coast of Cornwall. By 21 August, on Polstreath Beach, he finished the first act. A week later another act was completed. 'It springs into existence impetuously with leaps & bounds,' he told Trebitsch; 'the only trouble is to get it inked.'

He wrote everywhere, ending the third act on St Austell Station in Cornwall and starting the fourth the same day after joining the train from Exeter to London. He came to the end of this act at the village of Moulsford in the Thames Valley, then started the last on the train from Reading to London. The first draft was completed at twenty minutes past six in the evening aboard a steamer on the Thames, as it docked at Cherry Garden Pier below Tower Bridge.

Shaw's revisions ('a slower job than the writing was') persisted, through rehearsals, almost up to opening night on 20 November. From the Carfax Gallery the Court leased pictures by Augustus John, William Orpen and Will Rothenstein, suggesting an extraordinary diversity in Dubedat's style.

Again the critics were divided. But Shaw himself noticed how they were beginning to compare him somewhat unfavourably to himself. 'In the future, instead of abusing the new play and praising the one before, let them abuse the one before and praise the new one,' he recommended. He was genuinely anxious for the press to act as a helpful patron to the

Court. The 'atmosphere of good humour' which the newspapers could promote, he told Vedrenne, was 'next to an atmosphere of solid money' the most precious possession they could own. He felt a commitment to their enterprise not simply because it had given him an audience and made his name as a dramatist of performable plays, but because it represented a step towards establishing the theatre in England. 'It is a huge factory of sentiment, of character, of points of honour, of conceptions of conduct,' he wrote later when appealing for the building of a National Theatre, 'of everything that finally determines the destiny of a nation.'

*

Barker used these years at the Court to test some of the ideas he and Archer had proposed in their book, *A National Theatre: Scheme and Estimates*. This book, 'the blueprint and the bible for the National Theatre movement', envisaged a large repertory of plays, both ancient and modern, foreign and English. The Court was more avant-garde than anything that, for pragmatic reasons, they were recommending to the general public. But its success was an excellent advertisement for the scheme. Privately printed and circulated before the Court pilot project began in October 1904, their book was published shortly after the Vedrenne–Barker management left the Court in June 1907.

Barker and Shaw had introduced repertory into the London theatre and achieved what the young actor Hesketh Pearson called 'the most famous epoch in theatrical management since the days of the Globe on Bankside'. But besides Barker and Laurence Housman, none of the contemporary playwrights (who included Galsworthy, St John Hankin, John Masefield and W. B. Yeats) wrote work that was really popular. The only outstanding success was G.B.S. himself. Of the thirty-two plays by seventeen dramatists presented at the Court over almost three years, eleven were his; and of the 988 performances altogether, Shaw's plays made up 701. Everything could be explained away as having depended upon one man. After June 1907, when *Don Juan in Hell* and *The Man of Destiny* were presented in a double bill, Shaw's portfolio was pretty well exhausted. There was a feeling that he had been rather too successful. John Quinn, the American patron and collector, reported that the theatre was 'brimming over with Shaw and Shaw's plays at present . . . Yeats says he will soon become a public nuisance.'

But the reputation of the Court partly owed its solidity to 'the prudent pessimism' of Vedrenne. 'Barker, aiming at a National Repertory Theatre, with a change of program every night, was determined to test our enterprise to destruction as motor tyres are tested, to find out its utmost possibilities,' Shaw wrote. 'I was equally reckless. Vedrenne . . . was like a man trying to ride two runaway horses simultaneously.' Vedrenne wanted to make money out of the theatre. Barker felt constantly balked by his subtle economies, his greeting of all fresh ideas with extravagant horror. Shaw represented their mutual dislike as a miraculous bonus. 'The partnership of V & B has every aspect of permanence: you are exactly on the terms which bind men to one another for ever & ever,' he promised Vedrenne, 'each with a strong grievance against the other to give interest & life to what would otherwise be a tedious & uneventful routine.'

Everything was enlivened by what Barker felt to be Vedrenne's 'vendetta' against Lillah McCarthy. 'My position between you is very fearful,' Shaw warned Lillah. 'I ask myself repeatedly Is Lillah the greatest liar known to history, or is Vedrenne?' And he cautioned Vedrenne: 'You will end by busting up Vedrenne & Barker.' Under this pressure they were all driven to abuse each other. 'What with Barker gradually losing all desire to act, and Vedrenne gradually losing all desire to do anything else but act, the position has become more & more impossible,' complained Shaw. 'If I could only get V on the stage & B off it, I should amaze the world.'

In Shaw's opinion, the job of producing plays was ruining Barker's acting. But Shaw minimized Barker's distaste for public performance. 'I do believe my present loathing for the theatre is loathing for the audience,' he was to write a decade later. 'I have never loved them.' He wished to retire and write for a more refined theatre – the National Theatre of his imagination. Shaw's advice seemed partly to assist the first step in this retreat. 'The next thing *you* have to do is to finish the play [*Waste*] & produce it,' he had urged in the summer of 1906; 'then publish it with Ann Leete & Voysey in a single volume.'

But Barker needed money to write at his ease and produce his plays fastidiously. By 1907 two possibilities lay open to him. 'There is to be a new theatre in America financed by 23 millionaires; and I have been asked whether Barker will go over and manage it,' Shaw announced to Lillah. This Millionaire's Theatre, between 62nd and 63rd Streets on Central Park West, was being built to run on the repertory principles described in Barker and Archer's blueprint, and it offered Barker an opportunity to cut free from Vedrenne and join a more intellectual partnership with Archer. 'America looks rather real at moments,' he wrote to Archer, 'and it would be a correct sequel to the blue book if we went together.'

But the Millionaire's Theatre was still under construction and other arrangements had to be made for the coming season of 1907–8. Shaw believed that repertory meant playing in London for advertisement and then playing on tour for money. Vedrenne wanted to capitalize on their success at the Court by advancing straight into the West End of London. Perhaps because touring was such a helter-skelter business, Barker mainly supported Vedrenne and together they leased the Savoy Theatre in the Strand. Shaw did not intend to join their partnership: 'I shall act simply as usurer,' he told them. To enable the Savoy season to open he put up £2,000 (equivalent to £94,500 in 1997) at five per cent interest – to which was added £1,000 each from Vedrenne and Barker who were both to draw salaries of £1,000 a year. 'My own salary – another thousand – ' added Shaw, 'is to be taken out in moral superiority.'

The Savoy was twice the size of the Court and had become celebrated for its Gilbert and Sullivan productions. But the audiences from the Court never took to the Savoy where the management actually played the National Anthem and made them stand up. In his excitement Vedrenne appeared to Shaw to have thrown aside all his prudence; while Barker, his hopes focused on New York, would have been content with Restoration comedy. Shaw complained of his reluctance 'to tackle anything but easy plays and easy people – easy, that is, to his temperament'. He also objected to the many revivals of his own plays, which were losing their sparkle. 'The thing to aim at now,' he insisted to Barker, 'is a season without a single Shaw evening bill.' He wanted Galsworthy's new play *Joy* and Barker's *Waste* to take up the running. But Galsworthy's sentimental work was a disappointment; Barker's *Waste* was banned by the Censor; and even the weakly cast production of Gilbert Murray's version of Euripides' *Medea* appeared lustreless. The Savoy season, which closed on 14 March 1908, had turned out a failure.

Immediately afterwards Barker took off with Archer for New York. But they found the New Theatre, 'with an enormous, gaping, cavernous proscenium', to be 'fit only for old-fashioned, nineteenth century spectacle'. They returned in disappointment to London.

In the spring of 1908 Vedrenne leased another theatre, the Haymarket, to present Shaw's new 'dramatic masterpiece' *Getting Married*. This was to be followed in the summer with *The Chinese Lantern* by Laurence Housman whose *Prunella* (in collaboration with Barker) had been one of the Court's non-Shavian successes, and a new play called *Nan* by John Masefield whose *Campden Wonder* Shaw felt had been seriously underrated at the Court.

'The Vedrenne and Barker enterprise then is as much alive as ever?' Shaw made a *Daily Telegraph* reporter ask him in May 1908 – to which he answered: 'it seems to be immortal.' In fact Barker and Vedrenne longed to be free of each other, but (being so heavily in debt to him) could not come to any arrangement without Shaw's consent. And Shaw, reluctant to announce their separation, succeeded in delaying it until early in 1911. Barker had by then written *The Madras House*, directed a season of plays at the Duke of York's Theatre with the American producer Charles Frohman and begun a theatrical partnership with his wife. Vedrenne was starting on a new partnership, 'Vedrenne and [Dennis] Eadie', at the Royalty Theatre. To reunite them was no longer possible. Shaw, who had advanced £5,250 to them over the years and arranged for Barker to be repaid his loans first, agreed to accept £484 3s. 10d. (plus some assets from the sale of scenery) as a final settlement.

It had been 'worth the cost a hundred times over,' he declared; 'but the cost fell on us, and the benefit went to the nation'. In 1909 he had joined the Organizing Committee of the Shakespeare Memorial National Theatre, and converted his Vedrenne & Barker loss into an investment in the campaign. What could be done by private enterprise, he argued, had been exhaustively tried at the Court. 'Messrs. Vedrenne & Barker were not rich men,' he wrote. 'They voluntarily forewent the opportunity of turning the enterprise into a lucrative commercial speculation and left themselves at the end with all their resources mortgaged. My own income falls very far short of the point at which the loss of sums of four figures becomes a matter of no importance . . . I had to stop.'

ELEVEN

I

SITTING TO RODIN

> Do you know Shaw's writings? That's the man who has quite a good way of coming to terms with life – of putting himself into harmony with it (which is no small achievement). He is proud of his work, like Wilde or Whistler but without their pretension, rather like a dog that is proud of its master.
>
> Rainer Maria Rilke to Elizabeth von der Heydt (26 April 1906)

'We are in the agonies of househunting,' Shaw had appealed to Wells in April 1904. 'Now is the time to produce an eligible residence, if you have one handy.' Charlotte had grown more ingenious at braking her husband's flow of work. Early in 1906 she encouraged him to sit for his portrait by Neville Lytton. It was an extraordinary picture, owing much to an observation by Granville Barker that the Velázquez portrait of Pope Innocent X in the Doria Palace at Rome was uncannily similar to G.B.S. Working in imitation of Velázquez, and placing his subject in papal vestments and throne, Neville Lytton achieved what Shaw was to call a 'witty jibe at my poses'.

These poses multiplied over the last half of Shaw's career – as busts, statuettes, medallions, stamps, portraits in oils, watercolours, crayon and needlework; as wooden marionettes, caricatures on posters and in papers, on film, as photographs (poised either naked or eccentrically tailored) on land, in cars, under parasols, at sea; and as likenesses rendered in stained glass, from a simple stick of shaving soap, as a brass door-knocker or waxwork tricyclist and, most extreme of all perhaps, in grisaille with hands held to ears on a Chinese *famille rose* vase decorated with dense peony, chrysanthemum, lily and vine . . .

People were aghast at Shaw's Everest of vanity. But, admitting his addiction to public attention, he tried to employ it usefully. His commissioned portraits and busts may be seen as evidence of generous patronage. He was curious too about the public phenomenon he had manufactured to replace the unloved Sonny.

But Charlotte was not amused. Taking advantage of a visit to England by Rodin, she invited the French sculptor to visit her at Adelphi Terrace on the afternoon of Friday 1 March 1906. He came, they talked, and the consequence was that, as Shaw wrote to Trebitsch later that day, 'my wife insists on dragging me to Paris for twelve days at Easter so that Rodin may make a bust of me!!!!!'

They stayed at the Hôtel Palais d'Orsay, and after meeting Rodin on 16 April began the sittings at his private studio in Meudon. 'He had, I believe, a serious friendship for us,' Shaw was to write. They were at his house all day, most days, until they left France on 8 May. Talking to Rodin as he was preparing to begin, Charlotte complained that other artists and photographers had automatically produced the sort of mephistophelean figure they assumed her husband to be, without taking the trouble to look at him. Rodin replied that he knew nothing of Shaw's reputation: 'but what is there I will give you.'

G.B.S. was determined to prove a champion sitter, putting immense vitality simply into standing still. 'The portrait makes tremendous strides, thanks to the energy with which Shaw stands,' wrote Rainer Maria Rilke, then Rodin's secretary. 'He stands like a thing which has the will to stand, over and above its natural capacity for it . . .

'Shaw as a model surpasses description. He . . . has the power of getting his whole self, even to his legs and all the rest of him, into his bust, which will have to represent the whole Shaw, as it were, that Rodin has before him something quite unusually concentrated, which he absorbs into himself and into his work (you can imagine with what zest).'

Rodin's studio seemed transformed into a theatre. Each day an audience assembled and sat in mesmerized silence as Shaw ('*ce modèle extraordinaire*') collected and concentrated himself and Rodin filled the place with 'his raging activity, his gigantic movements', and volleys of unintelligible sound. In the intervals Charlotte played about G.B.S. 'like a spring wind about a goat'. In a letter to his wife, Rilke sent a beautifully exact description of the work's development. 'After rapidly cutting out the eyebrows so that something like a nose appeared, and marking the position of the mouth by an incision such as children make in a snowman, he began to make first four, then eight, then sixteen profiles, letting the model, who was standing quite close to him, turn every three minutes or so . . .

'In the third sitting, he placed Shaw in a low child's chair (all of which caused this ironical and mocking spirit, who is however by no means an unsympathetic personality, exquisite pleasure) and sliced the head off the bust with a wire – (Shaw, whom the bust already resembled very strikingly, watched this execution with indescribable delight.)'

What appealed to Shaw was Rodin's monumental matter-of-factness. He never pretended to a knowledge of his plays ('he knows absolutely nothing about books,' Shaw commented, ' – thinks they are things to be read'), his eyes never twinkled, his hands did not gesticulate: he worked, and 'like all great workmen who can express themselves in words, was very straight and simple'. Shaw's words, according to Rodin, were less straight but even more simple: '*M. Shaw ne parle pas très bien*,' he said; '*mais il s'exprime avec une telle violence qu'il s'impose.*'

These *séances* at Meudon became one of the features of Paris's spring season. People as various as G. K. Chesterton and Gwen John were reported to have bulged or peeped in for a moment. From Vienna came Trebitsch to marvel and absorb the 'lofty mind' of Charlotte in 'profound talk about God and the universe'.

To other acquaintances – including the young American photographer Alvin Langdon Coburn – Shaw sent invitations for the unveiling of Rodin's sculpture 'Le Penseur'. Coburn had photographed Shaw two summers earlier, and in 1906 Shaw had written a preface to the catalogue for an exhibition of his work in which he compared Coburn's photograph of Chesterton to Rodin's statue of Balzac. The inauguration of 'Le Penseur' outside the Panthéon took place on the afternoon of 21 April. Next morning Shaw surprised Coburn with the suggestion that 'after his bath I should photograph him nude in the pose of Le Penseur' on the edge of his bath. With this parody of 'Le Penseur' he came close to sabotaging his purpose in going to Rodin for evidence of himself 'just as I am, without one plea'. He wanted to feel cleansed of the revulsion that periodically rose up in him over his own notoriety. But this Shavian fame arose from so deep a need that he sentimentalized his humility towards Rodin when famously remarking: 'at least I was sure of a place in the biographical dictionaries a thousand years hence as: "Shaw, Bernard: subject of a bust by Rodin: otherwise unknown".'

They went to Ibsen's *Canard Sauvage* and to the Grand Guignol with Trebitsch. The more blood-curdling these plays, Trebitsch observed, the more of an effort Shaw had to make 'not to burst out laughing'. He particularly enjoyed the guillotine. Nothing, it seemed to Trebitsch, could frighten G.B.S., not even the evening newspaper predictions of a revolution in Paris on May Day which he looked forward to as 'the next instalment of the horror-play we have just been seeing'. Shaw spent the afternoon of May Day with Charlotte on the Place de la République and afterwards sent a message to the *Labour Leader* commenting that the French Government wanted to win the General Election 'by suppressing a revolution. Unluckily there is no revolution to suppress. The Government therefore sends the police and the dragoons to shove and charge the lazy and law abiding Parisians until they are goaded into revolt. No use: the people simply WON'T revolt.

'But several respectable persons have been shoved and galloped over and even sabred. Surely it ought to be within the resources of modern democracy to find a remedy for this sort of official amateur revolution making. It is a clear interference with our business as scientific revolutionists.'

In a letter to Granville Barker he admitted there had been a little more activity, describing Charlotte as clinging to lamp-posts in order to see over people's heads and growing 'so furious when she saw a real crowd charged by real soldiers that she wanted to throw stones'. After being 'pushed roughly hither and thither' she was led back by Shaw ('by dignified strategy which did not at any time go to the length of absolutely running away') to their hotel 'bursting into fresh spasms of rage all the way'. They had quitted the field without wounds and Shaw insisted that Charlotte had 'rather enjoyed being part of a revolution'. 'We finished up in the evening with a very stirring performance of Beethoven's 9th symphony at the Opera,' he told Trebitsch; 'so the day was a pretty full one.'

On 8 May Shaw sat to Rodin for the last time, then he and Charlotte caught the four o'clock train back to London. She carried with her two pencil-and-wash sketches of herself inscribed by Rodin '*Homage à sympathique Madame Charlotte Shaw*'. From London she sent him chocolates and her photograph of him (none of Shaw's had come out) and in October the curiously tame marble bust arrived at Adelphi Terrace; '*maintenant je suis immortel*,' wrote Shaw in a letter to Rodin that was returned to him as insufficiently addressed.

Within six weeks of returning to London Shaw was turning his head to William Strang for a good tight portrait. The following year, 1907, began with a couple of quick sittings for a bust by Troubetzkoy and ended with a preliminary one for Epstein. Shaw was to use these busts (and others by Sava Botzaris, Kathleen Bruce, Joseph Coplans, Jo Davidson, Sigismund de Strobl and Clare Winsten) to pull faces at his 'reputation'. Prince Troubetzkoy, being paternally Russian, 'made me flatteringly like a Russian nobleman'; and in the hands of Jacob Epstein, an American expatriate, he later became 'a Brooklyn navvy . . . my skin thickened, my hair coarsened, I put on five stone in weight, my physical strength trebled'. It followed that his plaster reputation lay in the imaginations of other people, not within himself.

Charlotte welcomed the respite from work these sittings and standings and posings obtained for him. But Epstein's ungentlemanly bust (completed in 1934) was 'like a blow in the face' and she told everyone who mentioned it to her that if this object 'came into our house she would walk out of it'. As Rodin had not understood his humour so Epstein had overlooked his Shavian veneer: and 'without my veneer I am not Bernard Shaw'.

This veneer, he had sometimes argued, was his reputation. In these busts and portraits, Shaw often felt he recognized part of himself; but never could he find all parts combined. Perhaps there was no method, even in his own work, of allying the opposing forces within himself. At the age of fifty he had proposed 'to furnish the world with an authentic portrait-bust of me before I had left the prime of life'. The nearest he came to this was perhaps Strobl's work – Charlotte certainly thought so. But the search for comprehensive authenticity continued almost to the end of his life. It was impossible, H. G. Wells complained, to move around Europe without being stared at by these Shavian images which seemed at the same time to mock and celebrate his rising success.

In the summer of 1906, as if in sympathy with this success, Shaw ascended from Wandsworth Gas Works in a balloon (a happening he would later re-compose for his play *Misalliance*). He rose and floated and descended over two and a half hours, without Charlotte's knowledge yet in the company of her sister, Granville Barker and the aviator-actor Robert Loraine. Loraine was a combination of artist and man-of-action Shaw particularly admired. 'I was never free from the impression when Shaw was speaking to me,' Loraine had written in his diary, 'that he might at any moment ascend to Heaven like Elisha on a chariot of fire.' They were guided in their balloon by an aeronaut Percival Spencer (who was translated into Joey Percival in *Misalliance*) to a height of 9,000 feet. After forty minutes' drifting 'very pleasant and seraphic with nothing happening, except that Shaw would peer through a hole in the boarding at his feet which made him feel rather sick, we discussed landing,' Loraine wrote. '... I thought the people would be rather interested to receive visitors from the air, and especially flattered when they discovered Shaw's identity. "Don't be so certain," said Shaw. "They may think my works detestable."' In the event they bumped down in a field near Chobham and were met by a purple-faced landowner, unacquainted with Shaw's *oeuvre* and waving a shooting-stick. 'The welcome he gave us was a curt direction as to the quickest way off his property.'

2

A CAT AND DOG LIFE

I was born to do odd jobs.

Shaw to Beatrice Webb (9 December 1910)

Their agonies of house-hunting ended when they came across the Rectory at Ayot St Lawrence, not far from Wheathampstead in Hertfordshire. The Rector, who could not afford to keep up the grounds, had no need of such a large house himself, and Charlotte decided to rent it. She did not plan to stay there long. They continued renting the place for fourteen years and shortly after the First World War bought it – following which it became known as 'Shaw's Corner'.

Ayot was a remote twelfth-century village where 'the last thing of real importance that happened was, perhaps, the Flood'. It had two churches, one shop, no omnibus or train service and, even by the 1930s, no gas or water supply, no delivery of newspapers and no electricity – the Rectory itself making use of a private generating plant. The house, which had been built in 1902, was a plain dark-red building standing in a sloping two-acre plot with scraps of kitchen-garden, orchard, lawn and a belt of conifers. Besides the dining-room, study and a small drawing-room, there were eight bedrooms.

Shaw and Charlotte moved in at the beginning of November 1906, with a married couple, Henry and Clara Higgs, to look after them. Higgs took over the garden, with an odd-job man to help him; and Charlotte engaged two maids to assist Mrs Higgs indoors. The Higgses, who had already been with them at Adelphi Terrace, were to remain in their service for some forty years. 'Mrs Shaw looked upon my wife almost as a daughter,' Higgs reckoned; 'they were like a father and mother to us.' Shaw recognized their value to him with an inscription in one of his books: 'To Harry and Clara Higgs, who have had a very important part in my life's work, as without their friendly services I should not have had time to write my books and plays nor had any comfort in my daily life.'

The Rectory was a fairly comfortable, fairly dismal house. Charlotte filled it with stiff armchairs, bureaux, beds: lodging-house objects with hardly a good piece among them. They had grown tired of house-hunting and this was one of the few houses about which they were agreed: neither of them liked it. Every day at Ayot felt like a Sunday. Once they had settled in, they were free to move out and around.

*

They had kept their maisonette in Adelphi Terrace, went regularly between London and Hertfordshire, and erratically everywhere else. At the end of March 1907, Charlotte carried Shaw off to France and they whirled through town after town for twelve days of hectic relaxation. 'I shall go to Beauvais probably tomorrow or next day,' Shaw wrote from Rouen, 'and shall either do the cathedral in ten minutes & hurry on Lord knows where, or stay there a day or two.' But, he owned, 'the cessation of writing & talking has done me a lot of good'.

To lighten the load of correspondence he had devised in 1906 a series of five stereotyped postcard messages. Over the next years the range of these cards greatly expanded. He attempted to give them a series of coloured codes, though eventually running out of colours. His views on capital punishment, on temperance, and the forty-letter British 'alfabet' were to be relayed in tones of green, orange-brown and blue. Neat piles of these coloured cards lay on his desk and, as he read through his mail each day he was able to cap many letters with an appropriate card. Snap! Politely and with force, they spelled out his reasons for being unable to read and report on unpublished manuscripts, give spoken interviews, inscribe books that were not his personal gifts, or comply with requests from strangers for his signature (with or without a photograph); why he could not receive visitors, acknowledge gifts, encourage people to celebrate his birthdays, respond to appeals founded on the notion that he was a multi-millionaire, open bazaars, speak at public dinners, write prefaces, read or write letters. In short: why he could not do so many of the things he spent his life doing.

'The only way to avoid giving offence by refusing is to refuse everybody by rule.' But Shaw consistently disobeyed his rule – even his authoritative refusals to provide autographs were sometimes signed. The cards were a method of saving time. He invested many hours in drafting variant texts. But always there was an ample margin that he could fill with commentary, outwitting the purpose of a printed message.

In 1907 he engaged Georgina Gillmore, daughter of his mother's half-sister Arabella, as his secretary. Charlotte and Shaw were fond of 'Judy'. She was eighteen and lived with Lucinda Shaw in Fitzroy Square when she started work for G.B.S. He sent her to secretarial college and she worked for him until her marriage in 1912.

Even with her help, Shaw complained that only 'the fear of my wife' was keeping him from a breakdown. Throughout the year, more than fifty of his articles, statements, interviews and letters appeared in the newspapers. There was Shaw on disarmament in the *Evening Standard*, on polygamy in *The Times* and on diet in the *Daily Mail*. His most common subjects were marriage, censorship and women's suffrage. But readers of the *Daily Graphic* could pick up what he had to say on 'the imperfections of phrenologists'; and *Clarion* subscribers could learn about 'the Gentle Art of Unpleasantness', a social exercise in three parts. He fired off a piece on Delacroix to the *Saturday Review*; composed a famous essay on Belloc and Chesterton for the *New Age*; and published a review of A. R. Orage's book on Nietzsche in *Fabian News*. The variety seemed infinite, the quantity endless.

In July 1907 the Shaws and the Webbs went off to a large house in Llanbedr, a village on the Welsh coast between Barmouth and Harlech, where the first Fabian Summer School took place. The event was underwritten by Charlotte who saw it as a method of ventilating their studies with fresh air and a holiday atmosphere.

The Fabian Summer Schools, which later came to be seen as a foundation of the intellectual wing of the Labour Party, were originally designed to get country members to meet metropolitan Fabians, and grey-haired socialists to mingle with the Fabian nursery. Occasional romances glimmered, but the exhilarations were generally those of a 'joyous monastery'. The day would begin with Swedish Drill led by Mary Hankinson, a much-loved muscular games mistress and leading Fabian cricketer, who was to be a prototype for Shaw's St Joan. Breakfast, an experimental meal, was followed by a venture into co-operative washing-up. Cold baths were free (hot baths cost sixpence); rooms were set aside in which to practise silence, and no smoking was permitted (except, literally, in the smoking-room). There were courses of lectures available on the National Debt and the Modern Novel. Additional fixtures included swimming and tugs-of-war (Vegetarians versus Meat-eaters); and people were allowed to bring bicycles and eventually tennis balls – though never dogs or children. Highly organized games were discouraged, but there was always some tonic recreation such as country dances with the aid of Cecil J. Sharp's *The Country Dance Book* (3 vols.). Lights went out and doors were bolted at 11 p.m., and Fabians were requested 'to refrain from loud talk and noises' in the dormitories.

'The Fabian School is sleeping five in a room, and apparently enjoying it,' Shaw wrote to Granville Barker. G.B.S. was the chief attraction. He lectured on marriage, education and foreign politics; gave readings from his plays; and chatted with everyone. Thirty-nine Fabians camped in the old schoolhouse down the road from the Shaws, who had been joined in their house by Charlotte's sister and Robert Loraine. After one day's hike Shaw failed to return. Dressed in convenient drill-costumes and equipped with lanterns, a party of almost a hundred Fabians streamed across the mountains and valleys: and he was discovered asleep in a hotel.

More alarming were his exploits at sea. Each morning he swam and one morning, after a storm, almost drowned. Pressing him later as to what thoughts had come to mind during what might have been his last few moments alive, Loraine was told that he had been almost completely preoccupied by the business inconveniences of his death. How would Charlotte understand the arrangements with his translators? How would she cope with his lateness for lunch? 'Then my foot struck a stone, and instead of saying "Thank God!" I said, "Damn!" '

It was against this terrible capacity for endangering himself, and his instinctive 'Damn!' rather than 'Thank God!' on reaching safety, that Charlotte had to be so fiercely on guard. Increasingly, as Arnold Bennett noticed, she looked 'like the mother of a large family'. For Christmas she tucked Shaw up again in her sister and brother-in-law's house, where it was pretty well impossible for him to get into scrapes. And she kept him under her supervision and out of the country for three summer months of 1908 while the drains at Ayot were being replaced. First they went to Stockholm. To help preserve its exclusiveness, he promised to 'perpetrate the notion that Sweden is a frightful place, where bears wander through the streets and people live on cod liver oil'. He then descended to Bayreuth where he heard Richter conduct Wagner's *Ring* as well as 'the most perfectly managed performance [of *Parsifal*] I ever saw (and I had seen six before)'. Finally, Charlotte escorted him round the railway hotels of Ireland, from Galway to Dublin, where he was to present the Municipal Art Gallery with one of his Rodin busts.

The visit marked a change from their previous tours of Ireland when they had stayed with the 'Brandons and Castletowns and Kingstons & other Irish peers in their castles'. These families regarded G.B.S. as a jumped-up Dublin office boy. 'Charlotte seems perfectly happy and delighted with her cad,' reported Edith Somerville, 'for cad he is in spite of his talent.' For Charlotte's sake Shaw made himself 'very agreeable and quite affable,' as Edith Somerville admitted, but this affability cost him a good deal in patience and energy, and after 1907 (when he declined to accompany Charlotte to Castle Haven) they stayed at hotels or with more recent friends such as Lady Gregory.

Their motor tour of Europe had been an ambitious excursion. 'I was crushed, I am now exasperated,' Shaw cried out in a letter to Granville Barker, ' . . . another day's motoring will murder me.' But the next day's motoring near Rothenburg had almost murdered Charlotte, the motor having 'backjumped,' Shaw explained, '& sent Charlotte like a rocket to the roof of the car (a limousine, unluckily)'. Her symptoms (a bad throat) made her uncertain whether or not her neck was broken. 'She leans to the belief that it is,' observed Shaw who had the advantage, while she recuperated, of remaining four days in the same place. Pathetically he signalled his friends for business letters, and confided to Granville Barker how fed up he was with 'the cat and dog life I lead with poor Charlotte . . . Another month of it would end in a divorce.'

Their most curious holiday episode had been an encounter with Strindberg. 'I thought it my duty to pay my respects to a great man whom I considered one of the great dramatists of Europe,' Shaw afterwards remembered. 'People told me it was not of the slightest use. He is absolutely mad, they said, he won't see anybody, he never takes walks except in the middle of the night when there is nobody about, he attacks all his friends with the greatest fury. You will only be wasting your time.' Nevertheless, 'I achieved the impossible,' Shaw wrote to Archer. Strindberg was 'quite a pleasant looking person,' Shaw recalled, 'with the most beautiful sapphire blue eyes I have ever seen. He was beyond expression shy.' Shaw had prepared some conversational material in French, but Strindberg took the wind out of his sails 'by addressing me in German'. Their exchange developed by way of some embarrassed silences, a 'pale smile or two' from Strindberg and an undercurrent of polite French from Charlotte.

Strindberg had arranged for them to see that morning a special performance of *Miss Julie* at his Intimate Theatre, having summoned August Falck and Manda Björling back from their holiday in the archipelago to play the two protagonists. The absence of an audience and the presence of Strindberg had been unsettling – this astonishingly being 'the first time Strindberg had accepted to see the play in the 20 years of its existence,' Anthony Swerling records, 'so much did he shy from the theatre'. Though Strindberg had proudly shown the Shaws round his theatre beforehand, shortly afterwards, in a celebrated spasm of gloom, he consulted his watch and, noting it was almost half-past one, remarked in German that at two o'clock he was going to be sick. 'On this strong hint the party broke up.'

How much did they comprehend each other, the author of *Married* which Strindberg called 'the reverse side of my fearful attraction towards the other sex'; and the author of *Getting Married*, a tentative 'conversation' with feminist implications dramatizing the economic relations of marriage? Shaw was to describe what he had seen at the Intimate Theatre as one of Strindberg's 'chamber plays'. With the emotional intimacy of chamber music he had never felt easy. But generally he knew where Strindberg stood. 'I was born too soon to be greatly influenced by him as a playwright, but,' he was to write 'he is among the greatest of the great.' In the Preface to *Three Plays for Puritans* he had described him as 'the only genuinely Shakespearean modern dramatist', a resolute tragi-comedian, logical and faithful, who gave us the choice either of dismissing as absurd his way of judging conduct or else, by accepting it, concluding that 'it is cowardly to continue living'.

The suffering men and women inflict on each other in the name of love never appears in Shaw's work as it does in Strindberg's. Greatness 'implies a degree of human tragedy, of suffering and sacrifice,' wrote Thomas Mann. 'The knotted muscles of Tolstoy bearing up the full burden of morality, Atlas-like; Strindberg, who was in hell; the martyr's death Nietzsche died on the cross of thought; it is these that inspire us with the reverence of tragedy; but in Shaw there was nothing of all this. Was he beyond such things, or were they beyond him?'

Shaw's tragedy lay in the need to suppress such things; Strindberg's in the need to re-enact them. But Shaw felt the force of that re-enactment. He tried to persuade Beerbohm Tree to put on *Lycko Pers Resa* at His Majesty's (the play closest to Ibsen's *Peer Gynt*), but without success. Almost none of Strindberg's plays had been translated into English before Shaw's sister Lucy, with Maurice Elvey, produced a version of *Miss Julie* that was first presented in London by the Adelphi Play Society in 1912. That year, the Swedish newspaper *Dagens Nyheter* circulated a letter eliciting opinions of Strindberg's role in European culture to be published in the event of his death from cancer. 'Strindberg is a very great dramatist: he and Ibsen have made Sweden and Norway the dramatic centre of the world,' Shaw replied. '. . . Time may wear him out; but Death will not succeed in murdering him.' Strindberg died a fortnight later.

3

GETTING MARRIED AND STAYING MARRIED

> This multiplicity of motives is, I like to think, typical of our times. And if others have done this before me, then I congratulate myself in not being alone in my belief in these 'paradoxes' (the word always used to describe new discoveries).
>
> Strindberg, Preface to *Miss Julie*

'On the question of technique, I have, by way of experiment, eliminated all intervals,' wrote Strindberg in his Preface to *Miss Julie*. For *Getting Married* Shaw used a similar experiment. 'The customary division into acts and scenes has been disused,' he wrote, 'and a return made to unity of time and place as observed in the ancient Greek drama.'

By directing critics to the play's Aristotelian rules, Shaw swept their attention past an embarrassing parallel. For years in the *Saturday Review* he had made fun of the plays of Victorien Sardou, full of a 'bewildering profusion of everything that has no business in a play'. *Getting Married* is in places an ingenious adaptation of Sardou's *Divorçons*. The parallels are 'not only in the overall fusion of Farce with a genuine discussion of marriage and divorce,' observed the critic Martin Meisel, 'but in particulars and details'. Sardou's plan of playwriting, Shaw had written, 'is first to invent the action of his piece, and then to carefully keep it off the stage and have it announced merely by letters and telegrams'.

The Shavian play structure too moved the action off stage, and reversed the relationship between dialogue and incident. *Getting Married* progresses by means of a series of conversations: duologues and trios that form and dissolve one into another. It is as if a conventional well-made play were being performed backstage, and we witness the performers discussing its event-plot during the intervals. 'It is the wedding day of the bishop's daughter,' he wrote. 'The situation is expounded in the old stage fashion by that old stage figure the comic greengrocer, hired for the occasion as butler.

'The fun grows fast and furious as the guests arrive, invited and uninvited, with the most distracting malapropositу. Two are missing: the bridegroom and the bride. They have each received anonymously a pamphlet entitled "*Do you know what you are going to do? By one who has Done It*," setting forth all the anomalies and injustices and dangers of marriage under the existing British law. They refuse to get up and dress until they have read this inopportune document to the last word. When at last they appear they flatly refuse to face the horrors of the marriage law. Thereupon the whole company plunges into a discussion of marriage, and presently sits as a committee to draw up a form of private contract, as in the later days of ancient Rome, to supersede the legal ceremony. They are utterly unable to agree on a single article of it.'

Though Shaw claimed a classical provenance for *Getting Married*, it actually represented 'a new dramaturgy' as Eric Bentley wrote, 'and not, as its critics thought, a mere pamphlet in dialogue form'. Like *The Doctor's Dilemma*, it stages an institution. 'The play is about marriage as an institution and about nothing else.' His method of treating it was one that he had first attempted, and been persuaded to abandon, fifteen years before in the original last act of *The Philanderer*. It had been the celebrated divorcée Lady Colin Campbell who opened Shaw's eyes to 'the fact that I have started on quite a new trail and must reserve this act for the beginning of a new play'. With *Getting Married* Shaw finally started out on that trail.

The Philanderer had been one of Shaw's most directly autobiographical plays; with *Getting Married* he had grown more oblique. Nevertheless there is an autobiographical undercurrent. The scene in which the whole company sits as a committee ineffectually attempting to draft an English Partnership Deed comes from Shaw's memory of the contract Annie Besant presented to him over their piano duets.

More complex in derivation are the characters of Mrs George Collins and St John Hotchkiss. Mrs George, as she is called, is a mayoress, a coal merchant's wife and also 'Incognita Appassionata', the mysterious writer of love letters to the Bishop of Chelsea: altogether 'a wonderful interesting' woman, her brother-in-law the greengrocer tells everyone. The others believe she is 'too good to be true' until her appearance, described in Shaw's stage directions at the moment of her entrance as a 'triumphant, pampered, wilful, intensely alive woman . . . But her beauty is wrecked, like an ageless landscape ravaged by long and fierce war . . . The whole face is a battle-field of the passions, quite deplorable until she speaks, when an alert sense of fun rejuvenates her in a moment, and makes her company irresistible.'

She represents three women in one. Her age is approximately Charlotte's, but Shaw adds the qualities of two other women covered by Mrs Collins's other names. As 'Incognita Appassionata' she embodies the sexual passion that had been excluded from his marriage. For more than two years Shaw had been receiving a series of extraordinary letters from 'Poste Restante, Godalming', signed 'Miss Charmer'. He replied saying that love was an infinite mystery 'like everything else'; and that she had better 'marry and have children: then you will not ask from works of art what you can get only from life.' The result was that the girl, who revealed herself as Erica Cotterill, a cousin of Rupert Brooke's and daughter of a respectable Fabian schoolmaster, Charles Clement Cotterill, transferred her infatuation from the plays to the playwright whose unorthodox theories of sexual intercourse outside marriage for the procreation of babies she urgently wanted them to put into practice together. She challenged Shaw to confront all he had turned his back on: which he obliquely attempts to do by transferring them to Mrs Collins's correspondence with the Bishop.

Then as 'Mrs George' Shaw summons up a third woman: the figure of his mother who appeared in his dreams as 'my wife as well as my mother'. These dreams elevated his affection for Charlotte and intensified his feelings for his mother since, Shaw explained to Gilbert Murray, there was 'the addition of the filial feeling and the redemption of the sexual feeling from "sin" and strain'.

Shaw's practice of obscuring the self-portraits of his plays by giving the characters a superficial resemblance to other people – Marchbanks to

De Quincey, Tanner to H. M. Hyndman, Professor Higgins to Henry Sweet – extends to St John Hotchkiss who is ostensibly modelled on his fellow-playwright St John Hankin. But when the 'St John' falls away and he confesses to Mrs George that 'my own pet name in the bosom of my family is Sonny' the pretence becomes transparent. In Hotchkiss we may see something of the reaction that Shaw produced on his contemporaries: 'He talks about himself with energetic gaiety. He talks to other people with a sweet forbearance (implying a kindly consideration for their stupidity) which infuriates those whom he does not succeed in amusing.'

When Hotchkiss meets Mrs George on stage he recognizes her as the coal merchant's wife with whom ('when I was a young fool') he had fallen in love. 'I felt in her presence an extraordinary sensation of unrest, of emotion, of unsatisfied need,' he remembers. It is not fanciful to feel in this 'unsatisfied need' Shaw's own response to his mother when in Dublin. In *Getting Married* Shaw makes Hotchkiss run away abroad in place of his mother leaving for England. And now that they meet again, Hotchkiss again falls in love. The relationship is essentially that of an adopted son. 'I want to talk to him like a mother,' says Mrs George who tells Hotchkiss that 'Sonny is just the name I wanted for you'.

So Shaw provides another scenario for the Dublin *ménage à trois*, now that his mother, merged with the figure of Charlotte, has returned to him in his dreams. His sense of the incompleteness of his marriage pervades this play. It was an incompleteness for which Charlotte was to compensate with mystical hoverings comparable to Mrs George's Blakean 'inspirations'; and from which Shaw escaped by taking on the authority of the Bishop who wants to 'make divorce reasonable and decent'. From the abnormality of his own marriage he argues with the tolerant voice of the greengrocer Collins that 'theres almost as many different sorts of marriages as theres different sorts of people'.

The cast of characters has been assembled to illustrate this observation. At one level they are the stereotypes of the Victorian theatre: crusty old general, thundering priest, dashing philanderer and so on. But there is another level where they are shown, wearing their official costumes, as representatives of the Church, the Army and the Landed Gentry. Finally Shaw removes their masks to reveal them as ourselves and the people we know. He wants to show us the varieties of human nature that must share the earth. The individual temperaments range from the enemies of marriage to the personification of domesticity; from the woman who loves children but not men, to the woman who wants lovers but is not interested in babies. From the interweaving of all these public and private voices Shaw conducts his symposium and arrives at the conclusion that marriage as a legal institution must be reformed as part of the general transformation of our society.

*

'It will improve by keeping,' Shaw had told Granville Barker. But Vedrenne needed a new play and Shaw was persuaded to place the action of *Getting Married* on 12 May 1908, the day of its first performance at the Haymarket. Five days before the opening he published in the *Daily Telegraph* the most extreme of his self-drafted interviews. 'There will be nothing but talk, talk, talk, talk, talk – Shaw talk,' he promised.

'. . . Shaw in a bishop's apron will argue with Shaw in a general's uniform. Shaw in an alderman's gown will argue with Shaw dressed as a beadle. Shaw dressed as a bridegroom will be wedded to Shaw in petticoats. The whole thing will be hideous, indescribable – an eternity of brain-racking dulness. And yet they will have to sit it out . . . they will suffer – suffer horribly . . . I am not a vindictive man . . . We shall not be altogether merciless. The curtains will be dropped casually from time to time to allow of first-aid to the really bad cases in the seats allotted to the Press.'

Getting Married was greeted with what Shaw called a 'torrent of denunciation'. Desmond MacCarthy was to question how we could take seriously characters who are presented to us merely as knockabout figures of farce: why should we be attentive to their opinions or moved by the absurdity of their passions? The 'scenes between Hotchkiss and Mrs George seem to me deplorable,' MacCarthy was to write; 'too funny to be serious, and too serious to be funny'. Lord Alfred Douglas, under the heading 'For Shame, Mr Shaw' in *The Academy*, called for the censor to put a stop to such insidiously feminine work making 'serious inroads on the British home'. Shaw challenged anyone to name a play that was not all talk, and enquired whether they had expected ballet. 'The cast finds out more every time of what it is all about; and so, consequently, does the audience.'

Yet he was uncertain about *Getting Married*. 'Poor people!' exclaims the Bishop. 'It's so hard to know the right place to laugh, isnt it?' Max Beerbohm and Desmond MacCarthy judged that he had orchestrated the laughter in the wrong place. And J. T. Grein believed that the play traded on Shaw's peculiar weakness: 'His loquacity is literally torrential.' In the play he makes Reginald Bridgenorth impatiently exclaim: 'It's no good talking all over the shop like this. We shall be here all day.' In a work aiming to preserve all the unities of time and place, this spasm of impatience articulated a genuine qualm which he submerged in a battle with the critics.

4

SLAVE OF THE AUTOMOBILE

I am a slave of that car and of you too. I dream of the accursed thing at night.

Man and Superman

'I shall take to motoring presently,' Shaw threatened in the summer of 1908. He had already studied at the National Motor Academy and subjected himself to lessons from a professor of driving, H. E. M. Studdy, from whom Charlotte also took tuition. By the end of 1908 the household at Ayot St Lawrence stood ready to receive the Shaws' first automobile, a 28-30 hp Lorraine-Dietrich. 'It is a double cabriolet, with detachable hind part,' reported *The Autocar*. ' . . . The lines of the car are uncommon and graceful.' They became a little more uncommon after the first day when Charlotte, attended by Mr Studdy, crashed it mildly into a local obstruction, scattering the splashboards and other impedimenta; and Mr Studdy, accompanied by Charlotte, knocked off the paddle-box against the gate on their way back.

Since Charlotte's career as motorist was brief and Shaw was rather too fond of reading in the car, a trained chauffeur, Albert James Kilsby from Notting Hill, was employed. In Kilsby's opinion the De Dietrich was 'a proper bugger' to start. But the car was also, Shaw reckoned, awkward to stop, the accelerator pedal being placed on the left with the brake to the right of it. He never lost the habit of treading on the right pedal to arrest a vehicle.

The two men, dividing the fun-and-labour of it, would swap driver and passenger positions fairly evenly. After three weeks, it was reported that G.B.S. was seriously disabled. 'Say I'm dead,' he cabled the *Daily Mail*. He was extraordinarily chivalrous to the injured, especially when the fault was theirs. He was also shockingly reckless at the wheel, sometimes (when Charlotte was not travelling) giving lifts to tramps, and presenting them with money. The De Dietrich was a car for all seasons and subjects: a philosophical vehicle. He reported on its capacity to penetrate Swiss avalanches and its place in the future of Ireland; on its moral claims versus the road dog, its tax-generating properties, and the lessons it gave (such as 'How to Narrow a Road by Widening It') in Shavian engineering. Of the detachable wheels, movable hood and electric klaxon horn, its cork and brass, the invisible locks and variable speed dynamo, Shaw grew pedantically fond. For a man entering his mid-fifties this was more appropriate than the bicycle. He still used the train for long political journeys, but for serious holiday-making the car was essential.

They took it first to Algeria and Tunisia for five spring weeks: Kilsby and Shaw jostling up front; Charlotte and her sister Mrs Cholmondeley occupying the back. Among the luggage they had room for the Koran, but no spare parts. 'Now I come to think of it, it's a wonder we got anywhere,' Shaw remarked. At Biskra he rode for two hours on a camel and 'my seat on this most difficult of mounts was admitted to be superb'. Next day he was stiffly back in the driver's seat and, careering a hundred miles north into Constantine, achieved a dramatic change of climate (something inconceivable on a camel): 'rain in colossal blobs instead of drops; and a wind against which I had to hold the car straight by main force'. Kilsby's time was much filled with repairing burst tyres and then veering melodramatically away from wonderful seas with islands rising out of mirror-like waters and other mirages in which he could not bring himself to disbelieve.

For the summers of 1909 and 1910 they accompanied the car on holidays to Ireland, parking at an extraordinary turreted hotel, the Great Southern, by the woods of Parknasilla on the Kerry coast. It was a place of long sea views and intricate walks between ferns and fuchsias, rock and rhododendron, to burnt-out castles, and along the various fingers of land that pointed south-west into the Atlantic. Sometimes they would try out the Irish roads with an expedition to Lady Gregory at Coole or, on Shaw's fifty-fourth birthday, an exploration of the Giant's Causeway where 'I sat under my umbrella in my aquascutum, like a putrid mushroom,' he told Barker, 'whilst a drenched mariner rowed me round the cliffs and told me lies about them'. Further out to sea he was rowed by ten men in an open boat and landed on the legendary Skelligs. 'At the top amazing beehives of flat rubble stones, each overlapping the one below until the circles meet in a dome – cells, oratories, churches, and outside them cemeteries, wells, crosses, all clustering like shells on a prodigious rock pinnacle . . . An incredible, impossible mad place.'

Upon this cathedral of the sea, the man who generally seemed a stranger on the planet felt at home. Standing in the graveyards at the Skellig summit, he recalled the summers of his early years when Sonny roamed over the rocks and goat-paths of Dalkey, and gazed across the blue waters to Howth Head; or had lain on the grassy top of the hill above the bay – then raced down to the shore known as White Rock and plunged into the waves. Sonny had been a product of Dalkey's outlook: there was little place for him in the bustling world where G.B.S. moved. But he breathed again in the magic climate of this island. 'I tell you the thing does not belong to any world that you and I have ever lived and worked in,' Shaw wrote next day to Frederick Jackson, a political journalist and solicitor: 'it is part of our dream world.'

They rowed him back in the dark, without a compass, the moon invisible in the mists: two and a half Atlantic hours. Then he drove to Parknasilla, to Charlotte, and the world he lived in.

During April 1910, in more orthodox style, the car had taken them for a spin in France, Shaw having undertaken to write reports for the Royal Automobile Club. In the first five and a half days they whizzed along 660 miles, going for all they were worth despite Shaw's view that, owing to the lethally cambered roads, it was unsafe to pass anything without first slowing to a halt. 'I am already twice the man I was when I left,' he reported to Barker. Charlotte felt less cheery. 'G.B.S. does not allow us one moment of peace – we are *harried* from place to place!'

From their cards Barker could feel a struggle developing between Shaw and Charlotte. 'I drive half the day,' Shaw exulted; 'lie deliciously awake half the night; and am visibly waning towards my grave.' At each shattering explosion of the exhaust, his spirits soared. His plan appears to have been to cure Charlotte for ever of their compulsory holidays. 'Charlotte positively loathes me, and is, as usual pathetically unable to dissimulate,' he told Barker at the end of the month.

Back in England, Charlotte diverted some of her loathing from her husband to his car. Their next holiday abroad would be, not yet apart, but separated from his roving machine. As for Shaw, he reported to the Royal Automobile Club that motoring in France was rather like driving along the roof of St Pancras Station.

5

A TREATISE ON BIOGRAPHY

> People like to back a winner . . . However, nothing succeeds like failure . . . Even nonsense is sometimes suggestive.
>
> Shaw to Ensor Walters (1 November 1903), to Trebitsch (20 July 1903), to Lady Gregory (16 April 1920)

'The villagers all thought he was a rum one – a *very* rum one,' remembered his neighbour Mrs Reeves. Sitting bolt upright in his car, he would career very fast (over 20 miles per hour) through the village, leaving behind him a wake of grumbling. But Edith Reeves never heard of him knocking anyone down. Living so near, she had got to know the Shaws quite well. They would put the mown grass over the wall as fodder for the Reeves's livestock, and give them cabbages and other vegetables from the garden. And Mr Reeves sold the Shaws raspberries and cherries.

Mr and Mrs Reeves named one of their sons Bernard. Shaw and Charlotte took great interest in the small Reeveses. During Mrs Reeves's confinements, while Mr Reeves was out with his sandwiches working in the fields, they would send cooked meals in to her – chicken or fish with fresh vegetables from their garden. Charlotte confided that she would have liked children of her own: and Mrs Reeves was given to understand that it was on account of her asthma that she had none.

Shaw's fondness for animals was notorious. Mr and Mrs Reeves would feel quite uncomfortable loading their squealing pigs into the cart for market – though Shaw never said anything. He had a pigeon-cote and several hives of bees in the garden; and there was an erratic little white dog, Kim, which would streak in and out of the house, sometimes barking, sometimes rolling on its back. Shaw never bought a dog, though 'I always own a dog in the country'. He was glad there had been a dog in his home in Dublin since this put him on easy terms with what was often a pleasant extension of human society. 'I have no lies to tell about dogs,' he declared. He had a fellow feeling for them, as well as for cats: any species of animal in fact. But he did not claim to like all dogs and cats.

The Shaws were good neighbours but they minded their business; and, since they were often away, the villagers regarded them as 'characters' rather than native people. They attached little importance to Shaw's literary fame.

*

This fame, though it stopped short at Ayot, had been spreading round the world with the publication of several books about him. Eighteen critical and biographical volumes appeared before the war. The most brilliant of them was by G. K. Chesterton; the most persistent of his biographers was Archibald Henderson.

Henderson was twenty-five and an Instructor in Mathematics at the University of North Carolina when, early in 1903, he had been 'electrified' by a performance of *You Never Can Tell* in Chicago. He spent the next year studying Shaw's writings and then sent Shaw a letter threatening to write his life: 'it never occurred to me,' he afterwards admitted, 'that perhaps I was wholly unfitted for the job.' Shaw added Henderson's name to an extensive card index marked 'Disciples' and wrote a postcard asking him to 'send me your photograph!' Henderson put himself to a good deal of bother over this, all of which amounted to placing himself in line for a kindly Shavian joke: 'You look like the man who can do the job.'

'I began making notes,' Henderson noted. For the next fifty years he continued making notes that Shaw orchestrated into a semi-Shavian melody. Henderson's first book on Shaw (*His Life and Works*) appeared in 1911. By 1932, in his blockbuster *Playboy and Prophet*, he reported having published 'the eighth book of mine devoted, in part or in whole, to interpretation of your life, character and significance'. He reached his apotheosis six years after Shaw's death and seven years before his own in *Man of the Century*, when the century only had forty-four declining years to run. Of Henderson it may literally be said that no man could have done more. But why had G.B.S. encouraged him to do so much?

He wanted to use his biographer to re-create the life of G.B.S. 'who is up to the chin in the life of his own times'. In his fashion G.B.S. was a truth-teller; but the fashion was far from literal. It needed ingenious interpretation and independent checking – and neither temperamentally nor geographically was Henderson able to supply these. He was a 'disciple' rather than a scholar, who manufactured what Shaw himself was to call 'a colossally expanded extract from Who's Who', and then went on manufacturing it. The surviving galley proofs of *Playboy and Prophet* reveal how large a part of this narrative was actually drafted in the third person by G.B.S. himself. He did not do this for facile self-aggrandizement, but to provide his ideas with the endorsement of biographical authority. If his childhood had been 'rich only in dreams, frightful & loveless in realities' this was because the social and economic conditions of those times were frightful. After leaving Ireland, Shaw believed he had turned his back on dreams and set out through the body of his literary and political work in England to make the realities of his times less frightful. He feared that if his instincts, like a compass, were seen as having been eccentrically affected by his early experiences, then his thinking itself might be regarded as eccentric. He used biography therefore as adjustments to the rudder, keeping his work in the mainstream. From these secret collaborations he learned how to ghost his own life through later biographers until he became the very author of himself.

'You are threatened with more than one competitor,' Shaw had written to Henderson in 1907. The chief competitor seemed to be G. K. Chesterton. Shaw completed the comic circle by reviewing Chesterton's book in *The Nation*, describing it as 'the best work of literary art I have yet provoked'. This compliment was not all it appeared to be. Shaw separated art from information rather as he divided feeling from thought. Henderson had the information; Chesterton was the literary artist: one book complemented the other. He was reasonably happy with Chesterton's *Shaw* because, despite its title, it 'has little to do with me'. 'My last word must be,' Shaw concluded, 'that gifted as he is, he [Chesterton] needs a sane Irishman to look after him.' In other words, Chesterton needed Shaw to write the book for him. Reviewing it was the next best thing.

'I have found that if I invent all my facts on a basis of my knowledge of human nature I always come out right, whereas if I refer to documents and authorities they weary me and set me wrong,' Shaw was to write to another biographer, St John Ervine. 'Trust to your genius rather than to your industry: it is the less fallible of the two.' This is what Chesterton did – and what Shaw complained of his having done. He represented Chesterton's commentary as a washing-line on which hung all manner of crucified shirts and dancing trousers. But none of them fitted him. Indeed, some more nearly fitted G.K.C. For biographers, like portrait painters, 'put something of themselves into their subjects and sitters when there is anything of themselves to put in,' Shaw explained.

'The truth is I have a horror of biographers,' Shaw admitted to Frank Harris. Chesterton had loaded his gun with guesses, but from time to time his aim was true. In his review, Shaw gave a wonderfully clownish performance, trying on all the conjectures that were 'madly wrong'. On others he turned his back, leaving them strung out along the line of Chesterton's impressions:

'quick-witted [and] . . . long-winded . . . the very forest of the man's thoughts chokes up his thoroughfare . . . if there is anything that Shaw is not, it is irresponsible. The responsibility in him rings like steel . . . a kind of intellectual chastity, and the fighting spirit . . . Shaw is like Swift . . . in combining extravagant fancy with a curious sort of coldness . . . benevolent bullying, a pity touched with contempt . . . sincere, unsympathetic, aggressive, alone . . . He never gives his opinions a holiday . . . Socialism is the noblest thing for Bernard Shaw; and it is the noblest thing in him . . . he cares more for the Public Thing than for any private thing . . . This is the greatest thing in Shaw, a serious optimism – even a tragic optimism . . .'

Shaw recognized in Chesterton, as he had in Wells, a quality absent in himself. Wells, who claimed to 'have got Great Britain Pregnant', had the power of sexual attraction; Chesterton, as champion of the common people against intellectuals and politicians, could magically elicit affection. People adored him for his wit and extravagance, his whacking style. His creation of the jolly toby-jug Chesterton had similarities with Shaw's invention of the pantomime ostrich. These cheery images displaced for both what Chesterton called 'the morbid life of the lonely mind'.

Shaw developed a proprietary interest in Chesterton. In a discarded segment of *Back to Methuselah*, he pictures him as Immenso Champernoon, 'a man of colossal mould, with the head of a cherub on the body of a Falstaff . . . friendly, a little shy, and jokes frequently enough to be almost always either still enjoying the last or already anticipating the next'. Shaw thought of Chesterton as a marvellous boy who never grew up, a political innocent who, by prodigious literary journalism, had taken the position created in the eighteenth century by Dr Johnson. In short: he was 'the greatest publicist we possess'. For over a quarter of a century, Shaw struggled to convert him to socialism and creative evolution.

Their debates began in 1911. On 29 May, in the Victoria Assembly Rooms at Cambridge, Shaw addressed the Heretics Society on 'The Religion of the Future'. He told his audience that superstitious religion had died in the Middle Ages, though it was artificially kept in existence by the stimulants of idolatry and intimidation. The English, he declared, had no fundamental religion: they simply made idols of people who were capable of giving orders and resorted to the stage management of them. Such people were given crowns, or gold lace on their collars, a certain kind of hat, a different income and a particular kind of house to live in. Their sons and daughters could not marry common people: and we pretended to believe that they were agents of a loftier idol. But in our democratic age we were gradually getting rid of idols. 'As for my own position, I am, and always have been, a mystic,' Shaw announced. 'I believe that the universe is being driven by a force that we might call the life-force.

'We are all experiments in the direction of making God. What God is doing is making himself, getting from being a mere powerless will or force. This force has implanted into our minds the ideal of God. We are not very successful attempts at God so far, but . . . there never will be a God unless we make one . . . we are the instruments through which that ideal is trying to make itself a reality.'

'The Religion of the Future' was one of a series of heterodox sermons Shaw had started to give after the writing of *Major Barbara*. His new theology redefined the terms and vocabulary of Christianity. God was impersonally reshaped into the Life Force; the Trinity was interpreted as 'You are the father of your son and the son of your father'; and the Immaculate Conception made an everyday happening: 'I believe in the Immaculate Conception of Jesus's mother, and I believe in the Immaculate Conception of your mother.'

The effect of Shaw's addresses on the public was extraordinary. They sat appalled, fascinated, squirming and twisting in their seats. 'The sight of his tall, tense figure in the pulpit, electrical in its suggestion of vital energy completely under the control of his will . . . compelled a similar intensity of interest and attention from his hearers,' wrote a reporter on the *Christian Commonwealth*. ' . . . Several times I looked round upon my fellow-auditors to mark the effect of his words. I saw consternated faces, hostile faces, faces which bore an expression of alarm and even horror.'

Many who heard him were convinced that here was the finest public speaker in England. He was admired, especially by the young; but he was not loved. His intellectual authority on the platform provoked extreme reactions from the press. *The Academy*, which described his lecture as a 'Detestable Outrage . . . vile and blasphemous ravings', protested against his 'dissemination of poisonous theories amongst young persons' and regretted that Shaw had not been 'kicked out of the window, or . . . thrown into the Cam'.

When they invited Chesterton to reply with a speech entitled 'Orthodoxy', the Heretics at last found a Christian champion capable of standing up to Shaw. Chesterton delivered his reply on 17 November at the Guildhall, Cambridge, and the first thing he did was to defend his adversary from newspaper attacks. *The Academy* report had been 'not merely written by an idiot but by an idiot who had no belief in the Christian religion,' he pronounced. ' . . . How could Mr Shaw blaspheme by saying that Christ or the Christian religion had failed in England when the remark is obviously true.

'The majority of the governing classes believe in no religion. I have known many editors and newspaper proprietors but I have yet to meet one who believed in religion . . . Mr Shaw is living in a comparatively Pagan world. He is something of a Pagan himself and like many other Pagans, he is a very fine man.'

This was characteristic of the intellectual magnanimity existing between the two men. 'I enjoyed him and admired him keenly,' Shaw was to write of Chesterton in the late 1930s; 'and nothing could have been more generous than his treatment of me.' And at about the same time Chesterton was saluting Shaw in his autobiography. 'I have never read a reply by Bernard Shaw that did not leave me in a better and not a worse temper or frame of mind; which did not seem to come out of inexhaustible fountains of fair-mindedness and intellectual geniality.'

When they moved from religion to politics, the contest was between Shaw's socialism and Chesterton's distributism, of equality of income against peasant proprietorship. Shaw defined socialism as 'that state of society in which the income of a country would be divided exactly equally amongst all the people of that country, without reference to age, sex or character'. Chesterton warned against the totalitarianism and artificiality within socialism.

'You cannot draw the line across things and say, You shall have your garden hose, but not your garden; your ploughshare, but not your field; your fishing rod, but not your stream; because man is so made that his sense of property is actually stronger for such things as fields or gardens or water than for such comparatively unnecessary things as garden hoses or rakes or fishing rods . . . if you want self-government apart from good government you must have generally distributed property. You must create the largest possible number of owners.'

Shaw conceded that collectivism without socialism might indeed be a system of tyranny – the tyranny that was later to emerge as fascism. He suggested therefore that the difference between Chesterton and himself appeared to be that one wanted distribution of property and the other *equal* distribution of property. 'This is not the normal definition of the term [socialism],' Chesterton objected. 'That the State should be in possession of the means of production, distribution, and exchange was always called Socialism when I was a Socialist.'

It was a good and serious contest. Their jousting over the years developed into a perfect balance of contrasting styles, with breathtaking displays of analogy and tricks of paradox. Chesterton's bulky swaying presence matched the immense range of illustration he gave his ideas, lit up by a spirit of enjoyment and comic inventiveness. Shaw was more incisive, his emphatic eyebrows like two supplementary moustaches, an assured and wiry figure standing with arms folded who could speak with a force thrilling to all who heard it. But to Chesterton's eyes, Shaw's strengths were limited in their humanity. 'Shaw is like the Venus de Milo,' he declared: 'all that there is of him is admirable.'

Chesterton's conversion to Catholicism in 1922 showed how far he was from agreeing with Shaw. 'If I wandered away like Bergson or Bernard Shaw,' he wrote at the end of his life, 'and made up my own philosophy out of my own precious fragment of truth, merely because I had found it for myself, I should soon have found that truth distorting itself into a falsehood.' Chesterton's truth seemed to Shaw a blind alley up which he had been led by Hilaire Belloc, 'with the odd result,' Shaw wrote to Wells, 'that he is now dreadfully in earnest about beliefs that are intellectually impossible'.

The two warriors met for their last public exchange at Kingsway Hall in the final week of October 1927. Tumultuous crowds struggled in the corridors, burst open the doors, flowed round the building like hot lava. Belloc presided and the British Broadcasting Corporation relayed their words through the country. 'Do We Agree?' was the question they debated. Both spoke well. They spoke of socialism and distributism, income and property – of all they had spoken about sixteen years and one world war earlier in the Memorial Hall. And they said similar things. The change was in the audience, baying for good sport. 'This is not a real controversy or debate,' Chesterton admitted. What they said was what they could most effectively perform as actors. 'I suspect that you do not really care much what we debate about,' Shaw said, 'provided we entertain you by talking in our characteristic manners.' This they did. 'Obviously we are mad,' remarked Shaw, taking what seemed a good embarkation point for a voyage of agreement. But it was when Shaw drew on his reservoirs of optimism that Chesterton felt dispirited. Shaw insisted on agreement. 'I find that the people who fight me generally hold the very ideas I am trying to express.' He tried to wrap Chesterton up in a jacket of agreement. The agreement of two mad people (in the East they would be reverenced) was important.

'If you listen to them carefully and find that at certain points they agree, then you have some reason for supposing that here the spirit of the age is coming through, and giving you an inspired message. Reject all the contradictory things they say and concentrate your attention on the things upon which they agree, and you may be listening to the voice of revelation.'

And did they agree? 'Ladies and gentlemen. The answer is in the negative.' Chesterton did not agree with Shaw and 'nor does Mr Shaw'. And the people watching and listening did not experience a voice of revelation. The spirit of the age had moved from the platform to themselves: it would be heard in their interruptions, their urging for disagreement to flourish, and their belief that none of it any longer mattered. 'In a very few years from now,' Belloc concluded, 'this debate will be antiquated.'

6

SHEWING UP THE CENSORSHIP

> Success in the theatre is very largely a matter of being able to flirt with the public.
>
> Shaw to Maud Churton Braby (18 May 1908)

Shaw had joined a society 'for the Prevention of Cruelty to Authors' in 1897 when deciding to publish his plays as books. Soon afterwards he started making his views and experiences known through the Society of Authors' Journal. He paid *The Author* the compliment of treating it as a serious business paper. He wrote there of the beauties of phonetic spelling and simplified punctuation; warned schoolmasters against inflicting literature compulsorily on children; described the pathos of British bookselling, calculating that 'the average man wears out over fifty pairs of boots whilst he is reading a single book'; and he gave advice on publishers: 'Whenever a publisher gives me literary advice I take an instant and hideous revenge on him. I give him business advice . . . and I urge him to double his profits by adopting my methods.' Some of these contributions to *The Author* – such as his recommendations to novice playwrights on the submission of manuscripts – were printed as circulars.

In most matters of negotiation, it seemed to him, authors presented themselves as a flock of sheep bleating to be fleeced. 'Nothing will save the majority of authors from themselves,' he declared, 'except a ruthlessly tyrannical Professional Association.'

He had been elected to its committee of management in February 1905, and joined its dramatic subcommittee the following year. He took this work seriously, believing that the literature of a country created its mind since each country largely took its ideas from what it read. What he looked for within the Society was the creation of a corporate consciousness. In Shaw's perfect world there would have been no law of copyright, no advances or retreats, no giving or receiving of royalties (the very word sounded dreadful to a republic-minded person). Pending this, authors were necessarily capitalists and literature a sweated trade. As an artistic and learned profession, it had to be defended against the presumption that its interests must give way to the most trivial political consideration.

Authorship was a good example of a profession that was helpless without collective action. A writer who was poor, Shaw argued, had no means to defend himself; and when, suddenly, he became famous, his time was so valuable that it was not worth his while wasting it on bad debts. It was pitiable to see these 'professional men on whom the Copyright Acts have conferred a monopoly of enormous value unable to do for themselves what is done by porters and colliers and trade-unionists generally with no monopoly at all at their backs'. Although unionism was most practicable in trades where the members worked together in large bodies, lived in the same neighbourhoods and belonged to the same social class, Shaw believed that the Society of Authors should be careful how it disclaimed the idea of being unionized. He looked on trade unions as conspiracies against the public interest that would become unnecessary in a socialist society, but that acted meanwhile as a corrective to the capitalist account.

Shaw was prepared to spend hours drafting and revising documents. It was admirable: but did he succeed? On the whole, he concluded, the ten years he spent on the Society's 'two big committees' might have been passed at the top of Everest. Over such matters as the model treaty with West End managers, on which he negotiated interminably, no progress was made. His frustration led him eventually to lose faith in the validity of unrefined democracy. For who, in their efforts to make improvements, had used the democratic process more thoroughly than himself? Had he not earned the right to a dissenting opinion? In the interests of getting things done much had been suppressed and little accomplished. His deepest disenchantment sounded from suppression itself: the censorship laws. What a heartbreaking business it had been. 'I had ten years of it; and I know.'

*

Shaw was to write more than fifty articles against the censorship, reinforced with many speeches and letters to newspapers. As late as 1950 he could still be heard objecting to the appointment of 'an ordinary official with a salary of a few hundreds a year to exercise powers which have proved too much for Popes and Presidents'. In fact the Lord Chamberlain never read plays but delegated this job to a series of under-paid clerks. These officials fell back on making a list of controversial subjects (religion, sex) that must not be mentioned, and words that must not be used: they then worked to this list automatically. Professional pornographers soon learnt these inventories and how to get round them, with the result that the commercial theatre had become a prostitution market masquerading as theatre.

Shaw argued that the censorship was damned both by the pernicious trash it allowed, and by the good work it suppressed. Its purpose was to suppress immorality: but what it meant by immorality was deviation from custom. It was assumed that every Englishman knew the difference between wicked and virtuous conduct. But Shaw reasoned that what was wanted from dramatists, and all other writers, was a constant challenge to such accepted knowledge. The notion that everything uncustomary was wicked helped to keep people in line with their neighbours and gave Government what appeared to be a moral basis for penalizing change. But without change there could be no development. Progress depended upon the toleration of unexpected behaviour, and heresy was essential to the welfare of a community. A nation that did not permit heresy was stagnant.

Shaw realized that he must not only discredit this function of the Lord Chamberlain's office, but also propose a better control of the stage by the community. The alternative was not anarchy, he wrote, but control by local authorities. 'The municipality will not read plays and forbid or sanction them,' he explained. 'It will give the manager both liberty and responsibility . . . Let him manage how he pleases, knowing that if he produces utterly vile plays, he will find himself without a defender in council when the question comes up as to whether his licence shall be continued.' It was important, Shaw stressed, to license the management, not the theatre. A manager could then pursue his business as any other professional man, while the annual licensing system would ensure that he could be struck off like a solicitor. Shaw was therefore taking a moral line more democratic than the official guardians of morality by recommending a transference of the care of the nation's morals from a few paid clerks to the county councils and city corporations, with watch committees to warn them when managers were conducting their theatres as disorderly houses.

He was propelled into the front line when Granville Barker's new play *Waste* was refused a licence late that year. This ban, and another in respect of Edward Garnett's *The Breaking Point*, led to a renewed attack by the playwrights. 'Stiffen your back,' Shaw exhorted Gilbert Murray. Throughout 1908 he kept up this campaign, luring the censorship into a serious blunder.

*

For half a dozen years Beerbohm Tree had been prompting Shaw to write him a modern stage version of *Don Quixote*. As a rather startling variation on this theme, and reverting to his method in *The Devil's Disciple*, Shaw dashed off *The Shewing-up of Blanco Posnet* between 16 February and 8 March 1909. This one-act 'Sermon in Crude Melodrama', as he subtitled it, was commissioned for a matinée performance at His Majesty's to benefit a children's charity. 'I wrote a perfect triumph of this made-to-measure art for Tree in *Blanco Posnet*, and he was simply shocked by it, absolutely horrified,' he remembered. Tree was then three months short of his knighthood. What worried him were Blanco's references to God as 'a sly one . . . a mean one', and his statement that the chief witness in the trial had had 'immoral relations with every man in this town', including the Sheriff. He appealed to Shaw to 'cut that bit about God and that other bit about the prostitute'. But Shaw convinced him there was nothing to fear. If the Examiner of Plays passed the words, Tree would have obtained official blessing; and if he didn't the actor would never have to utter them. So Tree submitted the play to the Censor: and the Censor, on the grounds of blasphemy, refused to license it.

Set in a Town Hall 'in a Territory of the United States of America' sometime during the nineteenth century, *Blanco Posnet* is pervaded with an air of unreality. 'Let the imagination play,' Shaw advised Martin-Harvey. 'There never was no such place and no such people.' His own imagination was literary and showed its derivations from Bret Harte, Dickens and Tolstoy's play *The Power of Darkness.* What he wanted was a respectable provenance for a piece of moral propaganda that had as its point the protest of a horse-thief against his punishment for an admitted crime. From the consequence of this crime he would have escaped but for his yielding to the first good impulse of his life: the giving up his plunder to an unhappy woman in order to save her sick child. By using some phrases from the Lord Chamberlain's proscribed list, he adapted this blameless drama into a ten-inch gun in the censorship war. 'I have taken advantage of the Blanco Posnet affair to write a tremendous series of letters to The Times,' he informed Trebitsch that summer; 'and the result has been that the Prime Minister has promised to appoint a Select Committee of both Houses of Parliament to enquire into the whole question of Censorship.'

Shaw's methods were to harass the enemy as a dramatist by all ingenious means: then hurry to their rescue as a responsible committee man. The opportunity of performing *Blanco Posnet* to the maximum embarrassment of the Censor came after a visit by Lady Gregory to Ayot. Shaw gave her the play, and she took it back to Coole where Yeats read it and agreed to put it on at the Abbey Theatre – Dublin being the one place in Britain beyond the Lord Chamberlain's jurisdiction.

As soon as the Abbey production was announced, the Under-Secretary of the Lord Lieutenant of Ireland wrote from Dublin Castle threatening to revoke the Abbey Theatre's patent. Lady Gregory and Yeats were summoned to the Castle by the Viceroy Lord Aberdeen, and one of the Castle lawyers warned their solicitors that if *Blanco Posnet* was performed, the authorities would use against the theatre all the legal powers at their command. Yeats found himself forced into a position where he had either to abandon the principle of theatrical freedom or risk, by the closure of the Abbey, the livelihood of its players and the fruit of half a dozen years' work. He and Lady Gregory decided to confront the Lord Lieutenant's precautionary notice with a manifesto.

'If our patent is in danger it is because the English censorship is being extended to Ireland, or because the Lord Lieutenant is about to revive, on what we consider a frivolous pretext, a right not exercised for 150 years, to forbid at his pleasure any play produced in any Dublin Theatre . . . we must not, by accepting the English Censor's ruling, give away anything of the liberty of the Irish theatre of the future . . . what would sooner or later grow into a political censorship cannot be lightly accepted.'

The issue had now been adroitly spread from blasphemy to cover almost the whole area of Anglo-Irish politics. Having defied the Castle, Lady Gregory tactfully offered the Lord Lieutenant a small face-saver in the way of two tiny omissions. It was essential, Shaw pointed out, that such concessions should be ridiculous. As he explained in a programme note:

'To oblige the Lord Lieutenant, I have consented to withdraw the word "immoral" as applied to the relations between a woman of bad character and her accomplices. In doing so I wish it to be stated that I still regard these relations as not only immoral but vicious; nevertheless . . . I am quite content to leave the relations to the unprompted judgement of the Irish people. Also, I have consented to withdraw the words "Dearly beloved brethren", as the Castle fears they may shock the nation.'

The Shewing-up of Blanco Posnet opened at the Abbey, with Lady Gregory's *The Workhouse Ward* and Yeats's *Cathleen Ni Houlihan*, on 25 August 1909. It was Horse Show Week in Dublin, the peak of the summer season, which 'draws to the Irish capital a vari-coloured crowd, of many languages,' wrote James Joyce. ' . . . For a few days the tired and cynical city is dressed like a newly-wed bride. Its gloomy streets swarm with a feverish life, and an unaccustomed uproar breaks its senile slumber. This year . . . all over town they are talking about the clash between Bernard Shaw and the Viceroy . . . between the representative of the King and the writer of comedy . . . while Dubliners, who care nothing for art but love an argument passionately, rubbed their hands with joy.' Many people now entering a theatre for the first time in their lives were offering guineas for standing-room in the wings. Foreign newspapers had sent their critics – James Joyce sent in a review to *Il Piccolo della Sera*. Charlotte was there with her sister but G.B.S. stayed strategically in Parknasilla. Lady Gregory's fear was that there might be a hostile demonstration, or complaints from the Church, that would give the Viceroy an excuse for taking legal action.

The reception of the play must have disappointed many who had come looking for a disturbance. The audience took to *Blanco Posnet* enthusiastically, laughing at its humour, passing over the dangerous passages with sympathetic blankness, and at the curtain interrupting their applause with vain calls for the author. There was general agreement that Mr Posnet was a very mild-spoken ruffian in comparison with the reports of him; and some people questioned whether they had been victims of an Abbey hoax. 'There is no feeling in Dublin except amusement about the more or less false pretences by which a huge audience was attracted last night to the Abbey Theatre,' reported *The Times*. 'Everybody today is enjoying the story of Mr Shaw's cleverness and the Censor's folly . . . The play is perfectly innocuous; it could not shock the most susceptible Irish feelings.' The Churches refused to make a protest (some clergymen actually preached sermons celebrating the play); and the *Irish Times* commented that if ridicule were as deadly in Britain as in France, the censorship would be 'blown away in the shouts of laughter that greeted *Blanco Posnet*'.

Shaw sent his congratulations. 'You and W.B.Y[eats]. handled the campaign nobly,' he wrote to Lady Gregory. 'You have made the Abbey Theatre the real centre of capacity and character in the Irish movement: let Sinn Fein and the rest look to it.' The Abbey had vanquished the Castle, but no one could tell what effect this Irish victory would have on the Censor in England.

It was this that Shaw set out to test by applying for a licence to produce *Blanco Posnet* at Annie Horniman's repertory theatre, the Gaiety, in Manchester. The play was submitted in its Irish version which, as George Redford noted, was 'practically identical' to the text sent to him by Beerbohm Tree. Under these circumstances, Redford added, 'there is no ground on which I could ask the Lord Chamberlain to reconsider his decision'. But Shaw was able to remind him that plays could be considered more than once. The performance in Dublin, which had elicited good opinions from critics and clergymen, was ample evidence, he contended, that an error of judgement had been made. He therefore requested a resubmission to the Lord Chamberlain. This Redford was obliged to do: but the Lord Chamberlain gave the same decision. 'What the Censorship has actually done exceeds the utmost hopes of those who, like myself, have devoted themselves to its destruction,' Shaw wrote in *The Times*.

There was one more move for him to make. He allowed *Blanco Posnet* to be performed in London by the Abbey Theatre Company under the protection of the Stage Society. The English could now see for themselves that his reputedly blasphemous piece was no more than a 'sentimental tract,' as Desmond MacCarthy was to describe it. The whole affair, including Shaw's publication in a newspaper of the words to which the Lord Chamberlain took offence, had dramatized the full absurdity of the system. 'Let us all dance on the prostrate body of Mr Redford as violently as we can,' exhorted Max Beerbohm in the *Saturday Review*.

*

'Mr Redford has a fixed delusion that I am a dangerous and disreputable person, a blasphemer and a blackguard,' Shaw wrote to the manager of the Gaiety Theatre, Ben Iden Payne.

He used Payne for an extra skirmish that summer. Between the end of March and the beginning of May 1909, he had composed a one-act satirical farce called *Press Cuttings*. Exploiting his own fear of women and merging it with the general fear of a German war, he coupled the cause of feminism to his fight against the censorship by naming two of his characters General Mitchener and Prime Minister Balsquith (who enters dressed as a woman). On 24 June Redford returned the manuscript in order to give its author 'the opportunity of eliminating all personalities, expressed or implied'. He called attention to the rule: 'No offensive personalities, as representation of living persons to be permitted on the stage.'

This was what Shaw calculated would happen. In various newspapers, he assured the public that he had been 'careful not to express a single personality that has not done duty again and again without offence in the pages of *Punch*'. Privately he let it be known that he had used the name Mitchener 'in order to clear him of all possible suspicion of being a caricature of Lord Roberts'. As for the well-worn *Punch* figure of Balsquith, it was neither Balfour nor Asquith 'and cannot in the course of nature be both'.

Two 'private receptions' of the play were given under the auspices of the Women's Suffrage movement at the Court Theatre early that July. Shaw then altered the names of Mitchener and Balsquith to Bones and Johnson (the ringmaster and clown of the Christy Minstrels) and Iden Payne re-submitted the play which was licensed for public performance on 17 August, and opened the following month at the Gaiety in Manchester. 'In the crucial scene the Prime Minister forced his way into the War Office disguised as a militant suffragette,' wrote Iden Payne. '... When he had removed his woman's attire, Bones exclaimed, "Great Heavens, Johnson!" When the innocuous name was heard there was a roar of laughter, followed by loud ironic applause, which was repeated when Johnson could be heard to answer "Yes, Bones".'

There were some who felt that Shaw was prostituting his talent in these forays against the censorship. Yet many playwrights agreed that some liberalization of the law was needed. It was important that those interviewed by the Select Committee should speak with a reasonably unanimous voice. In various multigraphed letters to members of the Society of Authors, Shaw assigned to himself the job of voice-trainer. 'Witnesses must be careful not to put forward the contention that the freedom of the stage would be absolutely safe. The proper reply is that its risks would be no greater than the risks of the freedom of the press, freedom of speech, and freedom of public meeting . . . they are the price of liberty and progress.'

These letters to fellow-writers were accompanied by an 11,000-word statement that Shaw had prepared as his own evidence. His examination was to consist of questions on this written evidence which, at the Committee's invitation and his own expense, he had distributed beforehand. However, the Committee informed him that it could not admit his printed statement into the record since to do so would be acting against precedent. Shaw argued that some of the distinctions he wished to make were not easy to bring out simply in replies to questions, and he cited three precedents from the 1892 Committee which had accepted written evidence in favour of the censorship. At this the Committee cleared the room, discussed the matter in camera, and then repeated without explanation that 'it would not be permissible to print the statement as part of the evidence'.

Shaw was completely taken aback. 'The sudden volte face when I cited precedent, the dramatic secret conclave, the point blank refusal without reason given, are too good to be thrown away . . . I shall fly to the last refuge of the oppressed: a letter to The Times.'

Shaw's letter appeared on 2 August; and three days later, when he arrived to resume his evidence, he was told that the Committee 'have no further questions to ask you'. It was hard to conceal his resentment. He incorporated his rejected evidence, as a form of minority report, into his Preface to *The Shewing-up of Blanco Posnet* which Conrad judged to be 'somewhat imbecile – in the classical meaning of the word'. Shaw had sought to inflict imbecility on those members of the Committee who supported the censorship: to embezzle them of their wits. He was acting the modern Don Quixote Tree had wanted him to dramatize in *Blanco Posnet*, the man who 'is always right and always apparently wrong with smaller and more practical people round him'. He had turned his plays into the accoutrements with which the Don set out to fight his battles.

'I saw that I had to deal with a hostile majority,' Shaw excused himself, '. . . so I misconducted myself.' His words spilled out all over the place. He could not stop. The Committee had treated Redford – 'the filter that my life's work has to pass through' – most decorously. He felt aggrieved; he felt aggravated. He had made himself better informed on censorship than any member of the Committee. Then he had worked by the rules, won every round fairly and been counted out.

The Report was published on 8 November 1909. What comes out strikingly is the evidence of what Shaw would call the idealists. Theatre managers' organizations argued that censorship had not inflicted any injury on serious drama in England; actors' associations spoke of the desirability of maintaining a censorship which protected their members from taking unpleasant parts in undesirable plays; A. B. Walkley, drama critic of *The Times* and President of the Society of Dramatic Critics, believed the censorship to be justifiable because it reflected the common sense of the man in the street, while Lena Ashwell, lessee of the Great Queen Street Theatre and soon to play the Polish aviatrix in *Misalliance*, wanted the Censor as protection against the man in the street; W. S. Gilbert thought it imperative that audiences be protected against 'outrages' – the theatre was 'not the proper pulpit from which to disseminate doctrines possibly of anarchism, of socialism, and of agnosticism'. Many authors too, if they were doing well, did not really want to change the system. 'A censorship of any kind acts inevitably as a protection to the average author,' Shaw explained. 'He is never censored; and those who are censored are not only his commercial rivals, but are generally putting up the standard on him and changing the fashion.'

Archer, Granville Barker, J. M. Barrie, Chesterton, Galsworthy, Gilbert Murray and Pinero gave evidence against the censorship. Some of their recommendations were attached to the Report which proposed that future licensing be optional and that unlicensed plays take their chance in the courts; that music halls be treated equally at law; and that doubtful cases be referred to a special committee of the Privy Council. But no legislation was passed to implement these proposals. Instead, an advisory committee was appointed the following year to assist the Censor. So matters stayed as they were.

Shaw had tried to improve things by letter and by law: this was temperamentally the most natural way for him to act. He was a scholar-revolutionary. His tactics for changing society had not been to break its laws, but to obey them pedantically, ingeniously, literally, until by laughing consent they were finally rendered impractical. But for the first time it seemed as if all the thought and feeling of this work was issuing nowhere. He was in his fifty-fifth year; as he grew older this sense of powerlessness was to intensify. Looking back, he came to believe that it had been this Censorship Committee that altered his views on how to obtain political results. He was forced into a belief in the inevitability of violence: 'the whole ridiculous transaction,' he wrote, '. . . was a lesson to me on the futility of treating a parliamentary body with scrupulous courtesy and consideration instead of bullying them and giving them as much trouble as possible.' He had forgotten how much trouble he gave.

The philosophy of violence that makes its appearance in Shaw's later life was a product of his sexual and then his political neutering; a reaction to having been made to feel as ineffectual as his mother had believed him to be. This was the true misery of life, the being used up for no purpose. The means were not justified that brought no ends: he had no children and he had no power. Increasingly he was to find compensation in the world of his imagination. His fantasies of longevity and dictatorship, which in the actual world did harm to no one, brought some relief to his despair, acting like Prospero's prayer

> Which pierces so that it assaults
> Mercy itself, and frees all faults.

TWELVE

I

THE GODS AND *MISALLIANCE*

> I am a specialist in immoral and heretical plays. My reputation has been gained by my persistent struggle to force the public to reconsider its morals. In particular, I regard much current morality as to economic and sexual relations as disastrously wrong; and I regard certain doctrines of the Christian religion as understood in England today with abhorrence.
>
> Preface to *The Shewing-up of Blanco Posnet*

'To me God does not yet exist; but there is a creative force constantly struggling to evolve an executive organ of godlike knowledge and power; that is, to achieve omnipotence and omniscience; and every man and woman born is a fresh attempt to achieve this object,' Shaw wrote in a letter to Tolstoy accompanying *The Shewing-up of Blanco Posnet*. '. . . Whoever admits that anything living is evil must either believe that God is malignantly capable of creating evil, or else believe that God has made many mistakes in His attempts to make a perfect being.'

The incomprehensibility of life was comforting to Tolstoy on whom Shaw's 'intelligent stupidities' jarred painfully. 'Life is a great and serious affair,' he rebuked him. Whatever G.B.S. could not reduce to intelligibility, he expelled as a joke. 'Why should humour and laughter be excommunicated?' he had asked. 'The problem about God and evil is too important to be spoken of in jest,' answered Tolstoy. But as Shaw had previously told Henry James, 'Almost all my greatest ideas have occurred to me first as jokes.'

Shaw had made a similarly painful impression on Henry James. James's god was art. But Shaw 'would not lift my finger,' as he wrote to Tolstoy, 'to produce a work of art if I thought there was nothing more than that in it'. When the Reading Committee of the Stage Society rejected James's one-act adaptation, called *The Saloon*, from his story 'Owen Wingrave', Shaw was asked to write and tell James.

'Shaw's writing – Bernard Shaw,' he began. James's adapted ghost story about a young pacifist in a military family who dies from an act of self-assertion is an exploration of the irreversible forces of the past – 'one of the most "deterministic" [tales] James ever wrote,' his biographer Leon

Edel calls it. It was this horror of inevitability that Shaw found 'sticking in my gizzard ever since'.

James seemed a man of the past and Shaw of the future – the novelty of the future. James believed that the imagination of the artist reached back and, planting itself in unconscious motives, gave the artist psychological energy with which to create beautiful things. 'It is art that *makes* life,' he instructed H. G. Wells. James recognized in art a force as mysterious and unalterable as Tolstoy's God. It was this fatalism, breaking out at the word of Darwin in the 1860s, and purveyed through the novels of George Eliot and Thomas Hardy, that was gaining new intellectual ground and, so Shaw protested, persuading people who had lost their faith in a Tolstoyan God 'that Man is the will-less slave and victim of his environment'. Shaw wanted to replace God with a more positive substitute. 'What is the use of writing plays?' he demanded, ' – what is the use of anything? – if there is not a Will that finally moulds chaos itself into a race of gods with heaven for an environment.' To Tolstoy this was impious vanity. And to James, the advice that proceeded from it – that he stick on a happy ending to his play since he 'could give victory to one side just as artistically as to the other' – revealed a wholly 'shallow and misleading' conception of what art was.

Shaw wanted more control over his destiny. 'You have given victory to death,' he accused James. Tolstoy had given victory to the next world. But Shaw wanted to win battles for this world. *Blanco Posnet*, no less than *Widowers' Houses* or *Mrs Warren's Profession*, had been written for contemporary use – even *Press Cuttings* was a farce designed to blow up a farcical situation. Yet all Shaw's works, however topical, had been determined in form by precedents from the past.

The Bernard Shaw not writing to Henry James was a playwright who had lost his sense of pragmatic certainty as to what his plays were saying and whose unconscious processes filtered into these plays layers of suppressed autobiography. This mysterious *alter ego* was a ghost that mocked the champion of free will and floated free of the scholar bent over his theatrical formulas. He seemed invisible to the writer of prefaces. For he was not obviously an executive organ of a creative force, but a dreamer of the absurd, wondering whether 'the world were only one of God's jokes'.

*

In April 1909 advertisements had begun to appear for a new repertory scheme opening in the West End of London. The man behind this enterprise was a powerful Broadway impresario Charles Frohman and the man behind Frohman was J. M. Barrie. Frohman was 'my kind of man,' Barrie decided – someone shy and successful who had tumbled in love with the stage and converted one of his London theatres, the Duke of York's, to experimental repertory. Productions of plays new, revived, and unwritten were placarded there, including works by Granville Barker, Henry James, John Masefield, Somerset Maugham, Gilbert Murray, Pinero, Shaw and Barrie himself – though not Galsworthy's *Justice*, with which, almost a year later, the season actually began.

People had faith in Frohman. He was a man of sumptuous generosity and wonderful schemes. They entrusted their capital to him, confident that here was a hard-headed businessman who would look at nothing that didn't pay. 'If Mr Frohman were really that sort of man, I should not waste five minutes on his project,' wrote Shaw in a dissenting opinion. 'He is the most wildly romantic and adventurous person of my acquaintance.'

The play, called *Misalliance*, Shaw wrote for Frohman between early September and early November 1909, was a return from the melodrama Frohman had hoped for after *Blanco Posnet* to the disquisitory tactics of *Getting Married*. 'I have again gone back to the classic form, preserving all the unities – no division into acts, no change of scene, no silly plot, not a scrap of what the critics call action,' Shaw wrote.

According to Barrie's biographer, Andrew Birkin, Frohman 'worshipped mothers and children'. Shaw had chosen the theme of parents and children because it was close to Frohman's heart but treated it comically. 'We cant all have the luck to die before our mothers, and be nursed out of the world by the hands that nursed us into it,' says one of the characters mocking Frohman's reverence for the family. ' . . . No man should know his own child. No child should know its own father,' he adds, matching Shaw's doubts against Frohman's ideals.

Shaw told Archibald Henderson that *Misalliance* 'is on the plan of *The Taming of the Shrew*'. Characteristically he reverses matters. If Shakespeare's farce is the chastening of a woman whose moods tormented him, Shaw's 'debate in one sitting' is a humbling of men from the governing classes at whose homes he had felt miserably ill at ease when he came to England, and who had recently humiliated him over the censorship. *Misalliance* is also a re-working of Barker's play *The Madras House*. Barker used the metaphor of the drapery trade, with its *haute couture*, to represent the decadent culture of contemporary Western civilization: Shaw uses Tarleton's Underwear.

Contemporary critics, to whom these derivations were not apparent, responded to *Misalliance* as an oddly disintegrating work. 'The debating society of a lunatic asylum – without a motion, and without a chairman,' was *The Times* critic's description. Desmond MacCarthy, too, was to feel that Shaw 'had not a clear notion where his perceptions in this case were leading him. It is inconclusive.' And Max Beerbohm, on whom it produced 'a very queer effect', objected to 'the unreality, the remoteness from human truth, that pervades the whole "debate" '.

Monitoring a revival of the play in 1939, *The Times* critic commented: 'With the lapse of time inconclusiveness comes to seem a positive merit.' With a further lapse of time these qualities of unreality and madness, and the fracturing of standard plot procedures, may be seen as having affinities with the drama of Pirandello, where events 'erupt on the instant, arbitrarily,' as Eric Bentley described them, 'just as his characters do not approach, enter, present themselves, let alone have motivated entrances; they are suddenly there, dropped from the sky.'

The extravagant ideas and incidents that cluster within the second part of *Misalliance* – an abrupt descent from the skies of a Polish equilibrist demanding a Bible, music-stand and six oranges ('billiard balls will do quite as well'); the emergence from a portable Turkish Bath of a cringing homicidal clerk, pistol in hand, crying 'I am the son of Lucinda Titmus' – all help to establish Shaw's kinship with Ionesco (who was not born until late in 1912) and show him to be, in R. J. Kaufmann's words, 'the godfather, if not actually finicky paterfamilias to the theatre of the absurd'. G.B.S. was familiar with early modernist experiments and had his own agenda for clearing away the dominance of the well-made play.

The house of *Misalliance* (which owes something to his sister-in-law's home at Edstaston) is an arena where incompatible aspects of Shaw's personality confront one another. Julius Baker, alias Gunner, arises from the Turkish Bath, prophesying revolutions despite being unable to fire a single bullet, to speak for the loveless ineffectual Sonny. Bentley Summerhays exhibits Shaw's thin-skinned capacity when young for provoking dislike (and occasionally protectiveness) from others; Joey Percival shares with him the culturally advantageous experience of having three fathers (his natural one, a tame philosopher in the house and his Italian mother's confessor corresponding to George Carr Shaw, Uncle Walter Gurly and Lee); Lord Summerhays, the experienced man who feels 'still rather lost in England', voices some of Shaw's political convictions about government and reveals a shrinking Shavian sensitivity to sexual matters ('Can no woman understand a man's delicacy?'); John Tarleton has Shaw's money-making abilities and a self-educated obsession with book-learning ('Have you learnt everything from books?' he is asked); and his son and daughter, Hypatia and Johnny, convey something of Shaw's contempt for these Shavian characteristics, in particular the actionless vacuum with its polished walls of 'Talk! talk! talk!'

Into this Shavian mansion comes the heavenly invader Lina Szczepanowska (pronounced [fi]sh-ch[urch]-panovska). She comes in answer to Shaw's prayer for positive action as much as to Hypatia's plea for 'adventures to drop out of the sky'. Like a bird she lands from above: the authentic superwoman who, arriving from the future, is to have her second coming in *St Joan*. Lina's appearance 'in full acrobatic trapeze dress, as dazzling as possible, to make her effect when she throws off her masculine cloak' is the most astonishing entrance to be made in a Shaw play. Up to this point the audience has been at an Edwardian country house party and heard the capitalist middle class in conversation with the aristocracy. It is a conventional drawing-room comedy of manners – Johnny even has the celebrated query popularly supposed to have been coined in the 1920s: 'Anybody on for a game of tennis?' The old are divided from the young, the rich from the poor, men cut off from women, parents from children: almost everyone is inhibited from any kind of initiative.

Lina comes from a different world: she is a foreigner to the class system whose manners and values look absurd. 'Wont you take off your goggles and have some tea?' enquires Mrs Tarleton after Lina has crashed into the greenhouse. The tone of the play now changes from realism into magic realism. 'These woods of yours are full of magic,' exclaims the aviator Joey Percival to John Tarleton. 'I must be dreaming,' remarks John Tarleton. 'This is stark raving nonsense.' Mrs Tarleton agrees: 'Well, I'm beginning to think I'm doing a bit of dreaming myself,' she says. But their dreams explode the British class system into fragments of comedy. 'It should be clear by now that Shaw is a terrorist,' wrote Brecht. 'The Shavian terror is an unusual one, and he employs an unusual weapon – that of humour.'

The play is obsessed with action, though the characters themselves are unable to change anything. The captain of industry and the colonial administrator have grown obsolete. John Tarleton is incensed that his human destiny should be restricted to underwear. 'I ought to have been a writer. I'm essentially the man of ideas,' he insists. Lord Summerhays (the name deriving from Wells's Samurai) also feels redundant in the twentieth century. 'I dont understand these democratic games; and I'm afraid I'm too old to learn . . . Democracy reads well; but it doesnt act well, like some people's plays.' Tarleton's two children representing sex (Hypatia) and money (Johnny); and Lord Summerhays's son representing fear – the emotional and economic fear of growing up – are the poisoned fruits of capitalism.

Capitalism is threatened in *Misalliance* by two types of invader. Julius Baker, alias Gunner, comes as revolution fuelled by personal grievance and carried out by force of arms. 'I came here to kill you and then kill myself,' he tells John Tarleton, his mother's alleged seducer. In the behaviour of the various inhabitants of the house we see the tactics bourgeois society uses to tame potential revolutionaries – how it tricks and intoxicates them, how it torments them with assistance: 'Let me hold the gun for you,' John Tarleton politely offers. And when Mrs Tarleton hears of Julius Baker's attempt on her husband's life, she exclaims: 'Oh! and John encouraging him, I'll be bound!' In such a contrived atmosphere the political terrorist sounds ridiculous: 'Rome fell. Babylon fell. Hindhead's turn will come.'

Shaw's other invaders represent salvation from the future not the past, the air and not the earth. Lina brings Joey Percival, the best mate for Hypatia who demands that her father 'buy the brute for me'. This is the biological method of serving the Life Force. The intellectual method is advanced by Lina's invitation to take Bentley Summerhays off in the aeroplane. Bentley's terrified acceptance of this is comparable to the birth of 'moral passion' in Sonny, lifting him above the religious climate of Ireland.

The part of Lina went to Lena Ashwell. She was celebrated for playing heavily emotional roles that called upon her 'to bear an illegitimate child or stab someone to death and then suffer gorgeously for her sins'. But though Yeats believed she had brought to the role something 'extremely rare: *beautiful gaiety*', she disliked the goggles, tunic and pants, and felt thrown off balance by the craziness of the play. Her imperviousness to G.B.S. was warmly approved by Charlotte and she became one of the few actresses whom Charlotte befriended.

Frohman's season opened on 21 February 1910. Barker's production of Galsworthy's *Justice* was a major contribution to the campaign for prison reform – the impact of a wordless scene in a cell was used by Churchill when introducing a provision into Parliament for more humane legislation. But a play dealing with solitary confinement was a brave choice for an evening's entertainment in London's West End. Shaw's country house burlesque, opening two nights later, made a confusing contrast. *The Globe* judged it to be 'absolutely his worst play', and *The Standard* doubted whether it would have ever reached the stage if written by someone else.

Instead of the capacity houses he anticipated, Frohman was getting less than half. He sat there paralysed, amazed, caught between his investors who wanted quick returns and big profits, and his new colleagues in the drama who, explaining that repertory needed time to accumulate its audience, congratulated him on doing so well. A triple bill of two small plays by Barrie and a posthumous comedy, partly in verse, by Meredith, was introduced at the beginning of March, and followed nine days later by *The Madras House* which Barker had been slow in finishing. The confusion deepened. Desperately, Frohman fell back on two popular revivals, Pinero's *Trelawny of the Wells* and Barker and Laurence Housman's Court Theatre success *Prunella*, which helped to restore the confidence of his backers.

Eventually King Edward VII came to the rescue. He died. And Frohman, his commercial and sentimental interests at last coinciding, joined the general shutting-down of theatres.

The season had lasted ten weeks and *Misalliance* was performed eleven times, *The Madras House* ten. But Frohman grew proud of having created 'an imperishable monument of artistic endeavour'. In a lecture called 'The Theatre: the Next Phase' delivered in London on 9 June, Barker argued that Frohman's experiment had shown that, though a repertory theatre could not be made to pay in the commercial sense, 'the practicability of modern repertory had been proved'. In concert with this speech, Shaw published a self-drafted interview three days later in the *Observer.* 'The season at the Duke of York's was well worth doing,' he wrote, '. . . because I shall never be able to persuade English men of business to endow the National Theatre unless I am in a position to say that I have exhausted all the resources of private enterprise.'

2

FURTHER PARTICULARS ON MR WELLS

> I rejoice in life for its own sake. Life is no 'brief candle' to me. It is a sort of splendid torch which I have got hold of for the moment; and I want to make it burn as brightly as possible before handing it on to future generations.
>
> 'Art and Public Money', *Sussex Daily News* (7 March 1907)

H. G. Wells had been one of those to whom Shaw, emerging from the rough Welsh seas off the coast of the Fabian Summer School, had reported his near death from drowning. 'Wasted chances! You shouldn't have come out,' Wells returned. 'There you were – lacking nothing but a little decent resolution to make a distinguished end . . . As for me I could have sailed in with one or two first class obituary articles.'

Shaw claimed to be 'dead against this exhibition sparring' because 'I do it so well that the sympathy goes to my opponent'. But on this occasion Wells had done it better. Neither of them enjoyed these knockabouts for long – they turned too deadly. But Wells found himself pressed forward into the ring by a new supporters' club among the Fabians. His spirits rose: he felt game enough. His potent spell promised a new era for Fabianism. 'He is a man of outstanding genius,' wrote Edward Pease. '. . . his energy and attractive personality added radiance to the Society only equalled in the early days.' During 1907 the membership doubled.

There was an influx of younger women and men from the universities, many of them drawn by what Rupert Brooke called 'the wee fantastic Wells'.

The political climate of the country was changing. Shaw's plays and Wells's novels had helped to create a middle class with expectations of swift social change. The failure of Campbell-Bannerman's Government to initiate any policy of reform soon led to middle-class discontent with Liberalism and a swelling support for the Labour Party. It was this switch of allegiance by progressive intellectuals that had given rise to the new Fabian boom.

These new members were joining the Society of Shaw and Wells, rather than of the Webbs. This was one of the reasons why Beatrice suspected this sudden Fabian popularity. Their new recruits 'lived the most unconventional life,' she observed during the Fabian Summer School, 'stealing out on moor or sand, in stable or under hayricks, without always the requisite chaperon to make it look as wholly innocent as it really is'. Could she be certain that it was innocent? Their conversation was surprisingly free. And their gym costumes gave several of the elderly Fabians some bad quarters of an hour. Beatrice felt apprehensive, too, when the economics had to stop, of where their 'larky entertainments' could lead. There was danger in innocence. There was danger everywhere.

Beatrice knew the undiscriminating power of sex. She suspected Shaw and Granville Barker, no less than Wells, of letting themselves go 'pretty considerably' with women. But she had so curbed her 'lower desires' that she seemed unaware of how controlled the erotic motive was in Shaw's *Misalliance*, which she described as 'disgusting'. 'I think probably the revelations with the H.G.W. various sexual escapades largely suggested the play,' she wrote. She seemed to have no means of telling, as could the young Fabians, the difference in such matters between Shaw and Wells.

Among the young Fabians, Shaw behaved benignly, his conversation mixing instruction with unflagging public entertainment. 'He was personally the kindest, most friendly, most charming of men,' remembered Leonard Woolf.

'He would come up and greet one with what seemed to be warmth and pleasure and he would start straight away with a fountain of words scintillating with wit and humour . . . but if you happened to look into that slightly fishy, ice-blue eye of his, you got a shock. It was not looking at you . . . it was looking through you or over you into a distant world or universe.'

Wells's eyes were more penetrating and when they looked at you they looked at no one else. As if to make up for early emotional loss, he was hungry for sex. He seemed vulnerable; but even his uncertainties were endearing – so often they were your own. He appeared 'nearer and more sympathetic than other men,' wrote Dorothy Richardson.

Wells was happy among the young Fabians. They were mostly women. There was a good-looking flirtatious writer, Violet Hunt, whom he entreated to 'be nice to a very melancholy man'. There was Hubert Bland's plump and beautiful illegitimate daughter Rosamund, who was said to enjoy the admiration of men. 'I have a pure flame for Rosamund,' Wells admitted. There was Amber Reeves, sweet, pretty, coaxing, who loved visiting the Wellses at Spade House. 'She adores you both,' her mother confided to Jane Wells. Lucy Masterman too remembered her holiday at Sandgate as an 'impression of perpetual sunshine, health and ease'. 'I am ready to go on working for [socialism],' Wells wrote, ' . . . in the meantime having just as good a time and just as many pleasant things as I can.'

Women now numbered more than a quarter of the Fabian membership and they wanted the Society to turn its attention to supporting votes for women. Shaw was appointed to discuss the matter with the Fabian spokeswoman, Amber Reeves's mother Maud Pember Reeves. There were few differences between them: Shaw supported women's suffrage and believed that women themselves should have the principal place in the suffrage campaign. He therefore returned to the executive with a recommendation that it agree to the women's wishes. As a result, 'the establishment of equal citizenship between men and women' was added to the Objects of the Society. A Women's Group (with Jane Wells on its executive) was formed – also a Biology Group and a Socialist Medical League – and the Fabian women arranged themselves into a useful platoon in the fight for enfranchisement.

The backbone of Shaw's feminism was financial self-respect: he spoke in particular of equal pay for actresses and the economic independence of wives. He wanted the Fabian Society to stand for political equality as the universal relation between citizens without distinction of sex, colour, occupation, age, talent or hereditary factors; and he advocated 'the explicit recognition by legally secured rights or payments of the value of their domestic partners and to the State as housekeepers, child bearers, nurses and matrons'. He wanted to see them, in equal numbers with men, on all political organizations, including the House of Commons.

It was his political 'discovery' that 'a woman is just like a man', that enabled Shaw to replace the Victorian stereotype of the womanly woman with Woman the Huntress. But 'the pursuit has about as much sex appeal as a timetable,' complained Frank Harris. Though the sexual 'syringeing' of women by men had 'compensations which, *when experienced*, overwhelm all the objections to it,' Shaw admitted to St John Ervine, ' . . . I always feel obliged, as a gentleman, to apologise for my disgraceful behaviour'. This 'apology' infiltrated his writing, against which some women reacted even when admiring the moral elegance of his argument.

'I am a woman,' says the man in one of Shaw's plays to the girl; 'and you are a man, with a slight difference that doesnt matter except on special occasions.' Wells did not feel this difference to be slight, and the occasions were frequent. Like Shaw, Wells defended the rights of women, condemning conventional sexual morality and the marriage laws founded on it. But he dared to do what he advocated. Several rebellious young women, oppressed by Edwardian conventionality, sought him out. He was not simply on the side of the young, he was in many ways one of them.

Although no scandal about his affairs had yet broken into public view, Wells had been accused in the press of having manufactured through his books a paramour's Utopia. Shaw and the Webbs feared that 'Fabian Free Love' might set socialism back a decade – Wells was not at liberty to throw his emotional match-ends about in powder-magazines. There had almost been an explosion over his relationship with Rosamund Bland. The Society had hummed with rumours of how Hubert Bland had intercepted the pair at Paddington Station. But these rumours were confined within the Society and did not reach the public. Shaw had circled round emitting advice but, knowing few of the facts, he was not well employed. 'What an unmitigated moral Victorian ass you are,' Wells accused him. 'You play about with ideas like a daring garrulous maiden aunt but when it comes to an affair like the Bland affair you show the instincts of conscious gentility and the judgement of a hen . . .

'You don't know, as I do, in blood & substance, lust, failure, shame, hate, love & creative passion. You don't understand & you can't understand the rights & wrongs of the case into which you stick your maidenly judgment any more than you can understand the aims of the Fabian Society that your vanity has wrecked. Now go on being amusing.'

Only Shaw among the Fabian elders had really wished Wells to stay on the executive. Webb and Bland plainly wanted him to leave – and Wells too was eager to go: all they differed on was the manner of his going. At a by-election in the spring of 1908, Wells supported the Liberal candidate, Winston Churchill, whose 'rapidly developing and broadening mind . . . [was] entirely in accordance with the spirit of our movement'. His motives for this action seem to have been mixed between a natural preference for Churchill over a dull socialist candidate incapable of winning the contest, and a wish to strengthen opposition to the Tory candidate, William

Joynson-Hicks, who had accused him of being 'a nasty-minded advocate of promiscuous copulation'. At the annual meeting of the Fabian Society on 22 April 1908, Wells was accused of betraying socialism and took the opportunity to resign. 'It is to other media and other methods,' he wrote, 'that we must now look for the spread and elaboration of those collectivist ideas which all of us have at heart.' He would go back to writing novels.

This resignation, which the executive accepted ten days later, was an act of mercy. During the winter of 1908–9 what Beatrice called 'a somewhat dangerous friendship' developed between Wells and Amber Reeves. Amber graduated with a double first in moral sciences and conceived Wells's child at about the same time. What made it worse for Beatrice to contemplate was that they had enjoyed sexual intercourse, so she heard, in the girl's rooms 'within the very walls' of Newnham College. The events, as they emerged over the year 1909, began to unsettle Beatrice. First she was irritated that Wells could intermittently go on living with his wife as if nothing were wrong; she was also affronted when Amber ran for the cover of a marriage of convenience to a chivalrous barrister with the tautologous name of Blanco White, giving Wells's daughter a 'legitimate' birth; then she felt exasperated on hearing that they were persisting with the liaison following that marriage; finally the publication of *Ann Veronica*, Wells's novel advertising the affair, drove her frantic.

Amber's father was Director of the London School of Economics; her mother was prominent among the Fabian Women's Group; her lover was a Fabian; her husband was a Fabian; and she herself had been treasurer of the Cambridge University Fabians. Even Jane Wells, the complaisant wife, was on the Fabian executive. Worse still, it was the Webbs who had introduced Wells to the Reeves family. 'I wish we had never known them,' Beatrice exclaimed. Something would have to be done. Pulpits were shaking with denunciations of *Ann Veronica*, and the National Social Purity Crusade brandished the novel at the head of its campaign for formal censorship in circulating libraries. Reviewers who knew something of Wells's biography took the opportunity to treat Ann as if she were Amber. The criticism overflowed from the book and cascaded into Wells's life. 'I can't stand this persecution,' he cried out. 'He will disappear,' Beatrice predicted, 'for good, from reputable society.' He did resign from the Savile Club; and Jane was asked to quit the Fabian executive.

Beatrice felt intensely involved. She insisted that Wells would be permanently wretched. 'I doubt whether he will keep his health – and he may lose his talent'; and she believed that Amber was 'a ruined woman, doomed to sink deeper into the mire'. Once Beatrice had been anxious lest Wells, after his resignation from the executive, became a Fabian enemy like Ramsay MacDonald. 'Don't shake us off altogether,' she had appealed. 'It won't be good for either the Webbs or the Wells and will be very bad for the common cause.' But now he was a danger, an abomination. 'The end of our friendship with H. G. Wells,' she noted in her diary in the summer of 1909.

Beatrice had done what she could. She had written letters to Fabians with teenage daughters; she had spoken to Blanco White and counselled Amber. She had also been in touch with Shaw. But Shaw took a different view. Now that Wells was only a subscriber to the Fabian Society, it was permissible to view the affair as part of that fine art of private life which consisted in taking liberties. Wells excelled at this kind of social experiment. 'The situation can be saved by letting it alone,' he instructed Beatrice. ' . . . I aim at the minimum of mischief.'

Shaw had already written sympathetically to Wells. 'Occasionally,' Wells responded, 'you don't simply rise to a difficult situation but soar above it & I withdraw anything you would like withdrawn from our correspondence in the last two years or so.' For despite everything, there was part of Shaw that warmed to Wells's escapading. Some writers had to act foolishly in order to write well. 'Mr Wells does not shirk facts because they are considered scandalous, especially when the conventional foundation of that view of them is becoming more and more questionable,' Shaw was to write a dozen years later; 'but I cannot find in his books a trace of that *morbidezza* which . . . is very largely produced by the fact that the writers have no real experience of what they are writing about, and are the victims of a baffled *libido* rather than a Casanovesque excess of gallantry.' The mixed vocabulary of this tribute indicates the changing culture through which these Fabians were passing. In this shifting landscape it was difficult finding one's way. 'All this arises because we none of us know what exactly is the sexual code we believe in,' observed Beatrice, 'approving of many things on paper which we violently object to when they are practised by those we care about.'

*

Wells's place as Fabian activist was almost immediately occupied by Beatrice herself. Until recently she had not acted as much more than an aide to Sidney. Her deeper involvement arose in part from a changed attitude to the role of women in politics. Some twenty years before she had signed an anti-suffrage manifesto drafted by Mrs Humphry Ward. It 'is the spiritual function of a woman to be the passive agent bearing a man's life!' she had emphatically instructed Sidney before their marriage. Her impatience with some of the militant pioneers of women's suffrage was overtaken by a feeling of distaste over the 'coarse-grained things' being said by men opposed to emancipation. Towards the end of 1906 she sent Millicent Fawcett, president of the National Union of Women's Suffrage, her formal recantation.

Nothing did more to alter Beatrice's views than her experiences as a member of the Royal Commission on Poor Law. She had been appointed by Arthur Balfour during the last days of his Government at the end of 1905. Before that, as she admitted, 'I have never myself suffered the disabilities assumed to arise from my sex'. Three years' work on this largely man-dominated Commission left her wondering: 'Are all men quite so imbecile as that lot are? . . . It makes me feel intolerably superior.'

'Certainly the work of the Commission will be an education in manners as well as in Poor Law,' she wrote. She trained like an athlete for this work, rising for her cold bath and quick walk at six-thirty, feasting off bread and cheese and drawing on Sidney's 'blessed strength and capacity'. Yet her manners did deteriorate. 'From first to last she has declined whilst in the Commission to merge her individuality in it, but claims the right of unrestricted free action outside,' wrote the mild-mannered chairman. Her Minority Report, completed early in 1909, was signed by three other Commissioners.

Everyone had been dissatisfied with the ramshackle Poor Law of 1834. Some saw it as expensive and inefficient; others as inadequate and demoralizing. Beatrice wanted to break up the Poor Law altogether and replace it with a comprehensive scheme of welfare that allocated responsibilities for assisting those below a national minimum to a series of Government departments dealing with specific causes of poverty, such as chronic sickness, old age and unemployment. She was contemptuous of the Majority Report which sought by simple unemployment insurance to alleviate the circumstances only of the destitute and necessitous. Shaw sensed that the Minority Report was a more important document than most people realized. 'It may make as great a difference in sociology and political science as Darwin's "Origin of Species" did in philosophy and natural history,' he predicted. '. . . It is big and revolutionary and sensible and practicable at the same time, which is just what is wanted to inspire and attract the new generation.'

The Report lies somewhere between Bentham and Beveridge. Beatrice's collectivist scheme was to be a blueprint for the Welfare State, but it also retained something of the puritanism of Bentham who had believed in the utilitarian device of the workhouse to 'grind rogues into honest men'. Beatrice was haunted by this problem of the able-bodied unemployed. 'I dream of it at night,' she wrote, 'I pray for light in the early morning.' For those who lacked capacity she recommended compulsory training; and for those who lacked will, disciplinary supervision. Believing that a grant from the community should be conditional on reasonable conduct from the individual, she was later to express criticism of Beveridge's proposed extension of unconditional unemployment doles on the grounds that this would encourage malingering.

It was the Majority Report that got the better press. But from the Fabian point of view, the political situation appeared to have improved. After Campbell-Bannerman suffered a heart attack in April 1908, a new Government was formed with Asquith its Prime Minister – a man 'inclined to carry out our ideas,' Beatrice thought. But Asquith left much of this work to Winston Churchill (President of the Board of Trade) and Lloyd George (Chancellor of the Exchequer): and neither of them was sympathetic to the Webbs. Sidney and Beatrice therefore decided to deploy the Fabian Society on a national campaign. This was the sort of enterprise Wells had been urging on the Fabians before his resignation – it was 'quite after my own heart,' he told Beatrice. Here was the 'new start' Beatrice had promised the Fabians: a missionary crusade of 'raging tearing propaganda' to change the mind of the country about destitution.

'As a preparation I practise voice presentation between 6.30 and 8 a.m. every morning on the beach – orating to the Waves!' she wrote after the Fabian Summer School. ' . . . It is rather funny to start on a new profession after 50!' The turmoil rather thrilled her. Yet it was a 'curiously demoralizing life'. She spurred herself on to be an itinerant agitator. 'It is no use shirking from this life of surface agitation, from this perpetual outgiving of personality.'

Beatrice had published her Minority Report in two volumes totalling 946 pages. Though it was extraordinarily far-seeing, it proved difficult to expound to electors; and it was impossible to convince governments that a complex bureaucracy would not be needed to set it up. After the last Liberal election win in 1910, people preferred Lloyd George's simple National Insurance Bill.

'Lloyd George and Winston Churchill have practically taken the *limelight*,' Beatrice conceded. She had needed the talents of Wells and Shaw to combat such brilliantly effective slogans as Lloyd George's 'Ninepence for fourpence' advertising contributory social insurance. But Wells, though he joined the campaign 'very much as a drop of water, when it encounters a pailful, lines up with the rest', was too busy working at his caricatures of the Webbs in *The New Machiavelli*; whilst Shaw seemed to have 'lost the power of doing anything except in imperative emergencies'.

Beatrice's Minority Report had a formative influence on Shaw's political thinking. It broke from the commercial tradition of the nineteenth century and went straight to the issue of public welfare. It was not enough, the Report stated, to secure every man a minimum wage for the work he found to do. 'You must provide the wage anyhow, and enable him to find all the work that exists, and if there is no work available you must still spend the wage on him in keeping him fit for work when it does come,' Shaw wrote in a review of the Report. 'His right to live, and the right of the community to his maintenance in health and efficiency, are seen to be quite independent of his commercial profit for any private employer. He is not merely a means to the personal ends of our men of business; he is a cell of the social organism, and must be kept in health if the organism is to be kept in health.'

From the Webbs' national minimum wage, Shaw's mind moved on to an annual salary that would in effect be an equal share of the national product. Then, in or about December 1910, he came up with a new definition of socialism. Ideally it meant equality of income – 'a state of society in which the entire income of the country is divided between all the people in exactly equal shares, without regard to their industry, their character, or any other consideration except the consideration that they are living human beings . . . that is Socialism and nothing else is Socialism.'

Though Shaw did not have much confidence in imposing this 'remoter solution' on the Fabians, he felt that Lloyd George's plans for pensioning the elderly and taxing unearned income made it imperative for socialists to regain the initiative in radical thinking about the redistribution of income. Equality was fundamental to socialism, he argued, and without it all Lloyd George's schemes to take from the rich and give to the poor would seem predatory. For without equality nothing could be done except to organize capitalism on a more commercially profitable basis. Shaw replaced Lloyd George's old age pension with a life pension, substituting social service for private profit as a motive for human action. 'We must proceed by taxation as Mr Lloyd George does,' he told the Fabians: 'but our object should [be] . . . the reduction of all excessive incomes to the normal standard.'

When, after their crusade, Beatrice arranged to take Sidney on a sabbatical voyage round the world, G.B.S. saw an excellent opportunity for retirement. He had always intended to resign, he reminded Edward Pease, 'when I had completed my quarter of a century service; but what with Wells and one thing and another the moment was not propitious . . . if we do not resign now, we shall never resign.' Neither Bland, nor he himself, nor Stewart Headlam would stand again. The clearing out of the Old Gang would be pretty well complete – so why not make it complete and simultaneous? 'I think Sidney *must* retire,' Shaw advised. 'We must all go together, with the limelight on, and full band accompaniment.'

At the executive elections in April 1911, Webb came top of the poll and stayed on: Shaw, Bland and three other members resigned. Looking back some years later, Shaw wondered whether the Old Gang should not have left half a dozen years earlier and taken the risk of handing everything over to Wells. 'In a way he [Wells] was fundamentally right in seeing that he could do nothing unless The Society would definitely accept him and trust him, and get rid of us,' he wrote.

3

SKITS AND FARCES

I confess I am getting old and childish and easily amused.

Shaw to Greenhaugh Smith (29 December 1904)

In the half-dozen years before the war Shaw whipped up more than half a dozen one-act skits, farces, extravaganzas for the stage written mostly in a style which Virginia Woolf described as that of 'a disgustingly precocious child of 2 – a sad and improper spectacle to my thinking'. The event-plots of these pieces tell the story of Shaw's contribution to magic and absurdity, and rearrange fragments of his life into revealing patterns.

The Fascinating Foundling was knocked off early in August 1909 for a charity performance at the request of Elizabeth Asquith, daughter of the Prime Minister. Shaw provided the piece with a subtitle – 'A Disgrace to the Author'.

The story revolves round the destiny of orphans. A smart and beautiful young man forces his way into the ante-room of the Lord Chancellor's office, and engages his elderly clerk in a broadsword combat (fire tongs versus poker). This parody of a Shakespearian duel is interrupted by the indignant appearance of the Lord Chancellor. The young man explains that he is Horace Brabazon, a foundling, and has come to the Lord Chancellor as 'father of all the orphans in Chancery' to ask for a wife – 'someone old enough to be my mother,' he explains, ' . . . not old enough to be your mother . . . I attach some importance to that distinction . . . One mustnt overdo these notions.' After he leaves a second caller arrives. She is Anastasia Vulliamy, a superior foundling who had been discovered 'on the doorstep of one of the very best houses in Park Lane'. She too wants the Lord Chancellor 'to be a father to me' and find her a husband, 'someone I can bully'. Horace Brabazon returns for his walking-stick, and she proposes to him, recommending a three-week engagement: 'You are only on approval, of course.' He agrees because she is a foundling and will bring no family to make him miserable.

The Glimpse of Reality was a more sombre tomfoolery which took Shaw nearly eighteen months to complete and eighteen years to see performed, chiefly because he kept mislaying it. It is set in the fifteenth century and takes place at an inn on the edge of an Italian lake. A devout friar aged one hundred and thirteen is hearing the confession of a young girl, Giulia. He urges her to press close to him as he is deaf. She does so, telling him that in order to win a sufficient dowry for her to marry a fisherman she is to decoy young Count Ferruccio ('a devil for women') to the inn. The Count will then be killed by her father who will claim the reward. The venerable friar flings off his gown and beard and reveals himself as the young Count. Giulia's father, the innkeeper, and her fiancé, the fisherman, appear, and all four of them sit down to supper. The Count negotiates for his life, but in a complicated tactical game is defeated. 'There is nothing like a good look into the face of death,' he says, '. . . for shewing you how little you really believe and how little you really are.' With this glimpse of reality his terror of death falls away. He speaks so fearlessly that the innkeeper and fisherman, believing him mad and therefore under the protection of God, refuse to murder him.

Among the other playlets of this period were 'An Interlude', 'A Thumbnail Sketch of Russian Court Life in the XVIII Century', 'A Piece of Utter Nonsense', and 'A Demonstration'. The 'Interlude', which was Shaw's subtitle for *The Dark Lady of the Sonnets*, is a miniature work of art composed between 17 and 20 June 1910, to support the appeal for a British National Theatre.

It is a midsummer night on the terrace of the Palace at Whitehall, overlooking the Thames, in the spacious times of Elizabeth I. A Beefeater is approached by a ghost. 'Angels and ministers of grace defend us!' he cries. The cloaked figure stops and writes, then speaks. He is no ghost, but a man come to keep tryst with his Dark Lady. The Beefeater relaxes: he knows this dark lady well enough. She is always making trysts with men. 'You may say of frailty that its name is woman,' he casually remarks. The man turns pale at this information, yet luxuriates in the phrase and makes a note of it – at which the 'well-languaged' warder dubs him 'a snapper-up of such unconsidered trifles': and down that goes too on the man's tablet.

The Beefeater moves discreetly off and a sleepwalking lady wanders along the terrace cursing the cosmetics that have peppered her with freckles: 'Out, damned spot . . . All the perfumes of Arabia will not whiten this Tudor hand.' The man, enchanted by this word-imagery, mistakes her for his mistress, the mysterious 'woman colour'd ill'. He wakes her but discovers that she is a stranger. By way of introduction he tells her that he is 'the king of words', and rhapsodizes over her own word-skill – he has so bad a memory, he adds, he must catch them on his tablets. He puts his arms round her, but the two of them are knocked sideways by the Dark Lady who has been jealously listening. During this falling-about the three characters are revealed as Shakespeare, Queen Elizabeth and Mary Fitton.

Mistress Fitton is terrified. Only fear strikes any words out of her that Shakespeare finds worth taking down and she is eager to leave the scene of danger. But Queen Elizabeth is a *femme inspiratrice* and practically every word she utters is Shakespearian. 'I am not here to write your plays for you,' she eventually rebukes him. Prospero-like, Shaw has called her there, together with Shakespeare, as history's two most commanding witnesses to plead the cause of endowing a National Theatre.

To the play Shaw attached a Preface warning readers against using the past as a refuge from the present. Shakespeare lives in each of us and all Shakespearian criticism is a form of autobiography. Shaw's Shakespeare makes comedy out of his own misfortunes, is inspired by his love of music, grows immune to the weaknesses of passion and becomes superhuman. He is also a master of irony. 'I am convinced,' Shaw concludes, 'that he was very like myself.'

The 'state of levity' which Shaw insists buoyed up Shakespeare's life floats through almost all these playlets whose subtitles have a similar mutinous tone to Shakespeare's popular comedies – *Much Ado About Nothing*, *As You Like It*, *What You Will*. His 'Piece of Utter Nonsense', otherwise called *The Music-Cure*, is a topical skit written as a curtain-raiser for the play he had finally persuaded G. K. Chesterton to write. Chesterton's drama, which shows love miraculously conquering diabolical evil, was called *Magic*. Shaw's variety turn is a piece of magic realism suggesting that this miracle of love is a hallucination, like the concept of evil.

Lord Reginald Fitzambey, Under-Secretary in the War Office, cannot stand very much reality. 'I am not fit for public affairs,' he confesses. '. . . I have a real genius for home life.' But because his father is a Duke he has been obliged to enter Parliament, and is suffering from a breakdown. A doctor gives him some opium and he 'sees' a laughing crocodile about to play the piano with its tail – which is Shaw's unconvincing version of evil. The doctor concludes that he should double the dose after which 'if anything comes it will be something pretty this time'. He leaves, and a lovely lady pianist, Strega Thundridge, appears. She tells Reginald that his mother has engaged her for a terrific fee to play the piano in his room for two hours. There follows, as she plays Chopin's Polonaise in A flat, an optimistic essay on the effects of opium upon the romantic imagination. 'Ever since I was a child I have had only one secret longing,' declares Reginald, 'and that was to be mercilessly beaten by a splendid, strong, beautiful woman.' Strega Thundridge, whose natural strength has been marvellously expanded by her playing of left-hand octave passages, is that splendid creature. She too has a dream: 'It is a dream of a timid little heart fluttering against mine, of a gentle voice to welcome me home . . . of someone utterly dependent on me, utterly devoted to me' whom she would beat sometimes to a jelly, before casting herself into an ecstasy of remorse. They play the Wedding March, embrace fiercely and confront their terrible destiny together.

The Music-Cure, Shaw revealed, 'is not a serious play'. It took him almost nine months to bring himself to complete it, during which time (between 29 July and 13 August 1913) he had also written *Great Catherine*. She is, he tells us in his 'Author's Apology', the Catherine whom Byron had celebrated in *Don Juan*.

> In Catherine's reign, whom glory still adores
> As greatest of all sovereigns and w----s.

Shaw's Catherine is a woman set in authority over men. There is no real plot in the play. It is an eighteenth-century encounter, spread across four bravura scenes, between some extreme personalities. There is the genial and gigantic Shavian villain Prince Patiomkin; there is a caricature Englishman, the stiff and insular Captain Edstaston of the Light Dragoons (who is Britannus escaped from *Caesar and Cleopatra* and now named after Shaw's sister-in-law's house) and his invincibly snobbish fiancée Claire – all comic stereotypes with whom Shaw felt at ease. 'This is carrying a joke too far,' protests the Captain as the semi-drunken Patiomkin carries him into the Empress's *petite levée* and dumps him on her bed. And that is what Shaw is doing, carrying the joke as far as it will go and further. 'This is perfectly ridiculous,' says Claire surveying the Empress's court which, after Shaw's juvenile rearrangement, has been converted into a nursery. In this nursery the pain and fear of adult life evaporate. The Captain, though threatened with five thousand blows of the stick, with being skinned alive, having his tongue ripped out or his eyelids cut off, is actually trussed up and tickled by the Empress's toe.

That rulers behave like children is an adult observation and one that was confirmed when the Lord Chamberlain's Comptroller recommended (besides modification to the captain's uniform) that Patiomkin be made a teetotaller and Catherine a monogamist so as to avoid giving offence to Grand Duke Vladimir of Russia, a friend of the British Royal Family. Such absurdities support Shaw's point that 'the fiction has yet to be written that can exaggerate the reality of such subjects'. Yet Shaw did not so much exaggerate as overrule reality. His characters behave badly out of fear, and it is this fear that these playlets replace with fun and games. But they show too, in a childlike way, the sources of his fear: physical cruelty and the dominance of death, but also infant sexuality and its bearing on the adult operation of the sex instinct. In the secret place of Shaw's fantasies, all prescriptions against sex are inoperative. 'The truth is that a man (or a woman) should never take his (or her) innocence for granted in matters of sex,' he wrote to Edith Lyttelton, 'in which ANYTHING is possible and even probable.'

It is this guilty world of ANYTHING that these playlets invade. The role of Strega Thundridge, for example, was written for an actress who had started her career as a talented pianist whom Shaw had encircled with erotic dreams. This affair, which virtually began by her bedside while she was ill, is comically retold in *Great Catherine* after the fastidious Captain Edstaston is deposited on Catherine's bed by Prince Patiomkin.

Shaw had given a 'demonstration' of this affair in another of his short plays. Its first title, *Trespassers Will Be Prosecuted*, had been suggested by a notice posted on the gate of Edith Lyttelton's house (she being a confidante of Shaw's erotic actress). After three weeks' work in the summer of 1912, he finished the play on a 'Gt Northern train passing Holloway', removed the warning, *Trespassers Will Be Prosecuted*, and substituted *Overruled*.

He believed his little play to be 'really a work of some merit'. For years he had been objecting to the teasing versions of adultery presented on the stage. In *Overruled* he claimed to have dramatized marital infidelity and introduced the act of sexual intercourse itself (so far as this was practicable) to the theatre. Mysteriously no one noticed.

The plot of the play explains some of the mystery. It is a summer night at a seaside hotel. A lady and gentleman are sitting together on a chesterfield in a corner of the lounge. He throws his arms round her but suddenly he discovers she is married. She too is astonished to learn that he has a wife, particularly since they have been cruising round the world each believing the other to be single. At that moment they hear the voices of a man and a woman in the corridor, and spring to opposite sides of the lounge. These voices belong to their respective husband and wife who enter, occupy the still-warm chesterfield and begin to enact a similar love scene. It transpires that both married couples had decided to enjoy a holiday away from each other and go round the world in opposite directions. The second flirtation is interrupted by the first couple, and there follows what Shaw calls in his Preface to the play 'a clinical study' of how polygamy actually occurs 'among quite ordinary people'.

Conceived as a one-act burlesque of Sydney Grundy's fashionable three-act 'tissue of artificialities' *Slaves of the Ring*, which involved 'a quadrille of lovers instead of a pair', *Overruled* was offered as a 'model to all future writers of farcical comedy'. Twenty years later this option was to be taken up by Noël Coward in his own version of Shaw's world-cruising quartet, *Private Lives*, where the couples once again meet in a hotel with each other's partners.

Overruled demonstrates certain truths about the married man who was now entering his late fifties. 'You see, it's a great many years since Ive been able to allow myself to fall in love,' explains one of the husbands. '... I thought I had lost the power of letting myself fall really and wholeheartedly in love.' And the second husband confesses: 'Year after year went by: I felt my youth slipping away without ever having had a romance in my life; for marriage is all very well: but it isnt romance.' In his optimistic fantasy Shaw assigns the wives of these marriages a perfect tolerance of adultery. 'If you will be so very good, my dear, as to take my sentimental husband off my hands occasionally, I shall be more than obliged to you,' says one wife to the other who is perfectly willing to comply since, she says, 'I like to be loved. I want everyone round me to love me.'

But Charlotte was far from feeling this. Shaw's comedy was an outlet for his wishes rather than a clinical study of how polygamy was soon to threaten their marriage. In the Preface, where he maintains that those who profess advanced views are mostly 'the last people in the world to engage in unconventional adventures of any kind', he opposes the 'demonstration' of his play. Was the play to overrule the Preface, or the Preface overrule the play? The dilemma registers the tension and uncertainty with which he entered the great romance of his life, for which *Overruled* had served as curtain-raiser.

4

ON THE SUB-TEXT OF SUCCESS

> I can't stand people who will not believe anything because it might be false nor deny anything because it might be true.
>
> Shaw to Cliff Keene (12 June 1914)

The quantity of objects, duties, events from which Charlotte had to remove G.B.S. was mounting. 'Anything to avoid Christmas in England!' he had exclaimed on 23 December 1910. For a fortnight Charlotte and he rolled on the rough seas, arriving on the evening of 6 January at Kingston,

Jamaica. They were met by their old Fabian friend Sydney Olivier, the Governor-General, who put them up at his post-earthquake palace, 'a masterpiece of *nouveau* art' in reinforced concrete. 'I am taking photographs in 100th of a second through yellow screens & watching the lizards and dragon flies,' Shaw wrote to Granville Barker. '. . . The trees & mountains look pleasantly theatrical through the mosquito curtains.' After six days on the island, they embarked for another fortnight at sea. 'On the whole it was a good move, this,' Shaw concluded, though he'd hardly had time to get used to the novelty of 'bananas and sugar canes and coloured villages and eighty in the shade in January'.

An enormous parcel of work and his first commercial stage success awaited him in London. *Fanny's First Play*, which he finished on 5 March 1911, had been born of Shaw's interest in some of the most topical events in England. But he had worked on it anywhere but in England: in the remote Gothic hotel at Parknasilla on the south-west coast of Ireland; and at sea while steaming to and from Jamaica. One consequence of writing in such far-off places about up-to-the-minute issues seemed to be a strange unfastening of the theme from its treatment – a dislocation which was to produce what some critics would later see as 'the type of alienation which Brecht thought necessary to a dispassionate argument'.

The play depicts two middle-class families, the Gilbeys and the Knoxes, associated in business and by their strictly brought-up son and daughter, Bobby and Margaret, who are engaged to be married. After short spells of imprisonment for assaulting the police, they are released from their social prison and acknowledge that their feelings for each other are those of brother and sister. Bobby then marries a prostitute and Margaret a footman who (in characteristic Shavian reversal) reveals himself as the younger brother to a Duke. Both are acting in accord with the natural morality of sexual instinct rather than the rules of an enclosed system.

That was the complete play when Shaw and Charlotte arrived from their holiday in Jamaica at 10 Adelphi Terrace, and when Lillah McCarthy (who could spy their arrival from her rooms at 5 Adelphi Terrace) came to see Shaw. She told him that she had borrowed some money from Lord Howard de Walden; that she was setting herself up as an actress-manager at Gertrude Kingston's Little Theatre below her apartment: and she asked him for a play. *Fanny's First Play* was too short. But on the plan of *The Taming of the Shrew*, Shaw ingeniously added an Induction and an Epilogue, and early in March handed Lillah this 'Easy Play for a Little Theatre'. 'The idea of the Induction is this,' Shaw explained to Charles Ricketts who designed the costumes. 'A certain Count O'Dowda . . . loathes modern industrial England, and has spent his life in Venice, in the footsteps of Byron, Shelley, and the Brownings.

'He has lived the perfect artistic life, with his daughter, tolerating nothing later than the XVIII century. But he has consented to send his daughter to Cambridge for two years as it is his own university, and he feels quite sure that it is still untouched by the XIX century. The young lady . . . writes an ultra modern suffragette play – Fanny's first play – the performance of which nearly kills the unfortunate old gentleman.'

Fanny O'Dowda has persuaded her father to have her play anonymously performed, 'with real actors and real critics', at his country house for her nineteenth birthday. The differences separating father from daughter reinforce the conflict of the parents and children in Fanny's play; and the sexual liberation of the young people in her play is complemented by Fanny's intellectual liberation from the rule of the theatrical critics, who are a police force of the mind. In the Epilogue these critics debate the authorship of the play they have just seen, offering scholarly comparisons with *The Admirable Crichton*, *The Madras House* and *The Second Mrs Tanqueray*. 'I believe it's Shaw,' blurts out Flawner Bannal. 'Rubbish!' retorts Gunn. 'Rot!' exclaims Vaughan. They all agree that Shaw is incapable of writing a play. All he wants is to 'set us talking about him', which to their disgust he makes them do.

Fanny's First Play had evolved in much the same way as had the full version of *Man and Superman*, and it takes to the point of caricature the Shavian practice of ending the drama in the middle of the play and letting the discussion take over. 'I have not put my name to it,' he told Lillah McCarthy when handing her the typescript, and he urged her to reveal that the author's name began with a *B*, so encouraging the rumour that it was by Barrie.

Fanny's First Play by Xxxxxxx Xxxx opened at the Little Theatre on 19 April 1911. 'It was like old time at the Court,' Shaw told Vedrenne two days later, 'except for the void left by Vedrenne.' But this was not repertory: they ran the play continuously for as long as the public wanted it – the way Vedrenne had always wished to run Shaw's plays at the Court. 'It is really amusing – considering who wrote it,' Shaw admitted: and the public agreed. The Shavian drama seemed to have won through to genuine popularity. On 1 January 1912 it transferred to the Kingsway Theatre and later completed a run of 622 performances. 'I thought that . . . you touched your highest, often striking the human note,' wrote Herbert Beerbohm Tree.

*

The coronation celebrations of King George V and Queen Mary that summer provided a good incentive for Shaw and Charlotte to get abroad again. Shaw's diary lists some forty towns in France, Switzerland, Austria, Germany and Italy that he and Charlotte saw over the next sixteen weeks. They travelled with the patient Kilsby and his boisterous motor car and spent many hours motor-mountaineering along impassable tracks over the Alps and Dolomites. 'In the valleys, in the towns, in the hotels, in the hideous heat, I have been wretched,' he informed Trebitsch; 'but on the mountains I revive.'

He was back in harness in the second week of October. Charlotte kept him gently on the move between Ayot and Adelphi Terrace, then boarded him up at Edstaston with her sister and brother-in-law for Christmas and the New Year. Here, on 2 January 1912, he began a new play, 'a religious harlequinade,' he described it to Frances Chesterton. 'Do you know anyone who can play a lion well, with a practicable tail, for the Christian Martyr scene in the arena?' he asked Pinero three days later. The last of the seventy-eight pages of shorthand manuscript was finished on 6 February and sent to his secretary Judy Gillmore for typing.

Androcles and the Lion was an offshoot from *Major Barbara*. Desmond MacCarthy's description of it as a 'religious pantomime' recalls Count O'Dowda's execration of this genre in *Fanny's First Play*: 'that vulgar, ugly, silly, senseless, malicious and destructive thing the harlequinade of a nineteenth century English Christmas pantomime!' This was a view that Shaw could share, having as Corno di Bassetto written that, rather than sit out another pantomime, 'I should choose death'.

Death was the subject of Shaw's pantomime. MacCarthy believed that in *Androcles and the Lion* Shaw had invented a new form, the nearest equivalent to which were 'those old miracle plays in which buffoonery and religion were mixed pell-mell together'. Shaw, who subtitled the work 'A Fable Play', turned his Roman arena into a variety theatre with a Call Boy announcing the successive entertainments: 'Number six. Retiarius versus Secutor . . . Number eleven! Gladiators and Christians! . . . Number twelve. The Christian for the new lion.' It was a flourish of Shavian extravaganza.

Androcles and the Lion was born of two other plays. The first was J. M. Barrie's *Peter Pan*, written for idealized children and then in its first great vogue. Max Beerbohm had drawn a caricature of Barrie 'reading it to a circle of elderly people and children,' Shaw remembered. 'The elderlies were beaming with enjoyment; the children were all asleep. I agreed, and wrote "Androcles" to show what a play for children should be like.'

The play was also intended as an antidote to Wilson Barrett's enormously popular religious melodrama *The Sign of the Cross*. Shaw had reported on this production in the *Saturday Review*. 'The whole drama lies in the spectacle of the hardy Roman prefect, a robust soldier and able general, gradually falling under the spell of a pale Christian girl, white and worn with spiritual ecstasy,' he wrote. '. . . As she gradually throws upon him the fascination of suffering and martyrdom, he loses his taste for wine; the courtesans at his orgies disgust him; heavenly visions obsess him; undreamed-of raptures of sacrifice, agony, and escape from the world to indescribable holiness and bliss tempt him; and finally he is seen, calm and noble, but stark mad, following the girl to her frightfully voluptuous death.'

'Depend on it,' G.B.S. alerted readers of the *Saturday Review*, 'we shall see Mr Wilson Barrett crucified yet.' Prior to crucifixion, he had been festooned with praise by the most celebrated writer of the day, author of *The Sorrows of Satan*, Marie Corelli, who had found in his 'choice and scholarly' language, 'the unpurchasable gift of genius'. 'I must either hold my tongue or else re-write the play to shew how it ought to be done,' Shaw responded. Holding his tongue was never in the Shavian line.

Wilson Barrett's scripture-drama had traded on the whip, the stake and the lions. But the audience at *Androcles* is forbidden these sensations. 'It is a crime to gratify that passion,' the Roman Captain tells Lavinia. Shaw renounces too the fairy-tales of Christianity which had been the substance of *The Sign of the Cross* but which Lavinia, as she waits for death, finds 'fading away into nothing'. 'Are you then going to die for nothing?' the exasperated Captain demands. And Lavinia answers that she is dying for something greater than dreams, something too big to give a name to. This is the same undefined decision to die as Dick Dudgeon made in *The Devil's Disciple*. The fact that Shaw's spokesman and spokeswoman for the Life Force should both volunteer for death and be saved only by the improbabilities of extravagant event-plots, reflects a pessimism that needed the constant somersaulting of paradox to turn up at the surface so courageously cheerful – like the Christian prisoners in *Androcles* who are 'determined to treat their hardships as a joke'.

After leaving the Fabian executive Shaw fixed his imagination on far-off solutions to political problems. To Beatrice Webb, still active in the Fabian campaigns, he seemed fantastically impractical. But this was what Shaw meant by the term 'religious'. He set his gaze over the horizon at a time when Christianity would have expressed itself politically as communism; when our system of punishments had been abandoned; when we had established an equal income for everyone and could trust our future to a sense of fellow-feeling with all living beings. This distant view, imbued by what Shaw understood as the essence of Christianity, was what moved him to take up Aulus Gellius' ancient legend of Androcles and set his play some sixteen hundred years off from the contemporary world.

In the Shavian sense Jesus was one of a number of Supermen who appear in history to show us the future of human evolution. It was a future for which Shaw was to make his appeal in the sombre Preface to *Androcles*: 'Why Not Give Christianity a Trial?' Jesus had been the first Christian, but by choosing a death that was not to be avoided by any Shavian manipulations of event-plot, he had become the last Christian too. 'Christianity was a growing thing which was finally suppressed by the crucifixion.' Since then all civilizations had been elaborate organizations for the prevention of Christianity.

Shaw's imaginary journey gave him the distance to comment dispassionately on the twentieth century. The Roman centurions are our own police and soldiers; the Emperor, who is 'a divine personage', is our monarchy; Lavinia and Androcles embody aspects of a religious spirit, but 'the saint is always embarrassed by finding that the dynamiter and the assassin, the thief and the libertine, make common cause with him'. The powerful and choleric Ferrovius, whose 'sensibilities are keen and violent to the verge of madness', is a human lion in the prime of life whose kingdom is very much of this world: which is to say he belongs to the present. In the hour of trial he reverts from passive Christianity to the warrior's faith that sees God in the sword. 'Mars overcame me and took back his own,' he says. 'The Christian god is not yet. He will come when Mars and I are dust; but meanwhile I must serve the gods that are, not the God that will be.'

As the chocolate soldier gets the better of the professional cavalry officer in *Arms and the Man*, so the 'small, thin, ridiculous little' Greek tailor Androcles triumphs over the Roman Emperor who behaves like the Mayor of Toy Town. Androcles is a Wellsian hero, recognized by Wells himself in a letter to Shaw as 'one of your greatest creations, the holy silly man . . . I could almost find it in me to try an imitation.' The dreadful monster of death is reconstituted as a nursery animal called Tommy, a frisky, clever, coquettish creature which 'purrs like a motor car' and transforms the ghastly arena of death into a dance hall. 'What a pretty liony-piony situation it is, with no thought at all for the realities of Christian martyrdom,' Stevie Smith later wrote. 'And underneath there beats a heart of fear that cannot allow suffering.'

In the lion that 'holds up his wounded paw and flaps it piteously before Androcles', Brigid Brophy has seen a likeness to the literary lion who once boasted to Beatrice Webb he was 'untameable' and who had then been tamed by Charlotte into marriage 'on one leg' and led off for a honeymoon on crutches.

But there is another way of seeing the paradisiacal dance that Androcles and this wonderful animal perform in the forest at the end of the Prologue. Androcles is a long-suffering married man 'addicted to Christianity' (as his wife Megaera complains) in much the same way as Shaw was addicted to work. The journey through the forest with his wife has all the tension and bickering that were beginning to fill the Shaws' holidays. When Androcles 'embraces the lion' and 'the two waltz rapturously round and round and finally away through the jungle', he is expressing Shaw's desire to be off on some escapade. When he triumphantly dances again with the lion at the end of the play in the Roman arena, his wife Megaera has gone – no one cares where. Her last words of the Prologue – 'you havnt danced with me for years; and now you go off dancing with a great brute beast that you havnt known for ten minutes' – are a comic variation of a complaint Shaw was soon to hear from Charlotte.

*

Early in 1912 there had been an eruption of labour disputes among railway workers, cotton operatives and dockers. The coal miners were on strike; feminists were breaking windows; there was fresh agitation in Ireland for Home Rule and new legislation covering military emergencies. Shaw exercised himself over everything: making political speeches at Coventry and Southampton; discussing Ireland with Winston Churchill and corresponding with Keir Hardie; writing on free speech for the *Fabian News* and, as an illustration of free speech, letting it be known in the *Saturday Review* that he would be prepared to shoot industrial malingerers. Malingerers, of course, were not miners or feminists, but ladies and gentlemen living the lives of social parasites on unearned incomes. Their social disadvantages of family, public schooling and vaccination had given them little chance.

There was little time for Charlotte. When alone they hardly spoke; when they did speak they broke out into quarrelling. Charlotte was making a selection of passages from Shaw's writings. By April the work for this compilation, arranged alphabetically under a hundred and ninety-five headings, was pretty well complete, and it was obvious to her that the time had come for a resounding holiday. She proposed that they go to Rome – and G.B.S. said no. In the fourteen years of their marriage, this was unprecedented. Charlotte made it clear that she needed a change; but still he would not go with her. What she needed, he believed, was what they both needed: a change from each other. How stupid, then, to change everything – air, language, meals, habits, country – except that main condition of their lives, and to intensify that condition violently by isolating themselves in a foreign place where they knew practically no one else. Their nerves would never stand it. Eventually she decided to sail alone. 'She took leave of me,' Shaw told Beatrice, ' . . . in a way that left Charles I taking leave of his family simply nowhere.'

Charlotte sailed on 12 April, and Shaw spent part of the time 'motoring about the country'. As if to punish G.B.S. Charlotte clung to her coughs and colds. G.B.S. sent her every two or three days a narrative-through-letters of his motoring tour round England. 'I feel fearfully incomplete, though I rather like the novelty of being a bachelor too,' he told her the day before he set out.

The motor party consisted of co-drivers Kilsby and G.B.S., and passengers Judy Gillmore (who was shortly to get married to a naval officer and give up her job as Shaw's secretary) and Granville Barker who was to catch up with them later. They advanced, sometimes bounding forwards at the rate of a hundred miles per day, by way of Cambridge, Peterborough and Lincoln, to York, where they stopped to wait for Barker.

Shaw and Barker together were like two schoolboys, endlessly and idiotically quoting Shakespeare, while Judy had developed into a fast and indefatigable walker. 'She flies up hills, leaving us gasping and trudging after in our elderly manner.' At Windermere they went by motor boat down the lake and were caught in the tempest and uproar of the hydro-aeroplanes which 'nearly blew us into the lake'. Then Barker suspended himself from a nail to calculate his weight and 'fell with an appalling bang on his back on the stones'.

They pressed on as far north as Carlisle where Judy went down with an overwhelming cold; Barker limped off home exhausted; Kilsby was left with his 'pet bag of scrap iron' doctoring the car; and Shaw was struck down by a vigorous lumbago which he sent off to Rome to compete with Charlotte's influenza. 'Lumbago is a fearful thing. Possibly it is appendicitis. Possibly spinal paralysis.'

The perils of road-journeying grew extreme when at a fork in the road Kilsby found himself steering while his employer reversed, and the car toppled over a bank: 'she slid down gracefully like the elephant on the chute at the Hippodrome – backwards – without the slightest shock, except one of surprise to Kilsby . . .' But nothing deterred Shaw. Producing a map, he pointed to a road which looked all that a road should be, but which soon ascended so steeply that the car again refused. Shaw and Judy jumped out and began searching for stones to arrest the descent, but the monster rolled backwards over Judy's finger and she fainted. 'Kilsby got his shoulders under her like a fireman; I heaped her up on him,' Shaw recounted to Charlotte, 'and he carried her up the hill to an open place where we laid her down and laid our by no means clean handkerchiefs, dipped in mountain water mud, on her forehead . . . This is a shocking country for motoring.'

Proceeding more cautiously they came to Blackpool, which was in festivity. Princess Louise had opened a new promenade and everything was illuminated, 'a triumph of crimson and gold fire'. This was Blackpool's first taste of royalty. Thousands of dancers moved to the tempo of band music over acres of parquet floor. 'The sentimental solemnity of the waltzing is beyond description,' Shaw exulted. 'The two-steps are more joyous; and the lancers approach, by comparison, delirium . . . Kilsby says he will bring Mrs Kilsby here for their next holiday.'

To heighten Judy's morale Shaw introduced her to a socialist hairdresser. 'Judy is all right,' he predicted. But shortly afterwards she admitted that she wanted to return to London. Since her naval officer was soon to be landing there 'I did not dissuade her,' Shaw wrote, and reluctantly put her on the train back.

So now there were two. They raced on to Edstaston where 'Mrs Chum' and her husband, the Colonel, put Shaw to work chopping down gorse, adding cramp to his other ailments. But: 'the place is looking delightful, all leaves & blossoms, and soft summer airs,' he informed Charlotte.

Charlotte returned on 22 May and Shaw met her at Southampton. Now that they were together, what had their separation shown? Charlotte could hardly have envied Judy's predicament which might so easily have been her own. G.B.S. had endured the same headaches, cramps, accidents, lumbagos as ever. Nevertheless, the difference had been Judy. 'The chief fun of the tour is her enjoyment of it,' he had explained to Charlotte. 'I never realized how very staid she is as secretary in Adelphi Terrace until I saw her gambolling like a rabbit or a lamb in the open.'

By early June two ingredients had been added to Shaw's career: a new woman and a new play. The new woman was Ann M. Elder. Approved of by Charlotte – she put G.B.S. in mind of 'a very attractive bullfinch' – Ann took Judy's place as his secretary and was to work with him for seven years before marrying.

The new play was *Pygmalion*. Shaw took it round that month to read to George Alexander. The professor of phonetics appealed to him so well that he told Shaw he could settle his own terms and name any actress he liked for the flower girl – except the actress for whom Shaw had written it, Mrs Patrick Campbell. 'I'd rather die,' he appealed to Shaw. But Shaw had set his heart on her. Eliza Doolittle was as good a fit for Stella Campbell as Lady Cicely had been for Ellen Terry: 'for I am a good ladies' tailor, whatever my shortcomings may be'.

5

DEAREST LIAR

> I badly need some sort of humanizing . . . I have loved – and have survived it . . . I shall never quite get over it.
>
> Shaw to Mrs Patrick Campbell (20 March 1913, 8 February 1914, 23 October 1912)

He had been 'violently in love' with Mrs Patrick Campbell from the start: and fearfully on his guard. Her sexual power was more compelling than Ellen Terry's charm, and when he used it as a warning to Janet Achurch he had been warning himself.

He had seen her in many plays. 'It is impossible not to feel that those haunting eyes are brooding on a momentous past, and the parted lips anticipating a thrilling imminent future . . . Mrs Patrick Campbell is a wonderful woman.' She had been 'wonderful' as Juliet, though unable to act the part; and a disquietingly mad Ophelia; and he had been delighted by her also as the heroine of 'the celestial bed' in *Nelson's Enchantress*. 'You will tell me, no doubt, that Mrs Patrick Campbell cannot act,' he lectured his *Saturday Review* readers. 'Who said she could? – who wants her to act? . . . Go and see her move, stand, speak, look, kneel – go and breathe the magic atmosphere that is created by the grace of all these deeds.' She would cast an extraordinary glamour round such plays as *The Second Mrs Tanqueray* or *The Notorious Mrs Ebbsmith*. 'Clearly there must be a great tragedy somewhere in the immediate neighbourhood,' Shaw concluded. ' . . . But Mr Pinero has hardly anything to do with it.'

Shaw was envious of Pinero. He wanted Mrs Pat for his own play-world. He had written his Cleopatra for her, but she only read the copyright performance. She was better formed for the mature Cleopatra of Shakespeare's world than Shaw's marvellous child. *Caesar and Cleopatra* had been a dramatization of their relationship thus far as critic and actress. The dazzled Caesar who retains his full self-possession is G.B.S., sworn critic of the *Saturday Review*, who names Mrs Pat as Circe, and states his intention of making 'the best attempt I can to be Ulysses'. He believed that he had the antidote to romance; that he could, like Ulysses, drink from the cup unharmed – and without harming others. He wanted to re-enact the Greek legend, with no descent to Hades before sailing on escorted by favourable winds. He wanted to serenade his Circe, through his acts on stage – to direct her, fill her with his words.

As early as September 1897 everything 'has been driven clean out of my head by a play I want to write . . . in which he [Forbes-Robertson] shall be a west end gentleman and she an east end dona in an apron and three orange and red ostrich feathers'. Fifteen years later he wrote this play. The liaison between Forbes-Robertson and his 'rapscallionly flower girl' as Shaw had called her was long over, and Mrs Pat had returned briefly to the St James's. Sir George Alexander would have made as good a West End gentleman as Sir Johnston Forbes-Robertson: but what mattered to Shaw was that Mrs Pat should become the cockney flower girl: a Galatea to his Pygmalion.

But would she stand for such a vulgar role? Not daring to offer it to her directly, he formed a stratagem. This involved Mrs Pat's close friend Edith Lyttelton at whose house he arranged to read his play on 26 June 1912, when Mrs Pat was expected to be present. She came: heard Shaw's amazingly awful cries of 'Nah-ow' and even 'Ah-ah-ah-ow-ow-ow-ow!'; recognized his clever mimicry of her own voice: and realized that this part of Eliza Doolittle was meant for her. She might have interrupted. She could have left. But Shaw read with spellbinding power and she listened.

Next day she wrote to thank him for 'thinking I can be your pretty slut' and inviting him to come and discuss the business proposals for *Pygmalion*. 'I wonder if I could please you,' she wrote. ' . . . We said so little yesterday. I mustn't lose time – my days are numbered surely.'

He went at once to her house in Kensington Square. It was now her turn to put forth spells. Shaw scorned the danger. But taking his hand she touched his fingers against her bosom and 'I fell head over heels in love with her,' he confessed to Granville Barker, ' – violently and exquisitely in love – before I knew that I was thinking about anything but business.' They were together for an hour. He walked on air all afternoon and the next day 'as if my next birthday were my twentieth,' he told Ellen Terry. His beard was going white, he was on the verge of fifty-six but 'I have not yet grown up'. She was forty-seven and still beautiful. 'Is there no age limit?' he wondered. He was determined, however, that his infatuation should last no longer than a day, or perhaps two, and by the end of the month declared that G.B.S. was himself again. 'I did not believe that I had that left in me,' he acknowledged in a letter to Mrs Pat – or Stella as he was to call her. 'I am all right now, down on earth again with all my cymbals and side drums and blaring vulgarities in full blast; but it would be meanly cowardly to pretend that you are not a very wonderful lady, or that the spell did not work most enchantingly on me for fully 12 hours.'

Shaw's recovery was signalled by a frightful migraine and pages of 'horrid' business practicalities about producing *Pygmalion* 'behind which my poor timid little soul hides'. Yet his feelings kept interrupting his professional literary manner. 'I wish I could fall in love without telling everybody,' he wrote. He told Lillah and Barker; he told Barrie, Edith Lyttelton, Ellen Terry, Lady Gregory . . . and he told Charlotte. 'I must now go and read this to Charlotte,' he concluded one of his letters to Stella. 'My love affairs are her unfailing amusement: all their tenderness recoils finally on herself.'

*

Charlotte had already experienced enough recoil over the business of Erica Cotterill. G.B.S. had encouraged that young girl disgracefully, she sometimes thought. They had actually been forced to threaten her with the police. But Shaw felt Charlotte's accusations were unjust. Was it his fault that, having received his advice to 'join some Socialist Society', Erica had become a Fabian and followed him devotedly back from his lectures to Adelphi Terrace? Could he seriously be blamed for not having foreseen that, after accepting tickets to his plays, she would write a play herself in which the heroine declares her passion to have 'some gorgeous thing to live for and love with every atom of my whole soul', and that she would point to G.B.S. as this 'gorgeous thing' and hand the play to Charlotte? Had he acted wrongly by informing Erica that her letters (which he scrupulously showed his wife) were illegible, simply because she was to go off, employ a printer, and begin publishing her correspondence to him as a series of 'accounts' totalling a quarter of a million words, dedicated to Shaw 'whom I love'? And where was the harm in inviting her to lunch and introducing her to some friends – unless it had lain in her decision to camp in the woods nearby and come racing up to Ayot on her motor-bicycle under the trance-like conviction that Charlotte's house belonged to her? No: he had done no wrong.

Yet her exasperating naïveté touched him at times with its loneliness and oddity so that, after almost seven agonizing years, he was still locked in correspondence with her in the summer of 1912. Her hypnotic style, undivided, ecstatic, insistent, was as unstoppable as his own. She wrote in one key identified by Shaw as E flat minor. This was a letter missing from the Alpha and Omega of his own prose. Her pages were emotional orgasms: she lived upon the page as if it were her body. Reluctantly he counselled her to adopt literature as a profession. Shaw would have to guide her.

He sent for her: bullied her with his high-speed opinions. But: 'I didnt want to be scolded,' she wrote, 'I wanted to be loved, and perhaps I nearly cried.' Then something happened. He pulled away, and laughed. 'What would have come if you had not held me back and I had knelt down to you?' she wanted to know. 'Would you have laughed then? . . . would you have felt nothing . . . and what would have come if you had felt it? . . . were you hidden deep from your conscious mind *afraid* of feeling it?'

He sent her away: and started his correspondence course. 'Now listen to me.' She was an adult not a baby; strong not weak; and exquisite. But everything was made impossible by her nymphomania. He pointed to his wife, and the iron laws of domestic honour. Then he explained about seducers and socialist orators; and then about divine sparks and ultimate goals. And after the explanations poured forth the advice. She should marry; she should marry as quickly as possible. Marriage was an acquired taste, but if she chose someone by the same rule as (for example) she might choose a horse, someone of the right size, shape, complexion and (in the horsedealer's sense) without vices, she could become fond of him – after which she could put her energy into work. Then after the advice came the education. 'When an adult woman and an adult man caress one another, the result is entirely different from the result of your kissing your mother.' The person to whom she behaved in that perfectly happy way would lose all power of doing anything but the thing that would result in her having a baby. 'People who do these natural things are socially impossible.'

But Erica *was* socially impossible and the woman least fitted in the world to be Eliza Doolittle to his Henry Higgins. 'You hardly yet know how to behave yourself at all,' he complained. He identified Erica with Sonny. He had been 'just as shy & sensitive as you are'. So now he tried to give this 'terrified child' all the parental help he had missed himself. But no amount of Shavian coaching could change her. For she had her own insights: 'youre a child all the while acting that youre a man,' she countered. '*Why* do you act – what *use* is it – it deceives no deep parts . . .

'in all the whole stream of people that have come out of you theres not one that moves me first and last for itself – you watch and study and get behind and master things in them . . . and then you suddenly do a thing – you suddenly *use them* . . . *consciously* youre using them to expose some evil or falsehood or whatever its chosen to be called . . . cant you feel that everything of any kind that comes from you, work speeches plays letters . . . comes *at its root* from a pose or attitude of some kind.'

Erica would not smarten up her writing, or learn her biology, or master the simplest obligations of society. She wanted the creative fire to leap into activity within their bodies. The strain was too much. 'I would not stand it from Cleopatra herself.'

But, in Stella Campbell, he had become involved with a modern Cleopatra, and to Charlotte's mind there was no telling what he would not stand. Over the Erica Cotterill affair, she had interceded by sending a letter (drafted by G.B.S.) forbidding the girl her house and her husband. To separate him from Mrs Pat she reintroduced their motoring holidays with her sister and Kilsby on the Continent. This time Shaw could not refuse, and they started on 27 July.

*

'All I ask is to have my own way in everything,' Shaw had reasoned with Stella, 'and to see my Liza as often as possible.' Charlotte's tactics in removing G.B.S. were somewhat nullified when Stella's taxi had 'a blinding bang' with another vehicle and she decided to recover in France, leaving three days after the Shaws. For part of August they were tantalizingly close. 'I have only to push on to Tresenda,' Shaw wrote from Bad Kissingen, 'turn to the right, skirt Lake Como, hurry through Milan, dash through the Little St Bernard (being myself the Great St Bernard), make through Albertville to Chambery, and then be in your arms in an hour. But back I must turn for all that, leaving your arms empty.'

No one had their way that summer. The waters at Aix and the air of Chamonix were of little benefit to Stella who arrived back in London feeling less well than when she set out. Meanwhile, the tonics in Bad Kissingen proved poisonous to G.B.S. – one mouthful and he made a dash for the Alps, and at fall of evening on 6 August, ruptured the car. This was largely Stella's fault since, instead of minding the road Shaw had filled his head with a thousand letters he wanted to write her with 'millions of additional verses'.

They returned to Bad Kissingen and deposited the two women for three further weeks of voluptuous cures. Charlotte 'gasps in rarefied air whilst her sister wallows in mud,' Shaw notified Stella. '. . . Charlotte wants to get thin; and her sister wants to get plump; so they have both agreed to be asthmatic and have treatments.'

The two men then launched themselves across Europe until, ploughing through ruts of limestone mud, the car 'seemed to get its teeth full of paving stones . . . and finally reduced us . . . to admit that our journey was over . . . Tomorrow we shall attach a couple of brewery horses to her and have her hauled to the railway station.'

While the car was being put to rights at Luneville, Shaw and Kilsby waited twenty-seven kilometres off at Nancy where G.B.S. corrected the proofs of a new Prologue to *Caesar and Cleopatra*, and made final revisions to his study of marital infidelity, *Overruled*. 'It has an air of being outrageous,' he advised Charlotte; 'but it really does drive in its moral, which is that four reasonably amiable people in a matrimonial difficulty find themselves with nothing to guide them but a morality which will not work.'

His letters to Charlotte were regular, amusing, friendly, informative – he even asks her to send a rough proof of *Pygmalion* to Mrs Pat who 'now says that her notion of bliss is to travel for a year and have a letter from me every week'. Shaw's letters to Stella were of a kind that Charlotte had never received. 'Stella, do not ever bully me: you don't know how easily frightened I am,' he wrote from Nancy. '. . . Let us take life as it comes, and love and hate and work without dramatizing it more than we can help.' But it was impossible for Shaw not to dramatize it. He had been born with the instinct to show off which his mother, feeling no pride in his tricks, had stifled. His hunger for love fed on his imagination and found consummation in his dreams. 'If you knew all the adventures we have had already in the imaginary world which is my real world,' he told Stella, 'you would blush to the remotest contours of your enchanting person.' Stella fulfilled an important adolescent need in Shaw untended by the years of his marriage. 'You are a figure from the dreams of my boyhood,' he told her. Their relationship took him back to 'the indescribable heartbreak of Ireland' and reminded him of that 'bewitching Calypso' with the beautiful 'black tresses' with whom he had fallen in love shortly before leaving Dublin. 'Once, in my calfish teens,' he told Stella, 'I fell in love with a lady of your complexion; and she, good woman, having a sister to provide for, set to work to marry me to the sister.'

The Calypso whom he originally loved was married and, being taken care of in reality, able to inhabit his imagination freely. His retreat from the sister was in effect a flight from reality, with which his emotions could not cope. But Stella, alias Mrs Pat, seemed to represent both sisters and threatened to bring the real and his imaginary worlds into collision. His letters to Stella have none of the artistry of the Ellen Terry correspondence: Shaw's relationship with Ellen had been on paper. But to Stella 'I dont know why: I cant write. Writing is no use . . . It is past letter writing with me. There are things one cannot put on paper . . . All that paper love is nothing: the real thing is in the marrow of my bones and the roots of my nerves.' The spoken not the written word was Stella's art ('I have always been an odious letter writer'). Their love affair therefore 'was acted, not written' and the correspondence incidental. But 'I must break myself of this,' he wrote.

Stella 'was the beauty of the moonlight,' wrote Rebecca West, 'as Ellen Terry was the beauty of the sunlight'. Like him, she was reckless yet fundamentally respectable. He was attracted by strong women, she to weak men. She had married Patrick Campbell when she was twenty and pregnant. It seemed romantic, but however handsome he looked Patrick

Campbell was not a creature of romance. After his death she had not remarried, but recently, unknown to Shaw, involved herself with a well-connected, insolvent officer, 'a bit short on brains', called George Cornwallis-West, unhappily married to the famous American beauty Jennie Jerome, widow of Lord Randolph Churchill.

Mrs Pat wanted to be loved and she wanted to act great roles; but she was impossible to live with and almost impossible to act with. The late Victorian and Edwardian theatre had very few good roles for actresses. She needed a playwright who believed in the equality of women and men in the theatre to write for her. But though Shaw's child-play made her laugh, so that she nicknamed him Joey after Grimaldi the clown; and though she was attentive to the commercial undertones of what he wrote to her, she underrated the emotional fires she had lit up in him.

But it was a delightful game and Stella played it beautifully. As for Shaw, he was feeling his part so deeply he sometimes forgot they were on stage. 'Playing Romeo has given me an ill-divining soul,' he told Edith Lyttelton: 'I cannot foresee the happy ending.'

*

By the time they scrambled back to England, Shaw had made up his mind to sell the car. It was four years old, had covered 70,000 miles, and gave him lumbago. But being fond of it, he postponed the sale for another eleven years and added to his stable a brisk little motor-bicycle in green enamel. This machine which he rode 'like a thunderbolt' suited his new spirit of recklessness which seemed to gain in response to everyone else's illness. Stella was confined to bed: Charlotte had fallen down; neither seemed able to recover from their continental cures.

More serious still was his mother's illness. While at Nancy he had heard from his sister Lucy that 'the Mar' had suffered a stroke. Over the next six months, she had two more strokes. She had continued into her seventies as a peppery music teacher at the North London Collegiate School for Girls; and she had continued living at 29 Fitzroy Square until the lease gave out, when Shaw bought for her the lease of 8 Park Village West, near Regent's Park. In her retirement she became economically more dependent on G.B.S., as did Lucy. 'I have now stock enough of my own to secure my mother & sister against all contingencies,' Shaw told Beatrice Webb that summer. He wanted to revoke the marriage settlement which, should he die first (in a car or motor-bicycle accident perhaps), made his family dependent on his wife. It was inappropriate, especially since they disliked Charlotte. Not that Bessie and Lucy seemed troubled: they spared George their gratitude. However hard he worked he was still 'a dreadful procrastinator' to his mother and a 'prosperous idler' to his sister.

Yet Lucy could not help associating herself with her brother's success. She liked to claim that he stole his best witticisms from her. Fate ('with her usual inscrutable workings and apparent lack of discrimination as to deserts') had raised up the brother and 'dealt her blows' to the sister. It was difficult not to feel bitter. 'The good things of this world which have poured into George's lap in the last three or four years are rubbing the sharp edges and crisp individuality off his intellect,' she cautioned a friend. '. . . My worst dread about him is that he may become commonplace – I could stand anything but that. I still wish for his own sake that he had not married.' Such wishes derived from the sense of insult she felt after the break-up of her marriage. In her early forties she had got pneumonia, then pleurisy, 'and the result is tuberculosis'. She had spent her convalescence in Jenny Patterson's house. When the doctor broke the news to her that she might be going to die, her reaction had been 'absolute relief, rest and even exaltation'.

There seemed little to live for. She had lost her voice. For almost a decade she exiled herself in Germany while her husband, Charles Butterfield, carried on in London. Then, one October evening in 1908 shortly after returning to England, she had been stopped in the foyer of the Coronet Theatre, Notting Hill, and told by the manager, Eade Montefiore, that her husband had been living with an actress during Lucy's years abroad. 'Although I had taxed him with almost every failing a man could have, I never for one moment suspected him of infidelity.'

Shaw advised divorce and paid the costs – £91 13s. 8d. (equivalent to £4,200 in 1997) – needed to prevent Charles Butterfield from contesting the action. 'I can find money for you as soon as you want it,' he told her early in 1910. She needed some money to pursue good health. She spent much time by the sea but kept coming back to her mother's Park Village house.

Mother and daughter had a patchy but strong relationship. Bessie was 'a great old war horse' and could never see what Lucy was making such a fuss about. A disappointing career, a broken marriage, chronic ill-health, almost no money – these were hardly things to complain of. As for herself, Bessie put her trust in spiritualism. She preferred her friends when dead and would spend an hour each day chatting to them at the ouija board. They liked to tell her of the death of other friends: and she would hurry out for the wreaths. They told her, too, what she suspected: that the sort of success which had come to George 'doesn't count for anything up here'. Lucy too experimented with the planchette and received some extraordinary communications from Rajah Mahattan,

Knight Oliphant, Master Bariole and other unknown exotics on the subject of the planet Mars which she sent, with disappointing results, to the Astronomer Royal. Bessie when 'influenced' filled the house with drawings though she could hardly hold a pencil at other times. G.B.S. didn't trouble Bessie with his scepticism. But he had been somewhat useless to his mother, as men were. No wonder she had kept no 'photo of my son as a boy or child,' as she informed Archibald Henderson. '. . . Nor have I a single letter.'

Now as she lay dying she shocked everyone, getting 'ridiculously cured . . . by a Christian Scientist who broke into the house and meditated on her whilst she slept,' Shaw reported. This cure did not prevent her death. Lucy was with her most of the time, and George (who came and went) provided two nurses. 'I have been watching her trying to die for five weeks since the last seizure,' Lucy wrote. 'Her body and all her organs are so sound that she seems unable to get away . . . the strain has been terrible.' Shaw too, in his fashion, felt the strain: 'my mother is dying, they say, but *wont* die – makes nothing of strokes – throws them off as other women throw off sneezing fits,' he wrote to Lady Gregory. Lucy had reported on 6 December that 'it is a question of days or even hours now', but Bessie held on for another ten weeks. On 19 February 1913 Lucy telegraphed George with the news: 'All over.'

To Lucy it seemed as if all was over for her too. 'My mother's exit has made an astonishing abyss in our little kingdom,' she told a friend. '. . . consciously and subconsciously she guided and influenced everything I ever did. I feel as if the rock had vanished from under my house and I was tumbling about in the sand.' When her mother's body was taken from the house Lucy 'completely broke to pieces'. George put her in the care of a chest specialist and he insisted that she stay in bed. 'A halt had to be called if I did not want to follow Mama,' Lucy wrote, 'which I certainly did.'

She was not well enough to go to the funeral service and cremation at Golders Green on 22 February. Four people turned up: the chaplain, the undertaker, Shaw and Barker – whose presence revived the rumour that he was Shaw's natural son.

The only person to whom Shaw could write about this day was Stella 'who understands about one's mother, and other things'. The words of the burial service had been altered a little for a cremation. 'A door opened in the wall; and the violet coffin mysteriously passed out through it and vanished as it closed,' he told her. '. . . I went behind the scenes at the end of the service and saw the real thing . . . it is wonderful.

'I found there the violet coffin opposite another door, a real unmistakeable furnace door. When it lifted there was a plain chamber of cement and firebrick. No heat, no noise, no roaring draught. No flame. No fuel. It looked cool, clean, sunny, though no sun could get there. You would have walked in or put your hand in without misgiving. Then the violet coffin moved again and went in, feet first, And behold! The feet burst miraculously into streaming ribbons of garnet colored lovely flame, smokeless and eager, like pentecostal tongues, and as the whole coffin passed in it sprang into flame all over; and my mother became that beautiful fire.'

They were told they should return in thirty minutes. 'When we returned we looked down through an opening in the floor to a lower floor close below,' Shaw wrote that night to Stella. 'There we saw a roomy kitchen, with a big cement table and two cooks busy at it.

'They had little tongs in their hands, and they were deftly and busily picking nails and scraps of coffin handles out of Mamma's dainty little heap of ashes and samples of bone. Mamma herself being at the moment leaning over beside me, shaking with laughter. They swept her up into a sieve, and shook her out; so that there was a heap of dust and a heap of calcined bone scraps. And Mamma said in my ear, "Which of the two heaps is me, I wonder!" '

For the first time she was behaving as her son commanded. The relief was enormous. He realized how little he had known her. They made dust of the bone scraps, then scattered the remains over a flower bed. The day had had some 'wildly funny' moments and been 'a complete success'. He made a note to buy some shares in the cremation business. That afternoon he drove to Oxford and at Notting Hill Gate (the car being in 'a merry mood') 'accomplished a most amazing skid, swivelling right round across the road one way and then back the other, but fortunately not hitting anything . . .'

*

His mother's death seemed to promise him emergence from the long shadow of his Dublin childhood, as his sea holidays at Dalkey had once done. To Stella 'I opened the grave of my childhood'. He expected a miraculous resurrection. Stella became everything he had once looked for in Lucinda Elizabeth Shaw and tried to replace with Alice Lockett, Jenny Patterson, Florence Farr, Janet Achurch and Charlotte too. She was his Virgin Mother and his Dark Lady, his playmate and working-partner, his magical friend. He had become a mass of wants that now rushed out towards her. He wanted to 'have a woman's love on the same terms as a child's,' he implored, '... to hear tones in a human voice that I have never heard before, to have it taken for granted that I am a child and want to be happy ... and suddenly find myself in the arms of a mother – a young mother, and with a child in my own arms who is yet a woman: all this plunges me into the coldest terror as if I were suddenly in the air thousands of feet above the rocks or the sea ... And yet I am happy, as madmen are ...'

Stella's mysterious illness heightened their affair. She wrote saying that the doctor had forbidden her to see anyone except himself. He would go galloping up the stairs, three at a time, with beard flying, to 'my most agitating heart's darling'. He was 'most frightfully in love with you'. Sitting by the bed, he was allowed to put his arms round her waist, and they would kiss and kiss.

Sometimes, on account of her illness, she begged him to 'be patient with me', then she urged him on: 'I think if you don't come and see me rather soon there won't be me to see.' He went backwards and forwards. 'I love you for ever and ever and ever, Stella,' he wrote. Her deteriorating health made him desperately anxious. 'I will get into the bed myself and we shall perish together scandalously.'

Early in 1913 she had entered a nursing home in Hinde Street for an exploratory operation. Shaw continued to visit her whenever possible. At his most sympathetic, he charmed and flattered her, made her smile, made her forget the illness and the operation. 'Himself living in dreams,' she testified, 'he made a dream-world for me.' In return she let him play 'in the nursery of my heart' where he felt happy beyond reason – 'I shall never be unhappy again.' Had she been well perhaps she might not have let their fantasy-attachment go so far, but it was now too late, she acknowledged, 'to do anything but *accept* you and *love* you'. He basked in this acceptance. 'I have slipped out of the real world,' he told her.

But Stella never lost sight, as Shaw seemed to, of the traps in their relationship. Shaw wished to remain loyal to Charlotte while loving Stella. 'I throw my desperate hands to heaven and ask why one cannot make one beloved woman happy without sacrificing another,' he cried out. He recognized that Charlotte, with her sensitiveness, her susceptibility to worry, needed protection; and he had tried to explain this to Stella. Only that February Charlotte had said that she never knew where George spent his afternoons. Once she had given no thought to such things. Now she was full of doubts. So he told her what the rest of London already seemed to know: that he had been at Stella's bedside.

Charlotte was devastated. Shaw had not continued reading to her his correspondence with Stella. His wish to protect her seemed no more to Charlotte, however, than the keeping of a guilty secret. No wonder she had felt so anxious, had lain gasping in bed with asthma and bronchitis. She refused to meet this 'middleaged minx' or leave calling cards on her – and this offended Mrs Pat's sense of propriety. She began to grow hostile to what she called the 'suffragette' figure of Shaw's wife.

Early in March Stella left the nursing home and went to convalesce in Brighton. As she began to recover so the romance clouded. She resented this marriage-attachment of 'Mr and Mrs Mouse' and chided Shaw on his timidity. His advances could have led to love-making if – 'if only you'd eat red steaks and drink beer your spirit would be meet, I mean meet to mate – no I dont mean that . . .' But she did mean it. Since Shaw's 'Mother is dead & Charlotte is your wife I'll be your grandmother,' she mocked him.

'Dearest Liar,' Shaw addressed Stella, not wishing to believe some of the things she was saying to him. There was no need for him to warn her against falling in love with him as he had warned other women. He sensed that she could beat him at his own game 'and revenge his earlier victims'. He knew the unhappiness he risked. But 'I am still in love with Stella . . . Cannot help it,' he found himself writing, '. . . my first defeat, and my first success.'

Late in March Shaw and Charlotte left for two weeks in Ireland. It seemed a safe move: except that in this country of his childhood, 'all the old longing for beauty and blessing get stirred up in me' so that he switched his emotional focus back to 'my girl, my beauty, my darling, barefooted, dusty petticoated, or my mother of angels, or a dozen lovely wild things . . .'

They were staying not far from Dublin with Horace Plunkett, founder of the agricultural co-operative movement in Ireland, who 'devoted his life to the service of his fellow-creatures collectively; and personally . . . disliked them all,' G.B.S. later recalled. ' . . . He remained a bachelor for the sake of Lady Fingal, and was unquestionably in love with her; yet I never felt convinced that he quite liked her.' There seemed nothing for G.B.S. to do but 'work, work, work', and this now pleased Charlotte who suddenly got well and, he wrote to Stella, 'changed from a fiend into a green-eyed mermaid, smiling & fascinating & dressing in diamonds & generally dispensing charm and childish happiness . . . Dont grudge her.'

But Stella had not been pleased by Shaw's efforts to strike some balance between the two women 'I was born to love'. That April, after they had all returned to London, she began to exploit what she saw as the limitation of Charlotte's marriage to G.B.S.: its childlessness. Stella knew that Shaw felt a reverence before the fact of childbirth. 'A sort of pang goes through me from the base of my heart down to my very entrails,' he had written to Sylvia Brooke, Ranee of Sarawak, when she was pregnant with her first child. '. . . you are going to be torn to pieces and come to life again with a terrible contempt for fragile male things that would be broken by such creative miracles.'

Shaw had denied himself a share in this miracle, and been joined by Charlotte in a conspiracy of denial they called their marriage. Stella, who had 'suffered her suffering' and given birth to a son and daughter while her husband was alive, now informed Shaw that 'I could have 6 more children' when all he apparently wanted to create with her was a new play. Sometimes Stella could be merciless over his 'being addicted to work and neglecting your hearts love'.

Shaw had warned her that only on paper was he brave. Sometimes she felt pinned to his sheets of paper like a Painted Lady. She seemed to exist only in the make-believe of his mind. 'I think you are mad,' she told him. 'I think I am pretending to be what it amuses you to think I am.' He had been generous with offers of money, but she had no status in his life – all that belonged to Charlotte; and she had no future.

In the second week of June, Stella summoned Shaw to her house and told him that she was thinking of marrying George Cornwallis-West. He had touched her with his helplessness and dependence when Shaw had merely been amusing: besides he was prepared to divorce his wife and Shaw was not.

In the train travelling back to Ayot that night Shaw wrote that Stella's marriage to 'the other George' would cut him off for ever from what was still young in his humanity. 'I say he is young and I am old; so let him wait until I am tired of you,' he wrote. '. . . It is impossible that I should not tire soon: nothing so wonderful could last . . . I will hurry through my dream as fast as I can; only let me have my dream out.'

It was a relief to Shaw to leave the country at the end of the month and spend a few days in Germany with Granville Barker. Though there were still delightful moments with Stella – making up verses for her (though he was lost for any rhyme to her name except umbrella), or teaching her to jump from the ground on to a bench in Richmond Park as part of her convalescence – he had felt 'all torn to bits' behaving so artificially with Charlotte. She had accidentally come upon a list of meetings mischievously entered by Stella in Shaw's pocket diary and there were dreadful scenes. Another time Charlotte had caught him speaking to her on the telephone and flared up into an appalling rage. Seeing someone suffer like this gave Shaw 'a sort of angina pectoris,' he told Stella. '. . . It hurts me miserably . . . I must, it seems, murder myself or else murder her.'

To help her resist these lacerating scenes Charlotte had taken up with a spiritual healer. James Porter Mills was a bad-tempered old man who had travelled the world perfecting what he called the 'Teaching'. His personality had a profound effect on Charlotte. She felt a compulsion to apply his principles, whatever they might be, to the painful upheaval of her emotions. The result was that, in the middle of some terrible quarrels with G.B.S., she would convulsively recover her balance, smile dizzily, and be changed back into 'the happy consort of an easygoing man'. But damage had been done, and in the priority she gave to Dr Mills's 'Teaching' over Fabianism and the Life Force, Charlotte was being unfaithful to G.B.S. in the only way open to her.

'This is a terrific romance,' remarked J. M. Barrie, 'and at last Shaw can blush.' Living opposite G.B.S. in Adelphi Terrace, Barrie witnessed Mrs Pat courting them both for plays. That summer she decided to appear in Barrie's *The Adored One* which was to open in September – and Shaw was grateful. To go into rehearsals now with Stella in *Pygmalion* would 'probably kill me,' he had calculated. It was as much as he could do to go round to her house on his return from Germany. But she shut the door in his face. He had thought that he could only experience the suffering of others, never his own. But now he felt it, and he was shocked. A little later that July, he found to his astonishment that he was crying. Everything except his adoration of Stella seemed tedious. 'This clown misses Joey,' she relented. But she must be alone to study the Barrie play. 'I will hide in the sands somewhere.'

'When I am solitary you are always with me,' he answered. 'When you are solitary by the sea, where shall I be?' She did not want him with her. 'Its getting difficult not to love you more than I ought to love you,' she reassured him. ' . . . But by the sea I must be alone – you know.'

He did not want to know. On the afternoon of 8 August he took Charlotte to Liverpool Street Station to catch the boat train for Marseilles. He intended to join her at the end of the month for a six-week tour of France. On leaving the station he went straight down to the Kent coast where he knew Stella had borrowed the theatrical producer Nigel Playfair's cottage at Ramsgate. But she was not there. Answering the door late that night, the Playfairs' housekeeper informed him that Mrs Campbell, her maid, chauffeur and dog, had gone to the Guildford Hotel on Sandwich Bay. Shaw walked off into the dark, an exhausted figure in his Norfolk jacket, making his way back across the sands.

Stella was not pleased to see him next morning. He had made his entrance in the wrong scene. The Guildford Hotel was far from being the private tomb of love they had created in her London bedroom. She intended to marry George Cornwallis-West and Shaw's presence could be compromising. 'Please will you go back to London today,' she wrote to him, ' – or go wherever you like but dont stay here – If you wont go I must . . . Please dont make me despise you.'

But Shaw would not go. He had come so far and there would never be another chance like this, with Charlotte out of the country – a chance to spend some days with Stella and perhaps one or two nights. After reading the note he searched the hotel and went looking for her in the darkness along the sands. Eventually he found her and they ordered a nightcap. Tired herself, Stella noticed with irritation how sleepy he was. They arranged to meet next morning before breakfast for a bathe in the sea – though not before eight o'clock, she insisted. But by half-past seven she was speeding along the coast, with her chauffeur, maid and dog, towards Littlestone-on-Sea. At eight o'clock punctually Shaw knocked at her bedroom door. 'Come & bathe,' he called. A cheerful chambermaid answered, telling him that they had gone – and he pretended to have muddled the dates. She had left him a note: 'Goodbye. I am still tired – you were more fit for a journey than I – .'

He returned to his room and tried to write away his distress. 'I am deeply, deeply, deeply wounded . . . I cannot bring you peace, or rest, or even fun.' The world was horribly changed. He looked up at her room where he had imagined happiness, and there was nothing. 'I shall die of thirst after all.' The truth was inescapable. Of his fifty-seven years 'I have suffered 20 and worked 37'. 'Then I had a moment's happiness: I almost condescended to romance. I risked the breaking of deep roots and sanctified ties . . .' and now, on that desolate strand, 'what have I shrunk into?'

He kept mailing letters to Stella wherever she was: again that night ('Sandwich. Darkness') then next morning ('Another day that might have been a day!') and after he returned to London ('back from the land of broken promise'). It seemed to him that she had been gratuitously cruel, and he turned all the blame on her. She used her sex appeal irresponsibly, furtively, without care. He felt the need of some monstrous retribution. 'I have not said enough vile things to you.'

But Shaw's rhetoric was not hurtful for, as Stella understood, 'you have no claws'. Nevertheless she needed to defend her action, and her retaliation was more piercing than anything he had written to her. 'No daughters to relieve your cravings – no babies to stop your satirical chatterings, why should I pay for all your shortcomings,' she demanded. ' . . . You lost me because you never found me – I who have nothing but my little lamp and flame – you would blow it out with your bellows of self.' Yet the depth of his feelings startled her, and she felt his suffering as he had felt Charlotte's. 'You are trying to break my heart with your letters,' she appealed. ' . . . What other thing was there for me to do? I had to behave like a man.'

Because they were 'useless, these letters; the wound will not heal', she agreed to see him once they were both back in London. He occupied himself as best he could, swimming at the Royal Automobile Club, visiting the zoo and stroking a lion as part of the preparation for Granville Barker's production of *Androcles*. He was to join Charlotte in France in the second week of September and he welcomed this. For the romance with Stella had confirmed all his beliefs about love. It was a hideous business: 'the quantity of Love that an ordinary person can stand without serious damage,' he measured, 'is about 10 minutes in 50 years.'

THIRTEEN

I

CONCERNING FAME AND ANONYMITY

I am a Mr Jorkins on the New Statesman; Clifford Sharp is Mr Spenlow.
Shaw to St John Ervine (1912)

Beatrice Webb was one of those who had viewed this emotional business between G.B.S. and his 'somewhat elderly witch' with distaste. Charlotte had told her all about it: and the two women shook their heads.

Beatrice, in her fashion, felt caught up in the wreckage of this affair. During the summer of 1912, she had begun appealing to G.B.S. to help her and Sidney launch a new Fabian weekly journal. But he had displayed little enthusiasm. Unless they established in the mind of the railway traveller, he told them, a certainty that he would be amused and interested by their paper for the next hour of his journey they would never capture the sixpenny public.

It was as bait for this public that Beatrice wanted Shaw's name as a regular contributor. Yet he was reluctant to give up the time and energy. He would hand over some money, but 'I wont write'. He believed they were too old. 'Unless you can find a team of young lions . . . and give them their heads, the job cannot be done,' he answered Beatrice. '. . . I should not serve you by attempting to lag superfluous on the stage I once adorned.'

But Beatrice persisted. The *New Statesman*, as it came to be called, was to be a platform for the reformist middle class, and her and Sidney's last venture before their retirement. There was need for a well-informed pugnacious journal voicing Fabianism in the contemporary political debate – one that featured G.B.S., instead of leaving him to permeate their opponents.

So Shaw was persuaded. He became one of the *New Statesman*'s original proprietors and directors, put up (with a cheque for £1,000, equivalent to £43,000 in 1997) one fifth of its capital, purchased approximately 2,400 shares and sent out a series of letters soliciting subscribers. And Beatrice was pleased.

Almost everything, Shaw told Beatrice, would depend on the tact and dash of their editor. The Webbs had chosen Clifford Sharp whom Sidney thought a 'weak, timid and slow' man, but Beatrice believed to be 'a good man of business'. His credentials were faultless. He was a steadfast member of the Fabian executive, had married H. G. Wells's ex-love Rosamund Bland, and had helped the Webbs' anti-Poor Law campaign as editor of the *Crusade*. But no one really liked him. He was like 'an old, mangy, surly, slightly dangerous dog,' wrote Leonard Woolf. Imperialist by temperament, Sharp did not share many of the radical preoccupations of socialism such as removal of the House of Lords, and introduction of proportional representation; he was not pro-birth-control or anti-vivisection. But he was a thoroughgoing collectivist: and that was what mattered most to the Webbs.

'The first number has been a huge success,' Shaw reported following its publication on 12 April 1913. Not wishing to find himself presiding over a raucous weekly symposium, Sharp relied on the anonymity of his contributions to help him achieve a single tone and unity of style throughout the paper. 'It is not usual for a journal to communicate to the public the names of those of its staff who contribute unsigned articles,' he wrote in the first number.

'We feel, however, that, in view of the promises which have been made, and which have possibly induced many persons to subscribe to *The New Statesman*, we owe it to our readers to explain that Mr Bernard Shaw and Mr Sidney Webb will as a rule write editorially in our columns, and that the present issue includes, in fact, more than one contribution from each of these gentlemen.'

Shaw's unsigned contributions on feminism and income tax, the performance of motor cars, the ethics of prize-fighting and the duties of the poet laureate were too surreal to blend into the mood of didactic common sense that Sharp wanted to establish. The two of them, it was said, saw eye to eye on nothing except Ireland and Death Duties – 'we did not even agree about the Income Tax,' Sharp added. He therefore proposed that G.B.S. should be treated as an exception to the rule of anonymity and be allowed to sign his contributions. But Shaw refused. 'I have had enough of being the funny man and the privileged lunatic of a weekly paper.' As a result 'the *New Statesman* is in fact the one weekly in which Shaw's name never appears,' Beatrice complained in her diary that summer, 'and it is Shaw's name that draws . . . He will not cooperate on terms of equality.'

But he had agreed to co-operate on terms of equal anonymity. Collectivism did not mean to him a regimentation of opinion, but the release of differing individual talents for a generally harmonious purpose. Sharp reminded him somewhat of his father. He was a moral teetotaller who drank: a man of late hours and cloudy scandals. Though it was impossible for Shaw to trust him, 'I never felt inclined to resent in the least the good-humoured contempt which he never concealed,' Sharp told Beatrice. 'I think he is much the most generous and sweetest-tempered person I ever came across.' Sharp met the difficulties with courage and ingenuity. 'I am very favorably impressed by his standing up to me,' Shaw admitted.

The differences between the two men were to be exacerbated by the war, during which, Sharp wrote, the *New Statesman* represented Shaw's views 'in scarcely a single particular'. He needed fortitude against Shaw's magnanimous and subversive tactics. Their battle was for authority. Sharp believed that authority belonged to him as editor: but Shaw needed this authority for his iconoclastic opinions. 'The time has come for me to be old and savage,' he asserted. He used everything except his money and his position as proprietor in their struggle. His weapons were words.

Beatrice, though she and Sidney were themselves to sever their relationship with Sharp later on ('your turn will come,' Shaw predicted), tended to support the editor. 'The New Statesman enjoys the distinction of being the only paper in the world that refuses to print anything by me,' Shaw was to write in the autumn of 1916, ' . . . and I am compelled, as I have been more or less all my life, to depend for publicity on the more extreme Conservative organs of opinion.'

*

Beatrice had wished for closer intellectual intimacy with Shaw through the *New Statesman*. But his 'big brain', she became convinced, had been spoilt by Mrs Patrick Campbell. 'He is the fly and the lady the spider.'

Shaw had been unusually subdued during the autumn of 1913 as he flew round France on what Stella called his 'honeymoon' with Charlotte. 'I am horribly unhappy every morning,' he wrote to her, ' . . . you have wakened the latent tragedy in me.' On his return he tried to keep hidden from their friends the memory of Stella that 'tears me all to pieces'. Now that the affair had ended, Beatrice began to feel more sympathetic towards him. Instead of hanging around Mrs Pat's bedroom he 'has attended every one of our six public lectures, and taken the chair twice,' she approved. It was not wholly displeasing to Beatrice that Shaw's recent plays, of which she did not think much, had been unsuccessful. *The Music-Cure* was presented for just seven performances at the Little Theatre; *Great Catherine* ran for thirty performances at the Vaudeville and had not been very well reviewed. More surprisingly, Barker's production of *Androcles and the Lion*, with shimmering Post-Impressionist designs by Albert Rothenstein, had come off after fifty-two performances at the St James's Theatre. The play had puzzled people. 'An English audience has not as a rule sufficient emotional mobility to follow a method which alternates laughter with pathos, philosophy with fun, in such rapid succession,' explained Desmond MacCarthy in the *New Statesman*.

Everyone had loved the lion, a delicious beast with the most alluring howls and pussycat antics, and 'the one character in the whole range of Shavian drama,' commented A. B. Walkley warmly, 'who never talks'. But it was the lion's evening rather than the playwright's. The *Manchester Guardian*'s critic reported that the words 'vulgarity', 'blasphemy', 'childish' were to be heard at the end of the performance, and predicted that 'Mr Shaw's new play will scandalise . . . the most characteristic part of the English public [which] . . . cannot understand being passionately in earnest about a thing and in the same breath making fun of it.' And so it proved.

For Christmas and the New Year he went to Devon and Cornwall for a fortnight's tour with the Webbs. The scenery had 'an almost Irish charm'. Each day they would set off walking over ten or thirteen miles of researched country, with the car panting in attendance to take them, when exhausted, to the most luxurious hotel in the neighbourhood. 'Our old friend and brilliant comrade is a benevolent and entertaining companion,' Beatrice allowed. But he was 'getting rapidly old physically, and somewhat dictatorial and impatient intellectually, and he suffers from restlessness,' she observed. 'We talked more intimately than we have done for many years.'

Shaw's life was changing – everything was changing – from comedy to tragedy. From Cornwall he wrote to Charlotte: 'I miss you, as you would be happy here, and I like to be with you when you are happy.' From Devon he wrote to Stella, reminding her of their love a year ago: 'I believe we were both well then, and have been ill ever since.' He could not conceal these divisions from the sharp eyes of Beatrice. 'He is still fond of Charlotte and grateful to her,' she noted, 'but he quite obviously finds his new friend, with her professional genius and more intimate personal appeal, better company.'

Stella had taken little notice of Joey's letters this winter. 'I ought to have written,' she acknowledged. Barrie's *The Adored One* had not been a success. She began to look differently at Shaw. 'Be quite serious in your friendship for me,' she appealed. Though not knowing whether Shaw still wanted her to play Eliza, she had recently approached Beerbohm Tree about *Pygmalion*. Having already heard from George Alexander that this play was 'a winner', Tree asked Shaw to come to His Majesty's and read it to him. The reading took place high up in the dome of the theatre, and before the end of the third act Tree had made up his mind to stage it. Rehearsals were to begin in February 1914. Tree's 'admiration for you and the play is ENORMOUS,' Stella wrote to Shaw. 'I'll be tame as a mouse and oh so obedient – and I wonder if you'll get what you want out of me . . .'

2

THE HISTORY OF *PYGMALION*

> Ibsen was compelled to acquiesce in a happy ending for A Doll's House in Berlin, because he could not help himself, just as I have never been able to stop the silly and vulgar gag with which Eliza in Pygmalion, both here and abroad, gets the last word and implies that she is going to marry Pygmalion.
>
> Shaw to William Archer (19 April 1919)

Pygmalion marks the climax of Shaw's career as a writer of comedies. It is a return in feeling and form to the period of his *Plays Pleasant*, an integration of Faustian legend and Cinderella fairy-tale, a comedy of manners and a parable of socialism. Written so near to his mother's death and to the flowering of his romance with Stella, the play weaves together a variety of Shavian themes and obsessions, imaginatively rephrasing the relationship between his mother and Vandeleur Lee, and casting Mrs Pat as the emotional replacement for Mrs Shaw. Its vitality and charm endeared *Pygmalion* to audiences, with whom it has remained Shaw's most popular 'romance'. 'There must be something radically wrong with the play if it pleases everybody,' he protested, 'but at the moment I cannot find what it is.'

He enjoyed describing *Pygmalion* as an experiment to demonstrate how the science of phonetics could pull apart an antiquated British class system. 'The reformer we need most today is an energetic phonetic enthusiast,' he was to write in his Preface. This was Shaw's gesture towards removing the power for change from fighting men who were threatening to alter the world by warfare, and handing it to men of words whom he promoted as 'among the most important people in England at present'. In this context, the character of Henry Higgins (who appears as a comic version of Sherlock Holmes in Act I) takes his life from the revolutionary phonetician and philologist Henry Sweet, who had died while the play was being written. Writing to Robert Bridges in 1910 about the need for a phonetic institute, he had described Sweet as the man 'I had most hopes of'. It was Bridges who, the following year, retained Shaw to speak at the Phonetic Conference on spelling reform at University

College, London. 'It is perfectly easy to find a speaker whose speech will be accepted in every part of the English speaking world as valid 18-carat oral currency,' he wrote to Sweet afterwards, 'NOT that the pronunciation represented is the standard pronunciation or ideal pronunciation, or correct pronunciation, or in any way binding on any human being or morally superior to Hackney cockney or Idaho american, but solely that if a man pronounces in that way he will be eligible as far as speech is concerned for the post of Lord Chief Justice, Chancellor at Oxford, Archbishop of Canterbury, Emperor, President, or Toast Master at the Mansion House.'

It was this experiment that Shaw transferred to Higgins's laboratory in Wimpole Street, with its phonograph, laryngoscope, tuning-forks and organ pipes. This is a live experiment we are shown on stage, and as with all such laboratory work it is necessary for the Frankenstein doctor to behave as if his creation were insentient. 'She's incapable of understanding anything,' Higgins assures his fellow-scientist Colonel Pickering. 'Besides, do any of us understand what we are doing? If we did, would we ever do it?' When Pickering asks: 'Does it occur to you, Higgins, that the girl has some feelings?', Higgins cheerily replies: 'Oh no, I dont think so. Not any feelings that we need bother about. Have you, Eliza?'

Shaw conducts a second social experiment through Eliza's father, Alfred Doolittle, an elderly dustman of Dickensian vitality. Doolittle is any one of us. When asked by Higgins whether he is an honest man or rogue, he answers: 'A little of both, Henry, like the rest of us.' Being his name, he does as little as possible – some bribery here or there, a little blackmail, more drinking, an occasional change of mistress: and he provides positively no education at all for his illegitimate daughter 'except to give her a lick of the strap now and again'. Yet he has the quick wits and superficial charm of the capitalist entrepreneur. He is society's free man – free of responsibilities and conscience. 'Have you no morals, man?' demands Pickering. 'Cant afford them, Governor,' Doolittle answers. Undeserving poverty is his line: 'and I mean to go on being undeserving. I like it,' he adds. His disquisition on middle-class morality is intended by Shaw to have the same subversive effect as Falstaff's discourse on honour.

Yet this is the man whom Shaw chooses as the first recipient of what he calculates to be a reasonable income-for-all. As the result of Higgins's joking reference to Doolittle as the most original moralist in England in a letter to an American philanthropist, the undeserving dustman is left £3,000. In Act II he had made his entrance with 'a professional flavour of dust about him'. In Act V when his name is announced and Pickering queries, 'Do you mean the dustman?', the parlourmaid answers: 'Dustman! Oh no, sir: a gentleman.' He is splendidly dressed as if for a fashionable wedding. Shaw's point is not that a gentleman is merely a dustman with money in the same way as a flower girl with phonetic training can be passed off as a duchess: it is that moral reformation depends upon the reform of our economic system. As Eric Bentley writes: 'He was giving the idea of the gentleman an economic basis.' It is this that Doolittle dreaded and derided, and now finds himself dragged into. 'It's making a gentleman of me that I object to,' he protests. '. . . I have to live for others and not for myself: thats middle class morality.'

Under Higgins's tutelage Eliza becomes a doll of 'remarkable distinction . . . speaking with pedantic correctness of pronunciation and great beauty of tone', which Mrs Higgins tells her son is 'a triumph of your art and of her dressmaker's'. This dummy figure replaces the 'draggle tailed guttersnipe' whose life Higgins acknowledges to have been real, warm and violent. The classical Pygmalion had prayed to Aphrodite to make his ideal statue come alive so that he could marry her. Shaw's flower girl, whom Higgins has manufactured into a replica duchess by the beginning of Act IV, is transformed into an independent woman whom Higgins refuses to marry. However, the transformation scene, in which Higgins lays his hands on Eliza like a sculptor's creative act, is a struggle the implications of which are sexual:

'*Eliza tries to control herself . . . she is on the point of screaming . . . He comes to her . . . He pulls her up . . .* LIZA [*breathless*] *. . . She crisps her fingers frantically.* HIGGINS [*looking at her in cool wonder*] . . . LIZA [*gives a suffocated scream of fury, and instinctively darts her nails at his face*]!! HIGGINS [*catching her wrists . . . He throws her roughly into the easy chair*] LIZA [*crushed by superior strength and weight*]. HIGGINS [*thundering*] Those slippers LIZA [*with bitter submission*] Those slippers'

These stage directions contain many sado-masochistic undertones. But Higgins himself resists every innuendo. This was important to Shaw. For, remembering Sweet's genius for 'making everything impossible', he turned his mind to another 'genius' as a model for Higgins, the author of *The Voice*, Vandeleur Lee. Higgins's asexual association with Eliza is consequently authorized by Shaw's faith in his mother's 'innocence', and written as an endorsement of his own legitimacy. The platonic arrangement depends on the professional circumstances of their relationship. 'You see, she'll be a pupil,' Higgins explains to Pickering, 'and teaching would be impossible unless pupils were sacred.' Higgins's voice tuition of Eliza takes the place of the singing lessons Lee had given Bessie (Lucinda Elizabeth Shaw) and to reinforce this substitution Shaw provides Higgins's pupil with the same name as Lee's pupil:

HIGGINS Whats your name?
THE FLOWER GIRL Liza Doolittle
HIGGINS [*declaiming gravely*] Eliza, Elizabeth, Betsy and Bess,
They went to the wood to get a bird's nes'.

'I've never been able to feel really grown-up and tremendous, like other chaps,' Higgins tells Pickering. He explains the reason to his mother who has regretted his inability to fall in love with any woman under forty-five. 'My idea of a lovable woman is somebody as like you as possible,' he tells her. 'I shall never get into the way of seriously liking young women: some habits lie too deep to be changed.'

In his final act, Shaw was rewriting the legend of Svengali and his pupil Trilby. When Svengali dies of a heart attack, Trilby's voice is silenced, she cannot sing at her concert, and she follows Svengali into death. In Shaw's version Eliza's true voice is heard once she emerges from Higgins's bullying presence and walks out to a separate life. But other forces were at work in the final act obliging Higgins himself to speak increasingly with the voice of G.B.S., the public figure that had developed from Vandeleur Lee; while Eliza comes to represent the emotions that Stella Campbell was introducing into his life. Higgins's description of Eliza as a 'consort battleship' has something of the armoured impregnability Shaw attributed to his mother ('one of those women who could act as matron of a cavalry barracks from eighteen to forty and emerge without a stain on her character'). But no one else in the play regards Eliza in this light. Mrs Higgins calls her 'naturally rather affectionate'; Doolittle admits she is 'very tender-hearted'; and Eliza herself demands: 'Every girl has a right to be loved.'

What Higgins wants is less clear. He claims he has created an ideal wife – 'a consort for a king' – yet he must resist her emotional appeal: 'I wont stop for you . . . I can do without anybody.' The purpose of Higgins's experiment has been 'filling up the deepest gulf that separates class from class and soul from soul'. It is half successful, half a failure. The class gulf is filled at the garden party, dinner party and reception: the gulf between Eliza and Higgins remains. Eliza has changed, but Higgins admits 'I cant change my nature.' He seems 'cold, unfeeling, selfish' to Eliza. 'I only want to be natural,' she says. But can Higgins be natural? Where will things lead if she accepts his invitation to go back to him 'for the fun of it'?

The original ending of the play is carefully ambiguous, reflecting Shaw's uncertainties over his romance with Stella. He could not marry her: she could not remain for ever his pupil as an actress learning from his theatrical direction. But might they become lovers? The question is left open to our imagination:

MRS HIGGINS I'm afraid youve spoilt that girl, Henry. But never mind, dear: I'll buy you the tie and gloves.

HIGGINS [*sunnily*] Oh, dont bother. She'll buy em all right enough. Good-bye. *They kiss. Mrs Higgins runs out. Higgins, left alone, rattles his cash in his pocket; chuckles; and disports himself in a highly self-satisfied manner.*

This, as Eric Bentley argues, 'is the true naturalistic ending'. But Shaw's subsequent attempts to clear up its ambiguity have blurred the outline of its elegant structure. The faint poignancy of the ending lies in the half-emergent realization that there is to be no satisfactory marriage for this Cinderella; while a feminist reading tells us that Higgins cannot be approved of as a husband. But the public wanted the Miltonic bachelor to be transformed into the beautiful lady's husband. 'This is unbearable,' Shaw cried out. Once his love affair with Stella had ended, he could not bear to speculate on what might have happened when 'I almost condescended to romance'. 'Eliza married Freddy [Eynsford-Hill],' he told Trebitsch; 'and the notion of her marrying Higgins is disgusting.' In other words Eliza married a double-barrelled nonentity like George Cornwallis-West, and Higgins's agonizing boredom with the Eynsford-Hill family reflects Shaw's own impatience with the smart visitors who sometimes crowded him out of Stella's house.

The history of *Pygmalion* was to develop into a struggle over this ending. For the play's first publication in book form in 1916, Shaw added a sequel recounting 'what Eliza did'. Her decision not to marry Higgins, he explained, was well-considered. The differences between them of age and income, when added to Higgins's mother-fixation and exclusive passion for phonetics, was too wide a gulf to bridge. He told the story of Eliza and Freddy, Mr and Mrs Eynsford-Hill, as invitingly as he could: but the public went on preferring its own version. Shaw made his final version of the end on 19 August 1939:

MRS HIGGINS I'm afraid youve spoilt that girl, Henry. I should be uneasy about you and her if she were less fond of Colonel Pickering.

HIGGINS Pickering! Nonsense: she's going to marry Freddy. Ha ha! Freddy! Freddy!! Ha ha ha ha ha!!!!! [*He roars with laughter as the play ends*]

But by now this laughter sounded as hollow as Higgins's prediction, and even Shaw's printers had begun to query his intentions.

The English-language film of *Pygmalion* gave Shaw an extra opportunity to remove 'virtually every suggestion of Higgins's possible romantic interest in Liza'. His screenplay even omits the word 'consort' and leaves Higgins calling Eliza a 'battleship'. But the producer of the film hired other screenwriters who added a 'sugar-sweet ending' which Shaw found out for the first time at a press show two days before its première.

But one battle he apparently did win. 'Hamon, my French translator, says that it is announced that Lehar is making an operetta of Pygmalion,' he notified Trebitsch in the summer of 1921. '. . . Can you warn him that he cannot touch Pygmalion without infringing my copyright, and that I have no intention of allowing the history of The Chocolate Soldier to be repeated.' For almost thirty more years he made the same reply to all composers. 'I absolutely forbid any such outrage,' he wrote when in his ninety-second year. *Pygmalion* was good enough 'with its own verbal music'.

*

Pygmalion, which was first published in book form in Germany, Hungary and Sweden (plus an unauthorized edition in the United States), received its theatrical début at the Hofburg Theater in Vienna on 16 October 1913, and was played a fortnight later at the Lessingtheater in Berlin. *The Times* on 17 October 1913 reported that the opening night in Vienna 'met with an excellent reception from the audience, which among a number of distinguished personages included the Archduke Francis Ferdinand'.

Shaw described this première as a compliment paid to him by German and Austrian culture 'which I value very much'. *Pygmalion* had been performed in a beautiful theatre splendidly subsidized and free of rent. 'I am handsomely paid for my work,' he reported. 'In London, with an equally popular play, the ground landlord leaves less than nothing for me and for the management . . . Meanwhile, huge endowments are proposed for football, pedestrian races, and throwing the hammer.'

However, there was a small cloud floating over this foreign production.

The central situation of the play also appears in Shaw's novel *Love Among the Artists* where the Welsh Beethoven, Owen Jack, gives elocution lessons to Madge Brailsford. But an alert German critic pointed out the extraordinary resemblance of Shaw's story to the adventures of Smollett's hero with a sixteen-year-old beggar girl in Chapter 87 of his novel *Peregrine Pickle* – and the British press immediately took this up as the reason why Shaw had produced his play out of the country. It showed 'an amusing ignorance of English culture,' Shaw countered. 'The one place where I should have been absolutely safe from detection is London.' He had read *Peregrine Pickle* in his youth and not cared for it and he did not realize that 'Smollett had got hold of my plot'. Later he was to speculate on the likelihood of this incident having 'got lodged in my memory without my being conscious of it and stayed there until I needed it'. None of this affected the morality of his position. 'If I find in a book anything I can make use of, I take it gratefully,' he stated. ' . . . In short, my literary morals are those of Molière and Handel.' Shakespeare too had taken his goods where he could find them. 'Do not scorn to be derivative,' Shaw urged his friends, ' . . . the great thing is to be able to derive – to see your chance and be able to take it . . . Read Goldsmith on originality.'

There was a rumour that the actor playing Higgins in Berlin had introduced a 'horrible gag' suggesting that he and Eliza shared the same bedroom. In London, where Shaw was producing the play himself, such travesties would not be permitted. But when he turned up for rehearsals in the second week of February he found His Majesty's a madhouse.

Famous for his absent-mindedness, Tree was the despair of playwrights. He greeted Shaw warmly, but with obvious surprise. It was as if he believed himself to be the author of *Pygmalion*. His head hummed with plans. For he had experience of collaborating with other dramatists – for example, Shakespeare into whose *Richard II* he introduced a very effective pet dog, and whose *Twelfth Night* he had improved by the addition of four miniature copycat Malvolios. His performances were hugely entertaining to his fans, but they relied on a good deal of improvisation especially when he was not quick enough to reach the stage furniture in time and pluck from its niches the pieces of paper on which he had written out his more troublesome lines. He loved to disguise himself with beards, uniforms, vine leaves, ear-trumpets. In this respect, Professor Higgins was a disappointment. It seemed he was required to do little more than dress and speak normally: and this bewildered him. In vain did he plead with Shaw to let him take large quantities of snuff, to vault onto the piano from time to time, to indicate an addiction to port by walking with a limp and a stick.

Delays were often caused by Tree's brainwaves for taking over other roles (such as Doolittle) or filling the theatre with philosophical dustmen and flower girls. To Shaw's businesslike mind it seemed miraculous that any production ever took place at His Majesty's. Tree had with dignity assured him that 'I will not place myself in the position of receiving a rebuff', and was taken aback when Mrs Campbell hurled a slipper bang in his face. His morale shattered, he collapsed into a chair while the cast tried to get him to understand that this was part of the play. The worst of it was, Shaw wrote, that 'it was quite evident that he would be just as surprised and wounded next time'.

Shaw was strangely convinced that Tree was a tragedian and Stella a comedian. 'I am sending a letter to Tree which will pull him together if it does not kill him,' he informed Stella. But Tree reflected in his notebook: 'I will not go so far as to say that all people who write letters of more than eight pages are mad, but it is a curious fact that all madmen write letters of more than eight pages.'

In her fashion, Stella worked hard at Eliza Doolittle. Her prompt copy of *Pygmalion* was pencilled with encouraging scribbles: 'My hand is held out Joey . . . I'll do my level best . . . Your delicious play needs real greatness . . . gentle Joey.'

But Shaw was not always so gentle. Though often maddened by Tree, 'I could never bring myself to hit him hard enough,' he regretted. But on Stella he believed that 'no poker was thick enough nor heavy enough to leave a solitary bruise'. He had been partly persuaded of this by the knowledge that she thrived on conflict. She would put out her tongue, turn her back on Tree ('But it's a very nice back, isn't it?') and finally drive him screaming from his own stage.

Stella's tantrums masked a lack of confidence. She had never played in comedy before and she was thirty years too old for the part. 'Dreadfully middle-aged moments,' Shaw observed in his rehearsal notebook. Occasionally he did not keep such observations to himself. At one moment, as he knelt before Stella imploring her to speak the lines as he directed, she told the actors: 'That's where I like to see my authors, on their knees at my feet.'

Opening night was set for 11 April 1914. The week before was marked by two spectacular disappearances. Instead of going to the theatre on Monday 6 April, Stella took off for the Kensington Registry Office where she married George Cornwallis-West two hours after his decree absolute came through. From there they went on a three-day honeymoon to a golfing resort near Tunbridge Wells, returning in time for Stella to take part in the dress rehearsal at His Majesty's on Friday evening. 'Of *course* I knew about the marriage,' Tree lied to the press assembled in the dress circle bar, 'and I'm very happy for both of them, but naturally I was sworn to secrecy . . . contrary to popular rumour there have been no quarrels between us, in fact rehearsals have progressed with the most delightful smoothness & harmony.'

Shaw could reflect now on the consequences of his own timidity. The day before the news of Stella's marriage appeared in the papers, Charlotte had sailed for the United States. She did not know that her husband's affair with Mrs Pat was over – how could you ever tell such things? The long rehearsals of *Pygmalion* had been agony for her. She did not want to witness their first night climax. On 8 April she left England with her friend Lena Ashwell to join their guru James Porter Mills and his wife. These last months, while G.B.S. occupied himself at His Majesty's, Charlotte had been preparing an abstract of Mills's 'Teaching' which he persuaded her to publish as a business prospectus entitled *Knowledge is the Door: A Forerunner.* It was a comfort to her that Dr Mills was not brilliant or literary. She felt calmed by his assurance that '*there is no need to give way to human feeling* . . . we can gradually quiet the waves of emotion.'

There was a great swell of excitement round the first night. Shaw sat by himself in the teeming theatre: not far off was the other George, Stella's 'GOLDEN man'. The curtain lifted on the first act. All went smoothly and well. In the second act Edmund Gurney, who had been listening to Lloyd George's speeches in the House of Commons to pick up the right tone of contempt for the aristocracy, scored a colossal success as Doolittle. Stella 'ravished the house almost to delirium' throughout the third act, and 'Tree's farcical acting was very funny'. But Eliza's sensational exit line, 'Not bloody likely,' nearly wrecked the play. The audience gave a gasp, there was a crash of laughter while Mrs Pat perambulated the stage, and then a second burst of laughing. The pandemonium lasted well over a minute. 'They laughed themselves into such utter abandonment and disorder,' Shaw wrote to Charlotte in the United States, 'that it was really doubtful for some time whether they could recover themselves and let the play go on.'

Tree had been in a pitiful state of nerves, begging Shaw to substitute 'blooming' or 'ruddy' for Eliza's dreadful word. Now he felt frightfully pleased. He relaxed. He expanded. 'He was like nothing human.' Much of the dialogue between Higgins and Eliza held special meanings for Shaw – echoes from the controlling influence of his mother ('I cant change my nature') and overtones of his unhappy romance with Stella ('I hadnt quite realised that you were going away . . . I shall miss you Eliza'). Tree made it all absurd; 'For the last two acts I writhed in hell,' Shaw wrote to Charlotte. ' . . . The last thing I saw as I left the house was Higgins shoving his mother rudely out of his way and wooing Eliza with appeals to buy ham for his lonely home like a bereaved Romeo. I went straight home to bed and read Shakespear for an hour before going to sleep to settle myself down.'

Stella had followed his directions as if she were Eliza imitating Higgins. To thank her, and because he could not endure going backstage after the performance, Shaw invited her and her new husband down to Ayot next day. 'You *must* consent to receive Cornwallis-West in the country,' he wrote to Charlotte that night. 'He has a dog Beppo, a huge black retriever, who plays hide & seek, distinguishes between right & left when he is given instructions, takes people's hats off when ordered, and is withal a grave & reverend signor. I believe you would ask them both to stay for a month on condition that Beppo came too . . . They treat me as a beloved uncle.'

Shaw doubted if *Pygmalion* could succeed. Once its success became apparent, Tree chivvied him to come back and see it. But Shaw was adamant. 'Come soon – or you'll not recognize your play,' Stella appealed. But he would not. 'Never no more.' But at last he relented and came to the hundredth performance on 15 July.

It was awful. It was appalling. It was worse than anything he had imagined. His directions had been wonderfully circumvented. Instead of flinging the ring down on the dessert stand at the end of Act IV, Eliza on her knees clutched and gazed on it feelingly – there were no words because the emotion was obviously too deep. In the brief interval between the end of the play and fall of the curtain, the amorous Higgins threw flowers at Eliza, a theatrically effective gesture, as Nicholas Grene has observed, 'reversing the image at the end of Act I where Eliza threw her flowers at Higgins'.

Tree claimed that his improvements delighted the audience: and it was this public that Shaw really blamed. What had happened to its serious instincts, its sense of proportion? During these hot summer months there had been turmoil in Ulster over Asquith's Home Rule Bill, and hunger strikes among the militant suffragettes in London. Then on 28 June, the Archduke Franz Ferdinand, who had been at the première of *Pygmalion* in Vienna, was shot: and Europe moved to the edge of war. But for much of this time 'all political and social questions have been swept from the public mind by Eliza's expletive,' Shaw reported. The Bishop of Woolwich cried out for it to be banned; Bishop Weldon felt saddened that such a vulgar word had to be uttered by a married lady with children. Scholars and intellectuals duelled in the columns of *The Times* over the origin of 'bloody'. The Oxford Union met and voted in favour of a motion declaring 'a certain sanguinary expletive' to be 'a liberating influence on the English language', but the Debating Society at Eton deplored 'the debasement and vulgarization of the commercial theatre'. The *Daily Express* got hold of an authentic Covent Garden flower girl called Eliza, took her to the play and reported her as being shocked. At 10 Downing Street the Prime Minister received a letter of protest from the Women's Purity League.

The summer days persisted hot and sunny; the public continued to come to *Pygmalion*: but Tree was bored. He wanted a holiday and took off the play late that July. He had attributed the bloody rumpus over

Pygmalion to 'the flatness of the political situation'. 'Triviality,' Shaw wrote, 'can go no further.'

3

WHAT HE DID IN THE GREAT WAR

> As for going mad, dont you wish you could? The trying thing is to be sane with everyone else (except the rogues who are taking advantage of it) as mad as hatters.
>
> Shaw to Rowley (7 January 1916)

The Fabians were unprepared for war. Most of them believed that modern war was caused by the capitalist struggle for markets and could be discouraged by means of the General Strike. Besides, as Sidney Webb said, 'it would be too insane'.

Shaw also thought it insane – and all the more likely for that. Militarism in all countries had developed, he argued, 'not from the needs of human society, but because at a certain stage of social integration the institution of standing armies gave monarchs the power to play at soldiers with living men instead of leaden figures'. German culture in particular had got stuck in this obsolete *Roi Soleil* system. This was why Shaw did not favour unilateral disarmament. 'All nations should be prepared for war,' he was to write. 'All houses should be protected by lightning conductors.' Until there existed a European police force, Britain must be prepared 'to make war on war' if she wanted to exercise an effective foreign policy. Sidney Webb's pacifism was that of the sane man. But at a time of war 'sanity is positively dangerous'.

Europe was ready for fighting, as if surfeited with the material gains of the previous hundred years. Germany's militarism was apparent. Thomas Mann was to speak of the hearts of poets standing in flame 'for now it is war! . . . Nothing better, more beautiful, happier could befall them in the whole world.' In England, where Rupert Brooke was to thank God for matching us with His hour, romantic militarism was dressed up to fit the righteous Christian, the hard-headed businessman, travelling adventurer, puritan character-builder. In a letter to *The Times* Lord Roberts had written: ' "My country right or wrong and right or wrong my country", is the sentiment most treasured in the breast of any one worthy of the name of man' – which Shaw paraphrased as 'teaching a Christian to disobey Christ at the commands of a non-commissioned officer'. His

Preface to *Androcles and the Lion*, written late in 1915, amounted to a denunciation of war as a method of solving international disputes.

Once war started, countries surrendered every other consideration except victory. 'It is one of the horrors of war,' he reminded Carl Heath, secretary of the National Peace Council, 'that both parties abandon the ground of right and wrong, and take that of kill or be killed. That is a reason for making an end of war, and in the meantime keeping political power out of the hands of bellicose persons.' He hated the silence of diplomacy. Laughter was one of his devices for shattering this silence: the mystique that in the public interest the public must know nothing. Preparation for war necessitated so much lying on the part of belligerent Governments as to develop an unthinking habit: 'if anyone remarks at noon that it is twelve o'clock, some minister automatically articulates a solemn public assurance that there is no ground for any such suspicion,' Shaw later wrote, 'and gives private orders that references to the time of day are to be censored in future.'

The secret of Britain's foreign policy was that there was no foreign policy. In an article for the *Daily Chronicle* on 18 March 1913 he proposed one: a triple alliance against war by England, France and Germany, the terms being that 'if France attack Germany we combine with Germany to crush France, and if Germany attack France, we combine with France to crush Germany'. From that starting point, he continued, the combination might be added to from Holland and the Scandinavian kingdoms 'and finally achieve the next step in civilization, the policing of Europe against war and the barbarians'. He repeated this formula, which was another magical trinity for achieving self-integration, in an article on the comity of nations entitled 'The Peace of Europe and How to Attain It' in the *Daily News* on New Year's Day 1914. 'I want international peace,' he stated. Those barbarians within our frontiers, who advocated war as a tonic, should not be let loose on foreigners but rather sent for annual war sports to Salisbury Plain, he suggested, to 'blaze away at one another' until the survivors (if any) felt 'purified by artillery fire'.

Lunching with the German ambassador Prince Lichnowsky, Shaw asked what he thought of his peace proposals and was told that such problems were better left to politicians and diplomats – which might have been a better answer if politicians and diplomats were required to do the fighting. 'Can anybody suggest an alternative policy?' Shaw had asked. But there seemed no alternative. 'Complete failure of my campaign,' he noted. This failure, together with his feeling of isolation from other Fabians, contributed to the somewhat aggrieved tone and massive outpouring of Shaw's writings on the war. A war symposium published by the *Daily Citizen* on 1 August he described as 'about as timely and sensible as a symposium on the danger of damp sheets would be if London were on fire'. But, he added: 'it is important that our statesmen and diplomatists should understand that there is a strong and growing body of public opinion to which all war is abhorrent, and which will suffer it now only as a hideous necessity arising out of past political bargains in which the people have had no part and the country no interest . . . We muddled our way in and we may have to fight our way out.'

*

Shaw and Charlotte were at a hotel at Salcombe in Devonshire on 4 August. Shaw first heard of the declaration of war on coming down to breakfast. A middle-aged Englishman 'after a fairly successful attempt to say unconcernedly "I suppose we shall have to fight them" suddenly changed "them" into "those swine" twice in every sentence'. It was an early symptom of the epidemic that was soon covering the country: 'the ordinary war-conscious civilian went mad.' People rejoiced at the prospect of a first-rate fight. The excitement, the dread of being thought unpatriotic even by fools with white feathers for brains, was to leave the country at the mercy of anyone in authority. 'This is the greatest fight ever made for the Christian religion,' the Bishop of London declared, ' . . . a choice between the nailed hand and the mailed fist.' Kitchener's finger was to point at everyone. The upper and the upper-middle classes were exhorted to sacrifice their butlers, chauffeurs, gamekeepers and grooms for service at the front. Old men postdated their births, dyed their hair, and lined up at the recruiting offices; old women lamented that their ineligibility to serve as nurses would prevent their killing the German wounded; mothers hustled their sons into uniforms and off to the trenches; a fifteen-year-old cadet at the Royal Naval College was publicly flogged when he tried to go home.

People needed enormous doses of self-righteousness to endure the shock of war. A chauvinistic industry, manufacturing foreign monsters, quickly expanded. A general in France, writing to a journalist, apologized that 'there has been only one atrocity lately and that was not a good one'. Not everyone was so meticulous. Newspapers competed for German atrocities to answer the clamour of their readers – 'like the clamor,' Shaw reported, 'of an agonizingly wounded combatant for morphia'. The whole country buzzed with stories of Germans tossing babies on the points of their bayonets; Germans burning field hospitals full of British wounded; Germans going into battle driving crowds of women before them; Germans making collections of fingers. Shaw searched for some practical line of reasoning to set against this hell. Would it really encourage recruitment? Surely it was kinder to those who had sons and husbands at the front *not* to insist that they must be horribly mutilated if they fell into enemy hands? 'Since you expect to go out soon, I really refuse to leave you troubled in spirit by that man with his eyes gouged out,' he reassured George Cornwallis-West. It was amazing how this totally blinded refugee careered around – he was far too quick for anyone to have seen, though all had heard of him. Elsewhere, a number of Belgian nurses whose hands everyone knew to have been scissored off by the Huns had, he was glad to see, grown new ones.

Among the baying patriots were the British disciples of Dr Mills. They could not tolerate Charlotte's refusal to assist this righteous war in any capacity 'except that of a reluctant taxpayer'. Worst of all in their eyes were her anxieties over poor Trebitsch. She felt a spring of joy on hearing that he had failed his medical examination. 'You will die prematurely,' G.B.S. assured him, 'at the age of 98 in a hotel lift, from ascending too rapidly.'

Shaw felt concern for all his translators – those other selves shredded in conflict. 'YOU AND I AT WAR CAN ABSURDITY GO FURTHER,' he had wired Trebitsch on 4 August. 'MY FRIENDLIEST WISHES GO WITH YOU UNDER ALL CIRCUMSTANCES.' Next day he and Charlotte went on to Torquay where they were to stay for a couple of months at the Hydro Hotel. 'This suits me pretty well too, as I have a lot of work in hand,' he told Beatrice Webb.

In a statement, drafted on 6 August, he set out the predicament as he saw it.

'We shall have to fight and die and pay and suffer with the grim knowledge that we are sacrificing ourselves in an insane cause, and that only by putting up a particularly good fight can we bring ourselves out of it with credit . . . For the present time there is only one thing to be done besides fighting . . . And that one thing is to set to work immediately to draft the inevitable Treaty of Peace which we must all sign when we have had our bellyful of murder and destruction.'

He accused the generals and politicians of being unable to think further ahead than the length of a bayonet, and he urged Beatrice Webb and other Fabians to cultivate 'long range firing more than you do, or you will leave forts unreduced in your rear which will undo half your work later on'. The real enemy was not Germany, he maintained, but jingoists and junkers in all countries. Therefore, in moments of optimism, he would represent the war as an opportunity of victory for the Suffragettes, the Irish volunteers and socialists everywhere.

Shaw judged the responsibility for war as lying almost evenly between British commercial adventurers and Germany's militarists, and denied that violation of Belgian neutrality was a *casus belli*. Using his new American literary agent Paul Reynolds, he placed an 'Open Letter to the President of the United States of America' in *The Nation* and the *New York Times*, appealing to him as 'the spokesman of Western Democracy' to rally the neutral powers for the purpose of demanding both sides to withdraw from Belgium ('the effect of our shells on Belgium is precisely the same as that of the German shells') and fight out their quarrel on their own territories. Behind this invitation lay a warning that history would judge Germany to have been the wrong side on which to intervene, and that Washington ('still privileged to talk common humanity to the nations') would inevitably chair the world conference that settled the peace.

The British press had been eager for Shaw's war contributions. But after three months, when he had vented his disgust on England and Germany as 'a couple of extremely quarrelsome dogs' and advised the soldiers in both armies to 'SHOOT THEIR OFFICERS AND GO HOME', many newspapers blacklisted him. 'In any ordinary time I should have been delighted to publish your letter with every word of which I agree,' wrote the editor of the *Manchester Guardian*, C. P. Scott, 'but at this horrible time one has to consider so many things which one would like to ignore . . . your letter would be highly disturbing to many minds. That of course is the object of it and a very excellent object. But I suppose one's duty now is to encourage and unite people and not to exercise and divide.' Shaw recognized the power of this call for suspending controversy in the face of national danger, but countered it with the argument that able-bodied soldiers in the trenches depended on able-minded civilians at home to guard their constitutional liberties. Soldiers must be protected while their backs were turned from those abuses of power – such as the suspension of by-elections – not necessary for the defeat of the enemy.

'I have sat at England's bedside during her delirium,' Shaw was to write. He saw himself as a doctor who reluctantly admits that his horror-struck patient may need chauvinistic drugs, but believes that the quality of his recovery depends upon their withdrawal as soon as possible. 'I do not grudge a mother the shelter of a lie any more than I grudge a soldier the shelter of a clump of briars,' he wrote; 'but the more thoroughly we realize that war is war, and death death, the sooner we shall get rid of it.' After the monthly casualty figures began to arrive affecting almost every family in the country (already in November there were 89,954 British casualties), then people would need some antidote. His *Common Sense about the War* was a complicated prescription prepared for those emerging from these bloody fantasies. On 14 November it appeared as a monumental supplement to the *New Statesman*. 'I have told the truth about the war,' Shaw claimed; 'and stated the democratic case for it.'

*

Until noon each day Shaw worked in the roof garden of the Hydro Hotel. Before lunch he would swim and after lunch continue working in his suite. Sometimes he went for rides in the car along the coast; sometimes he went and listened to Basil Cameron's concerts at the pavilion. After dinner he read.

It was impossible to think of anything except the war. Never can there have been a war in which the belligerents had such correct cases. Austria had the assassination of an Archduke; Germany the mobilization of Russia and the threatening articles of the Franco-Russian alliance; Britain the impeccable Treaty of 1839. All the provocations were valid according to the most accredited precedents. Academically, on all sides, the war was perfectly in order. 'I had to slave for months getting the evidence,' Shaw wrote to Alfred Sutro. ' . . . It makes me sick to recollect the drudgery of it all.'

The mood of the country was beginning to infiltrate Torquay. When a depressed Granville Barker came down for a few days, he and Shaw were threatened with shooting by a panicky coastguard as they walked along the beach. The hotel porter, a German who had registered as an enemy alien, was suddenly handcuffed and 'deported to the innermost centre of Britain – to Exeter, in fact' – so that he could not signal to German submarines.

Shaw needed to feel up to his chin in what was going on. Neither Asquith nor Grey, he believed, were the real spokesmen of their times. He hated Grey – 'a Junker from his topmost hair to the tips of his toes . . . [with] a personal taste for mendacity' – for his part in the sensational horror at the Egyptian village of Denshawai in 1906, when the British colonial power administered floggings, hangings and penal servitude for life after a rumpus arising from some pigeon shooting. This governing class was above listening to him. Shaw wanted his own class of men, Chesterton and Wells, Bennett and Bertrand Russell, to rise at the head of a popular movement and replace Asquith with someone such as Winston Churchill. He recognized that Churchill's anti-German pugnacity was enormously more popular in the country than the moral babble of Asquith. So he kept his eye on Churchill. Meanwhile 'our job is to make people serious about the war,' he wrote to Bertrand Russell. 'It is the monstrous triviality of the damned thing, and the vulgar frivolity of what we imagine to be patriotism, that gets at my temper.'

Shaw's position in *Common Sense about the War* was that of the Irishman who, when asked for directions, replies that he wouldn't start from here. It was given the Shavian dimension by the fact that England had not asked for directions. He was therefore obliged to step out dangerously into the traffic and transmit unsolicited signals.

He attempted to answer the question: what is the war about? It had erupted from a prodigious evil: that of mounting wealth throughout Europe untapped by any corresponding equitable distribution of this wealth. Borne on the soils and sighs of monstrous inequality this war had become a crude method of advancing social organization. Politicians still believed it was a question of Union Jacks and tricolours and Imperial Eagles – but 'there are only two real flags in the world henceforth,' Shaw wrote: 'the red flag of Democratic Socialism and the black flag of Capitalism.' The militarists of Europe had used this energy of dissatisfaction for their sport of war, and all the adventurous young men joined in. Shaw reasoned that the militaristic case led to what the militarists themselves most dreaded – a dramatic example was to be the collapse of tsardom and the rise of communism in Russia. 'The Democratic case, the Socialist one, the International case is worth all it threatens to cost,' he predicted. 'Democracy without equality is a delusion more dangerous than frank oligarchy and autocracy.'

Shaw's long-term aim was straight. He foresaw that the enormous demand for coal, cloth, boots, army rations, weapons, ammunition, transport vehicles, ships and all other accessories of war, would arrest the huge exports of capital and transform them into wages – besides doubling taxation on unearned incomes. He pointed out how the Government had already taken control of railways, bought up all the raw sugar, regulated prices, guaranteed the banks and achieved many of 'the things it had been declaring utterly and eternally Utopian and impossible when Socialists advocated them'.

During war we live in a political truce; in peacetime the political war begins again. Shaw wanted socialists to prepare for this struggle by ensuring that on enlistment labourers found themselves better fed, paid, clothed than before. He recommended the appointment of working-class representatives to the War Office, and the reform of the 'tyrannical slave code called military law' so that the soldier could serve as a citizen with all his rights intact.

This was Shaw's case for open diplomacy, full civil rights, a fair livelihood for the soldier and his dependants, and genuine working-class democracy in place of Asquith's Mutiny Acts which, even in time of peace, 'imprison Labour leaders and muzzle the Labour Press'. In his thirty years of public work Shaw had seen 'man after man in the Labour movement sell out because he could not trust his future to the loyalty of the workers,' he wrote, 'and I should perhaps have had to sell out myself long ago if I had not possessed certain powers as a writer which made me a little more independent than others'. Armed with this independence, 'I have put my best brains and skill at the service of the Labour cause'.

*

Shaw had modelled his *Common Sense about the War* on Tom Paine's *The Rights of Man*, and it blew up a similar dust-storm of abuse. Libraries and bookshops removed his works from their shelves; newspapers instructed their readers to boycott his plays. The editor of *The Clarion*, Robert Blatchford, described his manifesto as 'the meanest act of treachery ever perpetrated by an alien enemy residing in generous and long-suffering England'. At the Royal Naval Division the Prime Minister's son, 'Beb' Asquith, announced that he 'ought to be shot'. And former President Theodore Roosevelt called him a 'blue rumped ape' and lumped him with 'the unhung traitor Keir Hardie' among a 'venomous' herd of socialists, all 'physically timid creatures'. 'You are not so loved here as you were,' Granville Barker reported from New York. 'The "Common Sense about the War" raised you up many enemies and turned some of your friends very sour.'

Feeling themselves implicated, some writers reacted dramatically. The best-selling novelist W. J. Locke suddenly sprang up screaming: 'I will not sit in the same room with Bernard Shaw!' J. C. Squire put it to his readers that G.B.S. should be tarred and feathered. In an open letter, subtitled 'A Manual for the Haters of England', Henry Arthur Jones blasted him with an enormous vituperative sentence:

'The hag Sedition was your mother, and Perversity begot you. Mischief was your midwife and Misrule your nurse, and Unreason brought you up at her feet – no other ancestry and rearing had you, you freakish homunculus, germinated outside of lawful procreation . . .'

More painful to Shaw was the response of those he loved. Archer's son, whom from childhood Shaw had known as 'Tomarcher', sailed home from New York on the first available steamer to rejoin his volunteer corps and was sent to Flanders. 'It is a sickening business this sending lambs to the slaughter,' Shaw commiserated. But Archer, fiercely patriotic, felt differently.

Shaw had also hoped to get support from G. K. Chesterton. But Chesterton, who had been ill during late 1914 and early 1915, was 'hungry for hostilities'. The war excited the dark side of his nature. 'I have always thought there was in Prussia an evil will,' he wrote to Shaw. 'Of course there is an evil will in Prussia,' Shaw agreed. 'Prussia isn't Paradise. I have been fighting that evil will, in myself and others, all my life.' Chesterton's hatred seemed to Shaw the product of a mind in which the war had lodged as medieval fantasy. And to Chesterton, Shaw appeared equally unreal. 'I think you are a great man; and I think your first great misfortune was that you were born in a small epoch,' he wrote. 'But I think it is your last and worst misfortune that now at last the epoch is growing greater: but you are not.'

Wells too chimed in with the public outcry, describing G.B.S. as 'one of those perpetual children who live in a dream of make-believe . . . that he is a person of incredible wisdom and subtlety running the world.

'. . . It is almost as if there was nothing happening in Flanders. It is almost as if there was no pain in all the world . . . [he] flings himself upon his typewriter and rattles out his broadsides. And nothing will stop him. All through the war we shall have this Shavian accompaniment going on, like an idiot child screaming in a hospital . . . He is at present . . . an almost unendurable nuisance.'

'If I were a German, I should criticize the Berlin Government with equal fierceness for having made the war,' Shaw wrote to Trebitsch. In fact he did write 'The German Case Against Germany' in May 1916, but by that time he was widely regarded as a German sympathizer. 'I am not what is called pro-German,' he wrote, ' . . . neither am I an anti-German.' He insisted that a gentleman refused to hate his enemy in wartime. But this attitude had no comfortable place in a country exulting in the announcement that all German music was to be banned at concerts. People reminded one another how he had championed Wagner. Even 'his Fabian ideas of social reconstruction,' claimed the *Daily Chronicle*, 'are inspired by Berlinese notions of symmetry'.

His reasoning was impeccable; his offence emotional. 'In the right key one can say anything,' he wrote to Bertrand Russell, 'in the wrong key, nothing: the only delicate part of the job is the establishment of the key.' But many writers felt he had gone off-key. Henry James, who was soon to become a British citizen, claimed that he had not been able to read Shaw's *Common Sense* at all because 'his horrible flippancy revolts me'. Arnold Bennett, too, described as a 'disastrous pity' Shaw's 'perverseness, waywardness, and harlequinading'.

Shaw's jokes, such as his tip to those who wanted unconditionally to smash Germany that they should go about killing all her women, were his natural method of expression. 'If we did not die of laughter at the humours of war we should of horror,' he admitted to Robert Loraine; and to his sister Lucy he confessed: 'one has to learn to laugh at such things in war or else go mad.' He asked those who objected that his jokes did not fit the hour to ignore the 'imbecilities' of his style and fix on the content. But this was impossible. 'Shaw is often ten minutes ahead of the truth,' wrote Woodrow Wilson's brother-in-law Stockton Axson, 'which is almost as fatal as being behind the time.'

He felt his isolation. 'Thanks for your friendly hail,' he wrote acknowledging a letter from Bertrand Russell. 'It really is necessary for people who can keep their heads to pass the time of day occasionally lest they should begin to fear that they, and not the others, are the madmen.' Most members of the Dramatists Club refused to meet him at their lunches; and when James F. Muirhead, editor of *Baedeker*, resigned from the Society of Authors, because 'I cannot consent that any part of my affairs should be in any way under the control of a man of whom I think as I do of you', Shaw stepped down himself from the two committees at the Society of Authors where for the past ten years he had been the chief source of energy and initiative. Muirhead was an admirer of Shaw, counting the shocks he had given Britain over the past thirty years 'among the most salutary influences brought to bear on that country'. But by 1915 he was writing of his 'myopia of genius . . . you really do not understand why you are at present a cause of offence to 99 out of every 100 people that I meet.'

It had needed courage to go on writing as he did. 'It was not easy,' Shaw admitted. 'I know of no other literary man of anything like his eminence who would have taken such treatment so good-naturedly,' wrote Desmond MacCarthy. Almost he seemed unperturbed. 'I am not afraid of unpopularity,' he told Beatrice Webb. He could not get angry with people he met – 'it breaks my back completely,' he explained in a letter begging not to be introduced to Lloyd George. But he was long-lastingly affected. Below the surface of his forbearance, layers of disillusion were forming. He would take imaginative revenge against this society by threatening it with his Zeppelin raid at the end of *Heartbreak House*, and by scoring victories over the 'Goddams' in the person of St Joan. He would recharge his optimism, too, by gazing through the heartbreaking facts into a haze of Shavian hypotheses. 'I don't expect anybody but myself to see as far as I do,' he told the Webbs – an expectation amply to be justified by the public's blindness over *Back to Methuselah*. Meanwhile, he kept his spirits whirring with colossal swanking. 'The longer I live the more I see that I am never wrong about anything,' he admitted to Wells.

He protected himself too with brighter paradoxes. The war, he complained, 'has made me excessively popular'. He became expert at converting every rebuff into another victory. 'All the forts opened fire on me,' he had reported to Stella Campbell who was touring *Pygmalion* in the United States; 'and they have capitulated one after the other . . . my enemies are my footstool.'

About those matters that might have stirred approval – his cheque for £200 to the Belgian refugees; his £20,000 (equivalent to £700,000 in 1997) contribution to the British War Loan – he kept uncharacteristically quiet. Partly it was a matter of self-respect, partly of outmanoeuvring those who wished to surround him with obloquy. 'Unless you make a reputation at once for being utterly impossible, implacable, inexorable, you are lost,' he was to advise his French translator, Augustin Hamon. But by making such a reputation, Shaw was becoming a lost man in politics.

'When war comes the time for arguing is passed.' But Shaw could not keep from arguing. He argued as other people in another war were to dig: for victory. Whenever he was criticized, he counter-attacked. When accused of giving propaganda ammunition to Germany he retorted that it was his accusers themselves who had done that, Germany having attacked him bitterly until it noticed similar attacks in England.

He had an answer for everything: often a wonderfully exasperating answer, formed in the conviction that it was as much his duty to face criticism as it was the soldiers' to face bullets. Full of the appalling slaughter at Neuve Chapelle and at the Gallipoli landing, he mocked the outcry that arose in the spring of 1915 over the sinking of a popular Atlantic liner, the *Lusitania*. Here at last was something small enough – the killing of saloon passengers – for the public imagination to grasp. He heartily welcomed it, and the execution of Nurse Edith Cavell, for the effect it would produce on the United States, the moral centre of the neutral world. 'I even found a grim satisfaction,' he afterwards wrote, 'very intelligible to all soldiers, in the fact that the civilians who found the war such splendid British sport should get a sharp taste of what it was to the actual combatants.' During the first Zeppelin raids he advocated that movable metal arches should immediately be placed in school playgrounds so that children might know where to run when the Zeppelins came. But before this suggestion was implemented, people accused him of defeatism, goading him into recommending a judicious bombardment of London. 'In fact if we had any sense we would bombard London ourselves, and demolish the Houses of Parliament and all the new government offices for aesthetic reasons just as we should demolish the slums for sanitary reasons.'

The most difficult long-term problem for Shaw was recruitment. There could be no denying that the Government's painting of the war as a simple scene of knight errantry, with England as Lancelot-Galahad, Germany as the wicked giant and Belgium as the beautiful maiden, had been wonderfully popular. But after three months of war fever, recruitment had begun to fall off, and with it, Shaw claimed, the justification for keeping the nation in its fool's paradise disappeared. 'The recruiting got on its feet again,' he wrote, once the War Office 'withdrew the silliest of its placards, and faced the necessity for higher pay and better treatment of recruits'.

Shaw wanted to bring the same people up to the same guns equipped with a far better arsenal of attitudes, motives, opinions; to place them in the same trenches looking forward without detestation to the soldiers opposite, and looking back with scepticism at the politicians who had arranged this grotesque firing line. 'The newspapers are so stupid that, simply because he's Mr Shaw, they won't report him – instead of running him as our leading patriot,' wrote Lytton Strachey.

The newspapers did send their reporters to his speeches, but only to see him hissed and mobbed. The German press had already described him as being persecuted in London, fearful of assassination, and living under house arrest with sentries at his doors. The failure of his speeches to provoke mobbing – 'reporters who were sent to see me torn limb from limb withdrew copyless' – was partly due to the nature of his audiences which mingled 'smart persons of the soulful type – Lady Diana [Manners] for example' with clusters of prominent Fabians. They were, in short, very like theatre audiences, full of young people in bright clothes, for whom he gave excellent performances without benefit of reviews.

Most people did not know by now whether he was a pacifist or a conscriptionist – in fact he was neither. 'It seems to me that all Socialists should advocate compulsory national service, both civil and military,' he wrote. 'But compulsory soldiering is another matter.' It was agonizing to see the short, red-faced, Cecil Chesterton got up in khaki and looking as if he could camouflage himself 'as a beetroot on a sack of potatoes by simply standing stock still'. Shaw himself would have cut a far sharper figure in uniform. In the first days of the war he had witnessed a company of volunteers come swinging along Gower Street and 'to my utter scandal I was seized with a boyish impulse to join them'.

As a 'superannuated person' he felt the inappropriateness of urging young people to take up arms. He criticized the Derby Scheme, which was bullying and cajoling men into voluntary service, for its 'appalling bad stage management' as well as the perverted economic and emotional basis on which it was founded. 'If the decision is to be Conscription, let it be faced, not as a temporary expedient,' he wrote in the *Daily News*, 'but as an advance in social organization.' But the second Conscription Act, which became effective on 25 May 1916, a week before the Battle of Jutland, was an emergency measure, with little considered legal character. Every military authority now became a press gang. The superstition that all Britons were free was kept up by a clause in the Act which reserved the liberty of people to refuse service on conscientious grounds, but neither the qualifications nor the treatment of this category of exempt person were defined. The result was that conscientious objectors were in practice rancorously persecuted.

All over the country there were cases of ill usage and vindictive sentences: and though Shaw 'should not have objected myself if I had been liable to serve', he was greatly exercised by this widespread maltreatment. He intervened in the case of an employee in the Education Department of the London County Council who was sent for miscellaneous duties to a military barracks, because the decision meant that 'public education is of no service to the country'. How could the Government reasonably claim that 'to take an educated man of special literary talent and aptitude from the work of national education, and to set him to sweep barracks, dig latrines, or wait at table on an officers' mess is to effect a stroke of national economy which will materially help to win the war'? He objected to the composer Rutland Boughton's work being described as 'not of the least national importance'. Despite all the musical entertainments for the troops it was as if military tribunals believed that fine art was frivolous and out of place in wartime, 'and that all a man needs to be a complete Englishman is football in peace, fighting in war, and a formula about his duty to King and Country to save himself the trouble of thinking'. He appeared as a character witness at a court martial on behalf of Clarence Norman, a journalist whom he had employed to make verbatim reports of his speeches in shorthand and who was imprisoned for two and a half years for ignoring his call-up papers. And he used the cases of two other conscientious objectors of recognized integrity, Stephen Hobhouse and Clifford Allen, to demonstrate the common misuse of the Government's legislation by military tribunals. 'If Mr Hobhouse is imprisoned for a single hour,' he wrote in Massingham's *Nation*, 'the law is broken and the good faith of the Government discredited.'

Shaw studied the evidence, took trouble to be legally exact, and chose each case with care. Repeated sentences for the same offence could with hard labour become sentences of death. A new crime had been created. 'It is worth noticing that Quakers have been persecuted with the utmost ferocity,' Shaw wrote, 'whilst pugnacious objectors who simply objected to this particular war and openly declared that they would fight in a class war have been treated with comparative indulgence.'

He also gave sympathetic advice to one or two deserters, destroying the letters for their protection and writing confidentially so as not to undermine his own position as 'an old advocate of compulsory service'. According to Rebecca West, he was like Swift rather than Shelley, and whatever he said, the effect of his words was to question rather than inspire the prosecution of the war. Watching him as he walked on to the platform and began speaking, she perceived that his virtue was getting thin with dilution. 'The passing of middle age has wiped the aggressive strangeness from his face, by mitigating with silver the redness of his hair and the pirate twist of his eyebrows, and has revealed a predominant quality of noble and unhysteric sensitiveness,' she wrote. 'In public life there is not time for such sensitiveness . . . when he began to speak, and the Irish accent shivered over his musical voice like the wind over a lake, one perceived another reason why he should not enter into politics.'

But Shaw always worked against the grain of his natural sensitivity. 'I go back to politics, religion & philosophy,' he had written to Stella Campbell. 'They give me frightful headaches, but satisfy my soul.' He felt that he knew now 'why Shakespeare and Swift were so bitter' after the wars against Philip II and Louis XIV. To overcome early bitterness he had removed himself from the intimate thing and forced his way into politics, but now felt uncertain of his place in public life: 'I no longer have any confidence in my notions of what this generation needs to have said to it,' he told Wells.

It seemed impossible to go on writing plays. In these days of clashing events, art could 'only be carried by the deaf,' Rebecca West acknowledged. 'And the artist who, like Mr Shaw, abandons it, at least shows that he has good hearing and is listening to the world.'

But he wanted a world that listened to him. The Fabian Research Department had commissioned Leonard Woolf to investigate the causes of the war. Against a background of Bloomsburgian scepticism, Woolf records, 'I did an immense amount of work on this.' His conclusions were published in 1916 as a book, *International Government*, to which Shaw supplied an American Preface.

Leonard Woolf argued that the first step towards the prevention of war must be the creation, as part of international government, of a supranational authority. His examination of the minimum requirements for such a body and his description of its probable structure comprised the first detailed study for the League of Nations. Shaw wanted to amplify this project. 'I find myself installed as a great prophet,' he pointed out. But he was a prophet without disciples, disestablished, needing affirmations. Shaw's League of Nations floats with its dreaming spires like an academy for supermen and superwomen, a sublime factory where Undershaft's weapons are manufactured by a professor of Greek and his wife, charged with defending democracy from those who, seeking mob popularity, sacrifice the eternal to the temporal. It is a Palace of Revolution, shimmering across the wilderness where Shaw preached, in which international matters are taken from those whose outlook is formed by official habits and given over to the welfare of us all. Finally, this visionary League stands as a temple for Shaw's paradoxes, his Abbey of Theleme, where all is magnificently opposed to the ordinary world.

4

TOURING THE TRENCHES

> To a man who has produced a modern comedy, a campaign is child's play.
>
> 'Joy Riding at the Front', *Daily Chronicle* (7 March 1917)

The ordinary world, over which crawled tanks, U-Boats and Zeppelins, appeared scarcely less fantastical than Shaw's *phalanstère*. At the end of 1916 Lloyd George's new War Cabinet rejected Germany's peace proposals: but public opinion was veering more sympathetically towards 'Dearest G.B.S. (who is splendid about the war)' as Ellen Terry called him.

He had always found some supporters. Keir Hardie had 'felt the thrill' of his *Common Sense* and there had been the suggestion that a popular edition should be prepared by Arnold Bennett. When purged of the satirical absurdities readers accepted so literally, Bennett believed that Shaw's writing, which contained 'the most magnificent, brilliant, and convincing common sense that could possibly be uttered', would inaugurate a period of open discussion. Nothing came of this plan, though Shaw himself endorsed it. 'You, and I and Wells and Webb should be working together,' he urged Bennett late in 1916. '. . . However, it can't be helped – we must do the best we can ploughing our lonely back gardens.' Shaw had looked for a coalition of the intelligentsia, believing it was the duty of representatives of art and literature in all countries to keep moral considerations above the nationalistic level of the war. But though these writers gained no authority beyond what each could separately extort by the persuasiveness of his or her pen, at least the atmosphere had eased. Both J. C. Squire and W. J. Locke had come up and shaken Shaw's hand. Wells, too, having gone through 'disillusionment about the beneficence of our war-making', had reached conclusions similar to Shaw's.

Adelphi Terrace had been damaged in an air raid; at Ayot St Lawrence an anti-aircraft station, with searchlights and soldiers' sheds, was put up.

Shaw continued, as in peacetime, to divide his weeks between the two places. The villagers suspected him of being a spy. After all, he had been there less than a dozen years. They knew his car and motor-bicycle well enough; they knew his dog Kim, 'the village terror': but they did not know what to make of his remarks about this 'most *maddening* war'. Their suspicions began to blow away after the famous Hertfordshire Blizzard of 1915. 'He came out and worked hard with the other menfolk for days on end, sawing up trees which had been torn up by their roots and lay blocking the road,' one of them remembered.

It was the Zeppelin raids above all else that gave everyone a subject of conversation. One Zeppelin, after voyaging majestically over the Shaws' house on its way to London, was shot down near Ayot on 1 October 1916. Next morning Shaw rode off through the rain to see the wreckage – two lumps of twisted metal framework in a watery field splashed over all day by happy crowds. 'The police were in great feather,' he reported, 'as there is a strict cordon, which means you cant get in without paying.' But admission was cheap and well worth the price. 'I didnt half cheer, I tell you,' Shaw heard one girl remark. Nineteen bodies lay in a barn at the edge of the field. 'May I go in?' asked one woman. 'I would like to see a dead German.'

He had been enchanted by the sky-spectacle against the stars, with its magnificent orchestration. Having seen the Zeppelin fall like a burning newspaper, 'with its human contents roasting for some minutes (it was frightfully slow)', he had gone back to bed and was asleep in ten minutes. Reflecting on this, he confided to the Webbs: 'One is so pleased at having seen the show that the destruction of a dozen people or so in hideous terror and torment does not count . . . Pretty lot of animals we are!'

Charlotte wrapped herself round with remoter preoccupations. She felt proud of her husband's fame, but shared few of his interests; was wreathed in smiles, but seemed out of it all. To Virginia Woolf she appeared like a 'fat white Persian cat', which had rolled itself up on a cushion of Indian mysticism and gone to sleep. 'When she got me alone she tried to convert me,' Virginia wrote after a weekend together in the summer of 1916, 'and lent me little books about the Seutras, which she had to hide from Mrs Webb.' Unluckily for Charlotte, Beatrice Webb spied these little books beside her bed and nosed out their contents. 'The thesis is that by continuous meditation, or self-hypnotism, you will rise above the self-conscious self and realize the "God Power" within you,' Beatrice noted sceptically. Charlotte confided to Virginia Woolf that Beatrice, though a wonderful person, 'had no idea of religion'. She reacted with irritation to Charlotte's easy answers and (according to Virginia) 'jeered at poor old Mrs Shaw'. But it was the spectacle of *rich* old Mrs Shaw that aggravated

Beatrice – this woman whose decent restlessness had been stilled by a religious placidity removing her from 'all efforts to make things better for those who are suffering from their heredity or environment'. Beatrice had felt sympathetic to Charlotte when she was suffering over her husband's intrigue with Mrs Pat: what antagonized her now was Charlotte's lack of suffering. It was exasperating to see her beaming with overflowing contentedness in the middle of this appalling war: she appeared so little *inconvenienced* by it all.

At the beginning of 1917 Shaw began a new diary. 'I am going to try to keep it for a year,' he noted, 'as a sample slice of my life.' Altogether he kept it for ten days, and the sample slice it cut from his Ayot routine shows why he did not prolong it. There was no time. Every morning he was hectically occupied pouring out his 'intolerable opinions' to readers of the *Woman's Dreadnought*, *Somerset County Gazette*, and much of the American press. In the afternoons he and Charlotte would go into the garden where she sawed logs and he split them with a beetle and wedges. Sometimes he hurried through the village with his West Highland terrier; when he needed to go further he would set off for a spin and a spill on his motor-bike, and come rushing back to tighten nuts on the front wheel. At half-past four he allowed himself a cup of chocolate, while Charlotte drank tea. Then he would press on with his writing, often dealing with letters that Ann Elder had sent down from London. The second interval of the day – called dinner – began at half-past seven: then he would read and end the evening singing and playing the piano – Strauss's *Elektra* and Liszt's transcription of Beethoven's Ninth Symphony, Gounod's songs, arias from Mozart and Wagner operas, and a good deal of miscellaneous Berlioz, Elgar and Schumann. Finally he would go up to Charlotte's room to say good-night, and retire to his own bed with the *Economic Journal*.

Early that month he received an invitation from Douglas Haig, Commander-in-Chief of the British army, to visit the Front. 'Charlotte said I must go, as I ought to see this terrible thing for myself,' he noted. 'I grumbled that I should see nothing except a conventional round on which all the journalists are sent; but . . . my interest increased as the day went on.' By the following week he had come to feel that he 'was not free to refuse'.

In the blunted landscape, with its splintered trees, its signposts without villages, Shaw found some devastating material. Privately he confided to Lady Gregory that his week at the Front had been 'a most demoralizing experience'. Publicly in the *Daily Chronicle* he reported: 'I enjoyed myself enormously and continuously.' Both statements contained truth, and were a shorthand for his translation of a demoralizing early life into a career of sustained and serious comedy. He set out to console those who had husbands, brothers, sons, friends in the trenches, or who were themselves in training for that ordeal, with a display of black entertainment. He confidently assured everyone that there was no inevitability at the Front of being killed. On the contrary, death was very uncertain: the gas was crazily blown in the wrong direction, the high explosives were so appallingly imprecise that the 'Somme battlefield was very much safer than the Thames Embankment with its race of motors and trams'. The devastation was terrific yet many of the old towns had been badly in need of demolition. The cathedral at Arras looked finer as a ruin than when he had last seen it intact; the Little Square, too, had been most 'handsomely knocked about' and many old buildings, such as the Cloth Hall at Ypres, would gain a more beautiful existence in the memory than they had ever achieved in actuality.

Drudgery was one of the hardships of war: but the military provided many colourful diversions. Whenever an aeroplane sailed across the blue, delightful white puff-balls blossomed in the sky around it. Every night was Guy Fawkes Night. The guns hurled their fiery shells joyously into the air and set up a bombardment finer than Tchaikovsky's *1812*. He had difficulty believing that the man lying by the roadside was not a tramp taking a siesta during the booming and whizzing of this band music, but a gentleman who had lost his head. Behind the lines bayonet practice was conducted without the least blood lost, and imparted a bank holiday air to the place which really looked magnificent in the snow and sunshine. The trenches were crammed with pacifists, socialists and internationalists, all freed from theoretical illusions, all damning the party politicians with the greatest heartiness, and despite uncomfortable conditions, 'no more hopelessly wretched than I'. Fighting men, Shaw explained, escape the perpetual money worries of their civilian counterparts and the egotism of their preoccupation with commerce. At the Front something exciting was always happening that satisfied man's heroic instincts.

The horror is forced invisibly between the lines of Shaw's writing. War could do many things, he argued, but it could not end war. 'A victory for anybody is a victory for war.' He predicted that economic rather than military forces would eventually end it all, and that the only benefits of this vast calamity would lie in the employment of military virtues for a decently organized civilian life. For in the army, instead of your hand being against every man's and every man's hand against you, 'you are continually trying to get things done in the best possible way for the benefit of your comrades in arms, of your country, of the whole of which you are a part . . . whereas commerce is normally competitive and places your individual pocket before all the higher objects of ambition'.

Shaw's 10,000-word report of his experiences as a war tourist revived questions of his loyalty. One Member of Parliament demanded if this were the sort of man who should be officially invited to the British front line. 'I have always found that when any gentleman visits the front in France,' replied the Government spokesman, 'he comes back with an added desire to help the British Army and is proud of it.' The House of Commons filled with cheers – this time on Shaw's behalf. Many who had accused him of German sympathies now wondered whether he was actually in the service of the British Government to advertise the country's celebrated freedom of speech. Observing him to be 'an interesting man of original views', Haig had taken G.B.S. to a demonstration of experimental weapons. But though he later voted Haig 'the most interesting new writer of the past twelve months', Shaw privately judged him to be an academician of war 'trained socially and professionally to behave and work in a groove from which nothing could move him, disconcerted and distressed by novelties and incredulous as to their military value, but always steadied by a well-closed mind and unquestioned code . . . He made me feel that the war would last thirty years, and that he would carry it on irreproachably until he was superannuated.'

Though he greeted the news of the first revolution in Russia that March as 'a gain to humanity', and described the entry of the United States into the war on 6 April as a 'first class moral asset to the common cause against junkerism', Shaw felt politically gloomy. The Prime Minister had struck out his name from the 'list of persons with ideas' proposed for the Reconstruction Committee to advise on post-war social problems. He was still an outsider.

That July he was sixty-one. 'Any fool can be 60,' he explained to Trebitsch, 'if he lives long enough.' Charlotte had taken off for Ireland that summer for the sake of her lumbago, leaving G.B.S. to revert somewhat to his bachelor ways. He was seeing much of Kathleen Scott, formidable widow of the Antarctic explorer Robert Falcon Scott – a model Shavian heroine 'adventurously ready to go to the ends of the earth at half an hour's notice with no luggage but a comb with three teeth in it, and always successful'. Her job was sculpting – she made a bust and full-length statuette of G.B.S. in bronze. During periods of grass-widowhood G.B.S. was sometimes allowed to stay with Kathleen, especially after her marriage in 1922 to Hilton Young. 'We got on together to perfection,' he recorded.

After Stella had gone off to marry Cornwallis-West 'I really thought I was a dead man,' Shaw admitted, 'until I recovered my sanity by going right back to my economics and politics, and put in a hard stint of work on this abominable war.' But by 1917 he had come to feel that 'my bolt is shot as to writing about the war', and that he 'must get away for a moment from Fabians & politics or I shall go mad'. He decided to make for Ireland and enjoy the open skies of Parknasilla where Charlotte had been staying with her sister.

He arrived on 10 September and early the following month reported that he had been 'boating and bathing and making butter in a dairy ever since'. Work was impossible. 'In the Atlantic air one grows big and rank and Irish,' he wrote to Beatrice Webb. '. . . this is the Land of the Free compared to England.'

5

THE RECRUITING OFFICER

The art of the dramatic poet knows no patriotism.

Preface to *Heartbreak House*

Early in the war Shaw's box office appeal had plummeted. 'The moment is not happily chosen for resuming the old Shavian capers, which were among the strangest by-products of the long peace,' declared A. B. Walkley in *The Times*. There were many who felt that theatres, museums and picture galleries should be converted into hospitals and barracks. To their surprise the stage grew incomparably popular between 1914 and 1918. Initially there were recruiting plays with patriotic songs which featured a harangue in the interval by the fire-eating chauvinist (and fraudulent financier) Horatio Bottomley. Shaw, who went to see one of Bottomley's perorations, reported: 'It's exactly what I expected: the man gets his popularity by telling people with sufficient bombast just what they think themselves and therefore want to hear.' For a specialist in the unexpected there was no audience. Producers and actor-managers ransacked their memories for out-of-date musicals and revues to exploit the bliss of soldiers who were happy to be no longer under fire and ready to be delighted by every young girl they saw, old joke they heard. London suddenly reverted to antique farces played in bedrooms with four doors and a window, identical to the bedrooms of flats above and below them, and all occupied by jealous husbands and wives mistaking one bedroom for another.

Shaw's contribution to this wartime theatre was four playlets that caricature, in juvenile fashion, the economic and social changes brought about in Germany, England and Russia by the Great War: and the lack of any change in Ireland. His characters are preposterously named –

Archdeacon Daffodil Donkin, Ermyntrude Roosenhonkers-Pipstein – and preposterously re-cast. Wives of fashionable architects take jobs as tea ladies; eminent medical men become waiters in hotels. Shaw made the plots of these playlets more ludicrous and their action more knock-about than any bedroom farce – then having appealed to the popular nonsensical mood, he tried to introduce a few moments of serious reflection. At the end of *The Inca of Perusalem*, for example, the absurd Inca, whose athletic moustache 'is so watched and studied,' we are told, 'that it has made his face the political barometer of the whole continent', ceases to be a lampoon on the Kaiser, and speaks in the tones of the Devil from *Don Juan in Hell*. Shaw wanted to remind his audiences that war had long been a favourite food of their imagination – when men had no battles to fight they played at war in their films and magazine stories. Since all of us were partly infected by the same passion, we could not simply blame one man, the Kaiser, for making us fight.

Shaw's satire against wartime England was an exaggerated stunt, *Augustus Does His Bit*, which he threw off in August 1916 to be performed in aid of the Belgians. This skit on high-born officialdom and crass bureaucracy at home (Lord Augustus Highcastle produces a bullet which had been flattened by contact with his skull) was well recognized at the Front, but it did not gain much recognition in London. 'He has simply evolved an idiot out of his own consciousness,' noted *The Times*, 'and ascribed to him the follies of his own imagination.'

Annajanska, his 'revolutionary romancelet', is a half-hour bravura piece written during three December days in 1917 – a month after the Bolshevik Revolution and a week before Russia signed an armistice with Germany. Shaw hands the derelict power created by the fall of tsardom back to a 'wild grand duchess'. He wanted to exploit the apparent paradox of the most radical event in his lifetime having erupted in the most politically backward country. The extravaganza may best be regarded as a present to Lillah McCarthy. It enabled her to make a startling entrance dragging in two exhausted soldiers, fire off several fusillades and dominate the Coliseum stage in a magnificent green and black Russian fur coat designed by Charles Ricketts. 'I went home very tired,' she wrote happily.

O'Flaherty, V.C. had been conceived in the summer of 1915 while staying with Lady Gregory at Coole ('the scene is quite simply before the porch in your house'). He had intended a four-handed light comedy (with small but important additional roles for a thrush and a jay) that would appeal to what he called 'the Irishman's spirit of freedom and love of adventure'. But as he wrote, a portrait emerged of the Irish character that 'will make the Playboy seem a patriotic rhapsody by comparison,' he apologized to Lady Gregory. '... *C'était plus fort que moi.* At worst, it will be a barricade for the theatre to die gloriously on.'

Having been asked by Sir Matthew Nathan, Under-Secretary for Ireland, for help over Dublin Castle's disappointing recruitment campaign, he had taken a famous recent Irish exploit – the killing of eight German soldiers and capture of fifteen others singlehanded by Private Michael O'Leary – and Shavianized it for the stage. 'Incomprehensible as it seems to an Englishman, Irish patriotism does not take the form of devotion to England and England's king.' More effective, he reckoned, would be to advertise the war as an opportunity to travel abroad at the British Government's expense.

The enlargement of O'Flaherty's experience at the Front induces in him an unbearable realism. 'Knowledge and wisdom has come over me with pain and fear and trouble,' he says. 'Ive been made a fool of and imposed upon all my life.' He sees everything for what it is: Irish patriotism is mindless ignorance; Irish family life grows more terrible than life in the trenches; his Irish sweetheart, no longer the angelic colleen, is ruthless and mercenary; and his mother becomes an appalling termagant whose 'batings' at home have proved good training for O'Flaherty's acts of bravery in the army.

Shaw's happy ending was hardly adequate compensation for a recruiting play that has its hero exclaiming: 'Dont talk to me or any other soldier of the war being right. No war is right.' And: 'Youll never have a quiet world til you knock the patriotism out of the human race.' This was not what Sir Matthew Nathan had been expecting. He consulted General Sir John French, Commander-in-Chief of Home Forces and soon to be made Lord Lieutenant of Ireland, and, having brooded on it with him, wrote to say that they both believed the production should be postponed. It was a tactful letter. Any performance, he suggested, might lead to 'demonstrations' smothering the 'fine lessons' of the play.

O'Flaherty, V.C. received its first presentation on 17 February 1917 at Treizennes in Belgium. Robert Loraine was O'Flaherty and the other parts were played by officers of the Royal Flying Corps, while the men put on a performance of *The Inca of Perusalem*. Later that year Shaw himself read the play to a hospital full of wounded soldiers near Ayot. 'They gave me three cheers, and laughed a good deal,' he told Lady Gregory; 'but the best bits were when they sat very tight and said nothing.'

Though *O'Flaherty, V.C.* was not performed by the Irish Players until it had softened into 'A Reminiscence of 1915' at the end of 1920 – and then only in London – Shaw's reputation seemed to have come alive in Ireland. After seven years without a Shaw production, the Abbey Theatre staged what amounted to an extraordinary festival – seven Shaw plays between the autumn of 1916 and the summer of 1917. And what was happening in Ireland appeared to be happening in other parts of the world. The American manager William Brady had presented *Major Barbara* in New York; the British-born actor William Faversham had broken the box office records set by *Pygmalion* with his United States tour of *Getting Married*. Throughout Europe all manner of Shavian productions were appearing – *Androcles* in Stockholm, *Candida* in Budapest, *Pygmalion* in Warsaw, *Mrs Warren's Profession* in Helsinki, *Widowers' Houses* in Prague and *The Devil's Disciple* pretty well simultaneously in Copenhagen and Vienna.

In Britain too there was a recovery of interest in his work – *Man and Superman* had been performed in its entirety in Edinburgh, and half a dozen other plays were touring the country from Plymouth to Birmingham. The London theatre stood ready at last for a new drama from G.B.S. But he felt oddly undecided. He had begun a shorthand draft of a play, provisionally called *The Studio in the Clouds*, on 4 March 1916. 'I dont know what its about,' he wrote to Stella over thirteen weeks later. By the end of that year he had written a first act, 'filling the stage with the most delightful characters under the pleasantest circumstances,' he told William Archer. ' . . . I have left them there for months and months, hopelessly stuck. This has never happened before.' Later he changed the title to *Heartbreak House*. 'We must be content to dream about it,' he advised Lillah McCarthy in the summer of 1918. 'Let it lie there to shew that the old dog can still bark a bit.'

6

ANGLO-IRISH POLITICS

> The government of one nation against its will by another nation raises no question of whether such government is good or bad: it is itself misgovernment, and would be bad even if it produced perfect order and mutual material prosperity . . . I object to being governed by a superior race even more than by an inferior one, so that the Englishman may take it as he likes, as superior, inferior or equal: I object to his governing me.
>
> Shaw to Sá (4 November 1917)

'If you want to bore an Irishman, play him an Irish melody, or introduce him to another Irishman,' Shaw had written. ' . . . Abroad, however, it is a distinction to be an Irishman; and accordingly the Irish in England flaunt their nationality.' His original motive for leaving Ireland, like his mother's, had been economic: 'a necessary transfer of my business to a European metropolis'. The Irish Renaissance had changed the literary business potential of Dublin. But Dublin was still the city of his discontent. Returning there after more than thirty years, he saw that 'the houses had never been painted since and the little shops had eggs in the windows, with mice and rats running over them'. Later, after reading parts of *Ulysses*, he was to congratulate Joyce: 'It is a revolting record of a disgusting phase of civilization; but it is a truthful one,' he wrote in a letter to the book's publisher Sylvia Beach; 'and I should like to put a cordon round Dublin; round up every male person in it between the ages of 15 and 30; force them to read it . . . I have walked those streets and know those shops and have heard and taken part in those conversations. I escaped from them to England.' He wanted to dissolve that squalid past into a radiant future: and he advised Ireland to cease puffing her sails with the rhetoric of stale grievances, and replace her preoccupation over national divisions with an overall political emancipation.

Shaw separated Dublin from Ireland and overlaid biography with history. 'I am an Irishman and I have not forgotten.' What other person could have demanded, but be refused, membership of the Irish Convention; be offered, but decline, nomination to the Irish Senate; and accept the first presidency of the Irish Academy of Letters. He recommended that Ireland be established as a sanatorium where the English should be sent to gain flexibility of mind: and advised Britain to sell Ireland to the United States in order to pay off her national debt. He was to leave the country to 'stew in her own juice' by not returning there after 1923: then registered as a citizen of the Irish Free State twelve years later.

His career was studded with illuminating acts of generosity to Ireland. He campaigned with Lady Gregory to recapture Hugh Lane's pictures according to the wishes expressed in an unwitnessed codicil to Lane's will; and he promised the Lord Mayor of Dublin a donation of 100 guineas as his contribution towards a good municipal gallery to house them. He presented the Assembly Rooms at Carlow, which he had inherited from his uncle Walter Gurly, to the Catholic Bishop of Kildare and Leighlin for conversion into a technical school and was largely responsible for the Technical College which later developed on that site. He attempted to set up an Irish film industry to which he offered to give *Saint Joan*, being 'desirous that his plays shall employ and develop the dramatic genius of his fellow-countrymen and make Ireland's scenic beauties known in all lands'. Later he would hand the manuscripts of his novels to the National Library of Ireland and finally leave the National Gallery of Ireland one third of his residuary estate.

But Shaw's words spoke louder than his actions. He described Ireland's political debates as 'baby talk', her papers 'comics', her history mere 'police news', and her education a hellish training that prolonged the 'separation of the Irish people into two hostile camps'. He condemned the Censorship of Publications Act as an 'exhibition of Irish moral panic', and castigated her lack of birth control and sex education as a monstrous folly. He ridiculed the Gaelic League for loosening the country's hold on a vital twentieth-century acquisition, the English language, and counselled all patriots 'to go to bed and stay there until the Irish question is settled'. Nevertheless the fact that he was an Irishman 'has always filled me with a wild and inextinguishable pride'. He would have preferred to be 'burnt at the stake by Irish Catholics than protected by Englishmen'. And as a cure for the bad blood flowing from the unhappy historical marriage of England and Ireland, he prescribed a parting by consent rather than absolute divorce, together with a legal wand of oblivion moved over all past warring. To nurture malice, Shaw warned, 'is to poison our blood and weaken our institutions with unintelligent rancor'.

Shaw used 'every device of invective and irony and dialectic at my command' to assuage Ireland's longing for freedom. He had merged the subjects of divorce legislation and the constitutional independence of nations when covering the Parnell scandal of 1890. Home Rule had suddenly come within reach when a majority of Irish Members of Parliament pledged to the issue had been returned to Westminster. But at the height of his leadership of the Irish Party, Charles Parnell had been cited as co-respondent in a divorce case involving the wife of another Irish Member of Parliament and his political future seemed ruined. In letters to *The Star*, Shaw had argued that 'the whole mischief in the matter lay in the law that tied the husband and wife together and forced Mr Parnell to play the part of clandestine intriguer, instead of enabling them to dissolve the marriage by mutual consent, without disgrace to either party'. He advised Parnell to 'sit tight' and urged the Irish Party to unite behind him – otherwise the Liberal Government would exploit the disunity and abandon its commitment to Home Rule. The verdicts of antiquated laws, he added, 'can produce no genuine conviction of its victims' unfitness for public life'. Similarly repugnant was the legally enforced tie between England and Ireland, he implied, where under the Coercion Act 'constitutional reformers are driven to employ all the devices of criminals'.

In the 'Preface for Politicians' which he attached to *John Bull's Other Island* in 1906, Shaw had predicted that 'we can do nothing with an English Government unless we frighten it . . . under such circumstances reforms are produced only by catastrophes followed by panics in which "something must be done".' Ireland's catastrophe was the 'ghastly' Easter Rising of 1916. Shaw made clear his support for 'any Irishman taken in a fight for Irish independence against the British Government, which was a fair fight in everything except the enormous odds my countrymen had to face'. He felt anxiety lest relations between the two countries be fatally poisoned by acts of reprisal from the frightened English Government. 'The men who were shot in cold blood after their capture or surrender were prisoners of war,' he objected, after twelve of the insurgents had been executed.

Shaw's most quixotic intervention into Anglo-Irish politics was on behalf of Roger Casement. Casement had taken advantage of the war to seek help from Germany for the cause of Irish independence, but on the eve of the Easter Rising he was captured by the British as he stepped ashore in Ireland from a German submarine. Feeling in England ran high against Casement who, as a British subject, would inevitably be found guilty of high treason. Much of the money for his defence was raised in the United States. In England writers as various as Conan Doyle and Arnold Bennett appealed for clemency on grounds that ranged from Casement's mental health to Britain's political expediency. Beatrice Webb noticed that, when Charlotte spoke in support of him, her 'eyes flashed with defiance'. So Beatrice took Casement's old friend, Alice Green, who was helping to organize his defence, to see the Shaws. It was a painful meeting. Alice Green desperately needed money to engage a first-rate defence lawyer: Shaw insisted that, since no credible denial of the facts was possible, paying lawyers to come up with technical ingenuities and exchange legal compliments would be throwing money down the drain. Instead he proposed a 'daring frontal attack on the position of the Crown'. Casement was to conduct his own case, admit the facts, plead not guilty and apply as an Irish Nationalist to be held as a prisoner-of-war. Alice Green explained that Casement was extremely ill and incapable of handling a court full of lawyers: in which case, Shaw retorted, 'we had better get our suit of mourning'. So the meeting broke up: Alice Green retiring in tears; Beatrice feeling a fool for having intervened; and G.B.S. striding into his study to compose a speech for Casement which would 'thunder down the ages'.

Beatrice accused Shaw of conceitedly playing word games with the life of this poor man as if it were a 'national dramatic event'. But Casement himself was delighted with the speech. 'I shall be so grateful if you will convey to Bernard Shaw my warmest thanks,' he told the Sinn Fein sympathizer Gavan Duffy; 'his view is mine, with this exception – that I should never suggest to an English court or jury that they should let me off as a prisoner of war, but tell them "You may hang me, and be damned to you".'

Such a man was beyond saving. Casement later regretted not using what he called 'the only defence possible, viz., my own plan and that of G.B.S.' There had been nothing to lose: but he was dissuaded by Alice Green and other friends, found guilty, and sentenced to be hanged. Only then did 'the virtually dead man' rise to make his own lengthy speech from the dock, using a portion of what G.B.S. had written for him. In the fortnight between the court's verdict and the date of sentence, Shaw tried hard to win Casement a reprieve. 'I cannot make matters any worse than they are,' he told H. W. Nevinson, 'and there is just an off chance that I might make them better.' He wrote to *The Times* which rejected his letter, published correspondence in the *Manchester Guardian* and the *Daily News*, and anonymously drafted a petition to Asquith warning him that hanging would make Casement a national hero. Casement was hanged on 3 August 1916.

To those claiming that the unification of Ireland would result in Protestants and Catholics cutting one another's throats, Shaw had replied that 'civil war is one of the privileges of a nation'. Such extermination was 'too much to hope for,' he added darkly, though mankind 'still longs for that consummation'. If 'hatred, calumny, and terror have so possessed men that they cannot live in peace as other nations do, they had better fight it out and get rid of their bad blood that way'.

'What I have dreaded all along,' he told Horace Plunkett, 'is the usual political expedient of a settlement that is no settlement.' To argue for his own federal solution, he accepted an invitation from the editor of the *Daily Express*, a newspaper specially hostile to him during the war, to tell its readers how to unravel the Irish problem. His series of articles, which were later issued in Dublin and London as a pamphlet, *How to Settle the Irish Question*, assembled a brilliant array of arguments for the inevitability of federation. This conclusion, which he described as 'Home Rule for England', possessed similar magical properties to the triple alliance in *Common Sense about the War*, and he frequently edged Wales out of the equation to achieve his mystical three-in-one – 'the federation of the three nations (four if you count the Welsh)'. He then reinforced this combination by building three parliaments – National, Federal and Imperial – in his imagination for 'the three kingdoms alike'.

After eight deliberating months Plunkett's Convention, which had been set up by Lloyd George, voted for an Irish Parliament with authority over the whole country. 'The story becomes more thrilling as it draws to an end,' Shaw wrote to Plunkett in March 1918 after reading the proof sheets of his secret report to the King. '. . . I await the report with some nervousness.' The moment came: the report made no sound. The Government had 'funked it', and Shaw was left feeling that it had been another instance of the unreality in Dublin politics.

The extreme nationalist party Sinn Fein, which had refused to participate in Plunkett's Convention, rapidly evolved into a political power as Parnell's old Irish Party passed away. Sinn Fein refused to attend Westminster and formed their own assembly (Dáil Éireann) in Dublin, representing a completely independent Republic of Ireland which was immediately declared illegal by the British Government.

Shaw had advocated federation as early as 1888 and he was still advocating it more than thirty years later. The flaw in his logic, as he had once expressed it himself, lay in the problem not being 'one of logic at all, but of natural right'. England's extreme procrastination had produced Ireland's extreme reaction, leaving Shaw's consistency as a remnant of historical academicism. He disliked Sinn Fein's glorification of nationalism: yet thirty years before he had written of nationalism being 'an incident of organic growth [which] . . . we shall have to accept'. The young Shaw believed that 'like Democracy, national self-government is not for the good of the people: it is for the satisfaction of the people.' The older Shaw warned against national independencies and neutralities which were set up 'not by the internal strength of a nation's position, but by the interested guarantees of foreign Powers'.

In his 'Preface for Politicians' he had diagnosed the condition of Ireland as being like that of 'a man with cancer: he can think of nothing else . . . A healthy nation is as unconscious of its nationality as a healthy man of his bones. But if you break a nation's nationality it will think of nothing else but getting it set again. It will listen to no reformer, to no philosopher, to no preacher, until the demand of the Nationalist is granted . . . That is why everything is in abeyance in Ireland pending the achievement of Home Rule.'

Ireland's cancer had worsened and now demanded the fiercer remedies of separatism. Shaw regarded the policies of Sinn Fein as symptoms of the disease and not parts of a homoeopathic medicine. 'Sinn Fein means We Ourselves: a disgraceful and obsolete sentiment, horribly anti-Catholic,' he wrote in *How to Settle the Irish Question*. ' . . . Ireland is the Malvolio of the nations, "sick of self-love", and . . . Sinn Fein's delight is to propagate this morose malady.'

Ireland eventually placed its future in the hands of the quacks and windbags of the two rival religions, and in tearing itself away from England tore itself apart. Watching this process was to be intensely painful for Shaw. In his fashion he was devoted to Ireland. But he had become the reformer, philosopher and preacher to whom no one listened.

7

CASUALTIES OF WAR

Literature should never be at war.

Shaw to Henry Newbolt (25 July 1920)

The Shaws did not enter the revelry on Armistice Day. They stayed at Ayot. These years of helplessness seemed to have made a cavity within G.B.S. 'Every promising young man I know has been blown to bits lately,' he told Lady Mary Murray; 'and I have had to write to his mother.' He had written to Stella Campbell at the beginning of 1918 when her son Alan Campbell was killed by the last shell from a German battery. 'My beloved Beo is killed,' she had scribbled to him – but he could not find words of polite consolation. 'I cant be sympathetic: these things simply make me furious,' he burst out. ' . . . Oh, damn, damn, damn, damn, damn, damn, damn, damn, DAMN DAMN! And oh, dear, dear, dear, dear, dear, dearest!'

A month later the news reached him that Robert Gregory had been shot down in his plane and was dead. In a letter prefiguring Yeats's two poems 'An Irish Airman Foresees His Death' and 'In Memory of Major Robert Gregory', he wrote consoling Lady Gregory: 'To a man with his power of standing up to danger – which must mean enjoying it – war must have intensified his life as nothing else could . . . I suppose that is what makes the soldier.' He used Alan Campbell's death – used Stella's reaction – to bring Augusta Gregory comfort. 'Like Robert he seemed to find himself in doing dangerous things. His mother thinks he got all the life he wanted out of the war and nothing else could have given it to him.'

'I was hoping for a letter from you,' Lady Gregory replied. 'I knew it would be helpful.'

Most griefs were beyond help. 'I know you will be very sorry for us,' J. M. Barrie had written after his much-loved godson George Llewelyn Davies had been shot dead near Ypres. Though also living in Adelphi Terrace, he could not bear to give the news in person, but pushed his note through the door of the Shaws' apartment. When he read it, Shaw wept.

William Archer was another who suffered bereavement. His son 'Tom-archer' was wounded at Mount Kearnel and died in a German hospital not long before the Armistice. 'He left his young widow to take his place in his parents' affection, the newly beloved daughter succeeding to the newly lost beloved son,' Shaw recorded. 'Yet Archer was loth to let the son go . . . and even experimented unsuccessfully in those posthumous conversations in which so many of the bereaved found comfort. And so, between daughter and son, the adventure of parentage never ended for Archer.'

And there were others, such as the hopelessly unsoldier-like Cecil Chesterton who had visited Shaw before leaving for the Front and died soon afterwards from trench fever. 'It is impossible to describe what I used to feel on such occasions.'

Whenever possible Shaw used his comic energy to overcome his feelings. He lectured Robert Loraine who had been shot in the small of his back ('the bullet coming out of his collar bone after going up through his lung and knocking his heart into his left elbow') on the importance of being kept 'in the lowest spirits, as laughing cannot be good for shrapnel in the lung'. In the summer of 1918 Loraine was again wounded, and his left kneecap being shattered, advised that his leg might have to be amputated. 'If the worst comes to the worst, I suppose one can play Hamlet with a property leg,' Shaw calculated. ' . . . an artificial leg of the best sort will carry you to victory as Henry V. If you . . . are lame, it means a lifetime of Richard III, unless I write a play entitled *Byron*.' As for flying, 'when it comes to aerial combat, the more of you that is artificial the better'.

Loraine's leg was saved. But to St John Ervine, who did lose a leg that summer, Shaw sent hasty congratulations on his being 'in a stronger position'. Having two available legs, when had Shaw himself ever groused because he did not have three? 'You will have all the energy you have hitherto spent on it to invest in the rest of your frame. For a man of your profession two legs are an extravagance,' G.B.S. assured him. ' . . . You are an exceptionally happy and fortunate man, relieved of a limb to which you owed none of your fame, and which indeed was the cause of your conscription; for without it you would not have been accepted for service.'

Such black parodies of the Shavian dialectic were 'the cheering remarks one makes now to the sacrifice of this horrible war'.

*

The war also finished off the marriage between Granville Barker and Lillah McCarthy. They had gone to the United States where Barker 'fell madly in love – really madly in the Italian manner'. The Helen who had enchanted him was an occasional poet and minor novelist, the wife of Archer Milton Huntington, heir of a railroad fortune, who had provided a guarantee against loss for Barker's theatrical season in New York.

Barker had returned to England in June 1915 promising Lillah that his affair with Helen Huntington was over. He was some £5,000 (equivalent to £170,000 in 1997) in debt, but £2,000 of this was owed in royalties to

G.B.S. who immediately wrote it off. After joining a Red Cross unit, Barker drove over to France – then in September headed off back to the United States, this time to give a series of lectures paying off his debts. He had made what Shaw called a resolution to devote himself to poverty and playwriting. 'I cannot very well remonstrate, as I have been for years urging him to stick to his own proper job of writing plays and leave production and management to people who cant do anything else,' Shaw explained to Pinero that October. '. . . Meanwhile Lillah is at a loose end.'

On his way to the States, Barker had written to Lillah: 'my dear wife – I love you very much if you please – and I'm not very far from you. Distance doesn't mainly count.' But he was also corresponding with Helen, and instead of returning to England at the end of the lecture tour he sent Lillah a letter asking for a divorce. She went, 'all frozen on a cold January night', to Shaw's flat in Adelphi Terrace. He 'made me sit by the fire. I was shivering . . . presently I found myself walking with dragging steps with Shaw beside me . . . up and down Adelphi Terrace . . . he let me cry. Presently I heard a voice in which all the gentleness and tenderness of the world was speaking. It said: "Look up, dear, look up to the heavens. There is more in life than this. There is much more."'

Back with the Red Cross in France, Barker asked Shaw to act as his agent to procure the divorce. Since Lillah had already made him her confidant, he was placed in an awkward position. He went to work instructing Barker to write Lillah a letter her lawyers could use, advising Lillah what he had done, what Barker was doing, and what she should do – which was to get someone to counsel her as he was counselling Barker. Accordingly she chose J. M. Barrie. He, like Shaw, believed that the domestic crockery had been too badly broken to be worth mending, but his advice was swamped by Lillah's emotionalism. Was it likely, she demanded, that Barker knew his mind better than his own wife did? Once this affair was over, he would be coming back to her. This put Barrie's and Shaw's arguments into perpetual check, for it was impossible to recommend anything without offering Lillah a 'vulgar insult'. Shaw tried to hand her the initiative. 'Quite seriously, I have come to the conclusion that you had better get rid of Harley . . . as you are now at the height of your powers, and . . . I gravely doubt whether Harley is fit for married life at all . . . It is in your power to demand your release; he cannot refuse it.'

Barker had expected everything to be cleared up by the spring. He sailed back to the United States and continued fuming impatiently. 'What in heaven's name she is waiting for I don't know. I really believe she has some idea in her head that no divorce is complete without a scandal.'

Poised between Lillah's obduracy and Barker's exasperation, 'I had a difficult time of it,' Shaw afterwards admitted. Once conscription was brought in, Barker returned to Britain, and went to an officer cadet school in Wiltshire. Many of these summer and autumn weekends he spent at Ayot nervily plotting divorce tactics with G.B.S. and Charlotte or with Barrie in London. Driven mad by the delay he implored Shaw to offer Lillah a settlement of five or six hundred pounds a year for life. Since Barker had no money, Lillah immediately realized that he must be in collusion with Helen – and informed the unsuspecting Archer Huntington. 'There was an almighty explosion at the other end,' Shaw later reported, 'and Helen never forgave me for being, as she thought, solely responsible for Lillah's letter.'

Barker's decree was made absolute in the late spring of 1917; Helen's in the summer of 1918. On 21 June that year G.B.S. and Helen met for the first time: and detested each other. 'The guilty pair are not yet married,' Shaw reported to Lillah. ' . . . When it happens I will let you know as soon as I know myself.' They were married on 31 July, but let Shaw know nothing. 'I surmise that you are married; but it is only a surmise,' he wrote to Barker on 26 August. 'It is desirable that your friends should be in a position to make a positive affirmation on the subject. An affectation of ecstasy so continuous as to make you forget all such worldly considerations is ridiculous at your age.'

Shaw was not to know that they had both altered their ages, Helen reducing hers by almost eight years, on the marriage certificate. They wanted to free their lives from the sort of considerations he was emphasizing, and start again. Charlotte disapproved of Barker's divorce as setting a precedent for G.B.S., and she blamed Helen for introducing such unpleasantness into all their lives. Shaw tried to take the long-term view and, during a visit to them near the end of 1918, read out part of his new play *Back to Methuselah*. But 'it has never seemed quite so tedious before,' he apologized afterwards to Barker; ' . . . it was rather hard on Helen to have such a depressing beginning of my playreading.'

It was the end rather than a beginning. 'Virtually we never met again,' Shaw wrote. After her marriage in 1920 to the botanist Frederick Keeble, Lillah pretty well left the stage. 'You must begin a new career as a new woman,' Shaw was to tell her. And she responded: 'Life begins again. I find new delights every day & am re-born.'

But it seemed to Shaw that Barker's seclusion was a genuine loss to the theatre: and then there was the personal loss. 'I could not intrude when I was not welcome.' He was prepared to keep out of their way 'for six months or six years' if necessary. But after six years, 'the devil entered into me'. Though he had not seen them during this time, he had picked up various reports. They had bought a Jacobean mansion in Devon called Netherton Hall (renamed by Shaw Nethermost Hell). Here, his name newly hyphenated, his socialism cast off, and attended by fifteen servants (including a liveried footman) Granville-Barker completed his perfectionist work on the sociology of the stage, *The Exemplary Theatre*, and an unperformed play called *The Secret Life*. 'We shall have to keep on insulting him for his sterility,' Shaw commanded St John Ervine, 'or he will be dead before he gets another play on to the stage.' He tried to stir him up by likening him to Swinburne at Putney; by spurring William Archer on to 'tell him to do something thoroughly vulgar: he needs contact with earth'; and by inventing a Barker Relief Expedition consisting of Lawrence of Arabia, Thomas Hardy and J. M. Barrie.

In May 1925 Shaw was asked to give a vote of thanks after Granville-Barker's address on the theatre at King's College in the Strand. 'I praised Barker's speech to the skies and said that his retirement from the stage to become a professor was inexcusable,' Shaw told Hesketh Pearson. Barker was now placed in a very ticklish position. Lord Balfour, who was in the chair, rose to the rescue with a clever closing speech during which Shaw suddenly began to feel in great pain – 'as if my backbone had turned into a red-hot poker' was how he described it to Lady Rhondda. He was determined to sit it out. Somehow he reached home on foot. 'I really thought I was done for.' Charlotte removed him to Ayot where he lay helpless on his bed until one day, a month later, with a great effort of will he decided to walk down the road – and instantly the pain vanished. Later on he related this experience to Lady Colefax who revealed that Helen Granville-Barker had been sitting exactly behind him, not three feet away, leaning forward with her eyes glued to his backbone. 'I have never seen such hate in any eyes before.'

This story enabled Shaw to cast Helen as a witch who had placed her spell on Granville-Barker so that 'he ceased to be the independent human being we had all known'. This was less disconcerting to him than the belief that they were both perfectly happy. In his position 'I should regard myself as a damned soul,' Shaw remarked to Archer. But Barker had been retreating into his 'natural Henry Jamesism' before he met Helen. She re-created him as a fairy-tale Prince. Every syllable Shaw uttered threatened to dissolve this fantasy. All communication with him was therefore shut down until early in the 1930s when Lillah McCarthy invited Shaw to contribute a Preface to her memoirs. He arranged for the publisher to send Granville-Barker this Preface (which contained a celebration of Lillah's historic stage collaboration with Barker, as well as biographical sidelights on their marriage and divorce). As a result Barker suddenly turned up at Ayot demanding that the book be withdrawn.

Barker wished to forget Lillah whose very name disturbed Helen. 'Let it alone,' he had written to Shaw. Rather to his dismay, Lillah's book was to appear without any reference to him: his past had been obliterated. Twenty minutes after leaving Ayot he returned to take an effusive farewell of Charlotte: and this was the last time they saw him.

Shaw could not quench his pleasure on learning of Helen's fury when, Frederick Keeble being knighted, Lillah became Lady Keeble. Helen wanted a glittering knighthood for her husband, but had she not cut him off from all commerce with the theatre might he not have been given one? Or so G.B.S. believed. 'Cannot you persuade Mr Granville-Barker to stay here and produce Shakespeare,' Raymond Mortimer was to ask Helen years later during one of her last visits to London. To his horrified embarrassment the old lady burst into tears. 'Everyone blames me,' she answered, 'but it is not my fault: it is Harley's.'

Shaw blamed Helen. When Barker died in 1946 the shock 'made me realize how I had still cherished a hope that our old intimate relation might revive'. In a letter to the *Times Literary Supplement* enclosing an old photograph of his friend he had taken in the days of their intimacy, he was to quote Swinburne:

> Marriage and death and division
> Make Barren our lives.

*

This was a good epitaph for a war whose survivors would always be avenging their wounds. Many people have died 'in simple horror, mercifully without quite knowing it,' Shaw wrote to Henry Salt whose wife Kate died early in 1919. Janet Achurch had also died. 'So that adventure is over,' Shaw wrote to Charles Charrington, '. . . Now Janet is again the Janet of 1889, and immortal. Better that than half dead, like me.'

Another casualty was Shaw's sister Lucy. She had never wholly recovered from the death of her mother. Suffering from a 'nervous irritation' she was looked after by Eva Schneider, the daughter of the German family she had lodged with in Gotha. Shaw helped to arrange Eva's exemption from deportation through repeated applications to the Home Office establishing her as his sister's permanent nurse-companion. Financially he was conscientious over Lucy's needs, though otherwise 'I am forced to neglect her as I am forced to neglect everything else'. He had seen most of her when he was seeing most of Stella. They had used Lucy's home as one of their meeting places, enabling Lucy to boast that 'among my most frequent visitors is Mrs Patrick Campbell'. Shaw complimented Stella on having 'brought out the nice side of Lucy that I haven't seen since she was a girl'.

Lucy's tuberculosis was no longer active but her apprehension over the Zeppelin raids seemed to be killing her. 'She is in bed, fearfully ill,' Shaw notified Stella. '... [Her] address for the moment is 2 Grove Park, Camberwell Grove ... Later, the Crematorium, Golders Green.' Kept alive by the devotion of Eva, she somehow pulled through and in the Easter of 1917 the two of them moved to Sussex Lodge, a pretty house on Champion Hill in south-east London. Lucy had reckoned that, being close to an anti-aircraft battery 'we shall always know when the Zepps are on the way' and this would be a comfort. She had not realized that they were also near a bombing exercise ground and within sound of the gun testing at Woolwich Arsenal. Amid the continuous din, 'we didn't know whether a raid was on or not'. The booming of the big defence gun in the next field 'which seemed to blow the house away every time it went off', the noise of exploding bombs and the terrifying sight of a Zeppelin descending through the sky in flames was too much for her. 'I could not stand the strain.'

Shaw then rented a house at Okehampton in Devon where Lucy and Eva travelled in the summer of 1917. Despite eating almost nothing and going nowhere she had become 'a very expensive person,' she remarked wryly – '*my brother indulges me in any extravagance I express the least wish for*'. Shaw kept on Sussex Lodge with a caretaker and, a few weeks after the Armistice, Lucy returned in an ambulance to London. She was slowly starving herself to death. Eva did what she could to persuade her, spoonful by spoonful, to keep alive; and Mrs Pat sent all sorts of delicacies from Fortnum & Mason.

After Lillah's wedding on Saturday 27 March Shaw went round in the late afternoon and sat by Lucy's bed. 'I am dying,' she told him. 'Oh no,' he replied conventionally: 'you will be all right presently.' He took her hand and they were silent. 'There was no sound except from somebody playing the piano in the nearest house (it was a fine evening and all the windows were open), until there was a faint flutter in her throat. She was still holding my hand. Then her thumb straightened. She was dead.'

The doctor informed him that she had been suffering from shell-shock and become anorexic. 'My body to be cremated if possible and the ashes scattered,' she had noted in her will. 'No funeral, no flowers, no mourning.' Shaw arranged for a private cremation, like their mother's, at Golders Green. But finding the church crowded with people, he made up 'a sort of funeral service' of his own.

Fear no more the lightning-flash
Nor the all-dreaded thunder-stone.

Remembering the Zeppelins and awful guns that had made her want to die, Shaw ended the service with the dirge from *Cymbeline*. Lucy burnt with a steady white light, like a wax candle.

FOURTEEN

I

SOME HINTS ON THE PEACE

> It is to be impressed on all officers and men that a state of war exists during the armistice.
>
> *The Times* (21 November 1918)

The Cabinet had already decided on a quick post-war general election. A few days after the Armistice, Lloyd George dissolved Parliament and announced 14 December 1918 as polling day. It was a degrading election, exploiting people's hatred of the Germans and their delirious gratitude for peace, to grab a renewed mandate for the old coalition of Tories and Liberals. To cries of 'Vote for the Man who won the War', and 'Make Britain a fit country for Heroes to live in', the electioneering was hurried through before the heroes themselves had a chance of getting their opinions known, or the opposition (silenced so long by the Defence of the Realm Act) make itself effectively heard. 'I feel physically sick when I read the frenzied appeals of the Coalition leaders . . . to hang the Kaiser, ruin and humiliate the German people, even to deprive Germany of her art treasures and libraries,' Beatrice Webb wrote in her diary. 'The one outstanding virtue of the Labour Party . . . is its high sense of international morality.'

Shaw, now in his sixty-third year, dropped almost all his engagements to go campaigning. He toured the country, speaking every day to enormous crowds of working people at Liverpool and Manchester, Birmingham and Wakefield, Leicester and Wolverhampton. He spoke in support of Ramsay MacDonald, who had preferred to resign his leadership of the Labour Party rather than endorse Grey's foreign policy. He warned the electorate against making it a Jingo versus Pacifist contest: voters must look for the solid brickwork under all that political whitewash. He gave them facts; he gave them figures: more than 50,000 German children had died in 1917 alone, the civilian mortality rate had increased by thirty-seven per cent – and 'these are only the deaths'. He was to call for the raising of the Allied blockade of Germany which Lord Balfour had declared 'cannot cause the death of a single civilian' but which later caused 763,000 persons to die of malnutrition, 'a polite name for starvation'. Did they want *more* revenge? 'When we break a German's leg with a bullet and then take him prisoner,' he explained, 'we immediately set to work to mend his leg, to the astonishment of our idiots, who cannot understand why we do not proceed to break his other leg.'

Britain was vibrating with exultation over the most magnificent military triumph in her long record of victories. It was enormously important, Shaw insisted, that she should check the evil that could easily fester after the guns had stopped, and 'set the world an example of consideration for vanquished enemies'. Surely we wanted to prosper by restoring trade with our best customer?

Shaw's series of campaign speeches that winter was 'my greatest platform success'. But on 14 December, Lloyd George's coalition careered back to Parliament with 516 seats – a huge majority of 340 over the other parties. Most of the Labour candidates Shaw had championed – including Ramsay MacDonald – lost their seats because of their opposition to the war. However, with sixty-two seats over the twenty-seven of Asquith's Liberals, Labour now sat in the House of Commons as the official Opposition.

Shaw ended the war as he had begun it: with a brochure. Ten thousand copies of *Peace Conference Hints* were published on 12 March 1919. Partly an admonition to Britain against exploiting her self-righteousness at the Versailles Peace Conference, and in part a collection of 'hints' to nerve President Woodrow Wilson against the wiles of Clemenceau and Lloyd George, the pamphlet represents a continuation of Shaw's election campaign and the summation of his political writings about the war. It is a story retold and completed.

When asking for a mandate for his peace offensive against Germany, Lloyd George had demanded: 'Is no one responsible? Is no one to be called to account? Is there to be no punishment? Surely that is neither God's justice nor man's?' Shaw's answer invoked another justice and brought the matter before a different court of morality. He believed that by fixing the guilt of history collectively or individually on others, Lloyd George was making a classic evasion of the human spirit. Through this duplicity of mind Britain risked restarting the mechanism that would bring the same tragedies back into people's lives.

Peace Conference Hints is a Bunyanesque tract on the moral consequences of the war. He surveys botched-up British diplomacy between 1906 and 1914 to strengthen his case for the international acceptance of new rules of conduct in war and peace. He grinds out a history lesson to sharpen a moral point. 'The moral cleaning-up after the war,' he states, 'is far more important than the material restorations.' The Versailles Peace Conference must be made a nucleus for the League of Nations. Like an illuminated picture, the League of Nations that appears in Shaw's missal is a 'very vigorous organization of resistance to evil', protected by an international police force but making conquests through the power of conscience. 'Principle is the motive power in the engine,' Shaw explains: 'its working qualities are integrity and energy, conviction and courage, with reason and lucidity to shew them the way.' This technology for human progress is shown being forced upon us not only by the inevitable march of civilization but by our fear of Armageddon. For the next war, if permitted to occur, 'will be no "sport of kings"'.

Having raised up his Architecture of Nations, Shaw tries to set up as its mystical prophet from the New World, President Woodrow Wilson. With the rusty accoutrements of his fourteen points, he resembles a benighted Quixote of the Peace. The week after Wilson was to lay his patched-up rag of a treaty before the United States Senate, Shaw was declaring that he had known all along the Versailles Conference would come to nothing and that 'in spite of anything that could be urged by the wisest and most powerful statesmen, the victorious side would skin the other alive . . . I had no illusions on that subject when I backed Wilson for all I was worth; and therefore I am not disillusioned nor disgusted now.'

He may have had no illusions; he did have hopes. Woodrow Wilson's godlike procession through Europe before the conference had stirred people's goodwill. 'Nothing like this had ever been seen before,' records one witness. 'The full-throated acclamation of Londoners, Parisians and Romans was not the normal cordiality which crowds accord to a visiting monarch. The ovation surged from the depth of the wounded contrite universal heart to a deliverer, the shaper of a new world.'

Some echoes of these aspirations, like distant trumpets, sound through Shaw's pamphlet. For if the war had not gained new moral territory for human beings, then it had been a defeat for everyone. The possibility of defeat is in his text. Pessimism and optimism are cross-stitched into the narrative, and in his subsequent reaction to the incompetent document Woodrow Wilson took away from Versailles may be glimpsed the extent of Shaw's hopes. 'The treaty of Versailles, which was perhaps the greatest disaster of the war for all the belligerents, and indeed for civilization in general,' he wrote, 'left nothing to be done in foreign affairs but face the question of the next war pending the consolidation of the League of Nations.'

Like Bunyan, Shaw had urged the peacemakers to climb the hill Difficulty. But they had fallen into the pit Destruction. At the end of that year another work of moral tension and stylistic force, Maynard Keynes's *The Economic Consequences of the Peace*, was published. After a succession of dreadful weeks at Versailles, Keynes had quitted 'the scene of nightmare' and written up his account of 'the devastation of Europe'. 'A great sensation has been made here by Professor Keynes of Cambridge, who was at Versailles as economic expert, and resigned that position and came home as a protest against the peace terms,' Shaw reported to Siegfried Trebitsch. 'He has now published a book in which he demonstrates that the indemnity demanded from Germany is an economic impossibility.' Keynes's demonstration was Shaw's vindication.

In the urgency of his despair, Keynes, the informed insider, became 'an outlaw from British official circles', while Shaw was to occupy the position of enemy rather than outlaw. 'He felt that capitalism had caused the war,' commented William Irvine, 'and that democracy had lost the peace.' Keynes dedicated his book to 'the new generation [that] has not yet spoken and silent opinion [that] is not yet formed'. But Shaw, being a generation older than Keynes, felt his precarious faith in this generation diminishing. At the peace table, over the heads of his colleagues, Woodrow Wilson had appealed to the conscience of the public. But the public's conscience had been subtly changed by the European free press; and the man whom no one dared criticize during the war was now openly jeered at and called a 'dangerous radical' by businessmen who controlled the newspapers. 'He stood in great need of sympathy, of moral support, of the enthusiasm of the masses,' wrote Keynes. '. . . And in this drought the flower of the President's faith withered and dried up.' Such personal reliance on applause, and journalistic manipulation of popularity, came as additional evidence to Shaw that government by the people was unworkable. Only 'government of the people and for the people' was practicable.

2

SHAW'S HEARTBREAK

> Is this England, or is it a madhouse?
>
> *Heartbreak House*

Shaw's response to the Great War is most deeply revealed in *Heartbreak House*. His depression had seeped into the play: his anger over what he saw at Versailles inflamed the Preface. It had 'begun with an atmosphere', the unjudgemental atmosphere of Chekhov's plays. 'An exquisite play by Tchekoff was actually hissed,' Shaw had reported to George Moore before the war. 'You cannot conceive how inferior we are (a small circle excepted) to the common playgoer.' He was to subtitle his own play 'A Fantasia in the Russian Manner on English Themes'. *Heartbreak House* is full of 'the same nice people, the same utter futility' as *The Cherry Orchard*. But, as the Preface makes clear, this is Shaw's view of 'cultured, leisured Europe before the war'.

At the centre of this atmosphere Shaw placed the supernatural story-book character of Captain Shotover. His model had been the actress Lena Ashwell's seafaring father, Commander Pocock, who in retirement went to live on a sailing vessel on the River Tyne, fitting out the stern as his own quarters, placing bars on Lena's nursery portholes, and equipping the upper deck with a drawing-room and greenhouse.

Heartbreak House was intended as tragedy. 'Behold my Lear,' he later gestured from his puppet play, *Shakes versus Shav*. He regarded *King Lear* as pure tragedy: 'even the fool in Lear is tragic'. Like Lear, Captain Shotover's heartbreak has apparently been caused by his two daughters, Ariadne and Hesione.

Ariadne Utterword, who is 'as strong as a horse', speaks for Horseback Hall which is mentioned in the Preface as 'the alternative to Heartbreak House', a very Irish alternative 'consisting of a prison for horses with an annex for the ladies and gentlemen who rode them'. At the age of nineteen, Ariadne escaped from the overheated atmosphere of Heartbreak House and became part of the wooden-headed, outdoor tradition of English life. The Preface prepares us for a Peacockian dialogue in the style of *Headlong Hall*. Having run away from the eccentricity of her upbringing and the world of her emotions, Ariadne has pursued respectability which is represented by her decorous 'numskull' of a husband, a colonial Governor of the British Empire. Sir Hastings Utterword could 'save the country with the greatest ease,' she boasts, once he was given the necessary powers and 'a good supply of bamboo to bring the British native to his senses'. Ariadne is an utter philistine. For much of the first act Captain Shotover has pretended not to recognize her. 'You left because you did not want us,' he eventually tells her. 'Was there no heartbreak in that for your father?'

Hesione is the opposite of Ariadne. As the chatelaine of Heartbreak House she is a siren of sexual infatuation who lures people into her web and leaves them suspended. She has disabled the two 'inventors' in the house, her husband and her father. Hector Hushabye is a man of action reduced from being a creator of exploits to an inventor of stories; Shotover is the thinker whose intelligence has been trivialized into money-making. 'Money is running short,' Hesione informs him after his patent lifeboat has failed to earn them more than £500. '. . . Living at the rate we do, you cannot afford life-saving inventions. Cant you think of something that will murder half Europe at one bang?'

Shaw's Cordelia is Ellie Dunn, a spiritual offspring of Shotover's rather than his blood relation. She has been invited to the house by Hesione, and her unsentimental education is the play's single continuous thread of narrative. When the curtain rises she appears as a solitary figure on stage dreaming over *Othello*, only to find a few minutes later that her own Othello, a man of wonderfully adventurous stories whom she has known by the name of 'Marcus Darnley', is actually Hesione's husband Hector. She passes rapidly in the stage directions from '*great distress*', through anger to look '*curiously older and harder*'. She had been going to marry a fifty-five-year-old 'perfect hog of a millionaire' nicknamed Boss Mangan, acting from sentimental gratitude for the financial help he had given her father. In Act II, as part of her disillusioning education, she learns that Mangan has in fact made a profit out of her father by assisting him into bankruptcy. But she is still determined to marry him, her motive now being to gain use of the money he has tricked out of her father, even though Mangan, who has followed her to the house, has fallen in love with Hesione.

In the last act Ellie reveals to Mangan that she 'never really intended to make you marry me . . . I only wanted to feel my strength.' She has reached a mystical union with Shotover, who lies in her arms as fast asleep as a baby while she tells the others that she has given 'my broken heart and my strong sound soul to its natural captain, my spiritual husband and second father'. Her emotional transformation-in-a-day is an accelerated dash through the long pilgrim's progress of his life. All the optimism of the play centres on Ellie. 'Heartbreak is not what I thought it must be,' she says. For her it is the process of growing up and 'the sort of pain that goes mercifully beyond our powers of feeling'.

But Shaw also makes his Goneril and Regan victims of heartbreak. Hesione suffers from the dangerous after-effects of a love that came once in her lifetime, then passed. What she shared with Hector, whom she has now reduced to the 'household pet' of their marriage, cannot be regained. All her flirtations and seductions will bring no more than fading reflections of that dream. She is forty-four and has no other interests; what can she do but cry to dream again? For her sister Ariadne heartbreak is paradoxically lack of heart. She is as fearful of emotion as Mangan is of poverty, and has fashioned herself into a rigidly conventional woman of the world whose tragedy is that 'her heart will not break'.

Both sisters, we are given to understand, have been damaged by their wayward upbringing. 'Old Shotover sold himself to the devil in Zanzibar,' Hector romances. 'The devil gave him a black witch for a wife; and these two daughters are their mystical progeny.' In a letter to Trebitsch, Shaw explained that by heartbreak he meant the chronic effects of heredity and childhood, rather than the setback of an unhappy love affair. Shotover is prevented from advancing to his 'seventh degree of concentration' by forces that swamped Shaw's own childhood. He describes Heartbreak House itself as 'my kennel' – the word Shaw used for his birthplace in Synge Street – and, having retreated into 'my second childhood', he is diverted by habitual rum-drinking from pursuing his thought 'so long and so continuously' that it issues into action. 'To be drunk means to have dreams' – or Shavian fantasies. 'You must never be in the real world when we talk together,' Ellie soothes him. But this incapacity of the most gifted characters to use their abilities in the real world has by the last act developed into the collective heartbreak of the play. 'We sit here talking,' cries Hector, 'and leave everything to Mangan and to chance and to the devil.'

*

At the beginning, the house is 'a palace of enchantments, as in the second act of Parsifal'. It contains light and dark, land and sea, sleeping and waking, fantasy and fact. The first act, with its complicated jigsaw of almost sixty entrances and exits, its ensemble playing of what appears to be a chaos of informality, is 'as dependent on atmosphere as any of Tchekov's' plays. Shaw felt he had seen in *The Cherry Orchard* a method of advancing the disquisitory technique of *Getting Married* and *Misalliance* – which preserved the unities and removed the action outside the theatre – with the odd dramatic break-in by pilot, burglar or would-be assassin. In later acts he made a number of further references to Chekhov: the 'splendid drumming in the sky' accords with the snapping of the string in *The Cherry Orchard*; and the topsy-turvy burglar is the equivalent of Chekhov's ominous tramp. But Chekhov's world, with its fusion of impressionistic touches, is naturalistic; in Shaw's house, which is full of surreal and disorientating episodes, 'the very burglars cant behave naturally'.

From the moment the curtain goes up and the audience sees Ellie Dunn's copy of *Othello* sink to her lap, as she dozes in slumber on the draughtsman's chair, the theatre has moved into a world of dreams. Asleep in her bedroom upstairs lies Hesione, the mistress of *Heartbreak House*, who has changed her name from Shotover to the somnambulistic Hushabye as the result of her 'enchanting dream' of love with Hector. In the second act Mangan is sent into a hypnotic trance, and in the third act, as the thunderous bombers approach, it is the Captain who sleeps. This sleeping and dreaming allows Shaw additional licence for exploring his characters' unconscious minds. In the pathetic scene in which Hector, left alone on stage, 'falls into a daydream' and performs a desperate duel with an imaginary opponent and then in 'another reverie' mimes a thrilling love scene with an invisible woman, we witness all the qualities of courage and imagination he has never been able to employ in waking life – qualities that, when Shotover enters, are immediately contracted into 'a series of gymnastic exercises'.

Growing-up becomes allied to a process of waking-up. Ellie Dunn has the strength to wake herself and the power to mesmerize Mangan so that he cannot resist hearing the truth about himself. He exhibits the essential babyhood of capitalism. This is a revelation to Hesione, who has accepted him as he has presented himself to the world: a businessman 'Boss' with plenty of money and no heart. 'It comes to me suddenly that you are a real person: that you had a mother, like anyone else.' But it is too late for Mangan to grow up.

'What is true within these walls is true outside them,' announces Shotover. Heartbreak House has splendid views of reality which no one inside can reach. For the Palace of Dreams is a revelation as well as a refuge, and recalls an earlier dream sequence in Shaw's plays: the hell scene in *Man and Superman*. Hector is the reluctant Don Juan of this hell and Hesione a Doña Ana who has long ago given birth to her children and now gives herself over to pleasure. Her house is a moral vacuum. 'What do men want?' she demands, reversing Freud's question on women. ' . . . Why are they not satisfied?'

Shaw shuffles the cards of identity with comic virtuosity. It is a matter of Shavian orthodoxy that every person should contradict the pose he adopts. 'The great question is, not who we are, but what we are,' sententiously remarks Mazzini Dunn, little realizing that he is to be shown up as a gullible sentimentalist wrong about everything except his daughter ('you become quite clever when you talk about her,' Hesione admits). Even comfortable Nurse Guinness, who asks disbelievingly: 'now is it likely I'd kill any man on purpose', is shortly afterwards demanding why the burglar (who turns out to be her husband as well as one of the Captain's old crew) had not been shot. 'If I'd known who he was, I'd have shot him myself,' she swears. Shaw has her running at the end of the play 'in hideous triumph . . . laughing harshly' to the gravel pit where her husband has been blown up.

For Mazzini Dunn, Shaw borrowed some of the trappings of Ebenezer Howard, idealistic pioneer of the Garden City Movement. It had been Ebenezer Howard's book *To-morrow, A Peaceful Path to Rural Reform* that Tom Broadbent had carried round with him as a blueprint of heaven and model for his business expansion scheme in *John Bull's Other Island*. And it had been Ebenezer Howard's dream-town that Shaw put on the stage as Perivale St Andrews, 'beautifully situated and beautiful in itself', in *Major Barbara*.

Mangan is possibly the least sympathetic character in all Shaw's work. He is the alternative captain to Shotover: a captain of industry who sees his job as getting the better of 'other fellows in other departments'. His announcement that the Prime Minister had asked him to 'join the Government without even going through the nonsense of an election, as the dictator of a great public department', provokes a dismay which is part of the general humiliation of Mangan in *Heartbreak House* before his miserable death in a gravel pit. Nurse Guinness's 'Serves un right!' is the signing-off of Shaw's revenge on Mangan who was based on Hudson Kearley, head of a wholesale grocery firm, whom Lloyd George had brought into his Government at the same time as he rejected Shaw for a place on the Irish Convention.

Hesione is Shaw's first portrait of Mrs Patrick Campbell since the end of their affair. Hesione's talent for incapacitating those she seduces makes Hector liken her to a vampire. 'When I am neither coaxing and kissing nor laughing,' she says, 'I am just wondering how much longer I can stand living in this cruel, damnable world.' Mrs Pat had predicted that her life 'is sure to be a short one. I wish it to be.' Being denied her wish, she was to demand pathetically in old age 'who is there here who still *loves* me?' and receiving no reply, ask: 'Why am I alive – what for?' It is this emptiness that Hesione conveys, foreshadowing the career of a great actress who was to die '*sans profession*'.

Nobody could speak Hesione's lines as she could, Shaw told Stella, 'or give the quality of the woman as you could if you would'. But she fancied playing the eighteen-year-old Ellie – and that was impossible. For Ellie was conceived from Shaw's memories of that hypnotic young girl, Erica Cotterill, who had lived in 'a fanciful world of her own' and now occupied a special place within the fanciful world of his plays. As 'Incognita Appassionata' in *Getting Married*, she had embodied the sexual passion lacking in his marriage; and as Ellie Dunn she is his spiritual intimate, which may be one reason why *Heartbreak House* was 'loathed by Charlotte'.

Charlotte's loathing of this play is reproduced in Ariadne's disapproval of the house. Ariadne's emotional rigidity, as well as her early determination to make a marriage unacceptable to her living parent, were Charlotte's attitudes. Shaw had entered the world of Horseback Hall on visits to Charlotte's friends and relations, when he put up in the castles and big houses belonging to the county families of Anglo-Irish society. But Ariadne's affinity with Charlotte is well-disguised. Her appearance, it has been suggested, was taken from Virginia Woolf.

The Shaws, the Woolfs and the Webbs had come together during the weekend of 17 to 19 June 1916 at a house called Wyndham Croft in Sussex. 'We talked quite incessantly,' Virginia remembered. '. . . I liked it better than I expected. At anyrate one can say what one likes, which is unusual with the middle aged.' In Shotover-style, Shaw slept, Virginia observed, 'and then woke up and rambled on into interminable stories about himself . . . Poor Mrs Shaw was completely out of it.' In the mornings Shaw would go into the garden where Leonard saw him writing his play 'on a writing pad on his knee'. From this garden could be heard the guns of the Somme offensive which he turned into the 'splendid drumming' that Mazzini characteristically identifies as the sound of a goods train.

This weekend, with its coming together of Bloomsbury and the Fabians, helped Shaw over some of his difficulties with the play – which he acknowledged in a letter to Virginia twenty-four years later when the bombs of the Second World War had begun to fall. Though the Bloomsbury Group had published and exhibited little of its work before 1916, the principles of aesthetic sensibility and personal relationships which animated that work, and to which it gave priority over the economic and political values of the Fabians, would have become apparent to Shaw during these days of incessant talking, and it is these Bloomsbury values which he now injected into the play. 'Shaw visits upon the age of Bloomsbury with its cult of sentimental personal relations the same scorn Carlyle visited upon the age of Brummel with its Byronism and its pococurantism,' commented the critic Louis Crompton. But the inhabitants of Heartbreak House are more convincingly made up from that coterie of gallants and graces known as 'the Souls', who were more aristocratic than Bloomsbury and went on polishing their veneer of culture, went on sipping the sweet life, even after the declaration of war. Shaw added Bloomsbury to his mixture so as to make his play contemporary, but he had earlier and better knowledge of the Souls than of Bloomsbury.

Shaw's pessimism had grown from his experience of contemporary history; his optimism was increasingly tied to a visionary future where the action of human will has broken the cyclical pattern of behaviour. *Heartbreak House* is less a visionary than a contemporary play, and Shotover wins only a misanthropic victory. 'I cannot bear men and women. I have to run away,' he cries out. '. . . Old men are dangerous: it doesnt matter to them what is going to happen to the world.'

The throbbing pessimism, bolts of anger, shivers of violence that build to the ambiguously explosive climax are also ingredients active in the great apocalyptic works of the war: Eliot's *The Waste Land*, Lawrence's *Women in Love* and Yeats's 'The Second Coming'. Shaw is in surreal territory several years before the arrival of the surrealists who courted loss of control to explore connections between dream and reality. The sudden spiralling of his wit, the curious patches of farce, the sideslips of tone (such as the nursery incantation at the end of Act I which seems to sound from the world of T. S. Eliot), all fill gaps in the play's organic unity. He had written a revenge tragedy without blood. As they drift in and out of this visionary house, these elemental characters seem to grow disembodied, as if made of air and fire. It is the play of an older man. 'I have children,' says Hector. 'All that is over and done with for me' – as it is for Hesione and Ariadne. Larry Doyle in *John Bull's Other Island* had longed for a place where the facts were not brutal and the dreams not unreal; but the brutality of the war had driven Shaw deeper into dreams. The love charades of *Heartbreak House* are the games that go on in 'the house of the unreal and of the seekers for happiness' which is Don Juan's definition of hell in *Man and Superman*. He had come as close as he dared to 'the blasphemous despair of Lear'.

*

Some 20,000 copies of *Heartbreak House*, *Great Catherine*, and *Playlets of the War* were published in North America and Britain during September 1919. In Britain the critical response was generally unfavourable. A. B. Walkley doubted whether the 'fun' of *Heartbreak House* 'would stand the glare of the footlights', and other critics shared this doubt. Eventually, in the summer of 1920, Shaw signed a contract with the newly incorporated Theatre Guild of New York, where his volume of war plays had been less condescendingly received. The world première took place at the Garrick Theater in New York on 10 November 1920. It was well reviewed, and the production ran for more than 100 performances over almost five months.

In Vienna, where Trebitsch's translation was staged later that November 'with great respect for the intentions of the author', Shaw's loquaciousness seemed to weaken the power of the play. 'The audience at first listened with great interest,' one critic wrote; '. . . later, however, the interest lessened visibly, the signs of impatience were not wanting at the end.'

Shaw was to learn something of this difficulty for himself a year later during rehearsals of the English production which he directed with the new leaseholder of the Court Theatre, the Irish playwright and manager J. B. Fagan. 'I am rehearsing Heartbreak House at the Court Theatre,' he wrote to Edward Elgar. 'It was like old times rehearsing John Bull there.' But there was a difference. 'The book of the words has been so widely read and so much discussed,' wrote the critic of the *Westminster Gazette*, '. . . that the real hush of expectation was absent.' In the old times, publication of Shaw's plays had sharpened the public's demand for their performance; now it seemed to dull the curiosity of an audience that already knew about the eccentricities of Shotover and the climax of the bombing raid. It was retitled 'Jawbreak House' and the play which took place in 'a private lunatic asylum with many patients and no keeper' was classed as being 'about the worst there ever was'. The only reputation to be significantly lifted was Chekhov's. 'Tchekov always has an atmosphere,' commented the *Sunday Times*; 'this play has only a smell.'

Shaw blamed the lack of rehearsal time and immediately set about cutting it – exactly what he had forbidden the American and Austrian directors to do. 'I never cut anything merely to save time,' he told St John Ervine, '. . . [but] there are always lines which are dud lines with a given cast. Change the cast and you get other lines dud.' This truth, however, obscured another truth: the play lacked the seventh degree of concentration. 'As an entertainment pure and simple it is dull and incoherent . . . [with] all the author's prolixities and perversities,' reported James Agate in the *Saturday Review*, and yet 'I found it quite definitely exhilarating and deeply moving, and it therefore ranks for me among the great testaments.'

3

MISS CROSS PATCH COMES TO STAY

You are becoming too famous.

Shaw to Blanche Patch

'Would you care to be my secretary?' Shaw enquired of a forty-year-old clergyman's daughter. Blanche Patch seemed perfect casting for the vacancy. In appearance she reminded Shaw of Harold Laski – and since he was a prominent socialist at the London School of Economics, this counted in her favour. It may even have influenced Charlotte on whom Miss Patch made a 'pleasant impression'. She had been a nurse, a hand-loom weaver, a pharmacist's assistant in Wales and was currently typing for a London optician. She was 'not a university woman', but came recommended by the Webbs. She knew pretty well nothing about the literary or political world.

As a non-Shavian, Miss Patch was unaware of her advantages. Shaw's 'quick, witty, friendly way . . . [which] was new to me then' increased her diffidence, and she wrote back declining his offer. Recognizing the uncertainty behind this refusal Shaw tried again. 'I hardly like to steal you away from another man. Still, I will not take your first No for an answer; so will you let me have a second one, or a Yes, before I let loose a general announcement that the post is vacant?'

This tactful renewal gave her confidence to do what she really wanted. She started work as Shaw's secretary at the end of July 1920 and remained with him until his death. During this time he treated her like a typewriter. 'Nothing that you could possibly write,' he told Stella Campbell, 'could produce the slightest effect on her.' Certainly nothing that he wrote ever affected her. She was completely 'Shaw-proof'.

Ann Elder had observed that 'my successor, Miss Blanche Patch, was older and more mature than I, but I'm not sure that her sense of humour was ever very strongly developed'. This lack of humour amused Shaw. 'Patch is a born comedian,' he insisted in a letter to Beatrice Webb, 'and shews me photographs of herself as a Pierrot.'

She had been nervous at first. 'Does he throw things at you?' she asked one of the maids. But what responsible employer would deliberately damage his office equipment? During her thirty years' employment only twice could she remember him losing his temper – and then it was not with her. 'Even-tempered he always was, and that made working for him easy; but never a word of praise came from him.' He was less a father to her than a maintenance inspector.

He never misused her, never spoilt her. 'No man knows your value better than I do,' he told her: and it was true she was wonderfully economic. 'Will you think £3–10s per week too much?' she had asked him and he immediately agreed to this, not telling her that it was ten shillings a week less than Ann Elder had been getting. Over the years, she was to witness him handing away many thousands of pounds, but such gifts were conferred 'without human warmth,' Miss Patch noted, and often to people she felt were undeserving. It struck her as odd too that he should be so spontaneous with strangers while remaining so cautious with herself. His scorn for capitalistic money-making affected her awkwardly. He had been paying Ann Elder more than union rates and would have paid her still more if she had asked. But by the time Blanche Patch took over he preferred to *calculate* his finances. These calculations, sometimes hampered by an elderly adding machine, seemed to her 'finicky'. 'The meaning to the ordinary worker of the increased cost of living never reached his conscious mind,' she complained. She was not to know that he added a codicil to his will in the late 1920s leaving her an annuity of £260, which he raised to £365 in the late 1930s and to £500 in 1950 (equivalent to £9,300 in 1997). For a long time she puzzled over his financial aberrations until it suddenly occurred to her that he simply had no head for numbers. 'He could never, for instance, remember how many brothers and sisters I had.'

Shaw had warned her that the Adelphi Terrace apartment was protected by a fortified obstacle giving it 'the appearance of a private madhouse'. When she had got through this barbed-wire gate, she ascended to the study, a long 'horribly pokey room' on the third floor overlooking the Water Gate arches upon Hungerford Bridge, with Shaw's desk at one end and hers at the other. His shorthand, which was without contractions or grammalogues, had all the vowel signs written in and difficult words spelt out in longhand, so it was easy for her to transcribe. He wrote 1,500 words of prime work a morning on blocks of water-lined paper with a green tint to rest his eyes, and would give her his shorthand draft in batches. 'I used to rest his manuscript on a stand, such as violinists have, placed behind my typewriter and raised to eye height,' she wrote. Very occasionally she made an error – 'the profiteers of the theatre' instead of 'the proprietors of the theatre', which struck Shaw as an improvement, and 'porter' for 'torture', which for some reason made him laugh.

Apart from swimming at the RAC, walking, motorcycling and motoring (with a little hedge-trimming and log-sawing in the country), Shaw did nothing but work, so far as Miss Patch could see. 'His industry was terrific,' she wrote. 'I have always thought that he wrote too much.' Privately she found *Back to Methuselah* 'hard pedalling' and *On the Rocks* 'dull', while *Too True to be Good* 'bored me a bit'. The first two plays she worked on were *Jitta's Atonement*, which was 'slight' and 'rather dismal', and *Saint Joan*, which she acknowledged to be not his best. She was still less enthusiastic about his non-dramatic work. 'He would be an uncommonly devoted Shavian who to-day would cheerfully set out again to read through *The Intelligent Woman's Guide*, followed by *Everybody's Political What's What* not to say explore once more the Sahara of the novels,' she wrote after Shaw's death.

Often she was obliged to put aside her 1,500 words of play-typing for the articles and long letters about Beethoven and Churchill, Walt Whitman and Santa Claus; on proposals for sex training and the question of rejuvenation by monkey glands, also whether dogs have an after-life and why he could not afford a peerage – all implacably typed out. Then there were the 'pests' and 'busybodies', who wanted autographs, prefaces, cheques, speeches, whom she would 'fob-off' with one of the printed cards from his coloured pack or a paragraph of careful explanation. 'To most of them,' she objected, 'he was much too polite.'

Miss Patch herself was not so polite. Some of those who had been enchanted by her name ('it suggests a vivacious person in a play by Sheridan,' proposed Charles Ricketts) were soon addressing her: 'Dear

Miss Cross Patch.' She referred to 'my pretended irascibility' as a necessary component of 'our firmness'. The only person who really exasperated her was G.B.S. himself. 'Oh, go away and write another play!' she would exclaim when he came pacing near her typewriter – 'he created a considerable draught as he swung past me'. His formal manners were invariably courteous, she admitted, but he was a shy man who shrank from people: how envious he must be of the way she herself got on with everyone. 'He always appeared to be astonished that I knew much more about the working classes than he did.'

But what exasperated her most was the way he took her for granted. 'I resented being looked on simply as a shorthand typist.' Normally he behaved as if she wasn't there at all. 'I might be away for a week or so with influenza and he would receive me when I returned to work as if I had been there all the time.'

Planted beneath the cool surface of their relationship was a perpetually unflowering seed of emotion. Although she never showed it openly, Charlotte was 'jealous of the fact that I had to read and transcribe his shorthand,' Miss Patch noticed. It didn't surprise her. Phonetic shorthand was a form of intimacy that 'a lonely type of person' like Charlotte would have loved. Miss Patch could appreciate that. What she could not appreciate was Shaw's behaviour when, from time to time, he passed on 'certain of my duties' to another woman – by which she meant his former secretary and relative, Judy Gillmore. That really put a spark in the gunpowder. Why G.B.S. should still feel so fond of Judy Miss Patch could never comprehend. Judy had made her bed with Harold Musters in 1912; and that should have been that. Then there was the matter of the big toe of her right foot. Miss Patch must have injured it in her school days, for it had stiffened over the years and by the time she settled down at Adelphi Terrace it had become an agony. News of her toe never failed to stimulate G.B.S. By way of experiment, he even sent her at his own expense to a 'Scandinavian Naturpath' who applied hot fomentations to almost every part of her body except the foot, bringing no relief whatever. Shaw was anxious that she avoid 'the operation panacea' but all the extra walking during the General Strike finally disabled her and she decided to go into St Thomas's Hospital to have her toe joint removed. It was when she went down to Frinton for what she hoped would be a peaceful convalescence that Shaw exploded his surprise. He had engaged Judy Musters as *locum tenens*, 'so you need not hurry back if your foot needs a little more rest'. She hurried back.

But to do him justice, he seemed greatly relieved to have her back. 'I am distracted and lost without you,' he had appealed, and he had 'footed' the bill for her operation. So they settled down again until the next upheaval. Miss Patch realized that some people thought her attitude to G.B.S. was unfriendly; one of them (probably St John Ervine) was to send her an anonymous card marked JUDAS when she published her reminiscences of him. But Shaw himself understood the nature of their partnership. He cared for her as he did for his paste and scissors, which also contributed to the manuscripts and proofs of his life. And she looked after him as a matron of a nursing home might look after a long-term patient – with detachment and efficiency, occasionally telling him off when his foolishness went too far. 'The faithful Patch,' he once called her. She prized this tribute from one who had the tribute of the world.

*

'Travelling is still very troublesome,' Shaw had written to Trebitsch in the summer of 1919. For more than six years following the war the Shaws did not travel outside the United Kingdom, though Charlotte regularly hustled G.B.S. over England, Scotland, Wales and Ireland on a series of purposeful holidays, theatrical tours and to Fabian Summer Schools. Kilsby, going off to make aeroplane engines at Woolwich, had taken a long farewell of them during the war, and in May 1919 Charlotte engaged Fred Day from Codicote as their new chauffeur. G.B.S. was still a fiery motorcyclist, and he egged on Day to 'ginger up' his two-stroke machine – after which it would hurtle away, bucking him off and sometimes landing on top of him. Before Day's arrival he had taken hypothetical instruction from the local chemist, E. P. Downing, on how to steer this motorcycle round corners, but he could not bring himself to accept the theory that it was necessary to slow down and to lean over at an angle. The chemist was impressed by Shaw's 'outstanding deficiency in mechanical sense' and had no more luck with his hints on reversing motor cars, Shaw once taking half an hour to turn the car round, and demolishing some flower beds while doing so.

The village had grown proud of Shaw's notorious road exploits. Local dogs, knowing him well, would play dead under his car while he anxiously crawled after them – when they would bounce out, barking triumphantly. In Fred Day's opinion his employer was 'rather reckless' at the wheel, though 'always very considerate' afterwards. Whenever anything happened, such as a bump or a crash, he would leap out, offer to pay all expenses, scoop up the other driver and passengers and drive them trembling home.

Fred Day stayed on for thirty-one adventurous years and owned that he 'would do anything for Mr Shaw'. Once, during a storm, Shaw noticed Day give a small wave to a woman and child at a bus stop. 'Who's that?' he asked. 'My wife,' Day answered. 'Stop,' Shaw commanded, ' – turn round. We must take them home.' Day had schooled his family never to recognize him if they met him on duty since 'in those days [1925] it was definitely not usual for the gentry to have anything to do with the staff socially. But Mr Shaw was different. He put his arm round her shoulders and helped her into the car. She was terrified.' Later on, Shaw offered to pay for his daughter to train as a schoolteacher though admitting 'I'd rather be a crossing-sweeper'.

It was an interesting job being the Shaws' chauffeur. You got to drive all sorts of machines – a Vauxhall or a Bianca with mechanical windscreen wipers, a straight-eight Lanchester with a harmonic balancer (which Mr Shaw spoke of as if he believed it to be a musical contraption), followed by a 'run-about' Lanchester ten, then a chocolate-coloured Rolls-Royce and finally a 25–30 m.p.h. Silver Wraith. Mr Shaw would ask Day's advice on cars – such as the A.C. coupé they bought in 1923 – quiz him about helical pinions or differential gears and take him to the dealers. He liked to ride next to Day up front, and take the wheel until lunch, while Mrs Shaw preferred sitting at the back. Mr Shaw had the back seat specially upholstered for her, with the compartment sealed from draughts and fitted with a heater. Mrs Shaw designed the front seat for him, with a cushion at the head propping him bolt upright. In this manner, at various speeds, they travelled the country, very slow when Mrs Shaw was with them, very fast when she wasn't and Mr Shaw was driving. His favourite trick, Day noticed, was to mistake the accelerator for the brake. Sometimes, when visiting their friends, his employers would travel by train and arrange for Day to follow with the bags. It seemed to him a funny sort of logic, using a Rolls-Royce for carrying luggage.

4

TRAGEDY OF AN ELDERLY GENTLEMAN

I am doing the best I can at my age.

Preface to *Back to Methuselah* (1921)

'Messrs Constable & Co have to announce the publication early in the forthcoming season of an important and even extraordinary work by Mr Bernard Shaw,' wrote Shaw in a press release for his publishers in the spring of 1921. The book would, he promised, 'interest biologists, religious leaders, and lovers of the marvellous in fiction as well as lovers of the theatre'. It was 'his supreme exploit in dramatic literature'.

He had begun this colossal affair, its 30,000-word Preface leading to a sequence of five plays under the collective title *Back to Methuselah*, more than seven months before the war was over, and completed it at the end of May two years later, though continuing to revise and prepare it for publication into the early months of 1921. Like *Heartbreak House*, it was struck out of him by the war; but where *Heartbreak House* exploits the forces of death, *Back to Methuselah* explores new powers of life. It is a vastly hopeful composition, and 'the last work of any vigor I shall produce'.

In his mid-sixties Shaw sensed the encroachments of age not in ill-health and sexual loss, but more obliquely as philosophical pessimism and financial threat, a sense of falling out of step with the contemporary world and losing contact with his audience. The Continent was miraculously transformed from a battlefield into a playground. Don Juan's picture of hell had been visited on earth. Below the whirling triviality, Shaw sensed a disillusionment. He was fighting disillusionment in himself. These terrible post-war years sometimes seemed to him more frightful than the war itself. Every day he received appeals to save babies who were starving overseas. Every week some unfortunate German author would 'write me the whole history of his life, more to console himself and persuade his wife that he was doing something that might bring them the price of a sack of coals, than in any real hope of escaping from his miseries,' he told the German playwright Julius Bab; '. . . it became part of the day's routine to hear that So and So and his wife were starving and that there was not a child under 7 years of age left alive in Poland.' Before the war Shaw had been remarkably generous to all manner of people who appealed to him for money. But the financial calamity now seemed beyond all reckoning. His generosity persisted but, seeming almost pointless, grew capricious – one tragedy more or less was hardly noticeable when the whole world was breaking up.

It was an immense relief to work in the futuristic world of *Back to Methuselah*, phasing out the miseries of life around him. The expectation of death (with which *Heartbreak House* concluded) had utterly exhausted people who had learnt to feel, think and act as if there were no future. In *Back to Methuselah*, Shaw struggled to discover what this discouraged generation needed to have said to it. He wanted to give it back a future with new prospects of living, and restore the certainty of his own position.

His cycle of plays is a metaphysical (or what he called a metabiological) enquiry into the causes of pessimism in the development of thought since Darwin, and a search for a legitimate philosophical basis on which to re-engage optimism. His political experience suggested that men and women were incapable of solving the social problems raised by their civilization and had therefore been doomed to the poverty against which socialism vainly protested. But he insisted that this was no reason to abandon socialism. 'I take the view that the worse a job is the more reason for trying to make the best of it,' he wrote. 'But my creed of creative evolution means in practice that man can change himself to meet every vital need, and that however long the trials and frequent the failures may be, we can put up a soul as an athlete puts up a muscle. Thus to men who are themselves cynical I am a pessimist; but to genuinely religious men I am an optimist, and even a fantastic and extravagant one.'

Back to Methuselah is the vision of an extravagant fantasist, a *Paradise Lost* and *Paradise Regained* which seeks to demolish our concepts of normality, reintroduces the imaginative quality of free will as an unconscious process, and treats the present as a passing phase of history in which crisis and even collapse might be interpreted as vital changes for the future. There was a peculiar satisfaction for Shaw in responding to what he believed were the needs of the present by removing himself into the future. 'The present occupies all my time,' he wrote. But his chief contact with the historic present comes through newspapers and his animosity towards journalism – which pretends to be an organ and not the exploiter of public opinion – is partly the awareness of its inadequacy as a primary source. He dreamed of a renewal of faith that would measure conduct by the longest conceivable perspective, and of an imaginative rather than academic lens through which to regard history. He wanted to go as far as thought, and much further than facts, could reach. An instinctively trained eye was needed to recognize the tiny shoots and buds sent out by the Life Force – for example, the natural tendency for people in the twentieth century to live longer. Maynard Keynes caught the mood of the moment when in 1923 he wrote that in the long run we were all dead. But what would happen if, in the long run, we were still alive?

*

'Our will to live depends on hope,' Shaw was to write; 'for we die of despair, or, as I have called it in the Methuselah cycle, discouragement.' Christ had reformed the vindictive morality of Moses with his perception of the futility and wickedness of punishment and revenge. But after almost two thousand years another Reformation was needed to adapt Christian morality to the mental habits of modern times. Shaw believed it was necessary to redistil religion by scientific methods. This meant a change in vocabulary: a matter of replacing the word God with the concept of an evolutionary appetite operating by trial and error towards the achievement of greater power over the environment. From our past it was easy to prove that mankind was incorrigible. But though all known civilizations had collapsed, and contemporary civilization was showing all the recorded symptoms of collapse, nobody could prove that men and women would not succeed this time, or next time, or sometime. And even if the human species were scrapped, like the megalo-organisms which were known through fossils, that was no cause for pessimism. 'Man may easily be beaten: Evolution will not be beaten.'

Shaw called for the same sort of admission that Copernicus, Galileo and Darwin had demanded. He too removed human beings from their central position as unique instruments through which a divine will operated, but he restored to them their own will. As subjects of literary biographies will collaborate with their unknown biographers in the future writing of their lives, so our general history may be considered as part of an unfinished narrative that did not cater for our self-interest, but would be influenced by individual acts and thoughts. This collaborative hypothesis restored the value of instinct and the use of intelligence as controls for human destiny.

'If I must explain what I dont understand,' Shaw wrote, 'I prefer to do it in an inspiring way and not in a stultifying one.' His treatise is a modernizing of the first five books of the Old Testament (he subtitled his play 'A Metabiological Pentateuch') in which the Garden of Eden is comprehensively weeded. *Back to Methuselah* is Shaw's version of *Gulliver's Travels*, with longevity replacing size, and the element of the future added as a preventative against morbidity. For it had been a crude blunder, he argued, to treat causation as a process by which the present was determined by the past and would determine the future. 'The true view is that the future determines the present,' he wrote. 'If you take a ticket to Milford Haven you will do so not because you were in Swansea yesterday but because you want to be in Milford Haven to-morrow.'

Shaw encouraged everyone to treat themselves, under a strictly impartial rent act, as tenant-caretakers of this planet. He regarded the isolated figure of Samuel Butler as a pioneer in the crusade against the environmental consequences of Darwinism. Butler had revealed his genius to Shaw in *Life and Habit*, the essay on evolution where he compressed his objections to the dogma of Natural Selection into six words: 'Darwin banished mind from the universe.' In 1887 Shaw had been sent Butler's *Luck or Cunning?* for review by the *Pall Mall Gazette*. 'I was indignant because the review was not printed at full length,' he remembered, 'presumably because the literary editor did not consider Butler important enough . . . From this time on I was acquainted with Butler's view of evolution, though I do not think I grasped its full significance until years afterwards when I had arrived at it in my own way.'

The review treats Butler's opinions as being of equal merit to Darwin's. 'The question at issue is – granted the survival of the fittest, were the survivors made fit by mere luck, or did they fit themselves by cunning?' he wrote. 'Mr Butler is for cunning; and he will have it that Darwin was all for luck.' Shaw leaves undecided the matter of whether the controversy was one of semantics or metaphysical truth. Yet the review had felt almost epoch-making to Butler himself. Butler 'admits pure luck as a factor in evolution,' Shaw wrote,

'but denies its sufficiency as an explanation of all the phenomena, and insists that organisms that have the luck to be cunning make further luck for themselves by the deliberate exercise of that cunning, and so introduce design into the universe – not design as we used to conceive it, all-foreseeing from the first, but "a piecemeal, *solvitur ambulando* design", which, as it becomes more self-conscious and intelligent, tends to supplant natural selection by functional modification.'

In the decade following this review, Butler and Shaw met on several occasions. In his *Notebooks*, Butler admits to having 'long been repelled' by Shaw, though 'at the same time attracted by his coruscating power'. At the Fabian Society, after Butler had advocated his ingenious theory that the *Odyssey* was written by a young woman living at Trapani, Shaw got up and 'spoke so strongly that people who had only laughed with me all through my lecture began to think there might be something in it after all. Still,' Butler continues, 'there is something uncomfortable about the man which makes him uncongenial to me.' Shaw did not mind being disliked: he had long been uncongenial to himself. He regarded Butler as the sort of person he himself might have turned into if he had not invented G.B.S. – someone who, having gone around 'undermining every British institution, shocking every British prejudice, and deriding every British Bigwig with irreconcilable pertinacity', was dismissed by the public as an oddity and a vulgarian, and could make no headway with his writings. 'He died in 1902,' Shaw wrote; 'and, outside a small but highly select circle, nobody cared.'

As 'one of the select few who read "Erewhon" and swore by it', Shaw counted himself within this circle. By suggesting that poverty should be attacked as a crime instead of being coddled like a disease, Butler 'made me reconsider a rather thoughtless contempt for money, and thereby led me towards the theme of Major Barbara,' he acknowledged. In the Preface to *Major Barbara* he had described Butler as being 'in his own department the greatest English writer of the latter half of the XIX century'. Thereafter he makes many references to Butler which reveal the kinship he felt for this uncomfortable man. He pictures Butler as being 'naturally affectionate' as a child, as having 'sought for affection at home' and gone on 'assuming that he loved his dear parents' whose good names he later slew in *The Way of All Flesh* 'so reasonably, so wittily, so humorously, and even in a ghastly way so charitably'.

In a letter to Butler's biographer Festing Jones, Shaw wrote: 'Butler can stand on his own legs and carry most of us on his shoulders as well.' It was as an evolutionist, and particularly in *Back to Methuselah*, that Shaw stood on Butler's shoulders. As a great moralist, a writer whose *Erewhon* Shaw called 'the only rival to Gulliver's Travels in English Literature', who used his instinctive knowledge of human nature instead of a collection of evidence based on guinea-pigs in laboratories, Butler had stood alone. But he had committed the strategic error of handling Darwin like a moral delinquent. In his *Methuselah* Preface Shaw comes to praise Darwin, not to dig him up and throw stones. He was 'an amiable and upright man' and an 'honest naturalist' who 'never puzzled anybody'. Shaw congratulates him on 'having the luck' to be everybody's good neighbour. 'Darwin, by the way, was no more a Darwinist than I am a Shavian,' he adds. But in order to separate Darwin from his followers and repair the damage done by Butler's insults, he advances into factual error. Darwin had declared himself 'convinced that Natural Selection has been the main but not exclusive means of modification'. Shaw paraphrases this by declaring that Darwin 'did not pretend' that Natural Selection 'excluded other methods, or that it was the chief method'. Taking this extra step enables him to get beyond range of Darwin and to concentrate on the Neo-Darwinians whose minds Darwin himself had influenced only 'unintentionally'.

In Shaw's Preface Charles Darwin becomes a figure from *The Doctor's Dilemma*: someone whose evolutionary 'discovery' had often been made in the past – by his own grandfather Erasmus Darwin among others. By describing Natural Selection as Circumstantial Selection, Shaw made it all seem rather unremarkable. He used all his dialectical skills to undermine the authority of determinism, accusing its adherents of having reduced Evolution to the level of external accident, 'as if a tree could be properly said to have "evolved" into firewood by the storm which blew it down'.

Shaw felt an aversion to 'the barren cruelties of the laboratories', and objected to 'manufactured evidence in a secret chamber' because it produced knowledge that, being based on constructed and controlled events, was necessarily mechanistic. If the central debate in a scientific age was to be limited to the laboratory findings of people who would 'guess eggs if they saw the shells', then he was once more the complete outsider. He wanted to erase the distinction between scientists and imaginative artists such as Leonardo and Goethe. 'I have made observations and experiments in the spacious laboratory of the world with a marvellous portable apparatus compactly arranged in my head.'

Shaw's Preface to *Back to Methuselah* is an example of that compound of Will and Hope called wishful thinking. He took his readers to a high place and made them look round. What better evidence was there of where a belief in the 'survival of the fittest' had led than the contest of a world war?

But was all this necessary? Shaw says not, if we regard such disasters as evidence of the results and not as evidence of the truth of Neo-Darwinism. For we are co-authors of our world and our 'imagination is the beginning of creation'. Organic Natural Selection was unrepeatable in our life-span. Shaw therefore used the time-scale of his imagination. But he thought less about the scientific origins than the social effects of Darwin, whose theory of competitive survival could so conveniently be used to justify individualistic capitalism. 'I argue out the statements until I reach a verdict – often comic in its simplicity – and then I give the verdict,' he declared. But Shaw's verdicts were to sound as predetermined and his statements, hammered out in the secret chamber of his head, as much 'put up jobs' as any laboratory trial.

'Posterity will believe what it wishes to believe; and if its wishes jump with my guesses I shall be among the prophets,' he concluded. 'If not, I shall be only Simon Magus.'

*

After this appeal to the intellect came a demand of the imagination. Even the history of science carried its tales of witchcraft and wonders, from Archimedes in his bath to Newton under his apple tree. Shaw had begun to make a dramatic parable of his religion in the dream sequence of *Man and Superman*; and in the science fiction of *Back to Methuselah* he attempted to provide it with an iconography. 'I abandon the legend of Don Juan with its erotic associations, and go back to the legend of the Garden of Eden,' he announced. 'I exploit the eternal interest of the philosopher's stone which enables man to live for ever.'

The hell scene in *Man and Superman* took a Mozartian form; the Methuselah cycle, though it quotes from Mozart, advances as a series of Wagnerian leitmotifs. 'Back to Methuselah is my Ring,' Shaw confirmed. Despite its machinery of ghosts and miracles, with a cast that includes a couple of lethal Pavlovian dolls, one huge badly-behaved egg, a hooded serpent and a terrifying Oracle, Shaw did not intend it as a work of remote antiquity or impossible futurism, but as a contemporary drama gathering up the styles of political satire and drawing-room comedy, disquisition and extravaganza he had developed in earlier plays, and pointing the way to his future mystical fantasies.

The long journey begins in the Garden of Eden, where Adam and Eve come across a fawn that has stumbled and broken its neck. It is their discovery of death, and Shaw's illustration of how accident controls dying rather than living. The discourse that follows this discovery between the two of them and the serpent is a wonderful seminar in which vocabulary and understanding advance together. In the beginning there was Lilith, the Mother of Creation. 'I was her darling as I am yours,' says the Serpent, which represents Shaw's evolutionary belief that all habits are acquired *and* inherited – inherited by infinitesimal instalments and, when discarded, recapitulated in leaps and bounds.

While Lilith remained alone, all humankind was vulnerable to extinction by a single accident. So, like the snake, she renewed herself and overcame death by the miracle of birth. She imagined; she desired; she dared; she willed – and then she conceived. But since the labour of renewing life was too dangerous for one, she divided herself in two and created Adam and Eve to share this burden in the future.

Adam and Eve are suspended between two terrifying possibilities – the prospect of living for ever, and the accidental extinction of themselves. But they have not been created equal. 'Fear is stronger in me than hope,' Adam says. 'I must have certainty.' But hope is stronger than fear in Eve. She identifies improvement with the species rather than with herself, and accepts uncertainty, even death, as an inevitable risk in the process of creation.

The first scene of the play ends with the Serpent whispering the secret of conception to Eve. The stage directions read: '*Eve's face lights up with intense interest, which increases until an expression of overwhelming repugnance takes its place. She buries her face in her hands.*' This passage was criticized by St John Ervine. Was it not more likely, he demanded, that Eve 'leapt with joy'? Shaw defended his representation of a woman 'in a state of complete pre-sex innocence as making a wry face when it was explained to her that in consequence of the indelicacy with which Nature, in a fit of economy, has combined a merely excretory function with a creatively ejaculatory one in the same bodily part (she knowing only the excretory use of it), she is to allow herself to be syringed in an unprecedented manner by Adam . . . It is true that the indignity has compensations which, *when experienced*, overwhelm all the objections to it; but Eve had not then experienced them.' Coming at the end of this magical first scene which shows life expanding in an atmosphere of strangeness, as idea gives birth to idea in the sunny stillness of that garden, Eve's repugnance is theatrically powerful.

In the second scene 'a few centuries later' at an oasis in Mesopotamia, Adam and Eve have given birth to their family. What had taken place is a series of moral descents. The moment Adam invented death, it was 'no longer worth his while to do anything thoroughly well'. That was the first step of the Fall; the second came as a result of inventing birth, before which Adam dared not risk killing Eve because he would have been 'lonely and barren to all eternity'. But the invention of birth has meant that anyone who is killed can be replaced. One of Adam's sons 'invented meat-eating. The other . . . slew his beefsteak-eating brother, and thus invented murder. That was a very steep step. It was so exciting that all the others began to kill one another for sport, and thus invented war, the steepest step of all.'

Which is the stage reached in Mesopotamia in 4004 BC. Adam's fear has stopped his development with the invention of the spade. Cain is an early example of the Superman who sets the standards for further human advancement. Like his brother Abel, whom he envied, copied and killed, he is 'a discoverer, a man of ideas, a true Progressive'. From his father he has inherited fear which he overwhelms daily with acts of courage and the ecstasy of fighting. From his mother, he has taken hope, but he has no imagination to make creative use of his will and daring. 'I do not know what I want,' he tells Eve, 'except that I want to be something higher and nobler than this stupid old digger.' In Cain, the first murderer, Shaw embodies his belief that what we have learnt to call evil is technically an error in the experimental process of trial and error by which the Life Force must advance.

Cain is the dominant man. His fearful inventions of murder and war are reducing life to its new brevity. 'Through him and his like,' Eve declares, 'death is gaining on life.' She blames Lilith's miscalculation in sharing the labour of creating so unequally between man and woman. 'That is why there is enmity between Woman the creator and Man the destroyer.'

The twentieth century is largely populated by Adam's successors. In 'The Gospel of the Brothers Barnabas', the second part of his cycle, Shaw stages his revenge on these mean material people whom he typifies in Joyce Burge and Henry Hopkins Lubin, his lampoons of Asquith and Lloyd George. These are his contemporary idealists. They have one quality, which is Will, necessary to the Life Force. But it is Will without imagination, loveless, and by itself destructive. 'The Gospel of the Brothers Barnabas' is designed as a humiliation of these two Liberal leaders who arrive at Franklyn Barnabas's house as a couple of campaigning political candidates. They have come on fools' errands, having carefully read between the lines of several newspaper reports and made the erroneous conclusion that Barnabas is going to enter politics and contest the approaching general election. Almost everything they hear they misunderstand; almost everything they say is trivial or untrue.

The play demonstrates the incompatibility between Adam's offspring and the children of Eve – that incompatibility which Shaw felt to be his own inheritance. Lubin and Burge cannot take a long view even of the possibilities of longevity. They imagine the gospel of Creative Evolution to be a marketable elixir ('The stuff. The powder. The bottle. The tabloid. Whatever it is. You said it wasnt lemons') which must be kept secret. When they discover it to be an idea (or 'moonshine'), they have no further use for it.

For half an hour in the third part of the cycle, 'The Thing Happens', almost no progress is detectable. We have edged forward another 250 years. The Lilliputian President of the British Islands is named Burge-Lubin, symbol of soldered fixity. Equally unchangeable is Barnabas, the Accountant-General with a likeness to his ancestor Conrad Barnabas, a bureaucrat who has made a god of statistics. Two other characters resemble figures in the previous play of the cycle: the Archbishop of York is 'recognizably the same man' as the Reverend William Haslam who was engaged to Franklyn Barnabas's daughter Cynthia; and the Domestic Minister, Mrs Lutestring, seems remarkably similar to Franklyn Barnabas's parlourmaid. A statistical survey leads accidentally to the dramatic revelation that they are indeed the same people, and since, 'like all revolutionary truths, it [longevity] began as a joke', this gives Shaw's absurdist talent excellent scope. He chose for this experiment two of the least promising candidates from 'The Gospel of the Brothers Barnabas' so as to demonstrate that the change would not take place as the result of individual self-interest. 'If the geniuses live 300 years,' Shaw explains, 'so will the chumps.' Since there are more chumps than geniuses, most of those to whom the thing happens will be ordinary people, like the parlourmaid.

It is the story of Adam and Eve once again, with a vital difference. When this new word is made flesh, the mother and father of the long-lived (their own ages presently totalling more than 557 years) are animated solely by hope. These two long-livers have experienced a hostility and strangeness among the short-lived that reflects Shaw's own isolation. 'I have been very lonely sometimes,' reflects Mrs Lutestring; and the Archbishop reveals that it is 'in this matter of sex [more] than in any other, you are intolerable to us'.

All this is reversed in the fourth part of the cycle, 'The Tragedy of an Elderly Gentleman', which propels us forward to a colony of long-lived people at Galway Bay in the year AD 3000. The deputation of short-lived visitors has come to consult their oracle. Among them is Napoleon, 'the finest soldier in the world' and Cain's most perfect descendant. 'War has made me popular, powerful, famous, historically immortal,' he explains. 'But I foresee that if I go on to the end it will leave me execrated, dethroned, imprisoned, perhaps executed. Yet if I stop fighting I commit suicide as a great man and become a common one.' The Oracle answers that his only escape is death, and he is immobilized. For this scene Shaw developed the electric emanation, Vril, with which the subterranean sages of Bulwer-Lytton's *The Coming Race* (a favourite book of his boyhood) slayed at sight. The invisible mesmeric field, naturally accumulating round the long-lived, is that same fantasy of intellectual power that Captain Shotover had struggled to invent. By using this force finally to arrest the progress of his own 'Man of Destiny', Shaw seals the destiny of the short-lived.

'The Tragedy of an Elderly Gentleman' is perhaps the weakest play of the cycle. It explains differences between the two species that could be more imaginatively charted through the use of differing languages. Shaw recognized this growing challenge of vocabulary: he would get round it in the final play by having an 800-year-old She-Ancient tell a three-year-old that 'we have to put things very crudely to you to make ourselves intelligible'. Yet the short tragi-comic scene with which the fourth play ends is peculiarly effective. This introduces the Elderly Gentleman who is Shaw's partial self-portrait. In the short-lived world he has prided himself on daringly advanced thinking which, in the long perspective, becomes mere obscurantism. At home in neither world, he must choose between the despair of living among people to whom nothing is real, and consenting to be phased out among the superior long-lived. 'I take the nobler risk,' he decides, like Gulliver seeking to escape the Yahoos. The Oracle offers him her hands. '*He grasps them and raises himself a little by clinging to her. She looks steadily into his face. He stiffens; a little convulsion shakes him; his grasp relaxes; and he falls dead.*'

The Elderly Gentleman's grasping of hands is a commitment to the spiritual future set out in the fifth and last play of the cycle. 'As Far as Thought Can Reach' combines past, present and future as paraded before a viewing platform set in the year AD 31,920. We are given 'a glimpse of the past' through a grotesque puppet play performed by two 'artificial human beings' that have been manufactured in the laboratory. This synthetic couple proclaim themselves to be the products of Cause and Effect, and offer a pantomime of the determinists' concept of human life. They are ourselves, motivated by fear, enveloped in illusions, playing fantastic tricks that kill their Frankenstein-creator, the fanatical scientist Pygmalion, and finally, though shrinking from death at any cost, dying of terror and discouragement.

The future is a stateless society inhabited entirely by the long-lived. They have been born from artificially hatched eggs in which they were incubated for two years, developing from all sorts of creatures that no longer exist, to emerge as newly-born human beings roughly equivalent to our sixteen-year-olds. Before them stretch four years of what is called childhood, devoted to arts, sports and emotional pleasures, during which they pass through the immaturity that members of the audience begin to shed at the age of fifty. But whereas the short-lived audience will soon die of decay, the long-lived cast are like the original Adam and Eve, and will evolve over hundreds of years into a breed of intellectual voluptuaries known as the Ancients, who are Shaw's version of Swift's Houyhnhnms.

Such a prospect appals the children, just as it appals the audience, for we cannot sense anything in the existence of these Olympians to enchant us. Shaw's artistic problem is one experienced by many creators of utopias. 'I could not shew the life of the long livers, because, being a short liver, I could not conceive it,' he wrote. The imaginative effect is handed over to the actors, directors and designers.

In the final minutes of *Back to Methuselah* the ghosts of Lilith, Adam and Eve, Cain and the Serpent appear. Cain acknowledges that there is no future role for his offspring in the world; Adam too can make nothing of a place where matter does not rule the mind. But the Serpent feels justified. She has chosen the knowledge of good and evil, and she sees a new world in which, hope having vanquished fear, 'there is no evil'. Eve too concludes that all is well: 'My clever ones have inherited the earth.' Finally, as an epitome of the whole cycle, Lilith delivers her testament.

'Is this enough; or must I labor again? . . . They did terrible things . . . I stood amazed at the malice and destructiveness of the things I had made . . . The pangs of another birth were already upon me when one man repented and . . . so much came of it that the horrors of that time seem now but an evil dream . . . Best of all, they are still not satisfied . . . they press on to . . . the whirlpool in pure intelligence that, when the world began, was a whirlpool in pure force . . . when they attain it they shall become one with me and supersede me, and Lilith will be only a legend . . . Of Life only is there no end . . . for what may be beyond, the eyesight of Lilith is too short. It is enough that there is a beyond.'

Earlier in the play, the She-Ancient defined art as a 'magic mirror you make to reflect your invisible dreams in visible pictures'. Lilith's speech is Shaw's magic mirror. Following his courting of disorder in *Heartbreak*

House, he had made a greater effort than in any play since *Major Barbara* towards a new coherence. The end of *Back to Methuselah* foretells the dissolution of matter and, with it, all that had vexed his mind. He sent his optimistic signal infinitely far beyond personal experience. The distant echo he received underscores Lilith's words with a poignancy that against all odds makes them perhaps the most moving of all Shaw's speeches for the theatre.

*

'The sale of the book here and in America has been greater than that of any other of my works,' Shaw told Karel Musek, his translator into the Bohemian language. *Back to Methuselah* seemed to answer a need of the times. 'Your mind was never more infernally agile, your intellectual muscle was never better,' William Archer reassured G.B.S. ' . . . When a man can walk on a tightrope over the Falls of Niagara, turning three somersaults to a minute, it's no use his appealing to the census paper to prove himself decrepit.' More surprising was Max Beerbohm's opinion – that *Back to Methuselah* was the best book Shaw had written because he had got away 'from representation of actual things . . . and thought out a genuine work of art'.

Shaw sent complimentary copies of the book to any number of old friends and comrades, including one inscribed to Lenin. Lenin seems to have found in the Preface confirmation of his view that Shaw was 'a good man fallen among Fabians'. In those places where the shortcomings of capitalism were exposed, Lenin wrote his favourite expression – '*Bien dit!*' – in the margin. But where Shaw appeared to be 'in the power of his Utopian illusions there are marks of disapproval'.

Almost everyone agreed with Shaw's eventual view that 'I was too damned discursive'. In the critical opinion of T. S. Eliot such garrulity had been a product of the 'potent ju-ju of the Life Force [which] is a gross superstition'. This 'master of a lucid and witty dialogue prose hardly equalled since Congreve, and of a certain power of observation,' he wrote, was now 'squandering these gifts in the service of worn out home-made theories, as in the lamentable *Methuselah*'.

Shaw had not counted on a performance in the theatre. He had calculated, however, without the 'lunatic' founder of the American Theatre Guild, Lawrence Langner, who came to Adelphi Terrace in the spring of 1921. He was examined, as Trebitsch had been, by Charlotte: 'a gentle gracious lady with plain, pleasant features,' Langner observed, 'of medium height and comfortable build'. G.B.S. had introduced her 'in the grand manner' as if she were a *prima donna*, then ostentatiously seated her in a chair and stayed unfamiliarly quiet. Once her mystic scrutiny of Langner was over, Shaw sprang from his chair and dashed 'like a sprinter to the door' which he held open 'with a deep bow until she had passed into the hall'. Herself being favourably impressed, Himself was free to give Langner a brief synopsis of his play, lasting two hours, at the end of which Langner concluded that 'Shaw had more than a touch of the fanatic about him'. But between fanatic and lunatic an oddly effective partnership developed. *Heartbreak House*, Shaw cautioned Langner, was like 'a musical comedy' compared with *Back to Methuselah*. But despite its eight changes of scene, a cast of forty-five characters, and a duration exceeding twelve hours, Langner decided it was 'just the kind of thing for the Theatre Guild to do'.

The rehearsals, which began early in 1922, called for a group of actors who were sufficiently talented to play several parts, and sufficiently flexible not only to play them on succeeding weeks but to rehearse them almost simultaneously – 'much as the Grand Central Station had to be built while the trains were run'. *Back to Methuselah* opened in New York on 27 February 1922 with a matinée of Part I and evening performance of Part II. The cycle was completed over three weeks. Over nine weeks, twenty-five performances of the complete cycle were given, at the end of which the financial loss had risen to $20,000. On the other hand, the Theatre Guild had nearly doubled its subscribers. 'The Garrick Theater was too small for us to make money out of the play,' Langner explained. 'If we had had a theater twice the size, there would have been a profit instead of a loss.' 'It isn't likely that any other lunatic will want to produce *Back to Methuselah!*' Shaw concluded.

He had seriously underrated his attraction for lunatics. Going up to Birmingham in 1923 for a matinée of *Heartbreak House* he met Barry Jackson, known locally as 'the Butter King' after the Birmingham Maypole Dairies founded by his father, from which he derived a large private income. Jackson's madness took the form of philanthropy: over a period of twenty-one years he was to spend more than £100,000 (over £2 million in 1997) of his own money on the Birmingham Repertory Theatre which he had founded in 1913. Jackson had been disenchanted by the fashion machine of the London West End theatre. His repertory staged both classical and contemporary plays including continental expressionist drama – he put on Georg Kaiser's *Gas* and the Čapeks' *Insect Play. Heartbreak House* was the ninth of Shaw's plays to be produced there since its opening, and Jackson now proposed a tenth, the impossible *Methuselah*. 'I asked him was he mad,' Shaw remembered. '. . . I demanded further whether he wished his wife and children to die in the workhouse. He replied that he was not married. I began to scent a patron.'

Barry Jackson's patronage between the wars became the equivalent in

England of Lawrence Langner's promotion of Shaw's plays through the Theatre Guild in the United States. Almost twenty-five years younger than G.B.S., Jackson inherited Granville-Barker's kinship of the stage. 'Elegant, urbane, unselfconsciously dominating, always seeming to be a head taller than his companions', he appeared like one of the superior long-lived among the short-lived inhabitants of Birmingham. Though his theatre was one of the happiest places in which to work, it offended Birmingham's respect for profit-making.

Jackson appealed to Shaw as someone whose speciality was to make the impossible take place: a conjuror converting dreams into reality. He therefore handed over *Back to Methuselah!* (which at that time ended with an exclamation mark) and saw it staged in the autumn of 1923, with sets by Paul Shelving and featuring a cast of 'provincial nobodies' that included Gwen Ffrangcon-Davies, Cedric Hardwicke, Raymond Huntley and Edith Evans (who played the Serpent, the Oracle, and the She-Ancient). 'It is a mighty work,' Gwen Ffrangcon-Davies wrote during the rehearsals, '... but opinion is divided about it in the theatre ... I do not myself know whether it will be as enthralling to see as it is to read.'

Four consecutively played cycles were performed at Birmingham and produced a loss of around £2,500 (equivalent to £62,000 in 1997), of which a little was recovered from a further four cycles put on at the Royal Court Theatre in Sloane Square early the following year. But Shaw was happy. 'This has been the most extraordinary experience of my life,' he declared after the first performance.

From the sequence of secrets and revelations in the Garden of Eden to the terrible cry of the Elderly Gentleman receding into the distance, there were thrilling moments. Desmond MacCarthy, who had been told that, though marvellous, the play was rather boring, listened with riveted attention to the final part. He had learnt that those of Shaw's ideas which 'first struck me as silliest were the ones which I subsequently found had modified my thoughts most', and he recognized that G.B.S. was placing his ghostly faith out of reach of human discouragement. This kind of drama, with its chords of inspiration, flashes of moral passion, and searching chaos, was rare in the theatre. 'The superb merit of the play is that it is the work of an artist who has asked himself, with far greater seriousness and courage than all but a few, what is the least he must believe and hope for if he is to feel life is worth living.'

5

HOME RULE FOR ENGLAND

> What we need is not a new edition of rules of the ring but the substitution of law for violence as between nations.
>
> Shaw to Jerome N. Frank (13 April 1918)

In the first four and a half years of Fred Day's employment, the Shaws made four journeys into Ireland. Usually they spent some weeks bathing, boating, walking and writing at Parknasilla, which Charlotte had known as a child and which to her mind always rejuvenated G.B.S. Near the opposite coast, they would stay with Horace Plunkett of Foxrock outside Dublin – 'the kindest and most helpful of my Kilteragh guests,' he called them.

'One reason that I am anxious to get him here,' Plunkett had told Charlotte, 'is that I feel it in my bones that the time has come for him to do his great service to Ireland.' It was difficult for Shaw to resist such unusual trust, and when Plunkett's new party, known as the Dominion League, was formed in 1919, he began numerous contributions to its paper, the *Irish Statesman* edited by AE.

In Shaw's imagination the Dominion League became a forum for all extremists whose opposing views could be beguiled into a visionary Irish Bill that none of the extremist factions could obtain separately. To pull off this amazing trick 'the ace is the public opinion of the world,' Shaw reckoned, 'especially the English-speaking world'. He promoted the League as a sensible way forward for businessmen, an attractive vehicle for patriots, and an honourable solution for the British Government. 'What the Irish want is the freedom of their country,' he declared. But no one could agree what freedom meant. Was it complete independence, or the gaining of a position similar to Australia and Canada, or the occupation of a place equal to England's within the British Commonwealth, or the beginning of a federated partnership of the United Kingdom?

Meanwhile Ireland continued to exist under a virtual state of martial law. 'Laws are enforced, not by the police, but by the citizens who call the police when the law is broken,' Shaw argued. '. . . But in Ireland nobody will call the police, nobody will give away another Irishman to the policeman.' The result was a miserably weak British regime holding on to power through Black and Tan coercion. In Ireland 'you have every sort of liberty trampled on,' Shaw told the Fabians. '. . . all these petty persecutions, annoyance, these flingings of men into jail, putting down newspapers, charging political meetings with bayonet and baton charges have produced a condition of the most furious revolt against the British Government and, of course, you have the governing class in this country quite deliberately and unmistakeably going on with that in order to provoke revolts against them which will enable them to say it is impossible to give Ireland self-government.' Amid the raids, ambushes and weekly acts of terrorism, the attempted assassination at the end of 1919 of Lord French, the Lord Lieutenant of Ireland, which appeared to shock the English, came as no surprise to Shaw.

But what did take him by surprise was the sudden action of Lloyd George who announced a Bill for the 'better government of Ireland', partitioning six of the nine Ulster counties from the twenty-six so-called 'southern' counties, north and south being provided with separate home rule and a local Parliament. Lloyd George's Bill led to the Anglo-Irish Treaty and semi-finalization of the partition of Ireland at the end of the year. The Dáil ratified the treaty, but the minority opposing it, led by Éamon de Valera, attracted the support of a majority section of the Irish Republican Army. The Anglo-Irish war had ended: in June 1922 the Irish Civil War began.

'This is an impossible situation,' Shaw wrote in the *Irish Times* that summer. It was literally impossible in the sense that the men he had always called 'marginal impossibilists' had won the day. The IRA was flushed with success – though to Shaw's eyes it represented only 'the stale romance that passes for politics in Ireland'. His purpose throughout all these complicated Anglo-Irish troubles had been to promote any act of grace that could sweeten the atmosphere of this war-tortured country. 'We must all, at heavy disadvantages, do what we can to stop explosions of mere blind hatred.'

After the ratification of the treaty, whatever skirmishes went on between IRA and Irish Free State Army troops, the country would have to govern itself, 'which means that her troubles are beginning, not ending,' Shaw warned. He continued to come over, keeping himself up-to-date with political developments. On 19 and 20 August 1922 he and Charlotte had stayed once more with Horace Plunkett at Kilteragh where they met Michael Collins, one of the most attractive of the Free State leaders. Collins had been a member of the Irish delegation that negotiated the Anglo-Irish Treaty and now, as Commander-in-Chief of the Free State Army, was leading the fight against some of his ex-comrades in the IRA. A few days before this meeting, following the death of Arthur Griffith, he had been appointed head of the new government of the Irish Free State. To be dining with Michael Collins at Kilteragh seemed entirely appropriate to Shaw. With the political realignment between Irishmen, Collins had been moving from extremism to the moderate centre until he now occupied Plunkett's old role – the very change that Shaw had looked for, by non-violent means, in his proposals for the Dominion League.

The Shaws left Kilteragh next day; and a day later Collins was shot dead in an ambush near Cork. 'How could a born soldier die better than at the victorious end of a good fight, falling to a shot of another Irishman – a damned fool, but all the same an Irishman who thought he was fighting for Ireland – "a Roman to a Roman"?' Shaw wrote to Michael Collins's sister. 'I met Michael for the first and last time on Saturday last, and am very glad I did. I rejoice in his memory . . . So tear up your mourning and hang up your brightest colors in his honor; and let us all praise God that he had not to die in a snuffy bed of a trumpery cough, weakened by age, and saddened by the disappointments that would have attended his work had he lived.'

It was a handsome letter, masking Shaw's own pessimism under its shining style. Shaw had returned with Charlotte to Ireland for a couple of months in mid-July 1923, burning up the thirty miles of mountainous Cork and Kerry roads between Glengarriff and Parknasilla 'in a new 23–60 h.p.'. Despite alarms in the papers, excursions across the south of Ireland were safer than anywhere else in Europe, he reported to *The Times*. There was some outdoor economic socialism-in-action – 'the loot from plundered houses has to be redistributed by rough methods for which the permanent law is too slow and contentious' – but none of this was exercised at the expense of the errant Englishman. 'The tourist's heart is in his mouth when he first crosses a repaired bridge on a 30 cwt. car, for the repairs are extremely unconvincing to the eye,' he wrote; 'but after crossing two or three in safety he thinks no more of them.

'Since I arrived I have wandered every night over the mountains, either alone or with a harmless companion or two, without molestation or incivility . . . there is not the smallest reason why Glengarriff and Parknasilla should not be crowded this year with refugees from the turbulent sister island and the revolutionary Continent, as well as by connoisseurs in extraordinarily beautiful scenery and in air which makes breathing a luxury.'

On 12 September he fell on some rocks along the Kerry coast, damaging two ribs and badly bruising himself. He came back to England six days later, like an Irish hero himself, to be attended by an osteopath, a surgeon and radiographer.

This was his thirteenth visit to his country since he had emigrated from Dublin almost fifty years ago, and he would not go back again. His last political hopes for Ireland had appeared to go up in smoke when Horace Plunkett's house Kilteragh was burnt to the ground by the Republicans earlier that year. He had already written his valediction.

'I am returning to England because I can do no good here . . . I was a Republican before Mr de Valera was born . . . I objected to the old relations between England and Ireland as I object to the present ones, because they were not half intimate enough . . . I must hurry back to London. The lunatics there are comparatively harmless.'

6

FREE WILL IN TRANSLATION

> Nature must have a relief from any feeling, no matter how deep and sincere it is.
>
> *Jitta's Atonement*

'The war is over,' Shaw wrote. ' . . . All the literary, artistic and scientific institutions should be hard at work healing up the wounds of Europe.' What he advocated as public policy he tried to implement in his private dealings, seeking to invest his German royalties in German industry. 'It is with great pleasure that I find myself able to correspond with my German friends again,' he had written to Carl Otto in the autumn of 1919. 'I need hardly say that the war did the most painful violence to my personal feelings.' He felt a special tenderness for Siegfried Trebitsch. For much of the war they had hardly been able to communicate at all, and even during the long months of the Armistice Shaw had to obtain official authorization to write Trebitsch a letter – all his correspondence to Austria and Germany being inspected to make certain it was confined to business and 'expressed in terms suitable to the existing political relations between our respective countries'. When Trebitsch moved for a time to Switzerland, Shaw vented his relief: 'At last I have got you in a country which I can write to without being shot at dawn.'

Shaw instructed Trebitsch to hold on to all monies due and use them for himself and his wife. 'Spend my money: *steal* it: do anything you like with it as if it were your own until you are in easy circumstances once more.' But Trebitsch could not get the hang of these economic reversals. Despite all Shaw's urgings, he would convey strange sums by dubious routes at odd intervals, imperilling their licence to trade. Because he was aware of Trebitsch's dismay at becoming principally known as 'Shaw's translator' ('my name as a writer in my own right faded away'), G.B.S. hit on the corrective paradox of translating his translator. When Trebitsch sent him a copy of his latest play, *Frau Gittas Sühne*, shortly after the war, he accepted it as an opportunity to make this singular counter-reparationary gesture with *Jitta's Atonement*. 'I have read Gitta,' he wrote in May 1920, 'though most of your words are not in the dictionary.' Within this tangle of difficulties there opened a beautiful advantage for Shaw: 'I had to guess what it was all about by mere instinct.'

He took a year over the translation. Using 'some telepathic method of absorption, I managed at last to divine, infer, guess, and co-invent the story of Gitta'. He had asked Blanche Patch's German-speaking *locum tenens* to provide him with a literal translation of the play which served as a helpful departure guide. 'I hope my tricks wont make you furious,' he wrote uneasily to Trebitsch after completing the first act. 'Charlotte says I have made it brutally realistic; but this is an unintended result of making the stage business more explicit for the sake of the actress . . .The stock joke of the London stage is a fabulous stage direction "Sir Henry turns his back to the audience and conveys that he has a son at Harrow".'

Sending him this first act, Shaw advised Trebitsch to 'tear the thing up if it is impossible', but not to do so 'merely because it is disappointing' since all translations were that. 'It is much better than the original,' gallantly responded Trebitsch who had learnt Shaw's politeness without its component of irony. He eagerly exhorted G.B.S. to complete his version which 'proves again your stage-genious', and add his name as co-dramatist to increase its chances of production. 'I feel a childish delight reading Trebitsch in English,' he wrote happily. ' . . . Please handle that play like your own.'

This, increasingly, is what Shaw did. At the end of the first act, the fifty-year-old Professor Bruno Haldenstedt lies dead of a heart attack on the floor of an apartment where he had been keeping an assignation with his mistress, Jitta Lenkheim, the wife of a medical colleague. 'I was horribly tempted to make Haldenstedt sit up after Jitta's departure, and make a comedy of the sequel,' Shaw warned Trebitsch. His struggle to resist these temptations weakened in the second act and was joyously abandoned in the third where the cast, with 'a paroxysm of agonizing laughter', evolves into a hilarious troupe of Shavians. 'The real person always kills the imagined person,' announces Jitta as Trebitsch's characters die away; and the dead lover's daughter, Edith Haldenstedt, agrees that it is 'such a relief' to be acting sensibly at last.

Studying the typewritten transcription from Shaw's shorthand turned out to be a strange experience for Trebitsch. 'I was puzzeled very much reading your bold alterations,' he admitted. '. . . The III Akt is in your version almost a comedy!' Shaw was quick to provide healing explanations. It was true, he acknowledged, that he had not done justice to Trebitsch's poetry. But Trebitsch would be overjoyed to discover that by making the characters rather less oppressively conventional, and then inserting a little mild fun into their lives, he had managed to rescue the hero and heroine from their dark fates of misery and despair. 'That is the good news,' he confirmed. Then he had been obliged to replace Vienna (which still lay in the romantic haze of Strauss waltzes) with London and New York (where the delicious anaesthetic of romance was only tolerated in Italian opera). The hopeless gloom into which Trebitsch flung everyone would be fatal to the play in Britain and America. 'Life is not like that here,' he explained. Trebitsch was surprised to learn that even with such artificial aids as black clothes, the British exercised a reaction against grief over death – an irresistible reaction into cheerfulness. Also 'nine tenths of the adulteries end in reconciliations,' Shaw notified Trebitsch, 'and even at the connivance of the injured party at its continuation'.

The delight that had initially flowed through Trebitsch was by now rather confused. To what degree was *Jitta's Atonement* his own work? The tragedy of his first act and the melodrama of the second act had been dissolved in the sparkling comedy of Shaw's ending. It was true that he had been invited to refashion the play if he found these treacheries unbearable – but he trusted Shaw's 'diabolical skill' and his estimate of the play's increased chances of performance. So he gave the go-ahead to prepare an acting version of the text. 'What could I do but agree?'

'You will find that in this final acting edition of the play I have committed some fresh outrages,' Shaw wrote. '. . . Nothing has been lost by this except the characteristic Trebitschian brooding that is so deliciously sad and noble in your novels but that I could never reproduce . . . My method of getting a play across the footlights is like revolver shooting: every line has a bullet in it and comes with an explosion . . . so you must forgive me: I have done my best.'

Lee Schubert's production in Washington and New York, with Bertha Kalich as Jitta, 'did not succeed even as a comedy,' Langner recorded. For two years Shaw held up *Jitta* in England in the hope of getting a West End production – then he handed it to Violet Vanbrugh who 'will try it at a rather nice suburban theatre at Putney Bridge, called the Grand Theatre'. Shaw was abroad for this first English production, but caught up with it two months later at Leicester. 'The funniest thing about it is that I was very much struck with your play when I saw it on the stage,' he told Trebitsch. Most of the reviews made it clear that (as the *Daily*

Telegraph reported) 'Mr Shaw conjugates the verb "to translate" very differently from most men'. But whenever the reviewers should have felt like 'holding up our hands in horror at the shameful way the original author has been manhandled,' wrote the *Nation & Athenaeum* critic, 'we are laughing too loud to remember to do so . . . it cannot possibly have been better entertainment.' One of those most deeply entertained had been Arnold Bennett. '*The thing is simply masterly*, & contains a *lot* of the finest scenes that Shaw ever wrote.' In his diary he recorded that the effect of re-engineering a machine-made drama with Shavian wit had been electrical. 'The mere idea of starting on a purely conventional 1st act and then guying it with realism and fun, shows genius.

'In the other acts there is some of the most brilliant work, some tender, some brutal, and lots of the most side-splitting fun that Shaw ever did – and he is now approaching seventy, I suppose. The "hysterics" scene of laughter between the widow and the mistress of the dead man is startlingly original. The confession scene between the mistress and the daughter of the dead man is really beautiful.'

Though none of his fantasies of film versions and West End triumphs became facts, Trebitsch had already decided that 'the play was indeed a success'. Shaw paid Trebitsch £100 (equivalent to £1,750 in 1997) for a perpetual non-exclusive licence to translate and publish *Frau Gittas Sühne*, and then diverted Trebitsch's interests elsewhere. 'Did I tell you that I am working on a play about Joan of Arc?' he asked. There was, he had supposed, 'no chance of your coming over here'. Not having seen Shaw now for some ten years, and feeling it was his 'destiny and privilege' to meet his friend again, Trebitsch swore 'a vow that in spite of all difficulties and all qualms I would receive the master's new work only from his own hand. *Saint Joan* summoned me, and I had to go and receive her.' Shaw provided information on the prices and standards of London hotels, added an unglamorous assessment of Ayot – 'a village where nobody dreams of dressing' – and noted some of the house rules: 'If you smoke cigars, you will give Charlotte asthma.' All the same, he conceded, 'I hope to be able to give you printed proofs of Joan'.

The main obstacle to his visit was what Shaw called 'a disgraceful Aliens Act'. The British Embassy had cautioned Trebitsch against trusting to his visa alone. To avoid the risk of being sent straight back across the Channel, he would need an authoritative letter from a British citizen. The letter Shaw sent him admirably fulfilled its purpose, disarming 'the austere passport control officials' at Dover with 'considerable merriment'. Shaw met him at Victoria Station, 'coming with long strides along the platform,'

Trebitsch remembered, ' . . . a laughing giant . . . I grasped the hand this long-missed man held out to me.' They drove to Ayot where, for the first time, Trebitsch heard Shaw read one of his own works out loud.

Afterwards they spoke of the dreadful war years – experiences, moods and opinions that could never have been sent through the mail. 'My generation has passed away and I shall soon have to follow its example,' Shaw said. The days passed all too quickly for Trebitsch. When they said *auf Wiedersehen* it seemed to him that the additional unspoken phrase 'in a better world' was plainly implied. He carried with him the latest work. 'There is no other new play,' Shaw told him: 'Joan is *the* new play.'

FIFTEEN

I

COLLABORATING WITH A SAINT

We want a few mad people now. See where the sane ones have landed us!

Saint Joan

Shaw had been long familiar with Joan of Arc in the theatre. In his Notes to *Caesar and Cleopatra* he had classed her with Nelson and Charles XII – all 'half-witted geniuses, enjoying the worship accorded by all races to certain forms of insanity'. Some ten years later, in the Preface to *Getting Married*, she is no longer a lunatic but gifted with 'exceptional sanity'. In the interval, Quicherat's factual testimony had been translated and published in England, providing authentic evidence of the real Joan.

Shaw does not seem to have considered adding to Joan literature himself until 1913 when, returning from Germany through the Vosges and 'pleasing myself as to my route, I took Domremy on my way for the sake of St Joan of Arc'. He had often travelled through 'Joan of Arc country', but never before visited Orléans. It was here, at the Musée Historique, that he saw the fifteenth-century sculptured head of St Maurice, traditionally believed by the inhabitants to have been modelled from Joan after her triumphant relief of their town from the English. Shaw was happy to embrace this belief. For the Gothic image showed a remarkable face – 'evidently not an ideal face but a portrait, and yet so uncommon as to be unlike any real woman one has ever seen,' he wrote. '. . . It is a wonderful face . . . the face of a born leader.' This was the image before Shaw ten years later when he presented Joan in the turret doorway of his play – '*an able-bodied country girl of 17 or 18, respectably dressed in red, with an uncommon face: eyes very wide apart . . . a long well-shaped nose . . . resolute but full-lipped mouth, and handsome fighting chin*'.

From Orléans he wrote to Stella Campbell: 'I shall do a Joan play some day.' He imagined it beginning with the 'sweeping up of the cinders and orange peel *after* her martyrdom', and ending with Joan's arrival in heaven. 'I should have God about to damn the English for their share in her betrayal,' he wrote, 'and Joan producing an end of burnt stick in arrest of Judgment.'

The play's epilogue, a bedroom cabaret in Charles VII's dream, has some affinities with Shaw's original fantasy. But more significant is the change of surroundings in which Shaw places his 'masterful girl soldier' after the First World War, and the different task he assigns her. The chronicle play he wrote in 1923 is his 'one foray into popular myth-making,' Irving Wardle has written, 'undefaced by his usual ironic graffiti'; while the epilogue is a Shavian revue sketch which does not remove Joan up to heaven, but brings her forward from the fifteenth into the twentieth century – a move implicit in the previous six scenes.

Shaw felt he recognized in Joan the spirit needed for the regeneration of society in the modern world. A quarter of a century earlier in *The Perfect Wagnerite*, 'Siegfried as Protestant' had anticipated Joan, the first Protestant. Siegfried and Joan both quell their fear of fire, and are transfigured by the flames. Describing Protestantism in the late fifteenth century as a 'wave of thought' that led 'the strongest-hearted peoples to affirm that every man's private judgement was a more trustworthy interpreter of God and revelation than the Church', Shaw concluded:

'The most inevitable dramatic conception, then, of the nineteenth century is that of a perfectly naïve hero upsetting religion, law and order in all directions, and establishing in their place the unfettered action of Humanity . . . This conception, already incipient in Adam Smith's Wealth of Nations, was certain at last to reach some great artist, and be embodied by him in a masterpiece.'

Saint Joan is Shaw's attempt at this masterpiece and the vehicle for a dialogue between ancient and modern worlds. If Joan's rehabilitation was an example of a modern show trial, the original court hearing seemed to Shaw one of history's secret trials – like those of the Star Chamber. 'Joan was killed by the Inquisition . . . The Inquisition is not dead,' he wrote in 1931. ' . . . when in modern times you fall behind-hand with your political institutions . . . you get dictatorships . . . and when you get your dictatorship you may take it from me that you will with the greatest certainty get a secret tribunal dealing with sedition, with political heresy, exactly like the Inquisition.'

The hero as victim transformed into saviour had been in Shaw's mind as early as the *Passion Play* he had started to compose at the age of twenty-one. Like Jesus, Joan was an agent for change inspired against the idealist *status quo* of the established Church. Cauchon's great cry – 'Must then a Christ perish in torment in every age to save those that have no imagination?' – makes the connection plain. So *Saint Joan* became Shaw's passion play and represents Joan's life as another coming of Christ to the world.

Shaw interprets Joan's voices as evidence of a living imagination – the 'inspirations and intuitions and unconsciously reasoned conclusions of genius' – which are miraculous not by virtue of their alleged source but because of exceptional consequences. These voices and visions, being the manifestations of Joan's instinct ('the voices come first,' she explains, 'and I find the reasons after'), operate similarly to Shaw's own methods of writing. 'I am pushed by a natural need to set to work to write down the conversations that come into my head unaccountably,' he had explained ten years before. 'At first I hardly know the speakers and cannot find names for them . . . Finally I come to know them very well, and discover what it is they are driving at, and why they have said and done the things I have been moved to set down.' By this telepathic process Shaw hoped to attune himself to Joan, he echoing her when following the court testimony, she echoing him when he departs from it, and together collaborating in the miraculous creation of the play.

To many it seemed that the miracle had been Saint Joan's transformation of G.B.S. Johan Huizinga claimed that she had brought Shaw 'to his knees'. But the wretched innocent who had 'talked with angels and saints from the age of thirteen,' Marina Warner reminds us, who had defended the 'external and objective reality of those voices' and 'turned to the Pope for help in her long and appalling trial', reappears in Shaw's play as a 'sharp-witted individualist, who attributes her motives and ideas to hard common sense . . . [and is a] protesting prophet, subverter, active agent of the Life Force, rational dresser'. To have succeeded in getting this 'pert spitfire' to enter English consciousness as the true Joan was the final miracle.

'The first thing he invariably does when his setting is in the past, is to rub off his period the patina of time,' wrote Desmond MacCarthy; '. . . he will scrub and scrub till contemporary life begins to gleam through surface strangeness and oddities.' Shaw worked fast, filled with relief at having lifted himself free from the post-war débâcle and entered a previous century to fight another war against English imperialism. He translated his own assertion of style into Joan's inspired efficiency of action – 'She is so positive, sir,' Robert de Baudricourt's steward says to account for her effect on everyone. Shaw presents her as the warrior-saint he had sometimes thought of dramatizing as Cromwell and Mahomet, and had looked for in a play about the Unknown Soldier. But after *Saint Joan* he needed to write none of these works. 'It's a stupendous play,' Sybil Thorndike wrote to him, '& says all the things that the world needs to hear at the moment.'

*

Sybil Thorndike had felt destined to act St Joan and in 1923 commissioned Laurence Binyon to write a play for her about the Maid. Shaw, too, had begun writing his *Saint Joan* that year. On 27 August, he was able to write: 'Saint Joan is finished (except for the polishing) . . . and I thought I should never write another after Methuselah!'

It was not until he had finished the play that Sybil Thorndike and Lewis Casson got to hear of it. In some consternation they wrote, telling him of Laurence Binyon's work-in-progress and asking what should be done. G.B.S. was flatteringly adamant: 'Sybil is to play my Joan; let someone else play Binyon's.' In the event, Binyon gracefully withdrew and the difficulty lifted.

Charlotte seems to have been instrumental in Shaw's choice of subject. 'Yes, I sometimes find ideas for plays for the Genius,' she conceded. 'If we can find a good subject for a play, he usually writes it very quickly.' The same proposal had also been made by the man he had named as his literary executor, Sydney Cockerell, curator of the Fitzwilliam Museum in Cambridge, to which, early in 1922, the Shaws had presented one of Augustus John's portraits of G.B.S. 'I have always been under the impression that I was in a small way responsible for St Joan,' Cockerell wrote to Shaw twenty years later, 'by giving you or introducing you to Douglas Murray's book containing the full proceedings at her trial and rehabilitation and suggesting that you might do something with it.'

There was yet another begetter, a teacher at St Mary's College, Hammersmith, called Father Joseph Leonard, whom the Shaws had met in 1919 on holiday at Parknasilla. Shaw later sent him a letter asking where he could find a record of the proceedings of Joan's canonization. 'What I want to know is how the Church got over the fact, which must have been raised by the *advocatus diaboli* if he did his duty to his client, that Joan asserted a right of private judgment as against the Church,' he explained. ' . . . I may write a play about her some day; and this is the only point on which I do not feel fully equipped.'

This letter initiated a long exchange between Shaw and the priest who became his 'technical adviser' on the play, though not all his advice was accepted. Shaw held Joan's private judgement to be inspired and the Church's judgement banal. He took the evidence from the court – often in Joan's words – and dramatized it in the theatre as the speeches of a natural rebel against the Church's authority. Father Leonard declared Joan's loyalty to the Pope to be of far greater significance than any number of eccentric voices, for 'the Church is large enough to contain all sorts of queer fish'. But to have made Joan a queer fish within the Catholic aquarium would have destroyed the Protestant purpose of Shaw's play, which was to bring a realist heroine before a perfectly conducted court of idealists.

The play seemed almost to write itself. More difficult was the revision, in which he eliminated many tempting digressions. This was well advanced by the late autumn when Sybil Thorndike and Lewis Casson came down to Ayot to hear G.B.S. read his play. 'He read it beautifully – he ought to have been an actor really and from the moment he started we couldn't move!' Sybil Thorndike wrote to her son John. The reading lasted three hours and three minutes. 'When it came to the Epilogue Lewis and I were in tears,' Sybil Thorndike recalled.

*

Though Sybil Thorndike was the theatrical vehicle Shaw had in mind for the role, he had used another model as Joan's contemporary equivalent – the middle-aged Fabian Mary Hankinson. Hanky, as she was known, had been born in Cheshire, physically trained in Kent and employed as Head of a Sunday School. For thirty years she acted as Spartan hostess at the Fabian Summer Schools, captaining their cricket teams, drilling their country dancers and policing their morals. She was vividly remembered for teaching Shaw to waltz backwards: 'an unforgettable sight!' She seemed entirely sexless, pouring her energies into gymnastics and flute-playing, and sharing her domestic life with her friend Ethel Moor. Shaw had attended the Summer School in 1919 at Penlee where Hanky had miraculously quenched a Fabian uprising. But though a rigid disciplinarian, this

'maid with silver hair
With school-boy heart and skipper air'

as John Dover Wilson serenaded her, inspired much admiration, for she was a woman of 'unusual good sense,' St John Ervine observed. When *Saint Joan* was published in 1924, Shaw presented her with a copy inscribed: 'To Mary Hankinson, the only woman I know who does not believe she was the model for Joan, and also the only woman who actually was.'

'It is difficult,' wrote the critic Maurice Valency, 'to understand in what way Miss Hankinson . . . could have served as a model for Saint Joan.' But her feminism, which modulated Joan's speech so that it sounded to Desmond MacCarthy like the voice of 'a suffragette and a cry from a garden city', was the influence to which T. S. Eliot took exception when criticizing Shaw for having created 'perhaps the greatest sacrilege of all Joans' by turning 'her into a great middle-class reformer . . . [whose] place is little higher than Mrs Pankhurst's'. Shaw may have had Eliot in mind when, delivering a radio talk in 1931, he stated that although no modern feminist was quite like St Joan, 'St Joan inspired that movement . . . If you read Miss [Sylvia] Pankhurst, you will understand a great deal more about the psychology of Joan.'

Shaw's play carries on the historical business of literature, reconstructing the roles of past figures and keeping the dead in perpetual employment. He uses Joan's symbolic dimensions to add credentials to his vitalist philosophy, as Voltaire and Anatole France had used her for their purposes, and as Shaw's contemporaries were themselves using her for opposing ends. Not long before, Charles Péguy had re-created Joan as a socialistic mystic and martyr who found her equivalent in the government-persecuted figure of Dreyfus; and Charles Maurras had rediscovered her as a proto-fascist emblem of the Action Française, reinforcing military and national authority as Joan had reinforced the French army and the King.

Shaw's Joan is the complete outsider who feels most lonely when she is in company with those who voice opinions of the day. Her own timeless voices echo her unworldliness and establish her kinship with the man who felt a stranger on this planet and at ease only with the dead. Shaw's methods of composition were too oblique and multifaceted for straightforward self-portraiture. To illustrate how the progress of humankind still depended on some people regarded by philistine society as sick and even lunatic, Shaw enlisted more than one contemporary parallel. In addition to Mary Hankinson there was Lawrence of Arabia.

Shaw had been introduced to T. E. Lawrence in March 1922 when Sydney Cockerell brought him along to help carry away the portrait by Augustus John. Shaw was one of Lawrence's heroes, and five months later he received a letter from Lawrence asking him to read 'or try to read, a book which I have written'. By the middle of September one of the eight copies of Lawrence's *The Seven Pillars of Wisdom*, cumbersomely printed on a linotype machine by the *Oxford Times*, arrived at Ayot. This awkward and prodigious work, 'about twice as long as the Bible', stood at the centre of Shaw's working life. 'You are evidently a very dangerous man: most men who are any good are,' he told Lawrence. ' . . . I wonder what, after reading the book through, I will decide to do with you.'

His detailed revisions (including virtuoso use of the semi-colon), which affected 'the spirit as well as the letter of the book,' Lawrence acknowledged, and 'left not a paragraph without improvement', were not completed until some two years later. But Shaw had read the book 'to the last morsel' much sooner. By the time he started on *Saint Joan* he had only forty pages left to read, and when he finished it early in the summer he felt convinced that here was 'one of the great books of the world,' he told Lady Gregory.

In the meantime he had found out some facts about this puzzling man. Lawrence had quit his Arabian adventures, left the Colonial Office, erased his old name and, having been discharged from the RAF following his public identification as 'Private Ross', enlisted in the Royal Tank Corps in Dorset using as his new alias – of all names – Shaw.

Lady Gregory visited Ayot St Lawrence that May, and her diary records that the two people most on Shaw's mind were Joan of Arc and Lawrence of Arabia. To some degree *The Seven Pillars of Wisdom* may be read as a cross-referring work to *Saint Joan*. Lawrence was what Shaw called 'a grown-up boy, without any idea of politics'. He had gone to the Paris Peace Conference expecting President Wilson to secure self-determination for the Arab peoples, and had come away full of the bitterness of defeat. His inspired leadership of the Arab revolt against the Turks, which kept the Arabs fighting for the Allies instead of among themselves, helped to redeem them from their Ottoman servitude. Like Joan, Lawrence had been 'in the grip of a nationalistic impulse to create a unified state from a feudal order, and to set a monarch representative of that unity upon the throne of the nation-state'. Joan had succeeded with the Dauphin and been martyred; Lawrence had failed with King Feisal and seemed, after Versailles, to be backing into oblivion.

As a man-of-letters in peacetime who became a man-of-action in war, Lawrence provided a living connection between G.B.S. and Joan that helped Shaw to bring his heroine 'close to the present day'. Lacking an adult sense of his identity, Lawrence invited his heroes to invade his character and link it with their own. His choice of Shaw's name, the opening he gave G.B.S. to edit and amend his vast first-person chronicle of the Arabian campaign, and the visits he began making that summer to the Shaws' village, the name of which so coincidentally sanctified his own, were part of the mechanics by which G.B.S. was encouraged to merge their destinies.

Already, by the beginning of 1923, Shaw was advising Lawrence to 'get used to the limelight', as he himself had done. Later he came to realize that Lawrence was one of the most paradoxically conspicuous men of the century. The function of both their public personalities was to lose an old self and discover a new. Lawrence had been illegitimate; Shaw had doubted his legitimacy. Both were the sons of dominant mothers and experienced difficulties in establishing their masculinity. The Arab revolt, which gave Lawrence an ideal theatre of action, turned him into Colonel Lawrence, Luruns Bey, Prince of Damascus and most famously Lawrence of Arabia. 'I note that you have again moulded the world impossibly to your desire,' G.B.S. wrote to him. 'There is no end to your Protean tricks . . . What is your game really?' It was natural to interpret it all as a Shavian game, and to see in the shy bird who had helped to carry the Augustus John portrait a version of Sonny. 'I was naturally a pitiably nervous, timid man, born with a whole plume of white feathers,' he confided to Lawrence; 'but nowadays this only gives a zest to the fun of swanking at every opportunity.'

But it is this swanking and fun that makes Shaw's Joan into the Principal Boy of a pantomime, and the play into a charade exhibiting 'all Shaw's most irritating stylistic habits,' as Irving Wardle wrote: ' . . . garrulousness, flimsy poeticism, and thick-skinned flippancy'. Like another of Pygmalion's experiments, he had constructed a likeness of Joan by grafting the eccentric muscle of Mary Hankinson, and framing her with the aura of 'an accomplished poseur with glittering eyes,' as Beatrice Webb described Lawrence. G.B.S. gave Lawrence several copies of *Saint Joan* – variously dedicated 'to Shaw from Shaw' and 'to Pte Shaw from Public Shaw' – but Lawrence, who mislaid these copies, was an unreliable chaperon for the rendezvous of G.B.S. with his saint and remained as much of a mystery to Shaw as Joan herself whom, he conceded, 'I do not profess to understand'.

*

'Mortal eyes cannot distinguish the saint from the heretic,' warns Cauchon in the Epilogue. From the perspective of history it may be easy to see that Joan is inspired and that the other fanatic, de Stogumber, who throws himself into Joan's chair after her burning, is heretical. But there exists a more sophisticated fanatic in the Inquisitor, who gives a warning of where the toleration of fanaticism may lead. His fearful condemnation of change is made with such idealistic sympathy that some critics have understood it to define G.B.S.'s own attitude. What Shaw intended to voice through this 'most infernal old scoundrel' was his audience's opinion of the Church and Empire, before demonstrating where such opinions led. The Inquisitor's attack on Joan's masculine dress is also a denunciation of Shaw's Jaeger costume. Changes in fashion exhibit how the unorthodoxy of one time becomes the convention of another, a point dramatically made in the Epilogue by everyone's amusement at the appearance of the clerical-looking gentleman wearing 'a black frock-coat and trousers, and tall hat, in the fashion of the year 1920'. The Inquisitor's court has reduced justice to the dictatorship of fashion.

Saint Joan is a tragedy without villains. The tragedy exists in human nature where the mad credulity and intolerant incredulity of religious and secular forces meet and fix the *status quo*. Against this social structure Shaw's heroine gains no victory; she can win a battle as Shaw can win a debate, but she will never change the social order until the world truly becomes a fit place for heroes to live in.

The Epilogue, which reflects the flames of Joan's burning in the summer lightning against the windy curtains and brings us into the present century, gave Shaw the chance to step forward and 'talk the play over with the audience'. What he tells us is that we too would burn Joan at the stake if we got the chance. It was not surprising that much of the hostile criticism of *Saint Joan* centred on this Epilogue, which 'shattered the historical illusion' – and made way for Brecht.

The historical illusion was cherished by the public. In vain did the American critics protest after the play opened in New York that it contained 'too little comedy' and 'a good deal of fustian', and was 'a mere historical scaffolding upon which the dramatist drapes the old Shavian gonfalons'. Alexander Woolcott warned readers of the *New York Herald* that 'certain scenes grow groggy for want of a blue pencil'; and in the *New Republic* Edmund Wilson was to complain that it had the characteristic over-explicitness of the social historian turned dramatist, giving the audience a sense 'that it is reading a book instead of witnessing a real event'.

On the opening night a number of these critics and some of the audience began leaving the theatre before the final curtain came down at 11.35 p.m. Lawrence Langner cabled urgently to Shaw stating that if he refused to shorten it, *Saint Joan* could not be a success. Shaw replied declaring the press notices, which had so frightened him, to be 'magnificent'. For it was true that Alexander Woolcott had also called the play 'beautiful, engrossing and at times exciting', and Edmund Wilson described it as 'a work of extraordinary interest'; that the *New York Times* critic who found the play 'monotonous' had nevertheless thought it a 'great triumph', that the *New York Post* critic who found it 'exasperating' still thought it 'brilliant'. All these favourable points seemed to have been gathered together in a long review for the *New York Times Magazine* by Luigi Pirandello. 'I have a strong impression that for some time past George Bernard Shaw has been growing more and more serious . . . he seems to be believing less in himself, and more in what he is doing,' Pirandello wrote. ' . . . In none of Shaw's work that I can think of have considerations of art been so thoroughly respected as in *Saint Joan* . . . There is a truly great poet in Shaw.'

Shaw ranked Pirandello as 'first rate among playwrights', believing that he had 'never come across a play so *original* as Six Characters'. He advised the Theatre Guild to recover its nerve. 'It is extremely annoying to have to admit that you are right,' Lawrence Langner replied the following January. 'People are coming in droves to see *Saint Joan*, and it is a great success.' The production had to be transferred from the Garrick to the larger Empire Theater, and ran for 214 performances before being sent on tour.

The English production at the New Theatre in St Martin's Lane marked the culmination of Charles Ricketts's partnership with Shaw which had begun in 1907 at the Court Theatre with his 'inscenation' of *Don Juan in Hell*. His costumes there, modelled on Velázquez, had stood blazing against a stage dowsed in black velvet and appeared magical to Shaw. 'If only we could get a few plays with invisible backgrounds and lovely costumes like that in a suitable theatre,' he had written, '. . . there would be no end to the delight of the thing.' He had again turned to Ricketts for *The Dark Lady of the Sonnets* in which Shakespeare, clothed in greys and russets, Queen Elizabeth in silver and black, and the Dark Lady, wearing crimson and black, appeared before an 'intense and abnormal starlit sky of a fabulous blue'. The following year Ricketts had attired the Venetian *père noble* Count O'Dowda after Thomas Lawrence's portrait of George IV and given his daughter a strict Empire dress to lend her the look of a fillette 'depicted on elegant pre-revolution French crockery' in the successful run of *Fanny's First Play*. The 'gorgeous white uniform, half covered by an enormous green overcoat trimmed with black fur' he designed for Lillah McCarthy's role as *Annajanska* seven years later had been so successful that Margot Asquith copied the overcoat for her dressing-gown.

For *Saint Joan*, Ricketts created costumes designed to be an 'intelligent blend between Pol de Limbourg and the Van Eycks, avoiding the bright fourteenth-century colour of the first and the rather prosy phase in dress in the second'. He 'flung himself into the job', authenticating heraldry on the magnificent tapestries, tents and curtains, designing the stained glass for Rheims Cathedral, and basing the sunny stone chamber in the Castle of Vancouleurs on the kitchen of a Norman keep at Chilham which he shared with Charles Shannon. In his history of British theatre design, George Sheringham was to describe the visual effect as being, within its conventions, 'one of the most beautiful things that has ever been seen on the London stage'.

Partly perhaps as a heritage from William Morris and partly in response to Gordon Craig's influence, Shaw had used artists such as Albert Rutherston and Ricketts to carry the theatre away from Victorian scene-painting into twentieth-century realms of stage design that could produce a style to match the director's view of a play. This had gradually become accepted as part of a Shaw play-in-performance by the time Barry Jackson took over the Vedrenne–Barker tradition and appointed Paul Shelving as his regular designer.

Both Shelving and Ricketts designed productions of *Saint Joan*. The public's delight in the beauty and vitality of Ricketts's designs for the first production helped to establish it as Shaw's most successful play. At last he had done what Archer had been goading him to do: he had written a realistic or symbolic work that 'should go to every city in the world and shake the souls of people'. In Berlin and Vienna, Max Reinhardt's production, presenting Elizabeth Bergner as Joan, scored 'the greatest theatrical success that I have ever known,' recorded Trebitsch. Before long, the play was being performed in Scandinavia, throughout Eastern Europe, and even in Paris where seven unsuccessful productions of his previous plays in the Hamons' translations were thought to have established complete 'barriers of language, thought and feeling between Shaw and the French'. The play's producer and star actress, George and Ludmilla Pitoëff, who were to revive it in Paris no less than a dozen times in ten years, had been appalled by the Hamons' version. In collaboration with Henri-René Lenormand they revised it so as to present a dreamlike vision of a miraculously sublimated Joan. For the first time, the French critics united in their praise of the Hamons' brilliant rendering; for the first time they praised Shaw for an innovative structure of hagiography that contrasted the saint with the farcical world of Shavian satire, and parodied the court in the manner of an Offenbach operetta, while leaving Joan spiritually uncontaminated. This original technique was hailed as an effective means of dramatizing the supernatural, and Shaw was credited with having invented a new type of historical drama.

'Woe unto me when all men praise me!' says St Joan in the Epilogue. Shaw greeted his own popularity with similar scepticism. He had sent out his play to rescue Joan from canonization and restore her heresy, but found it was to lead to his own canonization with the Nobel Prize for Literature. He had been put up, and turned down, for the Nobel Prize four or five times previously. But the literary adviser to the Swedish Academy, Per Hallström, was converted by *Saint Joan*: 'even if the real Saint Joan was a different figure,' he acknowledged, 'Shaw has created a great one.' Shaw was appalled. 'The Nobel Prize has been a hideous calamity for me,' he told Augustin Hamon. ' . . . It was really almost as bad as my 70th birthday.'

He had never encouraged prizes. 'You cannot give examination paper marks to works of art,' he had written in 1918. He had not changed his mind. 'If the prizes are to be reserved on Safety First principles for old men whose warfare is accomplished,' he wrote to his Swedish translator Lady Ebba Low, 'the sooner they are confiscated and abolished by the Swedish Government the better.' After politely describing the award as a reinforcement between British and Swedish culture that, especially after